LEGENDS OF PRO WRESTLING

LEGENDS OF PRO WRESTLING

150 YEARS OF HEADLOCKS, BODY SLAMS, AND PILEDRIVERS

TIM HORNBAKER

FOREWORD BY JIMMY "SUPERFLY" SNUKA

SPORTS
PUBLISHING

Sports Publishing books may be purchased in bulk at special discounts for sales promotion, corporate gifts, fund-raising, or educational purposes. Special editions can also be created to specifications. For details, contact the Special Sales Department, Sports Publishing, 307 West 36th Street, 11th Floor, New York, NY 10018 or sportspubbooks@skyhorsepublishing.com.

Sports Publishing® is a registered trademark of Skyhorse Publishing, Inc.®, a Delaware corporation.

Visit our website at www.sportspubbooks.com

10 9 8 7 6 5 4 3 2 1

Library of Congress Cataloging-in-Publication Data
Hornbaker, Tim. Legends of pro wrestling : 150 years of headlocks, bodyslams, and piledrivers / Tim Hornbaker ; foreword by Jimmy "Superfly" Snuka.
p. cm. Includes bibliographical references.
ISBN 978-1-61321-075-8 (pbk. : alk. paper)
1. Wrestling--Juvenile literature. I. Title. GV1195.3H67 2012 796.812--dc23

2012015014

ISBN: 978-1-61321-075-8

Printed in Canada

Cover photos courtesy of:
Top Row:
Andre the Giant by Pete Lederberg
Randy Savage by Dr. Mike Lano
Hulk Hogan by Pete Lederberg
The Rock by Dr. Mike Lano
John Cena by Mike Mastrandrea

Middle Row:
Mick Foley by Pete Lederberg
Ric Flair by Pete Lederberg
Ricky Steamboat by Pete Lederberg
Jerry Lawler by Pete Lederberg
Billy Graham by Pete Lederberg

Bottom Row
The Sheik by Pete Lederberg
Sgt. Slaughter by Pete Lederberg
Sting by Pete Lederberg
Stan Hansen by Pete Lederberg
Wahoo McDaniel by Pete Lederberg

To my grandmother Virginia and my mother Barbara, who are both an inspiration in strength, courage, and unyielding love.

TABLE OF CONTENTS

III. Heroes and Villains Wage War in the Sacred Territories

Foreword

The Superfly just loves wrestling—everything about it! Ever since my mother and I would watch guys like Sam Steamboat do battle on TV when I was little, I have just loved everything about it. Wrestling brought the two of us even closer then we were, and we were close to begin with, brudda! Even before I became a wrestling superstar in the World Wrestling Federation (World Wrestling Entertainment today), I would have my mother fly in to be at ringside so she could see the action up close. She just loved it!

Wrestling does that to you . . . it gets in your bones. You root for your favorite stars, then they become heels and you boo them. The same works the other way around when bad guys turn good. I should know— I've been both a bad guy and a good guy. I decided to become a wrestler to make a living at first, but fell in love with it right away. I was an athlete all my life and always played at the highest level. I always pushed the limits to be the best. I was also quite fearless. I used to dive off cliffs as a kid and always threw myself into things without giving it too much thought. I played a lot of sports and eventually started bodybuilding. My body was so jacked back then. I was entering bodybuilding competitions while starting to train to become a wrestler. My muscles had muscles, brah. Wrestling seemed like a good idea, so I started training to be the very best. That's why I jumped off the steel cage against Don Muraco at Madison Square Garden. No one had done it before and I wanted to stand out.

I talk about this and so much more in my upcoming autobiography (*Superfly: The Jimmy Snuka Story*), but you'll have to buy it when it comes out, brudda! The Superfly will reveal all! What I can tell you, though, is that wrestling just came naturally to me from the second I stepped into the ring for the first time. It was like putting on a glove. I just loved it, brudda. I loved everything about it; I loved working with other brothers in the ring; I loved the fans reacting to everything; I loved listening to the fans and working with my opponent to make it all work. I loved it all! Back in those days, we had a story to tell to the fans. We took it slow. We listened to each other and we gained an unbreakable trust. We all wanted to give the best matches for the fans, and the best ones were always the ones where the excitement built throughout the match. You can't rush a match like they do today. You need to tell a story. Everything today just moves too fast in wrestling. That's not the only way things have changed.

When I broke into the business, it was the kayfabe era. Fans in TV wonderland believed the storylines, and we kept them going by not being seen together in public. I remember back in the day people really hated Cpt. Lou Albano because they thought he stole from me. It was a storyline, but fans believed it, brudda! I used to love getting the fans excited. Back when I was a bad guy moving through the territories, I would taunt them and I would just love them hating me. When I was a good guy, I got such a high from hearing them cheer my name. It didn't matter if I was in Portland or Japan; the same was true all over.

When I wrestled it wasn't like it was today with entertainment and gimmicks. Like I said, things these days are more rushed. But, you know the Superfly still loves to watch. I loved watching my son Jimmy wrestle as Deuce, and enjoy seeing my daughter Tamina Snuka wrestle in WWE today. I also love watching my nephew Dwayne "The Rock" Johnson continue to be one of the greatest of all time.

I was wrestling in the golden age, whether it was in Charlotte or New York City, brah. Andre the Giant was a brother to me, as was Roddy Piper, Ricky Steamboat, and Rocky Johnson. I loved wrestling with Paul Orndorff, Captain Lou Albano, and many other brothers. I loved locking up with my Hawaiian brother Don Muraco, Bob Backlund, Jesse Ventura, Ray Stevens, and so many more—I can't list them all! This book has them all in here, brudda. It's a history of every legend who ever stepped into the ring. It tells you what they were known for, highlights their best matches, and details the titles they won. I'm in here too, bruddas. You can read about some of the things I've done— the matches, the moments I've had, and of course, the titles. Yes, this brudda has had some gold around his waist, but I was never about that. I wanted to be the best there was and I feel like I became the best. My only goal was making the best match there could be.

There are so many talented guys in the business now including Mick Foley, John Cena, Santino Marella, and CM Punk, but it's important to take a look at the past. There have been so many talented brothers in the history of wrestling, and I was lucky to have wrestled with and/or against many of them. Wrestling always changes and that's what makes it fun to watch. For example, it was so different in the era I wrestled in and long before the Superfly ever entered the ring. It's all in this book. *Legends of Pro Wrestling* is really for the die-hard fan who wants to know everything there is about all the brothers who worked so hard in the ring back in the day.

The fans always came first for me, and they do in this book. If you live and breathe wrestling like the Superfly does, you'll love reading this who's who of wrestling. You know the Superfly loves it, brudda!

Jimmy "Superfly" Snuka
April 2012

I. The Pioneers Blaze a Trail
Pro Debut Between 1850 and 1920

At the heart of the professional wrestling business, more important than the weekly television ratings, pay-per-view buy-rates, and even attendance numbers, are the wrestlers themselves, who, in many cases, have devoted their entire lives to the industry. At great personal risk, these men and women have stepped through the ropes to entertain audiences, and their profound love for the sport cannot be equaled by any other form of athletics. While grappling is a time-honored tradition of combat with roots in Ancient Greece and India, modern professional wrestling has rapidly evolved over the last 150 years, and the wrestlers themselves have transformed in many imaginative ways.

With courage and sensibility akin to bare knuckle fighters, wrestlers going back to the American Civil War were tough to the bone and adept at battling opponents in a raw, brutal fashion that ended with the toughest competitor winning. There was very little flashiness, no grand match entrances, and the wrestlers didn't achieve success because of their "look" or by the push of a promoter. At some juncture, and historians don't exactly know when, the sport went through an important metamorphosis, and wrestlers heightened their performance in matches with predetermined finishes. Audiences responded positively to the adjustment, although the modification of its genuineness was kept from fans. For those inside the business, the overhaul of the fundamental blueprint for wrestling was almost necessary to keep it relevant to the public. In fact, the implementation of creativity into what used to be exhaustively contested matches that could last hours turned wrestling into a multi-million dollar business.

Colonel McLaughlin, William Muldoon, Tom Jenkins, and Farmer Burns were key athletes during the latter part of the 1800s. They were world-class wrestlers in both the Greco-Roman and catch-as-catch-can styles and had a heavy influence on the next generation of wrestlers—which included Frank Gotch—the greatest American wrestling champion in history. Through shear invincibility and magnetism, Gotch garnered mainstream attention in the 1900s and 1910s, and made professional wrestling respectable for middle- to upper-class followers. He was an indomitable spirit, and his legitimate wrestling knowledge, quickness, and aggressiveness made him unbeatable. Gotch was also able to work matches and create tension-filled situations that kept fans on the edge of their seats. Gambling was prevalent during this time-frame, and Gotch was as informed as anyone when it came to making money.

The business turned toward three men during the mid-to-late 1910s: Ed "Strangler" Lewis, Earl Caddock, and Joe Stecher. Each brought a unique personality and talent to the ring, and continued to build upon the strengths forged by their predecessors. Forward-thinking promoters were trying to stay ahead of the game by implementing intriguing concepts and introducing new wrestlers who'd keep the sport popular. Gimmicks and vociferous hype were on wrestling's doorstep, and fans embraced both the perceived competitive nature of the sport and the theatrical atmosphere of vaudeville. It all combined to create a world-wide phenomenon that is still being appreciated today.

Make no bones about it, anyone who undertakes the painstaking journey as a pro wrestler should be lauded for their commitment. *Legends of Pro Wrestling* honors the men and women who have awed and inspired fans everywhere through their actions on the wrestling mat, and these heroes will forever be cherished.

AMERICUS - GUS SCHOENLEIN

Born:	December 25, 1883
Height:	5'10"
Weight:	210
Real Name:	August John Schoenlein
Career Span:	1902-1921
Died:	July 17, 1958, Bowleys Quarters, MD 74 years old

Titles Won:	At least 3
Days as World Champion:	55
Age at first World Title Win:	30
Best Opponents:	Frank Gotch, Stanislaus Zbyszko, Fred Beell

Americus

When Americus began wrestling in a Baltimore ring, fresh off a stint as an amateur grappler, he weighed in the neighborhood of 145 pounds. He was a courageous athlete, and throughout his career, displayed cleverness in matches against men of much greater size. Taking his name to disguise his occupation from his father, Americus advanced through the weight divisions and won the World Light Heavyweight Title twice, first over Fred Beell in 1908 and then over Charles Olson in 1910. On March 13, 1914, he beat Beell again, this time for the World Heavyweight crown in a match supported by the retired champion, Frank Gotch. While dominant, his reign as champ was brief, losing to Stanislaus Zbyszko less than two months after winning the crown. Upon his retirement, he worked as a building contractor and coached both the Maryland State Police in hand-to-hand combat and Princeton's wrestling squad.

Born:	January 17, 1876
Height:	5'6"
Weight:	170
Real Name:	Friedrich A. Beell
Parents:	Wilhelm and Augusta Beell
Wife:	Anna Beell
Military:	Company A, Second Wisconsin Regiment
Trained by:	Lee Tepfer, Louis Cannon, Evan Lewis, Farmer Burns
Nickname:	Wisconsin Wizard, Wisconsin Whirlwind
Career Span:	1896-1919
Died:	August 5, 1933, Marshfield, WI 57 years old

Beell, Fred

Titles Won:	At least 4
Days as American Champion:	16
Age at first American Title Win:	30
Best Opponents:	Frank Gotch, Tom Jenkins, Ed Adamson
Halls of Fame:	1

The upset of the century was pulled off when Marshfield, Wisconsin wonder Fred Beell, a classy grappler, beat Frank Gotch for the American catch-as-catch-can heavyweight championship on December 1, 1906 in New Orleans. It was remarkable because Beell had defeated perhaps the greatest wrestler of all time, and a man who outweighed him by 35 pounds. Beell was born in Saxony, West Prussia and came through the Wisconsin ranks, conquering wrestlers of all sizes and displaying extraordinary cleverness. He beat a laundry list of renowned foes to include Harvey Parker and Americus, and with his stunning win over Gotch, reportedly earned $4,000—with thousands more changing hands by gamblers. On December 17, 1906, Beell lost the title back to Gotch. He also held claim to the middleweight and light heavyweight crowns during his career. Known for his strength, Beell became a police officer and was killed in the line of duty when he confronted robbers at the Marshfield Brewing Company in 1933.

Photo Courtesy of the Pfefer Collection, Department of Special Collections, University of Notre Dame

Born:	June 5, 1867
Height:	5'6"
Weight:	125
Trained by:	William Brown
Finisher:	Scissors hold
Career Span:	1897-1918
Died:	November 20, 1954, Bronx, NY
	87 years old

Titles Won:	At least 2
Best Opponents:	Tom Jenkins, Harvey Parker, Eugene Tremblay

Bothner, George

New York City's George Bothner was perhaps the most famous lightweight pro wrestler in history. He won several AAU amateur titles and was proficient at a number of different styles, to include jiu-jitsu, catch-as-catch-can and Greco-Roman wrestling. A legitimate shooter, he took on all challengers while touring with bare-knuckle legend John L. Sullivan, and had a long-running feud with Harvey Parker. In 1901, he claimed the World Lightweight Title, and two years later, won the Richard K. Fox belt with a victory over Tom Riley of England. He trained hundreds of wrestlers at his gym in Manhattan and, upon retiring from active wrestling, refereed nearly every major match in New York City from Stecher-Caddock to O'Mahoney-Shikat.

Caddock, Earl

Born:	February 27, 1888
Height:	5'10 ½"
Weight:	190
Real Name:	Earl Charles Caddock I
Parents:	John and Jane Caddock
Wife:	Grace May Caddock
Military:	United States Army (WWI)
Amateur Titles:	National AAU Heavyweight Title (1915), National AAU Light Heavyweight Title (1915), AAU Light Heavyweight Title (1914)
Trained by:	Martin Delaney, Ernest Kartje, Ben Reuben
Nickname:	The Berea Tiger, Man of a 1000 Holds
Career Span:	1915-1922
Died:	August 25, 1950, Walnut, IA 62 years old

Titles Won:	3
Days as World Champion:	1,026
Age at first World Title Win:	29
Best Opponents:	Joe Stecher, Ed Lewis, John Pesek
Halls of Fame:	4

Pound for pound one of the greatest wrestlers in history, Earl Caddock was not a man who yearned for the spotlight. In fact, he was quite shy and reserved. He was immensely bright, and learned the ins and outs of the legit form of catch-as-catch-can grappling, building an exceptional genuine arsenal of holds. He was an unbeatable man when he was at the top of his game. Ironically, though, he was only in his finest form as a pro wrestler for three years, between 1915 and 1918, prior to being shipped off for duty to France during World War I. But in that time, he proved invincible, and on April 9, 1917, he beat Joe Stecher when the latter refused to continue, and won the World Heavyweight Title. Caddock went overseas to fight while still reigning as champion, and was gassed in the trenches. Despite his courageous efforts to resume his career, Caddock was never the same. He lost his title to Stecher in New York on January 30, 1920, wrestled until 1922, and then quietly retired.

Born:	September 2, 1884
Height:	6'0"
Weight:	225
Real Name:	Charles Leroy Cutler
Parents:	Wallace and Christine Cutler
Wife:	Marie Cutler
Trained by:	Frank Gotch, Jack Coleman
Identities:	Kid Cutler
Career Span:	1905-1930
Died:	December 25, 1952, Paw Paw, MI 69 years old

Cutler, Charles

Titles Won or Claimed: At least 6

Days as World Champion: 135 (plus unknown time for other claims)

Days as American Champion: Around 726

Age at first World Title Claim: 28

Best Opponents: Frank Gotch, George Hackenschmidt, Joe Stecher

When Charles Cutler claimed the World Heavyweight Championship in 1915, it initiated a new lineage, separate from the undefeated king Frank Gotch, and was ultimately recognized as the most prized title in the sport. Born near Coopersville, Michigan, he built his strength as a logger, and was a remarkable dual sport athlete in boxing and wrestling from a young age. Around 1906, he received attention as a touring partner of the legendary John L. Sullivan, and half a dozen years later, Gotch picked the talented Cutler to be his replacement as heavyweight champion. Cutler also won the American title at least four times. Before captivated sportswriters in the offices of the *Chicago Tribune* on February 20, 1915, he boldly asserted that he was the rightful world champion over and above anyone else. He ended up losing the title a few months later to Joe Stecher in Omaha, Nebraska. Notably, Cutler was an early manager and trainer for the "Great White Hope" Jess Willard, and his brother Marty was a sparring partner for boxer Jack Johnson.

Born:	October 22, 1886
Height:	6'0"
Weight:	205
Real Name:	William Diaman Demetral
Nickname:	Greek Demon
Career Span:	1904-1939
Died:	August 13, 1968, Oak Forest, IL 81 years old

Titles Won:	At least 2, claimed to be champion of Greece
Best Opponents:	Frank Gotch, Stanislaus Zbyszko, Adolph Ernst

Demetral, William

In 1927, William Demetral became known as a "trustbuster," when he publicly spoke out against a major syndicate, effectively breaking kayfabe, and confirming the crookedness of wrestling to many people who already suspected its dishonesty. It was a startling revelation from a distinguished wrestler who'd attained high status all over the United States, holding versions of the World Light Heavyweight and American Heavyweight Championships. Demetral, originally from Greece, was an idol for his countrymen, and developed his mat skills in Chicago athletic clubs. Over the course of his three decades on the mat, he had important matches against "Strangler" Lewis, Jim Londos, and many others, and was known for his athletic conditioning and strength.

Born:	June 3, 1887
Height:	5'9 ½"
Weight:	180
Real Name:	Clarence Gust Eklund
Parents:	August and Julia Eklund
Wife:	Florence Eklund
Trained by:	Farmer Burns
Career Span:	1908-1934
Died:	January 4, 1981, Buffalo, WY 93 years old

Titles Won:	14
Best Opponents:	Earl Caddock, Mike Yokel, Ad Santel

Eklund, Clarence

Legendary light heavyweight competitor, Clarence Eklund was a nine-time world champion and retired as the undisputed titleholder in 1930. Born near Miltonvale, Kansas, he left home and got a job as a teacher when he was just eighteen years old. However, Eklund had the spirit of a nomad, and went on the road, ending up at a Canadian lumber camp. It was there that he learned how to wrestle, and debuted as a pro a few years later He won titles in two weight divisions in Canada, and settled in Johnson County, Wyoming around 1916. With victories over A.A. Britt, Sam Clapham, and others, Eklund claimed the World Light Heavyweight crown in early 1917, and affirmed his claim by defeating Pet Brown in 1917. Over the next ten years, he lost and regained the title four more times, and then won a major tournament in Australia to determine the undisputed champion on November 20, 1928. Noted for his intelligence, speed, and leg holds, Eklund was known to also wrestle barefoot from time to time.

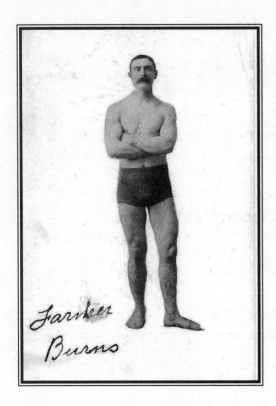

Born:	February 15, 1861
Height:	5'10"
Weight:	165
Real Name:	Martin Burns
Parents:	Michael and Mary Burns
Wife:	Amelia Burns
Career Span:	1869-1913
Died:	January 8, 1937, Council Bluffs, IA 76 years old

Titles Won:	At least 2
Days as World Champion:	920
Age at first World Title Win:	34
Best Opponents:	Evan Lewis, Dan McLeod, Tom Jenkins
Number of Wrestlers Trained:	Estimated at 1,600 over a forty-five-year period
Halls of Fame:	4

Farmer Burns

During the early 20th century, a vast number of people ordered the Farmer Burns School of Wrestling correspondence course, and paid one dollar a month to be provided with the same instruction the legendary Frank Gotch had received, albeit in the written form. Of course, the hands-on training Burns gave to hundreds of athletes was far more effective, and his lessons produced many superior grapplers. His name was synonymous with wrestling greatness and his reputation is still pristine today, 100 years later. The third of seven children to Irish immigrants, Burns grew up in Springfield in Cedar County, Iowa. Legend has it that he wrestled his first pro match as early as eight, competing with a schoolyard friend and winning fifteen cents. Quick and strong with a 20-inch neck, Burns dedicated himself to building his body into a machine, and refrained from alcohol and cigarettes. By the latter part of the 1880s, he had substantive backing for his claim to be the Iowa champion.

Helping popularize the catch-as-catch-can style in America, Burns won the world championship of that form when he beat the original "Strangler," Evan Lewis on April 20, 1895; although he would lose his title to Dan McLeod on October 26, 1897 in Indianapolis. Two years later, he met a youngster named Frank Gotch in Fort Dodge, Iowa, and was impressed by his natural strength and skill. He took Gotch under his wing and coached him to the American and World Heavyweight Titles, including two historic victories over George Hackenschmidt. Burns and Gotch traversed the country as part of an organized combine, working with a number of other top wrestlers of the era, and made bundles of money. Reportedly, Burns himself wrestled thousands of matches and crossed the continent twenty-seven times during his career. He was also known for his unusual hangman stunt that saw him survive a six-foot drop with a noose around his neck, which exhibited his extraordinary neck muscles and defied the laws of both gravity and rationality.

Born:	March 10, 1889
Height:	5'10"
Weight:	200
Olympics:	Greco-Roman Wrestling (1912) (Representing Italy) (DNP)
Career Span:	1914-1940
Died:	September 29, 1940, San Paulo, Brazil 51 years old

Titles Won:	None known, claimed Italian Title
Best Opponents:	Jim Londos, Joe Stecher, Ed Lewis

Gardini, Renato

Among the international contingent migrating to the U.S. in the 1910s to wrestle professionally was former Olympic star, Renato Gardini. Gardini was a highly recognized Greco-Roman grappler from Bologna, Italy, and arrived at Ellis Island in December 1914, just in time for the major tournaments in New York City in 1915. A hero for Italians across the nation, Gardini claimed the championship of his native country, and was a significant challenger for world titleholders Ed Lewis and Joe Stecher, as well as holding wins over Jim Londos and Wladek Zbyszko. He spent a lot of time in South America, where he helped promote shows and mentored many young wrestlers. While in Brazil, he suffered a fatal heart attack in 1940. Notably, *NWA Official Wrestling* called Gardini the "first millionaire wrestler" in its October 1952 issue.

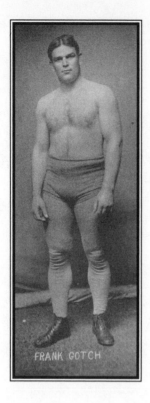

FRANK GOTCH

Photo Courtesy of the Pfefer Collection, Department of Special Collections, University of Notre Dame

Born:	April 27, 1877
Height:	5'11"
Weight:	215
Real Name:	Frank Alvin Gotch
Parents:	Frederick and Amelia Gotch
Wife:	Gladys Gotch
Finisher:	Toehold
Career Span:	1899-1917
Died:	December 16, 1917, Des Moines, IA 40 years old

Titles Won:	5 (Claimed other titles while barnstorming)
Days as World Champion:	3,544 (until death)
Age at first World Title Win:	30
Best Opponents:	George Hackenschmidt, Tom Jenkins, S. Zbyszko
Halls of Fame:	4

Gotch, Frank

Frank Gotch was an American wrestling icon. He was the first man to garner widespread celebrity status, and his popularity rivaled the top athletes from any other professional sport of his time. He was the face of wrestling as it evolved into a more socially acceptable form of entertainment, and was an invincible force of nature who dominated the profession. His unrelenting style of catch-as-catch-can wrestling inspired audiences from coast to coast, and there was no one, either home-grown or from an international location, who could beat him. Gotch's presence became so much that he demanded five figures per appearance later in his career, and his two defeats of strongman George Hackenschmidt will forever be part of wrestling lore. In terms of talent, he had it all, and reigned as the unconquered heavyweight champion of the world from 1908 until his death in 1917. Arguably, he is the most important American wrestler in history.

The ninth child born to German parents, Frank Gotch grew up in Springvale (later renamed Humboldt), Iowa, and was a child of the farm, building his muscles and stamina doing hard labor on the family homestead. In 1899, he matched up against the renown ex-champion Farmer Burns at Fort Dodge, and held his own, impressing the veteran so much that he took him as his apprentice. Gotch was rough around the edges and needed to zero in on the fundamentals, while retaining his natural instincts. Burns helped bring out the best in him and the two devised well-crafted plans to not only boost Gotch's reputation, but to make money. Gotch later admitted that he was only in the business to make a living, and understood from an early stage of his wrestling campaign that there were many different ways to earn cash. Some were in straight matches, while others were in bouts against members of his own touring troupe. There is no better example of this than Gotch's 1901 trip to the Yukon Territory during the gold rush.

Under the guise "Frank Kennedy," Gotch wrestled two of his partners, Joe Carroll Marsh and Colonel James McLaughlin in a series of matches, winning some and losing others, and there was a remarkable amount of gambling going on. When it was all said and done, Gotch earned as much as $30,000 during the tour. The lessons he learned on how to work the emotions of crowds, mixing athleticism and showmanship, and the substance of gambling in matches, were invaluable. On January 28, 1904, he beat Tom Jenkins for the first of three American Heavyweight Titles, defeating his opponent in two straight falls. Jenkins regained the championship at Madison Square Garden in New York on March 15, 1905, but lost it back to Gotch on May 23, 1906 in Kansas City.

Another example of Gotch's unparalleled mastery when it came to making money came on December 1, 1906 when one of pro wrestling's greatest upsets occurred. That evening in New Orleans, he was beaten by an opponent he outweighed by 30 pounds, and needless to say, was the heavy favorite going into the affair. An estimated $10,000 changed hands when Fred Beell, the "Wisconsin Wonder," won two of three falls and captured the title. Gotch and his cronies made a bundle of money and sixteen days later, he regained the American championship in Kansas City, winning with two straight falls.

The next major obstacle for Gotch was George Hackenschmidt, the World Heavyweight champion and a man he'd been after since 1905. Their supremely anticipated match occurred on April 3, 1908 in Chicago, and Gotch won the undisputed championship when the "Russian Lion" gave up after more than two hours of action. There was no denying that he was the best wrestler in the world and his fame increased to a level not seen by any professional wrestler to date.Over the next few years, Gotch toured when he wanted to make money, and spent time on his farm when he yearned for life away from the public eye. A rematch against Hackenschmidt was the most logical moneymaker and Gotch agreed to it once he was guaranteed upwards of $21,000 for the September 4, 1911 bout. More than 25,000 people turned out to see the Chicago match, and once again, Gotch proved victorious, winning in two straight falls. The gate of $87,953 was the largest ever for a wrestling match.

Gotch announced his retirement from the mat numerous times, and after every instance, he returned for one last match . . . but he was smart, waiting for the right payday, and unfortunately for him, the wrestling landscape lacked another foe like Hackenschmidt. Rather than rushing into another match, Gotch bided his time, proclaiming other grapplers champion, and enjoyed farm life with his wife and young son. Just as Joe Stecher was rising to fame and a potential match of the century was on the horizon, Gotch suffered a broken leg in an exhibition, and then became deathly ill. He passed away in 1917.

Born:	Around 1878
Height:	5'7 ½"
Weight:	250
Real Name:	Ghulam Mohammad Baksh
Family:	Brother of Imam Baksh
Identities:	Gama Pahalwan
Nickname:	Lion of the Punjab
Career Span:	Debut unknown, retired around 1955
Died:	May 21, 1960, Lahore, Pakistan 82 years old

Titles Won:	2 (Indian and world championships)
Days as World Champion:	Claimed title for around four decades
Best Opponents:	Raheem Baksh Sultani Wala, Stanislaus Zbyszko

Great Gama, The

Modern stories of The Great Gama are almost folklore and it is difficult to separate fact from fiction when researching this cultural icon from India. The tales of his otherworldly commitment to training, the remarkable five-figure crowds that always attended his matches, and the way he beat his foes with such ease make him a figure of such unique importance to pro wrestling history. Even if only a quarter of the stories are true about Gama, he is still a no-brainer for any Hall of Fame. He was undefeated during his entire career, beating Dr. Roller and Stanislaus Zbyszko without any trouble, and wrestled into his early 70s, still claiming to be the undefeated World Heavyweight Champion. Although Gama never toured the U.S. or faced Frank Gotch when both were in their prime, his status as a wrestling legend is very secure.

Born:	February 19, 1896
Height:	6'3"
Weight:	200
Real Name:	Fred Joseph Grobmeier
Parents:	Joseph and Eva Grobmeier
Trained by:	Farmer Burns
Nickname:	Legs, Grubby
Finisher:	Figure four hook scissors
Career Span:	1918-1944
Died:	March 24, 1970, Harrison, AR
	74 years old

Titles Won:	None known, claimed regional honors in Iowa
Best Opponents:	Joe Stecher, Jim Browning, Jim Londos

Grobmier, Fred

Fred Grobmier of Harlan, Iowa looked more like a string bean than a wrestler, and throughout his career, sportswriters would comment on his tall and lanky appearance. His modest look and country boy attitude worked perfectly at carnivals and AT shows, where he wrestled and usually beat touring champions who assumed he didn't have an athletic bone in his body. Grobmier was an extraordinary shooter, able to twist his long legs around opponents like a vine and squeeze the courage out of them. During the 1920s, he was known primarily as an independent grappler, meaning that he wasn't tied to the syndicates and was sometimes referred to as a "trustbuster." He worked his way east and joined the major circuits, performing in a journeyman capacity, and made others look good in the ring. Grobmier mentored many wrestlers, including a young Buddy Rogers, and worked as a guard for the New York Shipbuilding Corporation during World War II.

Born:	July 20, 1877
Height:	5'9"
Weight:	230
Real Name:	George Karl Julius Hackenschmidt
Parents:	George and Ida Hackenschmidt
Wife:	Rachel Marie Hackenschmidt
Military:	Russian Army (WWI)
Trained by:	Vladislav von Krajewski
Nicknames:	The World's Strongest Man, Hack
Career Span:	1900-1911
Died:	February 19, 1968, London, England 90 years old

Titles Won:	2, won several tournaments and claimed various other championships
Days as World Champion:	1,065 (catch title only)
Age at first World Title Win:	27
Best Opponents:	Frank Gotch, George Lurich, Stanislaus Zbyszko
Halls of Fame:	3

Hackenschmidt, George

The "Russian Lion" George Hackenschmidt was a wrestling phenomenon at the beginning of the 20th century. He was also a noted strongman and weightlifting pioneer, often compared to the legendary Sandow. Between 1905 and 1911, he crossed the Atlantic from England to the United States four times and cemented his role in grappling history by meeting Frank Gotch in two of the most momentous matches ever staged. Of German and Swedish parents, Hackenschmidt was born in Dorpat, Estonia and possessed above average intelligence. In fact, he extensively studied psychology and philosophy and learned to speak six languages fluently. As an amateur wrestler at the Reval Athletic and Cycling Club in Estonia, he was a quick learner in the Greco-Roman style, and proceeded to win tournaments all over Europe. His extraordinary strength set him apart and he consistently improved in his weight training, developing his body into one of the most impressive physiques in the world.

By the time Hackenschmidt made his professional debut in June of 1900, he was already a feared matman, able to overcome his lack of experience with his remarkable power. That applied to matches in the catch-as-catch-can style as well since he'd primarily trained in the Greco-Roman form. Tom Jenkins, the Cleveland catch great, ventured to London to face Hackenschmidt in July 1904 and agreed to Greco rules, where Hackenschmidt won in two straight falls. They faced off a second time during "Hack's" first tour of the U.S.

on May 4, 1905 in a bout for the catch-as-catch-can World Title. The match, at Madison Square Garden in New York, was again won by Hackenschmidt in two straight falls. There wasn't a more acclaimed wrestler in the world, and it would be nearly three years before he returned to the United States to meet a credible opponent. Gotch, the American king, was a national hero to wrestling fans, and his prime challenger. The match was being promoted as the biggest in history—and it truly was.

Chicago's Dexter Park Pavilion hosted the April 3, 1908 contest and Hackenschmidt was extended two hours and one minute before he gave in, surrendering the title to Gotch. In October of 1910, he returned to the U.S. to rebuild his reputation, and beat many top stars in the hopes he'd land a big money rematch with Gotch. Some of the victories he logged were against Henry Ordemann, Americus, and Charles Cutler. Once the financial terms were established, the contest was staged on September 4, 1911, again, in Chicago. Little did the fans know that Hackenschmidt had suffered a severe right leg injury during training that should have postponed the bout. With so much money on the line, he decided to go forward despite his handicap, and lost in two quick falls, the first in 14:18 and the second in 5:32. It was an embarrassing performance and the audience of 25,000-plus, paying a record $87,953, was wholeheartedly disappointed. Hackenschmidt retired from the business and became a scholar.

Photo Courtesy of Tom Ellis

Born:	August 3, 1872
Height:	5'9 ½"
Weight:	195
Parents:	Thomas and Mary Jenkins
Wife:	Lavinia Jenkins
Nickname:	Ham, Pop
Career Span:	1891-1914
Died:	June 19, 1957, Norwalk, CT 84 years old

Titles Won:	At least 3
Days as American Champion:	1,146
Age at first World Title Win:	29
Best Opponents:	Frank Gotch, Dan McLeod, Farmer Burns
Halls of Fame:	3

Jenkins, Tom

An outstanding catch-as-catch-can grappling phenomenon, Tom Jenkins bridged the gap between the era of "Strangler" Evans and Frank Gotch. Training under Mark Lamb at the latter's Ontario Street gym in his hometown of Cleveland, Ohio, Jenkins made his debut at twenty years of age, and obtained his first real taste of fame when he downed the great Farmer Burns on November 17, 1897 in two straight falls. On

November 7, 1901, Jenkins met champion Dan McLeod in Cleveland and won in two straight falls, capturing the American Title. McLeod won a rematch on Christmas in 1902, but Jenkins regained the championship on April 3, 1903. He also traded the crown with Gotch in 1904 and 1905, and then lost a match for the vacant World Title against George Hackenschmidt in May of 1905. Gotch beat him for the American claim for the final time on May 23, 1906. Two months later, Jenkins became the wrestling instructor at West Point and taught over 13,000 cadets over his thirty-seven years at the military academy.

Photo Courtesy of John Ketonen

Born:	May 16, 1891
Height:	5'7"
Weight:	155
Real Name:	August Kallio
Career Span:	1916-1942
Died:	March 2, 1962, Monroe, LA
	70 years old

Titles Won:	8
Best Opponents:	Clarence Eklund, Charles Fischer, Jack Reynolds

Kallio, Gus

The quickness and technical abilities displayed by Gus Kallio turned the welterweight division upside down during the latter part of the 1910s, and his ability to counteract any maneuver was extraordinary. A devoted student of Farmer Burns, Kallio beat Jack Reynolds for the World Welterweight Championship on October 3, 1921, and he held the title for several years. By 1927, the Finnish superstar was a full-fledged middleweight, and with a decision over Charles Fischer in Chicago, he was recognized as the disputed champion of the middleweight division. Kallio later won a tournament in 1930 for NWA backing, and reigned as a claimant through the late 1930s, losing and regaining the title several times. He also promoted wrestling in Monroe, Louisiana for twenty years.

Photo Courtesy of the Collection of Libnan Ayoub

Born:	June 24, 1890
Height:	5'7"
Weight:	170
Real Name:	Alexander Karasick
Trained at:	Olympic Club in San Francisco
Nickname:	Russian Lion, Gentleman Al
Career Span:	1920-1936
Died:	May 24, 1965, Honolulu, HI
	74 years old

Titles Won:	At least 1, claimed others
Best Opponents:	Ted Thye, Walter Miller,
	Mike Yokel

Karasick, Al

Tied up in the jumble of top-quality light heavyweight wrestlers during the 1920s, Russian-born Al Karasick was a contemporary of Mike Yokel, Clarence Eklund, and Ira Dern. Karasick was a dancer for the Russian ballet prior to settling in Oakland and claimed local honors in the welterweight division initially, but soon the middleweight and light heavyweight classes as well. On December 30, 1925, his unorthodox style got the best of Ted Thye in Portland, and he won the World Light Heavyweight Title, but lost it two weeks later to Yokel. Karasick toured the world and made a home in Hawaii, where he promoted wrestling for several decades. He was also instrumental in the spread of American style wrestling to Japan.

Photo Courtesy of the Pfefer Collection, Department of Special Collections, University of Notre Dame

Born:	July 5, 1888
Height:	5'6 ¾"
Weight:	155
Real Name:	Waino Alexander Ketonen
Wife:	Selma Ketonen
Career Span:	1910-1934
Died:	December 1, 1974, Boylston, MA 86 years old

Titles Won:	At least 4, claimed others
Best Opponents:	Mike Yokel, Joe Carr, Billy Riley

Ketonen, Waino

A Greco-Roman wrestler of much prestige and winner of many medals, Waino Ketonen sailed to the United States from his hometown of Tampere, Finland in 1910. His stunning natural abilities helped him transition smoothly to the catch style and, by 1915, was a world middleweight title claimant. He was fierce, fast, and respected throughout the sports community for his outstanding wrestling knowledge. Very few at his weight measured up to his level of skill, and Ketonen had noteworthy matches against Mike Yokel, Ira Dern, and Joe Turner. In Europe during the early 1920s, he beat the invincible Billy Riley, and spent many years as a coach. Praised by the legendary Farmer Burns, Ketonen retired to his Rutland, Massachusetts farm.

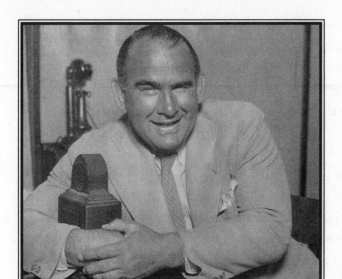

Lewis, Ed "Strangler"

Born:	June 30, 1890
Height:	6'1"
Weight:	210-290
Real Name:	Robert Herman Julius Friedrich
Parents:	Jacob and Molla Friedrich
College:	University of Kentucky
Military:	United States Army (WWI) (Physical instructor at Camp Grant)
Trained by:	Fred Beell, Billy Schober, Charlie Olson
Finisher:	Headlock
Managed by:	Billy Potts (1910), Jerry Walls (1912-1915), Billy Sandow (1915-1932)
Career Span:	1906-1948 (approximate debut year)
Died:	August 7, 1966, Muskogee, OK 76 years old

Titles Won:	At least 12, claimed others
Days as World Champion:	Over 1,927
Age at first World Title Win:	26
Best Opponents:	Joe Stecher, Stanislaus Zbyszko, Earl Caddock
Halls of Fame:	4
Movies:	5

The illustrious Ed "Strangler" Lewis was a physically gifted man who was known for being full of life. He tackled pro wrestling with an enthusiasm the sport lacked and leapt over all of his peers to become an icon, adored by fans and press alike. His outgoing personality got him places his wrestling ability couldn't, and was able to make connections throughout the sporting world so high that he was considered a peer of celebrities from other sports. It was recognition that mostly eluded professional wrestlers. Although Lewis wasn't the only superstar of his era, he received the best press, and his story has been told and retold so many times, some of it has become myth. Lewis was, without question, the truest of wrestling legends—a one-of-a-kind force that shaped the industry for decades. He also remained relevant even after stepping away from the ring himself. His story was atypical, but indicative of a sporting idol with far-reaching influence.

Born in Wood County, Wisconsin, Lewis was the third of five children, and a natural athlete. As a teenager, he played baseball with the Nekoosa city team and labored at Johanna Gutheil's general store in Nekoosa, handling stock and making deliveries. In early matches with locals, he displayed great strength and coordination, and with that, his confidence rose. He journeyed to neighboring states for contests with wrestlers of greater skill, and ultimately went to Lexington, Kentucky, where he adopted his trademark name, "Strangler Lewis." Sports writers in Chicago were soon calling him one of the great young stars in the sport, and Lewis' manager, Billy Sandow, a gregarious veteran, added that he was already better than world champion Joe Stecher. Lewis versus Stecher soon became the match everyone wanted to see. However, the two matches between them in 1915 and 1916 were horrible failures. The second, in Omaha on July 4, 1916, ended up going five hours to a draw and was an abysmal exhibition.

On May 2, 1917, Lewis beat John Olin for his first claim to the heavyweight title, albeit a secondary championship to the main line titleholder, Earl Caddock. Even after he lost to Wladek Zbyszko, Lewis and Sandow continued to claim he was champion, furthering their media manipulations. Over the next two years, he beat both Stecher and Zbyszko and held the strongest claim to the title outside Caddock, but then was defeated by Stecher in July of 1919. It wasn't until March 3, 1922 that Lewis regained the world championship, beating Stanislaus Zbyszko, and was finally universally accepted as the king of the heavyweights. For nearly three years, Lewis was champion, demonstrating time after time that his headlock could hospitalize opponents. He went out of his way to draw the ire of crowds, laying the foundation for heel wrestlers, and adding to the passion of frenzied audiences. This component was revolutionary, as was the way they used dramatic angles to prepare challengers in cities on their circuit.

In 1925, Lewis and Sandow propped up a former football player named Wayne Munn and temporarily passed the title to him in an attempt to resurrect declining houses. The idea went south when Munn was double-crossed out of the championship by Stanislaus Zbyszko, and in an instant, the momentum of the wrestling war shifted to an opposing faction. Lewis, in 1928, regained the World Title with a defeat of Stecher, and then sold the crown to Gus Sonnenberg. The loss to Sonnenberg was contingent on the basis that when he was ready to lose the title, he'd do so back to Lewis. That didn't happen, and Lewis had to shoot on Sonnenberg's successor, Ed Don George, to physically take the title back in April 1931. Ironically, Lewis himself was the victim of a shady deal in Montreal the following month, and lost the title to Henri DeGlane. Although he was suffering from an eye disease, trachoma, and had fallen far out of shape, he was still a box office attraction, and returned to the World Title again in New York in 1932.

Lewis was so important to the business that promoters utilized him whenever they could, either as a wrestler, referee, or ambassador to help with publicity and spike attendance . . . and this went on well into the 1950s. Of course, by that point, he was no longer lacing up his boots, but he still was on the road, teaching guys like Lou Thesz and Bob Ellis, and promoting whatever needed to be promoted. Financially crippled, Lewis relied on a special salary from members of the National Wrestling Alliance from 1949 to 1956, and eventually needed donations from old friends to help him survive. When he stepped away from the limelight, he was completely blind and often spoke about religion from the heart. His love of life was apparent, and what he brought to pro wrestling was unlike anyone else in history. Ed "Strangler" Lewis was a game changer, a man who added new levels of ingenuity to the sport, and defied the odds by leaving his small Wisconsin town and rising up to the utmost pinnacles of professional wrestling.

Photo Courtesy of the Pfefer Collection, Department of Special Collections, University of Notre Dame

Londos, Jim

Born:	January 2, 1894
Height:	5'8"
Weight:	210
Real Name:	Christopher Theophelus (many spelling variations)
Wife:	Arva Londos
Trained by:	George Miehling, Al Lavene, Pete Loch
Identities:	Chris Londos
Finishers:	Japanese sleeper, Airplane Spin
Career Span:	1914-1959
Died:	August 19, 1975, Escondido, CA 81 years old

Titles Won:	5, claimed various other titles
Days as World Champion:	Over 9,600
Age at first World Title Win:	36
Best Opponents:	Ed Lewis, Joe Stecher, Dick Shikat
Halls of Fame:	3

During the Great Depression, while people surged toward arenas to be absorbed by the colorful wrestling business and distract themselves from the harsh realities of life, Jim Londos was king of the mountain. He was the heart of the business as World Heavyweight Champion between 1930 and 1935, and was the catalyst for the largest period of growth wrestling had ever seen. His ability as a showman to draw around the country was extraordinary—everyone knew his name and even non-fans were stricken by the urge to see him in person. For Londos, a man who didn't know the proper way to spell his birth name or what year he was truly born, all the success was coming naturally after years of dedication to the sport he loved. Initially an amateur for the San Francisco YMCA and then the Olympic Club, Londos had the spirit to be a champion from day one. He captured the Pacific Athletic Association Light Heavyweight Championship in March of 1912 and made his debut as a professional two years later in Oakland.

Londos engaged in years of straight competition and picked up many tricks of the trade, effectively making him a dangerous shooter . . . the only drawback being his size. However, Londos was bigger than life, and overcame that obstacle time and time again. He began touring, picking up wins from many established wrestlers, even earning a two-hour-and-thirty-minute draw with the mighty Ed "Strangler" Lewis in 1918. Londos was mainly wrestling in secondary cities, and even though he was gaining respect, he didn't rise over the hump until he impressed the New York market with his January 5, 1920 victory over William Demetral.

However, promoters kept him out of the upper echelon, and throughout the 1920s, he bowed against the principal class of heavyweights, losing matches to "Strangler" Lewis, John Pesek, Joe Stecher, Earl Caddock, and others. He bided his time and gained key promotional allies in St. Louis, Philadelphia, and New York, which would catapult him to the top of the ranks.

On June 6, 1930, he beat Dick Shikat for the World Heavyweight Title, and was later recognized by the National Wrestling Association. Unlike his early years, Londos was now unbeatable, toppling opponent after opponent, and winning matches with a flamboyance that sealed his legendary status. His fame at this juncture was comparable to any superstar athlete in any other pro sport, and Londos drew thousands and thousands of fans regularly. He was a true icon during a terrible economic period. Jealousy reared its ugly head, and Londos was faced with a severe backlash after breaking from New York promoter Jack Curley to form his own syndicate in 1932. In retaliation, he was double-crossed in Chicago by a Curley wrestler, Joe Savoldi, on April 7, 1933—and Londos lost a match by pinfall in an unsatisfactory manner. The defeat did little to hurt his reputation.

Following the unification of rival promoters into the "Trust," matches that were previously off limits were being held across the nation, and on June 25, 1934, he beat the New York champion Jim Browning for local recognition. On September 20, he wrestled a dream match against Ed Lewis in Chicago. The affair set a new national gate record when 35,265 fans paid $96,302 to see Londos win. A substantial amount of money was needed for Londos to drop the title, and he was handsomely paid to lose to the "Trust's" next big thing, Danno O'Mahoney, on June 27, 1935 at Fenway Park, ending his reign at 1,847 days. Initially threatening to retire, he quickly changed his tune, and toured Europe and South Africa before returning during the summer of 1937. Within three months, he won a claim to the World Title and was once again doing his part to lure fans to arenas, especially those who'd turned their backs on the sport following the double-cross of O'Mahoney. Huge crowds turned out in Detroit, Philadelphia, and Los Angeles.

Because of his outstanding success, promoters had no other choice but to elevate Londos to the heavyweight throne once again. On November 18, 1938, he beat Bronko Nagurski to win the championship, and would never give up this claim to the world title—maintaining it until his retirement in 1959. Times had changed, and because of the down-slope of the marketplace, he was unable to recapture the same sort of glory he attained in the early part of the 1930s, although he continued to be successful. His athleticism and conditioning were always tip-top, which was surprising for his age, and he had a number of solid showings at the box office, particularly against Primo Carnera and Maurice Tillet. He initially retired in 1954, but had one final run five years later in Australia, of course, going undefeated. Londos' clean cut image and immortal legacy as the undefeated champion are as important to wrestling history as any other single figure to ever grace the ring.

Photo Courtesy of Scott Teal

Born:	March 17, 1897
Height:	5'11"
Weight:	210
Real Name:	Joseph Malcewicz
Parents:	Anthony and Helen Malcewicz
Family:	Brother of Frank Malcewicz
High School:	Utica Free Academy (NY)
Identities:	The Black Terror
Nicknames:	Utica Panther
Finisher:	Flying Scissors
Promoted:	San Francisco, California (1935-1962)
Career Span:	1913-1938
Died:	April 20, 1962, San Francisco, CA 65 years old

Titles Won:	At least 3, claimed several others
Days as World Champion:	Claimed World Title three times for unknown period of time
Age at first World Title Claim:	Around 24
Best Opponents:	Ed Lewis, Joe Stecher, Earl Caddock

Malcewicz, Joe

The San Francisco territory thrived for more than twenty-five years under the expert leadership of Joe Malcewicz. During that time, the payoffs to wrestlers were honest and fair, the booking was intelligent, and fans repeatedly displayed their appreciation of his hard work by packing the Auditorium to see his live shows. A wrestler himself since 1913, Malcewicz was from Utica, New York and trained under an old pro named Herbert Hartley. He served in World War I, earning the rank of sergeant, and by 1920, even the top superstars were impressed with his abilities. Press accounts attributed three claims to the World Heavyweight Title for Malcewicz, but none of them held any real weight. His most substantial claim came as a result of champion Joe Stecher walking out on a match in Boston in 1926. Malcewicz was also the California Champion twice.

Photo Courtesy of the Collection of Tim Hornbaker

Born:	June 30, 1891
Height:	5'11"
Weight:	310
Real Name:	Frank Simmons Leavitt
Identities:	Soldier Leavitt
Nickname:	Hell's Kitchen Hillbilly
Career Span:	1916-1940
Died:	May 29, 1953, Norcross, GA 61 years old

Titles Won:	None known
Best Opponents:	Jim Londos, Ed Lewis, Vincent Lopez
Movies:	8

Man Mountain Dean

A giant man with a giant personality, Man Mountain Dean was well-liked throughout the sports world. He was actually a monster grappler back when being mammoth was not an altogether positive attribute in pro wrestling, as promoters more often sought athleticism over the freakishly humongous. Initially known as "Soldier Leavitt," based on his military background, he was repackaged as "Man Mountain Dean" in 1932. Dean, who was from New York City, adopted a hillbilly gimmick, and grew a long beard. For his size, he knew his way around the ring, and could put on a good show. In Los Angeles in 1934, he was a huge box office smash, and his bout against Jim Londos set a California state record for attendance. Three years later, he broke his leg in a match and retired. Dean served in both World War I and World War II and worked as a policeman in Miami.

Born:	June 8, 1842
Height:	6'1"
Weight:	240
Real Name:	James Hiram McLaughlin
Parents:	Martin and Elizabeth McLaughlin
Military:	24th New York Cavalry (1864)
Career Span:	1859-1902
Died:	September 11, 1905, Fairbanks, AK 63 years old

Titles Won:	Won several, claimed others
Days as World Champion:	Held collar and elbow title for years
Age at first World Title Win:	27
Best Opponents:	James Owens, William Miller, Homer Lane

McLaughlin, Colonel James

James McLaughlin lived a full life; he was a railroad conductor, gold prospector, military leader, and, last but not least, a champion wrestler. After service in the Civil War, he wrestled all the greats over the next few decades, and in 1901, while in the Klondike, he faced Frank Gotch during their infamous gold-rush tour. McLaughlin scored impressive victories over Louis Ainsworth and Homer Lane early in his career en route to claiming the collar and elbow title of America. On March 10, 1870, he won a tournament in Detroit, capturing a diamond belt, one of the first ever produced. Along with his championships, he also had memorable matches against John McMahon, Henry Dufur, and James Owens. In February of 1874, McLaughlin had a notable bout in San Francisco versus a local hero named "Corduroy" Michael Whalen. Gamblers wagered an astonishing $15,000, but McLaughlin likely disappointed many of them when he won with two straight falls. He was on business in Alaska when he died, and was survived by his widow and daughter.

Photo Courtesy of the Collection of Libnan Ayoub

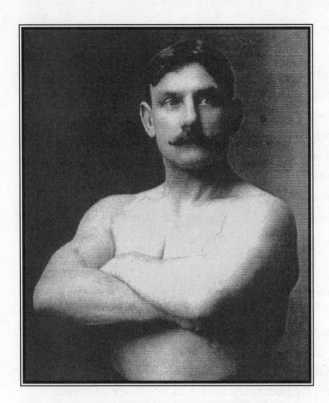

Born:	June 14, 1861
Height:	5'6 ¾"
Weight:	170
Real Name:	Daniel Stewart McLeod
Identities:	George Little
Career Span:	1890-1913
Died:	June 19, 1958, Los Angeles, CA 97 years old

Titles Won:	At least 3
Days as American Champion:	1,571
Age at first American Title Win:	36
Best Opponents:	Tom Jenkins, Farmer Burns, Frank Gotch

McLeod, Dan

Sturdy Dan McLeod was an authority of catch-as-catch-can wrestling at the turn of the 20th century. Born in Illinois to Scottish parents, McLeod enjoyed a whirlwind journey that took him across the U.S. and Canada, and ended up in San Francisco, where he awed contemporaries in the hammer throw, as well as on the mat at the famous Olympic Club. He worked out regularly with boxing champion James J. Corbett, and between 1897 and 1903, held the American Heavyweight Wrestling Championship twice—engaging in a spectacular feud with Tom Jenkins. McLeod's gracefulness in competition was inspiring, and many pros idolized him. As a trainer, he was just as influential, with Pet Brown and Cora Livingston among his students.

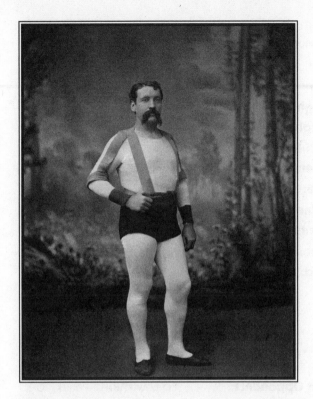

Born:	July 7, 1841
Height:	5'11"
Weight:	180-197
Parents:	Hugh and Bridget Owens McMahon
Military:	Company G, 13th Regiment, Vermont Volunteer Inf. (1862-1863)
Career Span:	1861-1892
Died:	April 3, 1911, Bakersfield, VT 69 years old

Titles Won:	At least 2, claimed several others
Days as World Champion:	Claimed collar and elbow title for over 2,900 days
Age at first World Title Win:	Around 38
Best Opponents:	Henry Dufur, James Owens, James McLaughlin

McMahon, John

Civil War veteran John McMahon of Vermont was an early American wrestling legend. He was a master at the collar-and-elbow style, and demonstrated his profound athletic prowess by throwing seventeen of his fellow soldiers one evening at Brattleboro. As a member of the Vermont Volunteer Infantry, McMahon served in combat for two years and gained his earliest fame as a grappler in 1873 when he won matches against Homer Lane and Perry Higley. In November of 1878, McMahon won an exciting contest from Colonel McLaughlin and then topped his cousin James Owens on August 6, 1879. McMahon claimed the World Title, and carried a belt to signify his status. He ran into perhaps his greatest opponent, Henry Dufur, in 1880. Dufur also claimed to be champion and their first match was a competitive six-hour draw. Their second bout in December 1883 ended when McMahon forfeited, and then Dufur won the title from him on September 3, 1887. McMahon retired in 1892 and suffered from rheumatism before passing away on his brother's farm. At the time of his death, McMahon still held his prized collar and elbow belt.

Born:	January 18, 1894
Height:	5'11"
Weight:	225
Real Name:	James Ervin Mondt
Parents:	Frank and Lula Mondt
Wife:	Alda Mondt
Trained by:	Farmer Burns
Identities:	The Masked Marvel, Tudor Mondt
Career Span:	1910-1932
Died:	June 11, 1976, St. Louis, MO 82 years old

Titles Won:	Claimed a variety of regional titles
Best Opponents:	Ed Lewis, John Pesek, Joe Stecher
Halls of Fame:	2

Mondt, Joe "Toots"

The history of Joe "Toots" Mondt is a complicated one, full of impressive achievements and dramatic catastrophes. Born in Iowa, Mondt grew up in Weld County, Colorado, and was one of eight children. Along with his brother Art, he appeared in vaudeville shows throughout the region, and featured exhibitions of strength and colorful wrestling demonstrations, which mixed light drama and comedy. Mondt gained a sense for entertaining audiences and fulfilling the desires of paying customers, playing to their emotions in the athletic realm. Soon, he was also wrestling in carnivals and testing his physical abilities in straight contests. These contests carved out the "shooter" he'd become, a dangerous wrestler in possession of genuine abilities. Mondt mixed his legitimate skills with fanciful showmanship, becoming a uniquely powerful figure in the business, particularly as it related to his position in the Ed Lewis combine between 1922 and 1927.

In addition to being a sturdy challenger to Lewis, Mondt was an intelligent force outside of the ring. His knack for drama helped conceive what are commonly known as "angles," devised to stir up interest through in-ring disputes or other means. This built up a system of challengers for Lewis throughout their circuit, creating a buzz and spiking attendance. His innovative ideas were embraced by top managers and promoters, and by the late 1920s, he was working behind the scenes in New York City. "Toots" spent time in Los Angeles before returning to New York in 1940, and managed a sizeable booking office, including lucrative operations at Madison Square Garden. By 1954, however, Mondt had driven his company into bankruptcy, and his infatuation with the race track was at the heart of his issues. Still looked to for wisdom, he acted in an advisory role in Vincent J. McMahon's WWWF (forefather to the WWF, then WWE). He retired to St. Louis in the early 1970s.

Born:	May 25, 1845
Height:	5'9"
Weight:	210
Real Name:	William H. Muldoon
Parents:	Patrick and Marie Muldoon
Family:	Brother of Martin Muldoon
Trained by:	Professor William Miller
Nicknames:	Solid Man
Career Span:	Early 1870s-1894
Died:	June 3, 1933, Purchase, NY 88 years old

Titles Won:	At least 3
Days as World Champion:	Over 2,700 days (not counting 1886-1890 claim)
Age at first World Title Win:	34
Best Opponents:	William Miller, Evan Lewis, Duncan Ross
Halls of Fame:	2

Muldoon, William

Perhaps no man has had more of an impact on both professional wrestling and boxing than William Muldoon. His influence was far reaching, inside the ring and out, and lasted more than fifty years. These statements are not embellishments of the facts, but revealing of a man, known as the "Iron Duke," who was known as the best Greco-Roman wrestler of his day and the czar of boxing. He didn't hold both distinctions concurrently, but did so over the span of his career. Beginning as a young man, Muldoon wrestled initially for the athletic challenge, later on for financial gain, and continued after becoming a police officer in New York City around 1876. He was versed in a number of different styles, but none more than the Greco-Roman, and began to make a real name for himself at the annual Police Athletic Games in 1877-1878. Taking a win from James Quigley, a patrolman on the force, he annexed the club's heavyweight "challenge" medal, only to vacate the title of champion to challenge the known professionals of America.

Muldoon won a gold medal with his January 19, 1880 victory over Thiebaud Bauer and claimed the World Heavyweight Title. He accepted the challenge of Professor William Miller two months later and the two men wrestled to a seven-hour draw at Madison Square Garden. His quickness and clever abilities fended off Miller's size advantage, and neither was able to secure a fall. Muldoon's conditioning was tested again in a six-hour match against Clarence Whistler the following January. He often wrestled in mixed-style matches and was occasionally defeated, but Muldoon remained the closest to undisputed Greco-Roman champion until June 28, 1886, when he was defeated by Evan "Strangler" Lewis in Chicago in a controversial bout. Upon losing the first fall and then winning the second, Muldoon gave Lewis the match, claiming to be sick.

However, it was also reported that Muldoon quit because the crowd was small, and that his title wasn't on the line. Lewis believed otherwise, but Muldoon continued to claim his title.

In 1889, Muldoon was the primary trainer for legendary bare-knuckle boxing champion John L. Sullivan, preparing the latter for his famous bout against Jake Kilrain. Their camp was at Muldoon's childhood home in Allegany County, New York. On May 28, 1889 in Cincinnati, the two men even wrestled an exhibition, and went ten rounds to a draw. Muldoon shaped Sullivan into a warrior, giving him the tools he'd need to withstand seventy-five rounds against Kilrain in Richburg, Mississippi. In 1891, Muldoon announced his intention to retire, specifically telling his longtime foe, "Strangler" Lewis that he wasn't going to defend the Greco-Roman title anymore. He touted his star pupil Ernest Roeber, his successor as claimant, and backed him financially. Muldoon ran an athletic combination for some time, appeared as an actor, and, in 1921, became an original member of the newly-established New York Athletic Commission. He remained a pivotal voice in athletics until his death in 1933.

Photo Courtesy of the Pfefer Collection, Department of Special Collections, University of Notre Dame

Born:	December 6, 1898
Height:	5'10"
Weight:	175
Real Name:	Clifford Hugh Nichols
Parents:	George and Lucile Nichols
Wife:	Elizabeth Nichols
Finisher:	Double Japanese toehold
Career Span:	1919-1938
Died:	December 15, 1956, Hollywood, CA 58 years old

Titles Won:	8, claimed others
Best Opponents:	Clarence Eklund, Ted Thye, Billy Edwards

Nichols, Hugh

Speedy Hugh Nichols was a rare breed of wrestler, capable of holding world championships in two separate weight divisions simultaneously. Born in Cedar Rapids, Iowa, he was discovered by Jack Reynolds, and further trained by the legendary Farmer Burns. Destined for greatness, Nichols ventured to Dallas and built a strong following of fans, and then beat Billy Edwards for his first World Light Heavyweight Title on March 7, 1927. The following September, he defeated Joe Parelli for a claim to the World Middleweight belt, becoming a double champion. Over the next decade, he'd win the light heavyweight championship at least five more times. In 1939, he became the matchmaker at Hollywood Legion Stadium and also promoted shows in San Diego until his suicide in 1956. During his career, he was an important and influential advocate for non-heavyweight wrestlers. His clever, scientific approach to wrestling was lauded, and yet he was willing to get down and dirty and fight with the best of them.

Born:	June 26, 1882
Height:	5'11"
Weight:	210
Real Name:	Henry Gyntner Ordemann
Wife:	Margaret Ordemann
Finisher:	Toehold
Career Span:	1907-1924
Died:	June 8, 1947, Minneapolis, MN 64 years old

Titles Won:	At least 3, claimed others
Days as World Champion:	Unknown
Age at first World Title Win:	32
Best Opponents:	Frank Gotch, Jess Westergaard, Stanislaus Zbyszko

Ordemann, Henry

Long before Verne Gagne ruled Minneapolis wrestling rings, Henry Ordemann was the local hero and a heavyweight sensation. Originally from Bergen, Norway, where he was an accomplished bicyclist and oarsman, Ordemann came to the United States in 1903. He built upon his strength as a blacksmith and joined a Minneapolis gym, training with well-known police wrestler John Gordon. In 1908, he met Frank Gotch and went on the road with the champion, learning many aspects of the business, including how to be successful with the toehold. Ordemann beat Dr. Roller, Fred Beell, and Charles Olson, and then won the American Title in 1910 when Gotch gave up the championship to the winner of Ordemann's bout with Charles Cutler. He'd win the title two additional times, plus claim the highly disputed World Title in 1914. Later on in his career, he'd lose matches to the leaders of the next generation of superstars: Ed Lewis and Joe Stecher.

Photo Courtesy of the Pfefer Collection, Department of Special Collections, University of Notre Dame

Born:	August 9, 1895
Height:	6'0"
Weight:	210
Real Name:	Nathaniel Greene Pendleton
College Ach.:	Two-Time Eastern Conference Champion (1914-1915)
Amateur Titles:	Two-Time AAU Champion
Trained by:	George Bothner
Finisher:	Japanese armlock
Career Span:	1920-1932
Died:	October 12, 1967, San Diego, CA 72 years old

Titles Won:	None
Best Opponents:	John Pesek, Wladek Zbyszko, Ivan Poddubny

Pendleton, Nat

Wrestler-turned-actor Nat Pendleton performed in more than 100 television and film projects, while wrestling professionally for a dozen years. Originally from Davenport, Iowa, he was educated at Columbia University and was an amateur grappler at the New York Athletic Club. He won a number of titles, and then took the silver medal at the 1920 Olympics in Antwerp. Later that same year, he turned pro, and began an impressive winning streak. In 1923, he confidently went to Boston to face an unknown wrestler promoted by a rival troupe, and was thrashed by "Tigerman" John Pesek, suffering torn ligaments in his leg during the brutal contest. The loss, his first on the pro mat, shattered the mystique of invincibility surrounding Pendleton, and Nat ultimately became more interested in what Hollywood had to offer. He acted alongside many legends of the screen to include Lionel Barrymore, James Stewart, Humphrey Bogart, and the Marx Brothers between 1924 and 1956.

Photo Courtesy of the Pfefer Collection, Department of Special Collections, University of Notre Dame

Born:	February 3, 1893
Height:	5'11"
Weight:	185
Parents:	Martin and Anna Pesek
Wife:	Myrl Pesek
Family:	Older brother of Charles Pesek, father of Jack Pesek Jr.
Trained by:	Clarence Eklund
Finisher:	Toehold, bar-arm wrist lock, double-wristlock
Career Span:	1913-1959
Died:	March 12, 1978, Ravenna, NE 84 years old

Pesek, John

Titles Won:	4, awarded and claimed others
Days as World Champion:	Over 3,816
Age at first World Title Win:	38
Best Opponents:	Ed Lewis, Joe Stecher, Earl Caddock
Halls of Fame:	4

In wrestling history, very few have had comparable talents to the "Tigerman," John Pesek of Buffalo County, Nebraska. Sporting cat-like reflexes and speed, and a mastery of holds, he was nearly unbeatable. Pesek's aggressive style had widespread box office appeal, and had wrestling been completely on the level, he would've been a hard man to topple from the mountain. At a time in which reputations were everything, Pesek was thoroughly respected by his peers for what he was capable of on the mat. One of seven children born to a Bohemian farmer, Pesek was naturally gifted and relied heavily on his instincts. His extraordinary ability shone through during his first couple years in the profession, and he was already far more advanced than the veterans in the region. Pesek showed no fear going into matches against opponents of greater repute or weight, and beat one after another. The vanquished reads like a who's who of pro wrestling: Clarence Eklund, Charles Cutler, and Wladek Zbyszko were among them.

Pesek joined the Ed "Strangler" Lewis combine in 1921 and became one of the top challengers to Lewis' world heavyweight championship. Lewis utilized Pesek's otherworldly talents as his protector against independent wrestlers, meaning that if an outsider wanted a crack at the title, they'd have to earn it by beating Pesek first—and that wasn't happening. Having Pesek around was a major deterrent. In 1931, after years of being dubbed the uncrowned champion, he was recognized as the MWA World Titleholder in Ohio, and he'd hold MWA recognition three separate times, and in September of 1937, he was also supported by the National Wrestling Association as World Champion. Away from the squared circle, Pesek was a champion greyhound racing owner, leading hall of fame dogs "Gangster," "Just Andrew," and "Tell You Why." During the last twenty years on the mat, Pesek was never defeated clean in the ring, and he's since been enshrined in four halls of fame, recognizing his remarkable achievements.

Photo Courtesy of the Pfefer Collection, Department of Special Collections, University of Notre Dame

Born:	July 20, 1887
Height:	6'2"
Weight:	240
Wife:	Lucritza Plestina
Trained by:	Charles Cutler, Farmer Burns, Frank Gotch, Pete Loch
Nickname:	Tarzan of the Mat, Marin the Mauler
Career Span:	1910-1939
Died:	December 26, 1945, Chicago, IL 58 years old

Plestina, Marin

Titles Won:	None, claimed world title in 1920
Days as World Champion:	Unknown
Age at first World Title Claim:	Around 32
Best Opponents:	Ed Lewis, John Pesek, Joe Stecher

   Out of middle of the chaotic Frank Gotch era came Marin Plestina, a Yugoslavian transplant to Chicago who was a common headliner, but played second fiddle to many of the more well-known heavyweights. Powerfully built, he worked out of the Gotch camp early in his career, gaining victories over Fred Beell and Ed "Strangler" Lewis, but losing to Joe Stecher, Charles Cutler, Earl Caddock, and Stanislaus Zbyszko. By 1918, Plestina had gained boisterous J.C. Marsh as his manager and announced that everyone of importance was dodging him. After failing to overcome the syndicate policeman, John Pesek, in two controversial matches, Plestina eventually decided to end the charade of being a trustbuster and went to work for the major troupes, but he never again made headlines like he did when he was besmirching every champion and declaring them unworthy.

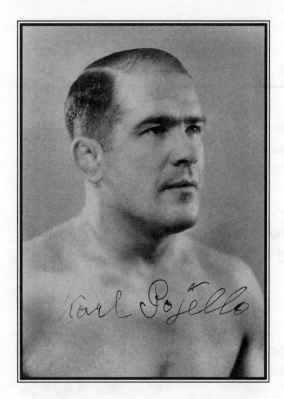

Born:	Around 1883
Height:	5'8"
Weight:	205
Real Name:	Karl Antonovich Pojello
Wife:	Olga Pojello
Career Span:	Unknown debut year-1945
Died:	August 3, 1954, Chicago, IL 71 years old

Titles Won:	Claimed at least two
Best Opponents:	Jim Londos, Jim Browning, Yvon Robert

Pojello, Karl

Commonly described as being unsuspecting in appearance, Karl Pojello was a dangerous wrestler with all the tools to break an opponent's bones with ease. Hailing from Steigvilai, Lithuania, he wrestled the Greco-Roman style exclusively before venturing westward across Siberia and into China and Japan, where he practiced jiu-jitsu and other combat forms. He toured the U.S. in the beginning in 1923 and was acknowledged as the Lithuanian Light Heavyweight Champion. As a member of the wrestling trust, he wrestled all the top names, and later discovered legend-to-be, "French Angel" Maurice Tillet in Singapore. Pojello trained many wrestlers and promoted smaller clubs in the Chicago area into the early 1950s.

Photo Courtesy of the Pfefer Collection, Department of Special Collections, University of Notre Dame

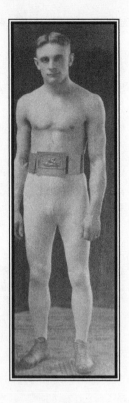

Born:	February 7, 1894
Height:	5'6 ½"
Weight:	145
Real Name:	Charles Voris Reynolds
Parents:	William and Nancy Reynolds
Wife:	Alice Dale Reynolds
Family:	Brother of Art Reynolds
High School:	Center Point High School (IA)
Career Span:	1910-1937
Died:	January 9, 1945, Covington, KY 51 years old

Titles Won:	15
Best Opponents:	Matty Matsuda, Bobby Chick, Robin Reed

Reynolds, Jack

The legendary Jack Reynolds usually entered the squared circle at about 145 pounds and was a standout welterweight for more than twenty years, claiming the world championship at least fourteen times. Clever, fast, and scientific, the Cedar Point, Iowa product was the youngest of seven sons, and trained with Farmer Burns and Frank Gotch early in his career. On January 8, 1914, he beat Cyclone Parker in Idaho Falls to capture his first welterweight title, and won his last title twenty-one years later. While an immensely talented grappler, Reynolds was also a capable showman, and he was a successful draw all over the country. In 1934, he was charged with second degree murder after a man died in a bar fight he was involved in, but he was later acquitted. Later in the 1930s, Reynolds ran a wrestling outfit of non-heavyweights on the West Coast, sometimes staging athletic (AT) shows at carnivals, and retired from the ring in 1937.

Photo Courtesy of Jane Byrnes

Born:	June 22, 1896
Height:	5'10 ½"
Weight:	175
Real Name:	William Harold Riley
Parents:	Patrick and Jane Riley
Wife:	Sarah Riley
Family:	Father of Ernie Riley
Trained by:	Billy Charnock
Trained:	Bert Assirati, Karl Gotch, Billy Joyce, Billy Robinson, Jack Dempsey, Roy Wood, and scores of others
Career Span:	1909-1968
Died:	September 15, 1977, Wigan, England 81 years old

Titles Won:	At least 2
Days as World MW Champion:	Reportedly claimed title for 18 years
Best Opponents:	Jack Robinson, Bobby Myers, Billy Moores

Riley, Billy

The "Old Master" Billy Riley taught the legitimate art of professional catch-as-catch-can wrestling at the renowned "Snake Pit" training center in England. He kept it up well after the need for real wrestlers had disappeared from the marketplace, as promoters sought hulking and colorful performers. It didn't matter to Riley. Some of his graduates were among the best catch grapplers in the world. From Wigan, Lancashire, Riley turned pro at fourteen and made a tour of the U.S. in 1923. A year later, he claimed the World Middleweight Title, and his *Wigan Observer* obituary stated that he remained champion for eighteen years. In 1933-1934, he toured South Africa, furthering his international exposure. Back at his gym, more and more youngsters learned his famous teachings, and his influence was felt in all corners of the wrestling world— and still is to this day.

Photo Courtesy of the Pfefer Collection, Department of Special Collections, University of Notre Dame

Born:	September 18, 1862
Height:	5'7"
Weight:	195
Real Name:	Ernst Roeber
Managed by:	William Muldoon
Managed:	Ernest Siegfried, Egeberg, Charlie Cutler
Career Span:	1885-1903
Died:	December 14, 1944, Auburndale, NY 82 years old

Titles Won:	At least 2, claimed others
Days as World Champion:	Around eight years
Age at first World Title Win:	29
Best Opponents:	Terrible Turk, Bech-Olsen, Tom Jenkins

Roeber, Ernest

Powerful German-born Ernest Roeber studied wrestling in recreation halls around his home in New York City and was respected for his outstanding Greco-Roman abilities as an amateur. He battled the likes of Young Bibby prior to turning pro and the famed William Muldoon mentored him late in the 1880s. On July 25, 1892, he beat Apollon for the Greco-Roman World Title and claimed global honors in addition to the American championship for the better part of the next eight years. Danish superstar Bech-Olsen took his World Title in March of 1900 at Madison Square Garden. Roeber retired and operated a pub until Prohibition, also working as a referee for the New York Athletic Commission.

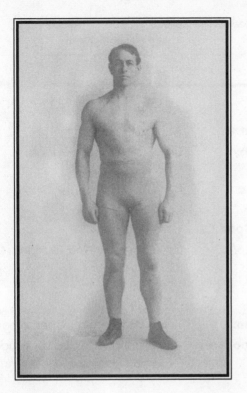

Photo Courtesy of the Pfefer Collection, Department of Special Collections, University of Notre Dame

Born:	July 1, 1876
Height:	6'0"
Weight:	210
Real Name:	Dr. Benjamin Franklin Roller
Parents:	Phillip and Emily Roller
Colleges:	De Pauw University, University of Pennsylvania
Trained by:	Frank Gotch, Joe Carroll Marsh
Identities:	Frank Roller
Career Span:	1906-1919
Died:	April 20, 1933, New York, NY 57 years old

Titles Won:	At least 3, claimed others
Best Opponents:	Frank Gotch, Great Gama, Stanislaus Zbyszko

Roller, Dr. B.F.

An unsung warrior of the early 20th century, Dr. Roller's success as a professional wrestler is usually obscured by the legend of Frank Gotch, as is the case for most heavyweights during that period. For Roller, of Newman, Illinois, he was a legitimate physician, a professional football player, and an intellect. Roller was in the wrestling business to make money, and he did so by playing to audiences, working gimmicks, and feeding into the athletic drama. His actions were no different than those of Gotch or anyone else. Roller traveled across North America and Europe, wrestling all the greats, including the Great Gama, and was, notably, one of George Hackenschmidt's trainers for his 1911 bout with Gotch. He claimed the American Heavyweight Title on several occasions, and intersected with every superstar wrestler from Farmer Burns to Earl Caddock.

Born:	April 7, 1887
Height:	5'9"
Weight:	185
Real Name:	Adolph Ernst Santel
Trained by:	Dick Sorensen, Joe Rogers, Charles Olsen
Identities:	Mysterious Carpenter, Otto Carpenter
Career Span:	1908-1933
Died:	November 10, 1966, Oakland, CA 79 years old

Titles Won:	At least 3, claimed others
Best Opponents:	John Pesek, Ed Lewis, Joe Stecher

Santel, Ad

Although he stood only 5'9", Ad Santel was a giant in the world of catch-as-catch-can wrestling. He began his career in Chicago after emigrating from Germany in 1907, and was an astute student of various wrestling and martial arts fundamentals. He was the only man to train with both Frank Gotch and George Hackenschmidt before their two legendary matches. By 1913, he claimed the World Light Heavyweight Title and affirmed his status as the rightful champion into the late 1920s. He successfully toured Japan in 1921, defeating jiu-jitsu expert Tokugoro Ito, and spread interest in American-style wrestling abroad. For over fifteen years, he made San Francisco his headquarters, and battled all the big names that toured through the city. In 1931, he partnered with his brother-in-law, Ernest Feddersen, to promote Oakland, and he would continue until the region was monopolized by Roy Shire thirty years later.

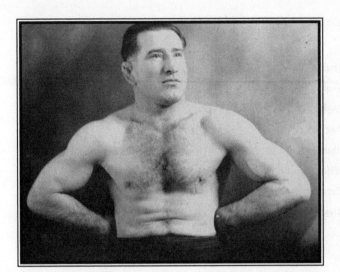

Photo Courtesy of Yasutoshi Ishikawa

Born:	October 18, 1894
Height:	6'0"
Weight:	225
Real Name:	Ivan Seric
Trained by:	Farmer Burns
Nickname:	Blackjack
Finisher:	Half-Nelson and scissors
Career Span:	1917-1950
Died:	October 11, 1969, Los Angeles, CA 74 years old

Sherry, Jack

Titles Won:	None known, claimed at least 3
Days as World Champion:	Unknown
Age at first World Title Win:	Around 26 when he claimed title in 1920
Best Opponents:	John Pesek, Ed Lewis, Henri DeGlane

Born in Yugoslavia and billed as an Alaskan Indian, Jack Sherry was a dangerous hooker, which in wrestling lingo meant that he had the ability to injure less capable opponents in matches. The reputation that preceded him came with a warning that he was a trustbuster and an independent, often unwilling to work for the mainstream promotional establishment. Sherry did conform at times, but he was definitely a rebel for most of his career. He claimed to be the uncrowned heavyweight champion until a comparable rival, John Pesek, nearly killed him in a match in Columbus in 1927. Six years later, he again proclaimed himself champion, stating that "Strangler" Lewis ran out on a bout with him at Philadelphia. Sherry wrestled all over the world and was recognized as titleholder during his tours of England. As late as 1948, Sherry was confidently issuing challenges, and nearly came to grips with Lewis for a shoot in Hawaii in January of that year, but it never happened.

Born:	January 11, 1897
Height:	6'1"
Weight:	225
Real Name:	Richard Scheckat
Family:	Brother of Joe and Paul Scheckat
Wife:	Ereka Schikat
Career Span:	1918-1953
Died:	December 3, 1968, New York, NY 71 years old

Titles Won:	3
Days as World Champion:	351
Age at first World Title Win:	32
Best Opponents:	Jim Londos, Ed Lewis, Stanislaus Zbyszko

Shikat, Dick

From Ragnit, East Prussia, Dick Shikat excelled in the Greco-Roman style of wrestling following his naval service in World War I. Along with Hans Steinke, he came to the U.S. on October 9, 1923 and quickly adapted to the American catch-as-catch-can ring method, proving to be a valuable asset to promoters. His quickness and aptitude earned him the respect of fans, and adding his size and strength, made him a top newcomer. In 1928, he received a significant push in Philadelphia, and, after taking "Toots" Mondt as his manager, was directly in line for a shot at the vacant World Heavyweight Title, supported by the Pennsylvania and New York Athletic Commissions. Before an estimated 30,000 fans at the Municipal Stadium in Philadelphia, Shikat took a popular victory from Jim Londos for the championship on August 23, 1929 and was presented with a belt valued at $5,000. Ironically, a few days later, Shikat left his new belt in the back of a New York City taxi and never saw it again.

The meteoric rise of Londos as a superstar in the industry was not ignored by promoters, and the Greek wrestler succeeded Shikat as the titleholder. Shikat's reign, lasting until June 6, 1930, was successful, and he reportedly made $250,000 while he was champion. For most of the next five years, he toiled around the wrestling circuit, drawing good houses in big matches, and performing as promoters expected. That would change on March 2, 1936, when he decided to lash out at the wrestling "trust" by double-crossing world champion Danno O'Mahoney at Madison Square Garden, and winning the title by submission. He remained champion until April 24, 1936, losing the championship to Ali Baba in Detroit. After his wife's unexpected death in early May 1936, Shikat scaled back his commitment to wrestling. He owned a bar in Buenos Aires for a time and became a Merchant Marine. On several ocean liners in the 1950s, he worked as a physical instructor and pool attendant.

Born:	April 5, 1893
Height:	6'0"
Weight:	225
Real Name:	Joseph James Stecher
Parents:	Frank and Anna Stecher
Wife:	Frances Ehlers Stecher
Military:	United States Navy (WWI)
Finisher:	Scissors leghold
Career Span:	1912-1934
Died:	March 26, 1974, St. Cloud, MN 80 years old

Titles Won:	6
Days as World Champion:	2,224
Age at first World Title Win:	22
Best Opponents:	Ed Lewis, Earl Caddock, John Pesek
Halls of Fame:	4

Stecher, Joe

On a very short list of greatest natural professional wrestlers in history, "Scissors" Joe Stecher, who held the World Heavyweight Title five times, including the undisputed championship in 1920, is most certainly one of them. He was a low-key athlete, very much unlike his number one ring adversary, Ed "Strangler" Lewis, who commanded attention. They were different in so many ways, from personality to body type, but when they faced off, there was a distinct struggle for superiority that neither wanted to give in to. Stecher, from Dodge, Nebraska, was one of ten children born to Bohemian parents, and worked on their farm in his youth. At the age of nineteen, he ventured to Iowa to labor on the farm of Frank Petit, and in April 1912, he opposed a local in a wrestling match at a hall in Berea. His opponent was none other than Earl Caddock, a future world champion himself—and one of Stecher's greatest all-time opponents. Before thirty-one people, Stecher won the first and third falls, garnered a few bucks, and became a pro wrestler.

Stecher trained exceptionally hard, focusing on his leg muscles, and developed his famous scissors hold that would finish off many of his rivals. He went on a tear following his debut, defeating opponent after opponent, and went undefeated for over four years. In the midst of his run, he toppled Charles Cutler for a claim to the World Heavyweight Title on July 5, 1915. Although he beat Cutler fair and square and was given a $3,000 gold belt emblematic of the championship, Stecher's rightful claim to the title was still somewhat disputed. That was because American hero Frank Gotch had never lost his title in the ring. Promoters tried every conceivable way to match the two, but Gotch suffered a broken leg in an exhibition, and died a year later, with Stecher versus Gotch being the best match in wrestling history that never happened. As the defending champion, and against all types of opponents, Stecher demonstrated his ring mastery, and lived up to expectations wherever he traveled.

However, there were exceptions, especially when it came to his first two pro losses. While on tour of the east, Stecher inexplicably walked out during a lengthy match against John Olin in Springfield, Massachusetts on December 11, 1916, and the defeat soured his reputation as a title claimant. On April 9, 1917, he was officially stripped of his World Title by Caddock, again, under somewhat dubious circumstances. Apparently, it was claimed that he told officials he was unable to continue, which was later denied. Nevertheless, Caddock was declared the champion. With victories over Wladek Zbyszko and Ed Lewis, Stecher regained a claim to the World Title in 1919, and waited for his return match against Caddock, who'd been injured during the war.

Things came together for a huge spectacular at Madison Square Garden in New York on January 30, 1920, pitting the rival championships of Stecher against Caddock. That night, Stecher became the undisputed titleholder after more than two hours of competition.

Lewis beat Stecher in December of 1920, and instead of continuing to chase the title, he went into semi-retirement, focusing more on baseball and other interests. He returned to beat Stanislaus Zbyszko for his fifth and final reign as World Titleholder on May 30, 1925, and held the championship until February 20, 1928, when Lewis won a three-fall encounter in St. Louis. Following his loss, Stecher took a backseat to the next generation of superstars and embraced a role as perpetual challenger. An injury in 1934 sidelined him, and Joe soon announced his retirement. In the years that followed, he was haunted by considerable financial problems. The *Associated Press*, on July 14, 1937, reported that the forty-four year-old Stecher was near death at a VA hospital in St. Cloud, Minnesota after suffering a nervous breakdown. Once an unbeatable force, Stecher was faltering mentally and physically, and never regained his health. He remained hospitalized until his passing in 1974.

Photo Courtesy of the Pfefer Collection, Department of Special Collections, University of Notre Dame

Steele, Ray

Born:	February 8, 1900
Height:	5'11"
Weight:	215
Real Name:	Peter Sauer
Parents:	Conrad and Catharina Sauer
Family:	Uncle of George Sauer
Wife:	Annie Sauer
Trained by:	George (Barnes) Sauer, Lloyd Carter
Identities:	Roy Steele, The Masked Marvel
Career Span:	1918-1949
Died:	September 11, 1949, Warm Lake, ID 49 years old

Titles Won:	7
Days as World Champion:	Around 580
Age at first World Title Win:	36
Best Opponents:	Jim Londos, Ed Lewis, Clarence Eklund
Halls of Fame:	3

Feared shooter Ray Steele was also a well-liked practical jokester, who was known for keeping things lively behind the scenes. However, his wrestling was anything but funny. Over the course of his thirty-one year career, he was highly successful and influential, winning championships in the ring and teaching others what he knew about the business. Born in Nokra, Russia, Steele was raised by an uncle and aunt in Lincoln, Nebraska, and took an interest in grappling after his older brother George began competing as a middleweight. Steele trained under Farmer Burns, and then wrestled as an amateur before making his pro debut as a teenager. Within a year, he'd travel to Wyoming and had several grueling matches against one of the best in the industry, Clarence Eklund. Despite his age, Steele was very impressive in his bout. Steele was already considered a future champion, and honed his skills in further training with John Pesek, the famed "Tigerman."

Victories over the British and Canadian claimants set up a rematch with Eklund in October of 1922 in Santa Paula, California, which Steele won and claimed the World Light Heavyweight Title. Around 1927, he adopted the name "Ray Steele," using it in certain cities and his real name in others. Heavyweight champion Jim Londos would become his greatest in-ring rival, and the two met numerous times before huge throngs of people. Little did people know that Steele, in fact, worked as Londos's "policeman," meaning that he protected the champion from rogue opponents. Steele was briefly World Champion in Ohio in 1937, and then won the National Wrestling Association championship from Bronko Nagurski on March 7, 1940—holding it for a little more than year. He also held the National Wrestling Alliance Title in Iowa in 1943-1944. The always competitive Steele was planning a comeback when he died unexpectedly in 1949.

Photo Courtesy of the Pfefer Collection, Department of Special Collections, University of Notre Dame

Born:	February 22, 1893
Height:	6'3"
Weight:	250
Real Name:	Johannes Steinke
Nickname:	The German Oak
Hollywood:	Appeared in the films, *Deception* (1932), *Island of Lost Souls* (1933) with Constantine Romanoff and Ali Baba, *Sweet Cookie* (1933), *Reckless* (1935—scenes deleted), *Once in a Blue Moon* (1935), *People Will Talk* (1935), *Nothing Sacred* (1937), and *The Buccaneer* (1938)
Career Span:	1919-1949
Died:	June 26, 1971, Chicago, IL 78 years old

Steinke, Hans

Titles Won:	Claimed several titles
Days as World Champion:	Unknown time as claimant
Age at first World Title Win:	35
Best Opponents:	Jim Londos, Dick Shikat, Ed Lewis

Exceptionally powerful, sometimes unruly, Hans Steinke of Stettin, Germany was an amateur Greco-Roman wrestling sensation in Europe around the time of World War I. In 1923, he ventured to the U.S., and adjusted to the American catch-as-catch-can form under the tutelage of Johnny Meyers and Wladek Zbyszko. He was embraced by promoter Jack Curley of New York City and pushed as a claimant to the world championship in 1928 after Curley's adversary Ed Lewis won the legit title. Steinke toiled as Jim Londos' policeman and worked the national circuit until retiring to Chicago in the 1940s. His brother Max was also a professional wrestler.

Photo Courtesy of the Pfefer Collection, Department of Special Collections, University of Notre Dame

Born:	January 6, 1887
Height:	6'1"
Weight:	220
Real Name:	John Taylor
Parents:	James and Euphemia Taylor
Military:	United States Army (WWI)
Career Span:	1911-1939
Died:	May 19, 1956, Edmonton, Alberta 69 years old

Titles Won:	At least 3, claimed variety of state titles
Days as World Champion:	90
Age at first World Title Win:	27
Best Opponents:	Joe Stecher, Ad Santel, John Pesek
Halls of Fame:	1

Taylor, Jack

Legendary Canadian heavyweight Jack Taylor was born in Greenock, Ontario, the second of six children. He made history when he beat Charlie Cutler in a controversial match in Winnipeg on November 25, 1914, defeating the latter by disqualification and taking a claim to the World Title. In February of 1915, he lost the championship to Joe Stecher. Taylor bought some land in Buffalo, Wyoming near the homestead of friend and mentor Clarence Eklund in 1917, and served in the Army during the war. He also faced and defeated many top names in the sport, including the Zbyszko Brothers, Ad Santel, and Bob Managoff. In the 1920s and early 1930s, he held the Canadian and British Empire Titles. A difficult man to beat, Taylor was instrumental in the careers of Earl McCready and Stu Hart.

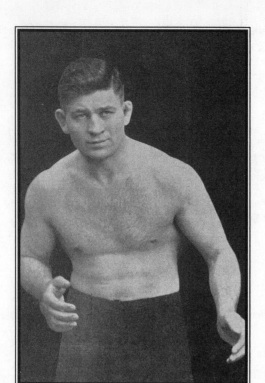

Born:	August 26, 1890
Height:	5'8"
Weight:	175
Real Name:	Theodore Thye
Parents:	Andrew and Bertha Thye
Trained by:	Dave Burns, Dr. John Berg
Career Span:	1915-1935
Died:	March 21, 1966, Portland, OR 75 years old

Titles Won:	7, claimed at least one other
Best Opponents:	Clarence Eklund, Mike Yokel, Walter Miller

Thye, Ted

Globetrotting Ted Thye was a celebrated wrestler, and in the 1920s, helped popularize the American style of grappling in Australia. Originally from Frederick, South Dakota, he migrated to the Pacific Northwest and took up wrestling at an amateur club in Spokane, Washington. By 1915, he was claiming the middleweight championship of the Pacific Coast. He beat Walter Miller, a career-long ring nemesis, in June 1919 for a claim to the disputed World Middleweight Title. Rarely did a sportswriter remark that a Thye match was anything but "thrilling," and he was overwhelmingly popular in his hometown of Portland. A master of leverage and proponent of the wristlock submission hold, Thye moved up to the light heavyweight division, and held the world title six times between 1920 and 1927. He first went to Australia in 1924, and in each of the next three years, returned to that country to headline, drawing huge crowds at shows. Later, he worked as a booking agent in the Pacific Northwest territory, Australia, and throughout the South Pacific.

Born:	February 28, 1882
Height:	6'2"
Weight:	220
Real Name:	Nels Jesse Reimer
Wife:	Anna Reimer
Managers:	Oscar Thorson, Emil Klank
Career Span:	1905-1925
Died:	Unknown

Titles Won:	3
Best Opponents:	Frank Gotch, George Hackenschmidt, and Stanislaus Zbyszko

Westergaard, Jess

The heartland of the U.S. was bursting with wrestling talent during the first quarter of the 20th century. Among them was Jess Westergaard of Des Moines, Iowa, a Swedish transplant and star heavyweight grappler. Having immigrated to the U.S. from Kristianstad in 1901 with a fine athletic background, Westergaard used his striking size and an education taught by Farmer Burns to tie up opponents. In 1911, he beat Charles Cutler for the American Heavyweight Title, and regained it in January of 1913 with a victory over Henry Ordemann. He built a strong Midwest following and trained regularly with world champion Frank Gotch. Westergaard stepped off the mat to serve as a Des Moines deputy sheriff, and later relocated to Houston.

Zbyszko, Stanislaus

Born:	April 1, 1879
Height:	5'9"
Weight:	240
Real Name:	Stanislaus Cyganiewicz
Parents:	Martin and Caroline Cyganiewicz
Family:	Older brother of Wladek Zbyszko
Nickname:	The Mighty Pole
Finisher:	Bearhug
Career Span:	1901-1932
Died:	September 23, 1967, St. Joseph, MO 88 years old

Titles Won:	3, claimed others
Days as World Champion:	Over 346 (unknown time for 1914 claim)
Age at first World Title Win:	35
Best Opponents:	Frank Gotch, Joe Stecher, Great Gama
Halls of Fame:	2
Movies:	2

When Stanislaus Zbyszko arrived in America in September of 1909, the wrestling landscape changed forever. Although he wasn't adept to the tricky American style of catch-as-catch-can grappling, he was a pure athlete and a proven champion. Born near Krakow, Poland, he began wrestling in 1897 as an amateur and took to the pro sport three years later in Charlottenburg, Germany. He became a world-class Greco-Roman wrestler and engaged in tournaments in Germany and France, and had wins over Ivan Podubny, Alex Aberg, Nouroulah, and George Lurich. He adapted quickly to the rules of catch grappling, using his intellect to outwit opponents, and when he displayed signs of inexperience, he could rely on his extraordinary strength. A prime-time superstar, Zbyszko wanted nothing more than a match with the unconquerable World Champion Frank Gotch. However, when he finally met Gotch on June 1, 1910, things went much different than he hoped—he was beaten in two straight falls and the first was scored in only six seconds.

Educated at the University of Vienna and able to speak eleven languages, Zbyszko was a signature wrestler in the era of Gotch and George Hackenschmidt, and following World War I, he returned to the U.S. to make a further impression on wrestling audiences. On May 6, 1921, he beat Ed "Strangler" Lewis for the World Title and held the championship until March 3, 1922, when he lost it back to Lewis. In a defining moment in the sport's history, he double-crossed Wayne Munn for the heavyweight title on April 15, 1925, and single-handedly seized power from one syndicate and gave it to another, of course for the right price. Zbyszko was briefly the matchmaker at Madison Square Garden in 1930 and made big news in 1932 when he issued a challenge to any college football team for a handicap wrestling match. He boasted that he could beat the entire team within an hour, claiming that he'd defeat the Princeton, Yale, and Harvard squads all in the same night. Zbyszko also appeared in several films, most notably portraying "Gregorius the Great" in the 1950 flick, *Night and the City*.

Photo Courtesy of John Pantozzi

Born:	November 30, 1891
Height:	6'0"
Weight:	230
Real Name:	Wladek Cyganiewicz
Parents:	Martin and Caroline Cyganiewicz
Family:	Younger brother of Stanislaus Zbyszko
Identities:	The Great Apollo (masked)
Nickname:	Polish Hercules
Military:	United States Army (WWI)
Career Span:	1911-1950
Died:	June 10, 1968, Savannah, MO 75 years old

Zbyszko, Wladek

Titles Won:	5
Days as World Champion:	126
Age at first World Title Win:	25
Best Opponents:	Ed Lewis, Joe Stecher, Earl Caddock
Halls of Fame:	2

Wladek Zbyszko is often overshadowed by his older brother, Stanislaus, but he too had a hall of fame career. Zbyszko was a claimant to the heavyweight championship at least four different times, and between 1916 and 1921, he was one of the best wrestlers in the world. Born in Krakow, he wrestled the Greco-Roman style in Europe before venturing to the U.S. in December of 1912. Like his brother, he adjusted to the catch-as-catch-can system of wrestling, and was a sensation on both coasts. In 1917, he beat Ed "Strangler" Lewis two separate times for the World Title, and did it again in March 1919. Owning a part of the Buenos Aires promotion, Zbyszko held his fourth title in Argentina in 1935. He settled in Northwestern Missouri and remained passionate about wrestling, even sending letters to regional promoters about the monopolistic actions he felt were threatening the sport.

II. Gimmicks and Ingenuity Rekindle Wrestling's Popularity
Pro Debut Between 1921 and 1950

A drop-off in attendance in the 1920s pushed innovators Joe "Toots" Mondt, Jack Curley, and Paul Bowser to enhance the sport with creative mechanisms that transformed things once again. The melding of wrestling and football was the most critical concept that was introduced, and former All-American Gus Sonnenberg was the man who revolutionized the business on the mat. His array of ring moves and likeable personality recharged the sport, and it became almost mandatory, regardless of the level of talent, for wrestlers to adopt his famous flying tackle as a finisher. It was so popular that fans demanded it, and the unpredictability of the move was very entertaining for audiences coast-to-coast.

With that said, no single wrestler was more popular than Jim Londos, and his success between 1930 and 1935 was unparalleled at that time. It wasn't until Hulk Hogan came along in the 1980s that Londos' remarkable run was similarly achieved. Londos was the hero that carried wrestling on his back through the Depression years, and even after stepping away from the limelight, promoters beckoned for his star power to reignite lagging arena sales. The late 1930s saw the rise of Lou Thesz to prominence and his legitimate wrestling aptitude was a throwback to the legends of yore. Thesz had all the qualities to dominate the heavyweight division and outside a few years of service during World War II, he did, and his supremacy continued well into the 1960s.

This time period saw the development of the first real wrestling villains, grapplers who purposefully antagonized audiences. Ed "Strangler" Lewis, during his reign as heavyweight champion between 1922 and 1925, drew the ire of crowds with his famed headlock stranglehold, and not only hospitalized opponents with the borderline illegal maneuver, but displayed arrogance in press interviews. Lewis's actions paled in comparison to the rowdy rule-breakers that emerged in the 1930s and 1940s, among them "The Golden Terror" Bobby Stewart and box office sensation "Wild" Bill Longson. The wrestling villain became a fundamental aspect of pro wrestling, and its relevance is as important today as it was seventy years ago.

For a number of reasons, the popularity of grappling went into a tailspin in the late 1930s and remained lackluster throughout North America during World War II with the exception of a few local divisions. The television boom did wonders for wrestling beginning around 1947 and sensational performers like Gorgeous George and Antonino Rocca were overnight phenomenons. Once again, wrestling was at the forefront of American entertainment, and this time around, there were many more intriguing characters on the circuit than at any time in history. Buddy Rogers, Killer Kowalski, and Verne Gagne were among the young stars ready to make a real dent in the industry, and with that kind of talent, wrestling's future looked immensely bright.

Born:	July 9, 1908
Height:	5'7"
Weight:	280
Real Name:	Bartolomeo Assirati
Wife:	Marjorie Assirati
Trained by:	Atholl Oakley, Henry Irslinger, Billy Riley at his famous Wigan Gym
Career Span:	1928-1960
Died:	August 31, 1990, Brighton, England 82 years old

Titles Won:	6
Days as World Champion:	237
Age at first World Title Win:	38
Best Opponents:	Dara Singh, King Kong Czaja, Henri DeGlane
Halls of Fame:	1

Assirati, Bert

An acrobat, strongman, and wrestler with an unprecedented reputation, Bert Assirati was a terrifically dangerous grappler. His offensive weapons of submission were occasionally hazards to rivals expecting to meet in worked affairs, as he was known to be uncooperative in some instances during bouts. With all that, Assirati was still one of the truest of pro wrestlers in the sense that he appreciated the legitimate art of the sport. Originally from London and of Italian parents, Assirati journeyed to the U.S. early in his career and competed at around 210 pounds. By the time he was in his prime, he weighed as much as 280. Standing only 5'7", he was a block of muscle with coordination and quickness to spare. In search of further conquests, Assirati toured the world from Germany to Singapore, and beat King Kong Czaja, Felix Miquet, and Maurice Tillet. He claimed the British Heavyweight throne for well over a decade and held the World Title following a tournament in 1947. Assirati was feared by opponents and beloved by fans that enjoyed his hard-nosed style and overall toughness.

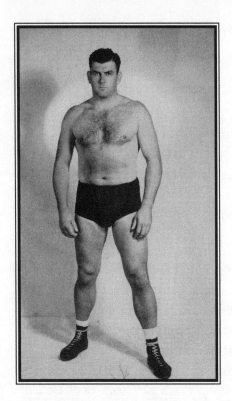

Born:	July 19, 1910
Height:	6'1"
Weight:	250
Real Name:	Robert Frederick Atkinson
Nickname:	Hard Rock from Down Under
Finishers:	Airplane Spin, Piledriver
Career Span:	1934-1964
Died:	May 15, 1988, Crystal Beach, Ontario 77 years old

Titles Won:	9
Best Opponents:	Billy Watson, Pat O'Connor, Don Leo Jonathan

Atkins, Fred

During his thirty-year career, Fred Atkins was a champion in Australia, Canada, and the United States. Originally from New Zealand, Atkins was a rugged individual in the ring, using his strength to overpower opponents, and relied on heel tactics, although he had the skill and ability to wrestle the pure catch style. He held the Australian national heavyweight championship for a number of years, and in 1949, he beat "Whipper" Billy Watson for the British Empire Title. Additionally, Atkins was an influential trainer, helping develop superstars like Giant Baba and Adrian Adonis.

Born:	September 14, 1901
Height:	5'6"
Weight:	205
Real Name:	Arteen "Harry" K. Ekizian
High School:	Pasadena High School (CA)
College:	Pasadena Junior College
Trained by:	Farmer Burns
Identities:	Harry Ekiz, Ali Yumid
Nickname:	The Terrible Turk
Career Span:	1924-1950
Died:	November 16, 1981, San Luis Obispo, CA 80 years old

Titles Won:	2
Days as World Champion:	63
Age at first World Title Win:	34
Best Opponents:	Ed Lewis, Ray Steele, Dick Shikat

Baba, Ali

Brawny, but small in stature, Ali Baba suffered the loss of both parents and his siblings during the early days of World War I and escaped to live with his uncle in Boston. He joined the U.S. Navy, where he wrestled competitively, winning various honors. Initially working under his real name, he was a successful middle and light heavyweight, until he took the guise of "Ali Baba" while wrestling in Detroit in 1936. On April 24, 1936, he upset Dick Shikat for the World Heavyweight Title in Detroit, and then beat him again on May 5 in New York. He was double-crossed by Dave Levin in Newark on June 13, 1936 and lost the championship, but since it was an unscripted event, he continued to claim the title until losing again to Everette Marshall later in the month. During his career, he obtained victories over Ed Lewis, Lou Thesz, Gus Sonnenberg, and Ray Steele.

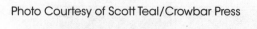

Born:	March 27, 1929
Height:	6'0"
Weight:	225
Parents:	John and Grace Barend
High School:	Jefferson High School (NY)
Finisher:	Airplane Spin
Career Span:	1948-1972

Titles Won:	23
Best Opponents:	Buddy Rogers, Johnny Valentine, Bobo Brazil

Barend, Johnny

Technically inclined because of his lengthy amateur background, Johnny Barend was a guy who could deliver an entertaining, personality-driven interview and then wrestle an exciting match. He was completely versatile, a headliner in singles and tag team bouts, and a proven commodity to promoters in need of a steady worker. Barend held U.S. championships in the WWWF and in Hawaii, holding World Tag Titles with Magnificent Maurice, Enrique Torres, and Ronnie Etchison, as well as the U.S. Tag belts with Buddy Rogers. A Navy veteran from Rochester, New York, he began grappling at eight years old and was trained by Olympian Ed Don George. Initially a clean-cut fan favorite, Barend morphed into a heel, known as "Handsome" Johnny in the late 1950s.

Born:	February 19, 1931
Height:	5'9"
Weight:	220
Real Name:	Rolland Garland Bastien
Parents:	Oliver and Helen Bastien
Military:	United States Navy
Trained by:	Einar Olsen, Henry Kolln
Identities:	Texas Red
Nickname:	The Flying Redhead
Finisher:	Sleeperhold
Tag Teams:	The Fabulous Redheads w/ Red Lyons
Career Span:	1949-1980

Titles Won:	22
Best Opponents:	Johnny Valentine, Verne Gagne, Maurice Vachon
Movies:	1

Bastien, Red

Born in Bottineau, North Dakota, Red Bastien began his professional wrestling career as a middleweight and was a fine showman from an early age. He was athletic to the bone, competently performing rapid maneuvers and was clever in the way he handled heavier opponents. He could chain wrestle and brawl, and his flying head-scissors leveled many foes with certain ease. Bastien grew up in Minneapolis, and was trained and learned the ropes from Verne Gagne and Joe Pazandak. Along with his faux brother Lou Bastien, he won the U.S. Tag Title from the Graham Brothers twice in 1960, and then traded the belts with the Fabulous Kangaroos. He also teamed with powerful Hercules Cortez to win the AWA Tag Title in May 1971. Cortez was killed in a car accident in July of that year and Crusher joined Red as his championship partner. As a singles grappler, Bastien held the Florida and Texas State Titles. He was a classy wrestler and appreciated for his unyielding gentlemanly behavior outside of the ring.

Born:	January 12, 1914
Height:	5'10"
Weight:	225
Real Name:	George Peter Becker
Finisher:	Alligator Clutch
Career Span:	1935-1972
Died:	October 25, 1999, Fort Walton Beach, Florida 85 years old

Titles Won:	25
Days as World Champion:	91
Age at first World Title Win:	32
Best Opponents:	Enrique Torres, Dave Levin, Ernie Dusek

Becker, George

The son of Russian parents, George Becker entered the business under the management of Jack Pfefer in the northeast in 1935 and competed for thirty-seven years. He won a claim to the World Heavyweight Title from Babe Sharkey on September 11, 1946 in Portland, and retained it until dropping a bout to Enrique Torres in Los Angeles in December. He also held the light heavyweight crown and the tag team title with his "brother" Bobby Becker. Becker became a mainstay in the Mid-Atlantic region until 1972. His wife, Joyce, was also a grappler for a short time.

Born:	November 20, 1906
Height:	5'8"
Weight:	200
Real Name:	Ralph Berry
Parents:	James and Ella Berry
Trained by:	Dutch Klem
Finisher:	Gilligan Twist, Stepover toehold
Managed:	The Fabulous Kangaroos (1957-1963), Hans Mortier (1963-1968), Max Mortier (1964), Gorilla Monsoon (1964-1968), Smasher Sloan (1964-1965), Tank Morgan (1966-1967), Bull Ortega (1966-1967), Professor Toru Tanaka (1967-1968)
Career Span:	1927-1965
Died:	July 28, 1973, Pittsburg, KS 66 years old

Berry, Red

Titles Won:	20
Best Opponents:	Danny McShain, Verne Gagne, Leroy McGuirk
Halls of Fame:	2

Nicknamed "Wild," Red Berry was as unrestrained and rabid as his moniker implied. In and around the squared circle, he was quick, devious, and was a tough foe against adversaries of all weight classes. He was primarily a light heavyweight, and won world championship claims in that division thirteen times between 1937 and 1947. Initially a boxer, Berry brought a lot of color to the light heavyweight class with his unorthodox methods, and he feuded violently with Danny McShain, Paavo Katonen, and many other talented grapplers. He was extremely verbose, lashing out at enemies with a flair more associated with promos seen in modern wrestling. Berry was ahead of his time, and his animated personality earned him both popularity and ire. He managed the legendary Fabulous Kangaroos and a stable of grapplers later in his career until retiring in 1969.

Blassie, Fred

Born:	February 8, 1918
Height:	5'11"
Weight:	235
Real Name:	Fred Kenneth Blassie
Parents:	Jacob and Anna Blassie
Family:	Gimmicked brother of Billy McDaniels, Jack Blassie and Mickey Blassie
High School:	McKinley High School (MO) (attended briefly)
Trained by:	Billy Hansen, George Tragos
Identities:	Bill Blassie, Freddie Beal, Fred McDaniels
Nicknames:	Sailor, Butcher Boy, Ayatollah, Fashion Plate of Wrestling
Finisher:	Neckbreaker, Atomic Drop
Tag Team:	The McDaniels Brothers w/ Billy McDaniels
Managed:	Waldo Von Erich (1975), Stan Hansen (1976), Muhammad Ali (1976), Tor Kamata (1976-1977), Baron Von Raschke (1976), Mr. Fuji (1977), Professor Tanaka (1977), Spiros Arion (1977-1978), Peter Maivia (1978), Victor Rivera (1978-1979), Nikolai Volkoff (1979), Swede Hanson (1979), Hussein Arab (1979), The Hangman (1980), Hulk Hogan (1980-1981), Stan Hansen (1980-1981), Tor Kamata (1980), Killer Khan (1981), George Steele (1981), Adrian Adonis (1981-1982), Jesse Ventura (1981-1982), John Studd (1983), Iron Sheik (1983-1984), Nikolai Volkoff (1983-1984), Kamala (1984), George Steele (1985), Cpl. Kirschner (1986)
Career Span:	1942-1985
Died:	June 2, 2003, Hartsdale, NY 85 years old

Titles Won:	41
Days as World Champion:	479
Age at first World Title Win:	43
Best Opponents:	The Destroyer, John Tolos, Mr. Moto
Halls of Fame:	3
Movies:	4

"Classy" Freddie Blassie was a Hall of Fame heel, a shrewd master of the squared circle who outsmarted his opponents and then talked trash about them in promos. He was a treasured wrestler to promoters around the world, literally for decades, and his act was as good in 1957 as it was in 1972. Blassie could draw immense heat from crowds and sold the intensity of feuds as well as anyone in the business. From St. Louis, he was a devoted athlete in his youth, training extensively at local gyms and athletic clubs. He initially majored in boxing, and rounded out his ring experience by learning holds and counters on the mat. In 1942, he not only joined the Navy, but turned pro, wrestling when he could break away from his duty station at Lambert Field in St. Louis. From 1944-1945, he served in the Philippines and weeks after his discharge in October 1945, he resumed his grappling career.

Blassie was known primarily as a fan favorite for the first half of the 1950s, respected for his scientific and clean style . . . but that changed as fans throughout the Southeastern U.S. were exposed to his rulebreaking antics. He feuded for years with Don McIntyre and Ray Gunkel and held the Southern Heavyweight championship more than ten times between 1954 and 1960. At points, he was part owner and booker of the Atlanta office. In 1961, he settled in Los Angeles and challenged Edouard Carpentier for the WWA World Title on June 12, drawing 13,200 fans and a gate of $40,000. Blassie won the championship in three falls and retained it in defenses against Ricki Starr, Primo Carnera, Antonino Rocca, and Dick Hutton. He'd trade the title with Rikidozan and The Destroyer over the next two years, and then win his fourth championship from Carpentier in January 1964. On April 22, 1964, Blassie lost the title to Dick the Bruiser. In addition to his collective body of work in Southern California, Blassie was a legend in Japan.

Blassie sold out Madison Square Garden in New York in matches against Bruno Sammartino and ended up passing the proverbial torch to John Tolos in their dynamic Los Angeles feud that culminated in a $140,000+ gate in August 1971. Blassie stepped away from the ring to become a manager in the WWWF during the 1970s and 1980s, and was a key ingredient in the promotion's success. His arrogance and verbal aptitude was still charging up fans and his color helped get comparatively colorless workers over with audiences. Outside the ring, he made a number of well-received TV and film appearances and wrote a telling autobiography in 2003 that revealed much about his life. He was honored by induction into the WWE Halls of Fame in 1994.

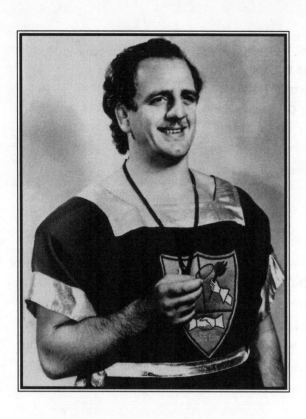

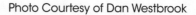

Born:	August 13, 1923
Height:	6'0"
Weight:	225
Real Name:	James Ranicar Blears
Identities:	Jan Blears, Mr. X
Nickname:	Tally Ho
Career Span:	1945-1973

Titles Won:	13
Best Opponents:	Lou Thesz, Sandor Szabo, Wilbur Snyder

Blears, Lord James

Twenty-two-year-old James Blears arrived in New York City on June 17, 1946 and hooked up with Al Mayer, the booking agent who'd arrange his first series of matches around the northeast. Blears, born in Tyldesley, England, served as a radio operator on a merchant ship during the war and barely survived a Japanese submarine attack that sank his vessel. In the ring, he was a skilled performer, and won the World Light Heavyweight Title from Red Berry in 1947. He adopted a royal heritage, took Capt. Leslie Holmes as his manager, and was a major television star on programs emanating from Los Angeles and Chicago. Along with Lord Athol Layton, he won a string of tag team championships. Blears was also an influential grappler and personality in Hawaii, where he made his home.

Born:	October 12, 1922
Height:	5'7"
Weight:	150
Real Name:	Alejandro Munoz Moreno
Wife:	Gregoria Moreno
Career Span:	1948-1988
Died:	December 16, 2000, Mexico City, Mexico 78 years old

Titles Won:	6
Best Opponents:	El Santo, Karloff Lagarde, Rayo de Jalisco
Halls of Fame:	1
Movies:	27

Blue Demon, The

An iconic wrestler with superhero status, The Blue Demon was a legend in his native Mexico. Originally from Rodriguez in Coahuila, he developed into a premier athlete under Rolando Vera, and first donned his famed blue mask in 1948. Extremely popular and inspiring, the Blue Demon won the NWA World Welterweight belt from Mexico's other lucha libre hero, El Santo, on July 25, 1953, and held it for over four years. He was also the Mexican National Welterweight Champion three times over. Dedicated to health and training, he was a real role model, and his protégé and namesake, Blue Demon Jr., upholds the same honorable traits he made famous—and is very successful all over the world, even winning the NWA World Heavyweight Title in 2008.

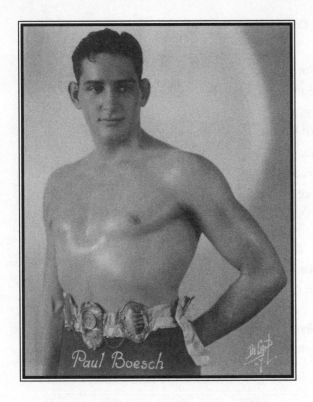

Born:	October 2, 1912
Height:	6'1"
Weight:	215
Real Name:	Paul Max Boesch
Parents:	Max and Delia Boesch
Wife:	Valerie Boesch
High School:	Long Beach High School (NY)
Military:	United States Army (WWII)
Military Unit:	G Company, 121st Infantry Regiment, 8th Division
Military Honors:	Earned two Silver Stars, two Bronze Stars, two Purple Hearts and the Croix de Guerre Award
Promoted:	Houston (1967-1987, 1988-1989)
Career Span:	1932-1965
Died:	March 7, 1989, Sugarland, TX 76 years old

Paul Boesch

Boesch, Paul

Titles Won:	Claimed at least 1
Best Opponents:	Bill Longson, Ray Steele, Buddy Rogers
Halls of Fame:	2

Popular Paul Boesch of Brooklyn, New York was a war hero, an author, lifeguard, wrestler, TV announcer, promoter, and genuinely nice guy. Discovered on the shores of Long Beach by promoter Harry Bloomfield, he was ushered into the business by Jack Pfefer in 1932. Pfefer sent him out onto the main New York circuit, and Boesch's speed and flawless execution were a big hit with fans. He ventured into Canada and landed in the Pacific Northwest, where he bought into the territory and acted as a promoter in Seattle throughout 1938. After service in World War II, where he distinguished himself on the battlefield and earned medals of valor, Boesch returned to the business, and was a valuable aide to Houston promoter Morris Sigel. Beginning in 1949, he was the voice behind the local TV program and took over the promotion when Sigel died. The always charitable Boesch ran Houston for two decades, and it was consistently a top-tier town because of his hard work.

Born:	September 19, 1923
Height:	5'10"
Weight:	325
Parents:	Alex and Angeline Bollas
High School:	Harding High School (OH)
College:	Ohio State University (1945-1946)
Trained at:	Al Haft's Gym in Columbus
Identities:	The Intercollegiate Dark Secret
Career Span:	1947-1968
Died:	January 28, 1977, Akron, OH 53 years old

Titles Won:	4
Days as World Champion:	42
Age at first World Title Win:	25
Best Opponents:	Lou Thesz, Verne Gagne, Buddy Rogers
Halls of Fame:	1

Bollas, George

Amateur wrestling great George Bollas was the son of Greek parents and the last of four children, born in Warren, Ohio. Weighing in excess of 300 pounds, he was a dominant collegiate grappler, winning two Big Ten championships and the NCAA crown in 1946 while attending Ohio State University. He became a pro wrestler, and in the summer of 1948, and adopted the famous gimmick of the "Zebra Kid," a masked, black-and-white striped mastodon. Booked by the famed Jack Pfefer, Bollas terrorized arenas all over the country and won the troupe's version of the World Heavyweight Title from Buddy Rogers in July of 1949. At the Wilmington Bowl in the Los Angeles area, he beat Sandor Szabo for the KECA-TV Wrestling Jackpot on December 23, 1952 and held onto honors until February, when Szabo won a rematch. The Zebra Kid also won the Hawaii Heavyweight crown and battled all the top heroes from Rikidozan to Lou Thesz. He was unmasked at least nine times in the ring and toured the world until an eye injury ended his career.

Born:	July 10, 1924
Height:	6'6"
Weight:	275
Real Name:	Houston Harris Sr.
Family:	Father of Bobo Brazil Jr.
Trained by:	Joe Savoldi, Rex Sheeley, Jimmy Mitchell
Finisher:	Coco Butt, Cobra Twist, Abdominal Stretch
Tag Team:	The Young Lions w/ Wilbur Snyder
Career Span:	1949-1993
Died:	January 20, 1998, St. Joseph, MI 73 years old

Titles Won:	52
Days as World Champion:	Around 520
Age at first World Title Win:	42
Best Opponents:	The Sheik, Dick the Bruiser, Buddy Rogers
Halls of Fame:	3

Brazil, Bobo

In interviews, Bobo Brazil affirmed that he drew great strength from cheering crowds, and that fans across the world were the catalyst for his courage against the biggest heels in the industry. When Brazil was fired up, he was aggressive in his approach and willing to utilize all parts of the ring to batter his opponents. Of all his maneuvers, the one he relied upon the most was his famed "Coco Butt," which was his version of the headbutt, and it was applied with such immense force that it usually floored his foe right then and there. Throughout his forty-four year career, he also displayed a wide assortment of technical moves, which counterbalanced his brawling attack. It didn't matter to the fans which style he used, as they were on his side regardless. Originally from the northeastern part of Arkansas, Brazil and his family relocated to Benton Harbor, Michigan after the death of his father, and he played some municipal baseball before taking to the pro wrestling mat.

Brazil was a quick learner and his lack of formal education didn't hinder him in the slightest. Initially wrestling as "Huston Harris," he adopted the signature name "Bobo Brazil" in 1950. A powerful African American, he was met with resistance by racist promoters unwilling to exploit his tremendous drawing ability. However, he made plenty of waves across North America from Toronto to Los Angeles and received national TV coverage. Brazil meant big money at the box office, and he chased NWA champion Buddy Rogers for a lengthy period of time, coming close to winning the belt many times. He captured the WWA World Title in both Los Angeles and Indianapolis and was an eleven-time United States Champion between 1961 and 1976, with violent feuds with Dick the Bruiser, The Sheik, and Abdullah the Butcher. Brazil was arguably the most influential African American wrestler in history and his legacy will forever be honored for all the positivity he brought to the business.

Born:	March 10, 1908
Height:	6'3"
Weight:	235
Real Name:	Orville E. Brown
Parents:	Clarence and Ellen Brown
Wife:	Grace Brown
Family:	Father of Richard Brown
Trained by:	Ernest Brown
Finisher:	Indian Deathlock, Piledriver, Stepover Toehold
Career Span:	1932-1950
Died:	January 24, 1981, Lees Summit, MO 72 years old

Brown, Orville

Titles Won:	17
Days as World Champion:	Around 5,734, including overlapping claims
Age at first World Title Win:	32
Best Opponents:	Lee Wykoff, Bobby Bruns, Jim Londos
Halls of Fame:	1

The most influential wrestler when the National Wrestling Alliance expanded in 1948 was Orville Brown of Kansas. As the group's initial heavyweight champion, he was expected to proudly represent the budding organization across a growing list of territories . . . and that's exactly what he did. His first taste of regional success came as a rookie when he dethroned Alan Eustace for the Kansas State crown in 1932. Within a few years, he was challenging Jim Londos for the World Title and doing shows all over the eastern part of the country. Around 1940, he returned to Kansas and established himself as the preeminent hero throughout the central states, gaining widespread popularity. In eight years at the top of the Kansas City promotion, Brown captured eleven Midwest Wrestling Association World Championships, and had sensational matches with Lee Wykoff, Bobby Bruns, Sonny Myers, and many others.

After years of being acknowledged as the "National Wrestling Alliance" champion in Iowa, Brown collaborated in an effort to expand the organization nationally, and his credibility as heavyweight champion was imperative as the new NWA tried to gain footing. Brown's group went head-to-head against National Wrestling Association champion Lou Thesz until the two entities made peace and it was agreed that both NWA titles would be unified in November of 1949. But weeks before his match against Thesz, Brown was nearly killed in a car accident, and his career as a wrestler was essentially over. He remained a booking agent, controlling a wide region in the central states until his power came into question during a real world feud with Gust Karras of St. Joseph, and, in 1963, he decided to walk away from the business. Brown's influence as a founder of the NWA and as its original ambassador has not, and will never, be forgotten.

Born:	March 31, 1903
Height:	6'2"
Weight:	240
Real Name:	James Orville Browning
Parents:	James and Anna Browning
Wife:	Mary Browning
High School:	Verona High School (MO)
Trained by:	Oscar Kimmons, Leo Dysart
Identities:	Young Stecher
Finisher:	Turnover Scissors
Career Span:	1924-1936
Died:	June 19, 1936, Rochester, MN 33 years old

Titles Won:	1
Days as World Champion:	490
Age at first World Title Win:	29
Best Opponents:	Ed Lewis, Jim Londos, Ray Steele

Browning, Jim

   Missouri's Jim Browning was a low-key champion during the Great Depression, the kind of man who was impressive in the ring, but not in terms of flamboyance. According to many of his peers, he was one of the greatest genuine wrestlers of all time. Browning's size and strength were overwhelming, and considering the years he spent as a carnival shooter early in his life, he was tough as nails. Winning New York recognition as world champion from Ed "Strangler" Lewis on February 20, 1933 was undoubtedly the greatest achievement of his career. He was titleholder when the new promotional alliance known as the "Trust" erased syndicate boundaries and he took on all his top challengers until losing the title to Londos on June 25, 1934 at the Madison Square Garden Bowl. An eye disease, trachoma, forced him into retirement before succumbing to illness at thirty-three years of age.

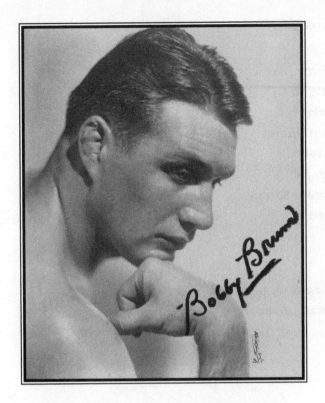

Photo Courtesy of the Pfefer Collection, Department of Special Collections, University of Notre Dame

Born:	July 12, 1914
Height:	6'1"
Weight:	225
Real Name:	Robert Harry Bruns
Parents:	George and Charlotte Bruns
Military:	United States Navy (WWII)
Nickname:	Bruiser, The German Apollo
Career Span:	1935-1967
Died:	January 23, 1983, St. Joseph, MO 68 years old

Titles Won:	13
Days as World Champion:	270
Age at first World Title Win:	25
Best Opponents:	Jim Londos, Lee Wykoff, Dick Shikat

Bruns, Bobby

Influential globetrotter Bobby Bruns sported a brilliant mind for the business and was a key booker in many cities during the 1950s and 1960s. Born in Chicago, he was the son of a railroad engineer and was an expert swimmer during his youth. He competed in amateur meets as a member of the Beilfuss Natatorium and was a lifeguard at Lincoln Park when he was called upon to train with Jim Londos prior to the latter's bout with Ed Lewis in 1934. Within a short period of time, Bruns made his wrestling debut, and soon thereafter, went to New York, where his career took off. On November 10, 1939, he beat Maurice Boyer for the World Light Heavyweight Title, which morphed into a "heavyweight" title claim for Jack Pfefer's enterprises. He lost the crown to his longtime rival, Orville Brown, on June 13, 1940. Bruns, in 1951, trained future legend Rikidozan and wrestled him in his pro debut in Japan. He was a booker all over the world, and was Sam Muchnick's main matchmaker in St. Louis for most of the 1960s.

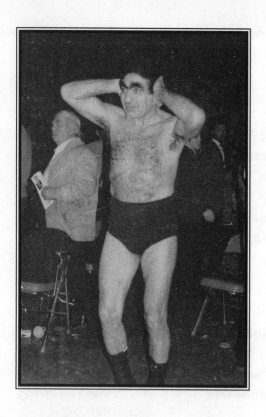

Born:	May 2, 1913
Height:	5'10"
Weight:	245
Real Name:	Fred Thomas Koury Sr.
Parents:	Nelson and Mary Koury
Family:	Father of Fred Curry
Career Span:	1932-1979
Died:	March 6, 1985, Columbus, OH 71 years old

Titles Won:	27
Best Opponents:	Bruno Sammartino, Johnny Valentine, The Sheik

Bull Curry

"Wild" Bull Curry was hardcore before the term was even coined. He was a gifted showman, known for his gigantic eyebrows, and gave fans their money's worth through a mixture of terror and excitement. Curry attended Hartford, Connecticut schools through the eighth grade, and joined a local carnival as a wrestler who'd take on all comers. Supporting his family after the death of his father, Curry joined a pro wrestling circuit in 1932, and for the next forty-seven years he brawled, gouged, and bludgeoned opponents with a distinctive zeal. He served as a police officer in Hartford and gained national attention for boxing Jack Dempsey in a Detroit exhibition, which he lost in the second round. Between 1953 and 1967, he held the Texas Brass Knuckles Title, a championship representing the "extreme" style, twenty times. He was also a two-time U.S. Champion.

Photo Courtesy of the Pfefer Collection, Department of Special Collections, University of Notre Dame

Born:	August 5, 1915
Height:	5'2"
Weight:	135
Real Name:	Mildred Bliss
Parents:	Bruce and Bertha Bliss
Family:	Adopted mother of Janet Boyer Wolfe
High School:	Manual High School (MO)
Nicknames:	Millie the Mauler, Wrestling Queen
Finisher:	Alligator Clutch
Managed by:	Billy Wolfe (1935-1952)
Career Span:	1935-1955
Died:	February 18, 1989, Northridge, CA 73 years old

Burke, Mildred

Titles Won:	4
Days as World Champion:	Around 7,000
Age at first World Title Win:	21
Best Opponents:	June Byers, Clara Mortensen, Nell Stewart
Halls of Fame:	2
Movies:	1

Long before the Divas and Knockouts took the spotlight, women wrestlers were generally considered a sideshow, there more for eye candy than presenting a sound athletic performance. By the 1930s, there were a handful of coordinated outfits featuring women grapplers on the pro circuit, usually centering around one particular superstar attraction who claimed to be the champion. It remained loosely organized until Billy Wolfe, a Missouri middleweight grappler, discovered a short teenage waitress named Mildred Bliss from Coffeyville, Kansas in 1934, and ultimately built an entire syndicate around her. Although he didn't know it at first, Bliss was his ticket to fame and fortune, and Wolfe put her through the wringer before realizing her potential. She went out on the carnival circuit and demonstrated her perseverance against men of all sizes, defeating virtually everyone she was matched against. She literally wrestled her way out from under circus tents and into arenas all across Missouri and into the surrounding states.

Wolfe changed her name to "Burke," and on January 28, 1937, gained her first big slice of national attention when she defeated Clara Mortensen in Chattanooga and claimed the women's title. She lost a rematch two weeks later, but returned to avenge the defeat on April 19, 1937 in Charleston. From that moment on, Burke positioned herself at the top of the women's pyramid, and helped build now husband,

Wolfe's stable of female workers into the best the sport had ever seen. She dominated her competition as a fighting champion and drew the largest crowds for any woman grappler in history. Her success continued into the early 1950s, and, in 1951, a web of personal issues between Mildred, Wolfe, and Wolfe's son, G. Bill, threatened the sustainability of their working arrangement. In September of that year, Burke was badly injured in a car accident while driving through the Mojave Desert, and things were further complicated when Wolfe demanded that Burke lose the World Championship to June Byers or Nell Stewart.

The personal war between Burke and Wolfe descended into chaos and Mildred was steadfast in her plight, protecting her championship and the value it meant to her. The situation was seemingly resolved when Burke paid Wolfe $30,000 for all of the latter's booking interests, but after the transaction, Wolfe refused to walk away from the business, reneging on his pledge to do so. He pushed Byers to the World Title in 1953 and conspired to taint Burke's good name every chance he got; but Burke was still the most widely recognized champion and her fiery demeanor was well appreciated by wrestling's faithful. She agreed to meet Byers in Atlanta to straighten out their rival title claims, and on August 20, 1954, they met in what was a deeply hostile shoot. Both of their reputations were on the line, and after Byers won the first fall, and the match was stopped before a result could be established in the second, the confusion in the feminine grappling ranks continued, especially as both walked away still claiming the title.

Burke was instrumental in spreading interest in women's grappling to Japan when she toured the country in late 1954. She never lost her championship in the ring and retired as titleholder. For sixteen years, between 1937 and 1953, she was the most well-regarded female wrestler in the business, and proved that women were not only sideshow attractions, but the main event. In many cities, she drew better than her male counterparts, and certainly was able to outperform men, giving audiences a more impressive wrestling display. Burke was a key figure in the evolution of women's wrestling and the dignity she brought to the ring and the championship paved the way for Moolah and every female grappler who followed. After leaving the ring, she operated a wrestling school in Southern California and also promoted on a small-time scale. The complete story of Burke's rise to superstardom and her trials and tribulations with Billy Wolfe is told in Jeff Leen's 2009 book, *The Queen of the Ring*.

Born:	May 25, 1922
Height:	5'7"
Weight:	150
Real Name:	DeAlva Eyvonnie Sibley
Parents:	Arthur and Ruby Sibley
Husbands:	G. Bill Wolfe, Sam Menacker
Trained by:	Shorty Roberts, Mae Young, Bobby Managoff, Karl Davis
Finisher:	Flying Dropkick
Career Span:	1944-1964
Died:	July 20, 1998, Houston, TX 76 years old

Titles Won:	5
Days as World Champion:	Around 3,400
Age at first World Title Win:	32
Best Opponents:	Mildred Burke, Nell Stewart, Lillian Ellison
Halls of Fame:	1

Byers, June

Women's wrestling was in turmoil after the relationship between celebrated champion Mildred Burke and the booker for the female troupe, Billy Wolfe, ended in 1953. That year, June Byers, a popular and talented veteran, became the primary wrestler for the Wolfe tribe, which included favorable booking connections across the NWA. On April 14, 1953, she won a tournament in Baltimore to become World Champion of the powerful Wolfe office. Since there was still controversy over who was the rightful queen, Byers faced Burke in Atlanta on August 20, 1954. Their infamous bout contained elements of a "shoot," because neither trusted the other. Byers ended up with a stained victory, and remained a claimant until 1964. Byers, who first learned about wrestling from her uncle in her hometown of Houston, was inducted into the Professional Wrestling Hall of Fame in 2006.

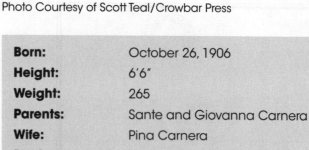

Born:	October 26, 1906
Height:	6'6"
Weight:	265
Parents:	Sante and Giovanna Carnera
Wife:	Pina Carnera
Pro Sports:	Boxing (1928-1937, 1945-1946)
Trained by:	Hardy Kruskamp
Nickname:	Da Preem, Alpine Atlas, Ambling Alp
Managed by:	Louis Soresi, Leon See, Bill Duffy, Walter Friedman, Harold Harris, Joe "Toots" Mondt, Babe McCoy, Hardy Kruskamp, and others
Career Span:	1945-1962
Died:	June 29, 1967, Sequals, Italy 60 years old

Carnera, Primo

Titles Won:	2 (claimed several others)
Best Opponents:	Jim Londos, Killer Kowalski, Verne Gagne
Boxing Record:	88-14 (72 by knockout)
Days as Boxing World Champion:	350
Age at first World Title Win:	26
Halls of Fame:	2
Movies:	15

Primo Carnera was a longtime member of the athletic community, first as a champion boxer and later as a wrestling sensation. Throughout it all, he was the pawn of a long list of managers, all of whom sliced up his pay and manipulated him to the utmost of extremes. Carnera took orders from parties with underworld ties and even from Fascist leaders of his native Italy. His push in boxing was incredible despite his less-than-stellar fighting skills, and on June 29, 1933, he beat Jack Sharkey in the sixth round for the World Heavyweight boxing championship. Carnera was titleholder until June 14, 1934, when he lost a landslide fight to Max Baer, getting knocked down eleven times. Barely surviving World War II, he returned to the U.S. in July 1946, and launched his mat campaign. He garnered a lot of attention based on name recognition and was even billed as a title claimant on occasion. Carnera was a successful international draw and remained a fixture on the circuit into the early 1960s.

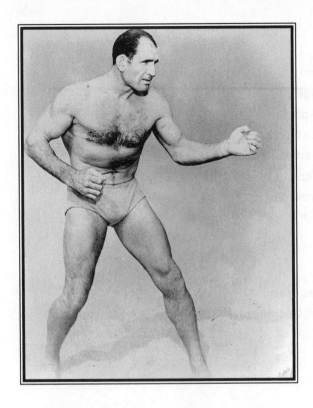

Born:	December 4, 1908
Height:	6'0"
Weight:	225
Real Name:	Stephen Casey
Parents:	Mike and Bridget Casey
Family:	Seven brothers including Jim, Paddy, Mick, and Tom Casey
Wife:	Mary Casey
Military:	United States Army (WWII)
Trained by:	Mike "Big Mick" Casey, Jack Albright
Finisher:	Kerry Crush, Killarney Flip
Career Span:	1933-1951
Died:	January 10, 1987, Brockton, MA 78 years old

Casey, Steve

Titles Won:	6
Days as World Champion:	1,680
Age at first World Title Win:	29
Best Opponents:	Maurice Tillet, Frank Sexton, Lou Thesz
Halls of Fame:	1

Based on the quality of advertising out of Boston promoter Paul Bowser's office, there were remarkably high expectations for the Irish newcomer, Steve Casey, in 1936. Casey was touted as better than his fellow countryman, former undisputed champion Danno O'Mahoney, and was reportedly undefeated in more than 200 matches. Fans responded positively to him from the start, and, unlike O'Mahoney's crash and burn, "Crusher" Casey could protect himself from a double-cross through sheer toughness. That attribute would benefit him through six AWA World Heavyweight Title reigns, the first beginning on February 11, 1938 when he beat Lou Thesz. He'd also win the championship from the likes of Gus Sonnenberg, Maurice Tillet, and his final victory in 1945 over Frank Sexton. In addition to his outstanding mat career, Casey was a champion rower with his brothers, and later ran a popular bar in Boston, appropriately named, "Crusher Casey's."

Photo Courtesy of Dan Westbrook

Born:	September 9, 1924
Height:	5'10"
Weight:	210
Real Name:	Christopher J. Clancy
Parents:	John and Mary Clancy
Nickname:	Irish
Career Span:	1945-1967
Died:	June 15, 1988, Tulsa, OK
	63 years old

Titles Won:	12
Best Opponents:	Lou Thesz, Verne Gagne, Fred Blassie

Clancy, Mike

A clever junior heavyweight who reigned supreme as NWA World Champion for the better part of two years, Mike Clancy was born in Woburn, Massachusetts and attended the Warren Academy. The son of Irish immigrants, he trained to be an amateur grappler at a local YMCA before taking to the pro circuit following his service in the Coast Guard during World War II. On April 10, 1956, he dethroned Ed Francis for the World Junior Title in Tulsa, and finally released his grip on the belt on February 28, 1958, when Angelo Savoldi defeated him in Oklahoma City. Clancy also held the World Tag Team Title with Oni Wiki Wiki and the Southern Junior Title. He retired to Tulsa, where he was a prominent businessman and county sheriff.

Born:	March 8, 1910
Height:	5'11"
Weight:	225
Real Name:	Elmer Claybourne
Parents:	James and Ella Claybourne
Identities:	The Black Panther, The Black Secret
Finisher:	Dropkick
Career Span:	1932-1958
Died:	January 7, 1960, Los Angeles, CA 49 years old

Titles Won:	3 (claimed several others)
Days as World Champion:	Unknown
Age at first World Title Win:	Around 33
Best Opponents:	Yvon Robert, Bobby Managoff, Billy Watson

Claybourne, Jack

Texas laws prevented African American Jack Claybourne from wrestling matches against Caucasian grapplers in the state in 1935 . . . so Claybourne went across the border to Juarez and became an overnight sensation. It was hard not to recognize his excellent repertoire of skills and fans responded with overwhelming positivity. Born in Mexico, Missouri, he was one of four children, and labored on local farms with his father and older brothers. He took to athletics, participating in organized baseball, and then became a wrestler on a small Missouri circuit. Not before long, he was competing in Kansas City and moved on to major metropolises across North America. He claimed the Negro Light Heavyweight and Heavyweight Titles, and reigned as titleholder in Hawaii from 1948-1949, having similar success in Australia, New Zealand, and Canada. Arguably, his dropkick was the best of the time period. Sadly, Claybourne committed suicide in 1960.

Born:	September 20, 1905
Height:	5'3"
Weight:	220
Real Name:	Abe Kelmer
Parents:	Shaya and Chevet Kelmer
Married to:	June Coleman
Career Span:	1928-1957
Died:	March 28, 2007, Fresh Meadows, NY 101 years old

Titles Won:	Claimed at least 1
Best Opponents:	John Pesek, Jim Londos, Ray Steele
Halls of Fame:	1

Coleman, Abe

Standing 5'3" Abe Coleman was an underdog through and through, and fans always wanted to see him score an upset against his usually larger foe. But Coleman's incredible strength and agility were a great equalizer, and he earned plenty of cheers for his competitive style. A Jewish grappler from Zychlin, Poland, he followed his brother to Canada in December of 1923, and later settled in the New York City area. He joined the wrestling circuit, appearing across North America and, in 1930, traveled to Australia. Often billed as the Jewish Heavyweight champion, Coleman was an early proponent of the dropkick, and in 2012, in celebration of his outstanding career, was inducted into the Professional Wrestling Hall of Fame.

Born:	December 14, 1919
Height:	5'10"
Weight:	225
Real Name:	Giacomo "Jack" Costa
High School:	Christian Brothers High School (Sydney, Australia)
Military:	Australian Army (WWII)
Trained by:	Jim Bonos
Managed:	Tony Charles, Les Thornton, Don Kent, John Heffernan
Career Span:	1939-1987
Died:	January 22, 2000, Clearwater, FL 80 years old

Costello, Al

Titles Won:	33
Age at first World Tag Title Win:	38
Best Opponents:	Lou Thesz, Bruno Sammartino, Edouard Carpentier
Wrestlers Managed:	11
Halls of Fame:	2

Many years before he became one half of the famous Fabulous Kangaroos tag team, Al Costello was being ushered by his parents toward a career as a singer, and had the tenor voice to do it. Instead, he graduated from his father's Australian fruit business and focused on the squared circle, where he fought and wrestled as an amateur, then as a professional grappler beginning in the late 1930s. Dedicated to weight-lifting and learning the scientific aspects of the business, Costello formed more of an identity as a showman after working with Dr. Len Hall, an established American grappler. He traveled around the globe, and in May of 1957, formed the Kangaroos with Roy Heffernan in Canada. Together, they were an unstoppable force of nature, winning World and U.S. Tag Team Titles from coast to coast, and their success as a duo was unrivaled to that point in history. Costello also teamed with Don Kent in a new version of the Kangaroos, and worked as a manager into the 1980s.

Photo Courtesy of Scott Teal/Crowbar Press

Born:	July 11, 1926
Height:	6'0"
Weight:	245
Real Name:	Reginald J. Lisowski
Parents:	John and Angeline Lisowski
Wife:	Faye Lisowski
High School:	South Milwaukee High School (WI)
College:	Marquette University
Identities:	Crusher Machine
Finisher:	Clawhold, The Neck Crusher, The Crusher Bolo
Career Span:	1949-1989
Died:	October 22, 2005, Milwaukee, WI 79 years old

Crusher, The

Titles Won:	29
Days as World Champion:	265
Age at first World Title Win:	36
Best Opponents:	Verne Gagne, Buddy Rogers, Nick Bockwinkel
Halls of Fame:	3

A former high school football letterman, Reginald Lisowski was stationed at Heidelberg Army Base in Germany and learned his first wrestling holds from a military athletic instructor. He added to his knowledge at the Milwaukee Eagles Club, training under two part-time pros: Ivan Racey and Bud Tassie. Early on, he appeared on a circuit based out of Chicago and was featured nationally on the ABC and DuMont networks. Lisowski formed one of the most formidable teams of the 1950s with Stan Holek, who used the moniker "Stanley Lisowski." Adopting the name "The Crusher," he captured both the Nebraska and AWA World championships in 1963. He'd win the AWA crown three times total. Partnered with the rowdy Dick the Bruiser, Lisowski took his fame to another level, and the Bruiser and Crusher were unstoppable. They won the AWA Tag Team Title five times and the WWA Title six times. The duo also went overseas to Japan and won the JWA International Tag Team Title in 1969.

Born:	August 1, 1917
Height:	5'10"
Weight:	220
Real Name:	Jose Jesus Becerra Valencia
Identities:	Apollo Anaya
Finisher:	Cobra Twist
Career Span:	1941-1960
Died:	January 4, 1999, Del Rio, TX 81 years old

Titles Won:	11
Days as World Champion:	Around 140
Age at first World Title Win:	31
Best Opponents:	Walter Palmer, Lou Thesz, Dory Funk Sr.

Cyclone Anaya

A sensational grappler from Quitupan, Jalisco, Mexico, Cyclone Anaya was initially discovered by an old pro named Joe Parelli, and won recognition in his home country before venturing to Chicago for promoter Fred Kohler in 1944. Within a few years, he was featured across Kohler's expansive television network and became an instant superstar. He held Kohler's local World Title in 1949, as well as the MWA Junior championship in Ohio. He also captured regional titles in Alabama and Texas. Seriously considered for a reign with the NWA World Junior Title, Anaya wrestled out of Houston until he was forced into retirement by a serious injury in 1960. From there on, he opened a chain of successful restaurants.

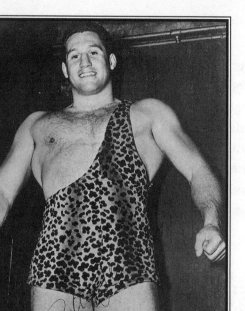

Born:	February 25, 1926
Height:	5'10"
Weight:	220
Real Name:	William Darnell
Trained by:	Buddy Rogers
Identities:	Billy Rogers
Nickname:	Leopard Boy
Finisher:	Airplane Spin
Career Span:	1943-1962
Died:	September 7, 2007, Maple Shade, NJ 81 years old

Titles Won:	8
Days as World Champion:	41
Age at first World Title Win:	22
Best Opponents:	Buddy Rogers, Ruffy Silverstein, Don Eagle

Darnell, Billy

In 1943, lifeguard Billy Darnell was mentored by a young Buddy Rogers, and both Camden athletes went on to have long, successful professional wrestling careers. Under the management of the quirky Jack Pfefer, Darnell held claims to the World Heavyweight and Junior championships. He then joined the Chicago syndicate, where he was booked by Jim Barnett and featured across the country on TV, where he teamed up with Bill Melby to capture the World Tag Team Title from Lord James Blears and Lord Athol Layton in July 1953. His career-long feud with his friend Rogers provided fans with scores of entertaining matches. Darnell retired in 1962 and worked as a chiropractor.

Born:	June 22, 1902
Height:	5'10"
Weight:	220
Real Name:	Henri Francois DeGlane
Wife:	Suzanne DeGlane
Amateur Wrestling:	French National Champion (1923)
Trained by:	Celestin Moret, Dan Koloff
Career Span:	1925-1948
Died:	July 7, 1975, Paris, France 73 years old

Titles Won:	At least 3 (claimed several others)
Days as World Champion:	647 (not counting European claims)
Age at first World Title Win:	28
Best Opponents:	Gus Sonnenberg, Ed Don George, Yvon Robert

DeGlane, Henri

French wrestling legend, Henri DeGlane was popular in the United States and Canada, as well as all across Europe. He was born in Limoges, France and trained extensively as an amateur. He won gold at the 1924 Olympics in Greco-Roman grappling and turned pro the following year. With high expectations, he arrived in New York in late 1927 and adjusted the flashier American catch-as-catch-can style. He won a controversial match against Ed Lewis on May 4, 1931 and captured the AWA World Heavyweight Title. The finish saw Lewis DQ'd after the "Strangler" reportedly bit DeGlane, but it was also claimed that DeGlane really bit himself to double-cross his opponent, but later lost the crown to Ed Don George on February 9, 1933. Later in the 1930s, he was recognized as the world champion in Europe and spent many years working as a firefighter in Paris after his career, and during World War II, he aided Allied soldiers as part of the French Resistance.

Dean
Detton

Born:	June 27, 1908
Height:	6'1"
Weight:	210
Real Name:	Dean Henry Detton
Parents:	Joseph and Hilva Detton
Family:	Brother of Dory, Reed, Gene, and Glen Detton
Trained by:	John Anderson, Ira Dern
Nickname:	Salt Lake City Flash
Finisher:	Airplane Spin
Career Span:	1931-1951
Died:	February 23, 1958, Hayward, CA 49 years old

Titles Won:	14
Days as World Champion:	274
Age at first World Title Win:	28
Best Opponents:	Ed Lewis, Jim Browning, Ray Steele

Detton, Dean

Raised in Idaho, Dean Detton was the second of eleven children, and was an above average wrestler and football player at the University of Utah. He also grappled for the famed Deseret Gym in Salt Lake City, and, in 1930, won the AAU Intermountain Titles in two different weight divisions. He turned pro in February of 1931, utilizing football tactics and technical skills in his matches, and earned the respect of many people in the business within a very short amount of time. By 1935, he was considered a top young prospect for the national "Toots" Mondt syndicate, and became the number one contender to the world title when he won a tournament in February of 1936. Detton beat Dave Levin for the heavyweight championship on September 28, 1936, and was recognized in more than twenty states. He was the kingpin until being pinned by Bronko Nagurski on June 29, 1937. Detton was a regional titleholder many times over and operated a tavern until his death.

Photo Courtesy of Dan Westbrook

Born:	December 24, 1923
Height:	6'1"
Weight:	225
Real Name:	Michael DiBiase
Parents:	John and Christine DiBiase
Family:	Husband of Helen Hilde, stepfather of Ted DiBiase
High School:	Omaha Tech High School (NE)
College:	University of Nebraska
College Ach.:	Three-Time Big Seven Heavyweight Champion (1947-1949)
Career Span:	1950-1969
Died:	July 2, 1969, Lubbock, TX 45 years old

Amateur Titles:	7
Titles Won:	30
Days as World Champion:	28
Age at first World Title Win:	43
Best Opponents:	Dory Funk Sr., Verne Gagne, Lou Thesz
Halls of Fame:	2

DiBiase, Mike

Out of the tremendous class of amateur wrestlers to turn pro in the early 1950s, one of the most spectacular was "Iron" Mike DiBiase. The son of Italian immigrants, DiBiase grew up in Omaha, Nebraska and was a standout tackle on his high school football team. In addition, he picked up two high school wrestling championships in 1941 and 1942. While serving in the Navy, he won the National AAU Title in 1946, and dominated the Big Seven Conference heavyweight division between 1947 and 1949 He was trained by famous welterweight Adam Krieger, and made his debut in April 1950. Over the next nineteen years, he won the Rocky Mountain, Southern, and North American Titles, the WWA World Title in Los Angeles, and tag team titles in the United States and Japan. He was also holder of the NWA World Junior Title in 1959. DiBiase, a hard-hitting and talented shooter, died of a heart attack during a match with Man Mountain Mike. He was married to women's wrestler Helen Hilde, and his son Ted DiBiase also grappled professionally, along with his grandsons, Mike, Ted Jr., and Brett.

Born:	November 8, 1914
Height:	5'9"
Weight:	215
Real Name:	Sterling Blake Davis
College:	Texas A&M University
Identities:	The Satin Kid
Nickname:	Dandy, Orchid, Gardenia
Career Span:	1935-1960
Died:	December 19, 1983, Rockwall County, TX 69 years old

Titles Won:	10
Best Opponents:	Ray Gunkel, Duke Keomuka, Red Berry

Dizzy Davis

A crafty, colorful grappler, Dizzy Davis was a graduate of the same Houston minor league circuit that Gorgeous George sprouted from. In fact, Davis was developing his own "dandy" gimmick when George made it famous and became a cultural sensation. Able to wrestle scientifically and brawl in the violent Texas style, he bucked the Houston wrestling syndicate in 1950, only to fall back into the good graces of the dominant combine. He won many regional championships and, in 1959, boxed Archie Moore in a losing effort in Odessa. Davis was a psychologist outside the ring and gained national news when he hired a commando to break his son out of a Mexican jail in 1976.

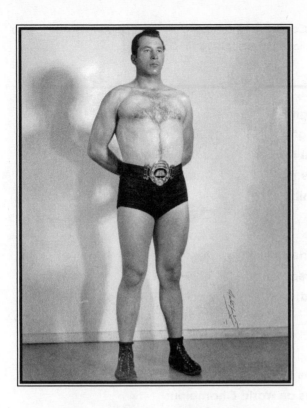

Born:	August 4, 1910
Height:	6'3"
Weight	230
Real Name:	Roy Harvey Dunn
Parents:	Laurence and Estella Dunn
High School:	Gate High School (OK)
Colleges:	Northwestern Oklahoma, Oklahoma A&M
Olympics:	Freestyle Wrestling (1936) (HWT) (Representing the U.S.) (DNP)
Amateur Title:	National AAU Title (1936) (HWT)
Career Span:	1937-1955
Died:	June 10, 2000, Holly, CO 89 years old

Titles Won:	3
Days as World Champion:	Around 3,700
Age at first World Title Win:	30
Best Opponents:	Ede Virag, John Pesek, Lou Thesz

Dunn, Roy

Roy Dunn was a magnificent wrestler, amateur and professional, and was one of the toughest independent grapplers in the business. Fresh out from the Olympics at Berlin, Dunn was confronted with the opportunity of turning pro after his teammate at Oklahoma A&M, Tom Hanley, made the jump. Dunn followed suit in 1937, and both men were coached by another ex-Aggie, Charles Strack. Dunn wrestled throughout the northeast early in his career before settling for a circuit closer to home, based out of Wichita. In January of 1941, he was named the inaugural National Wrestling Alliance Champion and remained titleholder until April of 1942, when he was defeated by Ede Virag. Dunn would regain the belt in April of 1946 and eventually retired as a champion. After the NWA expanded, he issued a challenge to Lou Thesz, its heavyweight king, but the challenge was ignored. Dunn retired from the ring in 1955.

Photo Courtesy of the Pfefer Collection, Department of Special Collections, University of Notre Dame

Born:	January 26, 1909
Height:	5'10"
Weight:	235
Real Name:	Ernest Hason
Parents:	Anton and Maria Hason
Family:	Brother of Rudy, Emil, and Joe Dusek
Wife:	Lillian Hason
Trained by:	Rudy Dusek
Career Span:	1929-1963
Died:	April 11, 1994, Omaha, NE 85 years old

Dusek, Ernie

Titles Won:	At least 14
Days as World Champion:	54
Age at first World Title Win:	30
Best Opponents:	Jim Londos, Ruffy Silverstein, Killer Kowalski
Halls of Fame:	2

Of the four members of the famous "Riot Squad" Dusek Brothers, Ernie was seen as the most marketable. He was the complete package; combining athleticism and showmanship, and was often identified with being excessively rough during his matches. He had the tendency to play outside the rules, which rubbed fans the wrong way, and earned him a reputation that sold tickets at arenas all over North America. He was such a big star that he was being considered as a replacement for undisputed World Heavyweight Champion Danno O'Mahoney in 1936. On August 8, 1939, he beat O'Mahoney in a tournament final to become the top challenger to the local Montreal crown, but after champion Cy Williams was stripped, Dusek was named titleholder. He was a multiple-time tag team champion with his siblings and held numerous regional titles, including the California and Nebraska State championships. In 1950, he beat Primo Carnera for the Omaha city title. After his retirement from active competition, Dusek became a referee on the Nebraska circuit.

Born:	January 25, 1901
Height:	5'10"
Weight:	220
Real Name:	Rudolph Hason
Parents:	Anton and Maria Hason
Family:	Brother of Emil, Ernie, and Joe Dusek
Trained by:	Tommy Ray, Farmer Burns
Promoted:	Was involved in booking of New York City area (1932-1957)
Career Span:	1922-1953
Died:	October 27, 1971, Passaic, NJ 70 years old

Titles Won:	At least 2
Days as World Champion:	73
Age at first World Title Win:	35
Best Opponents:	Jim Londos, Dick Shikat, Ed Lewis
Halls of Fame:	2

Dusek, Rudy

Although he didn't have an extensive formal education, Rudy Dusek was a bright man, and was able to successfully wield power over the rich New York City region for twenty-five years as a booking agent. Originally from Omaha, Nebraska, Dusek grew up along the banks of the Missouri River and was an avid outdoorsman. He wrestled as a member of the Omaha YMCA squad, and acquired the name "Dusek" during an early tour of Wyoming. In 1929, he landed in New York, and was a key figure in the various wrestling wars of the early 1930s as a wrestler and booker. Eventually, he became the lead matchmaker for more than fifty towns, extending up and down the east coast. In 1936, he took a victory from Danno O'Mahoney in Philadelphia by reverse decision and claimed the highly-disputed World Title. He was part of the group that brought wrestling back to Madison Square Garden in 1949 and remained a booker into 1957, when he was pushed out by rival promoters. Aside from promoting, Dusek also trained three of his eight brothers for the ring.

Born:	August 25, 1925
Height:	6'1"
Weight:	225
Real Name:	Carl Donald Bell
Parents:	John Joseph and Emma Bell
Family:	Son of Chief Joseph War Eagle (John Joseph Bell)
Indian Heritage:	Mohawk
Pro Sports:	Boxing (1947-1948)
Trained by:	Chief War Eagle
Finisher:	Indian Death Lock
Career Span:	1945-1964
Died:	March 17, 1966, Caughnawaga, Quebec 40 years old

Eagle, Don

Titles Won:	3
Days as World Champion:	Around 980
Age at first World Title Win:	24
Best Opponents:	Frank Sexton, Bill Miller, Buddy Rogers
Boxing Record:	15-4

Enormously popular, "Chief" Don Eagle was a fixture on television sets across the United States during the late 1940s and into the 1950s. A Native American from the Caughnawaga Reservation outside Montreal, Eagle performed a ceremonial war dance in the ring prior to matches and always wore his tribal headdress. The outward celebration of his heritage, along with his profound wrestling abilities, earned him sizable crowd support wherever he appeared. Eagle was adept in numerous sports as a teenager, including lacrosse and fencing. He followed his father to Cleveland to work as a structural iron worker and joined the Papke Athletic Club. In 1945, he participated in the local Golden Gloves tournament and proved victorious in the heavyweight division. A few short weeks later, he debuted as a pro wrestler. Jack Kearns, Jack Dempsey's former manager took notice of Eagle's potential, and signed him to a boxing contract in 1946. Over the next two years, he fought professionally, often appearing at the Marigold Arena in Chicago.

By September of 1948, he was back in the wrestling ring, and because of his exposure as a boxer, Eagle was a major draw in the "Windy City." Also proving valuable in Columbus, Ohio and Boston, Massachusetts, he received a consistent push into 1950, when he was booked against the AWA World Champion of five years, Frank Sexton. Their match occurred on May 23, 1950 in Cleveland at the Public Hall, and Eagle prevailed, winning the AWA crown. However, three nights later in Chicago, Eagle was caught in a politically-motivated double-cross staged by Kohler and perpetrated in the ring by Gorgeous George. Eagle seemingly lost the championship that night, but because it was an unscripted event, Haft and Bowser continued to recognize him as titleholder—and he even won a rematch over George on August 31. Around the middle of 1952, he suffered a serious back injury and forfeited the title in November. He continued his career, off and on, through the early part of the 1960s.

Born:	January 4, 1917
Height:	6'3"
Weight:	250
Real Name:	Floyd William Eckert
High School:	Soldan-Blewett High School (MO)
Identities:	Sandy O'Donnell
Career Span:	1935-1955
Died:	July 7, 1996, California, MO
	79 years old

Titles Won:	17
Best Opponents:	Lou Thesz, Enrique Torres, Sandor Szabo

Eckert, Ray

Born into a large family in St. Louis, Missouri, Ray Eckert began wrestling at a local boys' club and was competitive as a middleweight in high school and in AAU events. He grew into his size, developing into a 250-pound bruiser, and learned much from ex-champ Ed Lewis, who, at one point, bestowed upon Eckert the "Strangler" moniker. The redheaded Eckert wrestled both as a fan favorite and as a heel and had his greatest success in Northern California. In San Francisco, he was an eight-time Pacific Coast Champion and three-time World Tag Team Champion with Hard Boiled Haggerty, Frederick Von Schacht, and Fred Atkins.

Born:	September 23, 1917
Height:	5'8"
Weight:	215
Real Name:	Rodolfo Guzman Huerta
Parents:	Jesus and Josefina Guzman Huerta
Identities:	Rudy Guzman
Career Span:	1934-1982
Died:	February 5, 1984, Mexico City, Mexico 66 years old

Titles Won:	12
Best Opponents:	Blue Demon, Perro Aguayo, Bobby Bonales
Halls of Fame:	1
Movies:	54

El Santo

In all of history, few wrestlers have been able to transcend the business and become a national hero known casually by both fans and non-fans of the sport. El Santo did this in his native Mexico. He was embraced as a legitimate superhero, a bestowment that was fostered by his appearances in film, comic books, and other areas of popular culture. Becoming the masked El Santo in 1942, he proceeded to win the NWA World Welterweight and Middleweight Titles, and was a multiple time Mexican National Champion in three different weight classes. His last reign as National Middleweight Champion lasted just shy of four years. Between 1961 and 1982, he appeared in over fifty films and occasionally toured U.S. rings. His older brother, Black Guzman, was also a wrestler of note, and his son, El Hijo del Santo, is a top star known worldwide.

Etchison, Ronnie

Born:	May 6, 1920
Height:	6'1"
Weight:	230
Real Name:	Ronald Louis Etchison
Parents:	Everett and Lucille Etchison
Wife:	Almedia Etchison
High School:	Central High School (MO)
Trained by:	Warren Bockwinkel, Lou Thesz, Ray Villmer
Finisher:	Giant Swing
Promoted:	St. Joseph, MO (1976-1979)
Career Span:	1938-1980
Died:	March 4, 1994, St. Joseph, MO 73 years old

Titles Won:	31
Days as World Champion:	Around 70
Age at first World Title Win:	26
Best Opponents:	Orville Brown, Killer Kowalski, Gene Kiniski

Ronnie Etchison, a battle-hardened and popular ring veteran, wrestled in six different decades and won honors all over the wrestling spectrum. He began as a light heavyweight Golden Gloves boxer in his hometown of St. Joseph, Missouri and then turned pro under Gust Karras in 1938. Within a few months of his debut, he annexed the St. Joseph City trophy, and would later be given permanent possession of the title. During World War II, he served with the 6th Armored Division, and received four Bronze Stars and a Purple Heart. In October of 1946, he claimed to be "NWA" World Champion in Montana and gave the real titleholder, Orville Brown, many tough matches. On June 20, 1962, Etchison dethroned Killer Kowalski for another claim to the World Title in Saskatoon. He also held the U.S. and Missouri State Championships on a number of occasions. Following the death of Karras, Etchison took over as the promoter in St. Joseph in 1976.

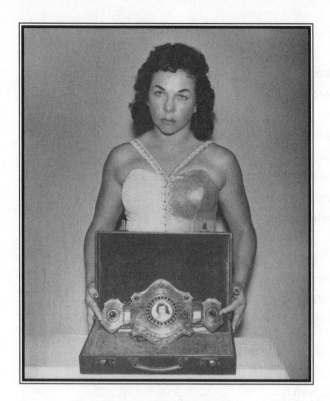

Photo Courtesy of the Pfefer Collection, Department of Special Collections, University of Notre Dame

Born:	July 22, 1923
Height:	5'5"
Weight:	138
Real Name:	Mary Lillian Ellisor (changed to Ellison)
Parents:	Henry and Mary Ellisor
Family:	Married to Buddy Lee
High School:	Columbia High School (SC)
Trained by:	Billy Wolfe, Mae Young
Identities:	Slave Girl Moolah, The Spider Lady
Nicknames:	Little Wildcat
Managed (Valet):	Buddy Rogers, The Elephant Boy
Trained:	She ran a women's wrestling school in Columbia, South Carolina and trained hundreds of aspiring athletes including Leilani Kai, Joyce Grable, Donna Christanello, and Vickie Williams.
Career Span:	1948-2005
Died:	November 2, 2007, Columbia, SC 84 years old

Fabulous Moolah, The

PPV Record:	4-0
WrestleMania Record:	1-0
WWE *Raw* TV Record:	3-2, 1 NC
WWE *Smackdown* TV Record:	1-2, 2 NC
Titles Won:	At least 13
Days as World Champion:	10,708
Age at first World Title Win:	33
Best Opponents:	Daisy Mae, June Byers, Judy Grable
Halls of Fame:	3

The internationally recognized Fabulous Moolah was the primary women's wrestling attraction for several decades, and held a claim to the world championship for nearly all of twenty-eight years between 1956 and 1984. Born in Kershaw County, South Carolina, she was the last of five children, and the only daughter of a hard working farmer, Henry Ellisor. This story is very different from the tale claiming that she had thirteen brothers and was originally from Johannesburg, South Africa, "facts" which were made up to spice up her wrestling persona. She attended high school in Columbia and became a pro wrestler in 1948 under the leadership of Billy Wolfe. Wolfe was the dominant force in women's wrestling, and booked several troupes of ladies throughout the country at any single time. Instead of putting up with Wolfe's controversial behavior, Moolah affiliated herself with another powerful booking agent, Jack Pfefer, and was just as successful. She had lengthy feuds with Darling Dagmar and Daisy Mae and reigned as junior champion.

On September 18, 1956 in Baltimore, Moolah won an 8-woman tournament and captured the World Title, and was presented with a belt by the chairman of the Maryland commission after the match. When the Wolfe circuit collapsed, she controlled the strongest troupe of women grapplers in the nation, and was able to travel from territory to territory with a stable of credible challengers to her title. Over the next twenty-eight years, she had three short breaks as titleholder, losing the championship temporarily before regaining it. In 1983, she made a financial deal to sell her title to the WWF, and lost her crown to the Cyndi Lauper-managed Wendi Richter on July 23, 1984. She won the title three additional times, the last in October 1999 over Ivory. All through the 1990s and up until several months before her death in 2007, she made many appearances on WWE television, mostly with her close friend, Mae Young. She was featured in the documentary *Lipstick and Dynamite* and inducted into the WWF Hall of Fame in 1995.

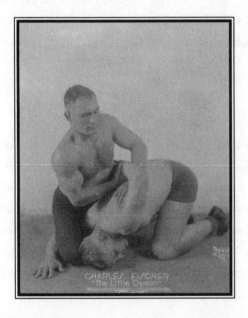

Photo Courtesy of the Pfefer Collection, Department of Special Collections, University of Notre Dame

Born:	January 2, 1898
Height:	5'3"
Weight:	165
Real Name:	Charles Berthold Fischer
Parents:	Berthold and Frances Fischer
Nickname:	Midget
Career Span:	1925-1954
Died:	November 16, 1982, Butternut, WI 84 years old

Titles Won:	5
Best Opponents:	John Pesek, Johnny Meyers, Joe Banaski

Fischer, Charlie

A remarkable athlete, Charles Fischer proved time after time that his stature (standing 5'3") was not a handicap, and had a compelling career as a wrestler. He began as an amateur in Chicago in 1924 and won several regional AAU honors. He then turned pro, and his quickness and deceiving strength took opponents of all weight classes by surprise. When he had his rivals worn down, he applied his famed piledriver, a move that he invented. In 1929, he won claims to both the World Middleweight and World Light Heavyweight Championships, and held them both simultaneously for years. He retired as champion in both divisions to his hometown of Butternut, Wisconsin.

Born:	March 24, 1925
Height:	6'1"
Weight:	230
Real Name:	Edward Andy Welch
Parents:	Roy and Alma Welch
Family:	Father of Robert and Ron Fuller
Trained by:	Roy, Lester, and Herb Welch
Career Span:	1947-1981
Died:	January 15, 1996, Pensacola, FL 70 years old

Titles Won:	20
Days as World Champion:	42 (excluding second Pfefer reign)
Age at first World Title Win:	38
Best Opponents:	Gene Kiniski, Lou Thesz, Eddie Graham

Fuller, Buddy

The eldest son of wrestler and promoter Roy Welch, Buddy Fuller spent his early years in Carter County, Oklahoma, and served as a Merchant Marine in World War II. He became a wrestler as a young man, often teaming with his uncles, Lester and Herb Welch. Not unusual, considering the success of his father, Buddy was also an enterprising promoter and restructured the Gulf Coast territory into a thriving region. He also bought booking rights to Louisiana in 1958. In Chicago, after Johnny Valentine walked out on Jack Pfefer, Buddy worked as "George Valentine," and won the vacant IWA World Heavyweight Title on October 4, 1963. He was a champion many times over throughout the southeastern United States before retiring in the early 1980s.

Born:	May 4, 1919
Height:	6'1"
Weight:	235
Real Name:	Dorrance Wilhelm Funk
Parents:	Adam and Emma Funk
Wife:	Betty Funk
High School:	Hammond High School (IN)
HS Ach.:	Two-Time Indiana State Wrestling Champion (1936-1937)
College:	Indiana University
Trained by:	Lou Thesz, Balk Estes
Finisher:	Spinning Toehold
Owned:	A percentage of the Amarillo promotion (1955-1973)
Career Span:	1942-1973
Died:	June 3, 1973, Amarillo, TX 54 years old

Funk, Dory Sr.

Titles Won:	52
Best Opponents:	Mike DiBiase, Fritz Von Erich, Lou Thesz
Halls of Fame:	4

An accomplished amateur and patriarch of the legendary Funk Family, Dory Funk Sr. grew up in Hammond, Indiana and was the son of a policeman. He initially wrestled on a Chicago-based circuit prior to joining the Navy in 1943, and resumed his career upon his discharge three years later. In January of 1948, he debuted in Amarillo, which would become his home base, and remained so until his death. Funk was an accomplished junior heavyweight, and won the NWA World Junior Title on June 5, 1958 from Angelo Savoldi. He was just as potent as a heavyweight, winning the North American crown two dozen times, and always giving any of the touring NWA heavyweight champions a tough match. The Amarillo circuit was known for its innovative matches and grueling contests, and blood was a normal sight on Thursday nights at the Arena. Funk trained his two sons, Dory Jr. and Terry to become top-flight champions themselves, and when he wasn't brawling around the ring, he was devoting time to the Boys Ranch, where he worked as a superintendent.

Gagne, Verne

Born:	February 26, 1926
Height:	6'0"
Weight:	225
Real Name:	Laverne Clarence Gagne
Parents:	Clarence and Elsie Gagne
Family:	Father of Greg Gagne
Wife:	Mary Gagne
High School:	Robbinsdale High School (MN)
HS Ach.:	High School State Championship (1943)
College Ach.:	Four-Time Big Ten Champion (1944, 1947-1949)
NFL Draft:	Chicago Bears (1947) (16th Round)
Trained by:	Joe Pazandak and Paul Boesch
Finisher:	Sleeperhold
Promoted:	American Wrestling Association (1960-1991)
Career Span:	1949-1986

Amateur Titles:	8
Titles Won:	34
Days as World Champion:	5,277 (including overlapping reigns)
Age at first World Title Win:	32
Best Opponents:	Nick Bockwinkel, Lou Thesz, Dick the Bruiser
Halls of Fame:	6

Few individuals in the annals of history have contributed to the legacy of professional wrestling like Verne Gagne. From the moment he first stepped into the ring, he was destined for greatness, and at a time in which many amateurs were breaking into the business, Gagne was at the head of the class. He became the foremost television superstar outside of Gorgeous George and Antonino Rocca, and one of the biggest draws of the 1950s. His accomplishments only grew from there, and between 1960 and 1981, he reigned as the American Wrestling Association World Heavyweight Champion ten times. His Minneapolis-based promotion sprouted roots throughout the Upper Midwest and westward to California, and was considered one of the "Big Three" organizations along with the NWA and WWWF. Gagne, at his training camp, coached a number of future champions to include Ric Flair, Sgt. Slaughter, Iron Sheik, and Ricky Steamboat.

Throughout his school years, Gagne was a proven winner, and his natural competitiveness was on display every time he stepped onto the mat or football field. His collegiate career at the University of Minnesota was broken up by service in the Marines during the war, and the few added years of life experience bolstered his confidence in route to three consecutive Big Ten championships from 1947 to 1949, and two NCAA titles in 1948 and 1949. Additionally, he was a member of the 1948 Olympic squad, but did not compete. A short time after winning the National AAU championship in 1949, he made his pro debut in Minneapolis, and was thrust into matches against NWA champion Lou Thesz and other heavyweights of impressive stature, like Killer Kowalski. Although Gagne only weighed around 200 pounds, his speed and science made it appear possible for him to beat any foe on any given night . . . he was just that good.

From 1950 to 1951, he brought much credibility to the NWA World Junior championship, and was fast becoming one of the biggest draws in the industry. Chicago was the site of Gagne's early success and the Saturday night TV show emanating from the Marigold Arena across the DuMont Network made him a national celebrity. He was a top challenger to Thesz's crown, and the two drew over 10,000 fans to the Amphitheater on January 25, 1952. Gagne held the champion to an hour draw and many fans anticipated him being Thesz's successor. He was booked in cities that carried the DuMont program and had enormous success from Milwaukee to Boston. At the 1953 annual convention of the NWA, members approved recognition of Gagne as United States champion, and he was presented with a belt emblematic of the title on September 12. Despite his status as one of the biggest box office attractions, he never succeeded Thesz as expected. In fact, Gagne never wore the NWA World Heavyweight Title.

Gagne's initial reign as U.S. Champion lasted thirty-one months, and he captured the title several other times. On August 9, 1958 in Omaha, he won his first claim to the World Title with a defeat of Edouard Carpentier for local recognition. He soon bought interest in the Minneapolis territory, and formed the AWA, which was integrated as the sanctioning body in 1960. An initial heavyweight champion of the AWA was declared, and it was Gagne, after it was claimed that the NWA titleholder Pat O'Connor failed to defend against him. Gene Kiniski was the first man to conquer him for the belt on July 11, 1961, but Gagne regained the title on August 8. Over the next two years, he won the championship four additional times, defeating Mr. M, Fritz Von Erich, and Crusher Lisowski twice. Another former Olympian, Maurice Vachon, beat him for the title in Minneapolis on October 20, 1964, and it took Gagne a few years, until February 26, 1967, to return to the top of the mountain.

His ninth reign started in 1968 after trading the belt with Dr. X and lasted an astounding 2,625 days until November 8, 1975, when Nick Bockwinkel beat him in St. Paul. On June 6, 1979, he teamed with his longtime rival, Vachon, to win the AWA Tag Team Title from Pat Patterson and Ray Stevens. Before a large crowd at Chicago's Comiskey Park on July 18, 1980, he won his final AWA World Championship, defeating Bockwinkel with his famous sleeperhold. Following his May 19, 1981 victory over Bockwinkel, Gagne retired as World Champion, something only a few others have ever done. He made a few appearances after that showing, his final on April 20, 1986 when he beat Sheik Adnan el Kaissey. A world champion in four different decades, Gagne was an impressive wrestler in every area. He was fundamentally gifted, intelligent, had quick reflexes, and was entertaining. He ranks, in terms of wrestling legends, as one of the very few legitimate icons of the sport.

Born:	March 19, 1907
Height:	5'11"
Weight:	220
Real Name:	Sam Curcuru
Parents:	Joseph and Lucy Curcuru
Family:	Brother of Chick, Ralph, Tony, and Joe Garibaldi
Career Span:	1928-1961
Died:	December 10, 1984, Los Angeles, CA 77 years old

Titles Won:	12
Days as World Champion:	29
Age at first World Title Win:	36
Best Opponents:	Jim Londos, Joe Stecher, Lou Thesz

Garibaldi, Gino

Gino Garibaldi grew up in DuQuoin, Illinois, the son of a coal miner, with four brothers and two sisters. He enjoyed training at the Rock Springs Athletic Club in St. Louis while in his early twenties, and worked out with wrestlers like Ray Steele, Billy Scharbert, and Joe Sanderson. Lloyd Carter trained him to be a pro wrestler and Gino debuted in 1928 under the name, "Vito Rinaldi." By 1929, however, he adopted the name "Gino Garibaldi," which had been recommended by a St. Louis sportswriter. During the 1930s wrestling boom, he was a strong challenger to champion Jim Londos, and had an ongoing feud with the Dusek Brothers, especially in the northeast. On May 12, 1943, he beat Yvon Robert for the Montreal World Title and held it a second time in 1944. His son, Leo, followed him into the business and they teamed up on many occasions. Garibaldi was a fatherly figure to many wrestlers, including a young Buddy Rogers and Nick Bockwinkel.

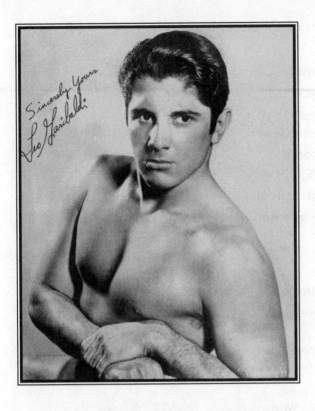

Born:	July 19, 1929
Height:	6'1"
Weight:	210
Real Name:	Leo Gino Garibaldi
Family:	Nephew of Chick, Ralph, Tony, and Joe Garibaldi
Wife:	June Garibaldi
High School:	New York Military Academy
Trained by:	Gino Garibaldi
Identities:	Frank Garza
Career Span:	1947-1961
Died:	May 12, 2008, Las Vegas, NV 78 years old

Titles Won:	10
Best Opponents:	Buddy Rogers, Johnny Valentine, Danny McShain

Garibaldi, Leo

The popular wrestling idol, Leo Garibaldi was a talented grappler and matchmaker. He was the son of veteran grappler Gino Garibaldi, and broke into the sport as a teenager in 1947. Born in St. Louis, he attended military school before joining the wrestling circuit, teaming often with his father during his rookie year. By the early 1950s he was a star, and won the World Junior Heavyweight crown three times, defeating Billy Varga twice and Michele Leone in Salt Lake City. In late 1951, he entered the Air Force and served four years, wrestling when he had the opportunity. A serious injury ended his active career and he went behind the curtain to promote in upstate New York and Austin, Texas. He was also a booker in Georgia and Florida. Garibaldi was well respected for his wrestling knowledge and brought many creative ideas to the business.

Photo Courtesy of Scott Teal/Crowbar Press

Born:	October 1, 1924
Height:	6′1″
Weight:	245
Real Name:	Robert Frederick Geigel
Parents:	Fred and Leota Geigel
Wife:	Vera Geigel
High School:	Algona High School (IA)
College Ach.:	Four-Time letterwinner in football (1946-1949), Three-Time letterwinner in wrestling (1947-1949)
Military:	United States Navy (WWII)
Promoted:	Kansas City (1963-1988), World Wrestling Alliance (1988-1989)
Career Span:	1950-1977

Titles Won:	33
Best Opponents:	Sonny Myers, Bob Ellis, Mike DiBiase
Halls of Fame:	1

Geigel, Bob

An All-American wrestler from the University of Iowa, Bob Geigel placed third in the 1948 NCAA tournament and was runner-up the following year in the National AAU tourney after losing a decision to Verne Gagne. In 1950, he broke into the business under the guidance of Alphonse Bisignano, and although he was primarily known as a Central States guy, he also found success in Minneapolis and in Amarillo. He won an abundance of championships during his career, including the AWA World Tag Team Title three times and the North American belt in West Texas. In 1963, he took over the Kansas City booking office from Orville Brown, and, with his three partners, ruled cities in Kansas, Iowa, and Missouri. He was elected president of the National Wrestling Alliance six times and was an influential member of the organization during the 1980s.

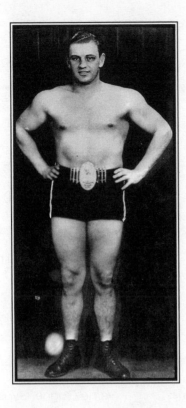

Photo Courtesy of Scott Teal/Crowbar Press

Born:	June 3, 1905
Height:	6'0"
Weight:	225
Real Name:	Edward Nicholas George Jr.
Parents:	Edward and Sarah George
Wife:	Joanne George
High School:	Canisius High School (NY)
Colleges:	St. Bonaventure College, University of Michigan
Amateur Titles:	AAU Title (1928-1929) (HWT)
Military:	United States Navy (WWII)
Trained by:	Fred Moran
Promoted:	Buffalo, New York (1947-1955)
Career Span:	1929-1942
Died:	September 18, 1985, Fort Lauderdale, FL 80 years old

George, Ed Don

Titles Won:	4
Days as World Champion:	1,194 (not counting European reign)
Age at first World Title Win:	25
Best Opponents:	Jim Londos, Gus Sonnenberg, Henri DeGlane
Halls of Fame:	5

The fourth place freestyle wrestler in the 1928 Olympics in Amsterdam was Ed Don George, a man who'd go on to grapple as a pro for thirteen years. Son of a Wyoming County, New York farmer, George demonstrated the class of a future Hall of Famer in that time, and won the World Heavyweight Championship four times. He was turned onto the business by New York neighbor Jack Albright, and with a push from the powerful Paul Bowser syndicate, George ended the reign of Gus Sonnenberg for his first AWA World Title on December 10, 1930. He was double-crossed by Ed Lewis on April 13, 1931 and lost the championship, but regained it on February 9, 1933 from another Olympian, Henri DeGlane. For more than two years, George remained titleholder, finally losing the crown to Danno O'Mahoney on June 30, 1935. In Paris, he beat Al Perreira for a European claim to the title in 1937. Once his active career ended, he promoted a circuit out of Buffalo that included a dozen cities and influenced many careers, including those of Johnny Barend and Mark Lewin.

Photo Courtesy of Scott Teal/Crowbar Press

Born:	January 3, 1918
Height:	5'8 ½"
Weight:	190
Real Name:	William Charles Goelz
Parents:	Leroy and Anna Goelz
High School:	Senn High School (IL)
Military:	United States Army (WWII)
Identities:	Stan Pesek
Finisher:	Stepover Toehold
Tag Team:	The G-Men w/ Johnny Gilbert
Career Span:	1936-1971
Died:	November 20, 2002, Port Charlotte, FL 84 years old

Titles Won:	16
Best Opponents:	Verne Gagne, Gypsy Joe, Al Williams

Goelz, Billy

Chicago mainstay Billy Goelz was a wrestler for more than thirty-five years, first as an amateur in the city parks system, and then as a professional. The son of a fireman, Goelz learned the trade from legend Lou Talaber and began wrestling as a teenager. At 190 pounds, he was a stellar junior heavyweight. He reigned as the Midwest champion of that division for most of the 1946-1955 time periods, and, in July of 1948, he was acknowledged as the National Wrestling Alliance World Junior Heavyweight Champion when the expanded union was formed. Goelz was also instrumental in the office of promoter Fred Kohler, working as a matchmaker and trainer, and owned a piece of the business. Always well liked by fans for his clean and scientific grappling skills, Goelz lived in Fox Lake most of his life, where he and his wife Ruth raised five children.

Born:	March 24, 1915
Height:	5'9"
Weight:	220
Real Name:	George Raymond Wagner
Parents:	Howard and Bessie Wagner
High School:	Milby Senior High School (TX)
Trained by:	Sam Menacker
Nickname:	The Toast of the Coast
Valets:	Jeffries, Cheri LaMonte, Jeeves
Career Span:	1932-1962
Died:	December 26, 1963, Los Angeles, CA 48 years old

Titles Won:	12
Days as World Champion:	97
Age at first World Title Win:	35
Best Opponents:	Billy Watson, The Destroyer, Lou Thesz
Halls of Fame:	4

Gorgeous George

With a style that has often been imitated, but never duplicated, Gorgeous George led a wrestling revolution and was an American entertainment legend. For years, he sauntered to rings around North America, his wavy blond hair uniquely nurtured, and his overwhelming arrogance a thorn in the sides of audiences. He provided the sport a stunningly crafted performance that had been seen in the act of a few other grapplers, but in smaller doses. George packaged all of it up and created the ultimate "bad guy," a villain who wore extravagant robes and spent at least fifteen minutes on his ring entrance, complete with music—just enough to grind into the nerves of fans. He was accompanied by an annoying valet, handed out "Georgie" pins (bobby pins), and even sprayed the ring area with his special perfume, all of which were electrifying to those who witnessed the spectacle. Gorgeous George forged a new style of wrestling heel that has since become textbook.

Despite his effeminate gimmick, George was no pushover. He'd endured a tough childhood and legitimately wrestled at the Houston YMCA and at an area carnival. At fifteen years of age, he worked as an attendant at a filling station and helped his struggling parents financially, then suffered the loss of his mother two years later. Around that same time, he was supplementing his income as a part-time grappler. He weighed only 165 pounds when he began appearing on a secondary pro circuit around Houston, and was notably popular because of his rapid maneuvers and clean style. He toiled as a journeyman before finding success in Oregon, a territory that specialized in non-heavyweight wrestlers, and won a number of regional championships. As early as 1940, he used the nickname "Gorgeous," but the actual gimmick of "Gorgeous George" wasn't perfected until about six years later.

Los Angeles wrestling fans saw him transition into a superstar in 1948. His cunning ring act lured many new enthusiasts to venues, and after he was seen on TV, he became the most talked-about performer in the industry. It wasn't long before he took his show on the road, crisscrossing the U.S. and cementing his place as a premier box office attraction. His exceptionally high level of showmanship made purists cringe, but George was part of the ever-changing wrestling atmosphere, and the dynamics of performers were becoming more outrageous. Fans responded, which, in turn, gave those in the business more motivation to continue raising the bar. He lived his ring character, legally changing his name to "Gorgeous George," and harbored some serious personal problems that weighed heavily on his health. His 1963 death wasn't a shock to people who knew the extent of his issues, but he was fondly remembered throughout wrestling and by the universe of fans who treasured their memories of the influential "Human Orchid."

Photo Courtesy of Pete Lederberg—plmathfoto@hotmail.com

Born:	January 15, 1930
Height:	5'11"
Weight:	225
Real Name:	Edward Gossett
Parents:	Jess and Velma Gossett
Wife:	Lucille Gossett
Identities:	Rip Rogers
Career Span:	1948-1980
Died:	January 21, 1985, Beach Park, FL 55 years old

Titles Won:	35
Days as World Champion:	70
Age at first World Title Win:	33
Best Opponents:	Great Malenko, Johnny Valentine, Lou Thesz
Halls of Fame:	4

Graham, Eddie

Tennessee roughneck Eddie Gossett became a professional wrestler in 1948 and remained involved in the sport until his death in 1985. He was a hard-fighting brawler and constantly on the most hated list after adopting the name, "Eddie Graham," one half of the infamous Graham Brothers tag team than began in 1958. However, he became a hero in Florida, which would be his home promotion for decades, and owned part of the exciting territory alongside his mentor, "Cowboy" Luttrall. In 1970, Luttrall retired, and Graham became the main operator in the region, running shows from Jacksonville to the Caribbean. Graham was also an influential member of the National Wrestling Alliance, and was elected president twice. He was a successful wrestling trainer, and his son Mike was one of his finest students.

Born:	January 11, 1921
Height:	5'9"
Weight:	195
Real Name:	Salvador Guerrero Quesada
Family:	Father of Chavo, Eddie, Hector, and Mando Guerrero, grandfather of Chavo Guerrero Jr., brother-in-law of Enrique Llanes
Wife:	Herlinda Yanez Guerrero
Trained by:	El Indio Mejia, Diablo Velasco
Identities:	Joe Morgan
Nickname:	Storm Bird
Finisher:	Gory Special, Camel Clutch
Promoted:	El Paso, Texas (1967-1975, 1977)
Career Span:	1937-1976
Died:	April 17, 1990, El Paso, TX 69 years old

Titles Won:	10
Best Opponents:	Rey Mendoza, Jack O'Brien, Tarzan Lopez
Halls of Fame:	1

Guerrero, Gory

Gory Guerrero began wrestling professionally as a teenager in Mexico and was involved in the sport as a competitor for nearly forty years. He was also the patriarch of the Guerrero clan, as his four sons and grandson followed him into the business. Gory was born in Ray, Arizona, where his father worked in a copper mine, and grew up partly in Los Angeles and in Mexico. He joined a local gym in Guadalajara, which is where he launched his wrestling career, fast becoming a sensation. Initially capturing the Mexican Welterweight and Middleweight Titles, he followed up with a victory over Tarzan Lopez for the World Middleweight Championship in 1946 and held the belt for two years. In 1951, he debuted in West Texas, where he won over the hearts and minds of local fans. His quickness and unabashed athleticism would become staples of the territory, and fans appreciated his technical ring work. He held the NWA World Light Heavyweight Title for over five years during the 1960s, and was one of the most popular luchadores in the United States.

Born:	February 16, 1924
Height:	6'2"
Weight:	230
Real Name:	Raymond Fred Gunkel
Parents:	Peter and Agnes Gunkel
College:	Purdue University
College Ach.:	Two-Time All-American (1947-1948)
Amateur Ach.:	Two-Time National AAU Champion (1947-1948) (HWT)
Trained by:	Billy Thom
Career Span:	1948-1972
Died:	August 1, 1972, Savannah, GA 47 years old

Titles Won:	33
Best Opponents:	Lou Thesz, Verne Gagne, Fred Blassie
Halls of Fame:	2

Gunkel, Ray

Son of a Chicago police officer, Ray Gunkel was an exemplary genuine wrestler, winning two National AAU championships as a heavyweight, and combined his legitimate talents with a solid performance in the ring. His "shooting" capabilities came in handy while in Eastern Texas when booking agent Morris Sigel used him as a "policeman" during the heated promotional war from 1953 to 1954, and Gunkel reigned as the state champion for over fourteen months. Immensely popular throughout Texas, he had a legendary feud with Duke Keomuka. Later in the decade, Gunkel planted roots in Georgia, and won the Southern Title seven times. He owned a percentage of the territory until his death, which occurred shortly after a match with Ox Baker in Savannah in 1972.

Born:	April 20, 1914
Height:	6'1"
Weight:	230
Real Name:	Clifton Orville Lowell Gustafson
Parents:	Charles and Gurina Gustafson
Wife:	Helene Gustafson
High School:	Gonvick High School (MN)
College Ach.:	Big Ten Heavyweight Title (1937), Two-Time All-American (1937-1938)
Amateur Title:	National AAU Title (1938) (UNL)
Career Span:	1938-1949
Died:	July 19, 2000, Bemidji, MN 86 years old

Gustafson, Cliff

Titles Won:	2
Days as World Champion:	389
Age at first World Title Win:	33
Best Opponents:	Bronko Nagurski, Sandor Szabo, Joe Pazandak

Often obscured by the more highly publicized wrestling champions of his day, Cliff Gustafson was a talented amateur and pro grappler, winning the localized Minnesota "National Wrestling Association" World Title on two occasions in the late 1940s. He captured the Big Ten Heavyweight Title while at the University of Minnesota and had two good showings in the NCAA tournament. He turned pro under Tony Stecher and went undefeated for several years. Ed "Strangler" Lewis helped put Gustafson over with the press, and he was very impressive as a straight wrestler in a world of gimmicks. On April 22, 1947, he beat Sandor Szabo in Minneapolis for the NWA Title, but lost it back two months later. Gustafson regained the belt on June 22, 1948 and retired as champion on May 21, 1949, a rare honor that most wrestlers don't get to see.

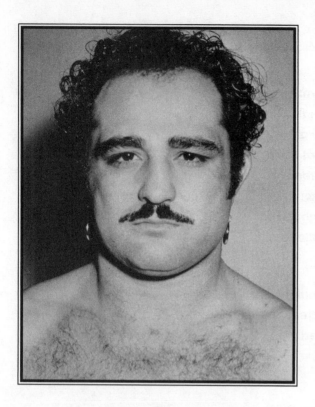

Born:	August 18, 1915
Height:	5'10"
Weight:	185
Real Name:	Ferdinand Carmen Muccioli
Managed by:	Lorraine Dorsetti (wife)
Career Span:	1936-1961
Died:	February 1986, Glendale, AZ 70 years old

Titles Won:	7
Days as World LHW Champion:	278
Age at first World LHW Title Win:	37
Best Opponents:	Billy Goelz, Verne Gagne, Pat O'Connor

Gypsy Joe

"Globetrotter" Gypsy Joe told the press that he was from Romania, but really hailed from Niagara Falls, Ontario. He initially wrestled as "Joe Dorsetti," which was in sync with his Italian heritage. However, he adopted the gypsy gimmick, and, along with his wife, wore customized costumes to highlight his new background. Ever colorful, Joe wrestled a rougher style than many fans liked, but it was never without success. He won the NWA World Light Heavyweight crown from Johnny Balbo on November 5, 1952 in Des Moines, and held an array of championships around the Great Lakes and the Pacific Coast Light Heavyweight crown in Oregon in 1948. Joe lived in Milwaukee most of his career, and retired to Arizona.

Born:	May 3, 1915
Height:	5'9"
Weight:	215
Real Name:	Stewart Edward Hart
Parents:	Edward and Elizabeth Hart
Military:	Canadian Navy (1942-1946)
Amateur Titles:	Canadian Amateur Wrestling Title (1940) (191)
Trained by:	Jack Taylor
Career Span:	1946-1979
Died:	October 16, 2003, Calgary, Alberta 88 years old

Titles Won:	2
Best Opponents:	Lou Thesz, Pat O'Connor, Fritz Von Erich
Halls of Fame:	3

Hart, Stu

In the basement of his Calgary home, Stu Hart trained an abundance of future wrestling legends, ranking him among the most influential mentors in history. If a wrestler wanted to learn about legitimate submissions, and if they had the guts, they'd enter Hart's "Dungeon," and receive the workout of their lives. Hart himself learned how to wrestle the hard way, stretched beyond the normal limits at the YMCA in his hometown of Edmonton, and carried his knowledge to a Canadian amateur championship in 1940. After service in the navy, he joined the pro circuit around New York City, where he met his soon-to-be wife, Helen. They had twelve children together, among them Bret and Owen Hart, and settled in Calgary. Hart bought the local promotion from Larry Tillman in 1951 and operated for the next three decades. He passed on his wrestling wisdom to his sons and the likes of Chris Jericho, Chris Benoit, Luther Lindsey, and many others. His impact was felt around the world as his pupils went out and entertained millions.

Born:	July 12, 1925
Height:	6'0"
Weight:	225
Real Name:	Lawrence Roy Heffernan
Parents:	Lawrence and Ida Heffernan
Trained by:	Lawrence Heffernan
Promoted:	International Promotions (1975-1977) (Australia)
Career Span:	1945-1971
Died:	September 24, 1992, Sydney, Australia 67 years old

Titles Won:	22
Best Opponents:	Dick Hutton, Antonino Rocca, Don Leo Jonathan
Halls of Fame:	2

Heffernan, Roy

Roy Heffernan, half of the legendary tag team of The Fabulous Kangaroos, was from New South Wales, Australia, the son of "Hugo the Strongman," an extraordinary weightlifter and staunch disciplinarian. His father's real name was Lawrence Heffernan, a railroad porter and sometimes wrestler. Roy began lifting weights at an early age, and was also taught many grappling tricks by his father. He turned pro, and by 1950, was known as "Mr. Australia" for his excellent physique and speedy mat work. That same year, he challenged Australian champion Al Costello, his future partner in the Kangaroos. It wasn't until seven years later that their partnership was actually formed in Canada and the tandem became a sensation across North America. They headlined everywhere, drawing tens of thousands in some places, and won a plethora of championships. Their influential work set a new template for teams to follow, and taught promoters that there was a lot of money to be made off the right combination of grapplers.

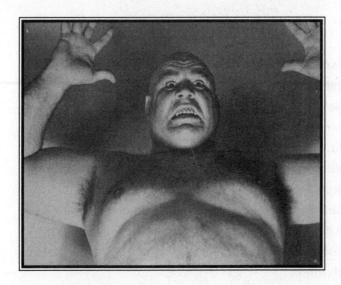

Photo Courtesy of the Pfefer Collection, Department of Special Collections, University of Notre Dame

Born:	October 19, 1903
Height:	6'3"
Weight:	365
Real Name:	Karl Erik Tore Johansson
Parents:	Karl and Lovissa Johansson
Wife:	Greta Johnson
Identities:	King Kong
Career Span:	1932-1954
Died:	May 12, 1971, San Fernando, CA 67 years old

Johnson, Tor

Titles Won:	None known
Best Opponents:	Bill Longson, Buddy Rogers, Antonino Rocca
TV Appearances:	Over 10
Movies:	32

Cult film icon Tor Johnson was a journeyman pro wrestler for more than twenty years. During his extensive international travels, he headlined in many towns, including Boston and Toronto, and his massive size struck a chord with audiences. With his face contorted to express his dramatic fury, Johnson was an imposing character of the mat, and had surprisingly good conditioning—even wrestling a ninety-minute match in 1937. Initially, Johnson tried his hand at boxing, but his huge bulk was much more appreciated on the wrestling mat. In the late 1940s, he worked as a member of the Jack Pfefer troupe, using the name "Super Swedish Angel." He was a performer in more than thirty films during his Hollywood career and gained a legion of admirers. A Halloween mask in his likeness was a bestseller for years.

Born:	April 29, 1931
Height:	6'6"
Weight:	315
Real Name:	Don Leo Heaton
Parents:	Jonathan and Leona Heaton
Wife:	Rosie Heaton
High School:	Cedar City High School (UT)
College:	Branch Agricultural College
Military:	United States Navy (1949-1956)
Trained by:	Brother Jonathan
Identities:	El Diablo, El Loco
Nickname:	Sonny, Mormon Giant
Finisher:	Mormon Sickle, Mormon Swing
Career Span:	1950-1980

Titles Won:	49
Days as World Champion:	Over 1,203
Age at first World Title Win:	24
Best Opponents:	Bruno Sammartino, Verne Gagne, Karl Gotch
Halls of Fame:	3

Jonathan, Don Leo

With the agility of a cruiserweight, the colossal Don Leo Jonathan never failed to surprise fans and foes alike. He was one of four children born to Mormon parents, and a second generation grappler from Hurricane, Utah. He was groomed to follow in his father, Brother Jonathan's footsteps from an early age, and his gymnastic background rounded out his athletic dexterity. When he finally stopped growing, he was 6'6", and weighed more than 300 pounds of pure muscle. He headlined all over the wrestling landscape from Madison Square Garden to the Olympic Auditorium and acted in the capacity of an aggressive and villainous heel and a popular babyface. Jonathan was also a nice guy outside the ring with an endearing love for the outdoors. Success in the ring came relatively early for him, as promoters were quick to utilize him in top positions. In early 1951, he held the Rocky Mountain Tag Team Title with his father, and then captured the regional single's championship from Joe Bennicasa on February 21, 1951.

Like his father, he served in the Navy, and upon returning to the circuit, won titles all over the wrestling map. North of the border, Jonathan won the Canadian Tag Title eighteen times. In 1955, he beat Pat O'Connor and Yvon Robert for two different runs with the Montreal version of the world championship. He beat Pepper Gomez for the Texas Title in 1957, and would regain the belt three years later from Torbellino Blanco. In Nebraska, he won the local World Title with a victory over Dr. X on January 7, 1961. The masked man won a rematch on March 2, but Don regained the title on April 7. He held the title until September 16, when Verne Gagne beat him in a special No DQ bout. In 1962, Jonathan was recognized as the World

Champion of the American Wrestling Alliance, a circuit of promoters which included Jim Barnett, Johnny Doyle, and Roy Shire. He lost the title to Karl Gotch on September 11, 1962. In 1969, he teamed with Antonio Pugliese to hold the IWA World Tag Team Title on two occasions during a tour of Australia.

Photo Courtesy of the Collection of Libnan Ayoub

Born:	June 23, 1901
Height:	6'0"
Weight:	230
Real Name:	Andrew Lutzi
Wife:	Frances Jones
Military:	United States Army Air Corps (WWII)
Identities:	John Paul Jones
Promoted:	Atlanta, Georgia (1944-1984)
Career Span:	1922-1944
Died:	April 17, 1988, Atlanta, GA 86 years old

Titles Won:	At least 3
Best Opponents:	Joe Stecher, Jim Londos, Ed Lewis
Halls of Fame:	1

Jones, Paul

Long before he was acknowledged as the heart of Atlanta's professional wrestling scene, Paul Jones was the Pride of Houston, a scientific flash who represented everything good about the sport. He was born in Saratov, Russia and grew up in Lincoln, Nebraska, wrestling at a local YMCA and gaining amateur honors as both a light heavyweight and heavyweight. He received unparalleled training from Clarence Eklund at the latter's Wyoming farm and, after competing under his real name, adopted the guise, "Paul Jones" while in Texas in 1923. In Houston, he was the central hero, and claimed the Southern Title after downing Charles Rentrop. He had a strong run in Los Angeles between 1926 and 1929, but returned to Houston, where he was an assistant in the office of Morris Sigel. When the opportunity to take over the Atlanta promotion came up in January 1944, he jumped at it, and remained a pivotal figure for four decades.

Photo Courtesy of Scott Teal/Crowbar Press

Born:	April 22, 1921
Height:	5'8"
Weight:	210
Real Name:	Hisao Martin Tanaka
Family:	Father of Pat and Jimmy Tanaka
Finishers:	Sleeperhold, Clawhold, Judo chop
Career Span:	1945-1971
Died:	June 30, 1991, Las Vegas, NV 70 years old

Titles Won:	35
Best Opponents:	Ray Gunkel, Verne Gagne, Killer Kowalski

Keomuka, Duke

Duke Keomuka drew intense heat in the years following World War II, as fans angrily reacted to his clever jiu-jitsu and Judo tactics in the ring. Although most press reports stated that he was from Honolulu, Keomuka was born in San Joaquin County, California, the son of Japanese parents. After service in the Merchant Marines, he joined the wrestling circuit and won the Hawaiian Junior Championship. He made a big splash in Texas, winning the state title five times and the tag belts on fourteen different occasions. In Florida, he captured the World Tag Team Title four times with Hiro Matsuda. Keomuka and Matsuda also had interest in the Tampa office from 1985 to 1987.

Born:	July 15, 1909
Height:	6'0"
Weight:	420
Real Name:	Emile George Zeimes
Identities:	Emile Czaja
Career Span:	1936-1969
Died:	May 15, 1970, Singapore
	60 years old

Titles Won:	9
Best Opponents:	Hamida Pahalwan, Aslam Pahalwan, Lou Thesz

King Kong Czaja

Born in Brasov, Romania, King Kong was the preeminent big man of his day; a wrestler whose reputation preceded him in his international travels. He was, however, much more than a hulking figure. He was an aggressive and talented athlete, and opponents were easily worn down by his strength and size. King Kong wrestled his way from Germany to Australia, and in Tokyo, he matched up against Rikidozan for the initial JWA All Asia Heavyweight Title on November 22, 1955, but was defeated. He also battled legends Lou Thesz and Bert Assirati and set an attendance record in India against Hamida Pahalwan with as many as 200,000 fans seeing their 1945 bout at Lahore. King Kong was one of the greatest box office attractions in the history of professional wrestling.

Photo Courtesy of Dan Westbrook

Born:	July 6, 1920
Height:	5'10"
Weight:	220
Real Name:	Arpad Sandor Kovacs
Trained by:	Stu Hart
Identities:	Mike Kovacs
Career Span:	1946-1972
Died:	June 30, 2004, Vancouver, B.C. 83 years old

Titles Won:	5
Best Opponents:	Don Leo Jonathan, Karl Gotch, Antonino Rocca

Kovacs, Sandor

Sandor Kovacs, a Hungarian athlete, migrated with his family to Canada around 1930, and he picked up amateur wrestling while in the navy. In 1946, he ventured to the U.S. with Stu Hart, his mentor, and joined the booking office of "Toots" Mondt. In the years that followed, he wrestled all over North America, and won regional championships in Los Angeles, San Francisco, Calgary, and Hawaii. He bought the Vancouver booking office along with Gene Kiniski and organized shows across British Columbia. Always appreciated by fans for his talents, Kovacs competed until retiring in 1972.

Photo Courtesy of the Collection of Libnan Ayoub

Born:	October 13, 1926
Height:	6'7"
Weight:	270
Real Name:	Edward Vladimar Spulnik
Parents:	Anthony and Marie Spulnik
Wife:	Theresa Kowalski
High School:	W.D. Lowe Secondary School (Windsor, Ontario)
College:	Assumption University
Military:	Canadian Army
Trained by:	Lou Thesz, Ed Lewis
Identities:	Masked Destroyer, Executioner I
Finisher:	Stomach Claw, Kneedrop
Career Span:	1948-1987
Died:	August 30, 2008, Malden, MA 81 years old

Kowalski, Wladek "Killer"

Titles Won:	45
Days as World Champion:	Around 3,621
Age at first World Title Win:	25
Best Opponents:	Yvon Robert, Buddy Rogers, Lou Thesz
Halls of Fame:	4

In 1948, a young man from Windsor, Ontario broke into pro wrestling, effectively beginning a legendary career. He was known at the time as "Ed Kowalski," but later assumed the more familiar name "Killer Kowalski," who was a megastar around the world and terrorized fans and foes alike. The twenty-two-year-old had already served in the military, played organized rugby with the Windsor Rockets, and tested his heart in pro boxing. With that background under his belt, and with the guidance of Bert Rubi of Detroit, he was prepared to gain the knowledge necessary to traverse the wrestling ring. Within two years, the sport was taken by storm, initially by "Tarzan" Kowalski, and then by the famed "Killer," initially adopting the latter designation while in Texas in the summer of 1950. He was seen as a vicious and cruel wrestler, out to maim opponents with no fear of anyone, and promoters pushed him into contests against their best workers, including important matches against NWA World Champion Lou Thesz.

Outside of the ring, Thesz had an influential role in Kowalski's career, to the point in which he had a say where and when he was booked. Thesz may have also been responsible for helping Kowalski navigate into Montreal, the site of many of Kowalski's greatest victories. In the Quebec province, Kowalski was recognized as World Champion twelve times, and feuded with the best in the business. Practically every great wrestler of the era came through Montreal to face him, and he welcomed each of them with intensive punishment.

On November 21, 1962, he took a one-fall victory from NWA World Champion Buddy Rogers after Rogers suffered a legit broken ankle, and assumed his schedule as a defending title claimant. His title was unified with Thesz in February 1963 at Houston. Kowalski was also world champion a number of times in Australia and won an abundance of other titles throughout his career. He retired from active competition in 1975 and opened a wrestling school, where he trained many current superstars, including future Hall of Famer, Triple H.

Photo Courtesy of the Pfefer Collection, Department of Special Collections, University of Notre Dame

Born:	January 3, 1903
Height:	6'0"
Weight:	240
Real Name:	Nicholas Kwariani
Parents:	Nestor and Caserines Kwariani
Career Span:	1928-1953
Died:	February 1980, New York, NY 77 years old

Titles Won:	None known (claimed Russian Title in 1929)
Best Opponents:	Jim Londos, John Pesek, Orville Brown

Kwariani, Kola

The bulky, bald man who instigated a memorable brawl in the 1956 Stanley Kubrick film *The Killing*, was none other than Kola Kwariani. Kwariani had been part of the wrestling scene in the U.S. since 1928, and was a Greco-Roman grappler in his native Russia before that. He was an intimidating figure, and his calculating mind made him a gifted chess player. When he wasn't actively touring North America, he was traveling around the world, entertaining audiences, and on the lookout for potential talent. In Argentina, he discovered Antonino Rocca, and toured for years as his road agent. At various times, he was involved in the New York City office, working with Joe "Toots" Mondt and the Johnston clan. Kwariani, who spoke half a dozen languages, was badly beaten outside of a chess club in Manhattan in 1980 and died a short time later.

Born:	August 20, 1920
Height:	6′5″
Weight:	270
Real Name:	Athol Alfred Layton
Military:	Australian Army (1943-1946)
Identities:	Ty Layton
Career Span:	1949-1976
Died:	January 18, 1984, Toronto, Ontario 63 years old

Titles Won:	8
Best Opponents:	Billy Watson, The Sheik, Lou Thesz

Layton, Lord Athol

A tall, former amateur boxer, Lord Athol Layton was born and reared in Australia. He entered pro wrestling while in Singapore in 1949, and was known as "Ty Layton" of California. He migrated to the U.K., and then to Canada where he wrestled for Frank Tunney in Toronto. By that time, he adopted the "Lord" gimmick, and was claiming to be a man of class and royalty from England. For the next twenty-plus years, he drew outstanding crowds, particularly in Toronto against Billy Watson and The Sheik. He won the U.S. Title twice and a number of other championships. Off the mat, he displayed his colorful personality while doing TV commentary in Detroit and Toronto.

Born:	June 8, 1909
Height:	5'9"
Weight:	215
Real Name:	Michele Leone
Parents:	Giovanni and Anna Leone
Wife:	Billie Leone
Trained by:	Michele Leone (uncle)
Finishers:	Bearhug, Roman neckbreaker
Career Span:	1933-1956
Died:	November 26, 1988, Los Angeles, CA 79 years old

Titles Won:	At least 5
Days as World Champion:	546
Age at first World Title Win:	41
Best Opponents:	Lou Thesz, Antonino Rocca, Enrique Torres

Leone, "Baron" Michele

Michele Leone was a Herculean performer during the early days of television and the medium helped transform him from a journeyman to superstar. On the many telecasts out of Los Angeles, Leone regularly showcased his affable personality and was striking as the "Baron," an Italian nobleman. He worked the ring like a master and turned many heads during his colorful out-of-the-ring interview segments that glorified his heelish characteristics. No one took him too seriously, and he was a rare breed who carried a strong fan base despite his "bad guy" image. Leone won the Los Angeles World Junior and Heavyweight Championships, and helped draw the sport's first $100,000 gate on May 21, 1952 against Lou Thesz in Hollywood. In the three years between 1949 and 1952, few wrestlers had more success than he did as a box office sensation, and in August 1953, Leone won the NWA World Junior Title. He'd reign until April 11, 1955, when he lost the belt to Ed Francis. Not much later, he retired to a quiet life in Santa Monica.

Levin, Dave

Born:	October 31, 1913
Height:	5'11"
Weight:	200
Real Name:	George William Wenzel
Parents:	George and Elizabeth Wenzel
Wife:	Virginia Wenzel
Trained by:	Herb Freeman, Bobby Managoff Sr.
Nickname:	Butcher Boy
Finishers:	Flying tackle, Airplane Spin
Career Span:	1934-1958
Died:	February 1, 2004, Oceanside, CA 90 years old

Titles Won:	At least 14
Days as World Champion:	Over 325 (excluding several Pfefer claims which may have amounted to more than a year)
Age at first World Title Win:	22
Best Opponents:	Buddy Rogers, Orville Brown, Dean Detton

An underrated superstar, Dave Levin was the prince of the traveling Jack Pfefer syndicate and a claimant to the world heavyweight championship at least nine times during his long career. Born in New York City, he was scouted by Pfefer and trained at Bothner's gym. An ex-butcher, Levin was very popular, and his worldwide notoriety increased measurably when he beat Ali Baba by DQ on June 13, 1936 and won the World Title. He added to his laurels by defeating Vincent Lopez on August 19, 1936 for recognition in California, giving him the strongest claim in the country, but lost the title to Dean Detton on September 28. The following January, Levin sustained rope burns in a match that developed into blood poisoning and nearly took his life. He needed seventeen blood transfusions, and was away from the ring for more than a year. In 1944, he won both the NWA and MWA belts and was often recognized by Pfefer as titleholder. He settled in Southern California, where he remained a fixture until the late 1950s.

Born:	April 18, 1934
Height:	4'3"
Weight:	92-130
Real Name:	Lionel W. Giroux
Parents:	Lucien and Lucille Giroux
Trained by:	Jack Britton, Sky Low Low
Career Span:	1950-1987
Died:	December 4, 1995, St. Jerome, Quebec 61 years old

PPV Record:	1-0
WrestleMania Record:	1-0
Titles Won:	At least 2
Days as World Champion:	Unknown, claimed title for years
Age at first World Title Win:	Around 23
Best Opponents:	Sky Low Low, Tom Thumb, Pee Wee James
Halls of Fame:	2

Little Beaver

The most famous midget wrestler in history, Little Beaver was internationally appreciated for his stylish Indian attire and colorful moves in the ring. Montreal's Jack Britton put together a troupe of four traveling little people grapplers in 1949, and soon thereafter, recruited fifteen-year-old Little Beaver of St. Jerome, Quebec. By the summer of 1950, Little Beaver was on the U.S. circuit, fascinating audiences with his agility and unrelenting offensive maneuvers. He reportedly patterned his in-ring techniques after Antonino Rocca and was often billed as the World Midget Champion. Off the mat, he was an entrepreneur, and notably, of his nine siblings, he was the only little person. Beaver was inducted into the Professional Wrestling Hall of Fame in 2003.

Photo Courtesy of Scott Teal/Crowbar Press

Born:	June 8, 1906
Height:	6'2"
Weight:	235
Real Name:	Willard Rowe Longson
Parents:	George and Alice Longson
Married to:	Althea Graves Longson
High School:	Granite High School (UT)
Amateur Ach.:	Intermountain AAU Wrestling Title (1928, 1931) (HWT)
Identities:	The Purple Shadow, Superman II
Finisher:	Piledriver, Atomic Drop
Career Span:	1931-1960
Died:	December 10, 1982, St. Louis, MO 76 years old

Titles Won:	13
Days as World Champion:	1,935
Age at first World Title Win:	35
Best Opponents:	Lou Thesz, Billy Watson, Yvon Robert
Halls of Fame:	3

Longson, Bill

"Wild" Bill Longson was as wild as they came; a master of mayhem and the definitive wrestling champion of the 1940s. He was the glue that held professional wrestling together in many parts of the United States during World War II, and was a consistent drawing card. Additionally, he was the first major heel to reign as the heavyweight titleholder, a job he performed well. He also had the talent to be able to work as a hero when his opponent was more hated than he was. The diversity of Longson came out as a young athlete in Salt Lake City, Utah, where he participated in football in high school, then joined the renowned Deseret Gymnasium, where he was instructed in wrestling by coach John Anderson. Longson was also on the boxing squad, winning the 1927 Intermountain AAU Heavyweight medal. No doubt influenced by the number of amateurs to become pros in the area, including Dean Detton, Longson earned his first paycheck for grappling at Salt Lake's McCullough's Arena on April 17, 1931, losing to Al Newman in twenty-one minutes.

A few months later, Longson boxed an exhibition against the former World Champion Jack Dempsey, but his real future was as a battler on the wrestling mat. Using his size to direct the tempo of matches, he was able to punish opponents with a variety of holds and maul them by resorting to unscrupulous tactics, which was fast becoming a needed ingredient in pro wrestling. Before he really got going, Longson suffered a broken back in a match against Man Mountain Dean in San Francisco in early 1937 and doctors predicted he'd never wrestle again. Longson was determined to return, and he did with a vengeance, capturing the Pacific Coast Heavyweight Championship three separate times. His remarkable comeback continued after relocating to the St. Louis area, where on February 19, 1942 at the Municipal Auditorium in St. Louis,

Longson beat Sandor Szabo and won the World Heavyweight Title, recognized by the National Wrestling Association.

Dethroned by Yvon Robert in Montreal on October 7, 1942, Longson regained the belt with a one-fall victory over Bobby Managoff in St. Louis on February 19, 1943. From that point on, he'd endure as titleholder for the next four years, an astonishing achievement, but indicative of the great success he was having. Longson was a proven box office success and made lots of money for promoters who used his services at the top of their program. Popular "Whipper" Billy Watson ended his lengthy run on February 21, 1947, beating Longson by disqualification when the latter punched the official. After the match, for good measure, "Wild" Bill socked the referee again—earning him a $50 fine. In St. Louis on November 21, 1947, he captured his third NWA World Title from Lou Thesz, using a reverse leglock to win the match in 25:15, however; Thesz regained the belt in July in Indianapolis. Longson owned points in the St. Louis promotion for years and also did some matchmaking and training of younger athletes looking to break into the business.

Photo Courtesy of the Collection of Libnan Ayoub

Born:	July 24, 1908
Height:	6'1"
Weight:	225
Real Name:	Daniel Vincente de Vinaspre
High School:	Meridian High School (ID)
College:	University of Idaho
Trained by:	Ed "Strangler" Lewis
Finisher:	Elbow smash
Career Span:	1933-1957
Died:	April 13, 1980, San Jose, Costa Rica 71 years old

Lopez, Vincent

Titles Won:	At least 5
Days as World Champion:	392
Age at first World Title Win:	27
Best Opponents:	Dean Detton, Ed Lewis, Dave Levin

A massive international tournament was staged in Los Angeles in 1935, and right from the beginning, Vincent Lopez, an amateur wrestling great who beat Bill Longson for the 1929 Intermountain AAU Title and contended for a spot on the 1932 Olympic team, was a sensation. He was billed as being from Mexico, although he was born in Meridian, Idaho. His parents were from Spain and he was able to appeal to a cross-section of the public. During the tournament, he beat a gaggle of big names, including Chief Little Wolf, Ed Lewis, and Man Mountain Dean in the finals to capture the California version of the World Title on July 24, 1935. Lopez received a special championship trophy the following April, then lost the title to rival title claimant Dave Levin on August 19, 1936. He added three Pacific Coast Championships to his resume and soon became a journeyman, wrestling all over North America until his retirement.

Photo Courtesy of the Collection of Tim Hornbaker

Born:	January 4, 1918
Height:	6'0"
Weight:	235
Real Name:	Robert Manoogian
Parents:	Avak (Robert Sr.) and Azniv Manoogian
Wife:	Eve Manoogian
High School:	Tuley High School (IL)
Career Span:	1937-1966
Died:	April 3, 2002, Chicago, IL 84 years old

Titles Won:	15
Days as World Champion:	818
Age at first World Title Win:	24
Best Opponents:	Bill Longson, Yvon Robert, Lou Thesz

Managoff, Bobby Jr.

Second generation superstar Bobby Managoff, Jr. was lightning fast, immensely bright, and managed to know every nook and cranny of the wrestling ring without having exceptional vision. He was born with double cataracts and familiarized himself with the squared circle through endless training, leaving no doubt that he could take care of himself against any opponent. The science of wrestling was something he'd learned from an early age, coached by his father Bob Managoff, a pro grappler as early as 1905 and the man who wrestled famous World Champion Frank Gotch in the infamous bout that saw the latter's leg broken in 1916. Bobby Jr. learned all the holds, the tricks to reverse maneuvers, and had the speed and agility to perform at the highest level. From day one, he was touted as a special athlete, and promoters gave him the room to grow, while at the same time expecting great things from him. Managoff didn't disappoint, and by the time he was twenty-four-years-old, he was ready to be a world champion.

In Houston on November 27, 1942, he beat Yvon Robert to score the National Wrestling Association Championship, and defended it proudly until February 19, 1943, losing a match in St. Louis to "Wild" Bill Longson. The following year, he held the Montreal version of the World Title, a belt he'd win five times in matches against Gino Garibaldi, Joe Savoldi, Yukon Eric, Robert, and Lou Thesz. He'd form a strong relationship with Montreal booker Eddie Quinn and own a percentage of the territory, as well as owning part of the St. Louis territory. Managoff was a regional champion in Texas, California, and Hawaii, and in his off time, he created spectacularly detailed wood carvings as a hobby. Managoff was good friends with Thesz, and their careers paralleled each other in certain respects. He was generally well-liked throughout the profession, and in 2000, was given the Frank Gotch Award by the George Tragos/Lou Thesz Professional Wrestling Hall of Fame.

Born:	November 4, 1905
Height:	6'0"
Weight:	220
Parents:	Claude and Pearl Marshall
Wife:	Harriet Marshall
High School:	La Junta High School (CO)
Trained by:	Mike Howard, Ed "Strangler" Lewis
Finisher:	Airplane Spin
Career Span:	1929-1947
Died:	February 10, 1973, Fort Collins, CO 67 years old

Titles Won:	14
Days as World Champion:	1,078
Age at first World Title Win:	29
Best Opponents:	Jim Londos, Ed Lewis, John Pesek
Halls of Fame:	2

Marshall, Everette

Known as the "Pride of the Rockies," Everette Marshall was a top heavyweight grappler who achieved national superstardom very early in his career. At about the time he was celebrating his first anniversary in the business, he was selling out the Olympic Auditorium in Los Angeles, and shortly thereafter, helped draw a $69,000 gate against champion Gus Sonnenberg. It was a remarkable start to an extraordinary career. Marshall was born outside La Junta, Colorado and played football in high school, leading his squad to the 1925 state title. In April of 1928, he won a freshman wrestling championship at the University of Iowa and, later that year, he beat a veteran grappler to capture a second school title. During the first part of 1929, he turned pro, and, on May 27, 1929, he defeated Joe Severini for the Rocky Mountain crown. Ed "Strangler" Lewis got wind of the young prodigy and brought him into his fold, expediting his push substantially.

In Los Angeles, Marshall was on course for a match against Sonnenberg and went over many veteran wrestlers, including Lewis himself. On May 5, 1930, Marshall and Sonnenberg drew over 17,000 fans and a gate of $69,745. Marshall remained a top contender to the championship, challenging Jim Londos a number of times, and the two even battled for three hours in 1934 before Marshall was defeated. He won his first World Title in June 1935 and bolstered his national standing with a variety of important victories in several states over the next two years. His biggest victory came over claimant Ali Baba on June 26, 1936. Lou Thesz ultimately beat him for the title on December 29, 1937, but because of his great record, Marshall was again named champion by the National Wrestling Association at its 1938 convention. Incidentally, Thesz was his conqueror this time as well, on February 23, 1939. Marshall wrestled until 1947, and competed mostly in the Central States region so he could tend to his Colorado onion farm.

Born:	July 31, 1918
Height:	6'1"
Weight:	230
Real Name:	Roy Lorne McClarty
Trained by:	Joe Pazandak
Finisher:	Sleeperhold
Career Span:	1948-1971
Died:	March 27, 1998, Vancouver, B.C. 79 years old

Titles Won:	At least 7
Best Opponents:	Verne Gagne, Killer Kowalski, Gene Kiniski

McClarty, Roy

Although Roy McClarty played the role of the babyface, popular throughout North America, he was as tough as any down and dirty brawler in the sport. For years, he was a defensive specialist in various Winnipeg hockey leagues and was never the kind of guy to back down from a fight. His competitiveness was also on display while an amateur grappler, and he was a member of the same club as talented George Gordienko. As a pro, he was remarkably athletic, and his blond hair and size made him a natural favorite of fans. He teamed with Pat O'Connor to win the World Tag Team Title twice in 1954 and in 1955, and was married to wrestler Shirley Strimple.

Born:	June 5, 1905
Height:	6'1"
Weight:	230
Real Name:	Earl Gray McCready
Parents:	Elgin and Lillian McCready
High School:	Central Collegiate High School (Regina, Saskatchewan)
College:	Oklahoma A&M
Trained by:	Dan Matheson (Regina YMCA)
Finisher:	Rolling cradle leg submission
Career Span:	1930-1955
Died:	December 6, 1983, Edmonds, WA 78 years old

Titles Won:	7
Best Opponents:	Yvon Robert, Billy Watson, Ed Lewis
Halls of Fame:	7

McCready, Earl

Sometimes the best wrestlers are not the ones displaying the most flamboyance. Guys like Earl McCready and Dick Hutton, two of the greatest amateur superstars to ever become professionals, were more stoic and subdued, relying more on genuine athletic abilities than outrageous showmanship. McCready's amateur credentials were unbelievable. He was both Canadian Dominion and the NCAA championship several times over, participated in the 1928 Olympics, and won gold at the 1930 British Empire Games. Once he was a pro, he beat Jack Taylor for the Canadian Title in 1933 and claimed the British Empire championship for most of his career, defending it in Canada, New Zealand, and England. A riveting grappler, he was full of speed, science, and strength, which ultimately made him a feared shooter. In terms of pure wrestling ability in the pros, Canada produced no one better than Earl McCready.

Born:	December 10, 1910
Height:	5'11"
Weight:	190
Real Name:	Leroy Michael McGuirk
Parents:	John and Anna McGuirk
High School:	Tulsa Central High School (OK)
Finisher:	Rolling double wrist lock
Promoted:	Tulsa, OK (1958-1982)
Career Span:	1932-1950
Died:	September 9, 1988, Claremore, OK 78 years old

Titles Won:	At least 6
Days as World Junior Champion:	3,886
Age at first LHW World Title Win:	23
Best Opponents:	Danny McShain, Red Berry, Buddy Rogers
Halls of Fame:	2

McGuirk, Leroy

The prodigious wrestling son of Oklahoma, Leroy McGuirk came up through the amateur ranks like a man on a mission, learning from extraordinary coaches and grappling his way to an NCAA championship in 1931. He took the ordinary route, wrestling in high school and in college—the latter under Ed Gallagher at Oklahoma A&M, and turned pro after failing to repeat as national champion in 1932. Within two years, he had captured the NWA World Light Heavyweight Title, and would meet all comers. Later in the decade, he graduated to the junior heavyweight class and won the National Wrestling Association World Championship from Johnny Swenski on June 19, 1939. He was the face of the division for over ten years, and it wasn't until he was blinded in a car accident in 1950 that his career came to an abrupt end. McGuirk's presence behind the scenes elevated, and he served as a booking agent in Tulsa before taking over the promotional reigns in 1958. He served in that position until the early 1980s.

McMillen, Jim

Born:	October 22, 1902
Height:	6'1"
Weight:	220
Real Name:	James W. McMillen
Wife:	Phyllis McMillen
High School:	Libertyville Township High School (IL)
College Ach.:	Two-Time All-American (1922-1923), Three-Time letterwinner (1921-1923)
Pro Sports:	National Football League—Milwaukee Badgers (1923) National Football League—Cleveland Indians (1923, 1931) National Football League—Chicago Bears (1924-1928) (1930-1931) (1935)
Military:	United States Navy (1941-1945)
Trained by:	Paul Prehn
Career Span:	1925-1950
Died:	January 27, 1984, Lake Forest, IL 81 years old

Titles Won:	At least 2
Best Opponents:	Jim Londos, Ray Steele, Dick Shikat

Football star Jim McMillen was inspired to become a pro wrestler after Wayne Munn had not only made the transition, but had won the world title in 1925. McMillen had starred at the University of Illinois and captained the 1923 undefeated team that also featured the legendary Red Grange as halfback. Having wrestled throughout college, McMillen was fundamentally skilled and proved to be a respected journeyman and a challenger to a number of heavyweight champions; with his highlight match being on January 26, 1931 against Jim Londos, which drew over 22,000 people to Madison Square Garden. Back home in Illinois, McMillen claimed the state championship until 1937. McMillen was a minority owner of the Chicago Bears and close associate of George Halas, and served as the mayor of Antioch, Illinois from 1952-1958.

Born:	October 30, 1912
Height:	6'0"
Weight:	190
Real Name:	Woodrow Wilson Shain
Parents:	Charles and Evelina Shain
Wife:	Sallee Lewin McShain
High School:	Glendale High School (CA)
Managed by:	Dick Lane (1937-1938)
Career Span:	1933-1967
Died:	July 14, 1992, Alvin, TX
	79 years old

Titles Won:	32
Days as World Junior Champion:	637
Age at first World Junior Title Win:	39
Best Opponents:	Red Berry, Leroy McGuirk, Johnny Valentine
Halls of Fame:	2

McShain, Danny

One of the most successful grapplers in history, Danny McShain engaged in mat battles for over thirty years and his matches were usually absolute, bloody mayhem. A captivating brawler who punished his opponents with an unmerciful flair, McShain was originally from Little Rock and grew up in Southern California, where he enlisted in the Army as a teenager and learned to box and wrestle at the Los Angeles Athletic Club. Between 1937 and 1947, "Dangerous" Danny held the World Light Heavyweight Title more than ten times, and on November 19, 1951, he won the National Wrestling Alliance World Junior Heavyweight belt. A legend in the "Lone Star State," McShain was a perennial state champion and defined what it meant to wrestle the brutal "Texas style," which was heavy on violence. He wore extravagant robes to the ring and carried himself with a confident swagger that grinded on fans. After hanging up his gear, McShain was a referee, and his presence was a constant reminder of his extraordinary career.

Wayne "Big" Munn.
6 ft 7 in
wt 265

Munn, Wayne

Born:	February 19, 1895
Height:	6'6"
Weight:	260
Real Name:	Wayne H. Munn
Parents:	Bethul and Loretta Munn
Family:	Brother of Glen, Monte, and Wade Munn
High School:	Fairbury High School (NE)
Military:	United States Army (WWI)
College:	University of Nebraska
Pro Sports:	Independent Team—Olson's All-Stars (Sioux City) (1921) National Football League—Kansas City Cowboys (1925)
Trained by:	Ed Lewis, Joe Mondt
Finisher:	Crotch and half Nelson
Career Span:	1924-1928
Died:	January 9, 1931, San Antonio, TX 35 years old

Titles Won:	1
Days as World Champion:	97
Age at first World Title Win:	29
Best Opponents:	Ed Lewis, "Toots" Mondt, Stanislaus Zbyszko
Boxing Record:	0-3

In terms of marketing, "Big" Wayne Munn of Jefferson County, Nebraska had three crucial aspects that made him a box office attraction: He was a football standout, had incredible size, and was a rookie sensation when he became a wrestler in 1924, which helped breathe life into a dreary industry. It was exciting to see Munn's newfangled approach to the sport, especially when compared to the monotonous work of many grapplers. Fatigued fans wanted something new; a breath of fresh air, and Munn provided it. On January 8, 1925, with only eleven months of experience, he beat Ed Lewis for the World Heavyweight Title. Immense buzz was created, and Munn's handlers protected him the best they could, building excitement for a financially rewarding rematch against Lewis. On April 15, 1925, however, Stanislaus Zbyszko preyed on Munn's inexperience, double-crossed him in the ring, and took the title in one of history's most infamous moments. In an instant, Munn's stock crashed and his career was never the same.

Born:	January 22, 1924
Height:	6'0"
Weight:	220
Real Name:	Harold Calvin Myers
Parents:	William and Sylvia Myers
Wife:	Elaine Myers
High School:	Pickett High School (MO)
Finisher:	Atomic Drop, Shoulder Scissors, Japanese Sleeperhold
Career Span:	1944-1975
Died:	May 7, 2007, St. Joseph, MO 83 years old

Titles Won:	32
Days as World Champion:	63
Age at first World Title Win:	23
Best Opponents:	Orville Brown, Lou Thesz, Bob Geigel

Myers, Sonny

A highly decorated regional champion, Sonny Myers was a major fan favorite in the central states territory and, at one point, was so successful on a tour of the "Lone Star State," that pundits began calling him "Mr. Texas." Myers played football at his St. Joseph, Missouri high school and entered wrestling under the guidance of promoter Gust Karras. Three years after his debut, on November 3, 1947, he beat Orville Brown for the local Iowa version of the National Wrestling Alliance World Title and held it for two months. In June of 1951, Myers was nearly killed by an irate fan after a bout in Angleton, Texas and received an 18-inch knife wound, requiring more than 100 stitches. He rebounded to have the best year of his career in 1952-1953, appearing on national TV and wrestling all over the country. Between 1955 and 1964, Myers was embroiled in an ongoing legal fight against the NWA and promoter Pinkie George over a claim that he was a victim of the Alliance's monopolistic practices. There was never a firm resolution to the matter.

Born:	November 3, 1908
Height:	6'2"
Weight:	230
Real Name:	Bronislau Nagurski
Parents:	Michael and Emila Nagurski
High School:	Bemidji High School (MN)
College:	University of Minnesota
Football Positions:	Tackle, Fullback
Pro Sports:	National Football League— Chicago Bears (1930-1937) (1943)
Pro Titles:	NFL World Championship (1932, 1933, 1943)
Career Span:	1933-1959
Died:	January 7, 1990, International Falls, MN 81 years old

Nagurski, Bronko

Titles Won:	7
Days as World Champion:	921
Age at first World Title Win:	28
Best Opponents:	Jim Londos, Lou Thesz, Ray Steele
Halls of Fame:	5

Canadian-born Bronko Nagurski supplemented his income during the 1930s by wrestling when he wasn't playing football for the Chicago Bears. Trained by Tony Stecher and Henry Ordemann, Nagurski made his debut in 1933 and took wrestling very seriously, learning the craft and relying on his strength and agility to beat opponents. His name value went a long way to sell tickets, and because of his ability to draw, promoters pushed him to the World Title throne four times, with the first time coming on June 29, 1937, when he beat Dean Detton. Nagurski won the NWA belt twice over Lou Thesz and Ray Steele, and then took a localized claim from Sandor Szabo in Minneapolis in 1948. Nagurski remained prominent into the late 1950s, appearing on TV and maintaining his solid reputation as a tough guy. Well-liked, he wasn't a boisterous self-promoter and achieved fame and fortune in sports like a real gentleman. He made his home in International Falls, Minnesota and was a charter member of the Pro Football Hall of Fame.

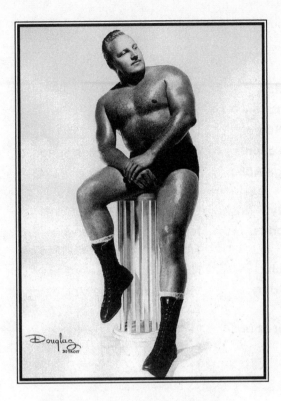

Born:	September 13, 1927
Height:	6'2"
Weight:	235
Real Name:	Arthur Nelson
Identities:	Art Nielsen, Art Neilson, The Destroyer, The Super Destroyer, The Phantom of the South, Red Raider, Golden Superman, Black Phantom, Avenger, Masked Hox and others
Career Span:	1947-1977
Died:	October 28, 1983, Las Vegas, NV 56 years old

Titles Won:	40
Best Opponents:	Pat O'Connor, Dory Funk Sr., Don McIntyre

Nelson, Art

Blond strongman Art Nelson was a masterful performer, having perfected the science of rule-breaking, and was undeniably tough. A Marine veteran, Nelson broke into the sport under Bert Rubi in the Detroit area, and was quick to adopt a trademark style. He became a well-known TV star in Chicago, and formed a championship tandem with Reggie Lisowski. Later on, he also had success with faux brother Stan Holek as the "Neilsons," and was a multiple-time World Tag Team titleholder—even winning the IWA belts in Australia with Ray Stevens. He had lengthy runs in the Georgia, Mid-Atlantic and West Texas territories, and after his death, was buried in Memory Gardens Cemetery in Amarillo.

Born:	June 19, 1924
Height:	6'3"
Weight:	255
Real Name:	Leo Joseph Nomellini
High School:	Crane Technical High School (IL)
College Ach.:	Two-Time All-American (1948-1949)
Military:	United States Marine Corps
Pro Sports:	National Football League—San Francisco 49ers (1950-1963)
Pro Ach.:	NFL Pro Bowl (10 selections)
Trained by:	Verne Gagne, Joe Malcewicz, Bronko Nagurski
Career Span:	1950-1962
Died:	October 17, 2000, San Francisco, CA 76 years old

Nomellini, Leo

Titles Won:	9
Days as World Champion:	115
Age at first World Title Win:	30
Best Opponents:	Lou Thesz, Sandor Szabo, Gene Kiniski
Halls of Fame:	4

Hall of Fame football player Leo "The Lion" Nomellini was also a distinguished pro wrestler. Following a reputable amateur career at the University of Minnesota, where he narrowly missed a Big-Ten mat title in 1950, Nomellini entered the pro ranks under promoter Tony Stecher. Recognizing his football talents, the San Francisco 49ers drafted him with their first round pick in 1950, and he set an NFL record by playing 159 consecutive games, and then retired after 174 straight games in 1963. Nomellini wrestled during the off season and participated in several high profile matches against NWA World Heavyweight Champion Lou Thesz in San Francisco. On March 22, 1955, he beat Thesz, capturing a claim to the NWA Championship, and toured the nation as a titleholder. The controversial situation also saw Thesz retain a claim until the strands were reunited a few months later in St. Louis. Nomellini was a sensational fan favorite on the West Coast and a successful box office attraction. His athleticism and durability were proven commodities in both sports.

Born:	August 22, 1924
Height:	6′1″
Weight:	235
Real Name:	Patrick John O'Connor
Parents:	John and Isabella O'Connor
High School:	Feilding Agricultural High School (N.Z.)
College:	Massey Agricultural College
Amateur Titles:	New Zealand National Title (HWT) (1948-1949), British Empire Games (Silver Medal) (1950)
Finisher:	Reverse Rolling Cradle, Spinning Toehold, Sleeperhold
Career Span:	1950-1987
Died:	August 16, 1990, St. Louis, MO 65 years old

O'Connor, Pat

Titles Won:	27
Days as World Champion:	1,196
Age at first World Title Win:	29
Best Opponents:	Buddy Rogers, Dick Hutton, Lou Thesz
Halls of Fame:	4

Pat O'Connor was a versatile heavyweight, boasting the intensity, speed, and size to be a thoroughly respected professional wrestler. As he departed the amateur ranks with two national championships and a silver medal in the British Empire Games, representing his home country of New Zealand, he was a highly touted prospect. He was scouted by Joe Pazandak and Butch Levy, and learned much from Verne Gagne and Tony Stecher in Minneapolis. Not wasting any time, O'Connor jumped on the circuit, appearing on national TV programs, and headlining big-time events all over North America. In matches, he applied the knowledge taught by his brilliant instructors, and incorporated his own aggressiveness and the fundamentals he picked up from amateur coaches Don Anderson and Anton Koolman back home in New Zealand. In 1954–1955, he won a slew of championships, including the Montreal World Title.

Many of the straight-laced characteristics Lou Thesz brought to the NWA were also seen in O'Connor, and his powerful backers gave him the time necessary to develop all sides of his wrestling persona, which particularly meant his outward personality, finding a way to connect to audiences and earn a reputation as a box office draw. When O'Connor was selected to replace Dick Hutton as the NWA World Champion, he was expected to improve attendance numbers and generate some excitement after a rough few years. Pinning the regeneration of the sport on the shoulders of one man was unfair, but the NWA's choice of O'Connor was a step in the right direction. On January 9, 1959, he beat Hutton in St. Louis and captured the championship.

Like his predecessors, he went out on tour, crisscrossing the nation, and appearing in cities of all sizes maintaining the prestige of the belt.

In the role of champion, O'Connor was a fan favorite and a heel, performing the necessary deed on any given night, and was very successful at the role. He defended his title against Thesz, Bill Longson, Fred Blassie, Dick the Bruiser, Johnny Valentine, Antonino Rocca, and tons of others, telling a different story in each match and walking from every arena a proud champion. On June 30, 1961, his reign came to an end against Buddy Rogers at Chicago's Comiskey Park in a contest that broke the national gate record, earning more than $120,000. Outside the ring, O'Connor invested in the Kansas City and St. Louis promotions, acting as a matchmaker in both territories simultaneously at certain times. He ended his active career in 1982 during a tour of New Zealand. A champion as an amateur and as a professional, on two continents, O'Connor made a tremendous mark on the business he loved, and influenced actions in front of audiences and behind the scenes for more than thirty years.

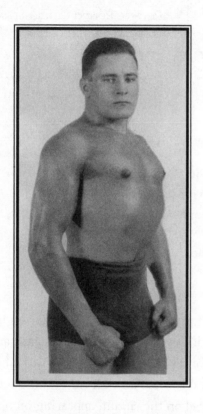

Photo Courtesy of the Pfefer Collection, Department of Special Collections, University of Notre Dame

Born:	September 29, 1912
Height:	6'2"
Weight:	225
Real Name:	Daniel Aloysius O'Mahony
Military:	Irish Free State Army
Trained by:	Jack McGrath, Fred Moran
Finisher:	Irish Whip
Career Span:	1934-1950
Died:	November 3, 1950, Maryborough, Ireland 38 years old

Titles Won:	3
Days as World Champion:	385
Age at first World Title Win:	22
Best Opponents:	Jim Londos, Ed Don George, Ed Lewis

O'Mahoney, Danno

A tall, twenty-two-year-old man arrived at Ellis Island on December 14, 1934 from Ballydehob, County Cork, Ireland. The individual was Danno O'Mahoney, who was entering the country to light the professional wrestling business on fire; and although he claimed to be a farmer, his agricultural days were over—indicated by the rush to get him to the airport that afternoon and onto a private plane to Boston, where he was introduced from ringside at the Garden. The newcomer was pushed to the moon, commencing a win streak that was unparalleled in history, and 195 days after his American landing, O'Mahoney conquered the unbeatable Jim Londos for the World Heavyweight Title. His championship win over the "Golden Greek," along with his victory over Ed Don George, gave him the strongest claim to the heavyweight throne seen in years. O'Mahoney's drawing power in many parts of the country was impressive, and he delivered a fine-tuned performance that wowed audiences.

O'Mahoney, however, was not an established veteran with the tools to protect himself in the ring. Instead, he was a young man with the weight of the world on his shoulders and a humongous target on his back. In a power hungry world, the inevitable happened on March 2, 1936, when Danno was double-crossed at Madison Square Garden by Dick Shikat, and forcibly stripped of his title in a shoot affair. The infamous match had a disillusioning effect on a great portion of the public after leaked information revealed ugly insider truths about the business. Additionally, the double-cross helped to fracture wrestling beyond repair, creating nothing but title claimants and chaos. O'Mahoney continued to wrestle, but his career was never the same. In 1950, after performing in several bouts in the Los Angeles area, he returned to Ireland, and was involved in a serious car accident. He suffered life-threatening injuries, and was taken to Maryborough County Hospital, where he died a short time later.

Born:	July 21, 1929
Height:	6'4"
Weight:	245
Real Name:	Robert Dale Orton
Family:	Father of Bob Orton Jr. and Barry Orton, grandfather of Randy Orton
Wife:	Rita Orton
High School:	Wyandotte High School (KS)
Identities:	Rocky Fitzpatrick, The Zodiac
Nickname:	The Big O, Wildcat Orton
Finisher:	Piledriver, Tornado Drop
Career Span:	1949-1976
Died:	July 16, 2006, Las Vegas, NV 76 years old

Orton, Bob Sr.

Titles Won:	25
Best Opponents:	Eddie Graham, Hans Schmidt, Bob Ellis

Orville Brown, one of the founders of the National Wrestling Alliance and an influential Central States booking agent, recruited Bob Orton around 1949 and considered him one of the best prospects he'd seen in years. Orton's size and strength made him a natural competitor on the heavyweight circuit, and during the early 1950s, was featured on the DuMont national television program out of Chicago. That kind of exposure opened up many job opportunities across the nation, and Orton went on the road. In the Kansas City territory, he feuded with Pat O'Connor and Sonny Myers, held the local championship several times, and challenged Lou Thesz for the World Title. Bruising opponents unmercifully, Orton was a fearsome grappler, and had plenty of success in New York and Florida, even using a controversial masked Zodiac gimmick. In 1976, he teamed with his son, Bob Jr. to win the Florida Tag Team Championship.

Photo Courtesy of Scott Teal/Crowbar Press

Born:	April 25, 1912
Height:	5'11"
Weight:	210
Wife:	Olga Palmer
High School:	Roosevelt High School (IL)
Colleges:	Crane College, Northwestern University
Trained by:	Lou Talaber
Identities:	George LaMarque, Red Ace, Ace Palmer, George LaMar
Finisher:	Spinning Toe Hold
Career Span:	1936-1954
Died:	July 10, 1998, Tucson, AZ 86 years old

Palmer, Walter

Titles Won:	At least 3, claimed a few others
Days as World Champion:	Unknown, maybe as much as several years
Age at first World Title Win:	Around 31
Best Opponents:	Lou Thesz, Ruffy Silverstein, Cyclone Anaya

Walter Palmer was the central babyface in the "Windy City" for a great deal of the 1940s and into the early 1950s, tending to business as the local hero and as a policeman for the territory. Having wrestled since he was in grade school, he gained experience in the parks system and considered training for the Olympics. He was a top contender to the junior light heavyweight title, then, as he gained weight, was billed as the uncrowned heavyweight champion. Based on his outstanding record, including remaining undefeated for several years, he claimed the Chicago World Title and held it multiple times between 1944 and 1949. At one point, he had to give the title up because of a severely broken leg. In 1951, the NWA recognized his career achievements by awarding him a special sportsmanship plaque, declaring him a credit to the sport.

Photo Courtesy of the Pfefer Collection, Department of Special Collections, University of Notre Dame

Born:	October 23, 1914
Height:	5'9"
Weight:	230
Real Name:	Joseph Eugene Pazandak
Parents:	Joseph and Caroline Pazandak
High School:	West High School (MN)
Amateur Titles:	Northwest AAU Championship (1935-1936)
Military:	United States Army (1941-1945)
Identities:	Joe Pazek, The Dark Secret (Masked)
Career Span:	1937-1960
Died:	December 2, 1983, Minneapolis, MN 69 years old

Titles Won:	At least 2
Days as "The Champ":	Around 300
Best Opponents:	Verne Gagne, Lou Thesz, Sandor Szabo

Pazandak, Joe

A combat veteran, amateur great, and trainer to the stars, "The Champ" Joe Pazandak was an influential and successful wrestler for over twenty years. Guided into the business by Minneapolis promoter Tony Stecher after winning two AAU championships and wrestling at the University of Minnesota, Pazandak was a fundamentally sound heavyweight. He was such an expert that Stecher relied on him to work the territory as a policeman and trainer, coaching dozens of future superstars to include Verne Gagne, Dick the Bruiser, and Roy McClarty. Perhaps his greatest in-ring fame came in Los Angeles as the defender of the TV wrestling jackpot known as "Beat the Champ" beginning in June 1951, and he successfully defended the money against top challengers for more than nine months. Pazandak also found success in Australia and New Zealand.

Born:	April 10, 1925
Height:	6'0"
Weight:	220
Real Name:	Angelo John Poffo
Parents:	Silvio and Egitina Poffo
High School:	Downers Grove North High School (IL)
Trained by:	Lou Talaber, Karl Pojello
Identities:	The Miser, The Question
Finisher:	Neckbreaker
Promoted:	International Championship Wrestling (1978-1984)
Career Span:	1949-1991
Died:	March 4, 2010, Largo, FL 84 years old

Poffo, Angelo

Titles Won:	10
Best Opponents:	Wilbur Snyder, Dick the Bruiser, Verne Gagne
Halls of Fame:	1

Born into a family of Italian immigrants, Angelo Poffo was raised in the Chicago suburb of Downers Grove and gained a real competitive spirit while serving in the Navy. On July 4, 1945, he undertook a challenge of breaking the world record for consecutive sit-ups and accomplished the feat with a total of 6,033, which was seventy-eight more than the previous mark. His achievement was featured in Robert Ripley's March 3, 1948 cartoon. After playing baseball in college, Poffo became a pro wrestler and won the U.S. Title from Wilbur Snyder on December 27, 1958. He was a significant player on the Barnett-Doyle circuit and gained wins from Bob Ellis, Yukon Eric, and Bobby Managoff. A man of convictions, Poffo trained his two sons, Randy Savage and Lanny Poffo, for the pro ring, and spotlighted them in his own promotion, ICW out of Lexington. In 1995, he was inducted into the WCW Hall of Fame.

Photo Courtesy of Viva Foy

Born:	November 26, 1917
Height:	5'10"
Weight:	180
Real Name:	Inman Curry Raborn
Parents:	James and Sarah Raborn
Wife:	Doris Raborn
Career Span:	1933-1958
Died:	August 31, 1968, Tulsa, OK
	51 years old

Titles Won:	At least 6
Days as World LHW Champion:	210
Age at first World LHW Title Win:	24
Best Opponents:	Verne Gagne, Red Berry, Billy Varga

Raborn, Billy

Across North America, Billy Raborn was cheered for his scientific style and blazing fast speed. He was purely athletic and his masterful wrestling knowledge was on display each time he appeared in the ring. Raborn was from Hephzibah, Georgia and was schooled by southern great Jack Ross. In 1937, he made his way to New York, where he was booked around the circuit by Jack Pfefer; and on August 24, 1942, he won the World Light Heavyweight crown from Red Berry in Tulsa. Days before he was set to enter the Army, Raborn lost the championship in Hollywood to Billy Varga on March 22, 1943. Raborn also won local titles in Texas and Florida. Always a gentleman, he retired to Cleveland, Oklahoma, where he worked as an insurance agent.

Born:	October 8, 1914
Height:	6'0"
Weight:	225
Family:	Older brother of Maurice Robert, father of Yvon Robert Jr.
Wife:	Leona Robert
Finisher:	Rolling short-arm scissors
Career Span:	1932-1957
Died:	July 12, 1971, Montreal, Quebec 56 years old

Titles Won:	18
Days as World Champion:	Over 3,336
Age at first World Title Win:	21
Best Opponents:	Lou Thesz, Bill Longson, Sandor Szabo
Halls of Fame:	1

Robert, Yvon

Montreal icon Yvon Robert was a pro grappler by eighteen years of age and a world champion by twenty-one. Originally from Verdun, he labored in a lumber camp as a teen and wrestled as an amateur prior to training under Emil Maupas, making his debut in 1932. Within two years, he was holding his own against established veterans and was primed to succeed Henri DeGlane as Montreal's leading superstar. On July 16, 1936, he beat Danno O'Mahoney for the first of his fifteen World Heavyweight championships, and over the course of the next twenty years, fought every major name from Lou Thesz to Buddy Rogers. It became a common theme for an American challenger to beat Robert for the local belt, and then have Yvon regain the title at a later date, of course after building lots of excitement and filling the Montreal Forum with adoring fans. In 1942, he added the National Wrestling Association prize to his collection with a win over Bill Longson. In the 1950s, he passed the torch to Johnny Rougeau and Edouard Carpentier.

Born:	April 13, 1921
Height:	6'0"
Weight:	225
Real Name:	Antonino Biasetton
Parents:	Antonio and Angelo Basso Biasetton
Wife:	Nellie Biasetton
College:	University of Buenos Aires
Trained by:	The Zbyszko Brothers
Finisher:	Argentine Backbreaker
Managed by:	Joe "Toots" Mondt, Vince McMahon, Fred Kohler
Road Agents:	Kola Kwariani, Harry Lewis
Career Span:	1940-1976
Died:	March 15, 1977, New York, NY 49 years old

Titles Won:	8
Days as World Champion:	42
Age at first World Title Win:	31
Best Opponents:	Lou Thesz, Killer Kowalski, Buddy Rogers
Halls of Fame:	4

Rocca, Antonino

A cultural icon, Antonino "Argentina" Rocca was the crown prince of pro wrestling for many years. He was the ultimate fan favorite and his enormous appeal transcended ethnic and social barriers during the late 1940s and early 1950s. His array of flashy maneuvers was ideal during the early days of television and helped wrestling attract scores of new viewers. At Madison Square Garden in New York City, there was no end to the support he'd receive in battle against an evil foe, and Rocca usually came out on top, pinning his opponent and leaving the ring as a massive celebration surrounded him. Rocca's superstar status was unmatched, particularly in the northeast, where he was worshipped and he became a household name, recognizable by even the casual observer. He was a likable showman, highly coordinated, acrobatic, and Rocca's fans were pleased by each and every performance.

Legend has it that Rocca was 18 pounds at birth, the sixth child of Italian parents, and migrated to Argentina after two of his brothers ventured there to work in construction. His wrestling debut came as early as 1940, recruited into the business by a veteran named Kola Kwariani, who was always on the lookout for high quality talent. Rocca established himself as a real comer before being brought to Texas by Nick Elitch in 1948. He received a hastened push and won the Texas State Heavyweight Title twice, receiving additional training from Paul Boesch along the way. Already the hottest young commodity in the sport, Rocca was at the heart of a struggle for his contract by promoters hoping to exploit him. The winner was "Toots" Mondt, who used Rocca to rebuild the northeastern circuit and booked him on major television outlets from coast-to-coast. Rocca's transition to full-fledged celebrity was relatively easy, and he met all demands, lived up to expectations, and delivered box office gold wherever he appeared.

From November 1956 to January 1961, Rocca headlined every Madison Square Garden wrestling show, only giving way to the phenomenon of Buddy Rogers. In terms of championships, Rocca didn't need a belt to garner attention, and in spite of that, he still won World Titles in Cleveland and Montreal, and held the United States Tag Team Championship with Miguel Perez in 1957 and 1958. He was featured in the comic book, *Superman* comic book, issue 155 entitled "The Downfall of Superman" in August of 1962. Under Vincent J. McMahon, wrestling was evolving in New York, and Rocca and Rogers were both eclipsed by the next superstar attraction, Bruno Sammartino, beginning in 1963. Rocca tried to run opposition to McMahon from Sunnyside Gardens, but couldn't keep pace with his major league rival. During the mid-1970s, he returned to the WWWF as a commentator, and then wrestled in Puerto Rico in 1976. Rocca, who was known for wrestling barefoot, passed away at the age of forty-nine on March 15, 1977 at Roosevelt Hospital.

Photo Courtesy of the Pfefer Collection, Department of Special Collections, University of Notre Dame

Rogers, Buddy

Born:	February 20, 1921
Height:	6'0"
Weight:	235
Real Name:	Herman Karl Rohde
Parents:	Herman and Freda Rohde
Family:	Father of Buddy Rogers Jr.
Identities:	Dutch Rhode, Wally Ward
Nicknames:	Nature Boy, Blond Adonis, Atomic Blond
Finisher:	Figure-four Leglock (Grapevine), Piledriver
Group:	The Mid-Atlantic Death Squad (1979-1980)
Managed:	John Studd (1979-1980), Jimmy Snuka (1980, 1981-1982)
Career Span:	1942-1983
Died:	June 26, 1992, Fort Lauderdale, FL 71 years old

Titles Won:	43
Days as World Champion:	Over 1,657
Age at first World Title Win:	26
Best Opponents:	Lou Thesz, Pat O'Connor, Bruno Sammartino
Halls of Fame:	3

Arguably the greatest wrestling villain of all time, Buddy Rogers set a standard so high that only the best of the best could come close. He was a pioneering blond heel that fans loved to hate, and his remarkable run as NWA World Heavyweight Champion between 1961 and 1963 drew millions of dollars. Tapping into the imagination of audiences, he also had his loyalists, but usually his snickering and taunting turned people off—just as he wanted, and Rogers was remarkable in the way he exhilarated arenas. As a performer, he was peerless; and because he was the complete package, Rogers would have been just as big a star today as he was then—perhaps even bigger.

Born in Camden, New Jersey, he was an athlete in high school, and wrestled at a local YMCA with his older brother, John. In November of 1939, he joined the Navy, but his father died suddenly a few weeks later, and Buddy was discharged the following March to help his mother. He served as a police officer in Camden, and began moonlighting as a professional wrestler in the beginning of 1942.

Taught by many veterans from the Philadelphia to New York circuits, Rogers learned from the likes of Joe Cox, Fred Grobmier, and the Dusek Brothers, picking up tricks of the trade that are only gained by experience. However, Rogers credited eccentric manager and promoter Jack Pfefer as giving him the push from mediocrity into the spotlight, telling Lester Bromberg of the *New York World Telegram* (3/15/50) that "He made me with the routine, and the costumes." By that time, he'd established himself as one of the premier attractions in the nation. His appearances in St. Louis helped turn the tides in the critical Sam Muchnick-Lou Thesz wrestling war, giving the former the edge and leading to a merger of the two sides. He was featured regularly on TV and claimed to have had "more television exposure than any wrestler in history" between 1947 and 1950. In 1951, incidentally, he broke from Pfefer, ending their long association and, needless to say, the minute manager was immensely bitter because of it.

This didn't matter, because Rogers could write his own ticket into any city he wanted, and promoters beckoned for him because it always meant big money. In the northeast during the late 1950s, Vincent J. McMahon was building an empire that depended on vibrant TV presentations, and bringing Rogers in was a concept that required little thought. His captivating style and overconfidence made him required viewing, and the powers that be crowned him NWA World Champion after he beat Pat O'Connor on June 30, 1961 in Chicago. The championship allure added to his drawing power, and although he was a divisive force within the NWA, he was responsible for boosting the public image of the title after a few less than stellar years. Some wrestlers, however, disliked Rogers' attitude and success. In the dressing room of a Columbus, Ohio arena on August 31, 1962, Rogers was confronted by Bill Miller and Karl Gotch, and the trio had words. The scene escalated into violence and Rogers was left bruised and battered.

A series of mishaps, injuries, and physical ailments plagued Buddy for the rest of his career. Stemming from the Columbus attack, he claimed that he'd developed a speech impediment. After a bout with Bobo Brazil, he reportedly lost forty percent of the vision in one of his eyes. He then broke his arm in Washington and followed that up by breaking his right ankle early in a bout with Killer Kowalski in Montreal . . . unfortunately, the worst was yet to come. In April of 1963, Rogers was hospitalized for chest pains, yet no one was positive whether or not he'd suffered a heart attack. Regardless, his health was more important than the business, and he performed all matches in a very restricted capacity. McMahon, at the time, was in the midst of branching out from the NWA, and despite Buddy's loss of the World Title to Lou Thesz on January 24, 1963, he still recognized him as the heavyweight champion. This changed upon news of Rogers' condition, and on May 17, 1963, the "Nature Boy" put McMahon's young star Bruno Sammartino over in less than a minute, and made the latter an instant hero.

Since that time, many rumors have circulated about what Buddy's role in the WWWF might have been had his health improved. There was also some talk that he was going to be a part owner of the organization, although none of this ended up happening. Rogers' attempt to break back into the sport as a promoter in Philadelphia was nixed by state officials, and when he did return to wrestling later in the 1960s, it was far from the heights he once knew. In the late 1970s, he again made a comeback in the Florida and Mid-Atlantic regions, even wrestling "Nature Boy" Ric Flair several times and trading victories. Perhaps his greatest match since 1963 occurred in a sandwich shop in the Fort Lauderdale area in 1989 when Rogers, then sixty-eight, pummeled a thirty-year-old man who was hassling employees. The legend of Buddy Rogers is still strong today through stories, memories, and plenty of wrestling folklore.

Photo Courtesy of the Collection of Libnan Ayoub

Born:	December 28, 1905
Height:	6'3"
Weight:	230
Real Name:	George James Hardison
Wife:	Mary Andrews Hardison
Trained by:	William O'Connell, Dick Stahl
Identities:	Ras Samara
Career Span:	1934-1956
Died:	Unknown

Titles Won:	At least 3, claimed others
Days as World Champion:	Unknown
Age at first World Title Win:	31
Best Opponents:	Lou Thesz, Everette Marshall, Jim Londos

Samara, Seelie

Pioneering African American Seelie Samara was billed as being from Ethiopia, but was really from Fort Valley, Georgia. To sell his gimmick to the public, promoters created an elaborate story for him, explaining that he had been a bodyguard for Emperor Haille Selassie. In reality, his size and athletic prowess opened doors for him as a boxer, followed then by a pro wrestler as the "Black Demon" in the New England region. Adopting the "Seelie Samara" persona in 1937, he claimed the World Heavyweight Championship of a secondary circuit in Boston. As his ring abilities grew, so did his showmanship, and he was often set up as a headliner. During a successful tour of Australia in 1946, he wrestled before crowds of 11,000 and 12,000 versus Jaget Singh and Jim Londos, respectively.

Born:	March 9, 1900
Height:	6'3"
Weight:	250
Real Name:	Edgar Civil
Military:	United States Army
Identities:	Eddie Civil, Bob Savage
Finishers:	Bearhug
Career Span:	1933-1960
Died:	January 7, 1967, Marion County, FL 66 years old

Titles Won:	At least 1
Days as World Champion:	355
Age at first World Title Win:	36
Best Opponents:	Ed Lewis, Danno O'Mahoney, Buddy Rogers
Boxing Record:	8-7
Movies:	1

Savage, Leo

The hillbilly gimmick was trademarked by Leo "Daniel Boone" Savage in 1934 after over a decade as a journeyman boxer. He reportedly received guidance from boxing legend Jack Dempsey to give wrestling a shot, and in less than two years, vaulted from obscure preliminary worker to being ranked as one of the ten best in the sport. Houston was the sight of his most noteworthy conquests and in May of 1936, he was recognized as the World Heavyweight Champion after Danno O'Mahoney ran out on a defense. Savage himself was stripped for the same reason when he failed to wrestle Chief Little Beaver in April of 1937. "Whiskers" was a household name in Texas, and because he appealed to the everyman, was a top attraction for many years.

Born:	April 21, 1914
Height:	5'9"
Weight:	215
Real Name:	Mario Fornini
Parents:	Felice and Camilla Fornini
Family:	Father of Joe and Mario Savoldi
Military:	United States Coast Guard (WWII)
Nickname:	Granite Chin
Career Span:	1937-1970

Titles Won:	At least 5
Best Opponents:	Danny Hodge, Bruno Sammartino, Dory Funk Sr.
Halls of Fame:	1

Savoldi, Angelo

As a villain who proved his resilience over and over, Angelo Savoldi disappointed fans who wanted to see him beat. He was in the upper echelon of junior heavyweights working the circuit, and even those fans who hated his in-ring behavior found it difficult to not appreciate his skill. He won the NWA World Junior Title five times between 1958 and 1964, topping Mike Clancy, Dory Funk Sr., Ivan the Terrible, Mike DiBiase, and Hiro Matsuda. Of all his feuds, his most headed was against Danny Hodge. In May of 1960, Hodge's father attacked Savoldi in an Oklahoma City ring with a penknife, and Angelo necessitated seventy stitches. The incident displayed the intense fervor of spectators during their rivalry. Savoldi was an influential veteran in the budding WWWF during the 1960s and 1970s, and turned ninety-seven years of age in 2011.

Savoldi, Joe

Born:	March 5, 1908
Height:	5'11"
Weight:	220
Real Name:	Giuseppe Antonio Savoldi Jr.
Parents:	Giuseppe and Celeste Savoldi
Wife:	Lois Savoldi
High School:	Three Oaks High School (MI)
Football Ach.:	Member of the Notre Dame National Champions in 1929 and 1930
Pro Sports:	National Football League— Chicago Bears (1930)
Military:	United States Army (WWII)
Trained by:	Ed Lewis, Joe Mondt
Promoted:	Benton Harbor, Michigan (1946-1949)
Career Span:	1931-1950
Died:	January 24, 1974, Cadiz, KY 65 years old

Titles Won:	At least 4
Days as World Champion:	136
Age at first World Title Win:	25
Best Opponents:	Jim Londos, Ed Lewis, Jim Browning

Innovator of the flying dropkick, a move that is still a fundamental part of the sport today, Italian-born "Jumpin'" Joe Savoldi was an All-American fullback at the University of Notre Dame under legendary coach Knute Rockne. After being thrown off the squad for getting a divorce, Savoldi briefly played for the Chicago Bears before he was courted into wrestling. With national name recognition, Savoldi used quick, football-like moves on the mat and became very popular. On April 7, 1933, he shockingly beat World Champion Jim Londos in Chicago, taking a pinfall from the previously unbeatable Greek in 26:20. The match was a double-cross, aimed at diminishing the drawing power of Londos, and both wrestlers left the match claiming the title. However, Savoldi's title had narrow support, and he eventually lost it to Jim Browning on June 12, 1933. Savoldi also held the Montreal World Title in 1945. He influenced the careers of Bobo Brazil and Verne Gagne, and taught high school science after retirement.

Born:	September 28, 1915
Height:	5'11"
Weight:	175-230
Real Name:	Francis Scarpa
Parents:	Carmen and Carmilla Scarpa
High School:	East Boston High School (MA)
Identities:	Gino Martinelli
Career Span:	1935-1969
Died:	January 25, 1969, Boston, MA 53 years old

Titles Won:	At least 7
Days as World Champion:	639
Age at first World Title Win:	51
Best Opponents:	Killer Kowalski, Bull Curry, Don Leo Jonathan

Scarpa, Frank

East Boston wrestling legend Frank Scarpa had a long and distinguished career. He was trained by amateur great George Myerson after showcasing his sports aptitude as a football player in high school and participated in several Boston Park Department amateur tournaments. In 1934, he won both the wrestling and boxing championships at 175 pounds. Under the name "Manuel Cortez," he was billed as being from Mexico, and used that gimmick for more than twenty years. Popular and aggressive in the ring, he wrestled all the greats of the time, and held the Boston area U.S. Title five times. On April 27, 1967, he won a tournament to win the Big Time Wrestling World Heavyweight Title, recognized by Tony Santos, and was presented with the old $10,000 Ed "Strangler" Lewis belt. The night before he passed away, Scarpa wrestled in North Attleboro and still reigned as the champion.

Born:	February 7, 1925
Height:	6'3"
Weight:	240
Real Name:	Guy LaRose
Identities:	Roy Asselin
Finisher:	Backbreaker, Piledriver, Neckbreaker, Clawhold
Career Span:	1949-1984

Titles Won:	17
Days as World Champion:	Over 302
Age at first World Title Win:	36
Best Opponents:	Verne Gagne, Wilbur Snyder, Edouard Carpentier

Schmidt, Hans

Hans Schmidt, the giant Nazi sympathizer, was one of the most hated men in the business. He perfected the performance of German stereotypes, cheated for victories, and criticized fans and opponents, drawing significant heat. Audiences were almost always furious with his actions and cheered wildly for Schmidt's opponent to give him the works. Schmidt was really Guy LaRose from Joliette, Quebec, a former amateur wrestler who adopted the German gimmick in 1952 upon advice from Boston promoter Paul Bowser. The career choice turned him into a million dollar draw. In places like New York City, Omaha, Montreal, and Chicago, huge crowds turned out to see him wrestle his dastardly style. The "Teuton Terror" annexed the United States Title from Wilbur Snyder on September 15, 1956 in Chicago, and by May 1957, he'd won the championship a total of four times. He also had five reigns as World Champion in Montreal between 1960 and 1966. Schmidt alarmed fans around the world for thirty-five years.

Born:	August 27, 1929
Height:	6'0"
Weight:	230
Family:	Older brother of Sandy Scott
Trained by:	The Dusek Brothers, Pat Murphy, Danno McDonald
Identities:	Benny Becker, The Great Scott
Career Span:	1949-1981

Titles Won:	20
Best Opponents:	Lou Thesz, Gene Kiniski, The Sheik

Scott, George

More committed to athletics at the Hamilton YMCA than to his schooling, George Scott was educated in the ways of pro wrestling, and developed one of the sharpest minds in the business. In his extensive travels, he absorbed knowledge like a sponge, learning what worked with audiences and what did not. He teamed with his brother Sandy to form a talented duo, and the pair won a number of world, international, and regional titles. As a matchmaker in the Mid-Atlantic region, he catapulted Ric Flair and Ricky Steamboat into household names. Later on, he served as an influential figure in the WWF, and was a force behind the scenes of the first two WrestleManias.

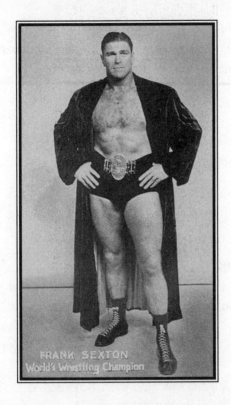

Born:	November 1, 1910
Height:	6'1"
Weight:	230
Real Name:	Francis Paul Sexton
Parents:	James and Elizabeth Sexton
Wife:	Opal Sexton
High School:	Sedalia High School (OH)
Identities:	The Masked Marvel, The Black Panther
Nickname:	The Sedalia Cyclone
Finisher:	Airplane Spin, Giant Swing
Career Span:	1932-1955
Died:	November 20, 1991, Columbus, OH 81 years old

Sexton, Frank

Titles Won:	11
Days as World Champion:	1,861, excluding multi-year European claim
Age at first World Title Win:	33
Best Opponents:	Steve Casey, Bill Longson, Jim Londos
Halls of Fame:	1

"Powerhouse" Frank Sexton was one of the longest reigning heavyweight champions at a time in which title switches and championship claimants were plentiful. It was a true testament of his ability to draw fans to arenas during the post-war years and the amount of esteem promoters had for him. A native of Sedalia, Ohio, Sexton was the youngest of eleven children and raised on the family farm. He starred in baseball and basketball in high school, and briefly attended Ohio State before the needs of his family called him back home. He was impressive during a wrestling session at a local circus and broke into pro wrestling under Columbus promoter Al Haft. On the wrestling circuit, he gained lots of experience, and many people whom he impressed along the way called him a future champion. After his breakout year in 1941, Sexton won the Pacific Coast Title in Northern California four times.

Sexton's final reign as Pacific Coast Champion lasted nearly two years. There was no question about it, he was a bonafide superstar and he added to his legacy by winning the Montreal World Title from local favorite Yvon Robert in 1944. In Boston on May 2, 1945, he beat Sandor Szabo for the AWA World Title, and then traded it with Steve Casey in June. Beginning on June 27, 1945 and over the course of the next 1,791 days, Sexton remained titleholder, a crowning achievement in a stellar career. During that run, he never shied away from opponents and met numerous rival champions, unafraid to mix it up in matches that could potentially develop into legitimate contests. He appeared in cities across the United States and included an undefeated tour of Europe, a rarity for most American champions, demonstrating that his claim was truly a "world" championship. In Cleveland on May 23, 1950, Sexton was dethroned by Don Eagle and his spectacular reign came to an end. Upon retirement, he owned and operated a construction company until 1972.

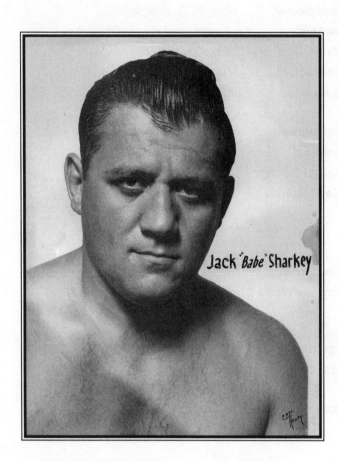

Jack "Babe" Sharkey

Photo Courtesy of John Pantozzi

Born:	November 20, 1912
Height:	6'4"
Weight:	250
Real Name:	Charles Kemmerer
Parents:	Marcus and Katie Kemmerer
High School:	Allentown High School (PA)
College:	Temple University
Pro Sports:	Reading Keys (Independent Pro Football Team) (1935)
Identities:	Tiny Cannon, Hard Boiled Hannigan
Nickname:	Texas
Career Span:	1940-1951
Died:	September 25, 1985, Santa Clara, CA 72 years old

Titles Won:	At least 1, claimed another
Days as World Champion:	Over 700
Age at first World Title Win:	31
Best Opponents:	Frank Sexton, Lou Thesz, Ed Lewis

Sharkey, Babe

Lehigh County, Pennsylvania's Charles Kemmerer went from being a relative unknown to a headliner across the country in a very short time. Around 1943, after three years in the business, he adopted the name "Babe Sharkey," and claimed he that was from Texas. He soon gained national notoriety when he boxed Tony Galento in Wilmington, losing in the third round. As a wrestler, Babe was nothing short of spectacular as a heel. He trounced opponents, using his size to dominate matches, and built-up an impressive win streak. On March 7, 1944, he triumphed in a 16-man tournament in Baltimore and a week later, beat Ed "Strangler" Lewis for the vacant World Title, recognized by the Maryland commission. He remained the titleholder until losing to Frank Sexton on January 29, 1946. A few months later, he was again billed as the champion in the Pacific Northwest, but lost his claim to George Becker on September 11 in Portland.

Born:	March 18, 1916
Height:	6'5"
Weight	265
Real Name:	Benjamin John Sharpe
Parents:	Digby and Margaret Sharpe
High School:	Westdale Secondary School (Hamilton, Ontario)
Olympics:	Rowing (1936) (representing Canada)
Career Span:	1944-1962
Died:	November 21, 2001, Palo Alto, CA 85 years old

Titles Won:	27
Best Opponents:	Lou Thesz, Rikidozan, Bobby Managoff
Halls of Fame:	1

Sharpe, Ben

"Big" Ben Sharpe was an outstanding athlete, an Olympic rower in 1936, and Hall of Fame pro wrestler. One of six children born to a Hamilton, Ontario detective, Sharpe was six years older than his brother Mike, and began wrestling just prior to service in the Royal Canadian Air Force during World War II. In 1950, Ben and Mike traveled to San Francisco, where their size and overbearing ring presence were valued by promoter Joe Malcewicz, and together they won eighteen World Tag Team Titles. They went to Japan several times, helping spread the American style of grappling to that country, and retired in 1962 after problems over pay arose with Malcewicz's successor, Roy Shire. The Sharpes were a revolutionary tag team, establishing a high standard for brother duos to come.

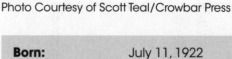

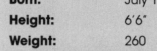

Born:	July 11, 1922
Height:	6'6"
Weight:	260
Real Name:	George Edward Sharpe
Parents:	Digby and Margaret Sharpe
High School:	Westdale Secondary School (Hamilton, Ontario)
Career Span:	1945-1964
Died:	August 10, 1988, San Joaquin Valley, CA 66 years old

Titles Won:	29
Best Opponents:	Lou Thesz, Killer Kowalski, Bill Longson
Halls of Fame:	1

Sharpe, Mike

The younger of the wrestling Sharpe Brothers, Mike Sharpe was the recipient of several notable pushes as a singles grappler in his career. In the late 1940s, he was a credible heavyweight in Toronto, and then was given matches against NWA titleholder Lou Thesz during his first major U.S. tour. Later on in San Francisco, he captured the Pacific Coast belt four separate times. However, he gained international attention as a tag team competitor with his sibling, Ben, and won eighteen World Tag Team Championships. They were startling figures because of their size, and were vicious in the ring, captivating viewers live and on TV. Mike also won the International TV and All Asia Tag Team Titles with Zebra Kid and Buddy Austin, respectively. His son, "Iron" Mike was also a wrestler.

Sheik, The

Born:	June 9, 1926
Height:	5'11"
Weight:	240
Real Name:	Edward George Farhat Sr.
Parents:	David and Eva Farhat
Family:	Father of Ed George, uncle of Sabu
Wife:	Joyce Fleser Farhat
College:	Michigan State University
Military:	United States Army (WWII)
Identities:	Sheik of Araby
Finisher:	Camel Clutch
Promoted:	Big Time Wrestling (1965-1978)
Career Span:	1949-1998
Died:	January 18, 2003, Williamston, MI 76 years old

Titles Won:	30
Days as World Champion:	Over 100
Age at first World Title Win:	41
Best Opponents:	Bobo Brazil, Verne Gagne, Bruno Sammartino
Halls of Fame:	3

Across a career lasting nearly fifty years, the Sheik faced all of the big name wrestlers and tried to gouge out the eyes of each and every one of them. Employing some of the cruelest tactics in pro wrestling history, he defined what it meant to be a roughhouse or extreme grappler. He was the opposite of Lou Thesz and Verne Gagne in terms of wrestling purity, and exemplified violence. In a world that showcased "bad guys," the Sheik was in dire need by promoters all over the world, and he sold plenty of tickets because of his thrilling gimmick. The Shiek broke into the sport under Bert Rubi in Detroit and was trained by Lou Klein. The Sheik immersed himself in his wrestling persona, rarely if ever breaking kayfabe. Fans were often thrown into a fury by his antics, and he never met a foreign object he didn't enjoy brutalizing his ring opponent with. He threw fire in the faces of rivals, bit them, and seemed to revel in being outside the ropes brawling rather than working within the confines of the squared circle.

His hardcore style was still in its infancy, but it was already scary and destructive to anyone who dared to wrestle him. All that being said, the Sheik was an exceptionally successful wrestler, and won titles in many territories. He won the United States belt more than ten times, feuding with the likes of Dick the Bruiser and Bobo Brazil, who was a lifelong adversary. In Montreal, he captured the local World Title three times between 1967 and 1974. With all of the chaos and mayhem came blood, naturally, and the carnage that was created by the Sheik resonated with fans that saw him perform live. Outside the ring, he bought hometown territory of Detroit in 1963 for a reported $50,000. He had a strong working relationship with Frank Tunney in Toronto, where he also worked as a matchmaker. It was in Toronto that he ran up a lengthy win streak, and constantly drew large audiences at the Maple Leaf Gardens. His 2003 passing was noted by the mainstream press and mourned by his longtime fans.

Photo Courtesy of Scott Teal/Crowbar Press

Born:	December 17, 1921
Height:	5'10"
Weight:	200
Real Name:	Roy P. Shropshire
Parents:	William and Amelia Shropshire
Family:	Gimmicked brother of Ray Shire
Wife:	Dorothy Shire
Promoted:	San Francisco, California (1961-1981)
Career Span:	1950-1961
Died:	September 24, 1992, Sebastopol, CA 70 years old

Titles Won:	At least 7
Best Opponents:	Dory Funk Sr., Frankie Talaber, Joe Scarpello
Halls of Fame:	1

Shire, Roy

Roy Shire lived and breathed wrestling and adhered to the unwritten code of protecting the business for thirty-one years. Two years after he retired, in 1981, he broke kayfabe in a major way, telling the press that he'd prearranged matches for years as a promoter in San Francisco. He talked about blading, the exaggerated effects of in-ring maneuvers, and even lambasted some of his peers. It was an astonishing series of revelations from the Hammond, Indiana product. Shire entered the business in Columbus and toured the country as the "Professor." He claimed to have several college degrees, and usually had a crooked manager helping him. Late in the 1950s, he partnered with a falsified brother named Ray Shire and won a claim to the World Tag Team Title. He invaded the Bay Area in 1961 and garnered a lot of attention. With sound booking, colorful TV programs, and top talent, Shire drove out his competition, and successfully promoted for the next twenty years. Among the highlights of his business was his popular annual 18-man battle royal.

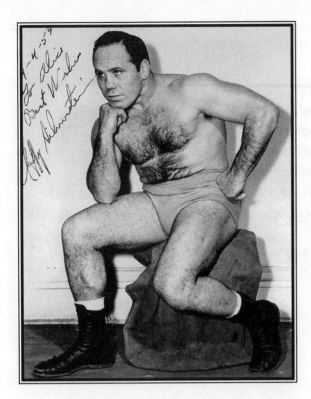

Born:	March 20, 1914
Height:	5'8"
Weight:	220
Real Name:	Ralph Silverstein
Parents:	Benjamin and Pauline Silverstein
High School:	Crane Technical High School (IL)
College:	University of Illinois
College Ach.:	Two-Time Big Ten Wrestling Champion (1935) (175), (1936) (HWT), NCAA Wrestling Title (1935) (175), All-American (1935) (175)
Military:	United States Army (WWII)
Finisher:	Abdominal Stretch
Career Span:	1937-1964
Died:	April 5, 1980, Maywood, IL 66 years old

Silverstein, Ruffy

Titles Won:	5
Days as World Champion:	Over 311
Age at first World Title Win:	37
Best Opponents:	Buddy Rogers, Bill Miller, Frankie Talaber

An expert in wrestling fundamentals, straight-laced Ruffy Silverstein won the Illinois State Championship in his first pro match, which basically laid the groundwork for a celebrated career. He ultimately won two AWA World Titles and was twice the WLW Television titleholder—credentials that added nicely to his Big Ten and NCAA amateur championships. Undefeated for many years, he mostly based his operations out of Columbus and Chicago, where his unparalleled proficiency was featured many times on national TV. Silverstein, to many people, represented the honest and clean style of pro wrestling, traits that were fast disappearing in a sport demanding chair shots and vast amounts of blood. Incidentally, the moniker "Ruffy" didn't derive from being a rough guy in the ring, but from a pet name his Russian mother had for him when he was a child.

Sonnenberg, Gus

Born:	March 6, 1898
Height:	5'8"
Weight:	205
Real Name:	Gustave Adolph Sonnenberg
Parents:	Fred and Caroline Sonnenberg
High School:	Marquette High School (MI)
Colleges:	Dartmouth College, University of Detroit
Pro Sports:	National Football League—Columbus Tigers (1923) National Football League—Buffalo All-Americans (1923) National Football League—Detroit Panthers (1925-1926) National Football League—Providence Steam Rollers (1927-1928, 1930)
Football Ach.:	NFL World Champion (1927-1928)
Trained by:	Dan Koloff, John Spellman, Pat McGill, Fred Moran
Career Span:	1928-1942
Died:	September 12, 1944, Bethesda, MD 44 years old

Titles Won:	2
Days as World Champion:	718
Age at first World Title Win:	30
Best Opponents:	Ed Lewis, Joe Stecher, Ed Don George
Halls of Fame:	3

The idea of exploiting football players in the world of wrestling was not new when "Dynamite" Gus Sonnenberg entered the business in 1928; but the way he presented himself in the ring revolutionized the concept. Instead of being a lumbering heavyweight with few visible athletic traits, he was quick-moving, crafty, and the originator of the most exciting finisher in sport: the flying tackle. The flying tackle, which saw Sonnenberg hurl himself at his opponent in a spear-like fashion, was extremely flashy, especially when compared to the dull moves usually seen on the pro mat. It was so instrumental to the sport that nearly all wrestlers utilized the move during matches, and it never failed to extract intense audience reaction. The business was rejuvenated by Sonnenberg, almost single-handedly, and on January 4, 1929, he beat Ed

"Strangler" Lewis in two straight falls for the World Heavyweight Title. In that instant, a lightning bolt electrified the entire industry, and Sonnenberg became the most coveted man in wrestling.

A former All-American and coming off a championship season as a member of the Providence Steam Rollers football team, Sonnenberg's lack of size was diminished by his dynamic performance and intensity. His championship reign coincided with a turbulent economic period, but that didn't stop sports fans from being attracted to his unique charisma, and Gus drew outstanding houses throughout the continent. But, with his success came jealousy and controversy. His promotional adversaries branched off and formed their own syndicate, and at one point, Sonnenberg was even attacked by a wrestler representing a rival troupe on the streets of Los Angeles. He reigned as champion until December 1930, then regained the title nine years later, and held it for thirteen more days. During World War II, he served as a physical training instructor at the Great Lakes Naval Center before becoming ill in December 1943. He died of leukemia that following September.

Photo Courtesy of the Collection of Tim Hornbaker

Born:	January 1, 1922
Height:	6'0"
Weight	225
Real Name:	Eugene Stanley Zygowicz
Family:	Brother of Steve and Loretta Stanlee
Career Span:	1946-1965
Died:	September 22, 2005, Redondo Beach, CA 83 years old

Titles Won:	2
Best Opponents:	Antonino Rocca, Buddy Rogers, Lou Thesz

Stanlee, Gene

Gene Stanlee was a popular showman in the early TV era, exhibiting a well-defined body that attracted viewers and a legion of female fans. During World War II, while in the Navy, he performed feats of strength for nearly a million sailors across the Pacific Theater. He was originally from Chicago, the tenth of twelve children, and upon his 1946 discharge from the Navy, he joined the pro wrestling circuit around the Great Lakes area. Stanlee's extraordinary physique was touted in promotions, and he benefited a great deal from joining a major New York booking office that marketed him nationally. Taking the nickname "Mr. America," Stanlee wrestled across the U.S., and was a top-selling card through the 1950s. He competed less and less, while still technically in his prime, and unceremoniously retired, disappointing his giant block of supporters.

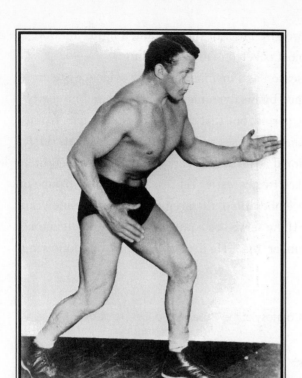

Born:	March 14, 1894
Height:	5'9"
Weight:	220
Real Name:	Henry Josef Steinborn
Family:	Father of Henry "Dick" Steinborn
Promoted:	New York City (1948-1952) (Manhattan Booking Agency), Orlando, Florida (1953-1978)
Career Span:	1922-1953
Died:	February 9, 1989, Orlando, FL 95 years old

Titles Won:	None known
Best Opponents:	Ed Lewis, Rudy Dusek, Ray Steele

Steinborn, Milo

Incredible strongman Milo Steinborn was a man who could perform an endless amount of impressive feats. He was a Greco-Roman wrestler and weight-lifter in Europe before landing in the United States after World War I, settling in Philadelphia, where he established three world lifting records. He learned the catch-as-catch-can style from George Bothner and wrestled throughout the world, competing against the likes of Ed "Strangler" Lewis, Jim Londos, and Primo Carnera, who he also managed. In 1944, he won a wrestling tournament in Philadelphia, beating Michele Leone in the final bout. After co-owning part of the New York booking office, he bought the Orlando franchise from Cowboy Luttrall for $1,000. He operated a famous gym at 2371 Orange Street in Orlando between 1960 and 1971.

Born:	March 7, 1912
Height:	6'3"
Weight	300
Real Name:	Robert Otis Stewart
Parents:	John and Susie Stewart
Identities:	Bob Weatherly, Hercules Weatherly, Robert Ashby
Career Span:	1932-1954
Died:	October 16, 1970, Austell, GA 58 years old

Titles Won:	1
Days as World Champion:	Around 10
Age at first World Title Win:	26
Best Opponents:	Jim Londos, Yvon Robert, Sandor Szabo

Stewart, Bobby

Throughout his career, the massive Bobby Stewart presented problems for his opponents, and if he didn't break every rule known to mankind during matches, he most certainly tried. He was despised by fans, yet his box office value, especially as the masked Golden Terror, was exceptionally high. Born in Stevenson, Alabama, Stewart lived a mysterious life, and newspaper writers always had trouble accurately reporting on him. In fact, he had a dozen or so hometowns and an abundance of aliases. Little did wrestling fans know that his trouble-making was as legitimate outside the ring as it was inside. His rap sheet was several pages long and he was wanted by the FBI at least two separate times. He also spent time in federal prison from 1956 to 1958 for the transfer of forged checks. Beyond that, there were claims that Stewart's outrageous behavior had gotten him blackballed by promoters. These issues, of course, were years after his superstar status faded. At his height, as the Terror, he briefly held the World championship in Baltimore, and was a constant main event attraction all across North America.

FRANK
STOJACK

Photo Courtesy of Scott Teal/Crowbar Press

Born:	February 11, 1912
Height:	5′10″
Weight:	180
Real Name:	Frank Nickolas Stojack
High School:	Lincoln High School (WA)
College:	Washington State University
Finisher:	Airplane Spin
Career Span:	1935-1958
Died:	August 30, 1987, Fox Island, WA
	75 years old

Titles Won:	12
Days as World LHW Champion:	At least 1,605
Age at first World LHW Title Win:	41
Best Opponents:	Andy Tremaine, Gypsy Joe, Danny McShain
Halls of Fame:	1

Stojack, Frank

Pacific Northwest luminary Frank Stojack was a tremendous athlete. He wrestled and played football in college, then turning pro in both sports in 1935, breaking into the wrestling business under Charles York in Spokane. The Brooklyn Dodgers signed Stojack in August 1935 and he played twenty-three games over two seasons. Upon returning to the Tacoma region, he continued his wrestling career and played semi-pro football in the Northwest Football League for the Tacoma Columbias (1939) and the Seattle Aero Mechanics (1941). He steadily held the Pacific Coast Junior Heavyweight Title and had big matches against the best in the region. On August 10, 1953, he beat Gypsy Joe for the World Light Heavyweight Title and was recognized by the National Wrestling Alliance, retiring as champion. He served as a Tacoma City Councilman, Tacoma Mayor, Pierce County Sheriff, and Commissioner of the Washington State Athletic Commission between 1950 and 1962.

Photo Courtesy of the Collection of Tim Hornbaker

Born:	October 16, 1906
Height:	6'1"
Weight:	240
Real Name:	Nils Filip Olofsson
Parents:	Alfred and Karolina Olofsson
Trained by:	Charles Hanson
Identities:	Phil Olson, Olaf Swenson
Nickname:	Popeye
Career Span:	1933-1952
Died:	February 9, 1974, Myton, UT 67 years old

Titles Won:	At least 2
Days as World Champion:	6
Age at first World Title Win:	37
Best Opponents:	Buddy Rogers, Ed Lewis, Orville Brown
Movies:	1

Swedish Angel, The

On the heels of the sensational rise of "The French Angel," Maurice Tillet, a journeyman worker with unique facial features, was also given a second "life" in wrestling. Promoter Jack Pfefer reinvented Olaf Swenson to be "The Swedish Angel," and the latter was a good box office attraction during the 1940s, winning the MWA World Heavyweight Title in December 1943 when he beat Orville Brown for the championship in Kansas City. Later in the decade, he became a matchmaker in Utah, and then bought out Jim Downing for the local promotion. The Angel ran the territory until December 1952, when he sold the business to Dave Reynolds.

Born:	January 4, 1906
Height:	6'1"
Weight:	225
Real Name:	Sandor Varga Szabo
Wife:	Lillian Szabo
Finisher:	Giant Swing
Career Span:	1930-1961
Died:	October 13, 1966, Los Angeles, CA 60 years old

Titles Won:	43
Days as World Champion:	Around 1,773, including overlapping reigns
Age at first World Title Win:	35
Best Opponents:	Jim Londos, Bill Longson, Yvon Robert
Halls of Fame:	1

Szabo, Sandor

Hungarian Sandor Szabo, a multi-time world heavyweight champion, was a dexterous grappler, successful in drawing heat from audiences as well as applause. In the ring, he combined speed with smarts, and was a compelling box office attraction throughout his long career. Szabo was a preeminent superstar all over North America, particularly during World War II, when he reigned as the world champion of both the NWA and AWA, plus in the realms of several independent state commissions. Born in Kassa, Czechoslovakia, he came to the U.S. after a successful amateur career as a Greco-Roman wrestler, and was still learning the American catch-as-catch-can trade when he debuted in 1930. On the northeastern circuit, he was an appealing young athlete and challenged Jim Londos for the heavyweight crown on a number of occasions. While he was making headway in New York, Szabo's real taste of fame and glory came in Northern California, where in 1937, he won the first of thirteen Pacific Coast Heavyweight championships.

The biggest win of Szabo's career occurred on June 5, 1941 in St. Louis when he beat Bronko Nagurski for the National Wrestling Association World Heavyweight Title. He held the belt until losing a February 1942 match to Bill Longson. In March 1944, he conquered The Golden Terror in Boston to win the "Duration" World Title, which was implemented after the rightful champion, Steve Casey, went off to serve in the Army. Later that year, he beat Yvon Robert to strengthen his claim and remained champion until suffering a loss to Casey on April 4, 1945. Szabo was able to win a rematch from Casey on April 25, 1945, and won the AWA World Title, but lost it to Frank Sexton the following week. In addition, Szabo was backed as champion in Minnesota four times between 1944 and 1948. A resident of Los Angeles, Szabo was an important figure in the local office for many years, training young grapplers, booking, and refereeing matches. Outside of the ring, Szabo was a talented swimmer and was well-liked and respected by his peers.

Born:	July 17, 1912
Height:	5'11"
Weight:	215
Parents:	Louis and Elizabeth Talaber
High School:	Lane Tech High School (IL)
Trained by:	Lou Talaber
Career Span:	1936-1964
Died:	September 7, 1994, Frankfort, IL
	82 years old

Titles Won:	20
Best Opponents:	Buddy Rogers, Don Eagle, Bill Miller

Talaber, Frankie

During the astronomical boom period created by the television medium in the early 1950s, Frankie Talaber was a leading star in the Columbus, Ohio territory and an influential matchmaker. Having learned all the fundamentals from his father, Lou, who was a former middleweight champion, he captured the Central AAU wrestling title and strengthened his showmanship as he went pro in 1936. Talaber hit his stride in Columbus while working for promoter Al Haft, and, between 1941 and 1954, he won the MWA World Junior Title ten times. In addition to booking, he was also an important trainer in Haft's famous gymnasium, and was a longtime favorite of crowds throughout the state. Featured regularly on TV, Talaber feuded with Buddy Rogers and Don Eagle and operated a restaurant in downtown Columbus, where many wrestlers spent their free time.

Born:	April 24, 1916
Height:	6'1"
Weight:	235
Real Name:	Aloysius Martin Thesz
Parents:	Martin and Katherine Thesz
Finisher:	Thesz Press, STF
Trained:	Mark Fleming
Career Span:	1934-1990
Died:	April 28, 2002, Orlando, FL
	86 years old

Titles Won:	26
Days as World Champion:	5,591 (excluding TWWA claim)
Age at first World Title Win:	21
Best Opponents:	Bill Longson, Verne Gagne, Buddy Rogers
Halls of Fame:	8

Thesz, Lou

As the National Wrestling Alliance unified promoters and booking offices in the late 1940s and into the early 1950s, the sport was facing many major changes. Television was providing a unique outlet for wrestling personalities, giving Gorgeous George and other colorful grapplers a platform to go through their motions of performance. On the other end of the spectrum, representing the NWA and the wrestling business as a whole was a dignified and straight-laced heavyweight champion named Lou Thesz. Thesz was the equivalent to the number one athlete in any other sport, called the "Babe Ruth of Wrestling" by one sportswriter, and heroically carried the weight of the NWA on his back. By refusing to play into the regular stereotypes that accompanied pro wrestling, Thesz commanded and received respect. Thus, the business benefited from having a champion of his caliber. With him, there was reason to believe that the best man was truly the world titleholder.

During Thesz's career, maintaining the illusion of wrestling's realness was the top priority for everyone involved. Thesz personally preserved that with his seriousness and legitimacy. Fans could plainly see it, writers understood it, and promoters coveted it. With all his success, the path to wrestling immortality wasn't cut in stone for Thesz. Over a career lasting fifty-six years, he earned everything that has been said about him. He was born in the Austrian community of Banat, Michigan, the son of hardworking parents, and grew up in St. Louis. Having attained the bug for wrestling from his father, Martin, who'd wrestled Greco-Roman in his youth, Lou worked out in local gymnasiums and became adept to the catch-as-catch-can style. His size and strength stood out on the semi-pro circuit in East St. Louis, and with formal training under Joe Sanderson and George Tragos, he was headed for bigger and better things.

Thesz's discipline for the fundamentals was ungodly. Instead of fixating on being the best grimacing heel, he worked on shooting and hooking opponents, training as if he was going to participate in square matches instead of exhibitions. He impressed promoters in the Central States before going out to San Francisco, where he was schooled by Ad Santel, who furthered his development measurably. By 1937, Thesz, after only three years in the business, was ready for a substantial push by his hometown promoter, Tom Packs, and on December 29, he beat Everette Marshall for the World Title. Rather than getting a real shot to display his talents as champion, Thesz was only a temporarily titleholder, losing the heavyweight crown to Steve Casey on February 11, 1938 in Boston. A victim of the sport's politics, he was quickly learning how to avoid being pushed around by promoters behind-the-scenes. He didn't want to be a pawn of greedy businessmen and wanted more control in the direction of his career.

On February 23, 1939, he returned to the heavyweight throne, topping Hall of Fame footballer Bronko Nagurski for the National Wrestling Association World Title in Houston. He reigned through June, and that following year, he won the Montreal version of the World championship. During the war, he worked as a shipbuilder before entering the Army in January of 1945 and wrestled when he could, maintaining his impeccable conditioning. He regained the NWA World Title in 1947, then again in 1948, but his real power came from ownership in the valuable St. Louis office, which came when Packs retired in June of 1948. Thesz also assumed control of the NWA championship, allowing him to dictate who was going to hold it and for how long. He topped Bill Longson on July 20, 1948 for the belt, and settled in as the king, a role he'd play for the next eight years. In November of 1949, the National Wrestling Alliance put their recognition behind him, giving Thesz the strongest claim to the championship in the world.

Thesz traveled extensively across a well-defined thirty-plus territory landscape and defined what it meant to be a reputable and esteemed titleholder. Demonstrating amazing stamina, he traversed the United States, Canada, Mexico, Cuba, and Hawaii, and successfully defended his title against every notable wrestler in the business. Controversial matches with Leo Nomellini and Edouard Carpentier purposely tainted his title run, executed to make money at the box office, but Thesz remained effective as a draw. Thesz ultimately lost the NWA Title to Dick Hutton on November 14, 1957, ending his lengthy run, and, having already sold out of St. Louis, was ready to control his own destiny as an independent grappler. By 1963, with the membership of the National Wrestling Alliance falling apart, there was a desperate need for stability in the wrestling ranks. The influential St. Louis booker Sam Muchnick coordinated Thesz's return to the throne, and on January 24, 1963 in Toronto, Lou beat Buddy Rogers for the NWA belt, his sixth world title.

Thesz was responsible for helping the NWA return to prominence between 1963 and 1966, and the organization's footing was much more stable when he lost the championship to Gene Kiniski on January 7, 1966 than when he started his run. In the years that followed, he maintained a full-time schedule for some years before slowly scaling back. Although he was getting older, his name recognition still sold tickets, and he was unwilling to give up the sport he loved. Thesz had his final match in Japan on December 26, 1990 against his protégé, Masa Chono. Chono won with an STF, a move Thesz made famous over the years. Over the course of his long career, he traveled an estimated sixteen million miles across the globe and participated in upwards of 6,000 matches. He was a heavyweight champion at twenty-one years of age and lastly, at sixty-two. Thesz's legacy as a wrestler and as an emissary for the sport left an indelible mark, and his influence is still being felt in the sport today.

Born:	October 23, 1903
Height:	5'9"
Weight:	275
Real Name:	Maurice Marie Joseph Tillet
Military:	French Navy
Career Span:	1937-1954
Died:	August 4, 1954, Chicago, IL
	50 years old

Titles Won:	3
Days as World Champion:	745
Age at first World Title Win:	36
Best Opponents:	Steve Casey, Bill Longson,
	Yvon Robert
Halls of Fame:	1

Tillet, Maurice

Of all the sports, only in the world of professional wrestling can a man with an advance billing of the "Ugliest Man on Earth" become a top gate attraction and superstar. Additionally, Maurice Tillet was called grotesque, bizarre, and a monster, which were endearing selling points to the wrestling crowd. Tillet was said to be the closest scientists had found to a Neanderthal, possessing a freakish looking head and powerfully built body. The son of French parents, Tillet was born in St. Petersburg, Russia, and was discovered in Singapore by a well-traveled Lithuanian wrestler named Karl Pojello around 1937. Pojello and Tillet immediately bonded and traveled to France, where the latter launched a successful run of 180 victories. Featured by *Life Magazine* and other mainstream press, Tillet was fast becoming wrestling's hottest commodity. People wanted to see his unique appearance in person and they surely weren't disappointed.

Keenly intelligent and with Pojello there to handle unscrupulous promoters, Tillet wasn't robbed regularly as other attractions like Primo Carnera and Antonino Rocca were. He was smartly pushed to the apex of Bowser's AWA, winning the heavyweight title from Steve Casey on May 13, 1940 and holding the title for two years. In that time, he conquered the likes of Bobby Managoff, Frank Sexton, Gus Sonnenberg, Ed "Strangler" Lewis, and many others who were considered the best in the business. Tillet used his amazing strength and signature bearhug to put opponents out, and his sound in-ring performance marginalized the freak factor as his only selling point to a certain degree. For two weeks in 1944, he reigned a second time as AWA World Champion after defeating Casey in San Francisco. Tillet, the "French Angel," spawned a host of other "Angels," that would roam the wrestling landscape, but none were as distinct as the original. He passed away only hours after his longtime friend, Pojello died, with his grief obviously overcoming him.

Born:	July 25, 1922
Height:	6'1"
Weight:	230
Parents:	Alfonso and Pomposa Torres
Trained by:	Benny Ginsberg
Career Span:	1946-1968
Died:	September 10, 2007, Calgary, Alberta 85 years old

Titles Won:	42
Days as World Champion:	1,442
Age at first World Title Win:	24
Best Opponents:	Fred Blassie, Lou Thesz, Gene Kiniski
Halls of Fame:	2

Torres, Enrique

In 1946, booker Johnny Doyle touted young Enrique Torres as the greatest Mexican grappler since Vincent Lopez, and Torres quickly lived up to the hype. Within months of his pro debut, he won the local World Heavyweight Championship on December 11, 1946 from George Becker in Los Angeles. He perpetuated a clean style and was extremely popular wherever he traveled. Born in Santa Ana, California, Torres was the oldest of six children, and his two younger brothers, Ramon and Alberto, also became grapplers. In addition to his nearly four-year reign as World Champion in Los Angeles, where he held the Pacific Coast Heavyweight Title and a number of tag team championships in San Francisco and Georgia. The Torres Brothers, combinations of the trio, were highly successful, and Enrique wrestled through 1968, when he retired from the business.

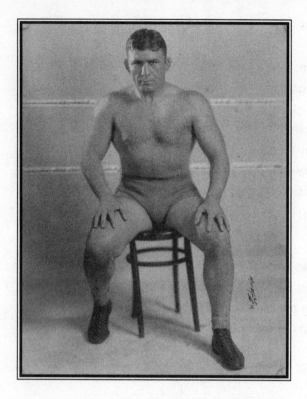

Photo Courtesy of the Pfefer Collection, Department of Special Collections, University of Notre Dame

Born:	March 14, 1897
Height:	5'9"
Weight:	215
Parents:	William and Stavroula Tragos
Amateur Ach.:	National AAU Title (1919) (158), Indiana State AAU Title (1921) (175)
Trained by:	George Pinneo
Identities:	George Kondylis
Career Span:	1922-1950
Died:	September 5, 1955, St. Louis, MO 58 years old

Titles Won:	None known
Best Opponents:	Ed Lewis, Ray Steele, Dick Shikat

Tragos, George

Eighty years ago, it was quite common for promoters to covet genuine wrestling "shooters" to humble the overconfident, punish the unruly, and test the greenhorns who wanted in to the business. In St. Louis, the promoter utilized the expertise of George Tragos, a world-class catch-as-catch-can wrestler, and Tragos not only acted as a training partner for every big name that entered the city, but tutored up-and-comers like Lou Thesz and Fred Blassie. With family in Chicago, Tragos migrated from Greece in 1910 and was a pivotal member of the Gary, Indiana YMCA, winning several AAU honors. He was also affiliated with the 1920 Greek Olympic wrestling team, although he didn't place In memory of his varied contributions to the sport, an Iowa wrestling Hall of Fame bears his name alongside his most famous student, Lou Thesz.

Born:	September 19, 1928
Height:	6'2"
Weight:	235
Real Name:	John Theodore Wisniski
Family:	Father of Greg Valentine
Wife:	Sharon Valentine
High School:	Tahoma High School (WA)
Identities:	Jimmy Valentine, Rocky Valentine, The Big O
Nickname:	The Blond Bombshell, Honest, The Blond Jet
Finisher:	Backbreaker
Career Span:	1947-1975
Died:	April 24, 2001, Near River Oaks, TX 72 years old

Valentine, Johnny

Titles Won:	64
Days as World Champion:	Over 140
Age at first World Title Win:	34
Best Opponents:	Lou Thesz, Buddy Rogers, Killer Kowalski
Halls of Fame:	5

As the television era courted an avalanche of colorful pretenders in the late 1940s, pro wrestling was running out of hard-nosed athletes who thought, behaved, and performed like wrestlers of old. Johnny Valentine filled the growing void, entering the sport with the knowledge and physicality of a veteran. Taught the traditional ways of the mat by two aging former champions, Stanislaus and Wladek Zbyszko, he was a stark contrast to those wrestlers who placed an emphasis on the dramatic side of the profession. A product of a broken Hobart, Washington home, Valentine began his training as a teenager and quickly absorbed the fundamentals. He also toughened his mind and body to not only dish out punishment, but to be able to take it. In 1947, he went to South America to make his professional debut, and traveled throughout Argentina, the Caribbean, and Florida. When he was ready, he returned to the U.S., quickly becoming a valuable box office commodity, and won regional championships nearly everywhere he went.

Able to wrestle technically and brawl until the last man was standing, Valentine had bloody feuds with Wahoo McDaniel, Great Malenko, and The Sheik that are embedded in wrestling lore. Never needing a gimmick to get over, he propelled himself into the top tier through hard work and dedication to the sport. Fans understood that when Valentine was coming to town, regardless of his opponent, they were going to get a sincere effort, sometimes in both science and brutality. He won the NWF World Heavyweight Title twice as well as the Montreal World crown. In the northeast, he teamed with Buddy Rogers, Bob Ellis, and Antonio Pugliese to capture the U.S. Tag Team Title. He held three different versions of the U.S.

Heavyweight Title, the Texas championship seven times, and the Missouri State belt. Valentine's career came to an abrupt end in October of 1975, when he was involved in a plane crash in North Carolina. At the time, he was still acknowledged as one of the toughest wrestlers in the world.

Born:	January 10, 1919
Height:	5'11"
Weight:	210
Real Name:	William Varga
Family:	Son of "Count" Joseph Varga
High School:	Hollywood High School (CA)
Finisher:	Abdominal Stretch
Career Span:	1940-1967

Titles Won:	9
Best Opponents:	Red Berry, Danny McShain, Joe Scarpello
Movies:	12
TV Appearances:	Over 10

Varga, Billy

Lauded by fans everywhere for his clean and scientific style, "Count" Billy Varga was a second generation grappler from Southern California. His father, Joe, began teaching him the art of catch-as-catch-can grappling when he was five years old; and after spending a number of years as an amateur, Billy turned pro in 1940. On December 1, 1941, he won the World Light Heavyweight Title from Red Berry in Hollywood and held it for three weeks. He captured it again two years later, and in 1954, he won the World Junior belt in Columbus, Ohio. Varga was one of the most popular wrestlers in the business and held the American championship for upwards of ten years, retiring as champion in the late 1960s. He appeared as the ring announcer in the classic film, *Raging Bull* in 1980.

Born:	April 22, 1912
Height:	6'1"
Weight:	225
Real Name:	Raymond Henry Villmer
Military:	United States Navy (WWII)
Career Span:	1935-1965
Died:	January 9, 2005, Tallahassee, FL 92 years old

Titles Won:	11
Best Opponents:	Buddy Rogers, Bill Longson, Lou Thesz

Villmer, Ray

Ray Villmer grew up in De Soto, Missouri but wrestled out of St. Louis. He was the son of a railroad switchman and, on the mat, he was exceptionally scientific and at times brutal. When his opponents came looking for a fight, Villmer was always ready to brawl, and he used his athleticism to prevail in matches throughout the territorial system. He wrestled from coast to coast and won a variety of regional honors, including the Central States, Southern, and Florida Heavyweight Titles. Villmer retired to Florida, ending his three-decade career, and passed away in 2005.

Born:	August 12, 1912
Height:	5'10 ½"
Weight:	230
Real Name:	Edward Ebner Virag
Wife:	Marguerite Virag
Military:	United States Army (1943-1945)
Finisher:	Full Nelson Suplex, Halsch Lock
Career Span:	1937-1951
Died:	October 20, 1951, near Kozani, Greece 39 years old

Titles Won:	2
Days as World Champion:	1,482
Age at first World Title Win:	29
Best Opponents:	Roy Dunn, Lou Thesz, Everette Marshall

Virag, Ed

Born in Budapest, Hungary, Ed Virag was an amateur wrestler of note, and placed first in the 1935 European championships in the freestyle division. He competed as a light heavyweight in the 1936 Olympics, but did not place. He ventured to the U.S. in 1937, became a citizen, served in the Army during World War II, and married a girl from Minnesota. During the 1940s, he scored victories over many well-known wrestlers, including ex-champions Ed "Strangler" Lewis, Wladek Zbyszko, and Everette Marshall. On April 27, 1942, he defeated Roy Dunn for a claim to the regional National Wrestling Alliance Championship and reigned for nearly all of the 1942 to 1946 time period. Virag, while touring overseas, was killed in a car accident en route to Athens, Greece and was buried in a Protestant Cemetery at Salonikia.

Born:	June 25, 1915
Height:	6'1"
Weight:	230
Real Name:	William John Potts
Parents:	John and Alice Potts
Family:	Father of Phillip Watson (Billy Watson Jr.)
Trained by:	Phil Lawson
Finisher:	Irish Whip, Canadian Avalanche
Career Span:	1936-1971
Died:	February 4, 1990, Orlando, FL 74 years old

Titles Won:	33
Days as World Champion:	302
Age at first World Title Win:	31
Best Opponents:	Lou Thesz, Bill Longson, Yvon Robert
Halls of Fame:	2

Watson, Billy

Wrestling legend "Whipper" Billy Watson was a hero of immense proportions in Ontario and throughout most of Canada. From the moment he debuted in Toronto on October 3, 1940 until his last bout there on November 28, 1971, he always gave fans something to cheer about, with his matches usually full of intense drama and colorful athleticism. The East York product initially gained experience while in England, and by the time of his first match in Toronto, he was ready to set the wrestling world ablaze. Claiming the Canadian and British Empire championships at different times, Watson became the centerpiece of Toronto's grappling scene, and promoter Frank Tunney specifically brought in heel after heel to declare war on him— maintaining his status as the hottest ticket in town. Watson made history when, on February 21, 1947, he beat "Wild" Bill Longson for the National Wrestling Association World Heavyweight Title. He held the belt through April 25, when he lost the prize to the great Lou Thesz.

Some years later, on March 15, 1956, he ended the seven-plus year reign of Thesz as National Wrestling Alliance World Champion when ex-boxing champion Jack Dempsey as special guest referee counted the latter out after more than thirty minutes and declared Watson the new king. While an amazing victory for Watson, Thesz was able to regain the title in November. In addition to his star qualities on the mat, he was a successful businessman, selling branded items featuring his name, and was invested in the Toronto and St. Louis promotions, including briefly in Seattle. On November 30, 1971, he was forced to retire from the ring after being hit by a car.

During his life, he dabbled in politics and was gracious with his time when it came to charities. He was not the kind of guy to walk by a child asking for an autograph, and if there were dozens of kids, he wouldn't leave until he'd signed them all. Watson's legacy goes well beyond the wrestling ring, and those who were touched by his kindness still remember him fondly today.

Photo Courtesy of Scott Teal/Crowbar Press

Born:	December 19, 1902
Height:	5'10"
Weight:	185
Real Name:	Roy Edward Welch
Parents:	Edwin and Birdie Welch
Trained by:	Edwin Welch, Cal Farley, Dutch Mantell
Family:	Brother of Herb, Lester, and Jack Welch
Career Span:	1929-1959
Died:	September 27, 1977, Trenton, TN 74 years old

Titles Won:	At least 6
Best Opponents:	Joe Gunther, Ike Chacoma, Tex Riley

Welch, Roy

A skilled athlete, animal handler, matchmaker, and promoter, Roy Welch wore many hats in the world of wrestling during a career that lasted over forty years. Originally from Sallisaw, Oklahoma, he was the oldest of four wrestling brothers and first gained fame as a light heavyweight in Oklahoma and Texas during the early 1930s. He toured many territories as the trainer of Ginger, a 350-pound wrestling bear, and claimed titles in both the light heavyweight and junior heavyweight divisions. Along with business partner Nick Gulas, Welch controlled wrestling in over three dozen cities and booked a couple hundred grapplers at a time between the 1940s and his death in 1977. His son Buddy Fuller and grandsons Robert and Ron Fuller also wrestled professionally.

Born:	July 27, 1910
Height:	6'2"
Weight:	230
Real Name:	Marvin Louis Westenberg
Parents:	August and Louise Westenberg
High School:	Lincoln High School (WA)
College:	University of Washington
Career Span:	1930-1950
Died:	August 20, 1978, Pierce County, WA 68 years old

Titles Won:	At least 1
Days as World Champion:	14
Age at first World Title Win:	28
Best Opponents:	Steve Casey, Yvon Robert, Ed Don George

Westenberg, Marvin

Westenberg was a twenty-year wrestling veteran, a heavyweight championship claimant, and a minority owner of a major promotion during his career. A native of Tacoma, Westenberg broke into the sport in early 1930 and found a strong mentor in Paul Bowser of Boston, where he first appeared in 1932. Under the guise of "The Shadow" and wearing a mask, he conquered the unbeatable Steve "Crusher" Casey on March 2, 1939 and won the AWA World Heavyweight Title—becoming the first masked wrestler to hold such a prestigious title. His reign only lasted two weeks, when he lost a rematch to Casey. For a time during his career, Westenberg was part owner of the Boston wrestling office, the location of his most important matches. In 1950, he suffered a serious head injury during a bout that prematurely and unfortunately ended his time on the mat.

Born:	November 6, 1907
Height:	6'2"
Weight:	265
Real Name:	Reuben Haz Wright
Family:	Brother of Jim Wright
Career Span:	1932-1961
Died:	November 9, 1983, Klamath County, OR 76 years old

Titles Won:	At least 2
Days as World Champion:	Unknown
Age at first World Title Win:	34
Best Opponents:	Ed Lewis, Everette Marshall, Sandor Szabo
Halls of Fame:	1

Wright, Rube

Big Rube Wright didn't follow in his father's footsteps by joining the clergy, but instead spent his time as a young man at the Hollywood Athletic Club. He was from Brown County, Texas, but grew up in Southern California and debuted after four years of amateur wrestling in 1932. A physical guy who was unafraid to mix it up in the ring, the gym, or on the streets, Wright wrestled around the world and gained his biggest fame when he won an international tournament on August 19, 1942 in Los Angeles and captured the California Title, which was initially a World championship. He also spent a number of years as wildman "Lu Kim," a wrestler claiming Manchuria as his homeland.

Photo Courtesy of the Pfefer Collection, Department of Special Collections, University of Notre Dame

Born:	March 10, 1898
Height:	5'11"
Weight:	225
Real Name:	Lee Arlo Wykoff
Parents:	Charles and Ethel Wykoff
College Ach.:	All-Kansas Football Honors (1920, 1922-1923)
Pro Sports:	National Football League—St. Louis All-Stars (1923)
Identities:	Big Bad Wolf (Masked)
Finisher:	Stepover toehold
Career Span:	1925-1947
Died:	April 30, 1974, Kansas City, KS 76 years old

Titles Won:	5
Days as World Champion:	Around 282
Age at first World Title Win:	43
Best Opponents:	Ed Lewis, Orville Brown, Everette Marshall

Wykoff, Lee

A scientifically skilled grappler from Osborne, Kansas, Wykoff made his mark from coast to coast and was legitimately feared for his exceptional shooting skills. He attended Washburn College in Topeka, where he earned a wide amount of respect for his athletic prowess on the football field. In the years that followed, he built his strength while working for the Missouri Pacific Railroad, and by 1926, he was traveling around the Central States as a professional wrestler. Finding that it was valuable to work the role of a heel during matches, Wykoff displayed rough tactics during tours of the east, and was a policeman for champion Everette Marshall in 1936. On August 13 of that year, he faced Ed Lewis in an infamous shoot match in New York. Their affair was marred by lengthy rest holds and tiresome inactivity and ended in a draw when both were counted out after more than two hours. In 1940, he won an international tournament in Los Angeles, and held claims to the World Title in the Kansas City region prior to retiring in 1947.

Born:	March 12, 1923
Height:	5'6"
Weight:	145
Real Name:	Johnnie Mae Young
Parents:	John and Lillian Young
High School:	Sand Springs High School (OK)
Trained by:	Billy Wolfe
Career Span:	1941-2010

PPV Record:	2-0
WWE *Raw* TV Record:	3-3, 2 NC
WWE *Smackdown* TV Record:	2-1, 1 NC
Titles Won:	4
Best Opponents:	Mildred Burke, June Byers, Nell Stewart
Halls of Fame:	2

Young, Mae

A pioneering, Hall of Fame wrestler, Mae Young has entertained wrestling audiences since 1941. In fact, she was wrestling professionally prior to the attack on Pearl Harbor and still makes the occasional appearance for the WWE. From the small town of Wekiwa, just west of Tulsa, Oklahoma, Young was the last of seven siblings, the daughter of a carpenter, and was taught how to wrestle by her brothers. She grappled on the boys' team in high school and made the acquaintance of women's wrestling impresario Billy Wolfe. Since then, she's toured the world, and was one of the roughest female grapplers in the business. She even demonstrated her indomitable spirit and toughness, at 77, when she was put through a table by the Dudley Boys on *Raw*, and partook in wild storylines—like giving birth to a hand—all for the profession she loves. Her unparalleled enthusiasm shows every time she appears on WWE programming, and she remains eternally popular with fans young and old.

Born:	April 22, 1916
Height:	6'1"
Weight:	275
Real Name:	Erick Holmback
College:	Washington State University
Finisher:	Backbreaker
Career Span:	1946-1965
Died:	January 16, 1965, Bartow County, GA 48 years old

Titles Won:	6
Days as World Champion:	266
Age at first World Title Win:	33
Best Opponents:	Killer Kowalski, Verne Gagne, Lou Thesz

Yukon Eric

Holmback was born in Monroe, Washington. He was the son of a logger and excelled in football as an adolescent, and spent much of his time weightlifting. Following a stint in the Army during World War II, he decided to become a wrestler and went pro. With an astonishing chest expansion measuring upward of 65 inches, he was initially billed as "The Chest," but matchmaker Al Mayer dubbed him "Yukon Eric," a lumberman from Alaska. In possession of a powerful bearhug, Eric toured extensively, winning the Montreal World Title over Bobby Managoff in 1950. On October 15, 1952, he suffered the loss of part of his cauliflower ear during a match with Killer Kowalski at the Montreal forum. He was rushed to the hospital and had surgery to repair the damage, and the event only served to strengthen their enduring feud. In Jacksonville on January 24, 1963, he teamed up with Don Curtis to win the World Tag Team Title from the Kangaroos. Eric was a popular superstar wherever he appeared, and the audience always left knowing they'd gotten their money's worth.

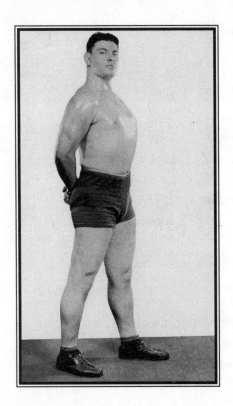

Born:	February 28, 1908
Height:	6'0"
Weight:	230
Real Name:	Theodore Vetoyanis
Parents:	Gust and Demitra Vetoyanis
Wife:	Babe Didrikson Zaharias
Trained by:	Milo Steinborn
Career Span:	1929-1948
Died:	May 22, 1984, Tampa, FL
	76 years old

Titles Won:	Claimed at least 2
Best Opponents:	Jim Londos, Ray Steele,
	Joe Stecher
Halls of Fame:	1

Zaharias, George

A product of Pueblo, Colorado, Zaharias was often known as a "bad guy" in the ring; but outside of the squared circle, he was very personable and popular among his peers. Today, people tend to associate the name "Zaharias" with the world renowned golfer, Mildred "Babe" Didrikson, who was George's wife from 1938 until her death in 1956. George and his two brothers, Chris and Tom and his nephew, Babe, were collectively known as the "Cripple Creek Terrors," and created chaos throughout the wrestling world. In addition to claiming the Colorado State Title, he was deemed the local successor to World Heavyweight Champion Danno O'Mahoney in January of 1936 by a group of cynical sportswriters. He promoted the Olympic Auditorium in Los Angeles and in Denver before leaving wrestling for the greener pastures of golf courses throughout the globe.

III. Heroes and Villains Wage War in the Sacred Territories
Pro Debut Between 1951 and 1975

Spurred on by the exposure of television, professional wrestling's esteem increased measurably in the early 1950s, and many viewers were fascinated by the colorfulness of its performers. The creation and expansion of the monopolistic National Wrestling Alliance helped streamline championships and made it easy for wrestlers to travel within its huge web of territories. Later in the decade, the Department of Justice found the NWA's ruthless actions with regard to outsiders to be illegal, and brought the hammer down—stopping short, though, of forcing the coalition of promoters to break up. The AWA and WWWF were established in the years that followed, and with the NWA, were collectively known as the "Big Three." The trio of organizations were the most noteworthy in the business for the next couple of decades.

The sport benefited greatly from a stream of credible amateurs who decided to turn pro. Former NCAA champions Verne Gagne, Dick Hutton, and Danny Hodge each made an impact soon after their debuts, and the likes of Jack Brisco followed in the mid-1960s. To the public, these individuals were shining examples of the genuine athletic marvels performing on a nightly basis around the country—and not all wrestlers were beastly figures with little to no legitimate sports ability. The varied gimmicks, particularly the behemoths, did make things lively and sometimes the crazier the worker, the more money it drew. For example, the maniacal Sheik displayed his riotous behavior across the globe and fans knew that when he was on the card, plenty of mayhem was to be expected. A mixture of authentic wrestlers and untamed brawlers gave the business a nice balance.

At the top of the heavyweight class, Bruno Sammartino, Gene Kiniski, and Dory Funk Jr. were fitting titleholders, and their multi-year reigns were nothing but successful. In terms of box office attractions, there was no one who quite matched up with the 6'11", 400-plus-pound Andre the Giant, and the "Eighth Wonder of the World" made a real impact wherever he traveled. Behind the scenes,, promoters Sam Muchnick and Vincent J. McMahon provided instrumental leadership that resonated throughout wrestling, and although the overall popularity waned at times, the territorial system thrived for the most part across North America. Likewise in Japan and Mexico, and with an abundance of superstars constantly touring and logical booking that made sense to enthusiasts, wrestling's reach continued to grow.

The squared circle was the center of attention in arenas around the globe, and grappling provided a nice escape from the cultural and social turmoil that people were dealing with on a daily basis. Into the 1970s, wrestling was facing some serious new challenges, particularly when confronted with the retirement or deaths of many older promoters who were the backbone of the territories. There was also the cable television factor, which made it easier for rival wrestling operations to present their brand in opposing regions. These critical avenues would soon be exploited by an enterprising third-generation promoter, and professional wrestling was never going to be the same.

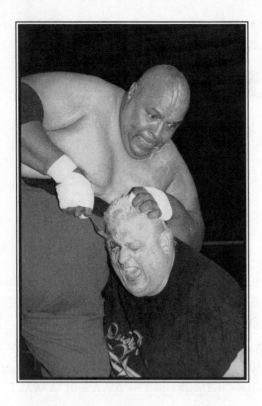

Abdullah the Butcher

Born:	January 11, 1941
Height:	6'1"
Weight:	360
Real Name:	Larry Paul Shreve
Parents:	George and Martha Shreve
Nicknames:	The Sudanese Madman, Madman from the Sudan, The Black Wizard
Finisher:	Elbowdrop
Career Span:	1966-2010

PPV Record:	1-2, 1 DCO
Titles Won:	45
Days as World Champion:	235
Age at first World Title Win:	31
Best Opponents:	The Sheik, Carlos Colon, Dusty Rhodes
Managers:	Over 25
Halls of Fame:	2

Long before being "extreme" was all the rage, there were only a few matmen with a penchant for hardcore violence and a longing for bloodshed. At the top of that short list was Abdullah the Butcher; a hefty, fork-wielding superstar from Windsor, Ontario who broke into the sport under the supervision of Detroit promoters Jack Britton and Bert Rubi. Initially known as "Zelis Amara," he adopted the "butcher" gimmick while wrestling in Vancouver in 1967 and regularly sent crowds into a panic with his out-of-control behavior, which failed to play by any of the old catch-as-catch-can rules. Abdullah was crafty in using Taekwondo martial arts, a style that he earned a seventh degree black belt in, even though he weighed over 350 pounds. An international phenomenon, Abdullah won world titles in the U.S., Puerto Rico, and Japan in his over forty years in the business. One way or another, his matches have always been memorable, and fans quickly learned that if Abby was heading toward them with fork in hand, it was best to flee in the opposite direction.

Born:	September 15, 1953
Height:	5'11"
Weight:	275
Real Name:	Keith A. Franke
Parents:	Kenneth and Kay Franke
Wife:	Bea Franke
High School:	Kenmore East High School (NY)
Trained by:	Fred Atkins
Nickname:	Adorable, The Golden Boy
Finisher:	DDT
Tag Team:	The East-West Connection w/ Jesse Ventura
Career Span:	1974-1988
Died:	July 4, 1988, near Lewisporte, Newfoundland 34 years old

Adonis, Adrian

PPV Record:	2-2
WrestleMania Record:	1-1
Titles Won:	8
Days as World Champion:	96
Age at first World Title Win:	29
Best Opponents:	Bob Backlund, Roddy Piper, Hulk Hogan

Adrian Adonis was a colorful wrestling personality with an incredible abundance of talent. Unusually nimble for his size, he competed in the 250-pound division while as a high school amateur grappler. He used his weight to his advantage once he turned pro, but it was also problematic when his weight reached over 300 pounds. He wrestled under the name "Keith Franks" in many territories prior to taking on the Adonis guise, which he adapted while wrestling in Georgia in 1978. During his stint in the AWA, he formed a successful alliance with Jesse "The Body" Ventura, and the two were awarded the World Tag-Team Title when the champs failed to appear for a defense in Denver on July 20, 1980. Adonis, wrestling in San Antonio in 1983, captured the SCW World Title, and, while in Japan a short time later, began teaming with Dick Murdoch. Adonis and Murdoch won the WWF World Tag-Team Title from Tony Atlas and Rocky Johnson in April of 1984, and held the belts until January 21, 1985, when they lost to Mike Rotundo and Barry Windham. Adonis tragically lost his life when he was in a car accident en route to a show in Newfoundland in 1988.

Born:	November 21, 1943
Height:	6'2"
Weight:	325
Real Name:	Afa Amituanai Anoai
Parents:	Amituanai and Tovale Anoai
Trained by:	Peter Maivia, Kurt Von Steiger, Rocky Johnson, Jerry Monti
Finisher:	Samoan Drop
Career Span:	1971-1994

Titles Won:	19
Best Opponents:	Andre the Giant, Hulk Hogan, Bob Backlund
Halls of Fame:	2

Afa

The brothers that made up the Hall of Fame Wild Samoans tag team performed with a brutal urgency in the ring, appearing to have absolutely no other mission in life than assaulting their opponents and forcing them to concede. Afa, one of eleven children born in American Samoa, served in the Marines and was influenced to join by watching fellow Samoan Chief Peter Maivia wrestle in San Francisco. He immediately turned pro, and then spent time mentoring his younger brother, Sika, and the two rampaged around the world, winning nineteen championships together. While in the WWF, they won the World Tag-Team Title three times, and later, Afa managed the Headshrinkers. Following his retirement, he turned to training athletes for the mat, and has taught many current superstars wrestling today.

Born:	October 4, 1939
Height:	6'0"
Weight:	230
Real Name:	Eugene Avon Anderson
Parents:	Royal and Pauline Anderson
High School:	South St. Paul High School (MN)
College:	North Dakota State College
Managed:	Jimmy Snuka (1979-1980), Ray Stevens (1980), Hussein Arab (1980), Masked Superstar (1980), Ivan Koloff (1981)
Career Span:	1961-1985
Died:	October 31, 1991, Charlotte, NC 52 years old

Titles Won:	27
Best Opponents:	Verne Gagne, Ricky Steamboat, Ric Flair
Halls of Fame:	1

Anderson, Gene

The famous Minnesota Wrecking Crew which was made up of Gene and Ole Anderson, won more than twenty championships between 1968 and 1981, establishing themselves as one of the best tandems in wrestling history. Gene was the only true "Anderson" in the hard-nosed clan of "siblings," which included Lars and Ole, and later Arn. Like Ole, he was from Ramsey County, Minnesota, and was a talented amateur grappler. Trained by the famous Verne Gagne, Anderson became a pro in 1961. Starting his career in the AWA, California, and Tennessee, he then moved on to have a prolonged career in the Mid-Atlantic territory in 1966. Teamed with Lars, the Andersons fought all the popular duos in very violent scraps, with Ole joining them two years later. Gene and Ole won the World Tag-Team Title seven times, plus a multitude of belts for the Crocketts and in Georgia. Of the two, Gene was the more reserved personality, but didn't hold back once he got in the ring. Outside of the squared circle, Anderson also worked as a matchmaker, trainer, and manager. His son, Brad, became a pro wrestler as well, and held the PNW Tag Team Title in 1991.

Born:	September 22, 1942
Height:	6'1"
Weight:	256
Real Name:	Alan Robert Rogowski
Parents:	Robert and Georgiana Rogowski
High School:	Alexander Ramsey High School (MN)
College:	University of Colorado
Groups:	The Four Horsemen (1985-1986, 1990, 1993)
Tag Teams:	The Minnesota Wrecking Crew w/ Gene Anderson
Career Span:	1967-1990

PPV Record:	0-1
Titles Won:	48
Best Opponents:	Antonio Inoki, Ricky Steamboat, Dusty Rhodes
Halls of Fame:	2
Published Books:	1

Anderson, Ole

The Anderson name has been synonymous with pro wrestling excellence since the 1960s, and Ole Anderson was not only one-half of the famous brother duo that ruled the tag team ranks, but was a member of the legendary Four Horsemen. From Roseville, Minnesota, he was an athlete in high school and college, served in the Marines, and went through the grueling training camp of Verne Gagne. He debuted as "Rock Rogowski," and was a tough competitor, wrestling throughout the AWA region until June of 1968, when he departed for the Mid-Atlantic area, and adopted the name "Ole Anderson." He teamed with his "brothers," Gene and Lars Anderson, and had a thirteen-year run with Gene as his partner. The Andersons captured the World Tag-Team Title seven times, the Mid-Atlantic championship five, and the Georgia Title on six occasions. Ole also held the Georgia Tag-Team Title an additional eleven times with six different partners (Jacques Goulet, Lars Anderson, Ivan Koloff, Stan Hansen, Ernie Ladd, Jerry Brisco). Behind the scenes, he was a first-rate matchmaker for the Crocketts, in Georgia, and for WCW. His son Bryant was also a wrestler, and competed in SMW and WCW in the 1990s.

Andre the Giant

Born:	May 19, 1946
Height:	6'11"
Weight:	520
Real Name:	Andre Rene Roussimoff
Parents:	Boris and Marian Roussimoff
Trained by:	Frank Valois, Edouard Carpentier
Identities:	Monster Eiffel Tower, Giant Machine
Nicknames:	The Eighth Wonder of the World, The Battle Royal King
Tag Teams:	The Mega Bucks w/ Ted DiBiase, The Colossal Connection w/ Haku
Managed by:	Bobby Heenan, Ted DiBiase
Personal Managers:	Frank Valois, Frenchy Bernard, Tim White
Career Span:	1964-1992
Size Notes:	Andre's height was commonly inflated to 7'4" during his career; he was also reported to have had a size 24 shoe, a 71" chest, a 21" Bicep, and a 24" neck.
Died:	January 27, 1993, Paris, France 46 years old

PPV Record:	3-8, 1 DDQ
WrestleMania Record:	2-3, 1 DDQ
Titles Won:	6
Days as World Champion:	0
Age at first World Title Win:	41
Best Opponents:	Hulk Hogan, Antonio Inoki, El Canek
Halls of Fame:	4
TV Appearances:	Over 10
Movies:	4

In and out of the ring, Andre the Giant was a superstar beyond words. His dominance as a performer, his humongous size and power, and the way he commanded the squared circle made him a peerless professional wrestler. At a weight that fluctuated upwards of more than 500 pounds, and at a height of 6'11", Andre was the largest man on the circuit. Whereas it might seem that someone of that bulk would be immobile, he was agile and athletic, being able to perform dropkicks and other impressive maneuvers. Andre had normal sized parents, but by the age of twelve, he was growing at a rate more in tune with his grandfather, who stood more than seven feet tall. A poor child from the Grenoble area of France, Andre was discovered at a local gym and brought to Paris, where he debuted as a wrestler in 1964. As he developed as a grappler, he toured Europe, and his reputation spread like wildfire. Soon after, he met Frank Valois, an influential Montreal wrestler, who taught a great deal to him.

In 1970, he went to Japan as "Monster Rousimoff," and traveled to the U.S. in the summer of 1971 under the guise, "Jean Ferre." He wrestled all over Canada, as well as for the AWA, but his life changed forever when Valois steered him toward cunning WWWF promoter, Vincent J. McMahon. McMahon knew how to maximize his potential, booking Andre throughout the world, and never in one territory too long. Thus, it kept his act fresh, and fans were always left in awe by his bigger-than-life appearance. Prior to the 1975 NFL season, the Washington Redskins expressed interest in Andre, but nothing more than publicity came from it. A year later, he beat boxer Chuck Wepner by count out in a special mixed match-up at Shea Stadium. When Vincent K. McMahon expanded the WWF into a national organization, Andre was a central part of the promotion. He beat Big John Studd in a $15,000 bodyslam match at the first WrestleMania, and was victorious in a battle royal at the second.

Andre turned heel against the popular Hulk Hogan in 1987, took Bobby Heenan as his manager, and went into the highly-anticipated WrestleMania III as Hogan's biggest WWF World Title threat to date. Before over 70,000 fans, Andre put Hogan over, helping catapult the latter into another league of superstardom, and was a remarkable passing of the symbolic torch. Andre finally beat Hogan on February 5, 1988, and won the WWF belt, but controversy saw the championship declared vacant. Andre held the WWF World Tag-Team Title with Haku from 1989-1990, but toned back his schedule, wrestling mainly in Japan after that. While in France for his father's funeral, Andre passed away at the age of forty-six. A&E ran a feature *Biography* on Andre, which was one of the highest rated shows in that program's history. Stories of his amazing consumption of beer, which was more than 100 bottles and up to 7,000 calories in a single day, are still marveled at. The "Boss," as he was known, was the first man inducted into the WWF Hall of Fame in 1993.

Photo Courtesy of the Collection of Libnan Ayoub

Born:	September 1940
Height:	6'3"
Weight:	240
Real Name:	Spiridon Manousakis
Parents:	Stauros and Konstantina Manousakis
Identities:	Arion Manousakis
Career Span:	1965-1985

Titles Won:	13
Days as World Champion:	320
Age at first World Title Win:	24
Best Opponents:	Jack Brisco, Killer Kowalski, Bruno Sammartino

Arion, Spiros

An international superstar, Spiros Arion was born in Egypt to Greek parents and migrated to Athens as a teenager, where he excelled in the Greco-Roman form of wrestling. Naturally charismatic and physically powerful, he trained to become a pro grappler and made an early mark on European mats, often billed as the "son" of his mentor, veteran Andreas Lambrakis. In 1965, he went to Australia and became one of the most popular wrestlers of the era. Arion won the IWA World Heavyweight Title five times and the Austra-Asian crown three times. Upon his arrival in the U.S. in 1974, he toured the WWWF and had a successful series against World Champion Bruno Sammartino at Madison Square Garden. Arion had partnered with Sammartino years earlier to capture the U.S. Tag-Team Title, a belt he held twice.

Born:	October 3, 1939
Height:	6'0"
Weight:	230
Real Name:	Joseph Melton James Jr.
Parents:	Joseph and Rebekah James
Wife:	Gail James
High School:	Sprayberry High School (GA)
Military:	United States Marine Corps
Identities:	The Bullet
Career Span:	1966-Present

PPV Record:	3-1
Titles Won:	61
Best Opponents:	Jack Brisco, Terry Funk, Ric Flair
Halls of Fame:	1

Armstrong, Bob

In 2011, forty-five years after his pro debut, "Bullet" Bob Armstrong is still appearing in professional wrestling matches. The father of a quartet of wrestlers and the 1967 NWA Rookie of the Year, Armstrong has been a longtime fan favorite and a perennial champion. He played high school football in his hometown of Marietta, Georgia, and became a fireman at the Fair Oaks station. A dedicated weightlifter, he was convinced to try his hand at grappling by local promoter, Elmo Chappell. Across the southeast, and wherever he traveled, he flourished, winning an extensive list of championships that included the North American, Southern, and Southeastern heavyweight crowns. Additionally, he was a matchmaker in the Georgia and Gulf Coast territories. In SMW and USWA, he acted as the commissioner, and was in an on-screen position of power in TNA in 2002. Armstrong remains semi-active on the indie circuit and was inducted into the WWE Hall of Fame in 2011. His four sons, Scott, Brad, Steve, and Brian, also had successful careers on the mat.

Born:	August 28, 1938
Height:	6'1"
Weight:	230
Real Name:	Joseph Hamilton
Parents:	Orville and Faye Hamilton
High School:	Benton High School (MO)
Trained by:	Larry Hamilton, Mike DiBiase
Identities:	Jody Hamilton, Mighty Bolo, The Flame
Career Span:	1956-1988

Titles Won:	61
Best Opponents:	Jack Brisco, Harley Race, Dusty Rhodes
Halls of Fame:	2

Assassin, The

In 1961, The Assassin appeared for the first time in Georgia, and wrestling fans were not too thrilled by his overt rule-breaking style. Under the mask, he was Joe Hamilton, the younger brother of Larry Hamilton. Like his sibling, Joe played football in high school and was an amateur boxer in his hometown of St. Joseph. The Hamiltons were successful in tag-team matches, but Joe, as the Assassin, would become an international sensation. Along with Tom Renesto as the second masked Assassin, Hamilton toured the globe and won many tag-team championships, including world titles in Australia, Georgia, and Florida. He was the main trainer at the WCW Power Plant and was inducted into the WCW Hall of Fame in 1994, as well as also running the Deep South promotion.

Born:	April 23, 1954
Height:	6'2"
Weight:	297
Real Name:	Anthony Gerald White
High School:	Patrick Henry High School (VA)
Bodybuilding Ach.:	Mr. Southern Hemisphere (1978), WBBG Pro Mr. U.S.A. (1979), and numerous other titles
Trained by:	Gene and Ole Anderson, Larry Sharpe
Identities:	The Black Atlas, Black Superman
Nickname:	Mr. USA, Mr. Universe
Finisher:	Powerslam, Full Nelson, Bearhug
Managed:	Mark Henry (2008-2009)
Career Span:	1975-2009

Atlas, Tony

PPV Record:	0-2
WrestleMania Record:	0-1
Titles Won:	18
Halls of Fame:	2

The widespread popularity and amazing strength of Tony Atlas made him a bright prospect when he debuted in 1975. Formerly a bodybuilder, Atlas heeded the advice of George and Sandy Scott to become a grappler. From Roanoke, Virginia, Atlas appeared all over the Mid-Atlantic region and into Georgia, and won many local championships. In 1979, in addition to winning the title of "Mr. USA," he joined the WWF, and his incredible physique and likeability got him over with fans just like it had in the south. He beat Hulk Hogan at Madison Square Garden in 1981, and two years later, won the WWF World Tag-Team Title with Rocky Johnson. Atlas also won championships in World Class, IWCCW, the CWA, and the WWC in Puerto Rico, but personal troubles ended up hurting his career. He returned to the WWF in 1991 as "Saba Simba," but it was short-lived. His off-camera struggles were featured on MTV's *True Life: I'm a Pro Wrestler*, a reality show that was initially broadcast in 1999. In 2006, he was inducted into the WWE Hall of Fame.

Born:	February 27, 1929
Height:	6′2″
Weight:	240
Real Name:	Wesley Austin Rapes
Parents:	William and Jewel Rapes
Career Span:	1956-1977
Died:	August 13, 1981, San Joaquin County, CA 52 years old

Titles Won:	15
Days as World Champion:	196 (excluding any claim in 1962)
Age at first World Title Win:	37
Best Opponents:	Buddy Rogers, Lou Thesz, Rikidozan

Austin, Buddy

Buddy Austin, an arrogant heel, was a terror of wrestling rings. Crowds generally reacted loudly to his riotous antics, especially if he was giving one of their favorites a rough going over. He grew up in Fulton County, Georgia, and learned the elementary methods of being a ruthless rule-breaker from a veteran of that style, Roy Graham. During his twenty-plus year career, he feuded with the best in the business. His foes included Bruno Sammartino, Buddy Rogers, Rikidozan, and Fred Blassie. Austin won titles in the U.S., Australia, and Japan and was a three-time WWA World champion in Los Angeles. To emphasize his violent and aggressive approach to the mat, Austin was nicknamed "Killer," and his piledriver was one of the most feared finishers of his time.

Born:	April 20, 1927
Height:	6'1"
Weight:	250
Real Name:	Wadi Youssef Ayoub
Trained by:	Tom Lurich, Chief Little Wolf, Jim Deakin
Career Span:	1953-1975
Died:	September 29, 1976, Australia 49 years old

Titles Won:	3
Best Opponents:	Dara Singh, King Kong, George Gordienko

Ayoub, Wadi

An impressive athlete with widespread popularity, Sheik Wadi Ayoub wrestled around the world, and it wasn't uncommon for tens of thousands to be in attendance for his matches. He began as an amateur Greco-Roman grappler in his native Lebanon, and, in 1951, moved to Australia, where he decided to go pro. Training extensively, he was a genuine force to be reckoned with on the mat, and proceeded to wrestle the best the sport had to offer throughout the South Pacific, India, and Europe. In 1965, Ayoub won a competitive Middle East tournament and was billed as the uncrowned world champion two years later in Singapore. He displayed his strength in a victory over King Kong for the Orient championship and also held the All-Asian belt.

Born:	January 23, 1938
Height:	6'10"
Weight:	320
Real Name:	Shohei Baba
Parents:	Kazuo and Mitsu Baba
Wife:	Motoko Baba
High School:	Niigata Prefectural Sanjo Industry High School (Japan)
Trained by:	Rikidozan, Fred Atkins
Owned:	All-Japan Pro Wrestling Co., Ltd. (October 1972-January 1999)
Career Span:	1960-1999
Died:	January 31, 1999, Tokyo, Japan 61 years old

Baba, Shohei

Titles Won:	24
Days as World Champion:	3,866
Age at first World Title Win:	35
Best Opponents:	The Destroyer, Jack Brisco, Billy Robinson
Tournament Wins:	16
Halls of Fame:	2

The legendary Shohei "Giant" Baba of Sanjo, Japan was a world renowned in-ring performer, known for his mammoth build, and an influential promoter. During the 1970s and 1980s, American fans were accustomed to reading about Baba's three NWA World Title victories in magazines, but there was much more to his legacy that went unrevealed by those kayfabe driven sources. Specifically, how his popularity kept wrestling hot following the stabbing death of Rikidozan, and his role as founder of All-Japan Pro Wrestling, one of the premier grappling institutions. A former baseball player for the Yomiuri Giants, Baba was courted into the business by Rikidozan and debuted in 1960. He toured the U.S. extensively early in his career, headlining some of the biggest venues from coast to coast, and faced off against Bruno Sammartino and Buddy Rogers while both were world champions. After several years of international touring, Baba returned to Japan and assumed a leadership role after Rikidozan died in 1963.

As a member of the Japan Wrestling Association, Baba won the International championship on three occasions and was victorious in the World League tournament six times. In October of 1972, he formed All Japan, as well as an important relationship with many American promoters. He also joined the NWA, which kept a free-flowing stream of imported talent for his company. On December 2, 1974, he dethroned Jack Brisco and became the first Japanese grappler to hold the NWA World Title. Baba reigned for only a week, but he won the belt a second time from Harley Race on October 31, 1979, and then captured his third title on

September 4, 1980, again from Race. As a mentor, Baba influenced the careers of superstars Jumbo Tsuruta, Toshiaki Kawada, and Mitsuharu Misawa, and maintained the success of All Japan until his death in 1999. Giant Baba was a cherished wrestling icon and his gentlemanly spirit will be remembered forever.

Photo Courtesy of Pete Lederberg—plmathfoto@hotmail.com

Born:	August 14, 1949
Height:	6'1"
Weight:	230
Real Name:	Robert Lee Backlund
Parents:	Normal and Bernice Backlund
Wife:	Corrine Backlund
High School:	Princeton High School (MN)
College:	North Dakota State University
Trained by:	Terry Funk, Danny Hodge
Finisher:	Cross face chicken wing, German suplex
Managed:	The Sultan (1997), Kurt Angle (2000)
Career Span:	1973-2007

Backlund, Bob

PPV Record:	3-8
WrestleMania Record:	0-2
WWE *Raw* TV Record:	0-1
WWE *Smackdown* TV Record:	0-1
Titles Won:	12
Days as World Champion:	2,086
Age at first World Title Win:	28
Best Opponents:	Billy Graham, Antonio Inoki, Harley Race
Halls of Fame:	2

The ultimate baby face, Bob Backlund was World Heavyweight champion for a total of 2,086 days over four different reigns. He's remembered mostly for his quality work as the technically proficient hero in the WWF from 1978 to 1983. A product of Princeton, Minnesota, Backlund was a grappler in high school and college and won NCAA Division II honors in 1971 at 190 pounds. He trained under Eddie Sharkey and made his professional debut in 1973. Early in his career, Backlund worked his way through many different National Wrestling Alliance territories and learned from guys like Danny Hodge and Terry Funk as he developed his ring skills and confidence as a professional. By 1977, he was considered one of the best up-and-comers, and impressed the hierarchy of the World Wide Wrestling Federation. Backlund's clean-cut appearance, amateur background, and popularity edged him into a unique position as top challenger to Billy Graham's World Title only weeks after beginning a tour of the northeastern region.

Wrestling fans were shocked, yet pleased, to hear that he dethroned the notorious "Superstar" Graham on February 20, 1978 in New York. In Japan, he was defeated by Antonio Inoki on November 30, 1979, but Inoki vacated the championship shortly thereafter and Backlund won a bout over Bobby Duncum to begin his second reign. The title was held up after a bout with Greg Valentine on October 19, 1981, and Backlund was victorious in the rematch. He overcame the challenges of Ivan Koloff, Ken Patera, George Steele, Peter Maivia, and many other big names throughout his years as titleholder. Finally, he was met with defeat on December 26, 1983 when his manager, Arnold Skaaland, tossed a towel into the ring, signifying his submission while locked in the Iron Sheik's camel clutch. Backlund had a strong showing at the 1993 Royal Rumble, and, on November 23, 1994, he turned in a heel performance to beat Bret Hart for his fourth WWF Title, though lost the belt three days later to Diesel. In 2000, Backlund ran for Congress in Connecticut and returned to the ring with appearances for TNA and the WWE in 2007.

Photo Courtesy of Pete Lederberg—plmathfoto@hotmail.com

Born:	April 19, 1934
Height:	6'5"
Weight:	330
Real Name:	Douglas Allan Baker
High School:	West Waterloo High School (IA)
Trained by:	Bob Geigel, Pat O'Connor, Buddy Austin
Managed by:	The Grand Wizard, Sir Oliver Humperdink
Managed:	The Russian Brute, The Nightstalker, Mark Callous
Career Span:	1964-1988

Titles Won:	25
Days as World Champion:	497
Age at first World Title Win:	40
Best Opponents:	The Sheik, Carlos Colon, Bruiser Brody
Halls of Fame:	1
Movies:	3

Baker, Ox

The potent Heart Punch was the dreaded finisher of Ox Baker, a former amateur grappler and boxer from Waterloo, Iowa. Baker participated in several Golden Gloves championships and, in February of 1964, won the Des Moines heavyweight crown. Soon after, Baker became a pro wrestler on the Central States circuit and capitalized on his impressive size and unique look to become an unforgettable villain. In 1974, he beat Bob Ellis for the WWA World Title and also held the WWC World Championship in Puerto Rico. Baker won belts in a number of territories from New Zealand to Los Angeles. In 1981, he appeared as the character "Slag," in the film *Escape from New York*.

Born:	August 11, 1934
Height:	5'8"
Weight:	145
Real Name:	Mary Ann Kostecki Weaver
Parents:	Frank and Clara Kostecki
High School:	Rosati Kain High School (MO)
Nickname:	Wow Girl
Career Span:	1954-1974
Died:	May 13, 2008, Mint Hill, NC
	73 years old

Titles Won:	6
Days as World Champion:	Around two years
Age at first World Title Win:	27
Best Opponents:	June Byers, Fabulous Moolah, Cora Combs
Halls of Fame:	3

Banner, Penny

Penny Banner was a credit to professional wrestling; a heroine who overcame obstacles and demonstrated the utmost bravery to become a sensational grappler. An athlete in high school, she was a waitress at the Arabian Lounge in St. Louis when convinced by promoter Sam Muchnick to try her hand at wrestling. With knowledge of judo, she ventured to Columbus, Ohio, where she trained for her 1954 debut. Before the end of her first year as a pro, she was already chasing World Champion June Byers. Banner teamed with Betty Joe Hawkins, Bonnie Watson, and Lorraine Johnson to capture the tag team championship, and, in August of 1961, she beat Theresa Theis in Angola, Indiana to become the initial AWA Women's World Champion. She wed wrestler Johnny Weaver and competed across North America into the 1970s. At the 1995 Senior Olympics, she won a silver medal in the 50-meter butterfly event and won another silver two years later in the discus event. She remained one of the more enjoyable personalities in the business until her 2008 passing.

Born:	January 13, 1932
Height:	6'6"
Weight:	265
Real Name:	Edward Michael Wright
Parents:	Edward and Lillian Wright
High School:	Omaha South High School (NE)
Boxing Trainers:	Bearcat Wright, Ralph Hayes
Finisher:	African Cannonball
Career Span:	1952-1975
Died:	August 28, 1982, Tampa, FL 50 years old

Titles Won:	19
Days as World Champion:	199
Age at first World Title Win:	29
Best Opponents:	Killer Kowalski, Buddy Rogers, Johnny Valentine
Boxing Record:	8-0

Bearcat Wright

In 1932, shortly after his newborn son Edward Michael Wright was born, noted African American boxer Bearcat Wright told an Omaha sportswriter that he would steer his child away from the fighting business. He was only somewhat successful. "Junior" Bearcat was a Golden Gloves boxer and won all eight of his professional fights before cutting his career short to become a pro wrestler in January of 1952. Tall and powerful, Wright was a popular matman, and his box office appeal was most impressive in 1960 when he headlined at stadiums in Chicago and Washington, D.C., drawing 26,000 and 16,000 respectively in bouts against Killer Kowalski and Buddy Rogers. On April 4, 1961, he beat Kowalski for a claim to the World Title in Boston and won the WWA belt on August 23, 1963 in Los Angeles. Wright also won the IWA Championship in Australia in August of 1966. Wright was a pivotal black wrestler during a time in which the industry was still trying to completely eradicate racial barriers and was a significant influence on many fans.

Born:	February 19, 1948
Height:	6'4"
Weight:	295
Real Name:	John William Minton
Family:	Father of Chip Minton
High School:	Butler High School (PA)
Identities:	Captain USA, Masked Superstar II
Groups:	The Mid-Atlantic Death Squad (1979-1980)
Career Span:	1972-1990
Died:	March 20, 1995, Burke, VA 46 years old

Big John Studd

PPV Record:	1-1
WrestleMania Record:	0-2
Titles Won:	15
Days as World Champion:	5
Age at first World Title Win:	35
Best Opponents:	Andre the Giant, Hulk Hogan, Bruiser Brody
Halls of Fame:	3
Movies:	8

The powerful and intimidating Big John Studd had the stature to stand toe-to-toe with Andre the Giant and Hulk Hogan and was always considered one of the best big men in the industry. He was a basketball star in high school and spent a lot of time on his family's Butler County, Pennsylvania, farm. Trained by Killer Kowalski, he debuted as "Chuck O'Connor" in 1972 in the northeast and donned a mask as one of the Executioners a few years later, teaming with Kowalski and Nikolai Volkoff in defenses of the WWWF Tag Team Title. In 1977, he adopted the "Big John Studd" gimmick and was managed by Gary Hart in memorable matches against the Von Erichs and others in Dallas. He won the American Heavyweight belt, and, among his other achievements, were the North American and Canadian Titles. In 1989, he eliminated Ted DiBiase to win the second ever WWF Royal Rumble. He worked with George Scott in the latter's NAWA promotion in 1990 and was a successful businessman prior to his death in 1995.

Photo Courtesy of the Collection of Tim Hornbaker

Born:	October 14, 1935
Height:	6'3"
Weight:	260
Real Name:	John Mortl Lanzo
High School:	DeLaSalle High School (MN)
College:	University of Minnesota
Identities:	Jack Lanza, Gino Lanza, The Texan
Career Span:	1962-1985

Titles Won:	10
Best Opponents:	Jack Brisco, Fritz Von Erich, Johnny Valentine
Halls of Fame:	1

Blackjack Lanza

The Blackjacks were a Hall of Fame-quality tag team in the 1970s and won world titles in the WWA and WWWF. The pair, made up of Blackjack Lanza and Blackjack Mulligan, shared a common characteristic— both were relentless heels with a shared appetite for brawling and rough tactics. Lanza grew up in Minneapolis and started in the business as a protégé of Verne Gagne. His longtime gimmick, however, claimed Albuquerque as his hometown, and he was known as the "Cowboy," a role he made famous. He was managed by Bobby Heenan for several years and held the AWA World Tag Team Title with Bobby Duncum for nearly a year in 1976-1977. After his retirement, he worked for the WWE behind-the-scenes as an agent and producer.

Blackjack Mulligan

Born:	November 25, 1941
Height:	6'6"
Weight:	235
Real Name:	Robert Deroy Windham
Parents:	W.R. and Nadine Windham
Family:	Father of Barry and Kendall Windham
High School:	Ector High School (TX)
Trained by:	Joe Blanchard
Identities:	Bob Windham, Big Machine
Finisher:	Clawhold, Boston Crab
Owned:	A percentage of the Amarillo promotion (1978-1980)
Career Span:	1969-1993

Titles Won:	18
Days as World Champion:	Around 380
Age at first World Title Win:	39
Best Opponents:	Verne Gagne, Bruno Sammartino, Fritz Von Erich
Halls of Fame:	1

Some wrestlers take a direct path to professional wrestling, but for Blackjack Mulligan, his Hall of Fame career came after playing two other sports and serving in the Marines. In high school at Odessa, Texas, he was a star basketball player and his awesome height was a great advantage. Following four years in the service, he was recruited to Texas Western College, where he played football. In 1966, he nearly made the New York Jets squad and played a few years in the Texas Football League. Mulligan, in 1969, debuted in wrestling, and was named the 1970 AWA Rookie of the Year. He officially took the "Blackjack Mulligan" moniker in 1971 during a run in the WWWF. While in the WWA, that same year, he began teaming with Blackjack Lanza, and in 1975, the duo won the WWWF Tag Team Title. For a majority of the 1975 to 1982 time-frame, he was a main star in the Mid-Atlantic region and feuded with Ric Flair, Ricky Steamboat, and Mr. Wrestling. In that territory, he won the U.S. Title three times.

Born:	January 22, 1954
Height:	5'11"
Weight:	225
Real Name:	Tully Arthur Blanchard
Parents:	Joe and Jackie Blanchard
High School:	Churchill High School (TX)
Colleges:	Southern Methodist University, West Texas State University
Trained by:	Joe Blanchard
Identities:	The Midnight Stallion
Finisher:	Slingshot Suplex
Tag Teams:	The Dynamic Duo w/ Gino Hernandez, The Brain Busters w/ Arn Anderson
Career Span:	1974-2008

Blanchard, Tully

PPV Record:	4-4, 1 Draw, 1 DDQ
WrestleMania Record:	1-0
Titles Won:	28
Best Opponents:	Magnum T.A., Wahoo McDaniel, Dusty Rhodes
Halls of Fame:	1

Four Horsemen alumni Tully Blanchard was a confident and slick performer. He could wrestle scientifically, brawl, and integrate high levels of psychology into his matches, making him one of the truly must-see grapplers of the 1980s. His father, Joe, was a well-known wrestler, and his biggest influence growing up. Tully was a star high school and collegiate quarterback, and wrestled during the off season. The same speed and cleverness that had helped him shine on the field were among his outstanding qualities on the mat. He held the SCW Championship eleven times and, after joining Jim Crockett Promotions, won the TV Title twice. He also captured the U.S. belt from Magnum T.A. and the World Tag Team Title on two occasions. Along with partner Arn Anderson, he went to the WWF and won tag title gold there as well. He went into semi-retirement, and made sporadic appearances, including a run in 1998 with Barry Windham as NWA Tag champs. He devoted his life to religion and acts as a preacher for prison inmates.

Born:	December 6, 1934
Height:	6'1"
Weight:	245
Real Name:	Nicholas Warren Bockwinkel
High Schools:	Canoga Park High School (CA), Jefferson Union High School (CA)
Colleges:	Valley Junior College, University of Oklahoma
Military:	United States Army
Trained by:	Warren Bockwinkel, Lou Thesz, Wilbur Snyder
Identities:	Dick Warren, Nick Warren, Nick Bock, Roy Diamond, The White Phantom
Managed by:	Bobby Heenan
Career Span:	1954-1993

Bockwinkel, Nick

Titles Won:	30
Days as World Champion:	2,990
Age at first World Title Win:	40
Best Opponents:	Verne Gagne, Lou Thesz, Curt Hennig
Halls of Fame:	3

A calculating and intellectual wrestler, Nick Bockwinkel was the definitive heavyweight champion heel of the 1970s. He stepped free of the tag team division to rule the AWA World Title from 1975 to 1980 for a total of 1,714 straight days, after dethroning the pride of the AWA, Verne Gagne. The son of wrestler Warren Bockwinkel, he was originally from St. Louis and attended several high schools while touring with his father—Jefferson Union High in the San Francisco area being one of them. While in school, he was a star fullback and earned an outstanding player trophy in 1953. An opportunity to continue his football success in college was sidelined because of injury, and in 1954, he made his professional wrestling debut in Southern California. Warren was entirely supportive of his son's athletic endeavors and coached him in all aspects of the mat, teaching him the technical skills that would serve him exceptionally well throughout his career.

Bockwinkel was a receptive student, even before he entered the business, learning the ins and outs of the road while traveling with his father and wrestler Yukon Eric. In the ring, he was able to adapt to the various styles of opponents and create his own sequence of maneuvers that were very popular. He toured the Great Lakes area, the Jim Barnett circuit, Pacific Northwest, and Hawaii, as well as also appearing in Japan. In 1969, he made a sharp change to his act, emphasizing a rule-breaking attitude that rubbed many fans the wrong way. Initially developing his newfound role in Georgia, Bockwinkel carried the disposition to Minneapolis and the AWA, where he really made his mark. He teamed with the talented Ray Stevens to capture the World Tag

Team Championship four times between 1972 and 1974, and on November 8, 1975 in St. Paul, he dethroned Gagne for the AWA World Heavyweight belt, initiating an exciting era for the promotion.

Bockwinkel was a distinctive champion, traveling throughout the U.S. and into Canada. He successfully defended his title against Billy Robinson, The Crusher, Edouard Carpentier, Maurice Vachon, and other big names. Gagne finally was able to regain the title at Chicago's Comiskey Park on July 18, 1980, ending Bockwinkel's lengthy run. When Gagne retired in May of 1981, Bockwinkel was awarded the belt because he was the number one contender, and in 1982, he traded the belt with Otto Wanz. On February 22, 1984, he lost the title to Jumbo Tsuruta. He was awarded his fourth AWA championship after Stan Hansen failed to defend on June 29, 1986 and Bockwinkel held it until losing a bout to Curt Hennig the following May. He wrestled his last match for the AWA in 1987 and came out of retirement in late 1990 to battle Masa Saito in Japan. Three years later, he drew with Dory Funk Jr. at WCW's Slamboree event. Bockwinkel also acted as WCW commissioner from 1994 to 1996.

Photo Courtesy of Pete Lederberg—plmathfoto@hotmail.com

Born:	August 6, 1948
Height:	6'1"
Weight:	248
Real Name:	Adolfo Bresciano
Wife:	Diane Bresciano
Nicknames:	The World's Strongest Man
Finisher:	Bearhug
Tag Team:	The Italian Connection w/ Gino Brito
Career Span:	1971-1992
Died:	March 11, 1993, Laval, Quebec 44 years old

PPV Record:	4-8
WrestleMania Record:	1-3
Titles Won:	17
Best Opponents:	Harley Race, Ric Flair, Nick Bockwinkel

Bravo, Dino

Powerhouse Dino Bravo found success in the wrestling ring as both a fan favorite and as an arrogant heel. He was a Canadian legend, although relocated from Italy, and based out of Montreal, where he learned a diverse repertoire of maneuvers from Gino Brito and Edouard Carpentier. Bravo was agile enough to pull off fast-paced moves, charismatic in revving up audiences, and impressively strong—able to bench over 600 pounds. On May 5, 1976, he teamed with Mr. Wrestling to win the NWA World Tag Team Title from the Andersons and two years later, he captured the WWWF Tag Team belts with Dominic DeNucci. In

Montreal, between 1980 and 1985, he won the Canadian Heavyweight Championship six times and was immensely popular. He returned to the WWF, turned heel, and hooked up with Frenchy Martin and Jimmy Hart. In 1990, he was a top rival for Hulk Hogan. Sadly, in March of 1993, he was shot to death in his Quebec home and his murder spawned heavy speculation to his ties to the illegal cigarette business.

Photo Courtesy of Pete Lederberg—plmathfoto@hotmail.com

Born:	September 21, 1941
Height:	6'1"
Weight:	225
Real Name:	Freddie Joe Brisco
Parents:	Floyd and Iona Brisco
Wife:	Jan Brisco
High School:	Blackwell High School (OK)
HS Ach.:	Oklahoma State Wrestling Champion (1958-1960)
College:	Oklahoma State University
College Ach.:	NCAA Wrestling Title (1965) (191)
Identities:	Tiger Brisco, The Masked Okie
Finisher:	Figure-four leglock
Career Span:	1965-1985
Died:	February 1, 2010, Tampa, FL 68 years old

Brisco, Jack

Titles Won:	53
Days as World Champion:	866
Age at first World Title Win:	31
Best Opponents:	Dory Funk Jr., Harley Race, Terry Funk
Halls of Fame:	4

The epitome of class and honor, Jack Brisco represented everything good about the business and particularly what was expected from a premier claimant to the World Heavyweight Title. There was no outrageous flamboyance or arrogance when it came to Brisco. He stuck to his pure athleticism in the ring, applying knowledge from his amateur days and throwing back the clock to an era in which fundamentals were the keynote to success. Brisco was respected by all corners of the industry and fans cheered on his efforts as he played by the rules and dismantled roughnecks with technical savvy. He was considered more of a "real" wrestler than his colorful counterparts, and was compared to legends and fellow NWA World Champions Lou Thesz and Dick Hutton. Like Hutton, Brisco was from Oklahoma, where he excelled in high school and collegiate wrestling and learned the essentials from Leroy McGuirk in Tulsa. Brisco was an NCAA champion and that distinction meant credibility in pro wrestling, regardless of his experience.

Beginning in 1965, Brisco proceeded along the circuit, learning the craft and helping support his family. He landed in Florida three years later and political cards were played by influential members of the National Wrestling Alliance in support of his candidacy for World Champion. After some wrangling and an injury to the heavyweight titleholder, Dory Funk Jr., a planned bout between Funk and Brisco that would see the latter win the championship was scrapped. Instead, Funk lost the title to Harley Race, and Brisco wrestled the belt away from Race on July 20, 1973 in Houston, becoming only the second man to have won both the NCAA and NWA titles in their career, with Hutton being the first. While in Japan in December 1974, Brisco lost the NWA Title to Giant Baba, but regained it back a week later. Finally, on December 10, 1975, he dropped the belt to Terry Funk in Miami Beach. His two reigns were saturated with spectacular matches across the grappling landscape, and, as the hero, he never failed to live up to his advance billing.

Brisco won the Missouri, Florida, Southern, Mid-Atlantic, and a number of other championships during his illustrious career. He also formed the famous Brisco Brothers tag team with his younger sibling, Jerry, and the two dominated competition for years. They won the NWA World Tag Team Title, plus belts in Florida, Georgia, and Puerto Rico. The Briscos were also part owners in the Georgia territory until selling out in 1984. They wrestled for a time in the WWF prior to Jack retiring in 1985, and when Brisco walked away, he walked away for good. His history was completely captured in his 2004 autobiography, *Brisco*, and he's been honored by several Halls of Fame. Recognized as one of the best the sport's ever seen, Brisco carried himself as a champion inside the ring and out, and was a true gentleman, a characteristic that contrasted very conspicuously against the murky backdrop of professional wrestling.

Born:	September 19, 1946
Height:	6'0"
Weight:	210
Real Name:	Floyd Gerald Brisco
Parents:	Floyd and Iona Brisco
Family:	Father of Wes Brisco
High School:	Stillwater High School (OK)
College:	Oklahoma State University
Identities:	Gerald Brisco
Career Span:	1967-2000

PPV Record:	0-1
WWE *Raw* TV Record:	5-6, 2 NC
Titles Won:	43
Best Opponents:	Dory Funk Jr., Harley Race, Jerry Lawler
Halls of Fame:	2

Brisco, Jerry

The talented Jerry Brisco teamed with his brother, Jack to win the World Tag Team Championship on three separate occasions between 1983 and 1984, and engaged in rough battles with the teams of Jay Youngblood and Ricky Steamboat and Wahoo McDaniel and Mark Youngblood. They discarded their usual hero roles to portray the "bad guys" across the Mid-Atlantic region and had a memorable run. Jerry, who was the younger of the two siblings, learned the ropes from Jack and entered the pro ranks in 1967 after several years of amateur grappling. In addition to his success as a tag team wrestler, Jerry won many singles titles and held the NWA World Junior Title in 1981. He had a backstage role with the WWF when, in 1998, he stepped back in front of the camera as one of Vince McMahon's faithful "stooges," along with Hall of Famer Pat Patterson. In 2000, he won the Hardcore Title twice and, along with Jack, was honored by induction into the WWE Hall of Fame.

Born:	October 16, 1938
Height:	5'11"
Weight:	255
Real Name:	Robert Harold Brown
Identities:	Bobo Brown
Finisher:	Backbreaker, Legdrop
Career Span:	1965-1996
Died:	February 5, 1997, Kansas City, MO 58 years old

Titles Won:	68
Best Opponents:	Harley Race, Dory Funk Jr., Bruiser Brody

Brown, Bob

A top-notch heel for decades, "Bulldog" Bob Brown grew up in Winnipeg, where he was a star amateur heavyweight grappler at the Westbrook Athletic Club. He won a number of club titles and developed his villainous act on semi-pro shows until leaving Canada for Kansas City in 1965. He learned much about the sport from Pat O'Connor and Bob Geigel and teamed with the latter to win the North American Tag Team Championship five times. He became a legend in the Central States territory, capturing the local heavyweight title twenty times between 1968 and 1987. In 1989, he partnered with his nephew Kerry Brown to win the International Tag Team belts in Calgary.

Bruiser Brody

Born:	June 14, 1946
Height:	6'4"
Weight:	275
Real Name:	Frank Donald Goodish
Wife:	Barbara Goodish
High School:	Warren High School (MI)
College:	West Texas State University
Pro Sports:	Texas Football League—San Antonio Toros (1968)
	Continental Football League—Mexico Golden Aztecs (1969)
	Continental Football League—West Texas Rufneks (1969)
	National Football League—Washington Redskins (1970) (camp)
	Continental Football League—Fort Worth Braves (1970)
	Canadian Football League—Edmonton Eskimos (1971)
Trained by:	Jack Adkisson, Buck Robley
Identities:	Red River Jack
Nicknames:	The Hammer, King Kong
Career Span:	1974-1988
Died:	July 17, 1988, Bayamon, Puerto Rico 42 years old

Titles Won:	30
Days as World Champion:	301
Age at first World Title Win:	33
Best Opponents:	Ric Flair, Harley Race, Antonio Inoki
Halls of Fame:	2

A one-of-a-kind wrestling performer, Bruiser Brody was a frightful sight for the unprepared viewer. He was an extraordinary brawler, taking violence to another level, and his great size and athletic ability added unique aspects to his colorful persona. Crowds around the world were captivated by his matches and he was known as an "outlaw" backstage for his shrewd business perspective. He was rarely without championship gold around his waist: In Indiana, he captured the WWA World Title, and won the AJPW International championship three times in Japan and the AJPW Tag Team Title with both Jimmy Snuka and Stan Hansen.

He also held numerous regional belts in Texas, Florida, and the Central States. During his career, he had memorable feuds with Abdullah the Butcher, Dick the Bruiser, The Von Erichs, and Jumbo Tsuruta. On July 16, 1988, prior to a show in Bayamon, Puerto Rico, he was stabbed by a fellow wrestler, Jose Huertas Gonzales, and died the following day. His life story has been told in two published biographies.

Born:	August 13, 1949
Height:	5'10"
Weight:	230
Real Name:	James Ewald Brunzell Jr.
High School:	White Bear Lake High School (MN)
College:	University of Minnesota
Football:	Manitowoc County Chiefs— Central Football League (1971)
Finisher:	Dropkick
Career Span:	1972-1994

PPV Record:	3-3
WrestleMania Record:	0-3
Titles Won:	9
Best Opponents:	Ric Flair, Jumbo Tsuruta, Ray Stevens

Brunzell, Jim

"Jumping" Jim Brunzell was an energetic and clean-cut wrestling hero. He was a football star in high school and college and was trained by the legendary Verne Gagne. Teamed with Verne's son Greg Gagne as the Hi-Flyers, Brunzell won the AWA World Tag Team belts on July 7, 1977 from Bobby Duncum and Blackjack Lanza. They reigned a second time from 1981 to 1983 after dethroning Adrian Adonis and Jesse Ventura. He also formed a popular tandem with Brian Blair in the WWF, known as the Killer Bees. As a singles performer, Brunzell held the Mid-Atlantic championship twice in 1979-1980. At the UWF Beach Blast show in 1991, Brunzell and Blair reunited to beat The Power Twins and Brunzell retired from the sport a few years later.

Canek

Born:	June 19, 1952
Height:	6'0"
Weight:	235
Real Name:	Felipe Estrada
Trained by:	Felipe Ham Lee
Identities:	El Canek, Principe Azul, El Principe Maya
Career Span:	1972-Present

PPV Record:	1-0
Titles Won:	20
Days as World Champion:	Over 7,000
Age at first World Title Win:	26
Best Opponents:	Lou Thesz, Vader, Andre the Giant
MMA Record:	1-0
Halls of Fame:	1

Powerful heavyweight Canek wrestled all the greats from Lou Thesz to Andre the Giant and was admired all over the globe. In the tradition of Mexico's finest lucha libra heroes, he wore colorful masks and attire and was the backbone of the Universal Wrestling Association since its inception. Canek reigned as UWA World Heavyweight Champion fifteen times between 1978 and 2004, dethroning Thesz for his first claim and also beating the likes of Tiger Jeet Singh, Riki Choshu, Tatsumi Fujinami, and Vader. He furthered his legacy in Japan as part of a talent agreement with Antonio Inoki's New Japan Pro Wrestling promotion and received worldwide attention for bodyslamming and pinning Andre the Giant. Many recognizable names went to Mexico to face him before stunning crowds, including Hulk Hogan, Billy Robinson, and Inoki himself. On June 18, 2004, he lost the UWA Title for the final time to Dr. Wagner Jr. in Mexico City. Canek still wrestles from time to time, continuing to add chapters to his legendary career.

Born:	July 17, 1926
Height:	5'9"
Weight:	225
Real Name:	Edouard Wieczorkwicz
College:	University of Sorbonne
Identities:	Eduardo Wiecezorski, Eddie Wiecz
Nicknames:	The Flying Frenchman
Career Span:	1952-1987
Died:	October 30, 2010, Montreal, Quebec 84 years old

Titles Won:	15
Days as World Champion:	Around 2,090
Age at first World Title Win:	30
Best Opponents:	Lou Thesz, Fred Blassie, Killer Kowalski
Halls of Fame:	3

Carpentier, Edouard

The lively acrobatics of Antonino Rocca initiated a trend in professional wrestling that was also capitalized on by the popular Edouard Carpentier of France. Carpentier, a former gymnast, was an innovator in the way he used a wide variety of tumbling maneuvers, displaying his amazing athleticism and craftiness. Standing about 5'9", he was one of the smaller grapplers, but he made up for his lack of stature with his quick feet and intellect. Carpentier matched up well with all the great monster heels of the time and his classy personality made him a ring idol for fans throughout the world. As a teen, he displayed extraordinary courage while fighting with the French Resistance and excelled on the rings and the trampoline, earning a spot as an alternate with the French national gymnastics squad at the 1948 Olympics. He trained for the mat under Henri DeGlane and launched his professional career in Europe. A few years later, he was scouted by Yvon Robert and debuted in Montreal in April of 1956.

Carpentier had no trouble adapting to the flashy North American style of wrestling and to the fame that came very easily to him. He succeeded Robert as the top draw in Montreal, drawing huge crowds to the Forum and the baseball stadium during the summers, and fought heated contests against Killer Kowalski, Gene Kiniski, and Buddy Rogers. The match he's most remembered for, however, was his disqualification win over NWA World champion Lou Thesz on June 14, 1957 in Chicago, which saw him proclaimed as the new titleholder. Unbeknownst to fans, the title switch was a political ploy to split the championship while Thesz was overseas, allowing NWA members to book him on the circuit in the interim. A squabble between promoters disintegrated the strategy a few months later, but Carpentier was a trooper and went about his business in rings all across North America in spite of the political shenanigans happening around him.

When Thesz eventually returned from his tour, he lost his official National Wrestling Alliance World Title lineage to Dick Hutton; but by that point, Carpentier was seen as a more valuable champion in terms of ticket sales. The one thing that Carpentier did not have was an out-of-control ego and he was willing to help a number of promoters across the nation establish new title lineages based on his 1957 win over Thesz. It began on May 3, 1958 in Boston when Carpentier dropped the championship to Killer Kowalski. A few months later in Omaha, he lost his title again to Verne Gagne on August 9, 1958. Finally, he was acknowledged as champion in Los Angeles in 1961 until being defeated by Fred Blassie on June 12, 1961 before 13,000 fans at the Sports Arena. In Montreal, he was a five-time champion and held tag team titles with both Bob Ellis and Bruno Sammartino. Carpentier was a strong mentor to many wrestlers and was credited with bringing Andre the Giant to North America from France.

Photo Courtesy of Dr. Mike Lano—Wrealano@aol.com

Born:	December 3, 1951
Height:	6'0"
Weight:	245
Real Name:	Mitsuo Yoshida
College:	Senshu University
Olympics:	Freestyle Wrestling (1972) (Representing South Korea) (DNP)
Trained by:	NJPW Dojo, Masa Saito
Finisher:	Lariet
Career Span:	1974-2010

Titles Won:	13
Days as World Champion:	Around 792
Age at first World Title Win:	30
Best Opponents:	Antonio Inoki, Tatsumi Fujinami, Keiji Mutoh
Halls of Fame:	1

Choshu, Riki

Riki Choshu was a preeminent figure inside the squared circle and out, wrestling countless great matches during his thirty-six year career and assisting in the charge of New Japan Pro Wrestling as a booker as it skyrocketed to record success during the 1990s. Additionally, his invasion of All-Japan in 1984 set off a dynamic feud and garnered a lot of worldwide attention. Choshu, as a singles competitor, has won three IWGP Titles, initially defeating Salman Hashimikov for the championship on July 12, 1989, as well as also dethroning Vader and Tatsumi Fujinami. Between 1988 and 1997, he held the IWGP Tag Team Title three times with partners, Masa Saito, Takayuki Iizuka, and Kensuke Sasaki, and in 1996, he won the G-1 Climax Tournament. Outside NJPW, he won the UWA World Title from Canek in Mexico in 1982 and captured the PWF World Title from Stan Hansen on April 5, 1986. He remained with New Japan from 1987 until 2002, and then operated the promotions Riki Pro and Lock Up. He was still semi-active as of 2010.

Born:	July 18, 1948
Height:	5'10"
Weight:	245
Real Name:	Carlos Edwin Colon Gonzalez
Family:	Father of Carlito, Primo, and Stacy Colon
Wife:	Nancy Colon
Trained by:	Red Beard
Identities:	Chief White Feather, Prince Kahulia
Finisher:	Figure-four leglock
Promoter:	World Wrestling Council (1974-Present) (Puerto Rico)
Career Span:	1966-2008

Colon, Carlos

PPV Record:		0-1
Titles Won:		68
Days as World Champion:	491	
Age at first World Title Win:	34	
Best Opponents:		Ric Flair, Harley Race, Terry Funk

A wrestling legend from Santa Isabel, Puerto Rico, Carlos Colon grew up in New York City. He was one of seven children and was influenced by the excitement of grappling throughout the area. Colon joined a gym frequented by legends Miguel Perez and Antonino Rocca, and learned the pro style, debuting on the circuit in 1966. He worked his way across the U.S. to California, and had extended stays in Montreal and the northeast. He returned to Puerto Rico and launched the WWC with Victor Jovica in January of 1974. Blending native workers with talent from around the world, Colon's WWC has been a hotbed for action, and he reigned as Universal champion twenty-six times, battling the likes of Abdullah the Butcher, Dory Funk Jr., and Ron Garvin. His long-running war with Abdullah is among the greatest feuds in wrestling history and perhaps the most violent. Colon was also a top challenger to NWA champions Harley Race and Ric Flair, and even pinned the latter in 1983, but was never acknowledged as an official titleholder.

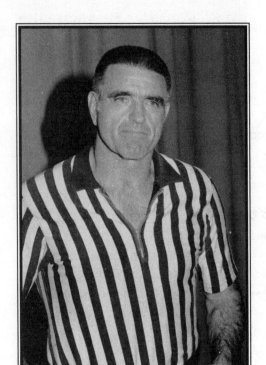

Born:	May 22, 1927
Height:	5'11"
Weight:	220
Real Name:	Donald Bain Beitelman
Parents:	Thomas and Helen Beitelman
Wife:	Dotty Curtis
High School:	Riverside High School (NY)
Trained by:	Lou Thesz
Identities:	Don Lutz
Finisher:	Sleeperhold
Career Span:	1951-1972
Died:	March 6, 2008, Jacksonville, FL 80 years old

Titles Won:	14
Best Opponents:	Lou Thesz, Johnny Valentine, Gene Kiniski
Halls of Fame:	2

Curtis, Don

A longtime crowd pleaser, Don Curtis was a superb athlete from Buffalo and had a long, successful career on the mat. While still a teenager, he served in the Navy on two submarines, the U.S.S. Skipjack and the U.S.S. Entemedor, attending the University of Buffalo upon his discharge. He was a standout football player in college, but it was his lightning moves as an amateur grappler that caught the eye of area promoter Ed Don George. He wrestled for six years under his real name, competing at length in the South Pacific, and debut in West Texas in January of 1957, where he debuted under the guise, "Don Curtis." He formed a renowned tag team with Mark Lewin, also of Buffalo, and won a number of championships in the Northeast and Florida. Altogether, Curtis won the World Tag Team Title five times and also reigned as the Southern champion. During the 1960s, he became an NWA-affiliated promoter in Jacksonville, but broke from the Tampa office in 1981 and formed an indie promotion, Sun Belt Wrestling.

Born:	April 7, 1932
Height:	6'1"
Weight:	245
Real Name:	Eduardo Ramon Rodriguez
Identities:	Lalo Rodriguez, Caribs Hurricane, Ciclon Negro
Career Span:	1960-1987

Titles Won:	33
Best Opponents:	Dory Funk Jr., Terry Funk, Ricky Steamboat

Cyclone Negro

Venezuelan Cyclone Negro appeared on the Texas wrestling scene in 1960 by wearing a mask, and quickly became one of the most popular grapplers in the territory. Formerly a boxer, Cyclone was exceptionally powerful, able to bench press more than 500 pounds, and held both the Texas State Heavyweight and Tag Team Titles simultaneously. When he was unleashed on the rest of the NWA, he ripped through territory after territory, capturing regional championships in Puerto Rico, California, Florida, and Japan. In 1974, he won the first of five International Titles. Cyclone Negro was very popular at times, but also was known as a talented heel. He competed into the 1980s and then settled down in Florida where he is retired.

Born:	June 15, 1932
Height:	6'2"
Weight:	260
Real Name:	Domenic D. Nucciarone
Trained by:	Tony Lanza, Jack Britton
Identities:	Masked Marvel, Dominic Bravo
Finisher:	Airplane Spin
Career Span:	1958-1988

Titles Won:	21
Days as World Champion:	Around 340
Age at first World Title Win:	32
Best Opponents:	Killer Kowalski, Ray Stevens, Waldo Von Erich
Halls of Fame:	2

DeNucci, Dominic

The immensely popular and influential Dominic DeNucci wrestled for three decades and left a dent wherever he appeared. Originally from Campobasso, Italy, he was an amateur Greco-Roman wrestler as a youth and turned professional in 1958, wrestling as the "Masked Marvel" in Montreal. For several years, he performed as one-half of the Bravo Brothers with Dino Bravo, and then took the DeNucci name. He captured the U.S. Championship in San Francisco, the NWF Title, and the IWA World Heavyweight crown in Australia four times between 1964 and 1970. He also held the WWWF World Tag Title on three occasions. At his Freedom, Pennsylvania wrestling camp, DeNucci trained Mick Foley, Shane Douglas, and many others.

Photo Courtesy of Dan Westbrook

© Dan Westbrook

Born:	July 11, 1931
Height:	5'11"
Weight:	230
Real Name:	Richard John Beyer
Family:	Father of Kurt Beyer
Wife:	Wilma Beyer
High School:	Seneca Vocational High School (NY)
Amateur Title:	Niagara District AAU Wrestling Title (1952) (HWT)
Military:	United States Army
Trained by:	Bill Miller, Ray Stevens, Dick Hutton
Finisher:	Figure-four leglock
Career Span:	1954-1993

Titles Won:	24
Days as World Champion:	470
Age at first World Title Win:	31
Best Opponents:	Fred Blassie, Rikidozan, Shohei Baba
Halls of Fame:	4

Destroyer, The

A white mask concealed the identity of the "Intelligent, Sensational" Destroyer as he toured the world and earned recognition as a living legend of the wrestling mat. He was technically sound, entertaining, and a box office smash wherever he traveled. Known outside the ring as Dick Beyer of Buffalo, he earned accolades for football and wrestling at Syracuse University and was guided into business by Ed Don George. In 1962, he adopted the "Destroyer" gimmick in Southern California and debuted in Japan the following year, garnering huge TV ratings for his match against Rikidozan. He was a huge attraction in the Los Angeles area, and won the WWA World Title three times. In 1968, he held the AWA World Title for a few weeks under the name, "Dr. X," while wearing a black mask. He wrestled his final bout in Japan in 1993, and taught education in Akron, New York. The Destroyer holds the distinction of having wrestled icons Gorgeous George and Rikidozan in their final matches.

DiBiase, Ted

Born:	January 18, 1954
Height:	6'2"
Weight:	245
Real Name:	Theodore Marvin DiBiase Sr.
Parents:	Mike and Gladys "Helen" DiBiase
Family:	Father of Mike, Brett, and Ted DiBiase Jr.
High Schools:	Creighton Prep (NE), Willcox High School (AZ)
Identities:	The Saint
Finisher:	Powerslam, Million Dollar Dream Sleeperhold
Groups:	The Rat Pack (1982-1983), The Million Dollar Corporation (1994-1995), The New World Order (1996-1997)
Tag Teams:	The Mega Bucks w/ Andre the Giant, Money Inc., w/ Irwin R. Schyster
Career Span:	1975-2007
Website:	www.milliondollarman.com

PPV Record:	9-16, 1 DCO
WrestleMania Record:	4-3, 1 DCO
WWE *Raw* TV Record:	1-0
Titles Won:	30
Best Opponents:	Randy Savage, Jack Brisco, Ric Flair
Wrestlers Managed:	16
Halls of Fame:	3

During the 1980s, few wrestlers had innate talent superseding that of Ted DiBiase. Both his mother, Helen Hilde, and adopted father, Mike DiBiase, were pro grapplers, and the business was in his blood. He spent a lot of time during his youth in Amarillo growing up in a wrestling town, and was heavily influenced by the Funk family. After his father's sudden death, he finished high school in Arizona and earned many accolades for his football prowess. After high school, DiBiase attended West Texas State and began training to be a pro wrestler with Terry and Dory Funk Jr. mentoring him. In the Mid-South territory, he garnered his first notable success, winning the North American Title. Two years later, he went to St. Louis and captured the prestigious Missouri championship. In 1987, he entered the WWF and adopted the gimmick "Million Dollar Man," claiming that "everyone has a price." DiBiase's powerful promos sold the unique character and he would often pay off spectators to perform embarrassing feats to earn cash.

In early 1988, he hired Andre the Giant to win the WWF World Title for him, and a controversial match on the *Main Event* against Hulk Hogan ended with Andre winning the belt—and DiBiase taking over as champion immediately afterward. Officials declared the title vacant, and at WrestleMania IV, DiBiase was in contention for the championship, but lost in the tournament finals to Randy Savage. Between 1992 and 1993, DiBiase held the WWF Tag Team belts three times with Irwin R. Schyster (IRS). DiBiase also had success in Japan, winning the PWF Tag Team Title twice in 1987 and the AJPW Unified World Tag Team Title in 1993. DiBiase often wore his custom Million Dollar Belt, a prize that demonstrated his riches. A serious neck injury ended his active career, but he remained involved in the WWF and WCW from outside the squared circle. In 2010, he was inducted into the WWE Hall of Fame.

Photo Courtesy of the Collection of Tim Hornbaker

Born:	June 27, 1929
Height:	6'1"
Weight:	260
Real Name:	William Franklin Afflis
Parents:	William and Margaret Afflis
Family:	Father of Michelle Replogle, father-in-law of Spike Huber
Wife:	Louise Afflis
High School:	Lafayette High School (IN)
Colleges:	Purdue University, University of Nevada
Trained by:	Leo Nomellini, Verne Gagne, Joe Pazandak
Finisher:	Stomach claw
Promoted:	World Wrestling Association (Indiana) (1964-1988)
Career Span:	1954-1988
Died:	November 10, 1991, Largo, FL 62 years old

Dick the Bruiser

Titles Won:	57
Days as World Champion:	Over 2,300
Age at first World Title Win:	34
Best Opponents:	Wilbur Snyder, Bob Ellis, Bruiser Brody
Halls of Fame:	4

No matter if it was singles or tag team wrestling, Dick the Bruiser was going into the ring for a fight. A brawler of the highest degree, Bruiser took the action from pillar to post and did everything in his power to cripple his opponent. The style he employed riled up crowds and his aggressiveness was as fierce as a tiger going after prey. He was hard-hitting and his roughness earned him as many cheers as it did jeers throughout his legendary career. His personality was also very apparent when he'd counteract howling from the audience with his own, often comical, posturing.

Dick the Bruiser was a standout football player in high school and college, and was drafted by the Green Bay Packers in 1951. He played forty-eight games over the next four years, and then hung his cleats up for wrestling boots and dedicated his life to grappling. Between 1957 and 1963, he won the United States Heavyweight Title thirteen times and engaged in many violent and bloody matches with Wilbur Snyder and Bob Ellis.

Bruiser formed a Hall of Fame tag team with Crusher Lisowski and they won the AWA World Tag Team Title five times and the WWA championship six. They also captured gold while in Japan in 1969. As a singles competitor, Bruiser beat Fred Blassie for the WWA World Title in 1965 and took the championship back to Indianapolis, where he formed the World Wrestling Association, a regionally-based promotion. Late in 1965, he teamed with Snyder to buy the Chicago territory, expanding their business significantly. Bruiser would win the WWA Title ten times during his time on the mat and promoted shows throughout Indiana, Illinois, and Michigan, as well as in St. Louis, where he won the Missouri Title three times. One of Bruiser's most noteworthy incidents occurred in 1963 when he brawled with football star Alex Karras in the latter's Detroit bar. It was a chaotic scene that promoted their upcoming mat showdown perfectly. The "World's Most Dangerous Man" proved that he was, without question, as unpredictable outside the ring as in it.

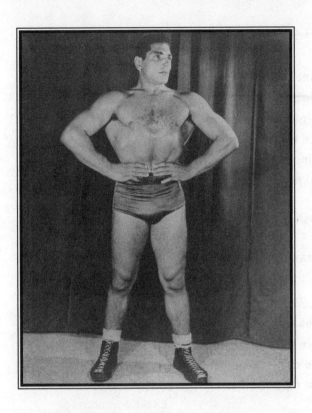

Born:	November 8, 1926
Height:	6'2"
Weight:	250
Real Name:	Ilio P. DiPaolo
Wife:	Ethel DiPaolo
Trained by:	Joe "Toots" Mondt, Dick Beyer
Career Span:	1951-1965
Died:	May 10, 1995, Buffalo, NY
	68 years old

Titles Won:	8
Best Opponents:	Gene Kiniski, Don Leo Jonathan, Buddy Rogers
Halls of Fame:	2

DiPaolo, Ilio

A popular hero and genuinely great guy, Ilio DiPaolo was a class act in a tough profession. He rose above the demoralizing aspects of the business to shine in every way possible, inside the ring and out. Originally from Introdacqua, Italy, DiPaolo was scouted by Joe "Toots" Mondt in Venezuela, and arrived in the U.S. on July 31, 1951. Soon thereafter, he found a permanent home in the Buffalo area, where he married the daughter of promoter Pedro Martinez. He won over audiences with his strength and likeable personality and formed popular tag teams with Bruno Sammartino, Sandor Szabo, and Billy Watson. In Canada, he was a six-time tag team champion and also found success during tours of Texas, California, and Japan. He opened a restaurant in Blasdell, New York and formed close bonds with many members of the Buffalo Bills football team. For his community leadership, he was named "Citizen of the Year" for 1978 in Blasdell and honored by the Professional Wrestling Hall of Fame with the New York State Award.

Born:	February 1, 1935
Height:	5'9"
Weight:	220
Real Name:	Dorrel Dixon
Trained by:	Rafael Salamanca
Nicknames:	El Gigante de Ebano (The Ebony Giant), Black Bullet
Finisher:	Jamaican Flying Bodyblock, Dropkick
Career Span:	1955-1983

Titles Won:	11
Days as World Champion:	35
Age at first World Title Win:	28
Best Opponents:	Buddy Rogers, Lou Thesz, Duke Keomuka

Dixon, Dory

The "Calypso Kid," Dory Dixon was a Jamaican transplant to Mexico, and was competing as a weightlifter when he was scouted by promoter Salvador Lutteroth who encouraged him to become a professional wrestler. With soaring popularity, he beat Al Kashey in Mexico City for the NWA World Light Heavyweight Championship on February 13, 1959, and shortly thereafter, began to steadily tour the Texas circuit. He won numerous regional titles and was always a solid challenger for the touring NWA champion. On March 28, 1963, he won his only world heavyweight title when he beat Rogers for the WWWA Title in Cleveland. Exceptionally conditioned and quick on his feet, Dixon was an excellent box office attraction throughout his career, which ended in Mexico during the 1980s.

Born:	October 24, 1943
Height:	5'7"
Weight:	215
Real Name:	William Cruickshanks
Family:	Father of Jamie Dundee
Identities:	Sir William Dundee
Nickname:	Superstar
Finisher:	Flying Press, Sleeperhold
Managed:	Lord Steven Regal (1993-1994)
Career Span:	1967-Present

Titles Won:	63
Days as World Champion:	44
Age at first World Title Win:	36
Best Opponents:	Jerry Lawler, Dutch Mantel, Billy Robinson
Published Books:	1

Dundee, Bill

A charismatic grappling legend, Bill Dundee was a bright spot in the Memphis Territory for decades. Born in Scotland, he migrated to Australia in 1961 and worked in a circus as a trapeze artist. He debuted as a local grappler in 1967 and then came to the U.S. eight years later along with George Barnes, wrestling throughout the Mid-America territory. Over the course of his career, he held more than sixty championships, including the CWA and USWA World Titles. He was AWA Southern titleholder nine times and an AWA World Tag Team Champion twice with Jerry Lawler. He also teamed with Lawler, and his son Jamie, to hold the USWA Tag Team belts in 1996. His autobiography was released in November 2011.

Born:	December 5, 1958
Height:	5'8"
Weight:	225
Real Name:	Thomas Billington
Other Sports:	Boxing
Trained by:	Ted Betley, Stu Hart
Career Span:	1975-1996

PPV Record:	5-3, 1 Draw
WrestleMania Record:	1-2
Titles Won:	24
Best Opponents:	Tiger Mask, Tatsumi Fujinami, Randy Savage
Halls of Fame:	2

Dynamite Kid, The

The influential Dynamite Kid was heralded around the world for his stunning moves, quickness in the ring, and overall technical abilities; with that skill set, he was considered one of the best wrestlers of his era. From Goldborne in Lancashire, England, he won championships in his native country, Canada, Japan, and the U.S. In February of 1984, he beat The Cobra for the WWF Junior Heavyweight Title. Later in the year, Dynamite joined the WWF full-time, forming a popular tag team with cousin Davey Boy Smith, known as the British Bulldogs. The Bulldogs annexed the World Tag Team Title from Brutus Beefcake and Greg Valentine at WrestleMania II on April 7, 1986. Later that year, Dynamite suffered a devastating injury and needed surgery to have two discs removed from his back. He displayed his fortitude in returning to the ring to lose the belts to the Hart Foundation in January of 1987. He wrestled his last match on October 10, 1996 in Tokyo, competing in a six-man tag team bout along with fellow legends Mil Mascaras and the original Tiger Mask, his greatest opponent.

Born:	December 27, 1946
Height:	6'2"
Weight:	300
Real Name:	William Reid Eadie
High School:	Brownsville High School (PA)
Trained by:	Newton Tattrie, Boris Malenko
Identities:	The Medic, Bolo Mongol, Super Machine, Ax, Axis
Career Span:	1972-Present

Titles Won:	31
Days as World Champion:	Unknown
Age at first World Title Win:	37
Best Opponents:	Rick Steamboat, Andre the Giant, Wahoo McDaniel
Halls of Fame:	1

Eadie, Bill

Track sensation Bill Eadie grew up south of Pittsburgh and attended West Virginia University. He graduated from a wrestling school taught by Newton Tattrie and partnered with his mentor as the Mongols, which made the rounds from the WWWF to the IWA. In 1976, he became the Masked Superstar in the Mid-Atlantic region and displayed his versatile style. His effective interview segments were also a sight to behold, and the Superstar wowed fans from Charlotte to Tokyo with his ring mastery. He claimed the IWA World Title during the summer of 1984 and held the National Heavyweight crown three times. Eadie formed the successful Demolition tag team with Barry Darsow, as Ax and Smash, respectively, and won a trio of WWF World Tag Team Championships between 1988 and 1990. With wrestling still in his heart, he still makes the occasional appearance on indie shows.

Born:	March 15, 1929
Height:	6'3"
Weight:	240
Real Name:	Robert Al Ellis
Parents:	John and Rose Ellis
High School:	San Angelo High School (TX)
Identities:	Bob Elliott
Finisher:	Bulldog Headlock
Career Span:	1956-1978

Titles Won:	25
Days as World Champion:	Over 340
Age at first World Title Win:	35
Best Opponents:	Buddy Rogers, Dick the Bruiser, The Sheik
Halls of Fame:	1

Ellis, Bob

The tall "Cowboy" from San Angelo, Bob Ellis was a popular brawler, and his toughness was on display every time he stepped through the ropes. He boxed as an amateur and played both high school and college football—the latter for McMurry College after service in the Army. After finishing college, Ellis was signed to play football by the Philadelphia Eagles in 1954. His pro football days didn't last long, and, after opening up a gym in his hometown and developing his physique, he entered the wrestling profession. By 1958 he was already a box office sensation. He engaged in many violent matches with Dick the Bruiser and beat the latter three separate times for the U.S. Title. Buddy Rogers was another important rival, and Ellis contended for the NWA Championship in the early 1960s. In 1964, he beat the Destroyer in California for the WWA World Title and, in 1973-1974, won the WWA (Indiana) World Championship twice. Ellis was a headliner nearly everywhere he appeared, including Madison Square Garden and the Olympic Auditorium in Los Angeles.

Born:	June 26, 1930
Height:	5'10"
Weight:	230
Real Name:	Henry Leonard Faggart
Parents:	Lewis and Delma Faggart
Family:	Brother of Sonny Fargo
Nicknames:	Wildman, Fabulous
Career Span:	1951-1999

Titles Won:	60
Days as World Champion:	Around 1,550
Age at first World Title Win:	30
Best Opponents:	Jerry Lawler, Gene Kiniski, Bruno Sammartino
Halls of Fame:	1

Fargo, Jackie

The legendary Jackie Fargo of China Grove, North Carolina was an exciting performer for many different reasons: He was a talented wrestler in the ring, a superb interviewer, and a box office sensation. As a tag team grappler, he won many championships with his faux brother Don Fargo (Don Kalt). He claimed the World Heavyweight Title for Jack Pfefer's troupe for most of the 1961-1966 times frame. In Houston, Pfefer put up a $50,000 offer for a unification bout between Fargo and NWA champion Lou Thesz, and goaded the latter in the press. Even with all the publicity, the big match never happened. Fargo was a real hero in Memphis, where he dominated headlines for years. He mentored and feuded with Jerry Lawler, and was a perennial champion throughout his career.

Born:	October 20, 1958
Height:	5'10"
Weight:	235
Real Name:	David John Finlay
Identities:	Belfast Bruiser, Fit Finlay
Finisher:	Celtic Cross
Career Span:	1974-Present

Finlay, Dave

PPV Record:	9-28, 1 NC
WrestleMania Record:	0-4
WWE *Raw* TV Record:	5-13
WWE *Smackdown* TV Record:	57-56, 2 Draws, 3 DDQ, 7 NC
Titles Won:	26
Best Opponents:	Chris Benoit, Booker T, William Regal

The no-nonsense Dave Finlay was a longtime pupil of amateur wrestling in his Northern Ireland hometown. Taught by his father, Dave Sr., Finlay excelled on the mat, and it wasn't before long that he combined a deep scientific knowledge of the catch-as-catch-can style with his own innate, old-fashioned toughness. He won middleweight, light heavyweight, and heavyweight championship honors in Europe prior to making his WCW debut in 1995. Three years later, he beat Booker T for the World TV Title. Finlay joined the WWF in 2001 and was an influential coach to many up-and-comers. While on *Smackdown*, he won the U.S. Title in the summer of 2006 at the age of forty-seven, and remained an important figure in the organization until leaving the WWE in 2011.

Flair, Ric

Born:	February 25, 1949
Height:	6'1"
Weight:	240
Real Name:	Richard Morgan Fliehr
Parents:	Richard and Kathleen Fliehr
Family:	Father of David and Reid Flair
High School:	Wayland Academy (WI)
College:	University of Minnesota
Trained by:	Verne Gagne, Billy Robinson
Nicknames:	Nature Boy®, Naitch, Slick Ric
Finisher:	Figure-four leglock
Groups:	The Four Horsemen (1986-1989, 1990-1991, 1993, 1996-1998), The Millionaires Club (2000), Team Package (2000), The Magnificent Seven (2000-2001), Evolution (2003-2005), Fortune (2010-2011), Immortal (2011)
Managed:	Hunter Hearst Helmsley (2002-2003), Batista (2002-2003)
Career Span:	1972-Present

PPV Record:	52-56, 1 Draw, 1 DCO, 1 NC
WrestleMania Record:	1-4
WWE *Raw* TV Record:	55-70, 1 DCO, 5 NC
WWE *Smackdown* TV Record:	6-4
Titles Won:	44
Days as World Champion:	3,721
Age at first World Title Win:	32
Best Opponents:	Ricky Steamboat, Harley Race, Randy Savage
Managers:	9
Halls of Fame:	5

Every generation has a "greatest wrestler," and Ric Flair is arguably the best seen by wrestling fans in the last fifty years. He was a masterful grappler—full of charisma, arrogance, and technical savvy, and was normally on the top of his game when delivering an enthusiastic promo or wrestling an important contest. His matches were always entertaining and it didn't matter if he was facing a comparable athlete or a dead weight, Flair could always make the bout interesting. His pacing and style, which set a standard for others to emulate, was extraordinary. At his height as the NWA World Heavyweight Champion, he'd wrestle more than 20-times a month, sometimes twice in a single day, and never missed a beat—performing well above his peers in an industry that respected his dedication and the honor he brought to the mat. Flair would wear his extravagant robes, strut around the ring, and wrestle like there was no tomorrow, leaving an indelible mark on audiences around the world.

Flair is a twenty-time World Heavyweight Champion, having won the National Wrestling Alliance World Title ten times between 1981 and 1993, the WWF World Title twice in 1992, and the WCW World Title eight times between 1991 and 2000. Those honors are emblematic of a surefire Hall of Famer, and he's since been enshrined in five separate institutions. The journey from motivated upstart to wrestling's "God" was winding, and it almost ended before it got started when he was nearly killed in a plane crash on October 4, 1975 on a flight from Charlotte to Wilmington, North Carolina. By this juncture, he'd graduated from the famous wrestling school of Verne Gagne and jumped from the AWA to Crockett promotions in the Mid-Atlantic territory and was establishing himself as a real up-and-comer. The accident broke Flair's back and immediate reports were that he would never wrestle again.

Defying the odds, he returned in late January of 1976 and continued his ascent to the top of the sport. Flair waged a long feud with Wahoo McDaniel, which saw them battle in many brutal and bloody matches. During his early years, he learned a great deal from veterans Rip Hawk, Johnny Valentine, and Tim Woods, and formed a successful tag team with Greg Valentine. Impressing the leaders of the National Wrestling Alliance, Flair was soon supported as a candidate for the heavyweight belt, and at thirty-two years of age, on September 17, 1981, he beat Dusty Rhodes for his NWA World Title in Kansas City. He immediately assumed a hectic schedule, wrestling throughout the globe and taking on a wide variety of competitors. After 631 days on top, Flair lost the belt to Harley Race in St. Louis on June 10, 1983. In the main event of the first Starrcade, Flair regained the belt in a special cage match.

The next seven years was a remarkable time for professional wrestling and for Flair. He was considered the opposite of Hulk Hogan, as Ric was the more finely-tuned grappler who appealed more to the serious wrestling enthusiast. During that time, he won the NWA World Title five additional times, beating both Race and Rhodes again, Kerry Von Erich, Ron Garvin, and Ricky Steamboat. He led the illustrious Four Horsemen, headlined Starrcade events, and proved his durability an endless amount of times. In 1989, he had two classic feuds against Steamboat and Terry Funk, and battled an old rival, Lex Luger all over the map the following year. Sting beat him for the NWA championship on July 7, 1990, but Flair regained it at the Meadowlands in East Rutherford, New Jersey on January 11, 1991, making him an eight-time titleholder. Flair also traded the crown with Tatsumi Fujinami before departing for WCW during that summer.

The WWF was his next stop, and on January 19, 1992, he entered the Royal Rumble at number three and remained in the bout for more than an hour. He outlasted his competitors to win the event and the vacant World Title. Flair became the second man in history to have won the NWA and WWF Titles after the original "Nature Boy," Buddy Rogers. He ended up losing the title to Randy Savage at WrestleMania, but regained it from him on September 1 of that year. Finally, he dropped the belt to Bret Hart at a house show in Saskatoon, Saskatchewan on October 12. In 1993, he returned to WCW and won his tenth and final NWA World championship from Barry Windham. On December 27, 1993 in Charlotte, he defeated Vader for the WCW World Title and a few months later, he resumed his longstanding feud with Steamboat. On July 17, 1994, he lost his title to the newly arriving Hulk Hogan.

Seven years later, after many memorable performances, Flair matched up against one of his greatest rivals, Sting, on the emotional final episode of WCW *Nitro* in March of 2001. Their bout was acknowledged as a fitting farewell to the promotion. Flair appeared in the WWF before the year was out, and engaged in a war for control of the organization with Vince McMahon as a purported co-owner. They took their bad blood into the ring at the Royal Rumble, which saw Flair win a street fight, but McMahon won a bout later on for full ownership. In 2003, he joined a group known as Evolution along with Triple H, Batista, and Randy Orton. On December 14, 2003, he captured the World Tag Team Title with Batista and regained the belts from Rob Van Dam and Booker T for a second reign as champion. At Unforgiven on September 18, 2005, he beat Carlito for the Intercontinental Championship. His reign lasted until February 20, 2006, when he lost a bout to Shelton Benjamin on *Raw*. Flair also teamed up with Roddy Piper to win the World Tag Team Title from the Spirit Squad in November 2006, but they lost the belts a week later in England.

A decree was made announcing that the next match Flair lost would force his retirement and "Naitch" did his best to remain active against many tough opponents. On March 30, 2008 in Orlando, he met his match, Shawn Michaels, and was defeated. The crowd and his peers the next night on *Raw* all gave him the respect he deserved. He remained employed by the promotion through the summer of 2009, and then left for greener pastures. Flair joined a tour led by Hulk Hogan in Australia later in the year and debuted for TNA on January 4, 2010. He began to mentor a younger crop of grapplers starting with A.J. Styles and later named his group, Fortune. Regardless of how many retirement matches he participates in, Flair won't leave the sport he loves willingly, and nor should any outside force decide for him. The same heart of a champion that was displayed so freely throughout his career remains strong in 2011, and if his body can keep up with him, he'll be wrestling indefinitely—much to the delight of his true fans.

Born:	December 28, 1953
Height:	6'1"
Weight:	200-235
Trained by:	Antonio Inoki, Karl Gotch
Identities:	Dragon Fujinami
Nickname:	The Dragon
Finisher:	Dragon Sleeper, Dragon Suplex
Trained:	Numerous athletes including Osamu Nishimura
Career Span:	1971-2011

Fujinami, Tatsumi

PPV Record:	0-2
Titles Won:	21
Days as World Champion:	887
Age at first World Title Win:	34
Best Opponents:	Riki Choshu, Vader, Antonio Inoki
Halls of Fame:	1

A superb technical wrestler who, in February of 2011, celebrated his fortieth anniversary in the business, Tatsumi Fujinami is credited with helping launch the junior heavyweight revolution in Japan. He was a pioneering figure in New Japan Pro Wrestling and was with the company when it started in 1972, being trained extensively by the legendary duo of Antonio Inoki and Karl Gotch. Fujinami took what he learned and spawned many classic matches throughout the course of his great career. On May 8, 1988, he won the vacant IWGP championship over Big Van Vader at Ariake Coliseum in Tokyo and wrestled a no-contest against Riki Choshu on May 27, which held up the title. Fujinami won the rematch on June 24, winning his second IWGP Title. On December 9, 1988, he beat Kerry Von Erich in a controversial IWGP-WCCW World Title unification match. A serious back injury forced him to surrender the IWGP Title in April 1989, but he bounced back to win his third championship on December 26, 1990 over Choshu.

In early 1991, Fujinami traded the IWGP belt with Vader, and then beat Ric Flair for the NWA World championship at the Tokyo Dome on March 21, 1991. The switch was never recognized in the U.S., but a rematch was staged on May 19, 1991 with Flair regaining the NWA crown. His longtime rival, Choshu, ended his reign as IWGP champion in January of 1992. In 1993, Fujinami won the G-1 Climax Tournament and captured his fifth IWGP Title from Shinya Hashimoto in April of 1994. It would be four years before he would win his sixth and final IWGP championship, on April 4, 1998, defeating Kensuke Sasaki during Inoki's retirement show. Between 1985 and 2001, he held the IWGP Tag Team Title four times with partner Kengo Kimura. Outside the ring, Fujinami worked as a booker and president for New Japan and was involved with the organization until 2006. On February 5, 2011, he wrestled Mil Mascaras to a ten-minute draw on a IGF show promoted by Inoki.

Funk, Dory Jr.

Born:	February 3, 1941
Height:	6'2"
Weight:	235
Real Name:	Dory Earnest Funk Jr.
Parents:	Dory and Dorothy Funk
Wife:	Marti Funk
High School:	Canyon High School (TX)
College:	West Texas State University
Trained by:	Dory Funk Sr.
Identities:	The Outlaw (Masked), Hoss Funk
Finisher:	Spinning Toehold
Managed:	Jesse Barr, Adam Windsor
Career Span:	1963-2008
Website:	www.dory-funk.com

PPV Record:	2-1
WrestleMania Record:	1-0
Titles Won:	44
Days as World Champion:	Over 1,660
Age at first World Title Win:	22
Best Opponents:	Jack Brisco, Harley Race, Gene Kiniski
Halls of Fame:	8
Movies:	2, plus a few documentaries

History was made on the evening of February 11, 1969 at the Armory in Tampa when Dory Funk Jr. forced champion Gene Kiniski to submit to his spinning toe-hold and won the NWA World Heavyweight Title. He won the most coveted championship in the business, and a belt that his father, Dory Sr. had chased for years. Funk would endure as champion for 1,563 days, the second longest reign the National Wrestling Alliance history. During that time, he met all contenders and performed admirably throughout the world. After an incredible run, he was finally beaten by Harley Race on May 24, 1973. Funk won regional championships throughout the NWA, from Florida to Japan, and teamed with his brother Terry to capture the AJPW International and World Tag Team Titles. They also won the Real World tournament in 1977, 1979, and 1982. Dory wrestled Terry on April 30, 1981 in Japan after being named International champion, and he came out victorious after a fifty-four minute match.

It may be hard to conceive, but Dory was actually a claimant to the World Heavyweight Title less than three months into his professional career. Ironically, the title victory also came at the expense of Gene Kiniski on March 28, 1963 in Amarillo. This version of the title, however, was regionally based, and was later merged with Lou Thesz's NWA championship. As a rookie, Funk was already conditioned enough to wrestle a broadway with Verne Gagne and challenge Thesz. He was a versatile athlete, and the family tradition of wrestling was carried forward to great success. Long affiliated with All-Japan Pro Wrestling, Funk acted as a booker for the promotion and did the same in Florida for a period. The Funk Brothers sold their interest in the Amarillo promotion in 1980 and he wrestled his last match in Japan in 2008. Dory operates the famous Funking Conservatory wrestling school in Ocala, Florida, where he's coached some of the best and brightest.

Photo Courtesy of Pete Lederberg—plmathfoto@hotmail.com

Funk, Terry

Born:	June 30, 1944
Height:	6'1"
Weight:	235
Real Name:	Terry Dee Funk
Parents:	Dory and Dorothy Funk
Family:	Brother of Dory Funk Jr.
Wife:	Vicki Funk
High School:	Canyon High School (TX)
Colleges:	Cisco Junior College, West Texas State University
Trained by:	Dory Funk Sr.
Identities:	Chainsaw Charlie
Nicknames:	Hardcore Legend
Finisher:	Piledriver, DDT, Spinning Toehold
Owned:	A percentage of the Amarillo promotion (1967-1978)
Career Span:	1965-2011

PPV Record:	10-15, 1 DDQ
WrestleMania Record:	2-0
Titles Won:	57
Days as World Champion:	724
Age at first World Title Win:	31
Best Opponents:	Ric Flair, Harley Race, Dusty Rhodes
Halls of Fame:	11
TV Appearances:	Over 20
Movies:	10, plus 7 documentaries

Terry Funk's love and passion for the business was apparent in every match he participated in, which goes back to 1965 and continues in 2011, where, at sixty-seven years of age, he's still giving it his all. The "Funker" grew up around the business, watching intently as his father Dory Funk Sr. did battle week after week at the Sports Arena in Amarillo. Terry, along with his brother, Dory Jr., not only also became pro wrestlers, but established themselves as legends in their own distinctive ways. For Terry, it was a natural affinity toward work as a tremendously brutal heel, drawing the anger from crowds and laying down the groundwork for the hardcore style that has become a significant part of the industry. He has held numerous wrestling championships across the globe, but perhaps his greatest accomplishment was winning the National Wrestling Alliance World Heavyweight Title in 1975, an honor that his brother also achieved six years earlier.

Hailing from the Double Cross Ranch near Canyon, Texas, Funk played football at West Texas State, and his anticipated wrestling debut came in December of 1965. The lessons of the Amarillo territory were vast, and included old-fashioned, no-holds-barred brawling. Terry was a quick learner and an enthusiastic competitor, displaying his fierceness in violent matches. He also knew the fundamentals that benefited him his entire career. In February of 1973, he won the Missouri Heavyweight Title in St. Louis, and two years later, he won the Mid-Atlantic version of the U.S. Heavyweight Title in a tournament. On December 10, 1975, at the Miami Beach Convention Center, he beat Jack Brisco for the NWA World Title, stunning the 5,000 fans in attendance. Funk remained champion until February 6, 1977 in Toronto, when he was defeated by Harley Race at Maple Leaf Gardens. Race preyed on Funk's injured knee and won the match with an Indian Deathlock in 14:10.

The Funk Brothers were also quite successful as a tag team, capturing the International Tag Team Title on several occasions, winning the AJPW Real World Tag Tournament three times in 1977, 1979, and 1982, and the WWC World Tag Team Title twice in Puerto Rico. Funk won a number of regional championships; the USWA and ECW World Heavyweight Titles, and the WCW U.S. Title in 2000. He had a memorable feud against Ric Flair in 1989 and great matches against Harley Race, Dusty Rhodes, Cactus Jack, and Sabu. He was instrumental in helping ECW gain notoriety and was the poster child for what it really meant to be "hardcore." His dedication to that "anything goes" style earned him respect from yet another generation of fans and influenced many of his fellow wrestlers. Although he's had a number of retirement matches, Funk has never completely walked away from the sport, competing in a match in 2011 in Japan.

Born:	November 27, 1948
Height:	6'1"
Weight:	220
Real Name:	Gregory Allan Gagne
High School:	Mound High School (MN)
College:	University of Wyoming
Finisher:	Sleeperhold
Career Span:	1973-1991

PPV Record:	1-0
Titles Won:	4
Best Opponents:	Nick Bockwinkel, Curt Hennig, Larry Zbyszko

Gagne, Greg

Popular second generation grappler Greg Gagne was not even a year old when his famous father, Verne, wrestled in his first pro match. For the next forty years, he was surrounded by the sport—from the promotional side of the AWA, to his own in-ring career. He was a talented quarterback in school and was trained by father and Billy Robinson for his 1973 professional wrestling debut. Along with Jim Brunzell, he formed the babyface tag team, The Hi-Flyers, and won the AWA World belts on two occasions. In 1987-1988, he also captured the AWA International TV Championship twice, and remained a main figure in the promotion until it went out of business. He worked for WCW and the WWE behind the scenes and had an influential affect on many careers. In 2006, he inducted his father into the WWE Hall of Fame.

Born:	September 25, 1952
Height:	5'11"
Weight:	230
Real Name:	James Williams
High School:	Leto High School (FL)
Trained by:	Joe Scarpa
Finisher:	DDT
Career Span:	1969-1999

PPV Record:	7-10, 1 Draw
Titles Won:	26
Best Opponents:	Ric Flair, David Von Erich, Rick Martel

Garvin, Jimmy

"Gorgeous" Jimmy Garvin's entertaining personality was always on display when he entered the ring. He was an engaging villain while touring with Precious on his arm and as a member of the Fabulous Freebirds. A talented amateur grappler in Tampa, Garvin broke into the business as the manager of Terry Garvin, and, under the name "Beau James," worked as a second for Ray Stevens. He, along with Freebird partner Michael Hayes, won a 1989 tournament for the NWA World Tag Team Title and later held the WCW World and U.S. championships. In addition to his Florida and Texas State Titles, Garvin also won the American Heavyweight crown on four occasions.

Born:	March 30, 1945
Height:	5'10"
Weight:	230
Real Name:	Roger Barnes
Family:	Stepfather of Jim Garvin
Trained by:	Pat Girard, Tony Santos Pro-Wrestling Camp
Identities:	Mr. Eau Gallie, Miss Atlanta Lively
Nickname:	Hands of Stone, One Man Gang
Finisher:	Indian Death Lock, Garvin Stomp
Career Span:	1962-1999

PPV Record:	2-5
WrestleMania Record:	0-1
Titles Won:	35
Days as World Champion:	62
Age at first World Title Win:	42
Best Opponents:	Ric Flair, Randy Savage, Tully Blanchard

Garvin, Ronnie

"Rugged" Ronnie Garvin of Quebec was a distinguished grappler for more than thirty-five years, displaying his toughness with his hands and feuding with the best in the business. He shocked the world on September 25, 1987 when he beat "Nature Boy" Ric Flair for the coveted NWA World Heavyweight Title. The victory, which came in Detroit, was inside of a steel cage, and Garvin reigned for sixty-two days, losing the belt back to Flair at Starrcade on November 26. Without question, that was the defining moment of his career, but Garvin won a number of regional championships in Florida, Georgia, and Tennessee, and formed a successful tag team with his "brother," Terry Garvin. He retired from the ring in 1999 and has occasionally worked as a referee for various indies. Nowadays, Garvin can be found in the cockpit of planes, as he is an accomplished pilot.

Born:	April 21, 1927
Height:	5'9"
Weight:	225
Real Name:	Joseph Serapio Palemino Gomez Jr.
Parents:	Joseph and Maria Gomez
Wife:	Bonnie Gomez
High School:	Roosevelt High School (CA)
Trained by:	Miguel Guzman
Finishers:	Stomach Claw, Airplane Spin
Career Span:	1953-1982
Died:	May 6, 2004, Oakland, CA 77 years old

Titles Won:	50
Days as World Champion:	154
Age at first World Title Win:	48
Best Opponents:	Lou Thesz, Buddy Rogers, Pat O'Connor

Gomez, Pepper

The "Man with a Cast Iron Stomach" was known to audiences as Pepper Gomez, a heroic superstar who fought the wrestling wars for twenty-nine years. Born in Los Angeles, Gomez was the son of a plumber, and was an athletic standout in high school and college. In 1950, the same year he was starring as a fullback at Los Angeles City College, he won "Mr. Muscle Beach" at Santa Monica for his impressive strength. Over the next six years, he participated in no less than thirteen amateur bodybuilding tournaments and was featured on the covers of *Strength & Health* and *Muscle Power*. Ed "Strangler" Lewis aided in his becoming a wrestler, and Gomez had no trouble finding a large base of fans throughout the country. He won the Texas State Title a total of fifteen times, the United States Title in California, and the WWA World Title in 1975. Feats like having a car drive over his midsection proved without a doubt that he had a "cast iron stomach."

Photo Courtesy of Dr. Mike Lano—Wrealano@aol.com

Gordy, Terry

Born:	April 23, 1961
Height:	6'4"
Weight:	285
Real Name:	Terry Ray Gordy Sr.
Parents:	Billy and Mildred Gordy
Family:	Father of Terry Gordy Jr., uncle of Richard Slinger
High School:	Rossville High School (GA)
Trained by:	James Kyle, Archie Gouldie, Afa
Identities:	Terry Mecca, Terry Meeker, Mr. Wrestling, The Executioner
Nicknames:	Bamm Bamm
Finisher:	Powerbomb
Career Span:	1974-2001
Died:	July 16, 2001, Soddy Daisy, TN 40 years old

PPV Record:	2-2, 1 Draw, 1 DCO
Titles Won:	37
Days as World Champion:	176
Age at first World Title Win:	25
Best Opponents:	Jumbo Tsuruta, Mitsuharu Misawa, Giant Baba

An agile 6'4" grappler with natural abilities, Terry Gordy was a well-rounded performer and a headliner around the world. He grew up in Rossville, Georgia and had the size and athletic competency to become a professional wrestler at the age of thirteen, initially working for his uncle's promotion. In 1978, he formed the legendary Freebirds with Michael Hayes, and, along with Buddy Roberts, won the World Six-Man Tag Team Title five times between 1982 and 1986, brutally feuding with the Von Erich Family. On May 30, 1986, Gordy beat Jim Duggan in a tournament final for the initial UWF World Heavyweight Title. While in Japan, he became the first foreigner to capture the coveted All-Japan Unified Triple Crown when he beat Jumbo Tsuruta in 1990. Gordy teamed with Stan Hansen to win the AJPW World Tag Team Title twice and with Steve Williams five times. He was a powerful, yet intelligent grappler, who was able to perform moves like a running dropkick with ease. At one point, he was among the best in the world.

Born:	June 4, 1937
Height:	6'6"
Weight:	350
Real Name:	Robert James Marella
Family:	Father of Joey Marella
High School:	Jefferson High School (NY)
College:	Ithaca College
Trained by:	Pedro Martinez, Stu Hart
Finisher:	Airplane Spin
Owned:	A minority share in the Capitol Wrestling Corporation
Career Span:	1960-1987
Died:	October 6, 1999, Mooresville, NJ 62 years old

Gorilla Monsoon

Titles Won:	7
Days as World Champion:	35
Age at first World Title Win:	30
Best Opponents:	Bruno Sammartino, Bill Miller, Bobo Brazil
Managers:	2
Halls of Fame:	3

The affable and insightful voice behind WWF programming during the 1980s and 1990s, Gorilla Monsoon was a talented Greco-Roman wrestler while in college, and during the summer of 1959, he toured with the national squad overseas. After turning pro, he was billed as being from Manchuria and was a convincing challenger to WWWF champion Bruno Sammartino. He also teamed with Killer Kowalski to lift the U.S. Tag Team Title from Brute Bernard and Skull Murphy. During a tour of Australia in 1968, Monsoon won the IWA World Title from Spiros Arion, and held the WWA World Tag Team Title twice in Indiana. In 1976, he made national news when he bodyslammed boxing legend Muhammad Ali. Away from the ring, he participated in many hilarious and sometimes oddball skits with Bobby Heenan on USA Network's *Prime Time Wrestling*. His straight-laced commentary worked perfectly alongside pro-heel talkers, Heenan and Jesse Ventura, and earned a spot in the WWF Hall of Fame in 1994.

Photo Courtesy of Dan Westbrook

Born:	August 3, 1924
Height:	6'1"
Weight:	235
Real Name:	Karl Charles Istaz
Trained by:	Billy Riley
Identities:	Karl Krauser
Finisher:	Atomic Suplex
Career Span:	1953-1982
Died:	July 28, 2007, Tampa, FL 82 years old

Titles Won:	5
Days as World Champion:	Over 727 (NJPW Real World Title claim is of unknown length)
Age at first World Title Win:	38
Best Opponents:	Antonio Inoki, Lou Thesz, Don Leo Jonathan
Halls of Fame:	3

Gotch, Karl

A student of the legendary "Snakepit" gymnasium in Wigan, England, Karl Gotch went on to become an astonishingly talented professional grappler. In fact, he was almost too much of an expert to be a pro wrestler in a world of flashy gimmicks and high drama. He was more in the league of a great Olympic champion, and had the ferociousness to beat nearly every opponent he stepped in the ring against. Born in Antwerp, Belgium, Gotch began wrestling at nine years of age, and was a perennial amateur champion. He represented Belgium in the 1948 Olympics in both the freestyle and Greco-Roman events, but did not place. By 1960, he was competing on the North American pro circuit and held the Ohio-based AWA World Title for nearly two years. Always displaying amazing scientific prowess, he earned international praise, particularly while in Japan, and trained many athletes in the pure art of submission grappling.

Born:	June 7, 1943
Height:	6'3"
Weight:	270
Real Name:	Eldridge Wayne Coleman
Wife:	Valerie Coleman
High School:	North Phoenix High School (AZ)
Pro Sports:	American Football League— Houston Oilers (1966)
Finisher:	Bearhug
Managed:	Don Muraco (1987-1988)
Career Span:	1970-1987

Titles Won:	12
Days as World Champion:	383
Age at first World Title Win:	31
Best Opponents:	Bruno Sammartino, Bob Backlund, Harley Race
Halls of Fame:	3

Graham, Billy

Displaying the frame of a bodybuilder, "Superstar" Billy Graham was a remarkable athlete and box office attraction. He was originally from the Phoenix area, where he was a track and field standout, specializing in the discus and shot put. Additionally, he boxed and participated in competitive arm wrestling. Already 6'3" and 200 pounds by the time he was fifteen, Graham was successful in every endeavor, even capturing the 1961 "Mr. Arizona" title for his impressive physique. In 1969, he was trained by Stu Hart in Calgary, and a year later, he adopted the signature "Graham" name while in Los Angeles—becoming a "brother" of Dr. Jerry Graham. Seven years later, he ended Bruno Sammartino's second run with the WWWF Heavyweight Title on April 30, 1977. He toured successfully as champion until February 20, 1978, when Bob Backlund beat him for the belt at Madison Square Garden. As a flamboyant grappler, Graham was outstanding and he established the standard for future muscle-bound heels to emulate.

Born:	December 16, 1931
Height:	6'0"
Weight:	275
Real Name:	Jerry Martin Matthews (legally changed to Jerry M. Graham)
Parents:	John and Mary Graham
Military:	United States Army (1947-1948)
Groups:	The Stable of Champions (1963-1965)
Career Span:	1952-1993
Died:	January 24, 1997, Glendale, CA 65 years old

Graham, Dr. Jerry

Titles Won:	13
Days as World Champion:	Unknown, briefly claimed in 1960
Age at first World Title Win:	28
Best Opponents:	Antonino Rocca, Bruno Sammartino, Bobo Brazil
Halls of Fame:	1

The one and only Dr. Jerry Graham was a chaotic figure inside and outside of the squared circle. He lived a life full of wrestling success, yet was troubled in his personal life to the extent that he had numerous run-ins with the law. He entered the Army at fifteen years of age in June 1947 and served with the 82nd Airborne Division at Fort Bragg as the driver for the famed General James Gavin. He returned to Phoenix, where he grew up, and participated in local athletics before being scouted and trained by Jim Londos. Large physically, Graham developed into a crafty worker, and was known as the wrestling hypnotist, claiming to own several college degrees, but was known to employ his own brand of psychology to manipulate both opponents and audiences. In 1958, he formed a punishing brother duo with Eddie Graham and won the U.S. Tag Team Title four times. Some type of controversy usually followed Graham wherever he went, and he wrestled into the 1990s on a part-time basis around Los Angeles. His legacy as an enjoyable villain is still celebrated today.

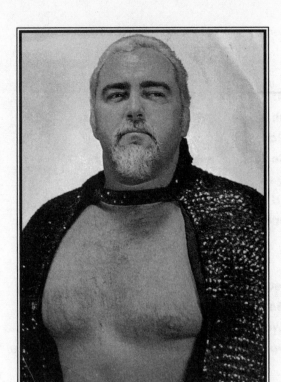

Born:	February 5, 1940
Height:	6'2"
Weight:	290
Real Name:	James Grady Johnson
Parents:	James and Grace Johnson
Identities:	Pretty Boy Calhoun, Pretty Boy Floyd, Mighty Yankee, El Lobo
Career Span:	1961-2001
Died:	June 23, 2006, Milledgeville, GA 66 years old

Titles Won:	22
Days as World Champion:	86
Age at first World Title Win:	25
Best Opponents:	Lou Thesz, Bruno Sammartino, Dusty Rhodes

Graham, Luke

The unpredictable Dr. Jerry Graham located a wrestler in 1963 that enjoyed chaos and carnage almost as much as he did. That man became Luke Graham, his "brother" in an ever growing clan of talented rule-breakers. Appropriately nicknamed "Crazy," Luke was from Union Point, Georgia, and wrestled around the southeast under a variety of gimmicks. The Grahams entered WWWF territory in 1964 and captured the U.S. Tag Team championship. A year later, in Los Angeles, Luke beat Pedro Morales for the WWA World Title, and won belts in Hawaii, Puerto Rico, and across the territorial system. In 1971, he was crowned, along with Tarzan Tyler, as the initial WWWF World Tag Team Champions. His antics drove audiences wild, and he always provided a colorful show worth watching.

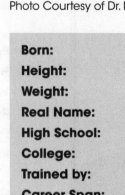

Born:	January 7, 1949
Height:	5'11"
Weight:	225
Real Name:	Salvador Guerrero III
High School:	Burges High School (TX)
College:	University of Texas
Trained by:	Gory Guerrero
Career Span:	1970-2011

PPV Record:	1-0
WWE *Smackdown* TV Record:	6-3
Titles Won:	48
Best Opponents:	Dory Funk Jr., Harley Race, Roddy Piper

Guerrero, Chavo Sr.

The first of four wrestling sons born to Gory Guerrero, Chavo Guerrero Sr. was an accomplished amateur grappler in El Paso. He went pro in 1970, initially using the name "Gory Jr.," but soon adopted the name that would carry him to international fame. In 1975, he had a breakout year in Los Angeles. The popular athlete won the Jules Strongbow Scientific trophy and the Americas Heavyweight and Tag Team belts. Over the next five years, he won the Americas championship sixteen times, and in 1977, held the NWA World Light Heavyweight crown, the same title his father had held years before. In May of 2004, as "Chavo Classic," he won the WWE Cruiserweight belt, taking the strap from his own son, Chavo Jr. on *Smackdown*.

Born:	April 1, 1931
Height:	6'3"
Weight:	250
Parents:	Orville and Faye Hamilton
High School:	Benton High School (MO)
Identities:	Rocky Hamilton, The Missouri Mauler, Casey McShain
Career Span:	1951-1980
Died:	July 20, 1996, St. Joseph, MO 65 years old

Titles Won:	22
Best Opponents:	Jack Brisco, Gene Kiniski, Dory Funk Jr.

Hamilton, Larry

St. Joseph, Missouri was a hotspot for professional wrestling under promoter Gust Karras for forty years, and among his greatest protégés was Larry Hamilton. Hamilton was captain of his high school football team, a talented amateur boxer, and a top grappling prospect when he debuted in 1951. He was physically big, and his oversized presence made him a natural heel, which Hamilton developed over the course of his career. By the late 1950s, he was a major personality. He was successful in tag teams with his younger brother Jody and Tom Renasto, and won many regional championships in the Central States, Florida, and the Mid-Atlantic territory.

Born:	August 29, 1949
Height:	6'3"
Weight:	320
Real Name:	John Stanley Hansen II
Parents:	John and Nella Hansen
Wife:	Yumi Hansen
HS Ach.:	All-State Football Player (1966-1967)
College Ach.:	Letterman (1968-1970), Team captain (1970)
Trained by:	The Funk family
Nicknames:	The Lariet, The Badman from Borger
Finisher:	Lariet Clothesline, Brazos-Valley Backbreaker
Tag Team:	The Superpowers w/ Vader
Career Span:	1973-2000

Hansen, Stan

PPV Record:	1-1, 1 DDQ
Titles Won:	37
Days as World Champion:	1,846
Age at first World Title Win:	34
Best Opponents:	Kenta Kobashi, Jumbo Tsuruta, Mitsuharu Misawa
Halls of Fame:	2

Hard-striking Stan Hansen was a brutally tough wrestler and an international legend. Engaging in mat battles for twenty-seven years, with over 120 tours of Japan, he was an aggressive competitor and unleashed awesome blows that could cut down even the largest foe. His brawling skills were intense, and the cowboy hat and tobacco dripping from his mouth added to his mystique. No one was safe around him and his career was full of memorable matches and championship victories. He was a high school football standout for the Las Cruces Bulldogs under coach Ed Boykin and was awarded the Prep All America Football Award. He continued his exceptional football career as a linebacker at West Texas State and had a tryout with the Baltimore Colts in July of 1971, but was cut the following month. Hansen broke into the business, learning from many ring veterans in the Amarillo area, and visited a few territories before working for All-Japan for the first time in 1975.

Managed by Fred Blassie, Hansen turned up in the WWWF the following year and broke Bruno Sammartino's neck with his lariat clothesline on April 26, 1976 at Madison Square Garden. The angle built up to their June 25, 1976 bout at Shea Stadium, where an estimated 32,000 fans turned out to see Sammartino exact revenge—and that's exactly what happened. On February 8, 1980, Hansen beat Antonio Inoki for the

NWF belt and three years later, topped Shohei Baba for the PWF championship, becoming the only man to have beaten both Japanese legends for titles. He made Rick Martel submit to capture the AWA World Heavyweight Title on December 29, 1985 and held the coveted AJPW Unified Japanese Triple Crown four times. During his career, he had memorable matches with Jumbo Tsuruta, Terry Funk, Genichiro Tenryu, and Hulk Hogan, and formed a vicious tag team with Bruiser Brody. From 2001 to 2007, he acted as the PWF Commissioner for All-Japan, adding another dimension to his wrestling resume.

Photo Courtesy of the Collection of Libnan Ayoub

Hard Boiled Haggerty

Born:	April 2, 1925
Height:	6'1"
Weight:	265
Real Name:	Donald Joseph Stanisauske (changed to Stansauk, then to Haggerty)
Parents:	Joseph and Josie Stanisauske
High School:	Franklin High School (CA)
Colleges:	Texas Christian University, Denver University
Military:	United States Navy (WWII)
NFL Draft:	Detroit Lions (1950) (18th Round) (226)
Pro Sports:	National Football League— Green Bay Packers (1950-1951)
Trained by:	Danny Loos, Tom Zaharias
Identities:	Don Sparrow, Mr. M, The Masked Executioner
Finisher:	Clawhold
Career Span:	1951-1969
Died:	January 27, 2004, Malibu, CA 78 years old

Titles Won:	22
Days as World Champion:	Unknown
Age at first World Title Win:	31
Best Opponents:	Verne Gagne, Fred Blassie, Gene Kiniski
TV Appearances:	Around 30
Movies:	Over 20

Recognizable Hollywood actor Don Haggerty was known by a variety of names throughout his life. In the ring, he was the most famous as the third "Hard Boiled Haggerty," a villain of the highest order, who wreaked havoc throughout the territories from the early 1950s until the late 1960s. One of his crowning achievements occurred in 1956 when he beat Killer Kowalski for the World Heavyweight Title in Montreal. The youngest of six children, Haggerty grew up in Los Angeles, took drama classes in high school and college, and developed the range of his characters in the squared circle—snarling at opponents and crowds, and drawing the ire of everyone who saw him wrestle. Wearing a trademark mustache, he performed in more than twenty films and made dozens of TV appearances. He was also a longstanding member of the Cauliflower Alley Club.

Photo Courtesy of Pete Lederberg—plmathfoto@hotmail.com

Born:	August 3, 1934
Height:	6'2"
Weight:	600
Real Name:	William D. Calhoun
Career Span:	1956-1980
Died:	December 7, 1989, McKinney, TX 55 years old

Titles Won:	4
Best Opponents:	Buddy Rogers, Johnny Valentine, Bruno Sammartino
Movies:	1

Haystacks Calhoun

In 1989, professional wrestling lost a true great: the giant Haystacks Calhoun of McKinney, Texas. Calhoun, a world-renowned hero of the industry, was recognized in the mainstream for his appearances on *The Tonight Show* and *Art Linkletter*, and his awesome 600 pounds were carried well inside of the squared circle. He entered the mat field in 1956 as Billy "The Blimp" Calhoun, but soon adopted the moniker, "Country Boy Calhoun," and took Count Pietro Rossi as his manager. "Haystacks" was his guise by 1958 and after many successful performances throughout the east, he was highly sought after by promoters and television producers. Calhoun won the WWWF Tag Title in 1973 with Tony Garea and kept up his popular act until 1980. His overalls, horseshoe, and bare feet were trademarks of the legendary big man.

Born:	January 29, 1936
Height:	6'0"
Weight:	275
Real Name:	Lawrence Henry Hennig Jr.
Parents:	Lawrence and Gertrude Hennig
Wife:	Irene Hennig
Family:	Father of Curt and Jesse Hennig
High School:	Robbinsdale High School (MN)
HS Ach.:	Minnesota High School State Wrestling Title (1954) (HWT)
Nicknames:	Pretty Boy
Career Span:	1957-1985

Titles Won:	10
Best Opponents:	Verne Gagne, Nick Bockwinkel, Dory Funk Jr.
Halls of Fame:	1

Hennig, Larry

The father of "Mr. Perfect" Curt Hennig, Larry Hennig was a hall of fame grappler himself. Throughout his career, Hennig was known as a rough customer and was a guy who couldn't be pushed around. He was a high school heavyweight wrestling champion in Minnesota, and his diverse knowledge of holds along with size advantage made him a feared battler. He was schooled by Verne Gagne and Joe Pazandak, two excellent coaches, and went on to capture the AWA World Tag Team championship on four occasions. Hennig teamed with Duke Hoffman to win a tournament for the vacant title on January 15, 1962, but his most successful partnership came with Harley Race. The duo dethroned the legendary Bruiser and Crusher on January 30, 1965, traded the belts with Crusher and Gagne, and then triumphed over Bruiser and Crusher for the final time in 1967.

Born:	July 7, 1932
Height:	6'2"
Weight:	315
Real Name:	Alfonso Carlos Chicarro
Identities:	Pepe Cortes, Hercules Romero, Raoul Romero, Mighty Hercules
Career Span:	1955-1971
Died:	July 24, 1971, Near St. Cloud, MN 39 years old

Titles Won:	At least 4
Days as World Champion:	Over 14 (unknown time for 1964 claim in Europe)
Age at first World Title Win:	Around 32
Best Opponents:	Killer Kowalski, Hans Schmidt, Nick Bockwinkel

Hercules Cortez

Entering the sport in his native country of Spain, Hercules Cortez toured the world, and his remarkable strength made a real impression on the fans of North and South America, Asia, and Australia. Cortez benched over 540 pounds and demonstrated his power in the ring on a nightly basis. In 1958, he appeared throughout the northeastern U.S. as "Pepe Chicharro," and also used the name "Claude Dassary" in Canada. In 1958, he was a popular challenger to Killer Kowalski's World Title in Montreal, and the latter, incidentally, was the man who ended Cortez's reign as IWA World Champion in Australia in 1965. Cortez teamed with Red Bastien to win the AWA World Tag Title in 1971 and was still champion when he tragically lost his life in a car accident.

Photo Courtesy of Pete Lederberg—plmathfoto@hotmail.com

Born:	May 13, 1932
Height:	6'0"
Weight:	215
Real Name:	Daniel Allen Hodge
Parents:	William and Hazel Hodge
Wife:	Dolores Hodge
High School:	Perry High School (OK)
HS Ach.:	Oklahoma State High School Wrestling Title (1951) (165)
Amateur Titles:	Three-Time National AAU Champion (1953-1954, 1956) (174) (Freestyle), National AAU Champion (1956) (174) (Greco-Roman)
Military:	United States Navy (1951-1953)
Trained by:	Leroy McGuirk, Ed Lewis
Career Span:	1959-1976
Magazine Cover:	*Sports Illustrated* (April 1, 1957)

Hodge, Danny

Amateur Titles:	12
Titles Won:	16
Days as World Junior Champion:	4,176
Days as World HWT Champion:	Unknown (TWWA World Title in 1968)
Age at first Junior Title Win:	28
Best Opponents:	Angelo Savoldi, Hiro Matsuda, Lou Thesz
Boxing Record:	7-2
Halls of Fame:	6

The remarkable Danny Hodge was arguably, pound-for-pound, the most skilled professional wrestler in history. He was an extraordinary athlete, winning Olympic honors as a wrestler, a national boxing championship, and for seventeen years, traveled the highways and byways as one of the most acclaimed pros in the industry. Hodge, from just outside Perry, Oklahoma, won nearly every amateur match he participated in from 1952 to 1957, including both Olympic Games during that period and during his stretch at the University of Oklahoma, with his losses being counted on a single hand. His amateur achievements began in junior high school when he took the Oklahoma State title in 1948 at 145 pounds, then won the high school championship in 1951. While in the Navy, he qualified and participated in the 1952 Olympic Games, but placed 5th overall. He then won Big Seven and NCAA Titles from 1955 to 1957, going undefeated all through college, and captured the silver medal at the 1956 Olympics.

III. HEROES AND VILLAINS WAGE WAR IN THE SACRED TERRITORIES

265

Hodge was not done showing the world the limits of his athletic prowess and entered the sport of boxing. He proceeded to go undefeated as an amateur, winning regional honors, and then taking to the National Golden Gloves heavyweight championship in March of 1958. His impressive foray into boxing continued as he stepped into the pro ring three months later and was victorious. Over the next ten months, he won seven additional fights, and only losing two. Promoter Leroy McGuirk was instrumental in getting Hodge to shift to pro wrestling and he made his debut later in 1959. During his career, he captured the NWA World Junior Heavyweight Title six times with wins over Angelo Savoldi, Sputnik Monroe, Hiro Matsuda, and others, and displayed his ring mastery and unnatural strength against opponents of all sizes. On March 15, 1976, he was injured in a car accident, and his days as a wrestler came to an end. If wrestling was decided by legitimate means, Hodge would've been an unconquerable force at his weight.

Photo Courtesy of the Collection of Tim Hornbaker

Born:	October 4, 1923
Height:	6'1"
Weight:	285
Real Name:	Richard Heron Avis Hutton
Parents:	Bailey and Gladys Hutton
High School:	Daniel Webster High School (OK)
College:	Oklahoma A&M University
College Ach.:	Three-Time NCAA Heavyweight Wrestling Champion (1947-1948, 1950), Four-Time All-American (1947-1950)
Military:	United States Army (WWII)
Trained by:	Leroy McGuirk, Ed Lewis
Nickname:	Cowboy
Finisher:	Abdominal Stretch
Career Span:	1953-1964
Died:	November 24, 2003, Tulsa, OK 80 years old

Hutton, Dick

Titles Won:	7
Days as World Champion:	421
Age at first World Title Win:	34
Best Opponents:	Lou Thesz, Pat O'Connor, Billy Watson
Halls of Fame:	3

Terrifically gifted, Dick Hutton of Oklahoma was as fierce and competitive in the world of pro wrestling as he was in the amateur ranks. A veteran of the 1948 Olympics and winner of three NCAA titles, he was seen as a potential future champion from day one. Low-key in terms of flamboyance, he let his aptitude speak for itself and his profound knowledge of the pure form of catch-as-catch-can grappling earned him the utmost respect from fans and peers. After only four years in the business, he defeated Lou Thesz for the NWA World Heavyweight Title on November 14, 1957, and displayed poise much greater than his experience. Facing many obstacles as titleholder, including a decline of wrestling's popularity in many territories, Hutton performed commendably as the straight-laced champion, but altogether, his reign lacked any overly defining moments. He met his match on January 9, 1959, and lost the NWA Title to Pat O'Connor in St. Louis. Upon retiring from wrestling, he was inducted into a handful of Halls of Fame, one of them being the National Wrestling Hall of Fame in Stillwater, Oklahoma.

Photo Courtesy of the Collection of Libnan Ayoub

Born:	September 15, 1937
Height:	6'3"
Weight:	350
Real Name:	Curtis Piehau Iaukea III
High School:	Punahou School (HI)
Identities:	Chico Garcia, King Curtis
Career Span:	1959-1979
Died:	December 4, 2010, Honolulu, HI
	73 years old

Titles Won:	29
Days as World Champion:	Around 296
Age at first World Title Win:	30
Best Opponents:	Mark Lewin, Johnny Valentine, Ray Stevens
Halls of Fame:	1

Iaukea, Curtis

Curtis Iaukea was a highly-touted football player at the University of California, Berkeley, and played three seasons in the Canadian Football League. While in the San Francisco area, he broke into pro wrestling and learned much from ex-footballers Leo Nomellini and Don Manoukian. He returned to his native Hawaii and was a key superstar in Honolulu throughout the 1960s. It was only natural that he'd also venture to Australia, where he became a household name, and won the IWA World Heavyweight Championship four times between 1967 and 1970. Two years later, he teamed with Baron Mikel Scicluna for the WWWF World Tag Team Title. Iaukea portrayed a cruel rule-breaker throughout his career, and when he dropped his 350-pound Hawaiian Splash, it usually marked the end for opponents. His son Rocky also made a career as a pro wrestler.

Inoki, Antonio

Born:	February 20, 1943
Height:	6'3"
Weight:	230
Real Name:	Kanji Inoki
Parents:	Sajiro and Fumiko Inoki
Identities:	Tokyo Tom
Nickname:	Moeru Toukon
Tag Team:	B-I Cannon w/ Shohei Baba
Owner:	New Japan Pro Wrestling Co., Ltd. (1972-2005)
Promoter:	Tokyo Pro Wrestling (1966-1967) (w/ Toyonobori), New Japan Pro Wrestling (1972-1989), Universal Fighting-arts Organization (1998-2002), Inoki Genome Federation (2007-Present)
Career Span:	1960-1998
Website:	www.antonio-inoki.com

Titles Won:	23
Days as World Champion:	1,031 (not counting time as Real World Champion)
Age at first World Title Win:	29
Best Opponents:	Karl Gotch, Stan Hansen, Riki Choshu
Tournament Wins:	17
MMA Record:	16-1, 3 Draws
Halls of Fame:	6

Perhaps no single man has been more influential in professional wrestling on a worldwide scale than Antonio Inoki. He was an admired wrestler for thirty-eight years, taking on the best in the business and beating the likes of Andre the Giant, Ric Flair, Stan Hansen, Hulk Hogan, Vader, and Sting. Adding credibility to the profession by his willingness to participate in legitimate contests against athletes from other sports, Inoki went to a fifteen-round draw against boxing legend Muhammad Ali in 1976. Outside the ring, he founded New Japan Pro Wrestling, a hugely successful promotion, and was crucial in the presentation of wrestling in places like the Soviet Union and North Korea, where it had rarely been seen. In fact, Inoki's appearance in the latter country drew the largest single attendance for a wrestling show ever—at a reported 190,000 people for his April 29, 1995 bout against Flair in Pyongyang. Rightfully enshrined in a number of Halls of Fame, Inoki is the standard-bearer for pro wrestling excellence.

The pupil of the legendary Rikidozan, Inoki made his pro debut the same day his longtime rival Giant Baba did in 1960 and toured the U.S. early in his career. Late in the 1960s, after his first attempt to run his own organization ended, Inoki rejoined the Japan Pro Wrestling Association (JWA) and formed a successful tag team with Baba. In late 1971, he departed from the promotion and again went out on his own, kick-starting New Japan on March 6, 1972 in Tokyo. He headlined the inaugural show and lost to Karl Gotch. In December of 1973, he beat Johnny Powers for the NWF World Heavyweight Title, a championship that would become the primary belt for NJPW until the early 1980s. Inoki would have four reigns as titleholder. He formed a strong relationship with the WWF and captured the heavyweight title of that promotion with a win over Bob Backlund on November 30, 1979 in Tokushima.

Inoki was also recognized as WWF World Martial Arts Heavyweight Champion and held the belt for nearly twelve years straight from 1978 to 1990. New Japan implemented the International Wrestling Grand Prix tournament and Inoki was knocked out in his finals match against Hulk Hogan on June 2, 1983 at Tokyo's Sumo Hall in an unscripted finish. In 1984, he beat Hogan to win the event and repeated the next three years. He vacated the IWGP championship in 1988 and made sporadic ring appearances after that. His "Final Countdown" series of matches led to his ultimate retirement on April 4, 1998 in Tokyo before an estimated 70,000 at the Tokyo Dome. He wrestled and beat Don Frye in his final match as two of his biggest rivals, Backlund and Muhammad Ali watched on. He sold his interest in New Japan in 2005 and two years later, he founded Inoki Genome Federation (IGF). A recognized icon throughout the industry, Inoki has been honored by the WCW, WWE, and Professional Wrestling Halls of Fame.

Photo Courtesy of Pete Lederberg—plmathfoto@hotmail.com

Born:	September 9, 1945
Height:	6'0"
Weight:	260
Real Name:	Hossein Khosrow Vaziri
Amateur Ach.:	National AAU Greco-Roman Title (1971) (180)
Identities:	Ali Vaziri, Great Hussein, Colonel Mustafa
Groups:	The Triangle of Terror (1990-1991)
Managed:	Sgt. Slaughter (1990-1991), The Sultan (1997)
Career Span:	1973-2010

PPV Record:	2-7
WrestleMania Record:	3-1
Titles Won:	16
Days as World Champion:	28
Age at first World Title Win:	38
Best Opponents:	Bob Backlund, Hulk Hogan, Ricky Steamboat
Halls of Fame:	2

Iron Sheik, The

In recent years, the wildly outspoken Iron Sheik has candidly voiced his opinion about pro wrestling on a slew of popular radio shows, revealing a side of his personality that many people did not know. He was much more identifiable by his work in the ring, an occupation he'd undertaken since 1973, and as an amateur before that. The Sheik's longtime pro-Iran gimmick and rulebreaking were real attention-getters, and he could turn a crowd against him within seconds. A former National AAU Champion while a member of the Minnesota Wrestling Club, he was trained by Verne Gagne and gained his greatest fame when he beat Bob Backlund for the WWF World Title on December 26, 1983 in New York City. He was an interim champion, losing the belt to Hulk Hogan on January 23, 1984. At WrestleMania X-Seven, Sheik won a special gimmick battle royal, and was inducted into the WWE Hall of Fame in 2005.

Photo Courtesy of Dr. Mike Lano—Wrealano@aol.com

Born:	August 24, 1944
Height:	6'2"
Weight:	255
Real Name:	Wayde Bowles
Trained by:	Billy Watson, Bobo Brazil
Identities:	Sweet Ebony Diamond
Career Span:	1965-2008

Titles Won:	33
Best Opponents:	Nick Bockwinkel, Billy Graham, Harley Race
Halls of Fame:	1

Johnson, Rocky

A boxer-turned-wrestler, "Soulman" Rocky Johnson launched his wrestling career in his native Nova Scotia in 1965 and wrestled across Canada in his first year. Four years later, he worked his way into California, where he became a household name in Los Angeles and San Francisco. He beat Paul DeMarco for the U.S. Title, and held the World Tag Team Championship three times with Pat Patterson. Johnson won state heavyweight titles in Texas, Georgia, and Florida, and other regional titles all over the map. In 1983, he teamed with Tony Atlas for the WWF World Tag Team Title. With wife Ata, the daughter of Peter Maivia, he had a son named Dwayne, better known to wrestling fans as The Rock. He was inducted into the WWE Hall of Fame in 2008.

Born:	June 28, 1942
Height:	6'0"
Weight:	230
Real Name:	Alfred Morris Frederick
Parents:	Daluck and Jessie Frederick
High School:	Thomas Jefferson High School (TX)
Nickname:	Number One
Career Span:	1964-1991

Titles Won:	33
Best Opponents:	Jack Brisco, Dory Funk Jr., Ric Flair

Jones, Paul

Having participated in Golden Gloves boxing for years, Paul Jones of Port Arthur, Texas was very adept to the squared circle and easily made the transition to wrestling in 1964 through promoter Morris Sigel in Houston. After tours of Hawaii, Japan, and Australia, Jones entered the Mid-Atlantic territory and won a cache of championships. He held the U.S. Heavyweight Title twice, the World Tag Team belts six times, and had some of the greatest matches of his career against the likes of Johnny Valentine, Terry Funk, and Jack Brisco. During his stay in Florida, he took his state championship belt and threw it off a Tampa bridge in one particularly hot angle. In the 1980s, he became a manager, and seconded the likes of the Assassins and Warlord and Barbarian.

Born:	January 23, 1957
Height:	5'7"
Weight:	165
Real Name:	Patricia Seymour Schroeder
High School:	Riverdale High School (FL)
Nickname:	Hawaiian Princess
Tag Team:	The Glamour Girls w/ Judy Martin
Career Span:	1975-2004

PPV Record:	1-2	
WrestleMania Record:	0-2	
Titles Won:	12	
Days as World Champion:		506
Age at first World Title Win:		28
Best Opponents:		Chigusa Nagayo, Madusa, Wendi Richter
Halls of Fame:		1

Kai, Leilani

Internationally known for her competitive spirit and skilled offensive ring attack, Leilani Kai was a world champion in the WWF and NWA. She grew up on the west coast of Florida and idolized great women grapplers Penny Banner and Ann Casey. At the age of seventeen, she attended the Fabulous Moolah's Columbia, South Carolina school, and was trained by Moolah's cadre, a group of experienced workers that included Susan Green. Kai was given a Hawaiian heritage and toured the world with Moolah's troupe. On February 18, 1985, she beat Wendi Richter for the WWF Women's World Title and holds the distinction of going into the first WrestleMania as the defending champion—although she lost the belt to Wendi Richter. Kai formed a championship tag team with Judy Martin and held the NWA Women's World Title for over a year in 2003-2004.

LEGENDS OF PRO WRESTLING

Born:	September 10, 1951
Height:	6'0"
Weight:	235
Real Name:	Stephen Paul Keirn
Parents:	Richard and Hazel Keirn
High School:	Robinson High School (FL)
Identities:	Doink the Clown
Nickname:	The Gator
Owner:	Florida Championship Wrestling (2007-Present)
Career Span:	1972-2007

PPV Record:	0-5
WrestleMania Record:	0-1
WWE *Raw* TV Record:	0-1
Titles Won:	58
Best Opponents:	Harley Race, Bret Hart, Terry Funk

Keirn, Steve

Tampa product Steve Keirn was friends with Mike Graham in his youth and entered the business under the tutelage of Mike's legendary father Eddie Graham and Hiro Matsuda. He won numerous championships and was named NWA Rookie of the Year in 1974. In 1986 and 1987, he won the U.S. Tag Team Title twice with Stan Lane as a member of the Fabulous Ones, and in 1989 he procured the PWF Heavyweight belt from Kendall Windham. Keirn took out a license to hunt alligators in Florida and after he joined the WWF in 1991, he took on a gimmick that played off that theme, known as "Skinner." Since the late 1980s, he's run a wrestling school in one form or fashion. For a time, it was known as the "Pro Wrestling School of Hard Knox," but now it is "Florida Championship Wrestling," a WWE Developmental territory. Graduates have included current WWE superstars Ted DiBiase Jr., Drew McIntyre, and Jack Swagger.

Photo Courtesy of Pete Leterberg—plmathfoto@hotmail.com

Born:	April 26, 1931
Height:	6'1 ½"
Weight:	270
Real Name:	Herbert Alan Gerwig
Trained by:	The Sheik, The Dusek Brothers
Finisher:	Brainbuster
Managed by:	Bobby Heenan
Career Span:	1955-1982
Died:	November 10, 2011, Dallas, TX 80 years old

Titles Won:	31
Days as World Champion:	54
Age at first World Title Win:	36
Best Opponents:	Dory Funk Jr., Jack Brisco, Dusty Rhodes

Killer Karl Kox

Killer Karl Kox held a master's degree in crowd psychology, and his ability to effectively rile up audiences was second to none. He grew up in Baltimore and played football for the Security Athletic Club in his teens. In 1955, following service in the Marines, he was taken under the wing of a local grappler named Fred Bozic in Cleveland. For the next six years, he wrestled under his given name, and then embraced the Kox gimmick in the early 1960s. He was an imposing heel, demonstrating his fine ring work and toughness all over the U.S., Japan, and Australia. In the "Land Down Under," he captured the IWA World Title three times. He was a regional champion in Florida, Texas, and Georgia, and held both the North American and National Titles.

Kiniski, Gene

Born:	November 23, 1928
Height:	6'3"
Weight:	250
Real Name:	Eugene Nicholas Kiniski
Parents:	Nicholas and Julia Kiniski
Family:	Father of Kelly and Nick Kiniski
High School:	St. Joseph's High School (Edmonton, Alberta)
Amateur Titles:	Canadian AAU Wrestling Title (1947-1948) (1952), AAU Title (1951)
Pro Sports:	WIFU—Edmonton Eskimos (1949, 1951-1953)
Identities:	Gene Kelly, The Mighty Canadian, Crimson Knight II
Nicknames:	Big Thunder, Canada's Greatest Athlete, Canadian Avalanche
Finisher:	Backbreaker
Owned:	A percentage of Northwest Wrestling Promotions (w/ Al Tomko)
Career Span:	1952-1992
Died:	April 14, 2010, Blaine, WA 81 years old

Titles Won:	52
Days as World Champion:	Over 1,650
Age at first World Title Win:	28
Best Opponents:	Lou Thesz, Verne Gagne, Bruno Sammartino
Halls of Fame:	6
Movies:	3

In terms of wrestlers on the pro circuit, Gene Kiniski was the cream of the crop; a perennial champion with an expressive personality, and a favored headliner throughout the world. Born in Lamont, Alberta, Canada, he grew up in Edmonton, where he was a standout amateur wrestler and football player. While attending the University of Arizona, he met promoter Rod Fenton, and the latter was eager to turn the big tackle into the next big grappling superstar. Kiniski had viable options to play pro football, but was found that the money in wrestling was better. He was aggressive in the ring and the kind of man who could chain together an endless amount of holds or brawl until the mat was red with blood. In June of 1957, he conquered Edouard Carpentier for the Montreal World Title, and on July 11, 1961, he went over Verne Gagne for the AWA World championship in Minneapolis. Kiniski was also regularly a champion in Toronto and booked as a title claimant in West Texas in 1962.

Versus Bruno Sammartino, Kiniski was spectacular and narrowly missed winning the WWWF World championship in 1964—actually carrying the belt for a short time after one controversial match. All of these accomplishments were setting the table for his greatest triumph on January 7, 1966 when he beat Lou Thesz for the National Wrestling Alliance World Heavyweight Title in St. Louis. For three years, he exceeded expectations by meeting all comers and upholding the dignity of the prized championship. His list of challengers reads like a Hall of Fame roster and include such luminaries as Bobo Brazil, Fritz Von Erich, Dick the Bruiser, Billy Watson, and Johnny Valentine. In November of 1968, he became the first NWA Champion to defend the title in Los Angeles in more than a decade. Dory Funk Jr. was the man to finally dethrone him, on February 11, 1969, in Tampa. Outside the ropes, Kiniski was well-liked throughout the industry, and he had his final match in 1992.

Born:	August 15, 1942
Height:	5'10"
Weight:	250
Real Name:	Oreal Donald Perras
Parents:	William and Blanche Perras
Wife:	Renae Perras
Identities:	Orwell Paris, Jim Parris, Red McNulty
Finisher:	Bearhug, clothesline
Career Span:	1965-1999
Website:	www.ivankoloff.com

PPV Record:	0-5
Titles Won:	45
Days as World Champion:	Over 170
Age at first World Title Win:	25
Best Opponents:	Bruno Sammartino, Pedro Morales, Verne Gagne
Halls of Fame:	1

Koloff, Ivan

Rulebreaking legend, Ivan Koloff had a storied career, and in 2011 was honored for induction into the Professional Wrestling Hall of Fame. It was recognition for years of hard work, battering opponents, and using his chain to brand foes with the famous stamp of the "Russian Bear." He was from the Ottawa Valley area of Ontario, not Moscow as it was usually claimed, and raised on a dairy farm. He was trained by an old grappler named Jack Wentworth and took the name "Ivan Koloff" while in Montreal in 1968. He scored a historic upset over Bruno Sammartino on January 18, 1971 at Madison Square Garden—ending Sammartino's seven-year-plus reign as WWWF World Champion. Ivan was dethroned by Pedro Morales a few weeks later. He headlined everywhere, and held the Mid-Atlantic version of the World Tag Team Title four times, as well as winning other numerous regional titles. In contrast to his wildman image, Koloff has always been a charitable and religious man outside the ring.

Ladd, Ernie

Born:	November 28, 1938
Height:	6'9"
Weight:	310
Real Name:	Earnest Lawrence Ladd
High School:	Wallace High School (TX)
College:	Grambling State University
Drafted by:	San Diego Chargers (AFL) (15th Round)
Pro Sports:	American Football League—San Diego Chargers (1961-1965) American Football League—Houston Oilers (1966) American Football League—Kansas City Chiefs (1967-1969)
Football Ach.:	AFL All-Star (1962-1965)
Trained by:	Hardy Kruskamp, Dick Beyer, Fred Blassie
Nicknames:	The Big Cat
Finisher:	The Taped Thumb
Career Span:	1963-1988
Died:	March 10, 2007, Franklin, LA 68 years old

Titles Won:	27
Days as World Champion:	43
Age at first World Title Win:	33
Best Opponents:	Bruno Sammartino, Fred Blassie, Lou Thesz
Halls of Fame:	6

Pro football's powerful lineman Ernie Ladd made a substantial contribution to wrestling for two decades, crushing foes with his strength and endlessly entertaining audiences. He was born in Louisiana, but reared in Orange County, Texas, and amazed football coaches all the way into the AFL in 1961. While playing for San Diego, he was approached to try his hand at wrestling, and agreed to give it a shot under promoter Hardy Kruskamp. Ladd, who reportedly made $13,000 a year in the AFL, doubled his salary in the ring and eventually quit the gridiron altogether. As an intimidating heel, Ladd was very successful on both coasts, and throughout the territorial system, winning the Mid-South North American championship five times between 1978 and 1984 and the NWF North American Title. Ladd had notable feuds with Dusty Rhodes and Andre the Giant and was, in the 1960s, a competitive eater—able to put away an unbelievable amount of food.

Lawler, Jerry

Born:	November 29, 1949
Height:	5'11"
Weight:	230
Real Name:	Jerry O'Neil Lawler
Parents:	Jerome and Hazel Lawler
Family:	Father of Brian Christopher and Kevin Christian, cousin of Carl Fergie and Wayne Ferris
High School:	Treadwell High School (TN)
College:	Memphis State University
Trained by:	Jackie Fargo
Finisher:	Piledriver, Fistdrop from the Second Rope
Tag Teams:	The Outlaws w/ Jim White, The Heavenly Bodies w/ Don Greene
Owned:	A percentage of the Memphis territory (1983-1997)
Career Span:	1970-Present

PPV Record:	8-21
WrestleMania Record:	0-1
WWE *Raw* TV Record:	26-17
WWE *Smackdown* TV Record:	2-1
Titles Won:	over 160
Days as World Champion:	2,275
Age at first World Title Win:	29
Best Opponents:	Jack Brisco, Curt Hennig, Bret Hart
Halls of Fame:	3

Many wrestlers through the ages have called themselves "King," but no man has worn the crown like Jerry Lawler. He has been involved in wrestling for the last forty-one years and has established himself as an icon in Memphis and throughout the WWE universe. In fact, he's wrestled as late as 2011, even competing against fellow broadcaster Michael Cole at WrestleMania XXVII on April 3, 2011. Perhaps Lawler's most notable feud was against comedian Andy Kaufman, which garnered mainstream attention in 1982. Their war of words became physical during an episode of *Late Night with David Letterman*, and the question of whether it was real or scripted remained for years. Lawler appeared as himself in the 1999 Kaufman biopic *Man on the Moon*, finally revealing that their "conflict" had been completely worked. Synonymous with wrestling in the "Music City," Lawler was the focal point of grappling on Monday nights at the Mid-South Coliseum since achieving his initial main event there in 1973.

In matches that were both scientific and violent, and in passionate feuds that meant something to fans, Lawler was worshipped to no end. He was champion most of his active career and may have held more titles than any single grappler in history. That includes the Southern belt forty-one times between 1974 and 1987 and the Unified World Title twenty-seven times between 1988 and 1997. He also held the CWA and AWA World Heavyweight Titles, the latter came as a result of a victory over Curt Hennig on May 9, 1988. The next day, the Memphis *Commercial Appeal* newspaper reported the news on its front page, representative of the local esteem showered upon him. As a commentator on WWE's *Raw*, he has been able to interject his decades of wrestling experience into the weekly storylines, showing his intellect and sense of humor. A talented artist, Lawler has also been an influential member of the community, and has donated lots of his personal time to charity.

Photo Courtesy of Pete Lederberg—plmathfoto@hotmail.com

Born:	March 16, 1937
Height:	5'11"
Weight:	235
Real Name:	Mark W. Lewin
Trained by:	Ed Don George, Danny McShain
Identities:	The Purple Haze
Nicknames:	Maniac
Finisher:	Sleeperhold
Career Span:	1953-1987

Titles Won:	37
Days as World Champion:	Around 220
Age at first World Title Win:	29
Best Opponents:	Dusty Rhodes, Lou Thesz, Terry Funk
Halls of Fame:	1

Lewin, Mark

Versatile Mark Lewin was the younger brother of Donn and Ted, the sons of a Buffalo jeweler. He became a pro wrestler as a teenager in Southern California and was a longtime idol to fans. Along with Don Curtis, he formed a Hall of Fame tag team and held the United States Tag Team championship in the northeast. In 1963, he adopted the mannerisms of a ring "bad guy," while remaining a fan favorite in some locations, including Australia, where he was a two-time IWA World Champion. Lewin also captured the WWA World Heavyweight Title with a victory over Lou Thesz in Los Angeles. Lewin's most memorable heel persona was the "Purple Haze," an exponent of sheer violence and madcap behavior.

Born:	August 29, 1933
Height:	6'1"
Weight:	245
Real Name:	Dale Folsom Lewis
High School:	Rib Lake High School (WI)
College:	University of Oklahoma
Trained by:	Verne Gagne
Identities:	Dr. Blood, Masked Medic I
Career Span:	1961-1979
Died:	August 31, 1997, Deschutes County, OR 64 years old

Titles Won:	19
Best Opponents:	Dory Funk Jr., Jack Brisco, Tim Woods

Lewis, Dale

Looking at his outstanding amateur credentials, one would guess that "Professor" Dale Lewis had wrestled from a young age . . . however, that is a false assumption. Lewis actually played basketball in high school and didn't begin grappling until joining the Marines. He earned a place on both the 1956 and 1960 U.S. Olympic squads, but did not place in competition. He added two Big Eight and NCAA heavyweight titles to his profile, and became a pro in 1961. Later that year, he won the AWA World Tag Team belts with Pat Kennedy. Additionally, he held state championships in Nebraska, Florida, and Georgia, and captured both the United National and Southern Heavyweight crowns.

Born:	December 30, 1924
Height:	5'7"
Weight:	235
Real Name:	Luther Jacob Goodall
Parents:	Luther and Ruby Goodall
Wife:	Gertrude Lindsay Goodall
High School:	Booker T. Washington High School (VA)
College Ach.:	All-CIAA (1948-1949)
Trained by:	Al Haft Gym trainers, Jack Ganson
Nicknames:	Juice, Bronze Bomber
Career Span:	1951-1972
Died:	February 21, 1972, Charlotte, NC 47 years old

Lindsay, Luther

Titles Won:	19
Days as World Champion:	Unknown
Age at first World Title Win:	Around 29
Best Opponents:	Lou Thesz, Dick Hutton, Buddy Rogers
Halls of Fame:	2

An exceptionally talented wrestler, Luther Lindsay was not only respected for his athletic abilities, but was admired for his kind personality. He is one of those guys in wrestling history who you never hear anything negative about—and was a definite legend on all accounts. Born in Norfolk, Virginia, he was a star football player in high school, and joined the Army in June of 1943. While in Italy, he saved the life of a fellow soldier in a swimming mishap and earned the Soldier's Medal. Between 1947 and 1949, he played football at Hampton Institute in Virginia and, in 1950, he had a stint as a pro with the Jersey City Giants. Mentored by Jack Ganson, Lindsay broke into pro wrestling and his skills were lauded by fellow grapplers, promoters, and the press. He conquered prejudices as he went forward, and worked his way up the card to title matches against NWA champion Lou Thesz, and performed spectacularly. He also won regional titles in Portland, Honolulu, and Calgary. Lindsay passed away after a match in Charlotte in 1972.

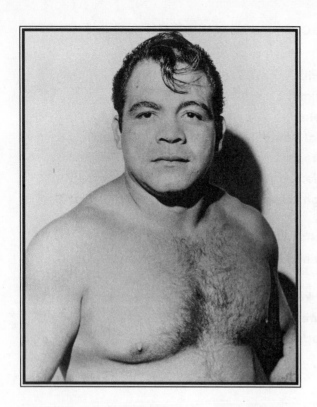

Photo Courtesy of the Collection of Tim Hornbaker

Born:	December 12, 1935
Height:	6'0"
Weight:	245
Real Name:	Guadalupe Garcia Robledo
Family:	Husband of Jean Lothario, father of Pete Lothario
Identities:	Jose Garcia, El Gran Lothario
Finisher:	Knockout Punch, Abdominal Stretch
Career Span:	1959-1985

Titles Won:	36
Best Opponents:	Johnny Valentine, Boris Malenko, Dory Funk Jr.

Lothario, Jose

Acknowledged as the man who helped shape "Icon" Shawn Michaels into a superstar, Jose Lothario was a talented and engaging grappler himself through a career lasting more than thirty-five years. He was scientifically knowledgeable, but also a cunning brawler, and competed in some hardcore matches for the Texas and Florida Brass Knuckles championships. A boxer before he became a wrestler, Lothario was originally from Mexico and settled in San Antonio, where he had two children with his wife Betty Jean. Lothario participated in many interesting feuds and won regional titles all over the United States, including the Texas State Title six times, as well as also capturing the world tag team belts in Florida and San Francisco. In 1997, Lothario appeared on WWF telecasts in Michaels' corner and feuded with manager Jim Cornette.

Born:	August 20, 1940
Height:	5'10"
Weight:	220
Real Name:	Kenneth Lucas
High School:	Mesa High School (AZ)
Trained by:	Lu Kim, Al Pago Pago, Art Nelson, Sputnik Monroe
Career Span:	1959-1998

Titles Won:	104
Best Opponents:	Jack Brisco, Harley Race, Ric Flair

Lucas, Ken

Ken Lucas was a superstar throughout the territorial system and a popular champion from West Texas to the Gulf Coast. Born in Pittsburgh but raised in Mesa, Arizona, he was a talented and disciplined athlete, entering the wrestling trade at the age of nineteen after working with many well-known grapplers. He began an impressive career that saw him win over 100 championships and battle the best in the business. He laid roots in the Pensacola region and captured eleven Gulf Coast Heavyweight Titles. He also held the U.S. Junior belt and regional straps in the Central States, Tampa, and Tennessee. Lucas teamed with Dennis Hall and Kevin Sullivan to become World Tag Team Champion as well. He was a top-tier wrestler and influenced peers and fans across the U.S.

Born:	April 6, 1937
Height:	5'10"
Weight:	235
Real Name:	Peter Fanene-Maivia
Parents:	Alfred and Peke Fanene
Wife:	Ofelia Maivia
Trained by:	Steve Rickard
Identities:	Peter Fanene Anderson
Finisher:	Samoan Stump Puller
Promoted:	Honolulu, Hawaii (1979-1982)
Career Span:	1960-1982
Died:	June 13, 1982, Honolulu, HI 45 years old

Titles Won:	15
Best Opponents:	Billy Graham, Bob Backlund, Pat Patterson
Halls of Fame:	1
Movies:	2

Maivia, Chief Peter

"High Chief" Peter Maivia was a preeminent wrestler from Western Samoa, supremely powerful, energetic, and full of charisma. He followed in the footsteps of Alo Leilani and Prince Maiava, two Samoan grapplers who went on to earn international recognition, and earned a name for himself in New Zealand before landing in United Kingdom in 1963. After developing his abilities on the rough English scene, he went to San Francisco, where he teamed with Pepper Gomez to win the World Tag Team Championship. He'd hold the straps four times in total, also teaming with Pat Patterson and Ray Stevens, as well as being the leading challenger to the local U.S. champion. During his career, he headlined at the Olympic Auditorium and Madison Square Garden. In 1979, he bought the NWA rights to Hawaii and promoted until his death in 1982. Maivia helped launch the Samoan wrestling revolution, and he had ties, bloodline or otherwise, to dozens of other wrestlers, including his grandson, The Rock.

Born:	July 8, 1933
Height:	5'10"
Weight:	235
Real Name:	Larry Simon
Family:	Father of Dean and Joe Malenko
Identities:	Larry "Crusher" Dugan
Nicknames:	Professor
Career Span:	1955-1980
Died:	September 1, 1994, Tampa, FL 61 years old

Titles Won:	21
Best Opponents:	Eddie Graham, Johnny Valentine, Wahoo McDaniel

Malenko, Boris

The Great Malenko was truly a terrorizing matman with incredible psychological powers. He was a proficient talker who made the bitter feuds he was involved in always sound legitimate, as if he really hated his opponents. His war with Eddie Graham in Florida was the model for viciousness, and every step of the way, in every city they worked the angle, it appeared to be genuine. Malenko did the same thing throughout his career, regardless of the gimmick he used, but as Boris Malenko, the Russian heel, he was masterful. He was originally from Irvington, New Jersey, where he learned the ropes at a local YMCA and trained with a number of talented coaches. He used numerous identities to include Otto Von Krupp, a Nazi sympathizer, and found his greatest fame as Malenko. Settling in Tampa, he was the mainstay bad guy, luring foes into violent Russian Chain matches and regularly winning regional titles. Malenko later opened up a wrestling school and taught many future stars, including both his sons, Marc Mero, and Barry Horowitz.

Born:	November 29, 1949
Height:	5'11"
Weight:	240
Real Name:	Wayne Maurice Keown
Identities:	Uncle Zebakiah (Zeb)
Groups:	Lawler's Army (1977)
Tag Teams:	The Kansas Jayhawks w/ Bobby Jaggers, The Desperados w/ Black Bart and Deadeye Dick
Managed:	Justin Bradshaw, The Blu Brothers
Career Span:	1973-Present
Website:	www.dutchmantell.com

PPV Record:	0-1
Titles Won:	47
Days as World Champion:	Over 85
Age at first World Title Win:	47
Best Opponents:	Jerry Lawler, Randy Savage, Bill Dundee
Published Books:	2

Mantell, Dutch

Sporting a distinctive look, capable of being a pivotal player in front of the camera and behind the scenes, and always an entertaining storyteller, "Dirty" Dutch Mantell has been a standout member of the wrestling community since 1973. A Vietnam veteran, Mantell was an outstanding brawler and a legend in Tennessee, where he won the Mid-America Title upwards of fourteen times. Also influential in the careers of Steve Austin and The Undertaker, Mantell has written two autobiographies full of wonderful stories and his insightful perspective of the business is a quality rarely seen. These reasons are why he's been successful as a creative player in the IWA and TNA, and widely respected by his peers. Mantell currently runs a wrestling school in Nashville, known as the "University of Dutch."

Martel, Rick

Born:	March 18, 1956
Height:	6'0"
Weight:	230
Real Name:	Richard Vigneault
Parents:	Fernand and Evelyne Vigneault
Family:	Brother of Michel Martel, uncle of Kevin Martel
Trained by:	Michel Martel
Finisher:	Boston Crab
Tag Teams:	The Can-Am Connection w/ Tom Zenk, The Strike Force w/ Tito Santana
Career Span:	1973-1998

PPV Record:	5-17, 1 DCO
WrestleMania Record:	2-4
Titles Won:	20
Days as World Champion:	595
Age at first World Title Win:	28
Best Opponents:	Ric Flair, Nick Bockwinkel, Stan Hansen

Rick Martel of Quebec City, Quebec played a variety of roles during his lengthy career on the wrestling mat. From his run as the smiling babyface with the science and strength to uphold the credibility of the AWA World Heavyweight Title, to the arrogant heel known as "The Model," Martel was successful, delivering countless entertaining matches and promos. His AWA Title win was, without question, his defining moment, occurring on May 13, 1984 when he took the strap off Jumbo Tsuruta in St. Paul. In the WWF, he held the World Tag Team Title three times, twice with Tony Garea in the early 1980s and again with Tito Santana beginning on October 27, 1987 when the duo beat The Hart Foundation. As a cunning rule-breaker, he had an intense feud with Jake Roberts after he temporarily blinded the latter with the cologne he usually doused the ring with. In 1998, he appeared in WCW and won the TV Title from Booker T, but lost a rematch at SuperBrawl VIII. That same year, he suffered an injury that forced him to retire from the mat for good.

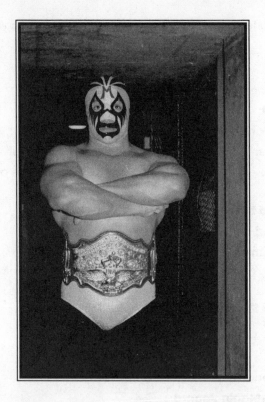

Born:	July 15, 1942
Height:	5'11"
Weight:	245
Real Name:	Aaron Rodriguez
Family:	Brother of El Sicodelico and Dos Caras
Trained by:	Diablo Velasco
Nickname:	The Man of 1,000 Masks
Finisher:	Flying Bodypress
Career Span:	1964-Present

PPV Record:	0-1
Titles Won:	17
Days as World Champion:	Over 14,000 (and counting)
Age at first World Title Win:	32
Best Opponents:	Black Gordman, The Destroyer, Canek
Halls of Fame:	3
Movies:	21

Mascaras, Mil

In wrestling history, there were individuals who were at the forefront of popularizing particular styles and in-ring methods that would later become commonplace. Mexican wrestler Mil Mascaras was the leader of an international revolution which saw audiences around the world accept and embrace the lucha libra style—and all of the high flying and athleticism that came along with it. His explosion on the U.S. scene in Los Angeles in 1968, then Texas in 1970, and Japan a year later was remarkable, and he was a unique trendsetter, indoctrinating fans worldwide to his quickness and aerial attack. His influence was immense, impacting fans who watched him and future wrestlers who wanted to emulate him. A regional champion in Los Angeles and Texas, Mascaras also was a World Heavyweight Champion in Mexico and for the upstart IWA indie promotion in 1975, still holding the IWA belt today. Additionally, Mascaras is a film icon in Mexico and continues to wrestle from time to time, further building upon his legacy.

Born:	July 22, 1937
Height:	5'11"
Weight:	220
Real Name:	Yasuhiro Kojima
Wife:	Judy Matsuda
Identities:	Ernest Kojima, Suhiro Kojima, The Great Matsuda
Finisher:	Sleeperhold, Judo Chop
Owned:	A percentage of Championship Wrestling from Florida (1985–1987)
Career Span:	1957-1990
Died:	November 27, 1999, Tampa, FL 62 years old

Titles Won:	18
Days as World Junior Champion:	387
Age at first World Title Win:	26
Best Opponents:	Danny Hodge, Lou Thesz, Jack Brisco

Matsuda, Hiro

Technical wrestling wonder Hiro Matsuda was universally respected across the industry and left a considerable imprint on the business. He was born in Yokohama, Japan, was trained under the celebrated Rikidozan, and spent time in Peru and Mexico prior to making his debut in the United States in the summer of 1961. Known as a Judo specialist, he wrestled as "Kojima Saito" in Texas and was renamed "Hiro Matsuda" by Bobby Bruns while in the Central States. He then went to Tampa, which would become his home base, and worked the Florida circuit, regularly teaming up with Duke Keomuka. On July 11, 1964, he beat a man who he'd have some of his most competitive matches against, Danny Hodge, for the first of two NWA World Junior Titles. The second reign began in June 1975 when he vanquished Ken Mantell. Matsuda came out of retirement to face Osamu Kido on December 26, 1990 in Japan. As a trainer, Matsuda schooled scores of future legends to include Hulk Hogan, Ron Simmons, and Lex Luger.

McDaniel, Wahoo

Born:	June 19, 1938
Height:	5'11"
Weight:	260
Real Name:	Edward Hugh McDaniel
Parents:	Hugh and Catherine McDaniel
High School:	Midland High School (TX)
College:	University of Oklahoma
AFL Draft:	Los Angeles Chargers (1960)
Pro Sports:	American Football League—Houston Oilers (1960) American Football League—Denver Broncos (1961-1963) American Football League—New York Jets (1964-1965) American Football League—Miami Dolphins (1966-1968)
Trained by:	Balk Estes, Johnny Heidman
Finisher:	Indian Deathlock, Double Underhook Suplex
Career Span:	1962-1996
Died:	April 18, 2002, Houston, TX 63 years old

PPV Record:	2-0, 1 NC
Titles Won:	39
Days as World Champion:	21
Age at first World Title Win:	35
Best Opponents:	Johnny Valentine, Billy Graham, Ric Flair
Halls of Fame:	3
NFL Games:	105

"Chief" Wahoo McDaniel was a powerful force on the wrestling circuit; superbly popular and undeniably tough. He could mix it up with the best in the business and brawl until the sun came up, all for the sake of earning a victory—or just giving the audience a good show. A dual-sport athlete, McDaniel was a standout football player, playing for the legendary Bud Wilkinson at Oklahoma, and then becoming a star in the American Football League. Around 1960, he was contacted by an old acquaintance named Balk Estes, who was also from the "Sooner State," and asked whether he wanted to give pro wrestling a try. McDaniel compared the potential earnings to be made in wrestling to what he was bringing in from football and noticed that some wrestlers made considerably more. He decided to jump into the grappling world on the trail of Estes' boss, Jim Barnett of Indianapolis, and began touring during the off season. His Indian heritage—part Chickasaw and part Choctaw—being a major part of his wrestling persona.

Sporting a headdress, performing a war dance, and delivering tomahawk chops to his opponents, Wahoo was a box office draw wherever he traveled. He had extended stays in the WWWF and AWA, plus Texas, Florida, and the Mid-Atlantic territory. On November 9, 1973 in Japan, he beat Strong Kobayashi for the IWA World Heavyweight Title, and then lost it back to the latter on November 30 of the same year. McDaniel made his home in Charlotte and was an icon for the Crocketts, winning numerous championships and feuding with the likes of Ric Flair and Roddy Piper. As the king of the Indian strap match and a hardcore warrior, he engaged in brutally violent and bloody matches, but never tarnished his image as the hero. Fans knew what to expect from him, and McDaniel lived up to expectations, dishing out punishment to the rule-breakers fans loved to hate. He held the World Tag Team Title three times in the Mid-Atlantic region and the U.S. belt a total of five times. He racked up numerous other regional titles and continued to wrestle through 1996.

Photo Courtesy of the Collection of Tim Hornbaker

Born:	June 5, 1927
Height:	6'5"
Weight:	275
Real Name:	Dr. William Merritt Miller, D.V.M.
Parents:	Dale and Dorothy Miller
High School:	Fremont High School (OH)
College:	Ohio State University
College Ach.:	Big Ten Heavyweight Wrestling Title (1950-1951), All-American Wrestler (1951)
Military:	United States Navy (WWII)
Trained by:	Ruffy Silverstein
Identities:	Dr. X, Mr. M, Crimson Knight
Finisher:	Neck stretcher, backbreaker
Career Span:	1951-1976
Died:	March 24, 1997, Reynoldsburg, OH 69 years old

Miller, Dr. Bill

Titles Won:	10
Days as World Champion:	1,108
Age at first World Title Win:	24
Best Opponents:	Verne Gagne, Bruno Sammartino, Ruffy Silverstein
Halls of Fame:	4

Only weeks after his successful collegiate wrestling career came to an end, "Big" Bill Miller was in a professional ring getting paid for grappling on the Ohio circuit by booker Al Haft. His debut occurred in April of 1951, and before the end of the summer, Haft's massive wrestling prodigy was claiming the AWA World

Heavyweight Championship and appearing on national television across the ABC network. It was a remarkable push, but Haft felt Miller's potential needed to be tapped immediately, as the former two-time Big Ten Heavyweight Champion had the word "superstar" written all over him. And Miller lived up to expectations, winning the Nebraska World Title, the coveted AWA World Title in Minneapolis in 1962, as well as capturing the IWA World Championship in Japan in 1971. Miller nearly annexed Bruno Sammartino's WWWF World belt on numerous occasions and their feud was very popular, of course, with Miller wearing the badge of the hated heel. Miller's brother Danny was also a professional wrestler for many years.

Photo Courtesy of Scott Teal/Crowbar Press

Moose Cholak

Born:	March 17, 1930
Height:	6'4"
Weight:	360
Real Name:	Edward S. Cholak
Parents:	Steve and Mary Cholak
Wife:	Arlene Cholak
High School:	Chicago Vocational High School (IL)
Military Sports:	All-Navy Boxing and Wrestling Heavyweight Champion (1952)
Identities:	The Golden Terror
Nicknames:	Golden, Yukon
Known for:	Wearing a moose head to the ring; his moose call
Career Span:	1953-1987
Died:	October 31, 2002, Hammond, IN 72 years old

Titles Won:	At least 6
Days as World Champion:	25
Age at first World Title Win:	33
Best Opponents:	Verne Gagne, Fred Blassie, Dick the Bruiser

A much-talked-about fixture on the Chicago amateur sports scene, super heavyweight Edward Cholak competed successfully for years as both a boxer and a wrestler. The son of Yugoslavian parents, he played freshman football at Wisconsin, and then joined the Navy, where he continued to demonstrate his toughness as a fighter. In 1952, he even advanced to the finals of National AAU boxing qualifiers. Cholak also appeared on the nationally televised program "Meet the Champ." A short time later, he was scouted by Don Eagle and trained to be a pro wrestler. He adopted the "Moose" gimmick, claiming to be from a fictitious town in Maine, but it was in his legit hometown of Chicago where he was recognized as IWA World Champion in 1963. He also held the WWA World Tag Team Title three times in Indiana, twice with Wilbur Snyder and once with Paul Christy.

Photo Courtesy of Pete Lederberg—plmathfoto@hotmail.com

Born:	October 22, 1940
Height:	5'11"
Weight:	235
Real Name:	Pedro A. Morales
Wife:	Karen Morales
Trained by:	Barba Roja
Identities:	Johnny Como
Finisher:	Dropkick, Boston Crab
Career Span:	1959-1987

PPV Record:	0-1
WrestleMania Record:	0-1
Titles Won:	24
Days as World Champion:	1,452
Age at first World Title Win:	24
Best Opponents:	Bruno Sammartino, Fred Blassie, Don Muraco
Halls of Fame:	1

Morales, Pedro

Renowned fan favorite Pedro Morales is a surefire Hall of Famer, a man who headlined steadily on both coasts, and accomplished goals that few peers have ever been able to duplicate. He was a hearty competitor, full of charisma, and extremely popular with people from many different backgrounds. A native of Culebra, Puerto Rico, Morales finished high school in Brooklyn and picked up wrestling at a local YMCA. He entered the business at seventeen years of age and, by 1960, he was traveling between the United States and Canada full time, wrestling steadily and learning the ropes from many established grapplers. In the northeast, his background was marketed specifically to lure Puerto Rican fans to the arena, and, to a lesser degree than Miguel Perez and Antonino Rocca, was responsible for doing so. He continued to build upon his ring talents and popularity in the Los Angeles area in 1965, and only a few months after arriving in the territory, he beat The Destroyer for the WWA World Heavyweight Title, starting the first of his two reigns.

On February 8, 1971, Morales made history when he dethroned the hated Ivan Koloff for the WWWF World Heavyweight Title at Madison Square Garden and held the title for over 1,000 days. He successfully defended it against some of the toughest heel challengers in the business, and it was commonplace to see over 19,000 fans at the Garden when he was at the top of the bill. After such a long and distinguished time as champion, Stan Stasiak finally ended his run on December 1, 1973. Some years later, Morales teamed with Bob Backlund to win the WWF World Tag Team Title and stopped Ken Patera for the Intercontinental belt, becoming the first man in organization history to hold the World, Tag Team, and Intercontinental Titles. In 1981, he traded the latter championship with Don Muraco, and lost the belt a final time to Muraco on January 22, 1983. Along with his WWF titles, Morales was also a four time co-holder of the WWA World Tag Team Title. Morales engaged in his final match in 1987.

Born:	May 4, 1935
Height:	5'10"
Weight:	250
Real Name:	Harry W. Fujiwara
Trained by:	Nick Bockwinkel
Career Span:	1962-1996

Titles Won:	21
Best Opponents:	Pat Patterson, Bob Backlund, Ricky Steamboat
Halls of Fame:	1

Mr. Fuji

A proponent of tossing salt into the eyes of foes and utilizing his walking cane as a weapon, Mr. Fuji was a prominent wrestler and manager for three decades. He entered the business in his native Hawaii, although billed from Japan, and devised his own trademark heel characteristics, which came to be quite successful across the globe. He won championships in Hawaii, New Zealand, Australia, and the United States, including the WWWF World Tag Team Title—becoming the first team to not only repeat, but three-peat as champions with Professor Tanaka in the 1970s. Fuji took to managing in the WWF, leading Demolition and Yokozuna to world titles. He retired to Tennessee and was inducted into the WWE Hall of Fame in 2007.

Born:	August 7, 1942
Height:	5'11"
Weight:	245
Real Name:	Masanori Saito
College:	Meiji University
Olympics:	Freestyle Wrestling (1964) (Representing Japan) (7th Place)
Identities:	Masa Saito
Managed by:	Captain Lou Albano (1981-1982), Masao Hattori (1983)
Career Span:	1965-1999

PPV Record:	2-2
Titles Won:	25
Days as World Champion:	57
Age at first World Title Win:	47
Best Opponents:	Antonio Inoki, Jack Brisco, Hulk Hogan

Mr. Saito

The famed Mr. Saito was an aggressive rule-breaker with a wide range of offensive weapons. His chops and suplexes were very effective and many times, opponents on the receiving end of his arsenal appeared to be in serious pain. A former two-time Japanese national amateur champion and Olympic veteran, Saito made history on February 10, 1990 in Tokyo when he beat Larry Zbyszko for the AWA World championship. He had a good run in the WWF, winning the tag title twice with Mr. Fuji, and held belts in Florida, Alabama, Los Angeles, San Francisco, and Vancouver. He was also a two-time IWGP Tag Team Champion in the New Japan promotion.

Born:	September 10, 1934
Height:	6'0"
Weight:	230
Real Name:	John Francis Walker
Wife:	Olivia Walker
College:	University of Hawaii
Trained by:	Tony Morelli, Pat O'Connor
Identities:	The Grappler
Career Span:	1956-2007

Titles Won:	51
Best Opponents:	Harley Race, Jack Brisco, Masked Superstar
Halls of Fame:	1

Mr. Wrestling II

The hooded hero, Mr. Wrestling II began his career as the contortionist Johnny Walker, a man who could escape any hold, and dubbed the "Rubberman." He grew up in Hawaii, the son of a sailor, and was involved in many sports while in high school. By the time he donned the white mask as a partner to the original Mr. Wrestling (Tim Woods), Walker had appeared all over North America and was well known for his athletic prowess. Since he was such a strong competitor, he was a natural for Woods' partner, and the two won the state tag team title on several occasions. As singles performer, he won the Georgia Heavyweight Title a total of ten times, and his most high-profile fan was none other than President Jimmy Carter. He feuded with many big-named superstars, challenged Jack Brisco and other NWA World Champions, and solidified himself as one of the greatest ever in the territory. He was also a spectacular draw in Florida, Alabama, and Tennessee, and won the Mid-South North American Title in 1984.

Photo Courtesy of Pete Lederberg—plmathfoto@hotmail.com

Born:	September 10, 1949
Height:	6'3"
Weight:	250
Real Name:	Donald T. Muraco
High School:	Punahou High School (HI)
College:	Glendale Junior College
Identities:	Dr. X, Magnificent M
Finisher:	Reverse Piledriver
Career Span:	1969-2005

PPV Record:	1-5, 1 DCO
WrestleMania Record:	1-2, 1 DCO
Titles Won:	16
Best Opponents:	Pedro Morales, Nick Bockwinkel, Hulk Hogan
Halls of Fame:	1

Muraco, Don

Most WWE fans today associate "The Rock" with Dwayne Johnson, but years before, Don Muraco of Hawaii used that moniker, and was exceptionally successful with it. Also known as "Magnificent" Muraco, he was a clever heel, utilizing strength, psychology, and was adept at the often forgotten form of telling a story in the ring. In 1967, he won a high school wrestling championship and trained at Dean Ho's gym, working out with many talented pros—with Lord James Blears being his greatest mentor. Named AWA Rookie of the Year, Muraco toured the territories and was a strong challenger for Bob Backlund's WWF crown before winning the Intercontinental Title from Pedro Morales in 1981. Muraco lost and regained the Intercontinental belt from Morales prior to losing it to Tito Santana in February 1984. In July of 1985, he won the first King of the Ring tournament and had well-received feuds with Ricky Steamboat and Hulk Hogan. Muraco was also a leading veteran in the budding ECW promotion that started out of Philadelphia.

Born:	August 16, 1946
Height:	6'2"
Weight:	265
Real Name:	Hoyt Richard Murdoch Jr.
Family:	Son of Hoyt "Frankie" Murdoch, nephew of Cecil "Farmer Jones" Murdoch
High School:	Caprock High School (TX)
Trained by:	Frankie Murdoch, Dory Funk Sr.
Identities:	Ron Carson, The Invader, The Tornado, Tornado Murdoch, Black Ace
Finisher:	Brainbuster
Tag Teams:	The Texas Outlaws w/ Dusty Rhodes
Career Span:	1967-1996
Died:	June 15, 1996, Amarillo, TX 49 years old

Murdoch, Dick

PPV Record:	1-2, 1 NC
Titles Won:	44
Best Opponents:	Harley Race, Ric Flair, Antonio Inoki
Managers:	8
Halls of Fame:	1
Movies:	4

Dick Murdoch of Canyon, Texas was a versatile athlete, but mostly remembered for being a ruthless, brawling heel. It was a role he performed well; drawing the ire of audiences and making fans believe that all of the violence they were witnessing was all too real. Wild disregard of all rules were commonplace in his matches, and Murdoch delivered thunderous blow after thunderous blow to his opponents, drawing blood, and never missing a beat as he pummeled foes into submission. Murdoch gained initial fame as a tag team partner of Dusty Rhodes in the late 1960s and early 1970s, and the pair captured championships in several territories. In the Mid-South region, he was a four-time North American champion and in St. Louis, the city he was born in, he won the Missouri crown three times. A regular in Japan and Puerto Rico, Murdoch also teamed with Adrian Adonis to capture the WWF Tag Team Title in 1984. He appeared in WCW in 1991 along with Dick Slater as one of the Hardliners, and was part of the WWF's 1995 Royal Rumble.

Born:	October 25, 1957
Height:	5'9"
Weight:	215
Trained by:	Giant Baba at AJPW Dojo
Identities:	Mr. Onita, The Great Nita
Nickname:	Namida no Karisuma (Charisma of Tears)
Finisher:	Thunder Fire Powerbomb
Promoted:	Frontier Martial-Arts Wrestling (1989-1995)
Career Span:	1974-2010

Onita, Atsushi

Titles Won:	16
Days as World Champion:	Over 641
Age at first World Title Win:	33
Best Opponents:	Tarzan Goto, The Sheik, Hayabusa
Halls of Fame:	1

In the early 1990s, many wrestling fans around the world heard stories of violent barbed-wire death matches taking place in Japan, but couldn't fathom the logistics of such a brutal contest taking place in their own squared circle. The man behind the innovative bouts was Atsushi Onita, a former high-flyer turned extreme warrior. Onita founded the FMW promotion in 1989 and launched a crusade against fundamental catch wrestling, turning the sport onto its head by engaging in bloody no-rope barbed wire bouts with explosions, electricity, and even fire. His ring wars against Tarzan Goto, The Sheik, Genichiro Tenryu, and Hayabusa were extraordinary for the amount of punishment the grapplers would take, and Onita, as the hero, would put his body on the line night after night in ways that made him almost appear supernatural. FMW drew huge crowds during its heyday and fans in all corners of the world wanted to see Onita's chaotic matches as a testament to his inventive style and charisma. Outside of the ring, Onita was also involved in Japanese politics.

Born:	November 10, 1950
Height:	6'1"
Weight:	235
Real Name:	Robert Keith Orton
Parents:	Robert and Rita Orton
Wife:	Elaine Orton
High School:	Ruskin High School (MO)
Finisher:	Superplex
Career Span:	1972-2009

PPV Record:	1-5
WrestleMania Record:	0-1
WWE *Smackdown* TV Record:	0-4
Titles Won:	23
Best Opponents:	Harley Race, Ric Flair, Bob Backlund
Halls of Fame:	1

Orton, Bob Jr.

An amateur background added to the knowledge taught by Jack Brisco, Hiro Matsuda, and the wrestling crew in Tampa provided "Cowboy" Bob Orton with the skills needed to handle just about any wrestling situation. A second-generation grappler, Orton went to Florida to learn the trade, initially working as a referee. He developed his in-ring and interview skills, and teamed with his tough father, Bob Sr., to capture the Florida Tag Team Championship in 1976. Orton had success as a singles grappler, winning regional titles, and then teaming up with Don Kernodle for the NWA World Tag Team belts in 1984. While a member of the WWF, he challenged both Bob Backlund and Hulk Hogan for the heavyweight title, and acted as a bodyguard for Roddy Piper. He also participated in the main event of the initial WrestleMania. One of his memorable gimmicks was wearing an arm cast to the ring and using it as a weapon during bouts. He returned to the WWE to assist his son Randy in his feud with The Undertaker and still occasionally wrestles on the indie circuit.

Born:	November 6, 1943
Height:	6'0"
Weight:	265
Real Name:	Kenneth Wayne Patera
Parents:	Frank and Dorothy Patera
High School:	Cleveland High School (OR)
Pan-Am Games:	4 Gold Medals (1971) (weightlifting)
Trained by:	Verne Gagne
Finisher:	Swinging Neckbreaker, Swinging Full Nelson
Tag Teams:	The Olympians w/ Brad Rheingans, The Sheiks w/ Jerry Blackwell
Career Span:	1972-1992

Patera, Ken

PPV Record:	0-4
WrestleMania Record:	0-1
Titles Won:	16
Best Opponents:	Andre the Giant, Nick Bockwinkel, Hulk Hogan

The ultra-competitive Ken Patera was one of five children born to a Portland baker and, like his three brothers, participated in multiple sports during his youth. At Portland State College, and later Brigham Young University, he established many records and was highly decorated in the shotput event. As a weightlifter, he won a number of AAU Titles, and at the 1970 tournament, he set four national records. In 1972, Patera became the first American to lift more than 500 pounds in the clean and jerk. That same year, he participated in the Olympics, but failed to place. Scouted by Verne Gagne, Patera dropped weight to become a wrestler, and was known as a charismatic heel on the AWA and NWA circuits. While wrestling the WWWF territory, he had many key matches against champions Bruno Sammartino and Bob Backlund, and was the second man to ever hold the Intercontinental Title, as well as also holding the AWA World Tag Team and Missouri State Championships. His 1977 third place showing in the World's Strongest Man competition is still occasionally broadcast on TV.

Born:	January 19, 1941
Height:	6'1"
Weight:	240
Real Name:	Pierre Clermont
Identities:	Lord Patrick
Nickname:	Killer, Pretty Boy
Groups:	The Corporation (1998-1999)
Tag Team:	The Blond Bombers w/ Ray Stevens
Career Span:	1960-2000

PPV Record:	0-1
WWE *Raw* TV Record:	4-4, 2 NC
Titles Won:	35
Best Opponents:	Ray Stevens, Bob Backlund, Gene Kiniski
Halls of Fame:	2

Patterson, Pat

Pat Patterson's behind-the-scenes influence helped develop many careers in the WWE and his creative mind established trademark concepts that the organization still uses, including the design of the Royal Rumble match. Before Patterson settled into a backstage role, he was a colorful and successful in-ring performer. Trained by Pat Girard at the latter's Rachel Street wrestling school in Montreal, Patterson worked in New England and in the Pacific Northwest early in his career. While wrestling in the San Francisco territory, he became a major star, capturing the local U.S. Title five times, the World Tag Team title nine times, and won the annual 18-man battle royal in 1975 and 1981. On June 19, 1979, he beat Ted DiBiase for the North American Championship, which was soon renamed the WWF Intercontinental Title. Nearly twenty years later, in June 2000, Patterson won the WWF Hardcore Title and was known as one of Vince McMahon's "stooges." He's served as a close advisor to McMahon and was inducted into the WWE Hall of Fame in 1996.

Born:	April 17, 1954
Height:	6'2"
Weight:	245
Real Name:	Roderick George Toombs
Trained by:	Tony Condello, Stu Hart
Identities:	The Masked Canadian
Nicknames:	Rowdy, Rowdy Scot, Hot Rod
Finisher:	Sleeperhold
Tag Team:	The Dream Team w/ Greg Valentine
Managed:	Paul Orndorff (1984), David Shultz (1984), Sean O'Haire (2003)
Career Span:	1973-Present

PPV Record:	12-18, 1 DCO
WrestleMania Record:	2-4, 1 DCO
WWE *Raw* TV Record:	3-1
WWE *Smackdown* TV Record:	3-2
Titles Won:	35
Best Opponents:	Hulk Hogan, Bret Hart, Greg Valentine
Halls of Fame:	3
TV Appearances:	over 30
Movies:	37
Published Books:	1

Piper, Roddy

The rowdy one, Roddy Piper has always been exceptionally unrestrained, straying far from the playbook—and rulebook for that matter. He was brutally honest and often funny in his rants, laying it out for the public to consume and driving up the intensity going into his next match. His outrageousness was the reason why he was loved and hated at the same time, and he was never at a loss for words. On those rare occasions when he had said enough, he would let his fists do the talking, as he was always ready for a brawl. Billed as being from Glasgow, Scotland, he was originally from Saskatchewan and was raised in Winnipeg. He represented Windsor Park Collegiate at the Manitoba High School wrestling championships and won the 165-pound title in March of 1971. Under the guidance of promoter Tony Condello, Piper broke into the business in 1973 and bounced around the Canadian independents with appearances for Verne Gagne in Minneapolis—including an early match against the future "Nature Boy" Ric Flair.

Breaking out into a star in Los Angeles, he feuded heavily with hero Chavo Guerrero and won the Americas championship five times. He left his mark in the Pacific Northwest before venturing east to the Mid-Atlantic territory, and was drawing intense heat everywhere he appeared. Piper's ability to inflame audiences was a promoter's dream. He won the U.S. Title twice for Crockett Promotions, and then jumped to the WWF in 1984. At the first WrestleMania, he partnered with Paul Orndorff in a losing effort against Hulk Hogan and Mr. T. That following year, he fought Mr. T. in a boxing match at WrestleMania II and was disqualified in the fourth round. His antics and violent behavior made feuds with Hogan and Jimmy Snuka exciting, and was responsible for helping bolster the WWF's exposure during a critical time in its history. In 1987, he retired to focus on his budding acting career, but returned to the ring two years later to feud with Rick Rude and Bad News Brown.

Piper won his first WWF championship when he captured the Intercontinental Title on January 19, 1992 from The Mountie, but ended up losing it to Bret Hart at WrestleMania VIII. Over the course of the next few years, he made sporadic appearances for the WWF and WCW. In the main event of Starrcade 1996, he beat Hollywood Hogan with a sleeperhold and three years later, toppled Hart for the U.S. Title with help from comedian Will Sasso. Piper retired again in 1999, but later worked as a WCW official. In March of 2003, he made his WWE homecoming, smashing Hogan with a pipe during the latter's bout with Vince McMahon at WrestleMania XIX, and then made an appearance for NWA-TNA, where he delivered an infamous shoot-style rant against Vince Russo. In 2005, he was inducted into the WWE Hall of Fame and has made a number of appearances for the promotion, including wrestling a handicap bout at WrestleMania XXV against Chris Jericho. He still shows up for the WWE a couple times a year, and always to a huge ovation from the fans.

Photo Courtesy of the Collection of Tim Hornbaker

Born:	March 20, 1943
Height:	6'4"
Weight:	245
Real Name:	Dennis Waters
Trained by:	Jack Wentworth
Identities:	Lord Anthony Lansdowne
Nickname:	Blond Adonis, Blond Bombshell
Finisher:	Powerlock
Managed by:	Bobby Davis
Career Span:	1963-1982

Titles Won:	14
Days as World Champion:	Over 324
Age at first World Title Win:	27
Best Opponents:	Antonio Inoki, Bruno Sammartino, Johnny Valentine

Powers, Johnny

In the summer of 1964, a blond-haired newcomer named Johnny Powers, reportedly fresh from a stint in Hawaii, appeared in the WWWF territory and challenged World Heavyweight Champion Bruno Sammartino. It was a remarkable ascension for the twenty-one-year-old Powers, who'd only made his pro debut the year before in the Detroit area. Originally from Hamilton, Ontario, Powers was incredibly strong, standing 6'4", and made the perfect foil for Sammartino. Powers went on to become a major superstar in the NWF, a territory extending from Cleveland to Buffalo, and held both their World and North American belts. He was also involved on the promotional side of both the NWF and the IWA, which was an indie promotion that ran between 1975 and 1978.

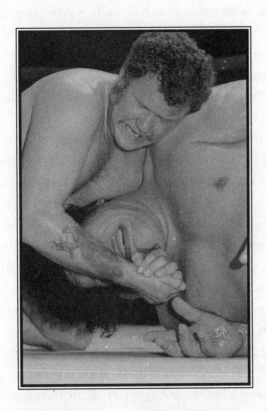

Photo Courtesy of Pete Lederberg—plmathfoto@hotmail.com

Born:	April 11, 1943
Height:	6'1"
Weight:	250
Real Name:	Harley Leland Race
Parents:	Jay and Mary Race
High School:	Quitman High School (MO)
Identities:	Jack Long, The Great Mortimer
Nicknames:	Handsome, Mad Dog
Finisher:	Indian Deathlock, Suplex
Managed:	Lex Luger (1991-1992), Mr. Hughes (1991-1992), Big Van Vader (1991-1995), The Super Invader (1993), Yoshi Kwan (1993), Steve Austin (1994)
Promoted:	World League Wrestling (WLW) (1999-Present)
Career Span:	1960-1993

Race, Harley

PPV Record:	3-3
WrestleMania Record:	1-1
Titles Won:	44
Days as World Champion:	Around 1,976
Age at first World Title Win:	30
Best Opponents:	Dory Funk Jr., Jack Brisco, Ric Flair
Halls of Fame:	7

Incredibly tough and intimidating, Harley Race was the classic professional wrestler in a day and age of corny gimmicks and characters. He was a solid force to be reckoned with, capable of dealing with a brawler in the same manner he'd take care of a technician: dismantling both with his power and skills. His overriding knowledge of holds and psychology gave him an advantage over his foes in the ring, but more importantly, put him in a place to be eternally successful in a business that coveted ring warriors of his ilk. In an era in which the National Wrestling Alliance World Heavyweight Championship was considered the most prestigious wrestling title in the business, Race won the belt not once, but eight different times. There is nothing more that needs to be said to affirm his Hall of Fame career. For some wrestlers, wearing the NWA belt even a few days was the high point of their career, but for Race, he stood tall as champion for 1,800 days.

Guided into the profession by St. Joseph promoter Gust Karras, Race studied the finer points of the art from old-school masters Stanislaus and Wladek Zbyszko, who had a farm in nearby Savannah, Missouri. Put through the wringer, Race was taught many lessons that were no longer commonplace among wrestlers because the sport had evolved with an emphasis on color instead of fortitude, which actually worked to give Race an advantage in terms of in-ring confidence. His core toughness and size made him unafraid of anyone in the ring, regardless of their reputation, and he was never unwilling to match up in a legitimate fight. Debuting as a teenager, Race suffered a career setback after being injured in a serious car accident after only a year in the business. He never gave up on trying to return to the ring, and set off on a whirlwind tour that took him all over the wrestling landscape. He was impressive in the ring and earned the respect of many influential NWA bookers who'd later support his candidacy for the World Title.

In Minneapolis, he formed a successful tag team with Larry Hennig and beat Bruiser and Cruiser for the AWA World Title, the first of three championship reigns, on January 31, 1965. Basing his operations in the Central States territory, Race won the regional heavyweight title nine times and the Missouri belt seven. His biggest achievement, however, occurred on May 24, 1973, setting off his decade-long relationship with the NWA World Heavyweight Title. That very first win came at the expense of Dory Funk Jr. with Race taking two of three falls. Even with it being a big win for his career, Race was only a transitional titleholder the first time around, losing the belt to Jack Brisco on July 20, 1973. That wasn't the case for his second reign. He dethroned Terry Funk on February 6, 1977 and remained champion for over two years, reportedly making over 700 successful title defenses. Race embodied the spirit of all his predecessors, fulfilling the rigorous demands of the NWA, and maintained the worldwide esteem for both the organization and the title itself.

Race went everywhere and met everyone, even battling WWWF champions Billy Graham and Bob Backlund in title vs. title contests. He was finally defeated by Dusty Rhodes on August 21, 1979, but regained the title five nights later. The next three title losses saw Race regain the belt within a week or less, including twice in Japan against Giant Baba. Race's seventh NWA Title victory came on June 10, 1983 against Ric Flair, and it was considered historic at the time because he was supposedly beating Lou Thesz's record six reigns as champ; Thesz, truth be told, was only a three-time wearer of the Alliance crown. In 1984, Race and Flair traded the belt once more, making Race an eight-time titleholder. A few years later, he became the "King" of the WWF after winning a King of the Ring tournament outside Boston. He later managed Lex Luger and Vader to gold in WCW, but unfortunately broke his hip in a car accident in 1995, which officially ended his active career. He currently runs a wrestling school in Eldon, Missouri, which he's been doing since 1999 and has taught many future pros the ropes.

Born:	October 12, 1945
Height:	6'2"
Weight:	275
Real Name:	Virgil Riley Runnels Jr.
Parents:	Virgil and Katherine Runnels
High School:	Johnston High School (TX)
College:	West Texas State University
Pro Sports:	Continental Football League— Hartford Charter Oaks (1967)
Identities:	Dusty Runnels, The Midnight Rider, The Midnight Cowboy
Tag Teams:	The Texas Outlaws w/ Dick Murdoch, The Superpowers w/ Nikita Koloff
Promoted:	Turnbuckle Championship Wrestling (2000-2003)
Career Span:	1967-2007

Rhodes, Dusty

PPV Record:	21-10, 2 NC
WrestleMania Record:	1-0
WWE *Raw* TV Record:	1-0
Titles Won:	57
Days as World Champion:	107
Age at first World Title Win:	33
Best Opponents:	Ric Flair, Harley Race, Randy Savage
Halls of Fame:	4

The legendary "American Dream," Dusty Rhodes was beyond popular during the height of his career. He was an icon, a naturally charismatic wrestling sensation that fought the good fight against heels from coast to coast. He'd verbally connect to the audience in promos, then play out a back-and-forth storyline in the ring, and rebound to grab the attention of all watching going into his finisher, the Bionic Elbow. He was an incredible lure to the box office throughout his time on the mat and his popularity is certainly on par with any of the other major stars of his era.

An actor in his high school drama club, Rhodes was a capable performer and confident in front of large crowds. After receiving words of encouragement from Fritz Von Erich, attending the Santos wrestling school in Boston, and learning from Joe Blanchard in San Antonio, Dusty was ready to make an impact on the business . . . and he did. Within his first year, he was already a headliner. Teaming with "Tornado" Dick Murdoch, he won a number of tag team championships as a rule-breaking heel.

Rhodes and Murdoch made a lot of noise in Toronto, Detroit, and Florida during their tenure together. In 1974, Dusty turned fan favorite in Florida and rampaged through the territory, building an army of supporters. Within a short time, there was no bigger superstar in the southeast. Rhodes kept the momentum going across other areas of the NWA, and his regular guy image was extraordinarily popular and was billed as the common man. Proven to be a box office success, he rose right to the top of the business and pinned Harley Race at the famous Armory in Tampa to capture the National Wrestling Alliance World Heavyweight Title on August 21, 1979. He had a matinee program in Jacksonville on August 26, and then appeared in Orlando at night, where he lost the belt in a rematch against Race. Rhodes became a two-time NWA Champion on June 21, 1981, winning again from Race, this time at the Omni in Atlanta. His reign lasted until September 17, when he lost a bout to his longtime foe, Ric Flair, in Kansas City.

During the 13th show of the Great American Bash tour, Rhodes captured his third NWA World Title from Flair in a cage match on July 26, 1986 in Greensboro. Flair regained the title on August 9, pinning Dusty while Rhodes was locked in a figure-four. Over the course of his career, Rhodes held many other championships, including two versions of the U.S. Title. In the Mid-Atlantic region, he worked as part of the behind-the-scenes staff as a booker where he had some of his most memorable moments. He feuded with Tully Blanchard over the TV Title, was double-crossed by the Road Warriors, and teamed with Nikita Koloff to win the second annual Jim Crockett Sr. Memorial Tag Team Tournament on April 11, 1987. They were victorious over Blanchard and Lex Luger and dedicated their win to the injured Magnum T.A. Dusty was a persistent challenger to Flair's crown, and they headlined Starrcade in both 1984 and 1985. In April of 1988, he was stripped of the U.S. Title after attacking Jim Crocket with a baseball bat.

Shortly after Starrcade in 1988, Rhodes returned to Florida and launched the PWF, a short-lived regional promotion with lofty aspirations. In 1989, he entered the WWF and Vince McMahon pushed Dusty's "son of a plumber" image, and the former NWA champion was decked out in polka dot attire. Although he gained a large following, Rhodes remained in the middle of the card and had strong feuds with Randy Savage and Ted DiBiase. It was during his war with the "Million Dollar Man" that Dusty's son, Dustin, was introduced to the national audience. Both father and son ended up in WCW, where Dustin found much success and Dusty worked as a commentator. In September of 1994, Rhodes came out of semi-retirement to team with his son and the Nasty Boys against the members of Colonel Parker's group in a War Games event. Rhodes would eventually make Parker submit to a figure-four and give his team the victory. A few years later, he shocked his followers by turning on Larry Zbyszko and joining the New World Order.

In 2000, he established an indie promotion known as Turnbuckle Championship Wrestling, which ran shows across the south. Many big name stars appeared for the promotion and Rhodes often laced up his boots and returned to the ring. His final stint in WCW came at its final pay-per-view on March 18, 2001 in Jacksonville. Dusty teamed with Dustin to beat Ric Flair and Jeff Jarrett.

An ironic fact: Rhodes was at Jim Crockett's first pay-per-view of Starrcade 1987 and WCW's last PPV, Greed. On January 8, 2003, Rhodes reunited with the Road Warriors in TNA in Nashville, and worked an angle with Nikita Koloff the following week. Since 2005, he's made a number of WWE appearances, including storylines with his up-and-coming son, Cody. Rhodes also had the honor of inducting the Funk Brothers and Eddie Graham into the WWE Hall of Fame, where he himself was enshrined by his sons Dustin and Cody in 2007.

Born:	July 26, 1956
Height:	6'0"
Weight:	245
Real Name:	Thomas Richardson
Trained by:	Dick Steinborn, Jerry Jarrett, Jerry Lawler
Finisher:	Sleeperhold, Thesz Press
Groups:	The York Foundation (1991-1992)
Tag Teams:	The Fabulous Ones w/ Eddie Gilbert
Managed by:	Jimmy Hart, Jackie Fargo, Paul E. Dangerously, Alexandria York
Managed:	The FBI (1997-1998)
Career Span:	1974-Present

Rich, Tommy

PPV Record:	5-4
Titles Won:	58
Days as World Champion:	4
Age at first World Title Win:	24
Best Opponents:	Harley Race, Jerry Lawler, Buzz Sawyer
Halls of Fame:	1

"Wildfire" Tommy Rich was one of the biggest names in the sport in the 1970s and 1980s. He was immensely popular, a "wide-eyed Southern boy" with charisma and appeal that never failed to pack arenas. A high school athlete from Hendersonville, Tennessee, Rich grew up around wrestling and committed himself to the business at the age of eighteen. Quickly embraced by fans throughout the region, he was steadily pushed by promoters, winning numerous championships, and eventually capturing the biggest prize of them all: the National Wrestling Alliance World Heavyweight Title. The victory came on April 27, 1981 at the Civic Center in Augusta, Georgia, when he pinned Harley Race in 27:22, making him the youngest NWA champion at that point. Although he was champion for only four days, losing it back to Race on May 1 in Gainesville, Rich had made history with it being a crowning achievement on a celebrated career. To this day, Rich makes independent appearances and can still light up an audience with his magnetism.

Born:	November 14, 1924
Height:	5'10"
Weight:	235
Real Name:	Mitsuhiro Momota
Family:	Father of Mitsuo Momota
Finisher:	Sleeperhold
Promoted:	Japan Wrestling Alliance (JWA) (1953-1963)
Career Span:	1951-1963
Died:	December 15, 1963, Tokyo, Japan 39 years old

Titles Won:	13
Days as World Champion:	119
Age at first World Title Win:	37
Best Opponents:	Lou Thesz, Masahiko Kimura, Fred Blassie
Tournament Wins:	5
Halls of Fame:	2

Rikidozan

Regarded as the "Father of Japanese Professional Wrestling," Rikidozan was originally from Korea and spent five years as a Sumo wrestler beginning in 1946. He spent some time working in construction at the Tachikawa Air Base before taking part on a show featuring a band of American wrestlers trying to build interest in the Western style of wrestling. The date was October 28, 1951, and Rikidozan made his debut, wrestling Bobby Bruns to a draw. Bruns, incidentally, had been his trainer, and was the liaison for the tour for Honolulu promoter Al Karasick, who had membership in the National Wrestling Alliance. Rikidozan was said to have dropped as much as six inches off his waist and had learned a great deal about the profession in a short amount of time. The appearance of an Asian grappler on the program was a welcomed sight, and from that point forth, he was more responsible for the spread of American wrestling in Japan than anyone else.

In 1952, Rikidozan appeared in Honolulu and then toured California, losing very few singles matches. Although he initially worked as a fan favorite, he altered his persona and became a heel, drawing the ire of fans with his illegal tactics. In Japan, however, Rikidozan was entirely popular. In fact, he helped foster the wrestling revolution in that country, propelling the sport into the public's eye. On December 22, 1954, he beat Masahiko Kimura to win the initial Japanese Heavyweight Title, winning the match by knockout. His televised matches drew record numbers and there was no debate who the most popular wrestler in the country was. He added to his fame with a victory over Lou Thesz for the International Title and also beat Fred Blassie for the WWA World Heavyweight crown in March of 1962. On December 8, 1963, Rikidozan was stabbed in the left side of his abdomen at the New Latin Quarter club in Tokyo. The thirty-nine-year-old international wrestling celebrity died a week later of peritonitis at Sanno Hospital.

Born:	May 30, 1955
Height:	6'5"
Weight:	250
Real Name:	Aurelian Jake Smith, Jr.
Family:	Son of Grizzly Smith, stepbrother of Sam Houston and Rockin' Robin
Trained by:	Grizzly Smith
Nickname:	The Snake
Groups:	The Legion of Doom (1983-1984)
Managed by:	Paul Ellering
Snake's Names:	Damian, Lucifer
Career Span:	1975-2011

Roberts, Jake

PPV Record:	12-18, 1 Draw
WrestleMania Record:	3-4, 1 Draw
Titles Won:	14
Best Opponents:	Ted DiBiase, Rick Rude, Randy Savage

Second generation star Jake Roberts of Cooke County, Texas was a colorful performer and the man who put the DDT finisher on the map. A cunning ring psychologist, he intimidated foes with his snake-like tactics, and the literal snake he carried to the ring added to his mystique. He was a capable heel and fan favorite and wore both hats while in the NWA, WWF, and WCW during the 1980s and 1990s. Roberts was a convincing brawler, and he had memorable feuds with Ricky Steamboat, Rick Rude, and Ted DiBiase. At one juncture, the massive wrestler Earthquake purportedly squashed his snake in a controversial angle that horrified witnesses—but really caused no harm to the animal. Roberts won the SMW heavyweight title in 1994, made occasional showings for ECW, and also wrestled in Great Britain and Mexico. Roberts reemerged in the WWF briefly in 1996 and in recent years has appeared for numerous indie organizations and for TNA. He officially retired from the ring in January of 2011. His out-of-the-ring trials were spotlighted in the documentary, *Beyond the Mat*, which came out in 1999.

Born:	September 18, 1938
Height:	5'11"
Weight:	235
Real Name:	William Alfred Robinson
Nickname:	Man of 1000 Holds
Finisher:	Double Arm Suplex
Career Span:	1958-1992

Titles Won:	18
Days as World Champion:	Over 719
Age at first World Title Win:	30
Best Opponents:	Antonio Inoki, Verne Gagne, Jumbo Tsuruta
Halls of Fame:	4

Robinson, Billy

Billy Robinson was a legendary catch-as-catch-can grappler. Influenced by his father and uncle, who were both boxers, he was instilled with a toughness at an early age and progressed through the amateur ranks in Britain, winning the national light heavyweight wrestling title in 1957. He trained for years at Billy Riley's infamous "Snake Pit" in Wigan, learning from some of the masters of the pure catch style. In addition to Riley, Robinson worked out with brothers Billy Joyce and Joe Robinson, Ernie Riley, and Jack Dempsey. He'd later beat trainer Joyce for the British championship in 1967. On December 19, 1968, he won a tournament in Japan for the initial IWA World Title and also teamed with Verne Gagne and The Crusher to hold the AWA Tag Title. During the 1970s, Robinson was one of the trainers at Gagne's wrestling school, coaching scores of future superstars. At one time, he was considered to be the best wrestler in the world, and his combination of science, strength, and unyielding ferociousness made him a dangerous and successful competitor.

Born:	May 24, 1931
Height:	6'0"
Weight:	220
Real Name:	Enrique Gregory Romero
Trained by:	Diablo Velasco, Dory Funk Sr.
Finisher:	Cannonball
Career Span:	1954-1983
Died:	January 15, 2006, Amarillo, TX 74 years old

Titles Won:	31
Best Opponents:	Dory Funk Sr., Gene Kiniski, Mike DiBiase

Romero, Ricky

For three decades, "Rapid" Ricky Romero was an undeniably popular hero of the wrestling world, being universally well-liked in and out of the ring. Originally from San Bernardino, California, Romero competed for several years under his real name, and his quickness and enthusiasm were keys to his success. He found a home in the Amarillo region and became a legend, winning the North American and Rocky Mountain Titles and often teaming with Dory Funk Sr. as the North American Tag Team champs. Romero, who played baseball when he was young, was a perfect foil to the heels in the territory and had the kind of charisma that people gravitated toward. His sons, Steve, Mark, and Chris were also grapplers, known professionally as the Youngbloods.

Born:	June 9, 1929
Height:	6'2"
Weight:	225
Real Name:	Jean Rougeau
Parents:	Armand and Albina Rougeau
Family:	Nephew of Eddie Auger, brother of Jacques Rougeau
High School:	Catholic High School (Montreal)
Trained by:	Eddie Auger, Yvon Robert
Promoted:	International Wrestling Association (IWA) (1964-1975)
Career Span:	1952-1971
Died:	May 25, 1983, Montreal, Quebec 53 years old

Rougeau, Johnny

Titles Won:	At least 8
Days as World Champion:	Over 725
Age at first World Title Win:	32
Best Opponents:	Killer Kowalski, Hans Schmidt, Ivan Koloff

Quebec legend Johnny Rougeau was influenced by professional wrestling early on his life, particularly by his uncle Edouard Auger, who'd turned to the grappling trade to earn a living in the late 1940s. Add the fact that the province was full of opportunities on a large scale at the Montreal Forum or on a secondary circuit, made becoming a wrestler was an easy choice for Rougeau after his goal of becoming a hockey player didn't pan out. Being a natural athlete, he took to wrestling easily, and by the summer of 1953, he'd defeated Harry Madison for the Canadian Junior Heavyweight Title. The following year, he dropped the championship and became a heavyweight. The popular hometown boy was an exciting part of the wrestling bill for Eddie Quinn's productions, and the latter brought in scores of top heels to wage war. Between 1965 and 1970, he won the International World Title six times and retired on August 2, 1971 to focus on his Laval Nationals Junior Hockey team, as well as to promote wrestling and boxing.

Born:	July 21, 1935
Height:	5'9"
Weight:	215
Real Name:	Nelson Combs
Career Span:	1955-1989
Died:	February 3, 2002, Mooresville, NC 66 years old

Titles Won:	17
Best Opponents:	Lou Thesz, Antonio Inoki, Dory Funk Sr.
Halls of Fame:	1

Royal, Nelson

Kentucky born Nelson Royal was a spectacular junior heavyweight wrestler and was a multi-time world champion. He studied under the legendary Indian grappler, Don Eagle, traveling with the "Chief" in 1955. By 1962, in Texas, he had developed a "Sir Nelson Royal" gimmick that claimed he was an aristocrat from England. Often aiming at the ire of the crowd, he even worked with a valet named Jeeves, which drove fans mad. Royal won many regional tag team championships in West Texas, Los Angeles, Pacific Northwest, and Mid-Atlantic territories, and held the NWA World Junior Title four times between 1976 and 1988. Royal, well-liked throughout the business, influenced many careers as a trainer and owned a western store in Mooresville, North Carolina.

Born:	October 6, 1935
Height:	5'10"
Weight:	265
Real Name:	Bruno Laopardo Franceso Sammartino
Parents:	Alfonso and Emilia Sammartino
Family:	Father of David Sammartino
Trained by:	Rex Perry, Ace Freeman
Finisher:	Bearhug, Backbreaker
Career Span:	1959-1987

PPV Record:	0-1
WrestleMania Record:	0-1
Titles Won:	9
Days as World Champion:	4,040
Age at first World Title Win:	27
Best Opponents:	Killer Kowalski, Bill Miller, Gene Kiniski
Halls of Fame:	4

Sammartino, Bruno

The "Living Legend" Bruno Sammartino is arguably the most important wrestler in World Wrestling Entertainment history. A case can be made that if it wasn't for the success of Sammartino as an outstanding fan favorite and box office attraction during the early days of the promotion, the WWE wouldn't be what it is today. His value to Vincent J. McMahon in the 1960s and 1970s cannot be measured. Audiences throughout the world treasured his magnetism and were brought to their feet as he stood toe to toe with the most vile rule-breakers in the industry. Fans wholeheartedly embraced McMahon's formula of importing in the biggest and baddest heels to challenge Sammartino, and Bruno, month after month and year after year, knocked them all back one at a time. The drama of each feud may have changed slightly, but the blueprint was written in stone, and Sammartino's ability to rise above each individual test only brought him closer to the people who were devoted to cheering him.

Born in Abruzzi, Italy, he developed his frame into that of a power-lifter and worked out at local Pittsburgh gyms with University of Pittsburgh wrestling coach Rex Perry, learning the finer points of amateur wrestling. His eagerness to excel was a selling point for Rudy Miller, an old wrestling promoter and manager, who scouted Sammartino for McMahon and brought him into the Capitol Wrestling fold in 1959. Green all over, Sammartino entered pro wrestling with an exceptional look and natural appeal, and McMahon found developing him into a fan favorite quite easy. Within a short time, however, there was some friction in Sammartino's northeastern run, and he ventured to Toronto, where his climb to the top of the wrestling rankings continued. Promoters and managers sought his contract with vigor, but McMahon pulled Sammartino back into the fold, setting the stage for the biggest match of Bruno's young career.

On May 17, 1963 at Madison Square Garden, 19,000 fans watched Sammartino crush the "Nature Boy" Buddy Rogers, the renowned champion and icon in less than a minute and win the WWWF World Heavyweight Title. The commanding victory pushed Sammartino into another realm of popularity, kick-starting his championship reign with flavor. The Sammartino era of dominance began that night, and McMahon wasted no time in lining up a stable of heels to push his young star to the limit. Guys like Dr. Bill Miller, Gene Kiniski, Fred Blassie, Gorilla Monsoon, Bill Watts, Waldo Von Erich, Stan Hansen, and Killer Kowalski all seemed like potential successors, and many times appeared to be the cusp of winning the prized championship. But Sammartino rebounded with Herculean strength, powering out the doldrums to pin his rivals. His knack for surviving perilous situations never got old, and his popularity was sustained throughout the northeastern territory for well over a decade.

Remarkably, Sammartino remained champion for more than 2,800 days and gave the WWWF major credibility against the NWA and AWA. When it was finally time to go in another direction, Ivan Koloff beat him for the title on January 18, 1971. A few years later, Sammartino was called upon again by McMahon to lead his company, and on December 10, 1973, he beat Stan Stasiak for his second WWWF World Championship. Bruno carried the belt until April 30, 1977, when he dropped the strap to Billy Graham in Baltimore. He wrestled into the 1980s, even appearing in a battle royal at WrestleMania II, and has since been honored for induction into several Halls of Fame. He established a high standard for heroes in the WWF/WWE, which Hulk Hogan, Bret Hart, The Rock, and John Cena had to follow and emulate, of course in their own individual ways. Sammartino laid the groundwork for each and every one of them, but to this day, has still not been honored for induction into the WWE Hall of Fame.

Savage, Randy

Born:	November 15, 1952
Height:	6'1"
Weight:	235
Real Name:	Randy Mario Poffo
Parents:	Angelo and Judith Poffo
High School:	Downers Grove North High School (IL)
Pro Sports:	Minor League Baseball—In system for the St. Louis Cardinals, Cincinnati Reds, and the Chicago White Sox (1972-1975)
Trained by:	Angelo Poffo
Identities:	The Spider, The Executioner, The Destroyer, The Graduate, Mr. Madness
Nicknames:	Rotten, Macho King
Finisher:	Flying Elbowdrop
Career Span:	1973-2004
Died:	May 20, 2011, Seminole, FL 58 years old

PPV Record:	38-31, 2 NC
WrestleMania Record:	7-4
Titles Won:	20
Days as World Champion:	Over 1,060
Age at first World Title Win:	26
Best Opponents:	Ricky Steamboat, Ric Flair, Hulk Hogan
Halls of Fame:	2
TV Appearances:	Over 15
Movies:	2

One of the most entertaining and influential wrestlers of the last thirty years, "Macho Man" Randy Savage has seen and done it all. He's delivered excellent matches, won World Titles, and established a legacy that is still fondly remembered by his conglomerate of fans. The son of wrestler Angelo Poffo, Randy was born in Columbus and grew up in the Chicago suburbs, where he was an outstanding baseball player in high school. After bouncing around the farm systems of several pro teams, he became a pro wrestler in 1973 under a mask. He wrestled in a number of territories to include Florida, Alabama, Detroit, and Toronto, and in 1977, he adopted the name "Randy Savage" upon the recommendation of Ole Anderson in Atlanta. Angelo and his two sons, Randy and Lanny, launched their own promotion, International Championship Wrestling in 1978 and it was known as an "outlaw" organization because it operated outside the global sphere of the National Wrestling Alliance.

A month after Randy beat his brother Lanny for the ICW World Heavyweight Title in July of 1979, the Poffos filed a $2.4 million federal antitrust suit against nine wrestling promoters to include Jerry Jarrett, Nick Gulas, Verne Gagne, and Jim Barnett. The Poffos claimed that the rival promoters prevented them from talent, blacklisted them, and damaged them financially. The ICW pushed forward and remained a strong independent force until 1983. Savage toured Puerto Rico and the Tennessee area before landing a job with the WWF. Appearing with his wife Elizabeth, who he married in 1984, he feuded with Bruno Sammartino, George Steele, and Ricky Steamboat. He beat Tito Santana for the Intercontinental Title on February 8, 1986, but lost it to Steamboat in a classic at WrestleMania III. During the summer of 1987, Savage became a fan favorite and won that year's King of the Ring tournament in September. At WrestleMania IV, he toppled four opponents in another tourney to win the vacant WWF World Heavyweight Title.

Jealousy over Elizabeth broke up the "Mega Powers" tag team he had formed with Hulk Hogan, and the two feuded until April 2, 1989 at WrestleMania V, when Hogan beat him for the belt. Now a rule-breaker, Savage partnered up with "Sensational" Sherri Martel and beat Jim Duggan to become "King" of the WWF. Three years later, he once again became World champion with a victory over Ric Flair at WrestleMania VIII, but lost it back to Flair that September. Savage divided his time as a wrestler and commentator until leaving the WWF in November of 1994. Only weeks later, he emerged in WCW, which had signed Hogan earlier in the year and once again feuded with Flair. He won the three-ring, 60-man battle royal known as "World War III" and captured the vacant WCW World Title on November 26, 1995. Flair beat him for the belt at Starrcade in December, but Savage regained it on January 22, 1996 with some unexpected help from Arn Anderson.

Flair beat Randy again on February 11 at SuperBrawl, this time in a cage match. On April 19, 1998 in Denver, Savage dethroned Sting for the WCW Title at Spring Stampede with interference from both Hollywood Hogan and Kevin Nash. The next day at the World Arena in Colorado Springs, Hogan defeated him and took the WCW Title. He had another single-day reign as titleholder beginning on July 11, 1999, when he won the title during a tag team match with Sid Vicious against champion Nash and Sting. Hogan again ended his title run the next day on *Nitro*. In 2002, Savage appeared in the box office hit *Spider-Man* as Bone Saw McGraw. He was also in several programs including *Mad About You; Baywatch; Arli$$, Walker, Texas Ranger; and Nikki*. To those outside of the wrestling world, Savage was known as the spokesman for Slim Jim. Other than a few appearances in TNA in 2004, Savage remained retired for the last decade of his life. He died tragically in a car accident in May 2011 at the age of fifty-eight.

Born:	August 27, 1948
Height:	6'6"
Weight:	290
Real Name:	Robert Rudolph Remus
Parents:	Rudolph and Florence Remus
High School:	Eden Prairie High School (MN)
Identities:	Bob Slaughter, Super Destroyer Mark II
Finisher:	Cobra Clutch
Groups:	Sgt. Slaughter's Army (1982-1983), The Triangle of Terror (1990-1991), The Corporation (1998)
Career Span:	1974-2011

Sgt. Slaughter

PPV Record:	5-7
WrestleMania Record:	1-2
WWE *Raw* TV Record:	1-9, 1 NC
WWE *Smackdown* TV Record:	0-1
Titles Won:	13
Days as World Champion:	64
Age at first World Title Win:	42
Best Opponents:	Bob Backlund, Hulk Hogan, Ric Flair
Halls of Fame:	1

Sgt. Slaughter was an extraordinary wrestling hero; a man who transcended the business with his immense popularity and becoming the real life inspiration for a G.I. Joe character. He grew up in Minnesota and served in the Marines prior to learning the ropes at Verne Gagne's camp in Chanhassen. In 1974, he made his debut and toured several territories as "Bruiser" Bob Remus. He gained success in the Central States and the WWF, and beat Ricky Steamboat for the vacant U.S. Title in the Mid-Atlantic region on October 4, 1981. A few years later, he became one of the most admired and recognizable pro wrestlers in the world. He promoted American patriotism and chants of "USA" were commonplace during his matches. That changed in 1990 when his character supported Iraq during the first Gulf War, and in January 1991, he beat the Ultimate Warrior for the WWF World Title. He regained his fan support and worked numerous roles in the WWE, including as commissioner and wrestled on *Raw* as recently as July of 2011.

Born:	May 16, 1921
Height:	5′9″
Weight:	230
Real Name:	Robert Kinji Shibuya
Parents:	Kinkichi and Kura Shibuya
Trained by:	Tetsuo "Rubberman" Higami
Identities:	Mr. Hito
Career Span:	1952-1975
Died:	May 3, 2010, Hayward, CA 88 years old

Titles Won:	22
Best Opponents:	Ray Stevens, Pepper Gomez, Dory Funk Jr.
Movies:	3
TV Appearances:	3

Shibuya, Kinji

Fondly remembered for his ruthless style inside the ring and his gentlemanly attitude out, Kinji Shibuya was a multitalented athlete. He was a standout high school and collegiate football player, starting guard at the University of Hawaii, and was convinced by Honolulu promoter Al Karasick to give pro wrestling a shot. He traveled across North America and developed a strong heel persona while in Minneapolis that helped him become a top box office attraction in the Bay Area in the 1960s and 1970s. Until his retirement in 1974, he drew extraordinary heat from crowds and knew how to push the right buttons to attain a powerful reaction. Shibuya held the San Francisco version of U.S. Title and World Tag Team championship three times each.

Photo Courtesy of Pete Lederberg—plmathfoto@hotmail.com

Born:	April 5, 1945
Height:	6'2"
Weight:	315
Real Name:	Leati Sika Anoai
Parents:	Amituanai and Tovale Anoai
Trained by:	Afa Anoai, Jerry Monti, Stu Hart
Career Span:	1973-2006

Sika

Titles Won:	19
Best Opponents:	Hulk Hogan, Bob Backlund, Jimmy Snuka
Halls of Fame:	2

Sika and his older brother Afa joined their "uncle" Peter Maivia in fostering a wonderful legacy for Samoans in professional wrestling. The trio of Hall of Famers were followed by relatives Yokozuna, Rikishi, and The Rock, as well as Sika's two sons, Matt and Joe, who are also involved in the business. The Wild Samoans, as Sika and Afa were known, won over a dozen regional and world tag team championships and their teamwork and timing were exemplary. As mammoth heels, they were intimidating to the utmost degree, and their coordinated attack not only left welts on opponents, but made an indelible mark on audiences around the globe.

Photo Courtesy of Pete Lederberg—plmathfoto@hotmail.com

Born:	May 19, 1951
Height:	6'1"
Weight:	240
Real Name:	Richard Van Slater
High School:	Robinson High School (FL)
College:	University of Tampa
Trained by:	Hiro Matsuda, Eddie Graham, Jack Brisco
Career Span:	1972-1996

Titles Won:	42
Days as World Champion:	391
Age at first World Title Win:	43
Best Opponents:	Ricky Steamboat, Ric Flair, Jack Brisco

Slater, Dick

Tampa roughneck Dick Slater was part of an exciting new crop of young talent coming out of the area in the early 1970s; a group that included Mike Graham, Steve Keirn, and later, his college wrestling teammate, Paul Orndorff. With nicknames like "Unpredictable" and "Dirty," Slater was a prototypical brawling heel, but that style mixed with his amateur background made him a standout. He was just as successful as his contemporaries, winning the Missouri Title from Jack Brisco in 1977 and the U.S. Heavyweight belt from Greg Valentine in 1983. He formed a brutal team with Dick Murdoch known as the "Hardliners," and also teamed with Bunkhouse Buck to win the WCW Tag Team Title in 1995. He also held the IWA World Title for over a year in Japan.

Born:	May 18, 1943
Height:	6'0"
Weight:	235
Real Name:	James William Reiher
Family:	Father of Jimmy Snuka Jr., Tamina Snuka
Trained by:	Frankie Laine, Danny Hodge
Identities:	Jimmy Kealoha, Great Snuka, Lani Kealoha
Groups:	The Mid-Atlantic Death Squad (1979-1980)
Tag Team:	The South Pacific Connection w/ Ricky Steamboat
Career Span:	1970-2009

PPV Record:	3-11, 1 DDQ
WrestleMania Record:	0-3
Titles Won:	34
Best Opponents:	Bob Backlund, Don Muraco, Ricky Steamboat
Halls of Fame:	2

Snuka, Jimmy

Seared into the minds of wrestling fans forever is the moment that Fiji Islander Jimmy Snuka launched himself from the top of a Madison Square Garden cage toward a prone WWF champion, Bob Backlund. The June 28, 1982 incident was one of the most dramatic moments in wrestling history, climaxing when Backlund moved at the last moment. Unfortunately for many other wrestlers on different occasions, they didn't have the luxury of moving out of the way, and Snuka landed his "Superfly" splash in spectacular fashion, putting them down for the count. With bodybuilder looks and stunning ring aerodynamics, Snuka proved to be one of the most popular wrestlers in the world throughout his career. He accompanied main eventers Hulk Hogan and Mr. T to the ring at the first WrestleMania in 1985 and returned to battle Chris Jericho in a handicap match at WrestleMania XXV in April of 2009. He was known for wrestling barefoot, and won regional championships in the Mid-Atlantic, Georgia, and Pacific Northwestern territories.

Snyder, Wilbur

Born:	September 15, 1929
Height:	6'2"
Weight:	235
Real Name:	Wilbur E. Snyder
Parents:	Firman and Lola Snyder
High School:	Van Nuys High School (CA)
College:	University of Utah
Pro Sports:	National Football League—Los Angeles Rams (1950-1951) WIFU—Edmonton Eskimos (1951-1953) Canadian Football League—Edmonton Eskimos (1952-1953)
Trained by:	Sandor Szabo
Finisher:	Cobra Twist
Tag Team:	The Young Lions w/ Bobo Brazil
Career Span:	1953-1983
Died:	December 25, 1991, Pompano Beach, FL 62 years old

Titles Won:	45
Days as World Champion:	Around 205
Age at first World Title Win:	29
Best Opponents:	Dick the Bruiser, Hans Schmidt, Verne Gagne

In 1953, the Southern California booking office revealed their newest superstar: an ex-football player named Wilbur Snyder. The fresh-faced giant of an athlete was an instant hit, and video of his matches circulated around the country, earning him a universe of fans who hoped to see him appear live. His legitimate football experience helped cement his push from promoters who sought such credentials in their advertising, and Snyder's charisma and physical ability pushed him over the top. He had two high-profile TV matches with NWA champion Lou Thesz in 1954, which helped expedite his path to superstardom. He would capture the U.S. Heavyweight Title no less than eleven times, the WWA World championship in Indiana, and the World Title in Omaha. In 1964, he partnered with Dick the Bruiser to purchase the Indianapolis promotion and the two launched the successful World Wrestling Association. Snyder remained an important member of the wrestling community, particularly throughout the Midwest, until his retirement in 1983.

Born:	March 24, 1940
Height:	6'4"
Weight	270
Real Name:	Donald Delbert Jardine
Identities:	Sonny Cooper, Super Destroyer
Career Span:	1955-1985
Died:	December 16, 2006, Wetaskiwin, Alberta 66 years old

Titles Won:	41
Days as World Champion:	35
Age at first World Title Win:	29
Best Opponents:	Lou Thesz, Harley Race, Fritz Von Erich

Spoiler, The

In 1955, the wrestling world was invaded by a New Brunswick teenager with the size and athletic coordination to match up against any of the decorated veterans. Taught by veterans Emile Dupre and "Whipper" Billy Watson, Jardine was quickly elevated to featured programs at major arenas in Canada. In the years that followed, he won the Nebraska Title and the World Tag Team belts with Dutch Savage under his real name, then donned a mask in Dallas in the summer of 1967, becoming the frightful Spoiler. From there on, he was an unstoppable heel and captured an abundance of state and regional championships; and in 1969, he held the IWA World Title in Australia for a little more than a month. While in the WWF, he reigned as the National champion after the Georgia promotion was purchased in 1984. Exceptionally influential, aspects of his ring style were adopted by other superstars—including by The Undertaker, who still uses the top-rope walking he learned from Jardine.

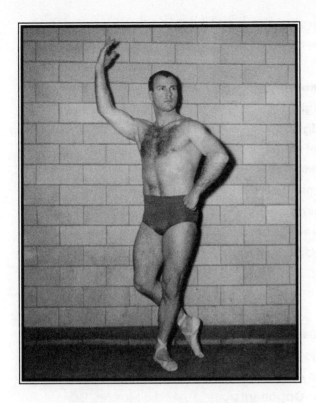

Photo Courtesy of the Pfefer Collection, Department of Special Collections, University of Notre Dame

Born:	1932
Height:	5'9"
Weight:	191
Real Name:	Bernard Herman
Parents:	Joseph and Margy Herman
Family:	Brother of Mark Starr
High School:	Soldan-Blewett High School (MO)
College:	Purdue University
Trained by:	Joe Herman
Career Span:	1952-1974

Titles Won:	3
Best Opponents:	Antonino Rocca, Gorgeous George, Fred Blassie

Starr, Ricki

A ballet performer turned wrestler, Ricki Starr pranced around the ring in pink shoes and displayed an outstanding combination of athleticism and showmanship. Even though his background was in dance, Starr was no slouch in terms of wrestling ability. In fact, he showed well in three National AAU tournaments from 1949 to 1951 and was a disciplined student of the sport in his hometown of St. Louis. He learned from his father, an ex-wrestler, and debuted in Texas in 1952. By the end of the decade, he was one of the biggest attractions in the sport. He spent a majority of the 1960s and 1970s in Europe, and the popular grappler eventually retired to London, where he maintains a quiet life outside of the spotlight he once commanded.

Born:	April 13, 1937
Height:	6'6"
Weight:	280
Real Name:	George Emile Stipich
Trained by:	Yvon Robert
Identities:	Stan Stasiak Jr.
Nicknames:	Stan the Man, Crusher
Career Span:	1958-1984
Died:	June 19, 1997, Portland, OR 60 years old

Titles Won:	29
Days as World Champion:	18
Age at first World Title Win:	33
Best Opponents:	Pedro Morales, Don Leo Jonathan, Bruno Sammartino
Halls of Fame:	1

Stasiak, Stan

Wrestling fans everywhere were saddened when mammoth heel Stan Stasiak dethroned the popular Pedro Morales for the WWWF Heavyweight Title on December 1, 1973 in Philadelphia. But for Stasiak, it was a defining moment in a career lasting twenty-six years. While it was an epic moment for him personally, he was only an interim champion, losing the title to Bruno Sammartino at Madison Square Garden nine days later. Well known throughout the Northeastern circuit, in Texas, and in the Portland territory, Stasiak was a powerhouse heel and his devastating heart punch was a frightening finisher. In Australia in 1970, he held the IWA World Heavyweight Title and captured the Pacific Northwest Title six times. Although he was occasionally billed as the son of the original Stanley Stasiak from the 1920s and 1930s, he had no relation. He passed away in June 1997 at the age of sixty. His son Shawn also became a professional wrestler.

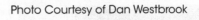

Born:	May 4, 1934
Height:	6'0"
Weight:	225
Real Name:	Samuel Kauaawa Mokuahi Jr.
High School:	Roosevelt High School (HI)
Trained by:	Lou Thesz
Career Span:	1956-1978
Died:	May 2, 2006, Honolulu, HI
	71 years old

Titles Won:	23
Best Opponents:	Don Leo Jonathan, Giant Baba, Gene Kiniski

Steamboat, Sam

The immensely popular Sam Steamboat was a longtime hero of fans throughout the territorial system, and particularly in his native Hawaii. In high school and at Weber College in Utah, he was a talented lineman in football and NWA champion Lou Thesz was credited with discovering him. In Texas and the Mid-Atlantic region, he was commonly seen battling the crooked villains, but he gained his biggest fame in Florida. He teamed with Eddie Graham to win the World Tag Team Title three times in the "Sunshine State," and captured the belts two additional times with Jose Lothario and Ronnie Etchison. Steamboat and Graham were also champions in Georgia and Florida. In Hawaii, he held the state championship twice and the North American crown on four occasions.

Born:	April 16, 1937
Height:	6'2"
Weight:	285
Real Name:	William James Myers
Trained by:	Bert Rubi, Gino Brito
College:	Michigan State University
Identities:	The Student (masked)
Groups:	The Oddities (1998)
Career Span:	1963-2000
Website:	www.georgesteele.com

PPV Record:	0-3
WrestleMania Record:	0-2
WWE *Raw* TV Record:	0-1
Titles Won:	2
Best Opponents:	Bruno Sammartino, The Sheik, Gorilla Monsoon
Halls of Fame:	3

Steele, George

George "The Animal" Steele was a memorable character of the wrestling ring. As his nickname implied, he acted much like an untamed beast, creating carnage wherever he appeared. Steele would take time out of a match to chew on a nearby turnbuckle or blast his foes with a foreign object. When he wasn't an unabashed wildman performing his gimmick, he was calm, articulate, and demonstrated his level of education. In fact, he was a teacher for more than twenty years, only wrestling part-time for the extra money. Originally from Michigan, Steele entered the WWWF and was a strong challenger to Bruno Sammartino's World Title in the late 1960s. He is often remembered for his wanton displays of affection toward Miss Elizabeth in the WWF in the late 1980s. Steele even appeared in film, performing the role of Tor Johnson in the Tim Burton classic, *Ed Wood*. Retired to Cocoa Beach, Florida, he still makes the occasional wrestling appearance as a manager.

Born:	September 28, 1933
Height:	6'1"
Weight:	220
Real Name:	Richard Steinborn
Family:	Brother-in-law of Jerry Oates
Trained by:	Milo Steinborn
Identities:	Dickie Gunkel, Mr. High, Mr. Wrestling, White Knight
Career Span:	1951-1984

Titles Won:	34
Days as World Champion:	7
Age at first World Title Win:	29
Best Opponents:	Buddy Rogers, Lou Thesz, Killer Kowalski

Steinborn, Dick

Started in the pro ring at seventeen years of age, Dick Steinborn, the son of strongman Milo Steinborn, was destined for greatness; and during his three-decade career, he won championships in at least nine different territories. A former amateur grappler, he was a legitimate force to be reckoned with on the mat, and crowds applauded his ring work in every city he wrestled. Steinborn toured the U.S. endlessly and also worked Puerto Rico, Canada, and Australia. In 1962, he teamed with Doug Gilbert to win the AWA World Tag Team belts and the following year he briefly wore the Georgia version of the World Heavyweight crown, as well as also holding the Southern and Texas Titles.

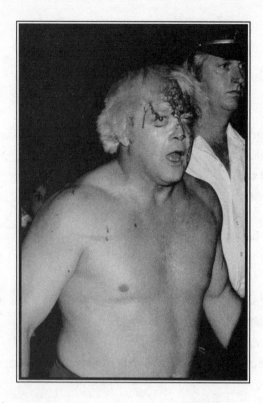

Born:	September 5, 1935
Height:	5'11"
Weight:	235
Real Name:	Carl Raymond Stevens
High School:	North High School (OH)
Trained by:	Bill Miller, Buddy Rogers, Roy Shire
Identities:	Ray Shire
Tag Team:	The Blond Bombers w/ Pat Patterson
Career Span:	1952-1988
Died:	May 3, 1996, Fremont, CA 61 years old

Titles Won:	41
Days as World Champion:	Unknown
Age at first World Title Claim:	26
Best Opponents:	Bruno Sammartino, Pepper Gomez, Bob Ellis
Halls of Fame:	2

Stevens, Ray

A football player in high school, Ray Stevens got the attention of influential promoter Al Haft and made his wrestling debut in Columbus. He was touted as a future superstar in his rookie year, and lived up to all expectations. He morphed into "The Crippler," an influential heel grappler, and teamed with faux brothers Roy Shire and Don Fargo. He was briefly billed as the world champion in Los Angeles in 1961, and six years later, defeated Bruno Sammartino by countout in San Francisco to claim the WWWF World Title. Aside from all of his singles achievements, Stevens was one of the most successful tag team wrestlers of all time. He won World Titles with Shire, Nick Bockwinkel, Pat Patterson, Peter Maivia, and others. His "Bombs Away" kneedrop from the top rope was a stunning finisher that always had devastating results. With all of his talents as a wrestler, Stevens never rose above being willing to help younger wrestlers, and lived life to the fullest. For a period in wrestling history, arguably, there was no better pro in the business than Ray Stevens.

Sullivan, Kevin

Born:	October 26, 1949
Height:	5'11"
Weight:	250
Real Name:	Kevin Francis Sullivan
Family:	Brother of David Sullivan, ex-husband of Woman
College:	Boston University
Identities:	Kevin Caldwell, Lucifer, The Taskmaster
Nicknames:	Games Master
Groups:	The Varsity Club (1988-1989, 1999), Sullivan's Slaughterhouse (1990) Dungeon of Doom (1994-1995)
Tag Team:	Butch Cassidy and the Sundance Kid w/ Mike Graham
Managed:	The Purple Haze (1983-1984), Elijah Akeem (1983), Kareem Muhammad (1983), Buzz Sawyer (1984), The Lock (1984), Fallen Angel (1984), Oliver Humperdink (1984), Billy Graham (1984), Mike Davis (1984), The Aug (1984), The Chairman of the Board (1984), Kharma (1984), Jim Duggan (1984), Angel Vachon (1984), Abdullah the Butcher (1990), Cactus Jack (1990), Black Blood (1991), Zodiac (1994-1995), Meng (1995), Kamala (1995), Barbarian (1995), The Giant (1995), The Shark (1995)
Career Span:	1970-2009

PPV Record:	7-17, 1 NC
Titles Won:	32
Best Opponents:	Dusty Rhodes, Chris Benoit, Mick Foley

A popular fan favorite, a hated heel, and a creative force behind the scenes, Kevin Sullivan has done it all in the world of professional wrestling. Mostly remembered for his "Prince of Darkness" role that had him leading a pack of Satan worshippers, Sullivan began his career in 1970 after being trained in the Boston area by Ron Hill. He ventured through the Southeastern territories, getting over with crowds, and his stock continued to rise while in the WWWF. Sullivan turned his image around during the early 1980s and, as a commandant of a possessed group of souls, he earned widespread recognition for his gimmick. Sullivan, with his painted face and live snakes, entered a longtime war with hero Dusty Rhodes in Florida, and their matches were full of brutality and bloodshed. In 1997 and again in 2000, he worked as a booker for WCW, and later for the short-lived XWF. Since his retirement, he has operated Froggy's Fitness gym with his wife in the Florida Keys.

Born:	January 6, 1930
Height:	6'1"
Weight:	270
Real Name:	Charles J. Kalani
High School:	Iolani High School (HI)
Colleges:	Weber Junior College, University of Utah
Military:	United States Army (1955-1966)
Career Span:	1966-1980
Died:	August 22, 2000, Lake Forest, CA 70 years old

Titles Won:	30
Days as World Champion:	92
Age at first World Title Win:	36
Best Opponents:	Bruno Sammartino, Pedro Morales, Fritz Von Erich
TV Appearances:	Over 15
Movies:	22

Tanaka, Professor Toru

Professor Tanaka, in addition to being a well-known heel grappler with a menacing presence, was a recognizable actor, having performed in over thirty TV and film projects. Originally from Hawaii, he attended college in Utah, and was a football All-American honorable mention in 1951 as an offensive guard and kicker. He briefly boxed professionally, but his heavyweight stature didn't equate to immediate success. He worked as a policeman in Honolulu, and in the summer of 1954, he was given a tryout with the San Francisco 49ers. With knowledge of martial arts, Tanaka was often billed as a Japanese karate expert on the wrestling circuit. It didn't matter that he wasn't Japanese, but that he filled an important role as an Asian "bad guy" and intimidated crowds with his size wherever he appeared. He won two IWA World Titles in Australia and four WWWF Tag Team Titles with partners Mitsu Arakawa and Mr. Fuji. In 1987, he appeared in the film, *The Running Man*, starring Arnold Schwarzenegger, performing the role of stalker, Subzero.

Born:	April 6, 1927
Height:	6'2"
Weight:	240
Real Name:	Camille Tourville
Parents:	Amedee and Esmeralda Tourville
High School:	Montreal High School
Trained by:	Manuel Cortez, Edouard Carpentier, Dr. Bill Miller
Career Span:	1956-1982
Died:	December 24, 1985, Laurentides Park, Quebec 58 years old

Titles Won:	22
Days as World Champion:	42
Age at first World Title Win:	36
Best Opponents:	Lou Thesz, Bruno Sammartino, Verne Gagne

Tarzan Tyler

The youngest of eight children, Tarzan Tyler was born and raised in the Montreal area, and played football in high school. With expert coaching, he became a grappler under the alias, "Tarzan Tourville," until adopting his more famous name in 1961. He spent a considerable amount of time in Florida and feuded with Jack Brisco and Bob Orton over the Southern and Florida State championships. While wrestling in Atlanta in 1963, he captured the localized version of the world title twice with victories over Eddie Graham and Dick Steinborn. In 1971, he teamed with Luke Graham to hold both the WWWF International and WWWF World Tag Team Titles, becoming the first tandem to be recognized as the latter. He was also a top challenger to champions Bruno Sammartino and Pedro Morales. After his retirement, he managed King Tonga and Masked Superstar in the Montreal promotion, and in 1985, he was killed in a car accident with two others following a wrestling show in Chicoutimi.

Photo Courtesy of Scott Teal/Crowbar Press

Born:	October 28, 1940
Height:	5'10"
Weight:	220
Real Name:	Leslie Alan Malady
High School:	Central High School (OH)
Career Span:	1960-1980

Titles Won:	15
Best Opponents:	Danny Hodge, Hiro Matsuda, Don Curtis
Halls of Fame:	1

Thatcher, Les

Personable Les Thatcher was still a teenager when he left his Cincinnati home for Boston to train at promoter Tony Santos' wrestling camp. He was successful across the circuit, winning an assortment of regional championships and earning the NWA Rookie of the Year trophy in 1967. In November of 1968, he teamed with Dennis Hall to win the World Tag Team belts and became a serious contender to the NWA World Junior Title. Thatcher hung up his boots to work as an announcer, promoter, and booker, and was also an influential trainer at a camp he operated in Ohio. Many superstars have a wealth of knowledge today because of the lessons they learned from Thatcher, and his contributions to the sport will continue to be seen for many years to come.

Born:	January 30, 1924
Height:	6'4"
Weight:	255
Real Name:	Arthur Thomas
Parents:	Alfred and Jessie Thomas
High School:	Madison Vocational School (WI)
Finisher:	Bearhug
Career Span:	1957-1987
Died:	March 20, 2003, Fitchburg, WI
	79 years old

Titles Won:	7
Days as World Champion:	56
Age at first World Title Win:	48
Best Opponents:	Buddy Rogers, Johnny Valentine, Killer Kowalski

Thomas, "Sailor" Art

African American superstar, "Sailor" Art Thomas was the hero to legions of fans over a career lasting twenty-six years. He was born in Arkansas and raised in Madison, Wisconsin, working at the Northland Greyhound garage when he joined the Merchant Marines in 1944. Devoted to weightlifting, he added 25 pounds of muscle mass by 1950, and was one of the most talked-about bodybuilders in the state. Thomas performed public demonstrations of strength, participated in competitions, and caught the eye of promoter, Jimmy Demetral, who tutored him in the art of wrestling. Shortly after his debut, he was booked along the major Kohler-McMahon circuit from Chicago into the northeast, and his imposing size and personality got him over with audiences in cities big and small. He went to war with the likes of Buddy Rogers and The Sheik, and maintained his credibility as a potential champion, even winning a claim to the WWA World Title in the Midwest in 1972. Known as a class act, Thomas left a lasting impression on those who saw him in the ring.

Photo Courtesy of Pete Lederberg—plmathfoto@hotmail.com

Born:	April 29, 1935
Height:	5'9"
Weight:	225
Real Name:	Leslie Thornton
Identities:	Henri Pierlot, Checkmate
Career Span:	1957-1990

Titles Won:	17
Best Opponents:	Ricky Steamboat, Tiger Mask, Tatsumi Fujinami
Halls of Fame:	1

Thornton, Les

The Florida territory was honored by the presence of a man dubbed "The Professional" in 1983; an individual who featured an endless array of submission holds, counters, and exemplified technical savvy in the ring. He was Les Thornton of Salford, Lancashire, England, a former amateur boxer and graduate of Billy Riley's "Snake Pit." Thornton, by that time, had won the NWA World Junior Heavyweight Championship four times and competed around the globe, from Calgary to Sydney. Legend has it that he turned the tables on hooker Stu Hart during one of the latter's well-known stretching sessions. Thornton was a masterful grappler, and fans were treated to his excellent athletic performances until his retirement in 1990.

Photo Courtesy of the Collection of Libnan Ayoub

Born:	April 3, 1944
Height:	6'3"
Weight:	260
Real Name:	Jagjit Singh Hans
Family:	Father of Tiger Ali Singh
Finisher:	Cobra hold
Career Span:	1965-1997

Titles Won:	15
Days as World Champion:	Over 325
Age at first World Title Win:	30
Best Opponents:	Antonio Inoki, The Sheik, Terry Funk

Tiger Jeet Singh

Tiger Jeet Singh of India relocated to Ontario and debuted at Toronto's Maple Leaf Gardens as an understudy of Fred Atkins, who doubled as his interpreter. Singh and Atkins, playing the roles of the heels, formed a successful tag team in 1966. The following year, Singh dethroned Johnny Valentine for the U.S. Heavyweight Title. Singh, in Japan, kick-started a feud with Antonio Inoki, and it garnered huge attention for the sport and his career. A wild man comparable to The Sheik and Abdullah the Butcher, he wrestled many gory matches in the hardcore style and won championships in Australia and Mexico. In the latter country, he was a two-time UWA World Champion, defeating El Canek and Inoki in 1980.

Born:	April 5, 1931
Height:	6'2"
Weight:	245
Identities:	The Coach
Tag Teams:	The Canadian Wrecking Crew w/ Chris Tolos, Big and Little Murder w/Jack McDonald
Managed:	Cactus Jack (1991), Bob Orton Jr. (1991), Mr. Perfect (1991), The Beverly Brothers (1991)
Career Span:	1953-1992
Died:	May 29, 2009, Los Angeles, CA 78 years old

Titles Won:	50
Best Opponents:	Fred Blassie, Killer Kowalski, Victor Rivera
Halls of Fame:	1

Tolos, John

Known as the "Golden Greek," John Tolos was a fantastically talented wrestler, combining a sincere wrestling ability with the personality traits that made him a superstar. Originally from Hamilton, Ontario, he and his older brother Chris trained at a local YMCA under pro wrestler "Wee" Willie Davis in the early 1950s. Within a short period of time, the Tolos Brothers were headlining throughout North America; and by the end of the decade, were appearing on the biggest stage in all the land, Madison Square Garden. They were villainous yet multi-faceted, and delighted as many fans as they repelled. Their toughness was spelled out on the foreheads of their opponents and they collected championship belts in several territories. As a singles wrestler, John was just as successful, winning the Americas Heavyweight Title nine times in the Los Angeles territory. His bloody feud with Fred Blassie culminated in a $142,000 box office gate in 1971. Other matches against Victor Rivera, Rocky Johnson, and the Sheik are still fondly remembered.

Born:	March 25, 1951
Height:	6'3"
Weight:	260
Real Name:	Tomomi Tsuruta
High School:	Hikawa High School (Japan)
College:	Chuo University
Olympics:	Greco-Roman Wrestling (1972) (Representing Japan) (7th Place)
Career Span:	1973-1999
Died:	May 13, 2000, Philippines 49 years old

Tsuruta, Jumbo

Titles Won:	33
Days as World Champion:	659
Age at first World Title Win:	32
Best Opponents:	Mitsuharu Misawa, Genichiro Tenryu, Riki Choshu
Tournament Wins:	7
Halls of Fame:	1

Born in Yamanashi, Tsuruta was a Japanese amateur wrestling great and Olympian. He was guided into the professional ranks by Giant Baba and trained extensively under the Funk Brothers. In Amarillo on March 24, 1973, he made his debut, launching a hall-of-fame career that lasted nearly twenty-six years. Tsuruta was a fan favorite for a majority of his career, earning the respect of his peers and people across the globe. Highly decorated and still celebrated, he is on a very short list for best wrestler of the 1980s, winning the AWA World Heavyweight Title from Nick Bockwinkel on February 22, 1984 and the initial AJPW Unified Triple Crown in April of 1989 with a defeat over Stan Hansen. During the early 1990s, his matches with Mitsuharu Misawa were considered some of the best in the business. He also formed legendary tag teams with Genichiro Tenryu and Yoshiaki Yatsu.

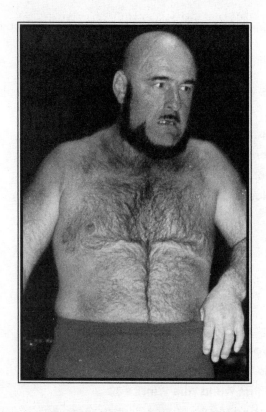

Born:	September 14, 1929
Height:	5'7"
Weight:	235
Parents:	Ferdinand and Marguerite Vachon
Family:	Brother of Paul and Vivian Vachon, uncle of Luna Vachon
Trained by:	Frank Saxon, Jim Cowley
Finisher:	Piledriver, Backbreaker
Career Span:	1952-1986

Titles Won:	34
Days as World Champion:	785
Age at first World Title Win:	34
Best Opponents:	Verne Gagne, Dick the Bruiser, The Crusher
Halls of Fame:	4

Vachon, Maurice

Successful amateur and pro wrestler, "Mad Dog" Maurice Vachon was a six-time World Heavyweight Champion. One of thirteen children born in Quebec, he trained at the Central YMCA in Montreal with brothers Paul, Guy, and Regis. Maurice made the national squad going to the 1948 Olympics and placed seventh at 174 pounds. As an amateur, Vachon collected a number of honors, including the 1950 British Empire middleweight crown. He turned pro in 1952, and was known for his shaved head and distinct beard. On May 2, 1964, he beat Verne Gagne for the AWA World Title, the first of five reigns for him between 1964 and 1967. Along with his brother Paul, he won the AWA Tag Team Title in 1969 from Bruiser and Crusher, and they remained champs until 1971. Vachon surprised many when he teamed with Gagne, his longtime archenemy, to win the AWA belts from Pat Patterson and Ray Stevens. He also held regional championships in Texas, Georgia, and Pacific Northwest.

Born:	September 20, 1950
Height:	6'0"
Weight:	245
Real Name:	John Anthony Wisniski
Identities:	Johnny Fargo, John Fargo, Hiroshima Joe, Johnny Valentine Jr.
Finisher:	Figure-four leglock
Career Span:	1970-2009

PPV Record:	6-16
WrestleMania Record:	2-5
Titles Won:	38
Best Opponents:	Roddy Piper, Ric Flair, Tito Santana
Halls of Fame:	1

Valentine, Greg

Greg "The Hammer" Valentine was a talented and successful second generation wrestler. As the son of Johnny Valentine, Greg possessed many of the qualities his father had made famous, and was a hard-hitting rule-breaker with trademark blond hair. He debuted in Canada after training under Stu Hart and developed further under the guidance of The Sheik in Detroit. In 1979, he was a top challenger to Bob Backlund's WWF Title and nearly won the belt on several occasions. He had a vicious feud with Roddy Piper in the Mid-Atlantic territory and held the U.S. crown twice and the World Tag Team Title four times. Back in the WWF, he captured the Intercontinental Title from Tito Santana in 1984 and wore the tag team belts with Brutus Beefcake. In 1989-1990, he had a memorable war with Ronnie Garvin and formed a comical team with the Honky Tonk Man, known as Rhythm and Blues. In 2009, he suffered a serious injury at a Chicago independent show and only occasionally wrestles today. The WWE inducted him into its Hall of Fame in 2004.

Born:	August 6, 1942
Height:	6'2"
Weight:	270
Real Name:	James Harold Fanning
High School:	Hammond Technical High School (IN)
Identities:	Jim Vallen, Jimmy Valentine, Charlie Brown
Nicknames:	Handsome
Career Span:	1964-2005

PPV Record:	1-0
Titles Won:	29
Days as World Champion:	Around 21 (WWA reign unknown length)
Age at first World Title Win:	Around 32
Best Opponents:	Jerry Lawler, Johnny Valentine, Jack Brisco
Halls of Fame:	1
Published Books:	1

Valiant, Jimmy

Entertaining for many reasons, Jimmy Valiant was an unorthodox performer and his style was unique all to himself. Needless to say, there was never a dull moment around him; from his days as one-half of the Valiant Brothers to his time as the popular "Boogie Woogie Man," he was a superstar who exuded charisma. From Hammond, Indiana, he was trained by Frank Zela, and took the name "Valiant" in Dallas in 1970. He partnered with John L. Sullivan, who became "Johnny Valiant," and the rule-breaking "brother" duo won championships across the U.S. On May 8, 1974, they won the WWWF World Tag Team Title under the guidance of Lou Albano, and held the belts for over a year. Valiant was also a World champion in the WWA and USWA. The Valiants were inducted into the WWF Hall of Fame in 1996.

Born:	July 15, 1951
Height:	6'3"
Weight:	245
Real Name:	James George Janos
Parents:	George and Bernice Janos
High School:	Roosevelt Senior High School (MN)
College:	North Hennepin Community College
Military:	United States Navy (1969-1973) (SEALs)
Trained by:	Eddie Sharkey
Nickname:	The Body
Career:	1975-1984

Titles Won:	7
Best Opponents:	Bob Backlund, Andre the Giant, Hulk Hogan
Halls of Fame:	1

Ventura, Jesse

A colorful athlete and television commentator, Jesse "The Body" Ventura left an indelible mark on the world of professional wrestling. In recent years, however, he's been committed to another realm of the sometimes unbelievable: American politics. Nowadays, most people have forgotten that he was even a wrestler at all, but his fans still enjoy the memories of him strutting around the ring—everlastingly confident—wearing his trademark feather boa. He was a multiple-time regional champion and one of his greatest moments came when he won the AWA World Tag Team Title on July 20, 1980 as part of the East-West Connection with Adrian Adonis. Ventura was physically imposing, using his brute strength to batter opponents, and was a top-notch brawler. Ventura and Adonis were champions for almost a year, losing the straps to Greg Gagne and Jim Brunzell on June 14, 1981. In the WWF, he was a serious challenger to Bob Backlund's heavyweight championship.

Ventura rechanneled his energy behind the microphone, where he was truly gifted. His ability to commentate added a unique spice to even the most ordinary bouts, and his chemistry alongside Gorilla Monsoon and Vince McMahon was extraordinary. Mostly pro rule-breaker, Ventura's quick wit and unconventional statements were sometimes out-and-out hilarious, especially with Monsoon and McMahon playing the straight man. Featured on *Saturday Night's Main Event* and WWF pay-per-views until 1990, Ventura spent some time in WCW, and appeared in a number of popular movies as an actor, including *The Running Man* and *Predator*. In 1991, Ventura was elected the mayor of Brooklyn Park, Minnesota, and became the 38th Governor of Minnesota in 1998 as a Reform Party Candidate. He made several wrestling appearances, and worked as a broadcaster for the short-lived XFL. Since then, he's been all over the media map, discussing politics and other important issues of the day. He's also written several books, including *Don't Start the Revolution Without Me!*, *American Conspiracies*, *63 Documents the Government Doesn't Want You to Read*, and his newest title, *Democrips and Rebloodlicans*.

Born:	October 14, 1946
Height:	6'4"
Weight:	290
Real Name:	Josip B. Peruzovic
Trained by:	Stu Hart, Newton Tattrie
Identities:	Joe Peruzovic, Bepo Mongol, Executioner, Boris Breznikov
Finisher:	Bearhug
Tag Teams:	The Mongols w/ Geto Mongol (Newton Tattrie), The Executioners w/ Killer Kowalski and Big John Studd, The Bolshevicks w/ Boris Zukhov
Career Span:	1967-2006

PPV Record:	3-11
WrestleMania Record:	2-4
Titles Won:	8
Best Opponents:	Bruno Sammartino, Hulk Hogan, Sgt. Slaughter
Halls of Fame:	1

Volkoff, Nikolai

A Yugoslavian weightlifter before turning pro wrestler, Volkoff reportedly once bench-pressed 500 pounds. He teamed with several partners to win the WWWF Tag Team Title, among them Geto Mongol, Masked Executioners (Killer Kowalski and Big John Studd), and the Iron Sheik. Around 1974, Volkoff was a strong challenger to Bruno Sammartino's WWWF heavyweight belt. Known for his anti-American gimmick, Volkoff regularly sang the Russian National Anthem before matches. That persona changed during the first Gulf War in 1990-1991 as a counter to Sgt. Slaughter, turning rule-breaker. Volkoff became an ardent U.S. supporter, and at the 1990 Survivor Series, led the popular team of Tito Santana and the Bushwhackers against Slaughter's Mercenaries. In the mid-1990s, he was lured into the Million Dollar Corporation and put into awkward and embarrassing situations by the group's rich manager, Ted DiBiase. Volkoff was inducted into the WWE Hall of Fame in 2005.

Born:	August 16, 1929
Height:	6'5"
Weight:	275
Real Name:	Jack Barton Adkisson
Parents:	Benn and Coren Adkisson
Wife:	Doris Smith Adkisson
Pro Sports:	American Football League— Dallas Texans (early 1950s)
Trained by:	Stu Hart
Nickname:	The Claw, Teutonic Terror
Finisher:	The Clawhold, Prussian Drop
Owned:	Southwest Promotions, Inc. (1966-1987)
Career Span:	1953-1984
Died:	September 10, 1997, Lake Dallas, TX 68 years old

Von Erich, Fritz

Titles Won:	36
Days as World Champion:	67
Age at first World Title Win:	32
Best Opponents:	Verne Gagne, Johnny Valentine, Lou Thesz
Halls of Fame:	4

The Von Erich legacy in wrestling was initiated by Jack Adkisson of Dallas, Texas, and remained strong for the next four decades. Graduating from Crozier Tech High School, Adkisson excelled in football and track. He went on to attend Southern Methodist University and gained a reputation as one of the nation's finest young football stars. In 1953, he made his Dallas Sportatorium wrestling debut, and within two years, was fully engaged in the business, even adopting a lifelong moniker that would impact his entire family and a nation of fans. Adkisson took the name "Fritz Von Erich," capitalizing on the anti-German sentiment after the war. It wasn't long before he was among the most hated wrestlers in the business. With impressive size and strength, he was a premier headliner throughout the territorial system, and seen as a menace to every regional and world heavyweight championship he challenged.

On July 27, 1963, he beat Verne Gagne for both the AWA and Nebraska World Heavyweight Titles. Three years later, he opened Southwest Promotions, Inc, an NWA affiliate, and promoted the Dallas region until December of 1987. He would win the American Heavyweight Title, the main belt of the territory, a total of fifteen times, battling the likes of Johnny Valentine, The Great Malenko, Bruiser Brody, and Ox Baker. A feud with manager Gary Hart's stable gained Von Erich fan support in 1967, ending his long run as a rule-breaker. Von Erich also held the U.S. and North American Titles. Fritz trained his five sons for the wrestling ring and they each made their debuts between 1976 and 1990. Four of them would pass away at a young age, and in 1997, Adkisson was buried next to his sons in Grove Hill Memorial Park in Dallas County. "Beloved Father" was carved onto his plot, as was the name he made famous, "Fritz Von Erich." In 2009, the entire Von Erich family was inducted into the WWE Hall of Fame.

Photo Courtesy of the Collection of Libnan Ayoub

Born:	October 2, 1933
Height:	6'1"
Weight:	250
Real Name:	Walter Paul Sieber
Trained by:	Red Garner
Identities:	Kurt Von Sieber, Baron Von Sieber, Wally Sieber
Career Span:	1954-1979
Died:	July 5, 2009, Kitchener, Ontario 75 years old

Titles Won:	16
Days as World Champion:	174
Age at first World Title Win:	38
Best Opponents:	Killer Kowalski, Bruno Sammartino, Destroyer
Halls of Fame:	1

Von Erich, Waldo

For fans of wrestling's popular heroes, it was bad enough when there was one "Von Erich" roaming the countryside—but in 1958, a second appeared, and was similarly committed to causing mayhem. Waldo Von Erich was really not from Germany as his gimmick implied, but rather from Toronto; and together, the Von Erichs were masters of disaster, winning championships in the Mid-Atlantic and Dallas territories. Waldo, on his own, won the NWF World Heavyweight crown twice, the Canadian championship, and the Texas State belt. During a tour of Australia, he captured the IWA World Tag Title, and not only won the U.S Tag belts while in the WWWF with Gene Kiniski, but was a leading challenger to Bruno Sammartino's World championship.

Born:	July 30, 1940
Height:	6'2"
Weight:	250
Real Name:	James Donald Raschke
High School:	Omaha North High School (NE)
HS Ach.:	Nebraska State Wrestling Title (1958) (HWT)
College:	University of Nebraska
College Ach.:	Big Eight Heavyweight Title (1962)
Olympics:	Qualified for the 1964 U.S. Olympic Wrestling Team (injured)
Military:	United States Army (1963-1965)
Nickname:	The Teuton Terror, The Clawmaster
Managed:	The Powers of Pain (1988)
Career Span:	1966-1993

Von Raschke, Baron

Titles Won:	21
Days as World Champion:	Over 1,004
Age at first World Title Win:	27
Best Opponents:	Verne Gagne, Dick the Bruiser, Edouard Carpentier
Halls of Fame:	3

Master of the clawhold, Baron Von Raschke was originally from Omaha, Nebraska, not Germany, as his gimmick indicated. He was an amateur Greco-Roman sensation, winning the bronze at the World championships in 1963, and a year later, while in the Army, he took home an Interservice title. His size and proven ability were significant factors in his warm reception into pro wrestling, and Verne Gagne took the lead in giving Von Raschke the tools he'd need to be successful. Adopting a pro-German attitude, he was immensely hated throughout the grappling community. In November of 1967, he beat Edouard Carpentier for a claim to the World Title in Montreal. He would win the WWA World Championship three times, and annexed numerous other belts in the AWA and NWA. Von Raschke is enshrined in several different wrestling Halls of Fame, recognizing his remarkable career as an amateur and pro.

Born:	June 13, 1943
Height:	6'2"
Weight:	360
Nicknames:	Big, King, Bulldog
Finisher:	The Steamroller
Promoted:	Catch Wrestling Association (CWA) (1977-2000)
Career Span:	1970-1990

Titles Won:	5
Days as World Champion:	4,015
Age at first World Title Win:	34
Best Opponents:	Antonio Inoki, Andre the Giant, Nick Bockwinkel

Wanz, Otto

Many fans were taken aback by the news that Otto Wanz had dethroned Nick Bockwinkel in St. Paul for the AWA World Heavyweight Title on August 29, 1982. The shock was mostly because Wanz was relatively unknown in the United States, but in his native country of Austria, he was a legend. A former amateur boxing champion, Wanz was awesomely powerful, able to tear a phone book in half, and his giant size made him an imposing figure of the squared circle. Only holding the title for a few months, Wanz dropped the AWA Title back to Bockwinkel on October 9, 1982 in Chicago. He was also a four-time CWA World Champion, defeating Jan Wilkens, Don Leo Jonathan, and Bull Power (Vader) twice. He retired as champion in 1990.

Watts, Bill

Born:	May 5, 1939
Height:	6′3″
Weight:	275
Real Name:	William Frederick Watts Jr.
Parents:	William and Emma Watts
High School:	Putnam City High School (OK)
College:	University of Oklahoma
Pro Sports:	American Football League— Houston Oilers (1961) United Football League— Indianapolis Warriors (1962) National Football League— Minnesota Vikings (1963)
Trained by:	Leroy McGuirk
Career Span:	1961-1993

Titles Won:	25
Best Opponents:	Bruno Sammartino, Harley Race, Lou Thesz
Halls of Fame:	2

The bruising "Cowboy" Bill Watts of Tulsa was a stellar wrestler and one tough customer. He followed up college and professional football with a lengthy career as a grappler, and had the size and grit to be a real success. Only a few years after his debut, he stormed through the northeast territory and was a vicious contender to Bruno Sammartino's WWWF Title—as the two drew huge numbers at Madison Square Garden. He won many regional titles and was a perennial North American champion. Behind the curtain, Watts was a matchmaker for his mentor Leroy McGuirk and, in 1979, branched off to form Mid-South Sports, which staged shows in Louisiana, Oklahoma, and Mississippi. A creative booker, he emphasized the importance of youthful talent on his shows, and pushed Steve Williams, Junkyard Dog, Jim Duggan, and Ted DiBiase early in their careers. Later on, he worked for WCW from 1992-1993. The WWE honored his career by inducting him into its Hall of Fame in 2009. His son Erik was also a wrestler.

Born:	July 28, 1934
Height:	6'0"
Weight:	230
Real Name:	George Burrell Woodin
High School:	Ithaca High School (NY)
College:	Michigan State University
College Ach.:	Two-Time Big Ten Wrestling Champion (1958) (177), (1959) (HWT)
Amateur Titles:	Two-Time AAU National Wrestling Champion (1955, 1957)
Career Span:	1962-1984
Died:	November 30, 2002, Charlotte, NC 68 years old

Titles Won:	24
Best Opponents:	Maurice Vachon, Blackjack Mulligan, Jack Brisco
Halls of Fame:	1

Woods, Tim

Ithaca's wrestling sensation, Tim "Mr. Wrestling" Woods, influenced a generation with his talent and popularity as a masked superstar. An amateur grappler in high school, Woods attended a handful of colleges from Cornell to Oklahoma A&M, and landed at Michigan State, where he won two Big-Ten championships, also placing second in the 1958 and 1959 NCAA tournaments. He began his pro career under the guidance of Bert Rubi in Detroit, wrestling as "Tim Woodin" in 1962. In the years that followed, he appeared throughout the territorial system, and his amateur background served him well. The arrival of "Mr. Wrestling" was a landmark for pro wrestling, and Woods' career vaulted to new highs—particularly in the southeast. He held the United States, Southern, and Georgia Heavyweight Titles, and nearly lifted the AWA World Heavyweight crown from Maurice Vachon in January 1966. He also won the Georgia Tag belts with Mr. Wrestling II three times. In 2001, he was inducted into the Tragos/Thesz Hall of Fame.

Born:	December 5, 1953
Height:	5'11"
Weight:	245
Real Name:	Larry Whistler
Family:	Son-in-Law of Verne Gagne
College:	University of Pittsburgh
Trained by:	Newton Tattrie
Finisher:	Bearhug, Boston Crab
Groups:	The Dangerous Alliance (1992)
Tag Team:	The Enforcers w/ Arn Anderson
Career Span:	1974-Present

Zbyszko, Larry

PPV Record:	8-7, 1 Draw
Titles Won:	15
Days as World Champion:	865
Age at first World Title Win:	35
Best Opponents:	Bruno Sammartino, Mr. Saito, Curt Hennig

Technically savvy with personality to spare, Larry Zbyszko was a cool, calculating heel and held the AWA World Heavyweight Championship twice. Originally from the Pittsburgh area, he stunned many fans when he turned on his mentor, Bruno Sammartino, leading to a historic feud. The payoff was huge, and over 40,000 fans witnessed their steel cage showdown in Shea Stadium on August 9, 1980, with Sammartino winning the match. In 1983, he "purchased" the National Title from Killer Brooks and won the Western States Heritage belt from Barry Windham in 1988. Zbyszko won his first AWA belt when he survived a battle royal on February 7, 1989 and held the crown for more than a year. He traded the title with Mr. Saito, and was the final AWA champion as the promotion folded in 1991. While with WCW, he worked as a TV commentator and won both the World Tag Team Title with Arn Anderson, as well as the TV Title. In 2008, he held the AWA Superstars of Wrestling World championship and still makes appearances across the U.S.

IV. New Legends Are Born: From Hulking Up to the G.T.S.

Pro Debut Between 1976 and Present

The ever-changing wrestling environment kept creative minds on their feet, and the wrestlers themselves had to adapt and adjust their ring personas to keep things fresh. A sudden heel turn for a renowned fan favorite was commonplace, or vice versa, and the flip was a spark enough to recharge an entire territory; of course, depending on the wrestler. Dusty Rhodes and Bob Backlund were among the most favored heroes of the late 1970s, and in the opposite corner were guys like Harley Race, Bruiser Brody, and a relative newcomer to the industry, the "Nature Boy" Ric Flair. Ultra arrogant with ring skills and personality to match, Flair was the standard bearer for technically proficient wrestlers and wore the NWA World Heavyweight championship ten times between 1981 and 1993. In recent years, Flair has performed many different roles in both the WWE and TNA, and is nearing his 40th anniversary in the business.

One of the most influential actions taken by any single individual involved with pro wrestling occurred during the first half of the 1980s, when Vincent Kennedy McMahon began a revolutionary raid on the traditional territories. His World Wrestling Federation (WWF) launched a campaign to "go national," and used television to garner local and national exposure for his creative cast of wrestlers. Directly opposing many old school promoters who were having a tough time upgrading their businesses to fit the times, McMahon's efforts made great headway, and in some places, he bought the entire territory to secure future dominance. Although he was following in the footsteps of his grandfather Jess and father Vincent J. in becoming a promoter, McMahon was doing things that no one had ever attempted before, and he was either going to sink or swim. Needless to say, he found a way for his company to not only survive, but thrive.

Incorporating and utilizing key talent was another major factor in McMahon's push. In addition to Andre the Giant, the Junkyard Dog, Randy Savage, and Roddy Piper, the WWF had the sport's biggest attraction, mega superstar in Hulk Hogan. Coming off a memorable role in *Rocky III* and a stint in the AWA, Hogan was as important to wrestling's remarkable growth as McMahon was, and his popularity was simply stunning. Arenas everywhere exploded on his arrival and as McMahon launched a blitz on the mainstream, annual WrestleMania events and regular pay-per-views, Hogan was the key to his success. World Championship Wrestling (WCW), which was spawned by Jim Crockett Promotions in the Mid-Atlantic region, was the WWF's main competition, and their head-to-head rivalry lasted until 2001 when WCW was purchased by McMahon.

Today, McMahon's World Wrestling Entertainment (WWE) is a publicly traded company that is broadcast in over 145 countries and is the clear leader in the industry. The wrestlers of the WWE continue to build upon the tradition that Bruno Sammartino, Hogan, and their peers established, and current stars

John Cena, CM Punk, and Triple H are as popular as ever. Other promotions like TNA and ROH offer an alternative product and the motivated young blood in pro wrestling are itching to show their talents to possibly one day solidify their place amongst the *Legends of Pro Wrestling*.

Abyss

Born:	October 4, 1969
Height:	6'5"
Weight:	350
Real Name:	Christopher J. Park
High School:	St. Joseph High School (OH)
College:	Ohio University
Trained by:	Roger Ruffin
Identities:	Original Terminator, Justice, King of Pain, Stone Mountain
Nickname:	The Monster
Finisher:	Black Hole Slam
Career Span:	1995-Present

PPV Record:	57-47, 4 NC
Titles Won:	21
Days as World Champion:	56
Age at first World Title Win:	37
Best Opponents:	Sting, Kurt Angle, A.J. Styles

Known as "the masked monster," Abyss has shown time after time that he has an affinity for violent matches with bizarre stipulations. He has always given his all to the wrestling profession, which has included wild bumps in bouts that featured thumbtacks, to barbed wire, and being able to brawl with the best of them. A football player in high school and college, Abyss made a name for himself in Puerto Rico and joined TNA full time in 2003. He engaged in some memorable mat wars against greats like Sabu and Mick Foley, and won the NWA World Heavyweight crown from Sting on November 19, 2006, yet lost the belt to Christian Cage the following January. In 2010, he formed a pact with Hulk Hogan and made a run for TNA champion Rob Van Dam's belt, but was unsuccessful. Known as an intimidating force, he even carried around a board with nails jutting out from all sides, which he referred to as "Janice." In 2011, he captured the TNA TV and X-Division championships and was a sturdy member of Hogan's Immortal group until leaving in October of that year.

Born:	February 10, 1955
Height:	6'1"
Weight:	230
Real Name:	Christopher Adams
Trained by:	Shirley Crabtree
Tag Teams:	The Dynamic Duo w/ Gino Hernandez
Trained:	Steve Austin, Khris Germany
Career Span:	1978-2001
Died:	October 7, 2001, Waxahachie, TX 46 years old

Titles Won:	25
Days as World Champion:	73
Age at first World Title Win:	31
Best Opponents:	Kerry Von Erich, Ric Flair, Jimmy Garvin

Adams, Chris

"Gentleman" Chris Adams was a world-class judo expert (along with his brother Neil), and won many championships in his native England. He switched gears to become a wrestler in 1978, and toured through several regions before finding a regular spot in the Dallas territory. Adams initially started his career as a fan favorite, but shortly became a heel opposite the Von Erichs. He held the American Heavyweight Title four times, and in July 1986, won the WCWA World Title from "Ravishing" Rick Rude. Owner of an impressive superkick, Adams also held various titles, including the Americas championship in Southern California and tag team titles with Gino Hernandez and Terry Taylor.

Born:	September 20, 1958
Height:	6'1"
Weight:	245
Real Name:	Martin Anthony Lunde
Parents:	Gary and Bobbie Lunde
High School:	East Rome High School (GA)
College:	Floyd Junior College
Nicknames:	The Enforcer, Double A
Finisher:	DDT
Groups:	Stud Stable (1983), The Legion of Doom (1983), The Four Horsemen (1986-1989, 1990-1991, 1993, 1996-1997), The Dangerous Alliance (1992)
Tag Teams:	The Brain Busters w/ Tully Blanchard, The Enforcers w/ Larry Zbyszko
Career Span:	1982-1997

Anderson, Arn

PPV Record:	9-30, 1 Draw, 1 DCO, 1 NC
WrestleMania Record:	1-0
Titles Won:	15
Best Opponents:	Ric Flair, Great Muta, Barry Windham

Always cool under pressure, Arn Anderson was a diabolical heel and the backbone of the Four Horsemen, an elite group of wrestlers during the 1980s and '90s. In the ring, it appeared that he was intent on hurting opponents and every move that he made was well thought out in advance. Anderson grew up in Rome, Georgia, and wrestled during his youth, as well as also playing organized baseball and football. Through weight-lifting and rigorous exercise, he increased his size from under 180 pounds to upwards of 230, and trained to be a wrestler under Ted Allen of Cartersville, Georgia. He spent time wrestling in Alabama, where he was known as the masked Super Olympia, and then the Mid-South, before becoming an "Anderson," a well-known family of grapplers, in the Mid-Atlantic territory. With Ole Anderson, he won the National Tag Team Title in 1985 and joined the dominant Horsemen. Arn won the NWA World Tag Title twice with Tully Blanchard and then won the WWF World Tag Team Title in 1989, as well as holding the NWA/WCW World TV Title on four different occasions. In 1997, he had neck surgery and announced his retirement from the sport. Today, he works for the WWE as a producer on *Raw*.

Angle, Kurt

Born:	December 9, 1968
Height:	6'1"
Weight:	232
Real Name:	Kurt Steven Angle
Parents:	David and Jacqueline Angle
Family:	Brother of Eric Angle
High School:	Mt. Lebanon High School (PA)
High School Ach.:	Pennsylvania State Wrestling Title (1987)
College Ach.:	Two-Time NCAA Heavyweight Wrestling Champion (1990, 1992)
Trained by:	Dory Funk Jr. and Dr. Tom Prichard
Finisher:	Olympic Slam, Anklelock Submission
Groups:	Team Angle (2002-2003), Angle Alliance (2007-2008), Main Event Mafia (2008-2009)
WWF Debut:	November 14, 1999, Detroit, MI, Survivor Series (TV Debut)
TNA Debut:	October 19, 2006, Orlando, FL, Interview Segment
Career Span:	1998-Present
College Record:	116-10-2

PPV Record:	69-64, 1 NC
WrestleMania Record:	3-5
WWE *Raw* TV Record:	61-62, 1 Draw, 7 NC
WWE *Smackdown* TV Record:	114-85, 2 Draws, 1 DCO, 2 DDQ, 14 NC
Titles Won:	20
Days as World Champion:	1,083
Age at first World Title Win:	31
Best Opponents:	Chris Benoit, Shawn Michaels, Brock Lesnar
Halls of Fame:	6

Olympic gold medalists are an extreme minority in professional wrestling with only a handful of grapplers ever earning top honors, which include Robin Reed, Russell Vis, John Spellman, Henri DeGlane, and Johan Richthoff. Of this elite grouping of superstar athletes, only one heavyweight with an Olympic gold medal in the freestyle event has transcended the amateur ranks and become a top pro grappler . . . and that is Kurt Angle. Angle, hailing from the suburbs of Pittsburgh, has been a premier superstar since his debut in

1998, initially for the WWF and currently for TNA. He is a twelve-time World champion and participated in many incredible and unforgettable matches. The same determined spirit that carried him through the Olympic experience has pushed him to the heights of pro wrestling, and there have been very few grapplers of his caliber on the trail—and that includes all of history.

Angle's outstanding amateur accomplishments began in high school, where he won a state title in 1987, and then captured a Junior National championship that same year. He went on to Clarion University, and captured two NCAA Titles and added the World Title in 1995. At the 1996 Olympic Games in Atlanta, Angle advanced to the 220-pound freestyle finals despite a severe neck injury and beat Abbas Jadidi of Iran, taking a referee's decision to win the gold medal. While his world-class amateur record didn't guarantee that he'd be a great pro wrestler, Angle adjusted without a problem and was seen to be a natural performer when he debuted for the WWF in 1999. He built a respectable undefeated streak and quickly won both the European and Intercontinental titles. Angle was victorious in the 2000 King of the Ring and headlined his first pay-per-view event in August of 2000 at SummerSlam. Finally, only about a year after his first televised showing, Angle beat The Rock on October 22, 2000, and won his first WWF World Title.

Aside from his in-ring work, Angle displayed plenty of personality, particularly when matched with Steve Austin, and the two had some humorous moments before entering into a bloody feud. On September 23, 2001, in his hometown of Pittsburgh, he won his second WWF Title in a grueling bout against Austin, and after the win, members of his family celebrated in the ring with him. Angle was drafted to *Smackdown* and had a long war with Edge. With some outside help from Brock Lesnar, he pinned Big Show for his third WWE championship on December 15, 2002. The anticipated Angle-Lesnar feud soon started thereafter. Often helped by his "Team Angle" partners, Charlie Haas and Shelton Benjamin, Angle remained the champ, going into WrestleMania XIX on March 30, 2003, but lost the belt to Lesnar. At Vengeance on July 27, he beat Lesnar and Big Show in a three-way bout for his fourth and final WWE Title, but was defeated a second time by Lesnar in a memorable Iron-Man bout in September of that year.

Over the next few years, he served as *Smackdown* General Manager, feuded with the likes of Eddie Guerrero, and had a classic WrestleMania match against Shawn Michaels in 2005. Following a run as World Champion in early 2006 and a stint in ECW, he jumped to TNA in October of 2006. He won the TNA championship on May 13, 2007 over champion Christian Cage and Sting, but because of the controversial finish, the championship was declared vacant. Angle won it again in a King of the Mountain bout on June 17, 2007, and before the end of the month, had added the IWGP championship to his list of credentials with a victory over Lesnar in Tokyo. In August of 2007, he topped Samoa Joe and captured both the TNA X-Division and World Tag-Team Titles, meaning that he held four separate championships at the same time. The two latter belts were lost at No Surrender and Sting won the TNA World Title on October 14, 2007. Angle defeated Sting in a rematch and took the belt back on *Impact* later in the month.

Neck problems were still hampering him, but Angle proved to be a relentless warrior and was fully dedicated to pro wrestling—often working through the pain. At the 2009 Slammiversary event, he won his fourth TNA World championship over champion Mick Foley, A.J. Styles, and Samoa Joe on June 21, 2009. Angle was a leading fan favorite through 2010 and into 2011, and engaged in a lengthy and very personal feud with Jeff Jarrett. Jarrett had married Angle's ex-wife, Karen, and the latter was worked into the storyline conflict. Angle and Jarrett wrestled numerous times, culminating in one final street fight that Angle won. Turning on the fans to join Immortal, he beat Sting for his fifth TNA World Title on August 7, 2011, withstood the challenge of Bobby Roode at Bound for Glory, and then dropped the belt in unexpected fashion to James Storm on October 18. Angle feuded with Storm through the end of 2011.

Animal

Born:	September 12, 1960
Height:	6'1"
Weight:	285
Real Name:	Joseph Michael Laurinaitis
Parents:	Joseph and Lorna Laurinaitis
Family:	Brother of Johnny Ace and The Terminator
Wife:	Julia Laurinaitis
High School:	Irondale High School (MN)
College:	Moorehead State College
Finisher:	Doomsday Device w/ Hawk
Groups:	The Legion of Doom (1983-1984), LOD 2000 (1998)
Career Span:	1982-2007

PPV Record:	27-18, 1 DDQ, 1 NC
WrestleMania Record:	3-0
WWE *Raw* TV Record:	0-2
WWE *Smackdown* TV Record:	12-9
Titles Won:	21
Best Opponents:	Ric Flair, Dusty Rhodes, Arn Anderson
Halls of Fame:	3
Published Books:	1

A twenty-two-year-old Minneapolis power-lifter entered the wrestling profession in 1982 under the guidance of Eddie Sharkey and adopted the signature name, "Animal," while in Georgia along with his friend, Hawk. The two debuted as the "Road Warriors," and were highly influential because of their outstanding display of strength and ferociousness, as well as their intimidating look. In fact, there was no team similar anywhere else in the world. They were the first duo to capture the AWA, NWA, and WWF World Tag Team Titles, and reigned as the AJPW champions in Japan in 1987-1988. All tag teams during the 1980s and 1990s were compared to the Warriors, and their iconic role in history has earned them a spot in several Halls of Fame. In 2001, Animal returned to WCW and challenged Scott Steiner for the World Title. He was also briefly a member of the Magnificent Seven group. Since Hawk's passing in 2003, Animal has appeared in the WWE and TNA in smaller capacities, and in 2011, released his autobiography. His son James is a pro football player for the St. Louis Rams.

Photo Courtesy of Dr. Mike Lano—Wrealano@aol.com

Born:	April 15, 1978
Height:	5'9"
Weight:	215
Real Name:	Daniel Healy Solwold Jr.
High School:	West High School (WI)
College:	Winona State University
Identities:	Austin Starr
Career Span:	2000-Present

PPV Record:	13-18, 1 Draw
Titles Won:	12
Days as World Champion:	419
Age at first World Title Win:	26
Best Opponents:	Samoa Joe, CM Punk, Jerry Lynn

Aries, Austin

Austin Aries burst onto the TNA wrestling scene in 2011, and the X-Division was energized by his slick maneuvers, flashy ring style, and cocky attitude. It actually marked his second stint in the promotion, but after two ROH World Heavyweight Title reigns and an endless string of top performances in matches around the world, Aries was ready to make a serious impact. The former baseball pitcher from Waukesha, Wisconsin broke into the business with friend Justin Leeper, training under Eddie Sharkey in 2000, and garnered considerable success for Ring of Honor out of Philadelphia. With years of experience behind him and moves like the pendulum elbow and brainbuster, plus a wealth of submission holds, Aries is a step away from becoming a mainstream wrestling sensation. He closed out 2011 as the dominant X-Division champion.

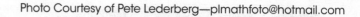

Born:	June 15, 1962
Height:	6'0"
Weight:	225
Real Name:	Robert Bradley James
Parents:	Joseph and Gail James
Family:	Brother of Scott, Steve, and Brian Armstrong
High School:	Wheeler High School (GA)
Trained by:	Bob Armstrong
Identities:	Mr. R., Fantasia, Arachnaman, Mr. K., B.A., Buzzkill
Groups:	No Limit Soldiers (1999)
Tag Teams:	The Lightning Express w/ Tim Horner, White Lightning w/ Tim Horner
Career Span:	1980-Present

Armstrong, Brad

PPV Record:	5-6
Titles Won:	26
Best Opponents:	Ric Flair, Ted DiBiase, Brian Pillman

Talented Brad Armstrong may never have reached his full potential in the wrestling business. He was a celebrated teenage rookie, a second generation star, and there were many high expectations for the Marietta, Georgia athlete. Throughout the southeast, he was adored by fans, and his quickness and mat knowledge were second to none. As he was gaining his wrestling experience, he teamed up many times with his father, Bob Armstrong. In January 1984, he won the National Heavyweight championship under the masked "Mr. R" guise, and then regained it from the Spoiler to begin a second reign. He also captured the MSWA North American Title that year, and along with Tim Horner, won the UWF World Tag-Team Title in 1987. Armstrong captured the WCW World Light Heavyweight Title in 1992, and while in that promotion, he used a variety of gimmicks to include a masked heel, Badstreet, and The Candyman, a hero who gave candy out to ringside youngsters. In 2006, he worked for the revived ECW, and has wrestled for many independent organizations since then.

Photo Courtesy of Dr. Mike Lano—Wrealano@aol.com

Austin, Steve

Born:	December 18, 1964
Height:	6′2″
Weight:	240
Real Name:	Steven James Williams
Parents:	Kenneth and Beverly Williams
High School:	Edna High School (TX)
Colleges:	Wharton Junior College, North Texas State University
Finisher:	Stone Cold Stunner, Stun-Gun Suplex off Ropes, Million Dollar Dream
Managed by:	Jeannie, Lady Blossom, Paul E. Dangerously, Col. Robert Parker, Harley Race, Ted DiBiase
Career Span:	1989-2003

PPV Record:	46-41, 2 Draws, 1 DDQ, 2 NC
WrestleMania Record:	5-2
WWE *Raw* TV Record:	37-16, 11 NC
WWE *Smackdown* TV Record:	15-8, 9 NC
Titles Won:	20
Days as World Champion:	529
Age at first World Title Win:	33
Best Opponents:	Bret Hart, The Rock, Triple H
Halls of Fame:	2
TV Appearances:	over 80
Movies:	8

One of wrestling's greatest all-time attractions, "Stone Cold" Steve Austin ruled the industry during the prime of his career, pushing the envelope of showmanship and delivering record box office and merchandise sales. Although he hung up his boots in 2003, Austin continues to appear on WWE programming in various capacities, as well as in feature films as an action star. His biting personality still captures the attention of audiences and his calculating behavior and beer drinking are still staples of his popular act. During the late 1990s, his rise to prominence helped the WWF shift momentum in the all-important Monday night ratings battle with WCW, and eventually overtook its rivals completely. Austin's image as the unpredictable "Texas Rattlesnake" and his crusade against his crooked boss, Vince McMahon, which the everyman could relate to, pushed him into a spot that no other wrestler in history ever reached, including Hulk Hogan.

A football player in high school and college, he graduated from Chris Adams' wrestling school, and began his career in 1989 at the famed Sportatorium. He wrestled on a circuit between Dallas and Memphis for the

USWA before joining WCW in 1991, and won the TV Title from Bobby Eaton within a few short days of his debut. Known as "Stunning" Steve Austin, he was managed by Lady Blossom and feuded with Dustin Rhodes and Barry Windham. He was a nice fit in Paul E. Dangerously's heel faction, The Dangerous Alliance, and went on to form the Hollywood Blonds, arguably the best tag team in the business, with Brian Pillman. In late 1993, he beat Rhodes to capture the WCW U.S. Title and reigned for eight months. He dropped the belt to Ricky Steamboat on August 24, 1994, but regained it a few weeks later by forfeit when the latter was injured and unable to defend at Fall Brawl. Austin, however, was immediately thrust into a bout with newcomer Jim Duggan, who pinned him in less than a minute.

A triceps injury kept Austin off the mat and he was subsequently let go from WCW. Austin reemerged in ECW and displayed a newfound attitude that lashed out at his former employers. His shoot-style promos were raw and realistic, and with the platform to speak his mind, Austin did so without restraint. The wrestling world took notice, and on December 18, 1995, he made his first showing for the WWF at a TV Taping. Austin was managed by Ted DiBiase and known as "The Ringmaster," which emphasized his technical skills. He also used the "Million Dollar Dream" sleeper as his finisher, but the gimmick didn't last long. By June 1996, he had evolved into "Stone Cold," a wrestler whose aggressiveness and independence were earning as many cheers as boos. He spoke his mind in interviews, displaying his outward anger toward rivals, and utilized the easily applied Stunner as his finisher. His catchphrases caught on with crowds, and his popularity increased measurably within a short amount of time.

Austin entered a feud with Bret Hart that dominated 1997, and their submission match at WrestleMania XIII was historic. The spectacular back-and-forth contest saw Austin win the crowd's favor with an admirable performance, but lost when he passed out to the pressure of a sharpshooter. The war against Hart continued, and was brutally violent at times. That August, he won the Intercontinental belt from Owen Hart, but suffered a serious neck injury in the match and later vacated the title. He beat Owen again in November, but lost the title a month later to Rocky Maivia Jr. In early 1998, he confronted ex-boxing champion Mike Tyson, who was named the special enforcer for Austin's match against Shawn Michaels at WrestleMania XIV. At that show, Austin pinned his foe and captured his first WWF World Title. In the weeks that followed, his private war against Vince McMahon escalated, and on April 13, 1998, their face-off helped *Raw* beat WCW's *Nitro* in the ratings for the first time since the summer of 1996.

Between January and October of 1998, Austin participated in ten straight pay-per-view main events, from special referee to defending as World Champion. He lost his WWF championship to Kane on June 28, 1998, but regained it the next night. On September 27, he was defeated again by both Kane and The Undertaker in a controversial finish that left the title vacated. He entered the 1999 Royal Rumble at number one and McMahon was the second entrant. Shockingly, both were still there at the end, and McMahon scored the victory. They fought in a cage match in February with the winner going to headline at WrestleMania. Austin was victorious in a bloody match after the Big Show interfered. In Philadelphia at WrestleMania XV, he won his third WWF Title from The Rock. He traded the belt with The Undertaker, and then lost it in a three-way bout to Mankind on August 22, 1999. In November of that year, Austin stepped away from the business to have major surgery on his neck and remained away until September 2000.

Austin had a significant feud with Triple H and then won his fifth WWF Title at WrestleMania X-Seven, defeating The Rock. He also turned heel, and formed a surprising alliance with Triple H and McMahon. On October 8, 2001, Austin won his sixth and final WWF belt, defeating Kurt Angle. That December, he was dethroned by Chris Jericho. He had a memorable battle with Booker T in a California grocery store and made the word "What" into a popular catchphrase that is still relevant today. Austin participated in his final match at WrestleMania XIX, losing an epic battle to The Rock. Since that time, in addition to his work as an actor, he's been active as a guest referee, host, and in various other capacities on WWE telecasts. In 2009, he was inducted into the WWE Hall of Fame and in 2011, he was involved in the revived *Tough Enough* series. Despite being off the mat for eight years, the always unruly Austin remains to be one of the most celebrated personalities in wrestling and fans continue to beckon for one more match.

Photo Courtesy of Dr. Mike Lano—Wrealano@aol.com

Born:	September 4, 1977
Height:	5'9"
Weight:	270
Real Name:	Kia Michelle Stevens
High School:	Carson High School (CA)
Trained by:	Jesse Hernandez, All-Japan trainers
Identities:	Amazing Kong, Kharma
Career Span:	2002-Present

PPV Record:	6-13
Titles Won:	13
Days as World Champion:	943
Age at first World Title Win:	26
Best Opponents:	Ayako Hamada, Aja Kong, Gail Kim

Awesome Kong

Awesome Kong, a multiple-time world champion and one of the fiercest women's competitors in the business, entered the WWE in 2011, and her arrival jolted the Divas division. With a look that drastically differed from her peers and an aggressiveness that carried her to gold all over the U.S. and Japan, she was gearing up for a major run when she announced that she had to take a year off because she was pregnant.

Her accomplishments speak for themselves. In 2004, she won the WWWA World Title in Tokyo, and in 2007, she held both the AWA and NWA World championships simultaneously. She was also a TNA Knockout Champion, but her run in that promotion ended in 2010. Powerful and intelligent, Awesome Kong's return to the business is inevitable, and her mark on the rest of the WWE Diva lineup will be historic.

Born:	January 24, 1965
Height:	6'6"
Weight:	290
Real Name:	Michael Lee Alfonso
High School:	King High School (FL)
Nickname:	Mullet
Finisher:	Awesome Bomb
Career Span:	1989-2006
Died:	February 17, 2007, Tampa, FL 42 years old

PPV Record:	14-9, 2 NC
WWE *Raw* TV Record:	2-0, 2 NC
WWE *Smackdown* TV Record:	0-3
Titles Won:	12
Days as World Champion:	840
Age at first World Title Win:	30
Best Opponents:	Masato Tanaka, Taz, Hayabusa

Awesome, Mike

Incredibly strong, Mike Awesome performed a number of unbelievable moves for a man of his size and flattened many opponents with his devastating top rope splash and power-bomb. Awesome played football in high school and entered the sport under the tutelage of Steve Keirn in his hometown of Tampa, Florida. Overseas, in Japan, he wrestled as "The Gladiator" and won the FMW Independent World Title from Kanemura in 1996. He captured the ECW World Heavyweight crown twice in 1999, and departed the organization for WCW while still champion. In June 2001, he won the WWF Hardcore Title, becoming the first of the "invading" WCW employees to win a WWF belt. He also appeared for All-Japan, MLW, and TNA before retiring in 2006.

Photo Courtesy of Dr. Mike Lano—Wrealano@aol.com

Bad News Allen

Born:	October 22, 1943
Height:	6'2"
Weight:	260
Real Name:	Allen James Coage
High School:	Thomas A. Edison High School (NY)
Other Sports:	Fifth degree black belt in Judo, second degree black belt in Aikido
Judo Ach.:	1970 Judo Grand Champion, *Black Belt* magazine Judo Player of the Year (1970, 1977)
Pan-Am Games:	Judo (1967) (Gold Medal), Judo (1975) (Gold Medal)
Trained by:	Antonio Inoki, Stu Hart
Identities:	Buffalo Allen
Finisher:	Ghetto Blaster
Career Span:	1978-1999
Hall of Fame:	Judo Hall of Fame—Inducted in 1990
Died:	March 6, 2007, Calgary, Alberta 63 years old

PPV Record:	2-5, 1 DCO, 1 DDQ
WrestleMania Record:	1-0, 1 DCO, 1 DDQ
Titles Won:	13
Best Opponents:	Bret Hart, Hulk Hogan, Antonio Inoki
Halls of Fame:	1

By the time Bad News Allen became a pro wrestler in the late 1970s, he was already a world-class athlete. He'd won an Olympic medal and appeared in competitions around the world, demonstrating his talent and dexterity in Judo. Allen began his whirlwind Judo training around 1964 and took to it naturally, despite not being an athlete in high school. He was from Queens, New York, and labored as a baker to pay his bills as he advanced into national tournaments. He captured four AAU championships, and then won the bronze medal at the 1976 Olympics. Two years later, he debuted as a wrestler and based on his Judo discipline and profound toughness, he carried with him an aura of distinction that rookies rarely saw. He won a number of titles in Calgary, Florida, California, and Hawaii, and, under the name "Bad News Brown," was a threat to Hulk Hogan's WWF Title in 1989. He also feuded with Roddy Piper, culminating in their infamous match at WrestleMania VI. He continued to appear on the mat sporadically through 1999.

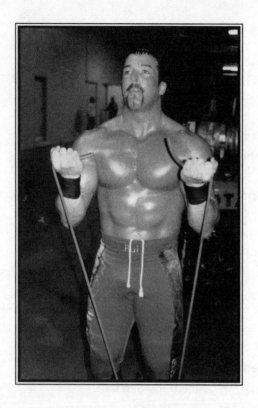

Born:	January 10, 1970
Height:	6'1"
Weight:	235
Real Name:	Marcus Alexander Bagwell
High School:	Sprayberry High School (GA)
Trained by:	Steve Lawler
Identities:	Fabulous Fabian, The Handsome Stranger
Finisher:	Buff Blockbuster
Career Span:	1990-Present

PPV Record:	22-30
WWE *Raw* TV Record:	1 NC
Titles Won:	21
Best Opponents:	Roddy Piper, Lex Luger, Dallas Page

Bagwell, Marcus

In the five years prior to joining the New World Order (NWO) in 1996, Marcus Bagwell was a popular hero. In a way, he represented the next generation of WCW superstars and won the World Tag Team Title on four occasions, twice with The Patriot and once with 2 Cold Scorpio and Scotty Riggs. Bagwell of Marietta, Georgia, adopted a more arrogant gimmick while as a member of the NWO, known as "Buff Bagwell," and teamed with Scott Norton as "Vicious and Delicious." Narrowly escaping a career-ending neck injury, Bagwell returned to the ring and won the WCW World Tag Team Title a fifth time with Shane Douglas in 2000. He wrestled briefly for the WWF in 2001, and outside several TNA appearances, he's been a mainstay on the indie circuit.

Born:	September 1, 1961
Height:	6'3"
Weight:	350
Real Name:	Scott Charles Bigelow
High School:	Neptune High School (NJ)
Identities:	Crusher Yurkof
Nickname:	The Beast from the East
Finisher:	Greetings from Asbury Park
Groups:	The Triple Threat (1997–1998), The New Jersey Triad (1999)
Career Span:	1985-2006
Died:	January 19, 2007, Hudson, FL 45 years old

Bam Bam Bigelow

PPV Record:	15-25
WrestleMania Record:	1-2
Titles Won:	13
Days as World Champion:	45
Age at first World Title Win:	36
Best Opponents:	Taz, Bret Hart, Rob Van Dam
MMA Record:	0-1
Movies:	5

Respected for his toughness and appreciated for his personable attitude, Bam Bam Bigelow was a frightening looking wrestler. His tattooed cranium was a daunting sight to fans as he approached the ring, but Bigelow was a kindhearted man and a genuine hero. In July of 2000, he risked his life to save several children from a dangerous brush fire and suffered burns over 40 percent of his body. Originally from Neptune, New Jersey, he wrestled as an amateur in high school and finished with a 26-1 record as a senior. He graduated from Larry Sharpe's Monster Factory and debuted at Studio 54 in New York City in 1985. Ten years later, he wrestled his biggest match against Hall of Fame linebacker Lawrence Taylor at WrestleMania XI, gaining tremendous national exposure. Bigelow's distinctive look and impressive agility made him a star across the globe and he captured titles in many promotions. In 1997, he beat Shane Douglas for the ECW World Heavyweight belt and also held the IWGP Tag and WCW World Tag Team Titles.

Barrett, Wade

Born:	August 10, 1980
Height:	6′5″
Weight:	260
Real Name:	Stuart Alexander Bennett
High School:	Llanishen High School (Cardiff, Wales)
Trained by:	Jon Richie, Al Snow
Identities:	Stu Sanders
Finisher:	Wasteland
Career Span:	2004-Present

PPV Record:	4-11
WWE *Raw* TV Record:	14-13, 1 DDQ, 2 NC
WWE *Smackdown* TV Record:	11-23, 1 DCO, 3 NC
Titles Won:	4
Best Opponents:	John Cena, Randy Orton, Sheamus

For months in 2010, a group of newcomers known as the Nexus ran rough shot over the WWE. Perpetrating acts of violence on popular stars such as John Cena, the rogue band gained real traction, and its leader, Wade Barrett, was pegged to be the next big thing. Barrett, a youthful athlete from Great Britain, was only six years into his pro career, and had trained in WWE developmentals since 2007. Possessing the size and attitude to be a top-level heel, he was a key figure in the explosive *Raw* debut of Nexus on June 1, 2010, in which the squad destroyed everyone and everything in sight. Barrett's ability to deliver promos advanced the important feud against Cena, which dominated headlines until December. He was also headlining pay-per-view events as a challenger to Randy Orton's WWE Title. Although he was unable to win the belt, he convinced many people that it was just a matter of time. In 2011, he formed a second group, The Corre, and won the Intercontinental Title from Kofi Kingston on March 22, 2011.

Photo Courtesy of Dr. Mike Lano—Wrealano@aol.com

Born:	January 18, 1969
Height:	6'5"
Weight:	275
Real Name:	David Michael Bautista Jr.
Parents:	David and Donna Bautista
High School:	Wakefield High School (VA)
Trained by:	Wild Samoan School, WCW Power Plant, WWE Ohio Valley Territory
Identities:	Kahn, Leviathan, Deacon Batista
Finisher:	Batista Bomb
Groups:	Evolution (2003-2005)
WWE Debut:	May 9, 2002, Bridgeport, CT, Taped *Smackdown*
Career Span:	1999-2010
Website:	www.demon-wrestling.com

Batista

PPV Record:	33-31, 1 DDQ, 1 NC
WrestleMania Record:	3-2
WWE *Raw* TV Record:	74-54, 9 NC
WWE *Smackdown* TV Record:	80-21, 1 Draw, 2 DCO, 10 NC
Titles Won:	11
Days as World Champion:	544
Age at first World Title Win:	36
Best Opponents:	The Undertaker, Triple H, John Cena
TV Appearances:	over 15
Movies:	5

Batista went a long way in a short period of time, and his forceful presence took him from a side role to the main event at WrestleMania. The honor of participating in the last match at the biggest event of the year went to him in 2005 at WrestleMania XXI, and fans saw him beat his former Evolution teammate Triple H for the World Heavyweight Championship. His rise to that position was years in the making, particularly as Batista built his body into a 290-pound mass of muscle. He carried himself with intensity, charisma, and had the look of a WWE superstar. In just three years, he transitioned himself from the bodyguard for Reverend D-Von to the top spot in the company. The Washington, D.C. native reigned as champion for nine months, and was only knocked off his perch when he suffered an injury in January of 2006 and had to step away from the active roster. At the 2006 Survivor Series, he beat Booker T for his second World Title, but was unsuccessful at WrestleMania XXIII, losing the belt to the Undertaker in Detroit.

Batista captured his third of four World Heavyweight Titles from The Great Khali at Unforgiven in September of 2007, winning a three-way bout over the latter and Rey Mysterio Jr. In December of that year;

IV. NEW LEGENDS ARE BORN: FROM HULKING UP TO THE G.T.S.   371

he was dethroned by Edge in Pittsburgh during the Armageddon pay-per-view. He beat Chris Jericho for the championship a final time on October 26, 2008, but lost it back to the former champ a short time later. During the summer of 2009, he took a cage match victory over Randy Orton and won the WWE Title, but had to vacate it again because of an injury. Batista went over John Cena for the WWE Championship a second time on February 21, 2010 when he took advantage of Cena moments after he'd retained his belt in an Elimination Chamber match. Cena had the last laugh, defeating him at WrestleMania XXVI to capture the belt, and taking the match by submission. Batista retired from wrestling a few weeks later and announced his intentions of becoming an MMA fighter. He is active in charities and can be followed on Twitter.

Benjamin, Shelton

Born:	July 9, 1975
Height:	6'2"
Weight:	245
Real Name:	Shelton James Benjamin
High School:	Orangeburg-Wilkinson High School (SC)
HS Ach.:	Two-Time State Wrestling Champion
JC Ach.:	1996 NJCAA Collegiate Champion (HWT)
College Ach.:	Two-Time NCAA Division I All-American
Trained by:	Ohio Valley trainers
Nickname:	The Gold Standard
Finisher:	450 Splash
Tag Teams:	Minnesota Stretching Crew w/ Brock Lesnar
Career Span:	2000-Present

PPV Record:	15-26
WrestleMania Record:	0-6
WWE *Raw* TV Record:	55-76, 3 NC
WWE *Smackdown* TV Record:	36-57, 1 NC
Titles Won:	13
Best Opponents:	Shawn Michaels, Triple H, Chris Jericho

Although amateur and professional wrestling great Shelton Benjamin never broke into a headliner role in the WWE, he demonstrated that he was of a rare breed of high-flying scientific grapplers. He was a standout Intercontinental Champion, which he held three times, and also reigned as the U.S. Titleholder for eight months. A product of the University of Minnesota and the teachings of J. Robinson, Benjamin broke into the business in 2000 and made his WWE TV debut in August of 2002. He joined Charlie Haas as a member of Team Angle and won the WWE Tag Team Title twice. On October 19, 2004 in Milwaukee, he beat Chris Jericho for his first Intercontinental Championship and also took title victories from Ric Flair and Rob Van Dam. He captured the U.S. Title from Matt Hardy on July 20, 2008 and retained the belt through March of 2009. Benjamin left the WWE in April of 2010 and has appeared in Puerto Rico for the WWC and also for Ring of Honor. He reunited with Haas to win the ROH World Tag Title in April of 2011.

Photo Courtesy of Pete Lederberg—plmathfoto@hotmail.com

Benoit, Chris

Born:	May 21, 1967
Height:	5'10"
Weight:	225
Real Name:	Christopher Michael Benoit
Parents:	Michael and Margaret Benoit
High School:	Archbishop O'Leary High School (Edmonton, Alberta)
Trained by:	Stu Hart and the Hart Brothers (Dungeon)
Identities:	The Pegasus Kid, Wild Pegasus
Nicknames:	The Crippler, Canadian Crippler
Finisher:	Flying Headbutt, German Suplex, Crippler Crossface
Groups:	The Four Horsemen (1995-1998), The Revolution (1999), The Radicals (2000)
Career Span:	1985-2007
Died:	June 24, 2007, Fayetteville, GA 40 years old

PPV Record:	54-60
WrestleMania Record:	3-5
WWE *Raw* TV Record:	81-48, 1 DCO, 8 NC
WWE *Smackdown* TV Record:	114-82, 1 Draw, 2 DCO, 2 DDQ, 6 NC
Titles Won:	32
Days as World Champion:	155
Age at first World Title Win:	32
Best Opponents:	Bret Hart, Kurt Angle, Chris Jericho
Halls of Fame:	2

In the wrestling ring, few were better than Chris Benoit. His sound technical abilities made him the favorite of scores of fans throughout the world, but his actions in June of 2007 demolished the respect people had for him and turned a influential life and career into one of horror. There is no getting past the fact that he killed his wife Nancy and seven-year-old son Daniel and all of his mat achievements are secondary to the sad truths of reality. The character of "Chris Benoit," a wrestler, who fans appreciated for his enthusiasm to the craft, always maintained a stoic personality and wrestled with a particular grit that few peers shared. He won world titles in WCW and the WWE, and engaged in many well-received bouts. At times, he was considered to be one of the best in the world. Prior to taking his own life on June 24, 2007, he murdered his wife and son in their suburban Atlanta home, and left the wrestling world in utter disbelief. To this day, it is still hard to comprehend what he did, and the perspective of his rightful place in pro wrestling history will forever be debated.

Photo Courtesy of Dr. Mike Lano—Wrealano@aol.com

Big Bossman, The

Born:	May 2, 1963
Height:	6'6"
Weight:	325
Real Name:	Ray Washington Traylor
Parents:	Ray and Maryland Traylor
Wife:	Angela Traylor
High School:	Paulding County High School (GA)
Trained by:	Ted Allen, Mickey Henry
Identities:	The Boss, The Guardian Angel, Big Bubba
Finisher:	Sidewalk Slam
Career Span:	1985-2004
Died:	September 22, 2004, Acworth, GA 41 years old

PPV Record:	19-35
WrestleMania Record:	5-1
WWE *Raw* TV Record:	10-30, 6 NC
WWE *Smackdown* TV Record:	10-16, 1 DCO, 3 NC
Titles Won:	6
Days as World Champion:	83
Age at first World Title Win:	23
Best Opponents:	Hulk Hogan, Rick Rude, Vader

Known by a variety of names, The Big Bossman was a sizable wrestler with outstanding athletic abilities. He made a dent in the profession shortly after his pro debut in Crockett Promotions as "Bubba Rogers," and won the UWF World Title from One Man King in April of 1987. In the WWF, he adopted the name, "Big Bossman," and was purported to be a prison guard from Cobb County, Georgia. He partnered with One Man Gang, now known as Akeem, as the Twin Towers, and had a memorable *Saturday Night's Main Event* bout against Hulk Hogan and Randy Savage in 1989 that caused the latter duo to break up. In 1993, he joined

WCW and remained there for five years, feuding with the members of the NWO late in his run. He rejoined the WWF in 1998 as a member of the Corporation and won the World Tag Team Title with Ken Shamrock, as well as winning the Hardcore belt four separate times. After leaving the promotion in 2003, he was a dedicated member of the Paulding County, Georgia community, and devoted lots time to charities and other causes.

Photo Courtesy of Dr. Mike Lano—Wrealano@aol.com

Born:	February 14, 1971
Height:	6'7"
Weight:	480
Real Name:	Nelson Lee Frazier Jr.
High School:	Eastern Wayne High School (NC)
Identities:	Nelson Knight, King V
Career Span:	1991-Present

Big Daddy Voodoo

PPV Record:	9-27, 1 DCO
WrestleMania Record:	2-1
WWE *Raw* TV Record:	15-35, 6 NC
WWE *Smackdown* TV Record:	7-14, 3 NC
Titles Won:	12
Best Opponents:	The Undertaker, Big Show, Kane
Movies:	2

Full of charisma, agile, and, not to mention weighing a monstrous 400-plus pounds, Big Daddy Voodoo is known by a variety of names, but is still the same powerful wrestler that has entertained audiences since the early 1990s. Taught by the famed Gene Anderson, Big Daddy of Goldsboro, North Carolina wrestled in the PWF and USWA, until he debuted in the WWF as "Mabel," along with "Mo," as the tag team, Men on a Mission, in 1993. The duo briefly held the World Tag Team Title during a tour of England in March of 1994. Since then, he's undergone several gimmick changes, including "Viscera" and "Big Daddy V." Among his other honors are victories in the 1995 King of the Ring tournament and the WWC Universal championship in Puerto Rico.

Born:	February 8, 1972
Height:	7'0"
Weight:	450
Real Name:	Paul Donald Wight Jr.
Parents:	Paul and Dorothy Wight
High School:	Wyman King Academy (SC)
Finisher:	Chokeslam
Tag Team:	ShowMiz w/ The Miz
Groups:	The Dungeon of Doom (1995-1996), New World Order (1996, 1997), The Union (1999), New World Order (2002)
Career Span:	1994-Present

Big Show, The

PPV Record:	57-78, 3 NC
WrestleMania Record:	3-8
WWE *Raw* TV Record:	114-91, 2 DCO, 19 NC
WWE *Smackdown* TV Record:	137-67, 1 Draw, 3 DCO, 1 DDQ, 21 NC
Titles Won:	21
Days as World Champion:	348
Age at first World Title Win:	23
Best Opponents:	Brock Lesnar, John Cena, Hulk Hogan
TV Appearances:	over 30
Movies:	7

When The Big Show was twelve years of age, he already stood 6'4" and was still growing. Today, he measures around the seven foot mark and weighs more than 400 pounds. In terms of size, he is this generation's Andre the Giant, and has thrived in the industry since 1995 with explosive charisma and impressive agility. An all-around athlete in high school, he was recruited by colleges around the nation and decided that he wanted to play basketball for Wichita State. He spent his freshman year at Northern Oklahoma Junior College and had a good season, making the All-Division first team, and then transferring to Wichita the following year. However, the death of his father and the departure of his coach made things rough on him, and he only averaged two points a game. He finished up at Southern Illinois and returned to Wichita, where he held down a number of different occupations, including as a club bouncer. He met Hulk Hogan at a charity event and, with the prospect of wrestling full time, attended WCW's Power Plant in Atlanta.

Using the name "The Giant," Show beat Hulk Hogan by DQ and won the WCW World Title on October 29, 1995. The belt was stripped from him on November 6 and declared vacant due to the controversy of his match with Hogan. He regained the title on April 22, 1996 when he beat Ric Flair on

Nitro and was champion until August 10, suffering a loss to Hogan. Before departing WCW in early 1999, he also held the WCW World Tag Team Title twice with partners Sting and Scott Hall. Defecting to the WWF, he made a high-profile debut on February 14, 1999 during Vince McMahon's cage match with Steve Austin. He feuded with Mankind and teamed with The Undertaker to win the WWF Tag Team Title twice. Show was a late substitution for the injured Steve Austin in a three-way bout against champion Triple H and The Rock on November 14, 1999, and ended the night as the new WWF World titleholder. His first reign ended on January 3, 2000 when he lost a bout to Triple H on *Raw*.

Show beat Brock Lesnar to win his second WWF Title on November 17, 2002, and Kurt Angle took the strap at Armageddon the following month. In October of 2003, he won the U.S. Title from Eddie Guerrero, and partnered with Kane in 2005 to hold the World Tag Team Title for five months. The ECW World Title was the prize for his July 4, 2006 win over Rob Van Dam, and the conquest made him the first man to capture a WWE, WCW, and ECW belt. He participated in a boxer vs. wrestler match against the 5'8" Floyd Mayweather Jr. at WrestleMania XXIV, and was defeated after the latter employed the use of brass knuckles. Since that time, he won tag team championships with Chris Jericho, The Miz, and Kane, and in 2011, he found himself in an increasingly violent war with the powerful Mark Henry—one that left him injured for several months. In December, he finally gained revenge on Henry, winning the World Title, but only to lose it to Daniel Bryan moments later after the latter cashed in his Money in the Bank briefcase.

Photo Courtesy of Dr. Mike Lano—Wrealano@aol.com

Born:	March 1, 1965
Height:	6'3"
Weight:	250
Real Name:	Booker Tio Huffman
Parents:	Booker and Rosa Huffman
High School:	Yates High School (TX)
Trained by:	Scott Casey
Identities:	G.I. Bro, Kole
Finisher:	Spinaroonie into an Axe-Kick, Book End, Missile Drop Kick
Groups:	The New Blood (2000), The Alliance (2001), New World Order (2002)
Tag Teams:	The Black Bombers w/ Stevie Ray, The Ebony Experience w/ Stevie Ray, The Harlem Heat w/ Kane
Career Span:	1989-Present
Wrestling School:	Pro Wrestling Academy (2005-Present) (Houston)
Website:	www.bookertonline.com

Booker T

PPV Record:	59-72, 1 DC, 1 DDQ, 1 NC
WrestleMania Record:	1-4
WWE *Raw* TV Record:	76-48, 5 NC
WWE *Smackdown* TV Record:	67-60, 2 Draws, 1 DCO, 1 DDQ, 10 NC
Titles Won:	40
Days as World Champion:	379
Age at first World Title Win:	35
Best Opponents:	Chris Benoit, The Rock, Kurt Angle

Booker T was long acknowledged as underrated, a potential superstar in a brother tandem with Stevie Ray—together known as Harlem Heat. In the late 1990s, he began to come into his own, revealing the depth of his abilities as a charismatic and entertaining grappler. His series with Chris Benoit in 1998 solidified his status as an up-and-comer and made naysayers believers. Finally, in 2000, he entered the upper echelon of WCW, winning the World Heavyweight Championship four times. Houston's Booker T hasn't looked back since, and has consistently been a leading figure in the industry. A student of Ivan Putski's wrestling school; he wrestled for the Dallas-based GWF prior to landing in WCW in 1993. Along with his brother Stevie Ray, Booker was a mainstay in the tag team division for years, feuding with the Nasty Boys, Public Enemy, and the Outsiders. On December 29, 1997, he beat Disco Inferno for the first of six WCW World TV Title victories and was a pointed moment in his career as a singles performer.

WCW was in complete turmoil in 2000, but one of the more responsible and appreciated decisions was the long awaited push of Booker T. During a controversial Bash at the Beach show on July 9, 2000, he pinned Jeff Jarrett and captured his first WCW World Heavyweight Title. Later that summer, he traded the title with Kevin Nash, and then lost the belt to Vince Russo on September 25 during *Nitro*. Russo vacated the championship and Booker won his third WCW Title on October 2 in a special four-corner "San Francisco 49er" bout. Late in November, Scott Steiner won the championship, but Booker regained it during the final edition of *Nitro* in March of 2001; and was also the WCW U.S. Champion during that time. Booker T emerged on WWF TV a few months later, and was still acknowledged as the WCW champion. He was quickly involved in feuds with the promotion's best, including Steve Austin, The Rock, The Undertaker, and Kurt Angle, and was an important figure in the Alliance vs. WWF war.

In 2002, he formed a comical team with Goldust, and the duo won the World Tag Team Title. Booker T won the Intercontinental Title from Christian, and also feuded with John Cena and Chris Benoit over the U.S. Title. On May 21, 2006, he beat Bobby Lashley to win the King of the Ring tournament, and two months later, pinned Rey Mysterio for the World Title. He feuded with Batista, successfully repelling his challenge until the latter won the belt at the 2006 Survivor Series. In October of 2007, Booker T joined TNA, where he was recognized as the Legends Champion. He joined a stable of grapplers known as the Main Event Mafia along with Sting, Scott Steiner, and Kevin Nash, and teamed with Steiner to capture the TNA World Tag Team Title. He remained in the promotion for two years and toured the indies until returning to the WWE at the 2011 Royal Rumble. Booker worked as a commentator on *Smackdown* and *Raw*, plus acted as a trainer for the *Tough Enough* reality series.

Brother Devon

Born:	August 1, 1972
Height:	6'1"
Weight:	260
Real Name:	Devon Hughes
Wife:	Yessenia Hughes
High School:	New Rochelle High School (NY)
Trained by:	Johnny Rodz
Identities:	Deacon, D-Von Dudley
Finisher:	3D w/ Bubba Ray Dudley
Groups:	The Alliance (2001), Front Line (2008-2009), EV 2.0 (2010)
Wrestling School:	Team 3D Academy in Kissimmee, FL
Career Span:	1992-Present

PPV Record:	47-72
WrestleMania Record:	0-4
WWE *Raw* TV Record:	54-64, 8 NC
WWE *Smackdown* TV Record:	60-53, 6 NC
Titles Won:	27
Best Opponents:	Eddie Guerrero, Rob Van Dam, Taz

Amassing a collection of twenty-three World Championships with partner Brother Ray, Brother Devon is one of the most prolific tag team grapplers of the modern era. Their combined achievements will never be duplicated, as well as their finely tuned cooperation in the ring, which set the standard for teamwork. Team 3D, also known as the Dudley Boys, were intense brawlers, doling it out as good as they could take it, and always taking it to the extreme. The duo first teamed in ECW and captured the World Tag Team Title eight times. They debuted in the WWF in 1999 and participated in the two famous WrestleMania TLC matches in 2000 and 2001. Feuding with the Hardys and Christian and Edge, they won the WWF Tag Team belts six times by the end of 2001. Before departing the promotion in 2005, the Dudleys added to their championship totals, winning the World Tag Team title twice more and the WWE Tag Team Title once. They turned up in TNA, and have been there ever since. In addition to their TNA and NWA title victories, they won the IWGP belts twice in 2009.

Born:	May 22, 1981
Height:	5'9"
Weight:	195
Real Name:	Bryan Danielson
High School:	Aberdeen High School (WA)
College:	Grays Harbor College
Trained by:	Tracey Smothers, William Regal
Identities:	American Dragon
Finisher:	Dragon Suplex, Cobra Clutch
Career Span:	1999-Present

PPV Record:	14-7
WWE *Raw* TV Record:	19-18, 1 NC
WWE *Smackdown* TV Record:	13-18, 1 Draw
Titles Won:	20
Days as World Champion:	475
Age at first World Title Win:	24
Best Opponents:	Samoa Joe, Austin Aries, Takeshi Morishima

Bryan, Daniel

Technically proficient, Daniel Bryan is recognized around the world as one of the best mat wrestlers in the professional ranks. A product of Aberdeen, Washington, he trained at Shawn Michaels' school in San Antonio, and further developed at MCW in Memphis and at the Inoki Dojo in Los Angeles. He was a legend on the indie circuit and was featured prominently on Ring of Honor shows beginning in 2002. In September of 2005, he beat James Gibson for the ROH World Title and held the title until December of 2006. In 2010, he joined the WWE as part of the NXT show, and after a brief layoff, returned to win the U.S. Championship from The Miz on September 19, 2010. Bryan, in July of 2011, won the *Smackdown* Money in the Bank ladder match, earning a future World Title shot, and announced that he'd cash in his briefcase at WrestleMania XXVIII. Instead, he used the briefcase to capitalize on newly crowned champion Big Show at the TLC PPV in December, and won the World Title.

Bully Ray

Born:	July 14, 1971
Height:	6'3"
Weight:	295
Real Name:	Mark Lomonica
High School:	Half Hollow Hills High School (East) (NY)
Trained by:	Sonny Blaze
Identities:	Bubba Ray Dudley, Brother Ray
Finisher:	3D w/ D-Von Dudley, Bubba Bomb
Groups:	Alliance (2001), Front Line (2008-2009), EV 2.0 (2010)
Wrestling School:	Team 3D Academy in Kissimmee, FL
Career Span:	1991-Present

PPV Record:	55-73
WrestleMania Record:	0-4
WWE *Raw* TV Record:	70-86, 9 NC
WWE *Smackdown* TV Record:	52-47, 6 NC
Titles Won:	32
Best Opponents:	Brock Lesnar, Chris Jericho, A.J. Styles

In 2010, the former Brother Ray emerged as "Bully Ray," a powerful and intimidating heel who used his size to dominate smaller competitors. The new gimmick was a refreshing turn for the ex-member of Team 3D and put a temporary hold on the long-running tag team with Brother Devon. Also known as the Dudleys, Ray and Devon established themselves as legends, winning twenty-three World Titles in the U.S. and Japan in ECW, the WWE, and NJPW. They were also two-time holders of the tag title in TNA, the organization they've been affiliated with since 2005. Gaining their initial fame in ECW, the Dudleys were famous for putting rivals through tables, and no one was safe from their Dudley Death Drop. Their success continued in the WWF beginning in 1999, and they participated in two classic Tables, Ladders, and Chairs bouts at WrestleMania. Team 3D broke up in 2010 when Bully Ray attacked his longtime partner and began an impressive singles run. He joined Immortal and feuded with Mr. Anderson and Abyss in 2011.

Candido, Chris

Born:	March 21, 1972
Height:	5'8"
Weight:	225
Real Name:	Christopher B. Candito
Family:	Brother of Johnny Candido
High School:	Red Bank Catholic High School (NJ)
Colleges:	Wellesley College, University of Tennessee
Trained by:	Larry Sharpe
Identities:	Skip
Nicknames:	Suicide Blond, Hard Knox, No Gimmicks Needed
Tag Teams:	The Suicide Blonds w/ Johnny Hot Body, The Bodydonnas w/ Zip
Groups:	Triple Threat (1996-1998, 2000)
Career Span:	1986-2005
Died:	April 28, 2005, New Brunswick, NJ 33 years old

PPV Record:	9-9
WrestleMania Record:	1-0
Titles Won:	24
Days as World Champion:	97
Age at first World Title Win:	22
Best Opponents:	Cactus Jack, Sabu, Terry Funk
Halls of Fame:	1

On April 28, 2005, Chris Candido, a gifted yet underrated wrestler, died in New Brunswick, New Jersey. He had participated in a tag team cage match for TNA only days before, and his unexpected passing shocked his peers and fans throughout the world. The Edison native was a veteran of many years of ring combat, and was the grandson of Chuck Richards, a former WWWF grappler. Candido competed all over the indie circuit and for major promotions, the WWF, WCW, and ECW. On November 19, 1994, he became the youngest NWA World Heavyweight Champion in history when, at twenty-two years of age, he beat Tracey Smothers in the finals of a tournament. He lost the title a few months later, on February 24, 1995, to Dan Severn. While in the WWF and ECW, he won World Tag Team Titles and held the XPW World Championship in 2000. In addition to his sound wrestling abilities, Candido was a mentor for many grapplers behind the scenes. His longtime partner and manager, Tammy, was inducted into the WWE Hall of Fame in 2011.

Photo Courtesy of Mike Mastrandrea

Born:	April 23, 1977
Height:	6'1"
Weight:	240
Real Name:	John Felix Anthony Cena
Parents:	John and Carol Cena
High School:	Cushing Academy (MA)
Football Ach.:	NCAA Division III 1st Team All-American (1998), Freedom Football Conference All Star (1998), Captain of the football team
Finisher:	Protobomb, Attitude Adjustment
Career Span:	2000-Present

Cena, John

PPV Record:	62-35, 1 NC
WrestleMania Record:	6-2
WWE *Raw* TV Record:	154-74, 1 DDQ, 21 NC
WWE *Smackdown* TV Record:	77-28, 2 Draws, 4 NC
Titles Won:	22
Days as World Champion:	1,163
Age at first World Title Win:	27
Best Opponents:	Shawn Michaels, CM Punk, Triple H
TV Appearances:	Over 50
Movies:	6

The biggest superstar in the United States today is John Cena with his popularity unrivaled. Each time his music plays and he steps from behind the curtain, thousands of adoring fans spring to their feet to cheer. His likeable personality, enthusiasm for the business, and commitment to an endless number of charities and the military make him the kind of hero that a promotion can be built around. While the entire WWE universe is not always enthralled by his every move, Cena constantly overcomes all the odds to prevail in the end. It doesn't matter who his opponent is, he's able to display wit in promos and cunning in matches. The sharpness of his character has kept people interested, and Cena's future status as a wrestling icon is forming before the eyes of fans on a week-to-week basis. The West Newbury, Massachusetts native was an All-American football player at Springfield College and a product of the Ultimate University wrestling school in Southern California. As "Prototype," he won the UPW heavyweight crown in April of 2000.

Featured in a cable documentary about wrestling, Cena gained some early publicity and the attention of the WWE. He graduated from Ohio Valley and worked his way onto the main roster in June of 2002. Before the end of the year, he developed a new image, a hip-hop gimmick, complete with in-ring rap performances and inspired wrestling gear. The role received mixed reviews, but Cena stuck to his guns and continued to add dimensions to his ring work and outward presentation. He beat the Big Show at WrestleMania XX for the U.S. Heavyweight crown and would win the title two additional times in 2004. He also switched gears by taking time off to film, *The Marine*, in which he had a leading role. Cena was garnering steam and ready to break into a headliner role in the organization. At WrestleMania XXI, on April 3, 2005, he beat JBL for his first WWE Championship, and soon introduced his famous spinning belt. For the remainder of the year, Cena remained champion, fighting off challenger after challenger.

Edge ended his reign as champion when he cashed in his Money in the Bank contract after Cena retained in a tough Elimination Chamber bout on January 8, 2006; Although Cena regained the belt at the Royal Rumble. On April 2, 2006, he forced Triple H to submit to retain at WrestleMania XXII and remained champion until June, when Rob Van Dam dethroned him in New York City. Cena won the WWE Title for a third time from Edge at Unforgiven, winning a TLC bout. This started an amazing reign as titleholder, which lasted more than a year and was the longest in the WWE since Hulk Hogan's first run. At WrestleMania XXIII, he beat Shawn Michaels to retain the championship in a classic bout and also warded off The Great Khali and Randy Orton in defenses. Unfortunately, he suffered a real-life injury in October and was stripped of the belt. Cena came back before he was expected at the 2008 Royal Rumble in the 30th spot, and eliminated Triple H to win the event. However, he wasn't able to win back the WWE Title at No Way Out or WrestleMania.

During the summer of 2008, he teamed with Batista to win the World Tag Team Title, and then feuded with the latter. A neck injury sidelined him again, but Cena returned with a vengeance at the Survivor Series, defeating Chris Jericho for his first World Heavyweight Title. Edge stripped him of the belt, but Cena regained it at WrestleMania XXV. Edge got the last word at Backlash, again defeating him in a Last Man Standing affair. Cena defeated Orton for the WWE championship on September 13, 2009, but Orton regained it less than a month later. They met again at Bragging Rights in a 60-minute Iron Man bout, which Cena won, and began his fifth reign as a WWE titleholder. Sheamus beat him in December 2009 in a tables match, but Cena won over Triple H for the Irish grappler's belt at February's Elimination Chamber show. There was no time for a celebration because Batista stepped into an impromptu bout and beat him for the belt in less than a minute. Cena beat Batista for the WWE Title at WrestleMania on March 28, 2010.

The year marked a long and twisted feud with Nexus, a band of upstarts looking for recognition in the WWE. Cena prevailed, as expected, and extracted revenge from its leader, Wade Barrett. In February of 2011, he entered a feud with a retired member of the WWE community, The Rock, and the two criticized each other around every turn. Finally, it was decided that the two would wrestle—but not until they could meet in the main event of WrestleMania XXVIII in April of 2012. In the meantime, Cena won the WWE Championship for the eighth time when he beat The Miz on May 1, 2011. He participated in an engrossing feud with CM Punk that captivated the wrestling universe during the summer, and Cena added two additional WWE Championship wins over Rey Mysterio and Alberto Del Rio. The last victory was his record-setting 10th WWE Title win, and occurred on September 18, 2011. He lost the belt in a three-way Hell in a Cell match on October 2 of that year, and found himself embroiled in an unexpected feud with Kane.

Chono, Masa

Born:	September 17, 1963
Height:	6'0"
Weight:	235
Real Name:	Masahiro Chono
Trained by:	NJPW Dojo, Lou Thesz, Stu Hart
Nickname:	Mr. August
Finisher:	STF
Groups:	New World Order (1997-1998)
Career Span:	1984-Present

PPV Record:	2-3
Titles Won:	13
Days as World Champion:	209
Age at first World Title Win:	24
Best Opponents:	Riki Choshu, Shinya Hashimoto, Kensuke Sasaki

A celebrated grappler who established himself in Japan and the United States, Masa Chono was actually a member of the NWO in both countries during its peak run. He was also the last man to wrestle the famous Lou Thesz. Chono has an astonishing list of accomplishments under the banner of New Japan Pro Wrestling, winning the IWGP Title from Tatsumi Fujinami on August 8, 1998 and the IWGP Tag Team belts seven times with partners Hiroyoshi Tenzan and Keiji Mutoh. He also proved victorious in the G-1 Climax World Tournament five times and won the vacant NWA World Heavyweight Title with a tourney win over Rick Rude in 1992, but would lose the title to Mutoh on January 4, 1993 in Tokyo. Early in his career, while wrestling for Bob Geigel in the Central States, he beat Mike George on February 26, 1988 to capture the WWA World Title in St. Joseph, although George regained the belt on March 17. Chono officially left New Japan in early 2010 and has made appearances for a number of different promotions since.

Christian

Born:	November 30, 1973
Height:	6'1"
Weight:	225
Real Name:	William Jason Reso
High School:	Orangeville District Secondary School (Ontario)
College:	Humber College
Trained by:	Ron Hutchison
Identities:	Christian Cage, Conquistador I
Nickname:	Canadian Rage, Captain Charisma
Finisher:	The Impaler, Frog Splash
Tag Teams:	Hard Impact w/ Edge, Suicide Blonds w/ Edge
Groups:	Thug Life (1997), Revolution X (1998), The Brood (1999), The Un-Americans (2002)
Career Span:	1995-Present

PPV Record:	54-68
WrestleMania Record:	4-5
WWE *Raw* TV Record:	84-119, 1 DDQ, 1 DCO, 12 NC
WWE *Smackdown* TV Record:	61-91, 1 DCO, 6 NC
Titles Won:	24
Days as World Champion:	522
Age at first World Title Win:	32
Best Opponents:	Kurt Angle, Chris Jericho, Edge
Movies:	2

Fierce, skilled, and wildly entertaining, Christian carries a lethal combination of characteristics that firmly solidifies his place among the top heavyweight contenders and/or champions in the sport today. Since 2006, he's won five World championships in TNA and the WWE, and continues to get better in both ring execution and promos, if that was even possible. Often compared to his longtime tag team partner, Edge, Christian has defined himself individually, and worked hard to achieve his own level of success. Three years after his pro debut, he went to Florida to train with the legendary Dory Funk Jr., and debuted in the WWF in 1998 along with Edge. Their longtime friendship translated to perfect compatibility in the ring, and Christian and Edge formed an incomparable tag team. They captured the tag team championship seven times, winning two WrestleMania TLC matches, and setting an early course for superstardom. Christian defined himself as a singles competitor and had a memorable feud with Chris Jericho in 2004.

In promos, he was able to mock opponents and tear on audiences with unusual flair, and fans were often mixed in reactions to his segments. Even while as a heel, he was still cheered. He joined TNA in November of 2005, and directed his focus toward NWA champion Jeff Jarrett. On February 12, 2006, he beat the latter for the crown and also warded off Abyss's stern challenge. He lost the belt in June in a King of the Mountain match to Jeff Jarrett. Christian, at the time, was known as a fan favorite, but turned heel when he attacked Sting in August of 2006 and beat Abyss and Sting in a three-way bout for his second NWA championship on January 14, 2007. He ended up losing the belt to Kurt Angle in May of that year. In 2009, Christian returned to the WWE and won the first of two ECW Titles from Jack Swagger. An injury sidelined him, but he rebounded to help Edge in the latter's war with Alberto Del Rio. When Edge retired in April of 2011, Christian faced Del Rio for the vacant World Title, and on May 1, captured the championship. Two days later, he lost it to Randy Orton.

Photo Courtesy of Mike Mastrandrea

Born:	October 26, 1978
Height:	6'1"
Weight:	220
Real Name:	Phillip Jack Brooks
High School:	Lockport High School (IL)
Trained by:	Danny Dominion, Ace Steel, Kevin Quinn
Finisher:	GTS (Go to Sleep), Anaconda Vice
Groups:	Straight Edge Society (2009-2010), New Nexus (2011)
Career Span:	1998-Present

CM Punk

PPV Record:	32-49, 1 DDQ
WrestleMania Record:	2-3
WWE *Raw* TV Record:	53-37, 1 DDQ, 4 NC
WWE *Smackdown* TV Record:	39-35, 4 NC
Titles Won:	28
Days as World Champion:	427
Age at first World Title Win:	26
Best Opponents:	Samoa Joe, John Cena, The Undertaker

Reputed to be the "Best in the World," CM Punk just may be that, demonstrating his exceptional versatility time and time again. While not an overly imposing figure, he has all the tools to be a dominant figure in any promotion, and currently reigns as the WWE champion. His ingenuity inside the ring and out, and the way he connects with audiences is extremely rare, and in 2011, his popularity skyrocketed. His credo is "straight-edge" all the way, refraining from the purported ills of society, and has two X-marks on his taped hands to represent his ideology. Having grown up in a suburb of Chicago, he attended a local wrestling school, and debuted in 1998. Punk's experience in martial arts, plus his athleticism makes for an entertaining show when he steps into the ring, and his personality-driven character completes the package. While working the independent circuit , he won the IWA Mid-South Title on five occasions between 2000 and 2004, beating Eddie Guerrero and A.J. Styles for two of his reigns. He also had lengthy feuds with Chris Hero and Colt Cabana that garnered a lot of buzz.

In the Ring of Honor promotion, he wrestled classic matches against Raven and Samoa Joe, including two sixty-minute draws against the latter in 2004. Despite his effort, he never overcame Joe for the ROH World Championship, but did beat Austin Aries for the belt on June 18, 2005. He dropped the title in August and went to Ohio Valley, a WWE developmental promotion. Punk beat Bret Albright for the local heavyweight title, and then debuted for the ECW brand in mid-2006, initiating a long win streak. He chased John Morrison for the ECW World Title, finally beating him on September 1, 2007, but lost it to Chavo Guerrero Jr. in January of 2008. At WrestleMania XXIV, he prevailed in an electrifying Money in the Bank ladder match. Three months later, on June 30, he watched as World Champion Edge was brutally beaten by Batista, and smartly cashed in his contract, capitalizing on the moment, and pinning Edge for the title.

At WrestleMania XXV, he won his second straight Money in the Bank ladder match, and on June 7, 2009, he cashed it in again at an opportune time, pinning Jeff Hardy after the latter's grueling match against Edge. In 2011, Punk was back at the top of his game and was outstanding in explosively candid promo segments that appealed both to the "smart" audience and the mainstream wrestling public. Even the non-wrestling sports community took notice of his dynamic performances. Punk beat Cena for the WWE Title on July 17, 2011 in a classic match, was stripped after apparently leaving the promotion, then beat Cena again to unify the two strands at SummerSlam. However, he was attacked by Kevin Nash after the bout, and then dropped the belt to Alberto Del Rio, who cashed in his MITB contract. On November 20, 2011, Punk forced Del Rio to submit, and regained the WWE championship. He ended the year still on top, and was constantly at odds with interim *Raw* General Manager John Laurinaitis.

Born:	May 29, 1973
Height:	6'1"
Weight:	220
Real Name:	Steven Eugene Corino
Family:	Brother of Allison Danger, father of Colby Corino
High School:	Perkiomen Valley High School (PA)
Trained by:	Tom Brandi
Finisher:	Old School Expulsion Neckbreaker, Northern Lights Bomb
Career Span:	1994-Present

Corino, Steve

PPV Record:	5-10
Titles Won:	79
Days as World Champion:	974
Age at first World Title Win:	27
Best Opponents:	Samoa Joe, Shinya Hashimoto, Dusty Rhodes

Leader of the "old school" revolution, Steve Corino has wrestled, toured, and represented a previous generation of pro grappling better than most of his contemporaries. He has over seventy-five wrestling championship victories, including the NWA and ECW World Heavyweight Titles. Born in Canada, Corino was raised in Trappe, Pennsylvania, northwest of Philadelphia, and entered the profession in 1994. Under 200 pounds, Corino was at a disadvantage early on, trying to wedge himself into a sport that spotlighted mostly behemoths; but he was persistent, and worked into contention for the ECW Title. On November 5, 2000, he beat Justin Credible to capture the ECW Title. The following April, he won the NWA belt from Mike Rapada, etching his name into the title lineage of many of the legends he admired. Corino remains a favorite wherever he appears, and if he continues at this rate, he'll have won more than 100 titles before he retires.

Born:	March 24, 1970
Height:	5'11"
Weight:	220
Real Name:	Daniel Christopher Covell
Parents:	Charles and Marcia Covell
Wife:	Lisa Covell
High School:	Pine Forest High School (NC)
Trained by:	Sam DeCero, Mike Anthony and Kevin Quinn
Identities:	Conquistador I, Curry Man, Suicide
Finisher:	Last Rites
Career Span:	1993-Present

PPV Record:	46-59, 1 Draw, 1 NC
Titles Won:	37
Days as World Champion:	182
Age at first World Title Win:	34
Best Opponents:	A.J. Styles, Samoa Joe, Kurt Angle
Halls of Fame:	1

Daniels, Christopher

Wrestling fans who appreciate athleticism, daring acrobatics, and technical savvy, respect the work and dedication of Christopher Daniels. A product of Fayetteville, North Carolina, Daniels graduated with a degree in theater from Methodist College in 1991. He attended Chicago's Windy City Pro Wrestling School and debuted as a grappler in 1993, and has since won over thirty championships across the Continental U.S., Puerto Rico, England, and Japan. He has won the TNA X-Division belt four times, the NWA World Tag Team Title six times, and held the ROH World Television crown from 2010-2011. In January of 2011, he made his return to TNA and aligned himself with the members of Fortune. Known as the "Fallen Angel," Daniels has consistently been among the best pro wrestlers on the circuit and continues to shine regardless if he's working an indie show before a few hundred or in a championship match on pay-per-view. His value as a wrestler is appreciated by his peers, audiences across the globe, and by promoters who benefit from booking him.

Born:	October 6, 1959
Height:	6'2"
Weight:	260
Real Name:	Barry Alan Darsow
Parents:	Melvin and Adeline Darsow
Family:	Father of Dakota Darsow
High School:	Robbinsdale High School (MN)
Identities:	Zar, Krusher Darsow
Tag Team:	The Mongolians w/ Gor
Career Span:	1983-Present

PPV Record:	9-15
WrestleMania Record:	3-3
WWE *Raw* TV Record:	0-1
Titles Won:	14
Best Opponents:	Randy Savage, Chris Benoit, Bob Backlund

Darsow, Barry

Teamed with Bill Eadie, Barry Darsow formed one of the most notable tag teams of the 1980s, Demolition. Darsow was "Smash," while Eadie was known as "Ax," and the pair won the WWF World Tag Team Title on three occasions. Their first reign lasted sixteen months, from March of 1988 to July of 1989. A product of Minnesota, Darsow played hockey in his youth and attended the camp of Eddie Sharkey after a few of his friends became pro wrestlers. Early in his career, he toured New Zealand as one of the Mongolians, and late in 1984, joined the Koloffs, Ivan and Nikita, as Russian "Krusher Khrushchev." He defended the NWA Tag Team Title, which the Koloffs had won previously, and also teamed with Ivan to capture the U.S. Tag Team belts. While in the WWF, following his run as a member of Demolition, he worked as the "Repo Man," and then as "Blacktop Bully" in WCW. At the Uncensored 1995 show, he wrestled Dustin Rhodes in the back of a moving truck. He's since reunited with Eadie on the indie circuit and is a successful businessman in Minnesota.

Born:	May 25, 1977
Height:	6'5"
Weight:	260
Real Name:	Alberto Rodriguez
Family:	Son of Dos Caras, nephew of Mil Mascaras
Trained by:	Dos Caras, FCW trainers
Identities:	Dos Caras Jr.
Finisher:	Cross Armbar submission
Career Span:	2000-Present

Del Rio, Alberto

PPV Record:	8-8
WrestleMania Record:	0-1
WWE *Raw* TV Record:	21-17, 2 NC
WWE *Smackdown* TV Record:	16-15, 2 NC
Titles Won:	3
Days as World Champion:	617
Age at first World Title Win:	30
Best Opponents:	John Cena, Edge, Ultimo Guerrero
MMA Record:	9-5

Many fans throughout the WWE Universe were pleasantly surprised that relative newcomer Alberto Del Rio won the 2011 Royal Rumble in Boston. A former amateur from Mexico, he was indisputably talented and his gimmick as an arrogant heel exhibited his charisma perfectly. His ring entrance saw him drive out in an expensive automobile and his own personal ring announcer alerted the audience of his arrival. For a number of years, he wrestled Greco-Roman for the Mexican national team and debuted as a pro in 2000, following in the footsteps of his father, Dos Caras. On July 8, 2007, he beat Universo 2000 for the CMLL World Heavyweight Title and held the belt until December of 2008. He went to Florida Championship Wrestling after signing a deal with the WWE and debuted in August of 2010, engaging in an early feud with Rey Mysterio Jr. After the Rumble, he continued his winning ways, adding *Raw*'s Money in the Bank contract, and then captured the WWE championship twice between August and October of 2011.

Born:	April 11, 1978
Height:	6'0"
Weight:	225
Real Name:	Elijah Burcks
High School:	Frank H. Peterson Academies of Technology (FL)
Identities:	Elijah Burke
Career Span:	2003-Present

PPV Record:	8-17
WrestleMania Record:	0-1
WWE *Raw* TV Record:	1-2
WWE *Smackdown* TV Record:	3-4
Titles Won:	1
Best Opponents:	Chris Benoit, CM Punk, Kurt Angle

Dinero, D'Angelo

A completely multi-dimensional wrestler with lots of potential, D'Angelo Dinero is one of the best current TNA superstars never to win a championship in the promotion. He's demonstrated skill behind the microphone and fluidity on the mat, and it seems like just a matter of time before he fights his way into the upper echelon of the promotion. Originally from Jacksonville, Florida, Dinero served as a corrections officer and boxed as an amateur before going to Louisville to train at Ohio Valley. While in the WWE from 2006-2008, he formed a partnership with Sylvester Terkay and nearly won the ECW championship on several occasions. After jumping to TNA, he prevailed in the 8 Card Stud Tournament in February of 2010 and feuded with Samoa Joe and Brother Devon.

Douglas, Shane

Born:	November 21, 1964
Height:	6'0"
Weight:	240
Real Name:	Troy Shane Martin
Parents:	George and Louise Martin
Wife:	Carla Martin
High School:	New Brighton Area High School (PA)
College:	Bethany College
Trained by:	Dominic DeNucci
Identities:	Troy Orndorff, Dean Douglas
Finisher:	Pittsburgh Plunge, The Franchiser
Groups:	Triple Threat (1997-1998), The Revolution (1999), The New Blood (2000)
Tag Team:	The Dynamic Dudes w/ Johnny Ace
Career Span:	1982-Present

PPV Record:	32-23, 1 NC
Titles Won:	21
Days as World Champion:	Around 1,000
Age at first World Title Win:	29
Best Opponents:	Terry Funk, Taz, Justin Credible

The "Franchise" Shane Douglas helped launch a revolution in 1994 when he denounced the NWA World Title and proclaimed himself the inaugural champion of "Extreme Championship Wrestling." It was a defining moment for the business as a whole and helped usher in a new era that influenced both the WWF and WCW. Douglas was a fan of wrestling as a young man and helped stage benefit grappling programs in his hometown of New Brighton, Pennsylvania while still in high school. By the mid-1990s, he was an experienced pro and the commanding figure behind ECW's rise to prominence. He held the ECW championship four times, feuding with the likes of Terry Funk and The Sandman, and always delivered heated promos, especially when he ranted about Ric Flair. At the tail end of WCW's run, Douglas won the World Tag Team and U.S. crowns. He competed for TNA in the beginning of 2003, and made his final showing in 2009. He's wrestled all over the indie map, and has won many belts to include the MLW and XPW World Titles.

Dreamer, Tommy

Born:	February 13, 1970
Height:	6'2"
Weight:	245
Real Name:	Thomas James Laughlin
Parents:	John and Susan Laughlin
Wife:	Trisa Laughlin
High School:	Iona Preparatory School (NY)
College:	Iona College
Trained by:	Johnny Rodz
Identities:	T.D. Madison
Finisher:	DDT
Career Span:	1989-Present

PPV Record:	15-20, 1 NC
WrestleMania Record:	1-0
WWE *Raw* TV Record:	11-25, 1 NC
WWE *Smackdown* TV Record:	0-4
Titles Won:	29
Days as World Champion:	49
Age at first World Title Win:	30
Best Opponents:	Raven, Rob Van Dam, A.J. Styles
Halls of Fame:	1

Tommy Dreamer is as passionate about pro wrestling as anyone involved in the sport today. His enthusiasm for the business is apparent every time he steps into the ring. Also known as the "Innovator of Violence," Dreamer displayed just how hardcore he was in August of 1994 during a Singapore caning session by the Sandman. He was the heart and soul of ECW and only left the promotion because it was sold in 2001. During his nine-year stay with the organization, he won the World Tag Team Title three times, and then on April 22, 2000, he beat Taz for the ECW World Heavyweight Title. After ECW folded in early 2001, Dreamer traveled to Ontario and won the vacant BCW Can-Am Heavyweight Title over Rhino and Scott D'Amore. He joined the WWF in 2001 and remained involved with the organization through January of 2010. While apart of the ECW "brand extension," he regained the ECW World Title. He emerged in TNA and was a member of the EV 2.0 troupe, then begrudgingly joined Immortal in 2011.

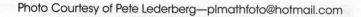

Born:	January 14, 1954
Height:	6'3"
Weight:	280
Real Name:	James Edward Duggan
Wife:	Deborah Duggan
High School:	Glens Falls High School (NY)
HS Ach.:	New York State High School Wrestling Title (1973) (250)
Pro Sports:	National Football League— Atlanta Falcons (1977–1978) (injured) Canadian Football League—Toronto Argonauts (1979)
Finisher:	Three-Point Football Stance into Clothesline
Groups:	Team Canada (2000)
Career Span:	1979-Present

Duggan, Jim

PPV Record:	18-21, 1 DDQ
WrestleMania Record:	2-1, 1 DDQ
WWE *Raw* TV Record:	5-15
Titles Won:	9
Days as World Champion:	Unknown
Age at first World Title Win:	50
Best Opponents:	Randy Savage, Ted DiBiase, Rick Rude
Halls of Fame:	2

The epitome of wrestling hero, "Hacksaw" Jim Duggan charged up audiences like few others, his explosive charisma inspiring chants of "USA," and his magnetism radiating to all corners of arenas. A high school wrestler and football star, he was a starting offensive lineman at SMU as a freshman, and was the team captain in 1976. He was trained by Jack Adkisson in Dallas and made his professional debut in 1979. A few years later, he formed the Rat Pack with Ted DiBiase and Matt Borne in the Mid-South territory, and then turned fan favorite in 1983. One of his first big title victories occurred when he defeated Buzz Sawyer for the North American crown in 1986. In the WWF, he won the very first Royal Rumble on January 24, 1988, and beat Haku to become "King" in April of 1989. While as a part of WCW, Duggan pinned Steve Austin in 27 seconds for the U.S. Title on September 18, 1994. Six years later, he found the WCW TV belt in the trash and held it for nearly two months. He's appeared in the WWE many times since 2005, maintaining his popularity, and was inducted into the WWE Hall of Fame in 2011.

Eaton, Bobby

Born:	August 14, 1958
Height:	6'0"
Weight:	235
Real Name:	Bobby Lee Eaton
High School:	Lee High School (AL)
Wife:	Donna Eaton
Trained by:	Tojo Yamamoto
Identities:	Earl Robert Eaton
Finisher:	Alabama Jam (Flying Legdrop)
Groups:	The Dangerous Alliance (1991-1992)
Tag Teams:	The Jet Set w/ George Gulas, Bad Attitude w/ Steve Keirn, The Blue Bloods w/ Lord Steven Regal
Career Span:	1976-2009

PPV Record:	14-17
Titles Won:	43
Days as World Champion:	7
Age at first World Title Win:	22
Best Opponents:	Ric Flair, Billy Robinson, Jerry Lawler
Managers:	9
Halls of Fame:	1

Highly respected by wrestling fans and peers alike, "Beautiful" Bobby Eaton of Huntsville, Alabama was the backbone of two versions of the famed Midnight Express tag team. He originally teamed with Dennis Condrey under the guidance of Jim Cornette, and beat the Rock and Roll Express for the NWA World Tag Team Title in 1986. The second incarnation saw Eaton partnered with another talented heel, Stan Lane, and this duo won the vacant U.S. Tag Team Title in a tournament. On September 10, 1988, while still holding the U.S. Title, they beat Arn Anderson and Tully Blanchard to win the World Tag Team straps. As a singles competitor, Eaton held the CWA World Title in 1980 and won the Mid-America belt eleven times between 1979 and 1983. In 1991, he captured the WCW TV Title and had an impressive, high-profile televised match against NWA champion Ric Flair. Eaton's son Dylan became a pro wrestler in 2006 and the two teamed up on several occasions.

Edge

Born:	October 30, 1973
Height:	6'4"
Weight:	240
Real Name:	Adam Joseph Copeland
High School:	Orangeville District Secondary School (Ontario)
College:	Humber College
Trained by:	Sweet Daddy Siki, Ron Hutchison, Dory Funk Jr.
Identities:	Adam Impact, Sexton Hardcastle, Damon Stryker
Nickname:	Rated R Superstar
Finishers:	Edgecution, Downward Spiral, Spear
Tag Teams:	Sex and Violence w/ Joe Legend, Hard Impact w/ Christian, Suicide Blonds w/ Christian, Rated-RKO w/ Randy Orton
Groups:	Thug Life (1997), The Brood (1999), La Familia (2007-2008)
Career Span:	1992-2011

PPV Record:	61-59, 1 Draw, 1 DCO, 1 NC
WrestleMania Record:	6-4
WWE *Raw* TV Record:	115-121, 1 DCO, 1 DDQ, 23 NC
WWE *Smackdown* TV Record:	102-90, 1 DCO, 12 NC
Titles Won:	35
Days as World Champion:	548
Age at first World Title Win:	32
Best Opponents:	The Undertaker, John Cena, Chris Jericho
Managers:	4
Movies:	2

Eight days after successfully turning back the top contender to his World Heavyweight Title at WrestleMania XXVII, Edge announced his retirement from pro wrestling on *Monday Night Raw* on April 11, 2011. The decision, made on the recommendation of his doctor, shocked fans everywhere and effectively ended his nineteen-year career at the age of thirty-seven. Since breaking out of the independents for the WWF in 1998, Edge has been a significant player, winning more than thirty championships, including eleven

World Titles. His cunning personality and skillful ring work made him a headline performer, and the angles he worked and the feuds he engaged in were some of the most memorable in recent years. Destined to be a WWE superstar, Edge had dreams of wrestling in high school and pursued training at a Toronto-area camp. He made his debut on the Canadian independent circuit and toiled away for the next six years before landing a full-time gig with the WWF. His childhood friend, Christian, also joined the promotion, and the two joined the Brood along with Gangrel in 1999.

The tag team made up of Edge and Christian was uniquely special, providing a high-flying and fast-paced style that matched well with two of the other dominant squads of the period: The Hardy Brothers and the Dudley Boys. They engaged in a 'Tables, Ladders, and Chairs" contest against their two rivals at WrestleMania on April 2, 2000 in Anaheim and won the lively match to capture the WWF World Tag Team Title for the first time. Over the next year, Edge and his partner won the championship five more times, and captured their seventh tag team title at WrestleMania X-Seven in Houston, once again defeating the Hardys and Dudleys in a dangerous, but exciting TLC bout. The adjustment to singles competition was easy for Edge and he won the King of the Ring tournament in 2001, as well as feuding with his former partner, Christian. He captured the U.S. Heavyweight Title from Kurt Angle, and unified it with the Intercontinental championship at the Survivor Series on November 18, 2001.

In 2002, he formed successful tag teams with Hulk Hogan and Rey Mysterio Jr., winning the WWE Tag Team Title with both partners, and a neck injury forced him from the ring in early 2003. At WrestleMania XXI, he won the initial Money in the Bank match, guaranteeing him a future World Title shot. That contract was cashed in on January 8, 2006 in Albany following champion John Cena's successful title defense in an Elimination Chamber bout. Edge capitalized on Cena's condition, and scored the pinfall for his first WWE championship. He'd end up losing it back to Cena at the Royal Rumble, but would regain it later in the year from Rob Van Dam. In 2007, he won the World Heavyweight Title after cashing in his second Money in the Bank contract and beating The Undertaker. That time around, he had to vacate the title because of another injury. He formed an on-screen relationship with Vickie Guerrero, the *Smackdown* General Manager, and benefited from her influence over the brand.

Edge was a five-time World Heavyweight Champion by the end of April 2009, having won the belt from Batista, Undertaker, Jeff Hardy, and John Cena. His relationship with Guerrero finally soured, but a legitimate injury forced him out of action yet again during the middle of 2009. When he returned in January of 2010, he came back with a vengeance, and won the Royal Rumble. It took him until December to win his sixth World Title in a TLC match over champion Kane, Alberto Del Rio, and Rey Mysterio. Guerrero stripped away his belt, but Edge regained it later in the same night from Guerrero's new cohort, Dolph Ziggler, capturing his record seventh World Title on February 15, 2011. He survived the Elimination Chamber, and then beat Del Rio at WrestleMania, all leading up to an unexpected announcement. Edge was suffering from spinal stenosis and, to prevent further injury, retired from the business as the reigning world champion.

Born:	June 7, 1965
Height:	6'3"
Weight:	270-290
Real Name:	Michael Francis Foley
Parents:	John and Beverly Foley
Wife:	Colette Foley
High School:	Ward Melville High Scholl (NY)
College:	State University of New York College at Cortland
Identities:	Jack Foley, Jack Manson, Dude Love
Finisher:	Double-arm DDT, Mandible Claw
Groups:	Sullivan's Slaughterhouse (1990), The Corporation (1999), EV 2.0 (2010)
Tag Team:	The Rock and Sock Connection w/ The Rock
Career Span:	1986-Present

Foley, Mick

PPV Record:	28-56, 1 Draw, 1 DCO, 1 DDQ, 1 NC
WrestleMania Record:	2-3, 1 DCO
WWE *Raw* TV Record:	23-17, 1 DCO, 7 NC
WWE *Smackdown* TV Record:	9-6, 5 NC
Titles Won:	28
Days as World Champion:	110
Age at first World Title Win:	33
Best Opponents:	The Undertaker, The Rock, Shawn Michaels
Halls of Fame:	1
TV Appearances:	Over 25
Movies:	3
Published Books:	9

Mick Foley took a unique route to becoming an international wrestling celebrity, a path that he forged through years of hard work. He overcame unfavorable odds, including promoters who didn't see the marketability in his ring persona, and set himself apart by always giving 100 percent of his body to a match. The reckless character that he turned into inside the ring never held back. His bumps were outrageously solid every time, and fans could see the legitimacy of his passion for the business. While other wrestlers have longevity on Foley, few could say that they gave as much as he did across the length of his career. Foley's matches were more like wrestling stunt shows with no regulator to limit the risks. He was a brawler on par with the "Hardcore Legend," Terry Funk, and adept to the psychological side of wrestling, getting feuds and angles over by talking on the microphone. Foley had a continued presence in TNA and the WWE in 2011, and his ability to sell major storylines is still very strong.

Trained by Dominic DeNucci, Foley wrestled in the USWA and WCW early in his career, and received his most significant push in 1992-1993 when he feuded with Ron Simmons, Sting, and Vader. During one Atlanta show in April of 1993, Foley was powerbombed on the floor of the arena and knocked out, setting up a long-running amnesia skit that saw him wandering aimlessly around Cleveland, lost. The angle displayed more of his personality and exhibited another dimension of his character. His mystique grew further when he lost part of his right ear during a bout in Germany against Vader on March 16, 1994—but yet continued to wrestle. He appeared in ECW later that year, and electrified the not-so-easily impressed Philadelphia audience in battles with The Sandman and Terry Funk, and took his rivalry with Funk to Japan, where he met the "Funker" in the finals of the IWA King of the Death Match tournament. Foley won that wild exploding barbed-wire bout. In early 1996, he began a new phase in the WWF as "Mankind."

Entering into a lengthy war with The Undertaker, Foley gave forth a monumental effort during their June 28, 1998 Hell in a Cell match, and his actions defied believability. He took two huge falls from the top of the 16-foot cage, and continued to fight until being chokeslammed on tacks, and finally tombstoned. Foley's ungodly commitment to the sport was evident, and made him an enormous superstar. From there, he won the WWF World Heavyweight Title three times and released his autobiography, which not only became a *New York Times* best-seller, but revolutionized the wrestling book business. He stepped away from the mat in 2000, but returned often to perform roles in both the WWE, and later TNA. Throughout this time, he's penned two additional autobiographies, three children's books, and two novels. On April 19, 2009, he returned to the ring to beat Sting for the TNA World Title and was positioned as the "network consultant" in 2011, but left the promotion before the angle got off the ground. He soon rejoined the WWE, and still makes the occasional appearance.

Photo Courtesy of Pete Lederberg—plmathfoto@hotmail.com

Born:	July 19, 1958
Height:	5'11"
Weight:	225
Real Name:	Ruben Chalker Cain Jr.
Family:	Younger brother of Ricky Gibson
Trained by:	Ricky Gibson
Promoter:	Pro Wrestling Connection (Northport, AL)
Career Span:	1976-Present

Gibson, Robert

PPV Record:	5-6, 1 DCO
WrestleMania Record:	0-1
Titles Won:	47
Best Opponents:	Ric Flair, Paul Orndorff, Ricky Morton
Halls of Fame:	1

The dynamic Rock and Roll Express made up of Robert Gibson and Ricky Morton was an explosively popular tag team in the 1980s and remains so to this day. They captured the hearts of young wrestling fans that admired their quick moves and likeable personalities, and won the NWA World Tag Team Title seven times between 1985 and 2000. Gibson grew up in Pensacola, Florida, and learned the trade from his older brother, Ricky. On July 9, 1985, the Express won their very first NWA championship from Ivan Koloff and Krusher Khrushchev, and over the next six years, they had memorable feuds with the Midnight Express and Four Horsemen. While in the Smoky Mountain territory between 1992 and 1994, the pair won the tag team belts ten times, and later in the decade, made appearances in the WWF as part of an NWA "invasion." In South Korea, they won their seventh NWA Title on April 12, 2000 over Steven Dunn and Jackie Fulton. Gibson continues to wrestle, reforming the famous Express with Morton on occasion.

Photo Courtesy of Pete Lederberg—plmathfoto@hotmail.com

Born:	August 14, 1961
Height:	5'10"
Weight:	220
Real Name:	Thomas Edward Gilbert Jr.
Parents:	Thomas and Peggy Gilbert
Family:	Grandson of Arlie Gilbert, brother of Doug Gilbert
High School:	Lexington High School (TN)
College:	Kennesaw State College
Nicknames:	Hot Shot, King Edward
Groups:	Hyatt and Hotstuff Incorporated (1986-1987), The First Family (1989)
Tag Teams:	The Fabulous Ones w/ Tommy Rich
Managed:	Jerry Bryant (1985), Playboy Frazier (1985), Mike Sharpe (1985), Dutch Mantell (1985), The Nightmare (1985), Sting (1986), Rick Steiner (1987-1988)
Career Span:	1979-1995
Died:	February 18, 1995, San Juan, Puerto Rico 33 years old

Gilbert, Eddie

PPV Record:	1-1, 1 Draw
Titles Won:	29
Days as World Champion:	137
Age at first World Title Win:	30
Best Opponents:	Jerry Lawler, Terry Funk, Tiger Mask
Managers:	13
Halls of Fame:	1

As a young man, Eddie Gilbert possessed the kind of brilliant wrestling mind only associated with well-traveled veterans. His innovative concepts were utilized throughout his career, giving promoters a charismatic wrestler in the ring and a superior asset behind the scenes. A third-generation grappler from Lexington, Tennessee, Gilbert entered the business as a seventeen-year-old prodigy, having studied under his father, Tommy, with the duo teaming together many times. In 1980, he formed a popular tandem with Ricky Morton, and in 1982, was a star on the rise in the WWF. He bounced back from a broken neck sustained in a car accident and had a good run in the Memphis territory. While in the UWF, he won the tag team title with Sting in 1986, and partnered with Rick Steiner to capture the NWA U.S. straps three years later. Among his other accomplishments were winning the USWA World Title on four occasions and the GWF North American crown. Gilbert was an influential creative force in nearly every territory he worked in from 1986 until his unfortunate death in 1995.

Born:	December 27, 1966
Height:	6'2"
Weight:	285
Real Name:	William Scott Goldberg
Parents:	Jed and Ethel Goldberg
Wife:	Wanda Goldberg
High School:	Tulsa Edison High School (OK)
NFL Draft:	Los Angeles Rams (1990) (11th Round) (301)
Pro Sports:	World League—Sacramento Surge (1992) National Football League—Atlanta Falcons (1992-1994) (14 games)
Career Span:	1997-2004
Website:	www.billgoldberg.com

Goldberg, Bill

PPV Record:	25-7, 2 NC
WrestleMania Record:	1-0
WWE *Raw* TV Record:	22-1, 5 NC
Titles Won:	5
Days as World Champion:	258
Age at first World Title Win:	31
Best Opponents:	Hulk Hogan, Triple H, Brock Lesnar
TV Appearances:	Over 25
Movies:	11

In seven years, Bill Goldberg made a sincere impression on the world of pro wrestling. He ascended the ranks like a bolt of lightning, bringing an intensity and determination that was unmatched, and achieved World championships in both WCW and the WWE. His popularity during his undefeated streak, which lasted through 173 matches, was enormous, and considering he was basically just a rookie, was simply remarkable. Throngs of fans chanted "Goldberg" as he approached the ring, and his matches were usually very quick, ending with a tremendous spear and jackhammer that planted his foe squarely on his back for the pinfall. The power displayed by the ex-football player was immense, and his streak was one of the hottest things in the sport in 1997-1998. Goldberg grew up in Tulsa, the youngest of four siblings, and attended the University of Georgia, where he shone on the football field as a defensive tackle. He logged 121 tackles his senior year and was drafted by the Los Angeles Rams in 1990 as the 301st pick (11th round).

An injury during preseason temporarily halted his football career, and the Rams cut him. But Goldberg rebounded to play in the World League, and then three seasons with the Atlanta Falcons. In 1997, he entered the WCW Power Plant, and made his debut in July of that year. He rapidly gained a following, as fans were fascinated by his enthusiasm and invincibility. Week after week, he demolished opponents with a certain ease, and as his unbeaten streak grew, as did his popularity. Before long, he was receiving the loudest reaction of anyone on the WCW roster. There was no denying it—Goldberg was a phenomenon. He won the U.S. crown in April of 1998, and a few months later, on July 6 at the Georgia Dome in Atlanta, he beat Hollywood Hogan for the World Heavyweight Title before more than 39,000 fans. His famous streak came to an odd end at Starrcade 1998 in a controversial match against Kevin Nash that saw a taser play a part in the finish. Missing months due to injury, he returned in late 1999, feuding with Bret Hart.

The remainder of Goldberg's stay in WCW was turbulent to say the least, and included a brief stint as a heel. His final showing came on January 14, 2001 in a tag team match with Dwayne Bruce against Lex Luger and Buff Bagwell. The stipulation was if Goldberg's team lost, he'd be forced to retire. They indeed were defeated, and he never returned to WCW. In March of 2003, he entered the WWE and debuted the night after WrestleMania XIX. He made his mark by spearing the Rock on *Raw*. On August 24, 2003, he nearly won the World Title from Triple H in an Elimination Chamber bout, and finally succeeded in doing so at Unforgiven on September 21. He remained the World Champion until December 14, 2003, when he lost the title back to Triple H in a three-way contest that also involved Kane. Goldberg won his final match against Brock Lesnar at WrestleMania XX and retired from the business. He has since acted as a commentator for MMA programs and appeared in several films. In 2010, he was featured on *Celebrity Apprentice*.

Photo Courtesy of Dr. Mike Lano—Wrealano@aol.com

Born:	October 20, 1970
Height:	5'10"
Weight:	220
Real Name:	Salvador Guerrero IV
Trained by:	Chavo Guerrero
Identities:	Lieutenant Loco, Kerwin White
Finisher:	Tornado DDT, Frog splash
Tag Team:	Los Guerreros w/ Eddy Guerrero
Career Span:	1994-Present

Guerrero, Chavo Jr.

PPV Record:	17-36
WrestleMania Record:	1-2
WWE *Raw* TV Record:	7-37, 1 NC
WWE *Smackdown* TV Record:	53-90, 1 Draw, 6 NC
Titles Won:	11
Days as World Champion:	68
Age at first World Title Win:	37
Best Opponents:	Eddie Guerrero, Rey Mysterio Jr., Chris Benoit

Talented third-generation wrestler, Chavo Guerrero Jr. is the son of Chavo Sr. and the grandson of Gory Guerrero. He started out in Mexico and Japan, finally gaining traction in WCW, winning the World Cruiserweight championship twice. For awhile, he carried around a toy horse, known as "Pepe," and regularly got on the nerves of his uncle, Eddie Guerrero. The Guerreros formed a winning tag team in the WWE, capturing the Tag Team Title twice in 2002-2003, and Chavo added four WWE Cruiserweight Titles to his resume. On January 22, 2008, he beat CM Punk for the ECW World Heavyweight Title, but lost it two months later at WrestleMania to Kane. Chavo departed from the WWE in June of 2011 and went to Puerto Rico, where he soon won the WWC Caribbean Title.

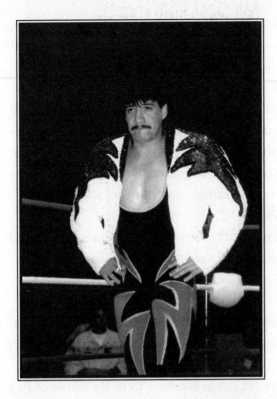

Photo Courtesy of Dr. Mike Lano—Wrealano@aol.com

Born:	October 9, 1967
Height:	5'8"
Weight:	220
Real Name:	Eduardo Gory Guerrero
Wife:	Vickie Guerrero
High School:	Jefferson High School (TX)
Identities:	Magic Mask, Black Tiger, Eddie Guerrero
Nickname:	Latino Heat
Groups:	Los Gringos Locos (1994), Latino World Order (1998), The Filthy Animals (1999-2001), The Radicals (2000)
Tag Team:	Los Guerreros w/ Chavo Guerrero Jr.
Career Span:	1987-2005
Died:	November 13, 2005, Minneapolis, MN 38 years old

Guerrero, Eddie

PPV Record:	34-42
WrestleMania Record:	2-3
WWE *Raw* TV Record:	25-28, 3 NC
WWE *Smackdown* TV Record:	92-73, 5 NC
Titles Won:	21
Days as World Champion:	133
Age at first World Title Win:	36
Best Opponents:	Dean Malenko, Rey Mysterio Jr., Chris Benoit
Halls of Fame:	3

The entertaining personality of Eddie Guerrero was a shining spot in wrestling, and he could always be counted on for an excellent match or amusing promo. His well-rounded abilities set him apart from his peers and his sudden 2005 death shocked the industry. There was no replacing a guy like Guerrero, who was finally hitting his stride in the WWE and getting his due in main events after years of hard work. The mainstream wrestling public had only been aware of his outstanding wrestling since 1995 when he debuted for WCW and made regular appearances on *Nitro*. Prior to that, however, he'd displayed the same heightened level of performance in Mexico, Japan, and ECW. The youngest son of wrestling superstar Gory Guerrero, Eddie grew up surrounded by wrestling in El Paso. Not only did his father wrestle and promote matches, but his three brothers, Chavo, Mando, and Hector, also entered the profession. Eddie was nineteen years younger than his oldest sibling, Chavo, and was heavily influenced by seeing his family perform.

His turn on the mat came in 1987 when he became a pro, and Guerrero spent his earliest years working in Mexico and Japan. In 1995, he was a fixture in the Philadelphia-based ECW promotion, and his unbelievable string of matches with Dean Malenko were among the best in the business at the time. He entered WCW and beat Dallas Page in a tournament final for the vacant U.S. Title on December 29, 1996. Guerrero also held the Cruiserweight title, but never broke through to the top level of the promotion's hierarchy—and WCW politics were to blame. In one emotional *Nitro* segment, he claimed Eric Bischoff was holding him back, and many people were left to wonder how much of the speech was true. After suffering serious injuries in a car accident, Guerrero ended up leaving WCW for the WWF in January of 2000 and took a commanding share of the spotlight upon arrival. He'd have stints as Intercontinental and European champion, and held the WWE Tag Team Title with nephew Chavo Guerrero Jr. and Tajiri.

Guerrero won the U.S. Title in the finals of a tournament on July 27, 2003, defeating Chris Benoit, and was champion until October. The biggest win of his career came on February 15, 2004 in San Francisco, when he pinned Brock Lesnar for the WWE Heavyweight Title after landing his patented frog splash. A month later at WrestleMania XX in New York City, he retained his belt over Kurt Angle in a memorable twenty-one-minute contest. Guerrero held back the challenge of John "Bradshaw" Layfield until losing the championship to him in a Texas Bullrope match on June 27, 2004 at the Great American Bash. A regular on *Smackdown*, Guerrero teamed with Rey Mysterio to win the WWE Tag Team Title from the Bashams in February of 2005, and then engaged in a personal war with Mysterio, even claiming to be the father of Rey's son. After several classic TV matches, Mysterio beat him for custody on August 21, 2005 at SummerSlam. The eternally charismatic Guerrero passed away in a Minneapolis hotel room on November 13, 2005.

Photo Courtesy of the Wrestling Revue Archives— www.wrestleprints.com

Born:	February 10, 1959
Height:	6'1"
Weight:	295
Real Name:	Tonga Uliuli Fifita
Parents:	Kelepi and Atiola Fifita
Wife:	Dorothy Fifita
Trained by:	Shohei Baba, Genichiro Tenryu
Identities:	Prince Tonga, King Tonga, Meng
Finisher:	Savate Kick, Tongan Death Grip
Tag Team:	The Islanders w/ Tomah, The Colossal Connection w/ Andre the Giant, The Faces of Fear w/ The Barbarian
Career Span:	1978-Present

PPV Record:	8-29, 1 DCO
WrestleMania Record:	1-3
WWE *Raw* TV Record:	2-3

Haku

The formidable Haku is not the kind of guy you wanted to run into in an alley on a dark evening. Luckily for anyone who actually met him, Haku is a nice, quiet, family man currently living in Florida. With that said, he's been more than successful in convincing the wrestling public that he's the opposite—a monster heel looking to demolish his rivals with his brute strength. The former Sumo wrestler from the Island of Tonga learned the profession while in Japan in the late 1970s, and traveled the globe honing his craft. He was given the title of WWF "King" after Harley Race was injured in 1988, and teamed with Andre the Giant to win the promotion's World Tag Team Title in late 1989. While in WCW, he was pushed as an unstoppable force and made it to the finals of the U.S. title tournament in 1995, but eventually lost to Sting. He held the WLW Title twice in 2000 and the WCW Hardcore belt in January of 2001. Every now and then, Haku still appears on the indie circuit.

Photo Courtesy of Dr. Mike Lano—Wrealano@aol.com

Hall, Scott

Born:	October 20, 1958
Height:	6'6"
Weight:	285
Real Name:	Scott Oliver Hall
High School:	American High School (Munich, Germany)
College:	St. Mary's College
Trained by:	Hiro Matsuda, Barry Windham
Identities:	Starship Coyote, Diamond Studd
Nicknames:	Magnum
Finisher:	Diamond Death Drop, The Razor's Edge
Groups:	New World Order (1996-1999, 2002)
Tag Teams:	The American Starship w/ Eagle (Dan Spivey), The Outsiders w/ Kevin Nash
Career Span:	1984-Present

PPV Record:	36-38, 1 NC
WrestleMania Record:	3-1
WWE *Raw* TV Record:	3-4, 2 NC
WWE *Smackdown* TV Record:	0-2
Titles Won:	19

Impressively built and full of charisma, Scott Hall performed in many entertaining contests during the 1990s. His ladder match against Shawn Michaels at WrestleMania X set the standard for all ladder matches to be compared, and had a significant role in the New World Order angle in WCW. In recent years, his life has been plagued by personal trials and tribulations that have kept him from a major role in pro wrestling and gotten him headlines for more dire reasons. Hall's contributions to the sport are considerable, and it is easy to remember him with his toothpick, parading around the squared circle as the Miami "Bad Guy," Razor Ramon. The son of a military father, Hall lived in many places when he was young, including Germany, Florida, and southern Maryland. He received his training in Tampa and entered the business, attaining his earliest fame in the AWA when he teamed with Curt Hennig to win the World Tag Team Title in 1986. He bounced around the business, working for WCW in 1991, and then was hired by the WWF.

As "Razor Ramon," Hall received a nice push, winning the vacant Intercontinental Title on September 27, 1993. On March 20, 1994, he beat Shawn Michaels to unify the latter's claim with his own, in a spectacular ladder match at WrestleMania. In 1995, he became the first three-time Intercontinental Champion, and followed up by winning his fourth in October over Dean Douglas. He left the WWF for WCW in 1996, initiating the NWO angle with his May 27, 1996 appearance on *Nitro*. A short time later, he was joined by his friend Kevin Nash and Hollywood Hogan, and the NWO turned the promotion on its head. Hall and Nash captured the WCW Tag Team Title five times between 1996 and 1999, and in 1997, he eliminated The Giant to win the World War III event. Hall briefly wrestled for the WWF again in 2002 and later worked for TNA, teaming with Nash to wear the World Tag Team Title in 2010. He often appears for various independent promotions.

Photo Courtesy of Bill Stahl

Born:	August 31, 1977
Height:	6'0"
Weight:	210
Real Name:	Jeffrey Nero Hardy
Parents:	Claude and Ruby Hardy
High School:	Union Pines High School (NC)
Identities:	Willow the Whisp, The Willow, Wolverine, Conquistador I
Nickname:	Charismatic Enigma
Finisher:	Swanton Bomb
Groups:	Team Xtreme (2000-2002), Immortal (2010-2011)
Career Span:	1993-Present

Hardy, Jeff

PPV Record:	50-57, 1 Draw, 1 NC
WrestleMania Record:	0-5
WWE *Raw* TV Record:	126-98, 2 DCO, 1 DDQ, 6 NC
WWE *Smackdown* TV Record:	74-58, 1 DCO, 1 DDQ, 10 NC
Titles Won:	31
Days as World Champion:	172
Age at first World Title Win:	31
Best Opponents:	The Undertaker, Rob Van Dam, CM Punk

Jeff Hardy brings many things to a wrestling match, including impressive ring savvy and mind-blowing high spots. His athleticism ranks among the best in the grappling world, and has carried him to main event status. Through his dedication to the business, magnetic personality, and unique appearance, he's acquired a legion of steady followers. His popularity has made it easy for the WWE and TNA to push him to the top level of their promotions, and Hardy has captured five heavyweight championships in those two organizations since 2008. The son of a tobacco farmer, Hardy grew up in the small town of Cameron, North Carolina, and was a fan of pro wrestling at a young age. Along with his older brother, Matt, he constructed a makeshift wrestling environment in their backyard, which included a trampoline, and practiced acrobatic moves incessantly. He was just sixteen years of age when he received his first preliminary match for the WWF in May of 1994, but it would be four years before he received a full-time contract.

The brothers received further training in Florida by the legendary Dory Funk Jr., and then came onto the WWF scene, albeit their push was slow at first. When it was time for them to shine, they did, particularly in big matches at WrestleMania that featured tables, ladders, and chairs. The TLC matches were spectacular displays of risky maneuvers that continuously set the bar higher and higher. There were no limits to what Jeff would do in the ring, above it from atop a tall ladder, or diving to the arena floor. The Hardys had a lot of success in tag team matches, winning a combined seven championships, and feuded heavily with Christian and Edge and the Dudleys. In 2001, as a singles performer, Hardy won the Intercontinental and Hardcore Titles, and was involved in a number of different angles before his sudden departure in 2003. During the middle of 2004, he resurfaced in TNA and challenged Jeff Jarrett for the NWA World Title.

Hardy made his way back to the WWE in 2006 and captured the Intercontinental Title three additional times. On December 14, 2008, he won a three-way match to win Edge's WWE Title, but lost it back to the latter at the Royal Rumble after his brother Matt interfered on behalf of his opponent. That led to a sibling rivalry, in which both brothers scored victories. Jeff beat Edge on June 7, 2009 for the World Title, but was the victim of CM Punk cashing in his Money in the Bank contract, and immediately lost the belt. The next month, Hardy regained the title, but Punk won it back at SummerSlam. He rejoined TNA in January of 2010 and won the vacant World Title at Bound for Glory with help from Hulk Hogan and Eric Bischoff. As the heel, he'd trade the title with Mr. Anderson before fading from the active roster after a controversial appearance at Victory Road in March of 2011, in which his main event match against Sting lasted less than two minutes. Hardy returned to TNA in August, and sought forgiveness for his actions from his peers and the fans.

Photo Courtesy of Dr. Mike Lano—Wrealano@aol.com

Born:	September 23, 1974
Height:	6'1"
Weight:	235
Real Name:	Matthew Moore Hardy
Parents:	Claude and Ruby Hardy
High School:	Union Pines High School (NC)
Trained by:	Dory Funk Jr.
Identities:	Surge, Conquistador II
Finisher:	Twist of Fate
Groups:	Team Xtreme (2000-2002)
Career Span:	1992-Present

PPV Record:	36-53
WrestleMania Record:	2-6
WWE *Raw* TV Record:	72-82, 2 DCO, 1 DDQ, 6 NC
WWE *Smackdown* TV Record:	126-123, 2 Draws, 1 DCO, 1 DDQ, 11 NC
Titles Won:	21
Days as World Champion:	127
Age at first World Title Win:	33
Best Opponents:	Edge, The Undertaker, Booker T
TV Appearances:	9

Hardy, Matt

An exciting grappler from Cameron, North Carolina, Matt Hardy teamed with his brother Jeff to form one of the most spectacular tag teams of this generation. The Hardys have come a long way since their days training on a backyard trampoline when they were kids, ascending up to the main stages of pro wrestling. They've defied the odds in the ring, leaping from turnbuckles and ladders, and constantly putting their bodies on the line. Together, they won the WWE World Tag Team Title six times and the WCW Tag Team belts once. After the Hardys went their own ways, Matt demonstrated that he was not to be pigeonholed as strictly a mid-card tag team worker, and stood out when he used the "Matt Hardy: Version 1.0" gimmick in 2002. He held both the U.S. and ECW World Titles, prevailing in a championship scramble bout in 2008 for the latter title and holding the belt for several months. In 2011, he debuted in TNA as a heel member of Immortal.

Hart, Bret

Born:	July 2, 1957
Height:	5'11"
Weight:	235
Real Name:	Bret Sergeant Hart
Parents:	Stu and Helen Hart
Family:	Brother of Bruce, Dean, Keith, Owen, Ross, Smith, and Wayne Hart, brother-in-law of Davey Boy Smith and Jim Neidhart
High School:	Ernest Manning High School (Calgary)
College:	Mount Royal College
Nicknames:	The Hitman
Finisher:	Sharpshooter
Groups:	The Hart Foundation (1997-1998), New World Order (1998), NWO 2000 (1999-2000)
Career Span:	1978-2011
Website:	www.brethart.com

PPV Record:	44-29, 1 Draw, 1 NC
WrestleMania Record:	8-6
WWE *Raw* TV Record:	2-0, 2 NC
Titles Won:	32
Days as World Champion:	710
Age at first World Title Win:	35
Best Opponents:	Steve Austin, Shawn Michaels, Owen Hart
Halls of Fame:	5
TV Appearances:	Over 20
Documentaries:	7

The "Excellence of Execution," Bret Hart was a preeminent superstar, one of the greatest Canadian wrestlers in history, and enormously popular throughout the world. Born into the business as the son of Stu Hart, Bret learned how to grapple in the basement of the Hart family home, known as the "Dungeon." The painstaking lessons he endured fostered a deep respect for the business and a laundry list of admirable qualities that he carried with him throughout his entire career. He broke free from a reputation as being strictly a tag team wrestler through hard work and consistently delivered first-class performances on the mat. The WWF recognized that he was ready for a substantial singles push, and Hart was capable of matching up against anyone in the promotion. Between 1991 and 1997, he was the backbone of the WWF, and won five World Titles, defining what it meant to be a traditional champion in a new era of wrestling shenanigans. Hart's smooth, calculating maneuvers set the standard very high for others to emulate.

The education Hart received from his father made his progression into the sport easy, and he stood out as an amateur in high school and college, even winning a Calgary city championship in 1974. Four years later, he made his pro debut, and was heavily influenced by wrestlers Mr. Hiro and Mr. Sakurada. He toured Puerto Rico, Amarillo, and Georgia in his first two years in the pro ranks, and feuded with the likes of Norman Frederick Charles III, Marty Jones, and Dynamite Kid in Calgary. He also teamed with brothers Keith and Bruce. From 1980 to 1982, he won the regional North American Title five times and had some grueling bouts with Leo Burke and Bad News Allen. Hart participated in a WWF Junior Title tournament for New Japan Pro Wrestling in early 1984 and teamed with Hulk Hogan on a few occasions. His explicit knowledge of technical wrestling drew the attention from WWF officials.

During the summer of 1984, Hart made his WWF debut and worked steadily as a preliminary grappler, often using a sleeperhold as a finisher. His role in the promotion was mainly undefined until becoming part of a heel tag team with Jim Neidhart known as the Hart Foundation, managed by Jimmy Hart in March of 1985. This was the central position he'd play for the next six years, although his talents would shine in the occasional one-on-one match. The Hart Foundation won the WWF Tag Team Title twice, the first in 1987 from the British Bulldogs, and the second in 1990 from Demolition. Hart went out on his own in 1991 and took the WWF by storm. He had two reigns as Intercontinental champion and wrestled a dynamic match against his brother-in-law Davey Boy Smith at SummerSlam in London on August 29, 1992 in which the latter captured the championship before 80,000 fans. Two months later, Hart dethroned Ric Flair for his first WWF World Title, and was champion until a loss to Yokozuna at WrestleMania IX.

On March 20, 1994, Hart beat Yokozuna for his second WWF championship, and participated in some of the most talked-about matches of the year against his brother, Owen. He'd lose the belt to Bob Backlund in November, but would regain it a year later from Diesel. At WrestleMania XII, he lost the title to Shawn Michaels in sudden death of an Iron Man match. Hart violently feuded with Steve Austin, and their explosive WrestleMania XIII submission match ended when "Stone Cold" passed out while in the sharpshooter. Hart's actions during the match drew the ire of fans, which led to his condemnation of U.S. audiences, effectively turning him heel—but maintaining his popularity north of the border. He reformed the pro-Canada Hart Foundation and, on August 3, 1997, beat The Undertaker for his fifth and final WWF Title. With his future in the promotion in doubt, Hart and Vince McMahon haggled over a match that would see Bret lose the belt to Michaels on November 9, 1997 at the Survivor Series in Montreal.

However, Hart didn't want to lose the belt in Canada, and went into the match believing that he'd drop the title on a later date. McMahon didn't want Hart appearing on WCW TV with the WWF belt, and had the referee call for the bell seconds after Michaels applied a sharpshooter. This event became known as the infamous "Montreal Screwjob." Hart departed the WWF for WCW, and over the next three years won the World Title twice, the U.S. crown four times, and had memorable matches against Chris Benoit and Dallas Page. A concussion received during a match forced him into semi-retirement in January of 2000. Two years later, Hart suffered a stroke after a bicycle accident and displayed an inspiring amount of courage in the recovery process. He made his WWE return as a wrestler in 2010, battling McMahon at WrestleMania XXVI, and beat The Miz for the U.S. Title. Hart dedicated his life to the business, understood the art of pro wrestling, and was a tremendous credit to the sport.

Photo Courtesy of Dr. Mike Lano—Wrealano@aol.com

Born:	May 7, 1965
Height:	5'10"
Weight:	225
Real Name:	Owen James Hart
Family:	Brother of Bret, Bruce, Dean, Keith, Ross, Smith, and Wayne Hart, brother-in-law of Davey Boy Smith and Jim Neidhart
High School:	Ernest Manning High School (Calgary)
College:	University of Calgary
Trained by:	Stu Hart
Identities:	The Avenger
Nicknames:	The Rocket
Groups:	The Hart Foundation (1997-1998), The Nation of Domination (1998)
Tag Teams:	High Energy w/ Koko B. Ware, The New Foundation w/ Jim Neidhart
Career Span:	1986-1999
Died:	May 23, 1999, Kansas City, MO 34 years old

Hart, Owen

PPV Record:	28-30, 1 DCO
WrestleMania Record:	5-2, 1 DCO
WWE *Raw* TV Record:	6-4, 1 DDQ, 1 NC
WWE *Smackdown* TV Record:	1-0
Titles Won:	13
Days as World Champion:	14
Age at first World Title Win:	28
Best Opponents:	Bret Hart, Shawn Michaels, Davey Boy Smith
Halls of Fame:	1

The youngest child of Stu and Helen Hart, Owen was an undeniable wrestling talent, able to match holds on the mat or scale the top rope and fly through the air. His repertoire of maneuvers was endless, and during his time in the industry, he played many roles. Unfortunately, there was one role in particular, a revisited gimmick from the past with a non-wrestling related stunt for an entrance, which ultimately cost him his life. Initially wanting to become a physical education teacher, Hart followed his brothers into the sport, in the footsteps of his father, Stu, and was a hot prospect in the latter's Calgary promotion. He displayed advanced skills for someone so young, and annexed regional gold. In 1988, he went to Japan and did the same, pinning

Hiroshi Hase in Sendai for the IWGP Junior Heavyweight Title. Owen also debuted for the WWF as the masked "Blue Blazer," which was a tough character to sell to the audience.

It really wasn't until he turned on his brother Bret and became a heel in 1994 that his stock in the WWF really began to rise. At WrestleMania X, Owen pinned his sibling and became a top contender for the World Title. A few months later, he won the King of the Ring tournament, and declared himself the "King of Harts." He received a title shot against Bret at SummerSlam and the two wrestled a thirty-three-minute classic with Bret retaining the belt. In 1995, he teamed with the massive Yokozuna to capture the WWF Tag Team Title and won the belts again with Davey Boy Smith (also known as the British Bulldog, and Owen's brother-in-law) the following year. Hart became a double-champion on April 28, 1997, when he beat Rocky Maivia Jr. for the Intercontinental Title. On May 23, 1999, Owen was booked in a match against The Godfather at Kansas City's Kemper Arena, and was going to make an elaborate entrance via the rafters above the ring. When his harness failed to hold him, he fell more than 70-feet to the ring below, and was fatally injured. His death left a hole in the industry that still hasn't healed.

Photo Courtesy of Dr. Mike Lano—Wrealano@aol.com

Hase, Hiroshi

Born:	May 5, 1961
Height:	6'0"
Weight:	225
College:	Senshu University
Olympics:	Greco-Roman Wrestling (1984) (Representing Japan) (9th Place)
Amateur Titles:	Two-Time World Freestyle Wrestling Champion
Trained by:	Riki Choshu, Stu Hart
Finisher:	Northern Lights Suplex
Tag Team:	The Viet Cong Express w/ Fumihiro Niikura
Career Span:	1986-2006

Titles Won:	8
Days as World Champion:	8
Age at first World Title Win:	32
Best Opponents:	Tatsumi Fujinami, Kenta Kobashi, Keiji Mutoh
Halls of Fame:	2

Olympian Hiroshi Hase was well-respected throughout the world for his technical abilities and has been a politician in Japan for the last sixteen years. With his stellar amateur background, his future was bright as he entered the business in 1986 and excelled as expected. He won the IWGP Junior Heavyweight Title twice, and then formed a successful tag team with Kensuke Sasaki. On November 1, 1990, they won the IWGP Tag Team Title from Keiji Mutoh and Masa Chono. The duo lost the belts in December of that year to Hiro Saito and Super Strong Machine, but regained it from them in March of 1991. Hase and Sakaki went head to head with the WCW champion Steiner Brothers on March 21 and lost the IWGP straps. Hase also won the IWGP belts with Mutoh as his partner on two occasions; as well as beating Rick Rude on March 16, 1994 to win the WCW International World Title, with Rude regaining the title eight days later. In 1995, he was elected to the Japanese House of Councilors, and in 2007, he became the chairman of the PWF.

Photo Courtesy of Dr. Mike Lano—Wrealano@aol.com

Born:	July 3, 1965
Height:	6'0"
Weight:	290
Family:	Father of Daichi Hashimoto
Identities:	Hashif Khan, Shogun
Finisher:	Jumping DDT
Promoted:	Zero-One (2001-2005)
Career Span:	1984-2004
Died:	July 11, 2005, Yokohama, Japan 40 years old

Hashimoto, Shinya

Titles Won:	11
Days as World Champion:	1,307
Age at first World Title Win:	28
Best Opponents:	Keiji Mutoh, Tatsumi Fujinami, Masa Chono
Halls of Fame:	3

On July 11, 2005, pro wrestling lost a genuine legend in Shinya Hashimoto, who died at forty-five years of age. The exciting ring warrior had thrilled fans across the globe since his debut in 1984 and accumulated a spectacular list of achievements. Hashimoto was much more dedicated than the average grappler; fine-tuning his skills early in his career under the guidance of the great Antonio Inoki. He then toured the U.S. and Canada, where he picked up additional knowledge from Stu Hart and Brad Rheingans, two of the best teachers in the sport. It's no coincidence that Hashimoto was a great wrestler as he had put in the time learning the trade, both the fundamentals and the electrifying maneuvers that would make him popular with crowds. He won the IWGP Heavyweight Title on three occasions between 1993 and 1997, and on October 13, 2001, he captured the NWA World Championship. Two years later, he became the fourth man in history to win both the IWGP and Triple Crown Titles when he beat Keiji Mutoh for the latter.

Hawk

Born:	January 26, 1958
Height:	6'3"
Weight:	277
Real Name:	Michael James Hegstrand
Parents:	Arthur and Margaret Hegstrand
Wife:	Dale Hegstrand
High School:	Patrick Henry High School (MN)
Trained by:	Eddie Sharkey
Identities:	Hawk Warrior
Finisher:	Doomsday Device w/ Animal
Groups:	LOD 2000 (1998)
Tag Teams:	The Hell Raisers w/ The Power Warrior
Career Span:	1983-2003
Died:	October 19, 2003, Indian Rocks Beach, FL 45 years old

PPV Record:	28-17, 1 DC, 1 DDQ, 1 NC
WrestleMania Record:	3-0
WWE *Raw* TV Record:	0-2
Titles Won:	22
Days as World Champion:	196
Age at first World Title Win:	34
Best Opponents:	Ric Flair, Keiji Mutoh, Masa Chono
Halls of Fame:	3

The international tag team scene was reinvigorated by The Road Warriors, made up of two friends from the Minneapolis area who were known to fans as Hawk and Animal. With spiked shoulder pads, intimidating haircuts and face paint, the duo actually appeared like warriors. Hawk grew up on the north side of Minneapolis, played football in high school, and was a devoted weightlifter. Along with Animal, he trained to be a grappler, and then proceeded to Georgia, where he joined Paul Ellering's Legion of Dome in 1983. During the summer of 1984, Hawk and Animal won the AWA World Tag Team Title and held the belts for over a year. They had a similar run in Japan with the AJPW International Tag Team Title as well. On October 29, 1988, they beat The Midnight Express for the NWA World Tag Team Title and in August of 1991, they became the first team to hold the AWA, NWA, and WWF belts when they toppled The Nasty Boys at SummerSlam. Hawk also teamed with Kensuke Sasaki to capture the IWGP Title twice and held the CWA World Title in 1992.

Born:	March 29, 1959
Height:	6'1"
Weight:	240
Real Name:	Michael Joseph Seitz
Trained by:	Afa
Identities:	Doc Hendrix
Nickname:	Pretty Boy, P.S. (Purely Sexy)
Finisher:	DDT
Music:	Lead vocalist on the album *Off the Streets*, including the song "Badstreet USA."
Career Span:	1977-2001

PPV Record:	7-12, 1 Draw
WrestleMania Record:	0-1
Titles Won:	25
Best Opponents:	Bruiser Brody, Kerry Von Erich, Rick Martel

Hayes, Michael

Wrestler and rock musician, Michael Hayes of Pensacola, Florida, entered the wrestling profession when he was still a teenager, gaining experience along the Mississippi circuit and early on in Germany. In late 1978, he bonded with another young athlete, Terry Gordy, and the two formed the basis for what would become the renowned Fabulous Freebirds. They garnered initial accolades while in the Mid-America territory and had many tough matches, among such legends as Jerry Lawler and Bill Dundee. While in the Mid-South territory in 1980, the duo added a third member, Buddy Roberts. In December of 1982, in Dallas, the fabled Freebirds-Von Erich feud commenced and lasted years. Later in the decade, Hayes turned fan favorite and won the U.S. belt from Lex Luger. He also reformed the Freebirds with Jimmy Garvin and captured the World Tag Team Title in 1989 and again in 1991. He remained in WCW until 1993, then joining the WWF as a commentator. His backstage duties increased until he was head of the creative team for *Smackdown* in 2006.

Born:	July 12, 1974
Height:	5'10"
Weight:	195
Real Name:	Gregory Shane Helms
High School:	East Wake High School (NC)
Trained by:	Hardy Boys, WCW Power Plant
Nicknames:	The Show, Serial Thriller, Sugar
Finisher:	Chokeslam
Career Span:	1991-Present

PPV Record:	18-19
WrestleMania Record:	1-1
WWE *Raw* TV Record:	24-57, 1 NC
WWE *Smackdown* TV Record:	22-40, 1 NC
Titles Won:	20
Best Opponents:	The Rock, Rey Mysterio Jr., Ric Flair

Helms, Gregory

Under a mask as the wrestling superhero "The Hurricane," Shane Helms earned widespread popularity. His sound ring work balanced out his character, and he was involved in many comical skits and entertaining matches. Hailing from Smithfield, North Carolina, he broke into regional independents as a teenager and got his first big break as a member of 3-Count in WCW. Days before the promotion folded, he won the Cruiserweight Championship, and took the belt with him to the WWF. He reigned as titleholder two additional times, including a reign that lasted more than a year, as well as teaming with Kane and Rosey to win the World Tag Team Title. He left the WWE in 2010 and rejoined the indie circuit where he first got his start.

Hennig, Curt

Born:	March 28, 1958
Height:	6'2"
Weight:	235
Real Name:	Curtis Michael Hennig
Parents:	Lawrence and Irene Hennig
Family:	Father of Michael McGillicutty and Amy Hennig
Wife:	Leonice Hennig
High Schools:	Robbinsdale High School (MN), Saguaro High School (AZ)
Colleges:	Normandale Community College, University of Minnesota
Trained by:	Verne Gagne, Larry Hennig
Groups:	The Four Horsemen (1997), New World Order (1997-1998)
Career Span:	1981-2003
Died:	February 10, 2003, Brandon, FL 44 years old

PPV Record:	14-35
WrestleMania Record:	1-3
WWE *Raw* TV Record:	1-6, 1 NC
Titles Won:	15
Days as World Champion:	373
Age at first World Title Win:	29
Best Opponents:	Bret Hart, Ric Flair, Nick Bockwinkel
Halls of Fame:	2

A profoundly scientific wrestler, Curt Hennig was admired by peers and fans alike for his adroit mat techniques. He was a first-rate grappler, gifted in the fundamentals and owning the right kind of mannerisms to get a crowd going. The son of Larry Hennig, Curt was destined for ring greatness, and since he grew up in the Minneapolis area, it was only fitting that he'd first become a superstar in the AWA, and on May 2, 1987, he defeated Nick Bockwinkel for the AWA World Championship. He held the title for a year and a week, until losing it to Jerry Lawler on May 9, 1988. In the WWF, he became known as "Mr. Perfect," a gimmick that he performed flawlessly, and beat Tito Santana for the first of two Intercontinental Titles on April 23, 1990. A back injury slowed his career, but he had a respectable run in WCW, where he won the U.S. and World Tag Team Titles with Barry Windham. He also had a string of success while wrestling on the indie circuit. Hennig had a second stint in the WWF and a run in TNA before his premature death in 2003.

Born:	June 12, 1971
Height:	6'3"
Weight:	375
Real Name:	Mark Jerrold Henry
Parents:	Ernest and Barbara Henry
High School:	Silsbee High School (TX)
Olympics:	Weightlifting (1992—Barcelona) (10th Place) Weightlifting (1996—Atlanta) (14th Place)
Trained by:	Stu Hart
Nicknames:	World's Strongest Man, Sexual Chocolate
Finisher:	Powerslam
Groups:	Nation of Domination (1998)
Career Span:	1996-Present

Henry, Mark

PPV Record:	18-34, 1 NC
WrestleMania Record:	0-3
WWE *Raw* TV Record:	54-58, 8 NC
WWE *Smackdown* TV Record:	45-46, 1 DCO, 6 NC
Titles Won:	3
Days as World Champion:	161
Age at first World Title Win:	37
Best Opponents:	Randy Orton, Big Show, The Undertaker

Prematurely born, Mark Henry grew to immense proportions, weighing 340 pounds while in high school. When he joined the U.S. weightlifting team, he was literally the biggest thing to hit the sport in decades. By nineteen years of age, he was considered a world-class lifter, and coaches marveled at his natural ability. Henry was more than just a mass of muscle; he was coordinated, flexible, and supremely athletic, able to slam dunk a basketball and capable of doing a split. He underachieved at the 1992 and 1996 Olympics, but took three medals—including a gold in the snatch event—at the 1995 Pan American Games. Signed to a ten-year contract by the WWF in 1996, Henry joined the Nation of Domination and participated in an odd angle with Mae Young, which saw the latter give birth to a hand. Winner of the 2002 Arnold Strongman Competition, Henry beat Kane for the ECW Title in June of 2008, and instituted his own "Hall of Pain" in 2011 en route to winning the World Heavyweight Title from Randy Orton at the September pay-per-view.

Hogan, Hulk

Born:	August 11, 1953
Height:	6'7"
Weight:	302
Real Name:	Terry Gene Bollea
Parents:	Peter and Ruth Bollea
Family:	Uncle of Horace Boulder
Wife:	Jennifer Bollea
High School:	Robinson High School (FL)
Colleges:	St. Petersburg Junior College, University of South Florida
Identities:	The Super Destroyer (Masked), Terry Boulder, Sterling Golden
Nicknames:	The Hulk, The Hulkster, Immortal
Finisher:	Big foot leading into the legdrop
Tag Teams:	The Mega Powers w/ Randy Savage, The Mega Maniacs w/ Brutus Beefcake, The Monster Maniacs w/ Randy Savage
Groups:	New World Order (1996-1999) (2002), The Millionaires Club (2000), Immortal (2010-2011)
Managed by:	Billy Spears, Fred Blassie, Johnny Valiant, Elizabeth, Jimmy Hart
Career Span:	1977-2011
Website:	www.hulkhogan.com

PPV Record:	52-27, 1 DDQ, 3 NC
WrestleMania Record:	8-3, 1 DDQ
WWE *Raw* TV Record:	6-1, 1 NC
WWE *Smackdown* TV Record:	9-4, 2 NC
Titles Won:	16
Days as World Champion:	3,362
Age at first World Title Win:	30
Best Opponents:	Randy Savage, Andre the Giant, Sting
Halls of Fame:	3
TV Appearances:	Over a hundred, including several TV series
Movies:	16
Published Books:	2

In wrestling history, only a handful of individuals have had the capability to step into influential roles and single-handedly broker revolutionary periods that affect an entire business. Hulk Hogan was one of those people, ascending into the national limelight in 1984 with his signature blond hair, bronze coloring, and massive build; immediately capturing the imaginations of the young and old. His free-flowing charisma attracted immense attention for the World Wrestling Federation, which was in the process of launching a national campaign on the sacred territories, and his role as the captain of the grapplers helped the promotion achieve goals that were once deemed unattainable. Hogan spearheaded an amazing crusade to expand the WWF into the first nationally-functioning promotion to endure the many pitfalls of such an endeavor. It also allowed the organization to transition into a culture of pay-per-view and mass marketing, and ultimately, enormous financial success.

Hogan's rise to iconic status went hand-in-hand with the growth of the WWF, and his box office power during those pivotal years was astonishing. Born in Georgia, Hogan grew up in Port Tampa, Florida, and was interested in baseball and music early in life. The exciting pro wrestling scene in the area caught his eye as a kid, and he attended local shows where he caught the attention of the Brisco Brothers. Hogan's impressive size got him in the front door of a local wrestling school, and his commitment to the craft was sincerely tested after Hiro Matsuda broke his leg during his initial workout. But Hogan was resolute, making his debut in 1977, and wrestling along the Florida circuit—competing under a mask as the "Super Destroyer" at times. Two years later, he went to New York for an impressive run as a heel in Vincent J. McMahon's WWF and adopted the name, "Hulk Hogan." His first stint in the WWF placed him in matches against Andre the Giant and his appearances at Madison Square Garden garnered international attention.

Overseas for New Japan Pro Wrestling, Hogan won the initial IWGP tournament and both teamed and opposed the legendary Antonio Inoki. He also went toe-to-toe with Sylvester Stallone in the film *Rocky III* as the mammoth "Thunderlips," and his performance left an imprint on audiences worldwide. Hogan was simply bigger than life, and his two-year tour of the Minneapolis-based AWA ended in late 1983 without the anticipated championship win over Nick Bockwinkel for the World Title. Instead, he took advantage of a job offer for Vincent K. McMahon, the son of his former boss and the enthusiastic new leader of the WWF. In less than a month in the organization, Hogan beat The Iron Sheik on January 23, 1984 and won the WWF World Heavyweight crown. The "Hulkamania" era was officially launched, and Hogan was the right man in the right place at the right time. Crowds loved him, and his promos, ring work, and overall mannerisms won over a whole generation of wrestling fans.

Hogan was the central character of McMahon's operations as the WWF expanded nationally, implementing an annual WrestleMania event, as well as semi-regular pay-per-view shows. At the box office, he was unrivaled as a draw, and Hogan remained the undefeated champion until 1988. At WrestleMania V, a year later, he regained the belt with a win over Randy Savage, and in 1990, he grappled fellow fan favorite, The Ultimate Warrior, in a rare losing effort. He'd return to the top spot at WrestleMania VII, defeating Sgt. Slaughter, and by 1993, he was a five-time WWF World Champion. In June of 1994, he signed a deal with WCW, and debuted on July 17, 1994 to capture the World Title from Ric Flair. WCW followed the WWF blueprint by relentlessly pushing Hogan, and his reign as champion lasted until October 29, 1995 when he was defeated by The Giant by DQ. In 1996, he shocked the industry by turning heel, becoming "Hollywood Hogan," and a member of the New World Order.

The NWO was a band of rebellious heels intent on causing problems within WCW, and the angle developed perfectly, helping the promotion maintain an advantage over the WWF in the ratings war. Hogan was always a main figure in the storyline, winning and losing the World Title and feuding with the likes of

Roddy Piper, Lex Luger, and Sting. In 1998, he lost the championship to the undefeated Bill Goldberg at the Georgia Dome before more than 41,000 fans. The stability of the promotion began to dwindle and Hogan left under odd circumstances following the controversial Bash at the Beach pay-per-view on July 9, 2000 . . . he'd never return to WCW. Two years later, he resurfaced in the WWF and had a memorable match against The Rock at WrestleMania X-Eight before a rowdy crowd of Hogan supporters. On April 21, 2002, he beat Triple H for his sixth WWE World Championship but lost it the following month to The Undertaker.

Hogan faced off and beat Randy Orton at SummerSlam on August 20, 2006, and toured Australia in 2009—where he feuded heavily with Ric Flair. On January 4, 2010, he debuted for TNA, and was working with Eric Bischoff to change the creative focus of the promotion. He took Abyss under his wing and worked a number of angles, including one in which he took over ownership of TNA from Dixie Carter. Outside the ring, he appeared in thirty-five episodes of the VH1 reality show entitled *Hogan Knows Best*, featuring his then-wife Linda and two children from 2005 to 2007. Over the next couple years, he faced many harrowing personal trials, documented in his second book, *My Life Outside the Ring*, and a 2010 A&E special, *Finding Hulk Hogan*. He has since made a number of TV appearances including on *American Idol* in 2011. He is still a pivotal player in TNA and maintains his unparalleled popularity. Hogan has impacted pro wrestling like no other.

Photo Courtesy of Dr. Mike Lano—Wrealano@aol.com

Honky Tonk Man, The

Born:	January 25, 1953
Height:	6'1"
Weight:	265
Real Name:	Roy Wayne Farris
Family:	Cousin of Jerry Lawler
High School:	Central High School (TN)
Trained by:	Herb Welch
Nickname:	The Greatest Intercontinental Champion of All-Time
Finisher:	Swinging Neckbreaker
Tag Team:	Rhythm and Blues w/ Greg Valentine
Career Span:	1977-Present
Website:	www.honkytonkman.net

PPV Record:	4-10, 1 Draw
WrestleMania Record:	2-1
Titles Won:	26
Best Opponents:	Ricky Steamboat, Randy Savage, Dusty Rhodes

A thoroughly entertaining wrestler, The Honky Tonk Man has made a career out of wearing jumpsuits, riding around in pink Cadillacs, and strumming guitars—much like another Tennessee icon, Elvis. His gimmick as a "musician" and grappler carried him to the longest reign in WWF Intercontinental Title history, a total of 454 days, and to center stage at WrestleMania. Born in Bolivar, Tennessee, he was a weightlifter at Memphis State and initially wanted to be a teacher. He coached high school athletics for two years before attending a wrestling camp in Dyersburg. He quickly found out that there was much more money to be made as a grappler than as a teacher, and began wrestling full time. On June 2, 1987, he beat Rick Steamboat for the Intercontinental Title and remained titleholder until August 29, 1988, when he lost it to the Ultimate Warrior in twenty-eight seconds. He performed a song at WrestleMania VI and often worked as a WWF commentator during the 1990s. He still wrestles on the indie circuit today.

Photo Courtesy of Dr. Mike Lano—Wrealano@aol.com

Born:	August 31, 1979
Height:	5'4"
Weight:	130
Real Name:	Mickie Laree James
High School:	Patrick Henry High School (VA)
Trained by:	Dory Funk Jr., Ohio Valley trainers
Identities:	Alexis Laree
Career Span:	1999-Present

James, Mickie

PPV Record:	16-22, 1 NC
WrestleMania Record:	1-2
WWE *Raw* TV Record:	71-51, 1 DDQ, 2 NC
WWE *Smackdown* TV Record:	10-6
Titles Won:	16
Days as World Champion:	496
Age at first World Title Win:	26
Best Opponents:	Trish Stratus, Tara, Madison Rayne

Currently one of the most talented and enthusiastic performers in women's wrestling, Mickie James of Virginia represents "Hardcore Country" in mind, body, and spirit. Her determination to rank among the best in the sport was second to none, and she graduated out of the indies and Ohio Valley to become a feature grappler in the WWE. Between 2006 and 2010, James held the WWE Women's championship on five occasions, and also captured the Divas Title from Maryse in 2009. The following year, she turned up in TNA and won the Knockouts belt twice in 2011, from Madison Rayne and Winter. As popular as ever, she is also a country singer.

Jannetty, Marty

Born:	February 3, 1962
Height:	5'11"
Weight:	220
Real Name:	Frederick Martin Jannetty
High School:	Hardware High School (GA)
Trained by:	The Oates Brothers
Identities:	Martin Oates
Finisher:	Showstopper
Tag Teams:	The Uptown Boys w/ Tommy Rogers, The New Rockers w/ Leif Cassidy
Career Span:	1984-Present

PPV Record:	6-18
WrestleMania Record:	1-2
WWE *Raw* TV Record:	1-2
WWE *Smackdown* TV Record:	0-1
Titles Won:	16
Best Opponents:	Shawn Michaels, Steve Austin, Kurt Angle

Rocker Marty Jannetty grew up in Columbus, Georgia and entered the business in 1984. While working in the Central States, he befriended Shawn Michaels and the two formed a remarkably compatible tag team able to perform colorful spots and garner loud crowd reactions—especially from younger fans. As the Midnight Rockers, they won the AWA World Tag Team Title in 1987. The following year, they jumped to the WWF, where their popularity intensified, but were obscured by the larger teams in the promotion. In October of 1990, they won the tag team title from the Hart Foundation, but the belts were returned to the latter on a technicality and the duo parted ways in 1991. On May 17, 1993, Jannetty captured Michaels' Intercontinental Title in a classic match on *Raw*. The following January, Marty and the 1-2-3 Kid won the WWF Tag Team Title. Jannetty has made a number of appearances for the WWE throughout the years, including a match on *Raw* against The Miz in October of 2009; a bout he lost. He is still a regular on the indie scene.

Born:	July 14, 1967
Height:	5'10"
Weight:	230
Real Name:	Jeffrey Leonard Jarrett
Parents:	Jerry and Deborah Jarrett
Trained by:	Jerry Jarrett, Tojo Yamamoto
Identities:	The Blue Blazer
Nicknames:	Double J, The Chosen One
Finisher:	The Stroke, Figure-four leglock
Groups:	The Four Horsemen (1997), New World Order 2000 (1999-2000), The New Blood (2000), The Magnificent Seven (2000-2001), Planet Jarrett (2005), Immortal (2010)
Owner:	J Sports & Entertainment (2002) (partner with Jerry Jarrett), TNA Entertainment, LLC (2002-Present) (minority shareholder)
Career Span:	1986-Present

Jarrett, Jeff

PPV Record:	83-84, 5 NC
WrestleMania Record:	1-1
WWE *Raw* TV Record:	15-11, 1 DDQ, 2 NC
Titles Won:	74
Days as World Champion:	1,620 (and counting)
Age at first World Title Win:	26
Best Opponents:	Kurt Angle, Booker T, Sting

Wrestling has come very naturally to Jeff Jarrett, a third-generation grappler; and his work over the last twenty-five years has been Hall of Fame quality, particularly when he's drawing the ire from just about everyone with his overwhelmingly heelish attitude. His ability to grind into the minds of wrestling fans catapults him to the head of the class in terms of wrestling psychology. It is hard not to lambaste his overly cocky persona and his brash and arrogant remarks. But his in-ring wrestling is textbook, covering many fundamental bases. Where his size could've been a handicap, Jarrett perfected the mental game, and that, along with his admirable wrestling skills, have carried him to great success. In fact, he's held the WCW, WWA, USWA, AAA, and NWA World Heavyweight Titles. He was a major performer in the WWF, WCW, and currently with TNA, where he still is able to inflame audiences, much like the top rule-breakers of yesteryear.

The grandson of Eddie Marlin and son of Jerry Jarrett, Jeff became a wrestler in 1986 and appeared in the CWA and USWA, where he amassed a full resume of championship victories. In 1993, he arrived in the WWF and received national exposure for the first time in his career. He was a perennial Intercontinental Champion and developed his heel country singer gimmick, much to the dismay of crowds. He used a guitar as a weapon, smashing it over the heads of foes, for which he drew a lot of heat. Jarrett jumped to WCW for a year term in 1996-1997, but then returned to the WWF. Finally, in 1999, he departed the WWF for the final time, burning a bridge in the process, and went to WCW, where he'd stay until the promotion was sold. It was during that period that he'd ascend to the World Heavyweight Title, initially winning a tournament for the vacant strap in April of 2000. Over the next few months, he lost and re-won the WCW belt three additional times. When WCW closed up shop, Jarrett had to look for opportunities other than the WWF for work.

Teaming with his father, Jerry, a veteran promoter, Jarrett established Total Nonstop Action in 2002. The new promotion was based out of Nashville, and was positioned to assume the number two promotional role in the U.S. with a weekly pay-per-view offering. On November 20, 2002, he beat Ron Killings for his first NWA World Title. Over the next four years, he'd win the belt five more times and participate in a long running feud with A.J. Styles. Two of his other major opponents during this time were Christian Cage and Sting. With those successes, Jarrett's most intense ring war came against Kurt Angle, which extended off and on for a period of years, and was rekindled in the latter stages of 2010. The grudge was given an extra boost of symbolism when Angle's ex-wife Karen married Jarrett, and the real life relationship was turned into a wrestling storyline involving Kurt. Their 2011 feud included many intense battles, and Jarrett returned to the title picture, this time in Mexico, when he won the AAA World Title on June 18, 2011 from El Zorro.

Born:	November 9, 1970
Height:	5'10"
Weight:	225
Real Name:	Christopher Keith Irvine
Parents:	Edward "Ted" and Loretta Irvine
High School:	Westwood Collegiate (Winnipeg)
College:	Red River Community College
Identities:	Super Liger
Nicknames:	Lionheart, Y2J, Living Legend
Finisher:	The Lion Tamer, Walls of Jericho, Lionsault
Tag Teams:	Sudden Impact w/ Lance Storm, The Thrillseekers w/ Lance Storm
Career Span:	1990-Present
Website:	www.chrisjericho.com

Jericho, Chris

PPV Record:	60-76
WrestleMania Record:	4-6
WWE *Raw* TV Record:	160-164, 2 DCO, 15 NC
WWE *Smackdown* TV Record:	74-88, 1 Draw, 1 DCO, 10 NC
Titles Won:	37
Days as World Champion:	219
Age at first World Title Win:	30
Best Opponents:	Shawn Michaels, Steve Austin, The Rock
Halls of Fame:	1
TV Appearances:	over 50
Movies:	3
Published Books:	2

A versatile entertainer, Chris Jericho can safely be called the "King of All Media" when it comes to professional wrestlers. He broached the usually impenetrable wall from wrestling into the mainstream media by performing on the wildly popular television show *Dancing with the Stars*, appeared in several films, wrote two successful books, and tours as the lead singer of a rock band, Fozzy. On top of all that, he's been an influential figure in wrestling for the last fifteen years, initially gaining rave reviews for his cruiserweight showings in WCW to becoming the first grappler to win the undisputed WWF World Heavyweight Title. Behind the microphone, he's delivered top-notch promos, setting himself apart from his peers, and it didn't matter if he was invoking the name "Bore-us" Malenko or going off on a tangent on Shawn Michaels, he always gained an intense fan reaction. This combination of being able to convey psychologically stimulating promos with his abundance of mat talent makes him a superstar in every sense of the word.

Jericho emulated his father, renowned NHL player Ted Irvine, by playing hockey in high school, but followed his interest in wrestling to the Hart Brothers camp in Calgary, where he was extensively trained. Physically able to perform high-flying maneuvers that few others could, he was very impressive from an early age, and gained experience in Japan and Mexico—two places that allowed the quicker non-heavyweights to thrive. It also gave him an opportunity to gain further experience before entering the U.S. indie scene in SMW, then in Philadelphia, for ECW. He advanced to WCW in 1996 and would remain in the promotion for three years. Despite his best efforts, he couldn't break out of the middle of the card, but distinguished himself as a four-time Cruiserweight champion and TV titleholder in 1998. He'd proven his value, and the WWF was ready to exploit his talents where WCW had failed to do so.

By the latter stages of 2001, Jericho had already won the WWF Intercontinental Title four times, plus the European and Hardcore championships. He defeated The Rock for the WCW World Heavyweight Title on October 21, 2001, and was soon entered in a four-man tournament to determine an undisputed titleholder on December 9, 2001. That night, Jericho unexpectedly went over both The Rock and Steve Austin and won the championship. Elevated to another plateau of wrestling success, Jericho went into WrestleMania X-Eight as the defending champion, but lost the title to Triple H. Jericho feuded with the likes of Rob Van Dam and Christian over the Intercontinental Title, and also battled Shawn Michaels and Goldberg. In August of 2005, he left the promotion to focus on his band and reemerged in November of 2007—appearing to not have missed a step. Jericho did battle with Randy Orton and JBL prior to kick-starting his longtime rivalry with Michaels. Jericho also won the Intercontinental Title two more times, giving him nine reigns in total.

Six years had passed since Jericho last held the Undisputed World Title, and on September 7, 2008, he prevailed in a championship scramble match and captured the belt once again. He lost the title to Batista on October 26, 2008, but regained it eight days later on *Raw* in a cage match. John Cena ended his reign at the Survivor Series on November 23. At WrestleMania XXV, Jericho won a handicap elimination contest over a trio of legends, Jimmy Snuka, Ricky Steamboat, and Roddy Piper, and held the Unified World Tag Team Title with The Big Show. In February of 2010, he won the World Title for a third time, but lost it to Jack Swagger in late March on *Smackdown*. He left the WWE again during the summer and participated in ABC's *Dancing with the Stars* in 2011, teaming with Cheryl Burke, and placing 7th. His second autobiography, *Undisputed*, a follow-up to his acclaimed 2007 book, *A Lion's Tale*, was released in early 2011. There were rumblings going into 2012 that Jericho was going to make his WWE return, but no one was certain.

Born:	December 12, 1952
Height:	6'3"
Weight:	275
Real Name:	Sylvester Ritter
High School:	Bowman High School (NC)
College:	Fayetteville State University
College Ach.:	All-CIAA (1975), All-NAIA (1975)
Pro Sports:	Ohio Valley Panthers (1975)
Trained by:	Sonny King
Identities:	Leroy Rochester, Big Daddy Ritter
Groups:	Dudes with Attitudes (1990)
Career Span:	1976-1993
Died:	June 2, 1998, Near Forest, MS 45 years old

Junkyard Dog

PPV Record:	6-5, 1 NC
WrestleMania Record:	1-3
Titles Won:	20
Days as World Champion:	21
Age at first World Title Win:	39
Best Opponents:	Ric Flair, Harley Race, Ted DiBiase
Halls of Fame:	2

One of the greatest stars of the "Rock and Wrestling" era, Junkyard Dog was extraordinarily popular, arguably second only to Hulk Hogan in the 1985-1987 time frame. A former footballer, he received NFL tryouts with Houston and Green Bay, and made headway in his quest to play for the Packers, but was sidelined when he suffered a serious knee injury. In November of 1976, he made his pro wrestling debut in Batesboro, South Carolina as part of the Southern Wrestling Association. He shuffled around the territories before landing in the Mid-South promotion for Bill Watts. It was there that he adopted his trademark gimmick as "JYD," and set a course for success. Entering the ring to "Another One Bites the Dust," he danced around the ring, and then preceded to headbutt and power-slam his opponents into submission. In addition to winning the Wrestling Classic tournament, the first pay-per-view in WWE history, he held the North American Title and USWA Unified World belt.

Kane

Born:	April 26, 1967
Height:	6'8"
Weight:	320
Real Name:	Glenn Thomas Jacobs
Wife:	Crystal Jacobs
High School:	Bowling Green High School (MO)
Identities:	Bruiser Mastino, Doomsday, Dr. Isaac Yankem
Finisher:	Chokeslam, Reverse Piledriver
Groups:	The Corporation (1998-1999)
Tag Team:	The Brothers of Destruction w/ The Undertaker, The Dynamic Duo w/ Al Snow
Career Span:	1992-Present

PPV Record:	55-71, 1 Draw, 1 DCO, 2 NC
WrestleMania Record:	5-8
WWE *Raw* TV Record:	147-119, 1 DCO, 1 DDQ, 25 NC
WWE *Smackdown* TV Record:	121-92, 1 Draw, 3 DCO, 14 NC
Titles Won:	19
Days as World Champion:	246
Age at first World Title Win:	31
Best Opponents:	The Undertaker, Steve Austin, Shawn Michaels
Movies:	2

The "Big Red Machine" Kane was never really burned in a fire, nor is he related in any way to The Undertaker. Glenn Jacobs is the man who portrays the unstoppable monster, and the success of the gimmick pushed him straight to the upper echelon of the WWF. Before turning to wrestling, the Pike County, Missouri athlete played basketball at Northeast Missouri State, establishing school records for field goal percentage for a single year and career. He was also a notable offensive lineman in football, but a knee injury caused him to fail his physical with the Chicago Bears in 1991. Within two years, Jacobs had made the decision to become a professional wrestler, relocated to Tampa to train with the Malenkos, and even made his first showing on national television as enhancement talent for WCW. He bounced around the independents before finding stable work for Smoky Mountain Wrestling in Tennessee as "Unibomb." An early WWF run as a psychotic dentist (Isaac Yankem, DDS) was unremarkable.

The immensely powerful Kane debuted at the WWF's Badd Blood pay-per-view in St. Louis on October 5, 1997, going to the ring with Paul Bearer to confront his "brother," the Undertaker during the latter's Hell in the Cell bout against Shawn Michaels, with Kane's interference costing the Undertaker the match. The feud between the "siblings" lasted for several years. On June 28, 1998, he beat Steve Austin and captured the WWF World Heavyweight Title— undoubtedly his most important career achievement to date. He lost the belt back to Austin the next night on *Raw*. Despite his English degree, Kane's verbal promos were limited because of the role he played, but ended up developing more over time. He won the Intercontinental Title twice, beating Triple H and Chris Jericho for the championship, and had lots of success as a tag team wrestler. He captured the World Tag Team Title nine times with various partners, including Mankind, The Undertaker, X-Pac, and Big Show. In June of 2003, he finally unmasked—showing the world that he really wasn't disfigured.

Throughout his time in the WWE, Kane has participated in a few borderline bizarre angles. One of them was the Katie Vick necrophilia storyline in 2002, along with Triple H and another was his "relationship" with Lita in 2004 that saw the latter impregnated and the two married. He stepped away from the squared circle to star in the film *See No Evil* and appeared on NBC's *Weakest Link*, where he won $83,500 for charity. He outlasted his foes in a special battle royal prior to the Wrestlemania XXIV broadcast, and then beat Chavo Guerrero Jr. in eight seconds for the ECW World Title. He lost the title to Mark Henry on June 29, 2008. In July of 2010, he won the Money in the Bank ladder match at Kansas City, and later in the night, cashed it in and went over Rey Mysterio Jr. for the World Heavyweight Title. His victory came in less than a minute. Kane remained champion until December, finally succumbing to Edge in a four-way bout at Houston. In 2011, he reformed his successful tag team with Big Show and won the WWE Tag Team Title.

Photo Courtesy of Dr. Mike Lano—Wrealano@aol.com

Born:	January 4, 1970
Height:	6'3"
Weight:	250
Real Name:	Christopher Klucsarits
Parents:	Jack and Barbara Klucsarits
High School:	Archbishop Molloy High School (NY)
College:	University of Buffalo
Trained by:	Pete McKay, Afa, Fabulous Moolah
Career Span:	1992-2010
Died:	April 2, 2010, Sunnyside, NY 40 years old

Kanyon, Chris

PPV Record:	8-11, 1 NC
WWE *Raw* TV Record:	2-2, 1 NC
WWE *Smackdown* TV Record:	4-6
Titles Won:	4
Best Opponents:	Dallas Page, Booker T, Mike Awesome
Movies:	2

Full of personality and potential, Chris Kanyon was a bright spot on the WCW roster during its final years, and carried his talent over to brief runs in the WWF. He grew up in Queens, New York, and was physically adept to play a number of sports because of his size and agility. Interested in pro wrestling, he attended the WCW Power Plant, and became known as "Mortis," managed by James Vandenberg. Later in his career, he gained attention as a member of the Jersey Triad with Dallas Page and Bam Bam Bigelow. Kanyon engaged in an entertaining war with Page, and adopted some of the latter's ring traits, including use of the "Kanyon Cutter," which he employed on many unsuspecting people—in a humorous way. He held the U.S. and Tag Team Titles in the WWF, but was plagued by injuries for most of his time there. He wrestled for indie promotions until 2010, the last appearance several months before he took his own life. His candid autobiography was released in 2011.

Photo Courtesy of Dr. Mike Lano—Wrealano@aol.com

Born:	December 8, 1963
Height:	5'11"
Weight:	230
Trained by:	Shohei Baba, Genichiro Tenryu
Identities:	Kio Kawata, The Black Mephisto
Nickname:	Dangerous K
Finisher:	Powerbomb
Career Span:	1982-Present

Titles Won:	18
Days as World Champion:	912
Age at first World Title Win:	30
Best Opponents:	Mitsuharu Misawa, Kenta Kobashi, Stan Hansen
Tournament Wins:	7
Halls of Fame:	1

Kawada, Toshiaki

A five-time All-Japan Unified Triple Crown Champion, Toshiaki Kawada was long the backbone of the promotion, even remaining steadfast after nearly all other wrestlers abandoned ship in 2000. He displayed unreal strength in title victories over Steve Williams, Mitsuharu Misawa, Keiji Mutoh, and reigned supreme in a tournament for the vacant title on September 6, 2003. Two of the reigns, ironically, were ended prematurely because of injuries. Kawada formed a legendary tag team with Akira Taue, and the pair held the AJPW Tag Team Title on six occasions. Once the All-Japan roster left to form Pro Wrestling NOAH under Misawa's leadership in 2000, Kawada and his remaining cohorts entered an interpromotional rivalry with New Japan—a long-awaited concept that helped keep AJPW alive. For a time in 2005, Kawada appeared for HUSTLE, but returned to All-Japan the next year. On October 24, 2009, he beat Masato Tanaka for the Zero-One World Heavyweight Championship, and reigned until April 11, 2010.

Photo Courtesy of George Tahinos

Born:	February 20, 1977
Height:	5'4"
Weight:	125
High School:	York Memorial Collegiate Institute (Toronto)
College:	University of Toronto
Identities:	La Felina

Kim, Gail

Career Span:	2000-Present
PPV Record:	15-12
WrestleMania Record:	0-2
WWE *Raw* TV Record:	28-46
WWE *Smackdown* TV Record:	5-4
Titles Won:	5
Days as World Champion:	161 (and counting)
Age at first World Title Win:	26
Best Opponents:	Awesome Kong, Mickie James, Trish Stratus

Awesomely talented, Gail Kim's athleticism radiates each time she steps through the ropes. Trained by Ron Hutchinson in her hometown of Toronto, she won the WWE Women's belt in her first televised match in the promotion on June 30, 2003. Kim beat out nine others for the initial TNA Women's Title on October 14, 2007, and regained it upon her return to the organization with a win over Velvet Sky on November 13, 2011. She also teamed with Madison Rayne to win the TNA Knockouts Tag Team belts. As a heel or fan favorite, she delivers top-notch ring performances, displaying the veteran qualities that make her one of the premier women grapplers in the world today.

Born:	November 7, 1955
Height:	6'3"
Weight	425
Real Name:	Christopher Alan Pallies
High School:	Washington Township High School (NJ)
Trained by:	Larry Sharpe
Identities:	Chris Canyon, Big Daddy Bundy, Boom Boom Bundy
Finisher:	Atlantic City Avalanche
Groups:	The Legion of Doom (1983-1984), Million Dollar Corporation (1994-1995)
Career Span:	1982-2007

PPV Record:	3-4
WrestleMania Record:	1-3
Titles Won:	13
Best Opponents:	Hulk Hogan, Andre the Giant, The Undertaker
Movies:	2

King Kong Bundy

Once you saw King Kong Bundy in person or on TV, you never forgot the image. The bald behemoth weighing more than 400 pounds with the fear-inducing scowl on his face was a terror of the wrestling ring, splashing victims into temporary comas, and demanding referees count to five for pinfalls instead of the customary three. Little did many fans know was that the "King" had a great sense of humor and has often performed as a stand-up comedian. A funny and light-hearted personality was far from the man crowds saw in feuds with the Von Erichs and Hulk Hogan, particularly in the run up to WrestleMania II, which Bundy co-headlined with the latter in 1986. He was ferocious in squash matches on TV, and footage of him manhandling opponents was either comical or frightening, depending on whom you asked. He was a regular on the indie circuit before returning to the WWF in 1995. In reruns, fans can still catch Bundy's two appearances on *Married . . . with Children;* particularly the episode in which he pulverizes "Bud Bundy" in a wrestling exhibition.

Born:	August 14, 1981
Height:	6'1"
Weight:	225
Real Name:	Kofi Sarkodie-Mensah
High School:	Winchester High School (MA)
College:	Boston College
Finisher:	Trouble in Paradise
Career Span:	2006-Present

PPV Record:	17-17, 1 NC
WrestleMania Record:	1-2
WWE *Raw* TV Record:	65-41, 1 DCO, 2 NC
WWE *Smackdown* TV Record:	37-29, 2 NC
Titles Won:	7
Best Opponents:	Chris Jericho, Jack Swagger, Kane

Kingston, Kofi

Supremely athletic and overwhelmingly popular, Kofi Kingston's progression as a pro wrestler has been nothing but remarkable. In his six years in the business, he's won two United States, three Intercontinental, and one World Tag Team championship. Born in Ghana, West Africa, Kingston attended high school in Winchester, Massachusetts and collected over 100 victories as an amateur grappler. He learned the fundamentals from Mike Hollow and Killer Kowalski, then working out at the Deep South and Ohio Valley WWE developmental organizations before his 2008 ECW debut. Later that year, he won the Intercontinental belt from Chris Jericho and gained two additional title victories from Drew McIntyre and Dolph Ziggler. His U.S. Title wins came at the expense of MVP and Sheamus, and in 2008, he held the World Tag Team belts with CM Punk.

Born:	March 27, 1967
Height:	6'2"
Weight:	250
High School:	Fukuchiyama High School (Japan)
Trained by:	Shohei Baba, Dory Funk Jr.
Nickname:	Orange Crush
Finisher:	Brainbuster
Career Span:	1988-2009

Titles Won:	17
Days as World Champion:	431
Age at first World Title Win:	29
Best Opponents:	Mitsuharu Misawa, Jun Akiyama, Stan Hansen
Tournament Wins:	8
Halls of Fame:	1

Kobashi, Kenta

Over the last twenty years, few wrestlers have engaged in as many instant classics as Kenta Kobashi of Japan. He's been a walking highlight reel, famously displaying his fine ability to tell a story in the ring, and working terrifically performed matches that resonate with fans across the world. His influence has been global, and only injuries could keep him away from the ring he's graced with his pure athleticism since 1988. A three-time AJPW Triple Crown Champion, Kobashi defeated Akira Taue for his first reign on July 24, 1996, and then Mitsuharu Misawa for his second in January of 1997. During his third run as champion in 2000, he joined a group led by Misawa, leaving All-Japan to form Pro Wrestling NOAH, and effectively vacated his title. He won the Global Honored Crown from Misawa on March 1, 2003 in Tokyo and held the respected title for more than two years In that time, his high level of performance was unrelenting, and Kobashi participated in some of the best matches anywhere in the world.

Born:	March 9, 1959
Height:	6'2"
Weight:	250
Real Name:	Nelson Scott Simpson
Parents:	Paige and Olive Simpson
High School:	Robbinsdale High School (MN)
Colleges:	Golden Valley Junior College, Moorhead State University
Trained by:	Eddie Sharkey, Ivan Koloff
Identities:	Mr. Wrestling IV
Nickname:	The Russian Nightmare
Finisher:	Russian Sickle
Career Span:	1984-1992
Website:	www.nikitakoloff.com

PPV Record:	6-2, 2 Draws
Titles Won:	7
Best Opponents:	Magnum T.A., Ric Flair, Lex Luger
Halls of Fame:	1

Koloff, Nikita

Wrestling was impacted by a Lithuanian nightmare in 1984 when powerful Nikita Koloff began to come into his own in the Mid-Atlantic region. A truly feared competitor, he was billed as the nephew of Ivan Koloff, and teamed with his uncle and Don Kernolde as part of the World Six-Man Tag Team Champions. However, in reality, young Nikita was from Robbinsdale, Minnesota, and had been a football player throughout high school and college. The Koloffs also reigned as World Tag Team titleholders twice in 1985 and 1986. Remarkably strong, Nikita was a gifted personality in a colorful industry, and his best-of-seven series against Magnum T.A. for the U.S. Title is still talked about today. After Magnum was injured in a car accident, Koloff turned fan favorite and teamed up with Dusty Rhodes to win the Crockett Cup Tag Team Tournament in 1987—dedicating the win to their fallen comrade. He retired a year later, but came back in 1991 to feud with Lex Luger and Sting in WCW before his career was ended after suffering a serious neck injury.

Konnan

Born:	January 6, 1964
Height:	5'11"
Weight:	235
Real Name:	Charles R. Ashenoff
High School:	Southwest Miami Senior High School (FL)
Trained by:	Rey Mysterio Sr., Negro Casas, Super Astro
Identities:	El Centurion, Max Moon, Konnan el Barbaro
Nickname:	K-Dogg
Finisher:	Tequila Sunrise, 187—Cradle DDT
Groups:	Los Gringos Locos, New World Order (Black and White) (1997-1998), New World Order (Wolfpack) (1998), The Filthy Animals (1999-2001), Authentic Luchadores (2003), 2 Live Kru (2003-2005), La Legion Extranjera (2006-2011)
Career Span:	1988-Present

PPV Record:	36-38, 2 NC
Titles Won:	17
Days as World Champion:	Over 295
Age at first World Title Win:	27
Best Opponents:	Cien Caras, Perro Aguayo, Ric Flair
Halls of Fame:	1

Exploding on audiences with outstanding charisma and the ability to rap, Konnan was a multitalented performer and a favorite everywhere he went. He was born in Cuba and raised in South Florida, served in the Navy, and broke into the business in early 1988. He had the size and athletic skill set to stand out very quickly and was a major star in Mexico during the early 1990s. Huge crowds saw him feud with Perro Aguayo and Cien Caras, and on June 9, 1991, he beat the latter to capture the CMLL World Title, and was also a headliner in the newly founded AAA promotion in 1993. In 1996, he entered WCW and quickly won the U.S. Title. He built a faithful following and was standout member of the NWO Wolfpack and Filthy Animals. Behind the microphone, he was always a great promo man, letting it fly off the cuff and giving the fans what they wanted to hear. He wrestled in TNA from 2003 to 2007 but was sidelined because of health issues. He is currently involved in AAA in Mexico.

Born:	September 1, 1961
Height:	6'0"
Weight:	235
Real Name:	William Ensor
Trained by:	Boris Malenko
Identities:	Buddy Roop
Finisher:	Superplex
Managed by:	Jim Cornette, General Skandor Akbar, James J. Dillon, Peaches
Career Span:	1979-2010

PPV Record:	0-3
Titles Won:	36
Best Opponents:	Shawn Michaels, Ric Flair, Jerry Lawler

Landel, Buddy

Similar to his "Nature Boy" counterparts, Buddy Landel was a blond and arrogant grappler with respectable mat abilities. From Knoxville, Tennessee, where he was a natural athlete in high school, he was destined for great things in 1985 when he was fired from Jim Crockett Promotions because of his outside-the-ring problems. Despite his personal issues, he won more than thirty wrestling titles to include the NWA National, USWA, SMW, and WWC North American Heavyweight belts. In 1991, he nearly squared off against Buddy Rogers in New Jersey, but the match was cancelled. Landel was terrific in promos and many of his interviews are must-see classics.

Photo Courtesy of Pete Lederberg—plmathfoto@hotmail.com

Born:	August 5, 1953
Height:	6'1"
Weight:	225
Real Name:	Wallace Stanfield Lane
High School:	Page High School (NC)
College:	East Carolina University
Career Span:	1978-2008

PPV Record:	6-7
Titles Won:	39
Best Opponents:	Dusty Rhodes, Jimmy Garvin, Dutch Mantel
Halls of Fame:	1

Lane, Stan

Trained by Ric Flair, Stan Lane of Greensboro initially worked as "Stan Flair," and also adopted the trademark "Nature Boy" moniker. He teamed with Steve Keirn to form the Fabulous Ones, winning the U.S. Tag Team Championship twice in 1986 and then reunited to capture the USWA World Tag Team Title in 1991. Lane also joined Bobby Eaton as a member of the famed Midnight Express, managed by Jim Cornette. The duo won the U.S. Title three times, and the World Tag Team belts in 1988. Later on, he partnered with Tom Prichard as the Heavenly Bodies and won the SMW Tag Team Title five times. Always displaying a good repertoire of moves, Lane has returned to the ring several times over the years, appearing at reunion shows alongside Eaton and Cornette.

Born:	December 27, 1969
Height:	5'10"
Weight:	180
Real Name:	Joan Marie Laurer
Parents:	Joseph and Janet Laurer
High School:	Penfield High School (NY)
College:	University of Tampa
Nicknames:	Ninth Wonder of the World, Amazon
Finisher:	Pedigree
Magazine Covers:	*Playboy* (November 2000), *Playboy* (January 2002)
Career Span:	1995-Present

Laurer, Joanie

PPV Record:	10-11
WrestleMania Record:	2-0
WWE *Raw* TV Record:	21-14, 5 NC
WWE *Smackdown* TV Record:	14-5, 1 Draw, 1 NC
Titles Won:	5
Days as World Champion:	214
Age at first World Title Win:	31
Best Opponents:	Chris Jericho, Jeff Jarrett, Masa Chono
TV Appearances:	Over 20, including recurring roles on several reality programs
Movies:	10

The spirited Joanie Laurer resurfaced in big-time pro wrestling in May of 2011 after a long hiatus of reality TV appearances and personal struggles. Her impressive size set her apart in a world of divas and knockouts, and she remains one of the most recognizable women grapplers in the business. Trained by Killer Kowalski, she entered the WWF in 1997 as "Chyna," and was a bodyguard for Triple H. She became the first woman to hold the WWF Intercontinental Title, a feat she repeated two additional times, on October 17, 1999 when she beat Jeff Jarrett. At WrestleMania X-Seven, she defeated Ivory for the WWF Women's Title. After leaving the WWF in 2001, she wrestled for New Japan and lost to Masa Chono on October 14, 2002 at the Tokyo Dome. Her return to wrestling for TNA alongside Kurt Angle in 2011 created a lot of interest, but lasted only one match.

Layfield, John "Bradshaw"

Born:	November 29, 1966
Height:	6'6"
Weight:	285
Real Name:	John Charles Layfield
Parents:	Richard Lavelle and Mary Layfield
High School:	Sweetwater High School (TX)
College:	Abilene Christian University
College Ach.:	1st team All-American (1989), 2nd team All-American (1988), 1st team All-Conference (1988, 1989)
Pro Sports:	National Football League—Los Angeles Raiders (1990) (camp) World League—San Antonio Riders (1991)
Identities:	Justin Hawk, John Hawk, Blackjack Bradshaw, JBL
Finisher:	Clothesline from Hell
Groups:	The Ministry of Darkness (1999), The Cabinet (2004-2005)
Career Span:	1992-2009

PPV Record:	34-46
WrestleMania Record:	3-6
WWE *Raw* TV Record:	63-64, 13 NC
WWE *Smackdown* TV Record:	56-65, 1 Draw, 7 NC
Titles Won:	30
Days as World Champion:	280
Age at first World Title Win:	37
Best Opponents:	Eddie Guerrero, John Cena, The Undertaker

A towering figure, John Layfield was a WWE superstar from 1996 until 2009 and graduated from the tag team division to reign as the heavyweight champion for nine months. He played offensive tackle in high school and college, and learned the ropes from Brad Rheingans. In 1995, he captured the North American belt from Kevin Von Erich, and the next year debuted in the WWF as "Justin Bradshaw." He partnered with Faarooq as the Acolytes and they won the World Tag Team Title three times between 1999 and 2001. Their often comical performances displayed Layfield's wit and diversified his on-air role. He won the Hardcore Title seventeen times and added the WWE Heavyweight Title to his resume with a victory over Eddie Guerrero in June of 2004. He remained champ until the following April, losing to John Cena at WrestleMania XXI. He retired from the business in 2009, and has been a prominent figure on cable TV as a financial analyst. He also released a book in 2003 offering his practical advice for money management.

Photo Courtesy of Dr. Mike Lano—Wrealano@aol.com

Leslie, Ed

Born:	April 21, 1957
Height:	6'3"
Weight:	270
Real Name:	Edward Harrison Leslie Jr.
Wife:	Barbara Leslie
High School:	Robinson High School (FL)
Identities:	Ed Boulder, Dizzy Hogan, Ed Hogan, The Butcher, The Man with No Name, The Zodiac, The Booty Man, The Disciple, Brute Force
Groups:	Dungeon of Doom (1995), OWN (1998)
Tag Teams:	The Dream Team w/ Greg Valentine, The Mega Maniacs w/ Hulk Hogan
Career Span:	1979-Present

PPV Record:	9-11, 1 DCO, 1 DDQ
WrestleMania Record:	2-3, 1 DCO, 1 DDQ
Titles Won:	8
Best Opponents:	Curt Hennig, Randy Savage, Hulk Hogan

Ed Leslie was a high school friend of Hulk Hogan and broke into the business under his pal's wing in the late 1970s. He achieved a great deal of superstardom using the name "Brutus Beefcake" in the WWF. The Tampa product was initially a heel and co-held the WWF Tag Team Title with Greg Valentine. But it was his tour as the "Barber" that carried him to immense popularity, and by 1990, he was one of the top fan favorites in the organization. His specialty was putting an opponent out with his sleeperhold, and then cutting his downed foe's hair. Leslie was challenging for Intercontinental belt when he was nearly killed in a freak parasailing accident. Proving doctors wrong, he not only made a comeback, but teamed with Hogan at WrestleMania IX. He'd also headline Starrcade 1994 in a bout against Hogan—which he lost. Leslie used an abundance of gimmicks while in WCW, and has wrestled on the indie circuit ever since. His fine showmanship and likable personality have been a staple in the business for over thirty years.

Lesnar, Brock

Born:	July 12, 1977
Height:	6'3"
Weight:	265
Real Name:	Brock Edward Lesnar
Parents:	Richard and Stephanie Lesnar
High School:	Webster High School (SD)
Trained by:	WWE Ohio Valley Trainers, Scott LeDoux (MMA), Greg Nelson (MMA)
Nickname:	The Next Big Thing
Finisher:	F-5
WWF Debut:	March 18, 2002, Montreal, Quebec, *Raw*
Tag Team:	The Minnesota Stretching Crew w/ Shelton Benjamin
Career Span:	2000-2007

College Record:	106-5
Amateur Titles:	5
PPV Record:	14-8, 1 NC
WrestleMania Record:	1-1
WWE *Raw* TV Record:	10-2
WWE *Smackdown* TV Record:	33-15, 4 NC
Titles Won:	7
Days as World Champion:	984
Age at first World Title Win:	25
Best Opponents:	Kurt Angle, The Undertaker, The Rock
MMA Record:	5-3
Days as UFC Champion:	707

Looking back at wrestling history, it's hard to find someone comparable to Brock Lesnar. The massive South Dakotan is the embodiment of exceptional genetics and intense discipline, and his success as a professional wrestler and MMA fighter put him in a category all by himself. In the worked environment of wrestling, he performed flawlessly, winning world titles in the United States and Japan. He then crossed over to the legitimate combat sport, mixed martial arts, where he proved that he was the real deal—a world–class battler with the heart and ability to become heavyweight champion in that realm too. Lesnar has cultivated all the tools necessary to stand out in any endeavor he chooses to undertake, and the wrestling world awaits his anticipated return, for one day he may step back through the ropes to reclaim a spot among the best in the business. This possibility may be even closer to reality now that he's retired from MMA, and no doubt rumors about a comeback will heighten.

A wrestler in high school, Lesnar learned from coach John Schiley, and with two consecutive third-place finishes at the state tournament, he was not recruited to a major university, and instead landed at Bismarck Junior College. It was there that he won his first significant amateur title, taking the NJCAA championship as a heavyweight in 1998, then proceeded to the University of Minnesota, where he won an NCAA championship in 2000. Lesnar opted not to pursue an Olympic medal and signed with the WWF, making his debut in August of 2000. He quickly outgrew his environment in the developmental promotion, and was on the fast track to glory by the summer of 2002, winning the King of the Ring tournament. On August 25, 2002, he became the youngest man in history to win the WWE Title when he beat The Rock for the belt at SummerSlam. His reign was disrupted on November 17 when his manager Paul Heyman turned on him, and allowed The Big Show to capture the championship.

Now a fan favorite, Lesnar prevailed at the Royal Rumble and wrestled another former NCAA champion, Kurt Angle, at WrestleMania XIX on March 30, 2003. The hugely anticipated match was full of high drama, and at one crucial moment, Brock sailed from the top rope attempting a dangerous shooting star press—and narrowly missed serious injury. Lesnar pulled through and won his second WWE championship. His feud with Angle continued that summer and they traded the title again. Their September 16, 2003 Iron Man match was a classic and saw Lesnar with five falls to his opponent's four. After losing to Goldberg at WrestleMania in 2004, he departed from the promotion and announced his intentions to play in the NFL. He played some preseason ball, but was cut by the Minnesota Vikings in August. Lesnar returned to wrestling for NJPW and won the IWGP Title in a three-way match against Masa Chono and Kazuyuki Fujita on October 8, 2005 at the Tokyo Dome.

While overseas, he made many successful showings, but was stripped of the title during the summer of 2006. Incidentally, he kept the belt and defended it against Kurt Angle on June 29, 2007 in what would be his final pro wrestling match to date, with Angle winning by submission. The options for Lesnar were wide open, and it was initially believed he'd return to wrestling in some capacity, but he instead announced his intentions to participate in mixed martial arts. He trained to diversify his fighting skills, and prepared for his June 2007 debut in Los Angeles, where he beat Min-Soo Kim. He lost his second match to Frank Mir, but rebounded to stop Heath Herring and then Randy Couture for the UFC Heavyweight Title on November 15, 2008. Following intensive recovery after a serious illness, Lesnar beat Shane Carwin, and then lost his title to Cain Velasquez on October 23, 2010 in Anaheim. In late December 2011, he retired from MMA after a first round loss to Alistair Overeem at UFC 141.

Born:	November 10, 1964
Height:	5'7"
Weight:	215
Real Name:	Keiichi Yamada
Trained by:	NJPW Dojo including Tatsumi Fujinami, Stu Hart
Identities:	Fuji Yamada
Finisher:	Liger Bomb, Shooting Star Press
Career Span:	1984-Present

Liger, Jushin

PPV Record:	4-7
Titles Won:	33
Days as IWGP Junior Champion:	2,245
Age at first IWGP Junior Win:	24
Best Opponents:	Great Sasuke, El Samurai, Ultimo Dragon
Tournament Wins:	9
Halls of Fame:	1
MMA Record:	0-1

Japanese marvel, Jushin "Thunder" Liger has been a leader of the wrestling high-flier community since the 1980s. His epic aerial display and athleticism carried him to world championships in Japan, the United States, Mexico, and Great Britain, and a record eleven IWGP Junior Titles. Always heroically performing risky maneuvers, Liger made a real impact on WCW fans in 1991, and has returned to the U.S. to wrestle many times. Originally from Hiroshima, he entered the business in 1984 and adopted the "Jushin Liger" character five years later for New Japan. He won his first IWGP Junior Championship from Hiroshi Hase on May 25, 1989 in Osaka. In the years following, he would win the belt from Naoki Sano, The Pegasus Kid, and two times from Norio Honaga. On December 25, 1991, he beat Brian Pillman for the WCW World Light Heavyweight Title, but lost it back to the latter on February 29, 1992. Their remarkable feud continued at the very first edition of *Nitro* in 1995, with Pillman winning that round.

On January 4, 1993, Liger beat Ultimo Dragon at the Tokyo Dome for his sixth IWGP Junior Title. He won his seventh before 64,000 on January 4, 1996 from Koji Kanamoto. A year later, Liger beat Dragon for the J-Crown Octuple Championship, which included his eighth IWGP Junior Title. Over the next two years, he won the belt from Shinjiro Ohtani and Kendo Ka Shin before Juventud Guerrera ended his reign on WCW *Nitro* on November 29, 1999. It was the first time the IWGP Junior Title changed hands outside of Japan. Guerrera was injured in the contest and unable to defend the title a week later in Milwaukee. Psicosis was allowed to defend against Liger and lost the championship. It was his eleventh and final IWGP Junior Title victory. Over the last decade, he's continued to make the rounds, appearing in TNA, ROH, and in Mexico. At this point, he is only building upon his incredible record and showing younger fans what their older counterparts already knew about his legendary status.

Lita

Born:	April 14, 1975
Height:	5'7"
Weight:	135
Real Name:	Amy Christine Dumas
High School:	Lassiter High School (GA)
Trained by:	Leilani Kai, Dory Funk Jr.
Identities:	Miss Congeniality, Angelica
Career Span:	1998-2006

PPV Record:	7-14
WrestleMania Record:	0-1
WWE *Raw* TV Record:	48-28, 3 NC
WWE *Smackdown* TV Record:	13-16
Titles Won:	4
Days as World Champion:	160
Age at first World Title Win:	25
Best Opponents:	Trish Stratus, Victoria, Ivory

Sporting reddish hair and an affinity for extreme spots, Lita stood out from most of the women grapplers on the WWE roster. She regularly performed the moonsault and top-rope huracanrana, and her athleticism made her highly popular with fans. Lita began her career in Mexico and worked in ECW in 1999, just prior to entering the WWF. She initially appeared at the side of Esse Rios, but was mostly known for her strong bond with the Hardy Boys. She won the Women's Title from Stephanie McMahon in August of 2000 and also beat Trish Stratus and Mickie James for the belt. She lost the title for the last time on November 26, 2006, to James, in what was her retirement match, and has since focused on her music career.

Photo Courtesy of Pete Lederberg—plmathfoto@hotmail.com

Born:	June 2, 1958
Height:	6'5"
Weight:	275
Real Name:	Lawrence Wendell Pfohl
High School:	Orchard Park High School (NY)
College:	University of Miami
Pro Sports:	Canadian Football League—Montreal Alouettes (1979-1981) National Football League—Green Bay Packers (1982-1983) (camp) United States Football League—Jacksonville Bulls (1983) United States Football League—Tampa Bay Bandits (1984) United States Football League—Memphis Showboats (1984-1985)
Finishers:	Torture Rack Backbreaker "Rebel Rack," Forearm Smash, Piledriver
Tag Teams:	The Allied Powers w/ Davey Boy Smith, Totally Buff w/ Buff Bagwell
Career Span:	1985-2006

Luger, Lex

PPV Record:	41-39, 2 Draws, 1 DDQ, 2 NC
WrestleMania Record:	2-1
Titles Won:	18
Days as World Champion:	242
Age at first World Title Win:	33
Best Opponents:	Ric Flair, Hulk Hogan, Sting
Managers:	8

With a bodybuilder physique, three-time World Heavyweight Champion Lex Luger was a pivotal player in wrestling for over two decades. He was pushed right from the beginning, shown by his Southern Title victory over Wahoo McDaniel only nineteen days after his pro debut. He had the size and strength to become a superstar, and promoters gave him the platform to sink or swim. Luger had winning potential, stepped up to the plate, and delivered a home run—successfully transitioning from the football field to the pro mat. The wise Hiro Matsuda and Bob Roop gave him the tools he needed to measure up to the hype, and he was capable, even as a rookie, of delivering a performance that the fans reacted positively to. As his stock rose, he joined the Four Horsemen and won the U.S. Heavyweight belt, the first of four title victories, from

Nikita Koloff at the 1987 Great American Bash. At the initial Clash of the Champions, he teamed with Barry Windham to capture the World Tag Team Title, but his partner turned on him a month later.

Throughout 1988, he chased NWA champion Ric Flair and came close to winning the belt innumerable times, but one technicality or another prevented him from walking away as the new titleholder. He beat Windham for the U.S. Title at the Chi-Town Rumble on February 20, 1989, and, incidentally, Chicago was always billed as Luger's hometown, although he was really from upstate New York. After trading the belt back and forth with Freebird Michael Hayes, Luger began a seventeen-month reign as U.S. Champion. It took Stan Hansen, a former AWA World Champion, to dethrone him at Halloween Havoc on October 27, 1990. On July 14, 1991, he won the WCW World Heavyweight Title, turning heel in the process, and took Harley Race as his manager. He ended up losing the crown to Sting the following February. Shortly thereafter, he left WCW to participate in the short-lived World Bodybuilding Federation, and, in 1993, he entered the WWF as "The Narcissist," an egotistical rule-breaker.

Fans took to Luger after he bodyslammed the humongous Yokozuna on the U.S.S. Intrepid, and while Luger rose to the top of the promotion, even co-winning the 1994 Royal Rumble, he never won gold in the WWF. On September 3, 1995, Luger worked a WWF house show, and the very next night, he appeared on WCW's first showing of *Nitro*. Luger's unexpected arrival brought a sense of spontaneity to *Nitro* that would linger for years. He won his second WCW Title from Hollywood Hogan on August 4, 1997, but lost it back to the latter five days later. In late 2002, he beat Sting for the vacant WWA World Title on a pay-per-view from Scotland, and reigned for a week before Sting won in a rematch. He went into semi-retirement and made varied showings for TNA between 2003 and 2006. In 2007, he suffered a spinal stroke that left him paralyzed. He has slowly recovered his ability to walk, and has devoted himself to the Christian religion, publicly speaking out against drug abuse.

Lynn, Jerry

Born:	June 12, 1963
Height:	5'10"
Weight:	215
Real Name:	Jeremy Clayton Lynn
High School:	Woodcrest Baptist Academy High School (MN)
Trained by:	Eddie Sharkey, Brad Rheingans
Identities:	Mr. J.L.
Nickname:	Dynamic, The New F'n Show
Finisher:	Cradle Piledriver
Career Span:	1990-Present

PPV Record:	49-58, 1 Draw, 2 NC
WWE *Raw* TV Record:	1-0
WWE *Smackdown* TV Record:	1-2
Titles Won:	Over 50
Days as World Champion:	106
Age at first World Title Win:	37
Best Opponents:	Rob Van Dam, A.J. Styles, Lance Storm
Halls of Fame:	1

A talented grappler from Minneapolis, Jerry Lynn was the World Heavyweight Champion twice in his career, and merits the respect he now receives wherever he appears on the circuit. With a background in gymnastics, Lynn was quick to grasp the wrestling trade, and bore all the characteristics of a future champion. His first significant milestone occurred at ECW's Anarchy Rules on October 1, 2000, when he beat Justin Credible for the World Title. While in the WWF, he won the light heavyweight championship and became a two-time NWA World Tag Team titleholder in TNA. Lynn also captured the prized X-Division belt twice. In Australia, on May 21, 2003, he won a tournament for the WWA International Cruiserweight Title. More recently, on April 3, 2009, Lynn topped Nigel McGuinness for the ROH World Heavyweight crown. He remained champion until June 13, 2009, when he lost the title to Austin Aries.

Born:	June 11, 1959
Height:	6'1"
Weight:	240
Real Name:	Terry Wayne Allen
Wife:	Courtney Allen
High School:	Norfolk Collegiate High School (VA)
College:	Old Dominion University
Trained by:	Buzz Sawyer, Eddie Graham
Nickname:	Tenacious
Finisher:	Belly-to-belly suplex
Career Span:	1981-1986

Titles Won:	11
Best Opponents:	Nikita Koloff, Tully Blanchard, Ric Flair

Magnum T.A.

Terry Allen had noticeable magnetism that radiated outward and, to promoters, it meant money. It is hard to ignore a young athlete in the world of wrestling with superstar qualities. Fans who were privy to the outward expression of his innate talents, supported him thoroughly, and made him the hero of the day. A 1977 VISWA amateur wrestling champion in high school, Allen took the name "Magnum T.A." while in the Mid-South region, and received a mighty push for the Crocketts a short time later. He won the U.S. Title on March 23, 1985, and traded the belt with Tully Blanchard. His second reign came to an abrupt end after he punched NWA President Bob Geigel and was stripped of the title. The title was put up in an exciting best-of-seven series between Magnum and Nikita Koloff, ending on August 17 when Koloff won his fourth match and the championship. On October 14, 1986, Magnum was severely injured in a car accident, and the career of the twenty-seven-year-old with the immensely bright future ended far too prematurely.

Malenko, Dean

Born:	August 4, 1960
Height:	5'9"
Weight:	220
Real Name:	Shelly Dean Simon
Family:	Brother of Joe Malenko
Wife:	Julie Simon
High School:	Jesuit High School (FL)
Identities:	Dean Solkoff, Cyclope
Nicknames:	Iceman
Finisher:	Texas Cloverleaf
Groups:	The Four Horsemen (1998-1999), The Revolution (1999), The Radicals (2000)
Career Span:	1979-2001

PPV Record:	21-22
WrestleMania Record:	0-1
WWE *Raw* TV Record:	14-18
WWE *Smackdown* TV Record:	14-13, 1 NC
Titles Won:	13
Best Opponents:	Eddie Guerrero, Chris Benoit, Chris Jericho

Dean Malenko, the son of the Great Malenko, and an enthusiastic student of the legendary ring master, Karl Gotch, earned the nickname "Man of 1,000 Holds" because of his endless repertoire of grips and methodical techniques. His knowledge of submissions and ability to down rivals with legitimate skills also warranted the moniker, "Shooter." There was never a question about his talent, but promoters were hesitant to use such a mild-mannered spokesman in a world of cockiness and brash attitudes. Simply, Malenko let his athletic prowess speak for itself, and finally, in 1995, he began to gain national attention in WCW. He held the U.S. Title and the World Cruiserweight Championship four times. He jumped to the WWF and became the first man to have held both the WWF Light Heavyweight and WCW Cruiserweight Titles when he captured the former championship from Esse Rios during *Raw* in March of 2000. After his retirement in 2001, he was hired by the WWE as an agent.

Born:	February 8, 1958
Height:	5'7"
Weight:	130
Real Name:	Sherry Lynn Russell Schrull
Nicknames:	Scary, Sensuous, Queen
Career Span:	1980-2006
Died:	June 15, 2007, McCalla, AL
	49 years old

PPV Record:	1-2
WrestleMania Record:	0-1
Titles Won:	6
Days as World Champion:	Over 926
Age at first World Title Win:	27
Best Opponents:	Fabulous Moolah, Candi Devine, Rockin' Robin
Wrestlers Managed:	23
Halls of Fame:	1

Martel, Sherri

The tough "Sensational" Sherri Martel, born and reared in Alabama, had a Hall of Fame career. She was initially a wrestler, trained by the Fabulous Moolah, and won the AWA World Title from Candi Devine on September 28, 1985. Two additional reigns followed, and Martel distinguished herself with her aggressiveness and outgoing personality. In the summer of 1987, she entered the WWF, where she won the WWF Women's Title from her old coach, Moolah, and reigned as champion for over a year. After Wrestlemania V, she joined Randy Savage, aiding in his victory over Jim Duggan for the title of "King" of the WWF, and becoming known as "Sensational Queen" Sherri. Martel and Savage feuded with Sapphire and Dusty Rhodes in 1990, and lost a mixed tag bout at WrestleMania VI when the latter duo received outside help from Miss Elizabeth. In the years that followed, she also acted in a managerial-type role for Ric Flair, Shawn Michaels, Shane Douglas, and Harlem Heat.

Born:	July 9, 1960
Height:	6'0"
Weight:	235
Real Name:	Marc Eric Mero
Parents:	Harold and Diane Mero
High School:	Liverpool High School (NY)
Family:	Brother of Joel Mero
Nicknames:	Marvelous, Wildman
Finisher:	Knockout Punch
Managed by:	Teddy Long, Sable
Career Span:	1991-2005
Website:	www.championofchoices.org

PPV Record:	25-18, 1 Draw
WrestleMania Record:	1-0
Titles Won:	4
Best Opponents:	Steve Austin, Triple H, Brian Pillman

Mero, Marc

In 1979, a young man from Liverpool, New York was looking to stay in shape during the hockey off season, and met Ray Rinaldi, the coach of the North Area Athletic Club. Rinaldi convinced the talented athlete, Marc Mero, to step into a boxing ring, and Mero agreed. In 1980, he won a gold medal in the Empire Games and took a victory in the Golden Gloves tournament the following year. Mero's pro boxing aspirations were sidetracked by an injury, and he took a chance at wrestling instead, training under the Malenkos in Tampa. He was hired by WCW and became known as "Johnny B. Badd," incorporating some boxing into his grappling repertoire. He won the World TV Title on three occasions between 1994 and 1996, and, after jumping to the WWF, captured the Intercontinental belt on September 23, 1996. After the Chris Benoit murder-suicide, Mero spoke out about the industry and today aspires to empower people to make positive life choices through his organization, Champion of Choices.

Born:	February 9, 1963
Height:	5'9"
Weight:	145
Real Name:	Debra Ann Miceli
High School:	Robbinsdale High School (MN)
Trained by:	Eddie Sharkey, Brad Rheingans
Finisher:	German Suplex (bridge)
Groups:	The Dangerous Alliance (1991-1992), Team Madness (1999)
Career Span:	1985-2001
Website:	www.madusa.com

PPV Record:	5-8
WrestleMania Record:	1-0
Titles Won:	8
Days as World Champion:	Over 1,349
Age at first World Title Win:	24
Best Opponents:	Sherri Martel, Wendi Richter, Bull Nakano

Miceli, Madusa

Born in Italy and raised in the Minneapolis area, the talented Madusa Miceli was a prominent wrestler for over fifteen years, capturing world championships in the AWA, WWF, WCW, and in Japan. She was a relentless worker, dedicating herself to the business after trying her hand at modeling and nursing, and was tough to the bone. She beat Candi Devine to capture the vacant AWA Women's World Title on December 27, 1987. Miceli then went overseas to wrestle for All-Japan and won the IWA World Title on two occasions in 1989, the second reign lasting until 1991. As Alundra Blayze, she captured the reactivated WWF World Title in a tournament final over Heidi Lee Morgan on December 13, 1993. She held it two additional times before appearing on WCW *Nitro* and dumping the belt in a trash can on December 18, 1995. In 1999, she held the WCW Cruiserweight Championship and retired from wrestling in 2001 to focus on her new career as a monster truck driver. It didn't take her long to find success in that realm as well.

Michaels, Shawn

Born:	July 22, 1965
Height:	6'0"
Weight:	225
Real Name:	Michael Shawn Hickenbottom
Parents:	Richard and Carole Hickenbottom
High School:	Randolph High School (TX)
College:	Southwest Texas State University
Nicknames:	The Heartbreak Kid
Finisher:	Sweet Chin Music (Superkick)
Groups:	D-Generation X (1997-1998, 1999, 2006, 2009) The Corporation (1998-1999), New World Order (2002)
Managed by:	Sherri Martel, Luna Vachon, Jose Lothario
Promoted:	Texas Wrestling Alliance (2000) (San Antonio, Texas)
Career Span:	1984-2010

PPV Record:	50-57, 2 Draws, 1 DCO, 1 DDQ, 3 NC
WrestleMania Record:	6-10
WWE *Raw* TV Record:	109-47, 2 Draws, 1 DCO, 1 DDQ, 10 NC
WWE *Smackdown* TV Record:	4-1, 1 NC
Titles Won:	22
Days as World Champion:	424
Age at first World Title Win:	30
Best Opponents:	Bret Hart, The Undertaker, Scott Hall
Halls of Fame:	2

By surveying the nicknames bestowed upon the shoulders of the great Shawn Michaels, you get the feeling that he is a well-respected guy in the wrestling industry. He's known as the "Showstopper," the "Icon," and "Mr. WrestleMania," and these descriptive monikers weren't done flippantly—but very astutely. Michaels has been one of the most influential and successful wrestlers of the last quarter century. He's had innumerable outstanding matches and constantly performed brilliant maneuvers with excellent timing. Michaels was committed to greatness, and in time, fans came to expect nothing less from him. He was born on a military installation southeast of Phoenix, the son of a decorated Air Force officer, and moved a number of times during his youth. In 1973, his father, Col. Richard Hickenbottom became commander of the 47th Air Base Group at Laughlin near Del Rio, Texas, and the family relocated again.

From a very sports-oriented family, Michaels took part in track events and was a standout on the Memorial Lobos football squad of the Val Verde Pee Wee Football League while in Del Rio. After his father was transferred to Randolph Air Force Base outside of San Antonio, he earned a reputation as a defensive marvel in high school, and in 1982, performed a wrestling skit with a friend at a talent show that suggested his real goal of becoming a pro grappler. Michaels was influenced by television broadcasts of Southwest Championship Wrestling and sought out legend Jose Lothario for training, becoming a pro at the age of nineteen. He spent his rookie season in the Mid-South territory for Bill Watts, then toured Kansas and the AWA, establishing himself as an up-and-comer with Marty Jannetty in a lightning quick tag team known as the Midnight Rockers. The Rockers were able to mix science with high-flying, and were idols to kids, possessing the right kind of look to draw the interest of younger audiences.

The appeal of Michaels and Jannetty was an attractive quality to promoters, and they received a push in the AWA to the top of the tag team ranks. On January 27, 1987, the Rockers beat Buddy Rose and Doug Somers for the World Tag Team Title and were champions through May 25, when they were defeated by Soldat Ustinov and Boris Zukhov. Later that year, they had an exceptionally brief stay in the WWF, and then turned up in the CWA before regaining the AWA World Tag Team Title in late December of 1987, by beating the Original Midnight Express. When the WWF came calling again in 1988, they were ready embrace the new adventure. Although the promotion had a heavy tag team field, the Rockers found their place, winning over fans, and extended their popularity from coast to coast. It was clear that Michaels had singles potential, and in December of 1991, after five years together, he turned on his partner, and attacked Jannetty. To mark the occasion, he threw the latter through a glass window on an edition of the "Barber Shop."

On October 27, 1992, Michaels beat Davey Boy Smith for the first of three Intercontinental Title reigns. Full of charisma and portraying a character as arrogant as could be, Michaels went a long way in a short period of time in establishing himself as a potential future World Champion. At WrestleMania X, he wrestled a classic ladder match against Razor Ramon, proceeded to win the 1995 and 1996 Royal Rumbles, then beat Bret Hart on March 31, 1996 to capture his first WWF World Heavyweight Title. Michaels lost the belt to Sid Vicious on November 17, but regained it on January 19, 1997. The belt was later declared vacant after Michaels suffered an injury. On November 9, he rebounded to challenge Hart in what is commonly known as the Montreal Screwjob match. Michaels won the controversial bout and his third WWF Title. 1997 was also the year that saw D-Generation X formed by Michaels, Triple H, Chyna, and Rick Rude, and the group established itself the rebellious backbone of the promotion.

Michaels lost the WWF Title to "Stone Cold" Steve Austin on March 29, 1998 at WrestleMania XIV and retired from the business to nurse a seriously injured back suffered earlier in the year. Back home in Texas, he operated a wrestling school and made sporadic appearances in the WWF, including as commissioner in late 1998 and as a member of DX in 1999. In 2000, he briefly made a comeback for his San Antonio promotion, and it wasn't until June of 2002 that he returned to the WWF as a full-time competitor. He feuded heavily with his former DX partner Triple H and won the World Title on November 17, 2002 at Madison Square Garden in an elimination chamber bout, beating "The Game" in the finals. A month later, he lost the belt to Triple H at Armageddon. Michaels also went to war against Chris Jericho, who he beat at WrestleMania XIX. A year later, he came up short in a three-way match against Triple H and Chris Benoit at WrestleMania XX, which Benoit won and captured the World Title.

On July 4, 2005, Michaels attacked Hulk Hogan, setting up a dream match for many fans at SummerSlam on August 21. The bout went more than twenty-one minutes before Hogan scored the win. Michaels beat Vince McMahon in a no-holds barred match at WrestleMania XXII and was unable to win the WWE

Title from John Cena at WrestleMania XXIII on April 1, 2007. He did force Ric Flair into retirement at WrestleMania XXIV on March 30, 2008 with his win. Staying on top of the sport, he feuded with Randy Orton and Chris Jericho again, maintaining his bigger-than-life presence in storylines, but went down in defeat against his old rival The Undertaker on April 5, 2009 at WrestleMania XXV in Houston. Later that year, he teamed with Triple H to win the WWE Unified Tag Team Title. With his own career on the line, Michaels tackled The Undertaker again at WrestleMania XXVI, and was defeated, ending his career. He was inducted into the WWE Hall of Fame in 2011, and while his active career ended, fans expect to see him from time to time, always adding an additional spark to WWE programming.

Photo Courtesy of Dr. Mike Lano—Wrealano@aol.com

Born:	June 18, 1962
Height:	6'1"
Weight:	245
High School:	Ashikaga-kodai High School (Japan)
Trained by:	Shohei Baba, Dick Beyer, La Fiera
Identities:	The Kamikaze, Tiger Mask II
Nickname:	Untouchable
Finisher:	Emerald Flowsion
Owned:	Pro Wrestling NOAH (2000-2009)
Career Span:	1981-2009
Died:	June 13, 2009, Hiroshima, Japan 46 years old

Titles Won:	20
Days as World Champion:	1,799
Age at first World Title Win:	30
Best Opponents:	Toshiaki Kawada, Kenta Kobashi, Stan Hansen
Tournament Wins:	8
Halls of Fame:	1

Misawa, Mitsuharu

Five days before his 47th birthday, wrestling legend Mitsuharu Misawa wrestled his final match in Hiroshima, Japan, participating in a tag team event. The routine situation turned tragic when Misawa was rendered unconscious following a move and later passed away. He'd been a recognized icon around the world for his superlative performances in matches, and was a leader during the wrestling boom of the 1990s. A former amateur wrestler, Misawa trained in the All-Japan dojo and was a noteworthy junior heavyweight, winning the NWA International Junior Title over Kobayashi in August of 1985. For six years he used the

Tiger Mask gimmick and unmasked in May of 1990 as part of a major push he was set to receive. Misawa competed in a number of spectacular bouts and held the AJPW Unified Triple Crown five times, carrying the promotion's banner and elevating the international repute for its main championship to immense proportions.

Among his title victories came over Stan Hansen (twice), Kenta Kobashi (twice), and Vader. His final win came on May 2, 1999 against the latter at the Tokyo Dome before an estimated 65,000 fans, during the Shohei "Giant" Baba Memorial Show. After the death of his mentor, Misawa became the President of All-Japan, a role he performed until May of 2000 when disagreements with members of the company's management saw him ousted. Misawa founded Pro Wrestling Noah, a new organization, a short time later. In the finals of a 16-man tournament, Misawa beat Yoshihiro Takayama for the initial Global Honored Crown World Heavyweight Title on April 15, 2001 in Tokyo. He would hold the championship two additional times. Misawa was a special breed of professional wrestlers, naturally capable of raising his game to the level of legends, and delivering extraordinary matches that will be heralded forever.

Photo Courtesy of Mike Mastrandrea

Born:	October 8, 1980
Height:	6'1"
Weight:	230
Real Name:	Michael Gregory Mizanin
Parents:	George and Barbara Mizanin
High School:	Normandy High School (OH)
Trained by:	UPW trainers, Bill DeMott, Al Snow
Identities:	The Calgary Kid (masked)
Nickname:	The Most Must-See WWE Champion in History
Finisher:	Skull-Crushing Finale
Tag Team:	ShowMiz w/ The Big Show
Career Span:	2003-Present

PPV Record:	15-29
WrestleMania Record:	2-0
WWE *Raw* TV Record:	55-67, 6 NC
WWE *Smackdown* TV Record:	31-27, 1 Draw, 4 NC
Titles Won:	10
Days as World Champion:	160
Age at first World Title Win:	30
Best Opponents:	John Cena, Randy Orton, Daniel Bryan

Miz, The

A number of reality TV entertainers have tried to cross over to wrestling, and many were put off by the difficulty of the transition. The Miz not only made the leap successfully, but rose to the top of the WWE to become a superstar. His dedication to the craft shows in his smooth ring work and his personality displayed behind the microphone. These traits accelerated his push and climaxed when he won the WWE Championship in 2010. From Parma, Ohio, The Miz participated in a number of sports while in high school, and attended Miami University until auditioning for the 10th season of the popular reality show, *The Real World* on MTV. During that program, viewers actually witnessed the first incarnation of "The Miz" character, and in the succession of reality programs that followed, his athleticism was displayed in physical exhibitions. He attended the UPW wrestling camp and participated in the WWE's 2004 Tough Enough series, but lost in the finals to Daniel Puder.

Despite the result, The Miz still found himself in the WWE developmentals. Learning from many skilled trainers, he sharpened his ring knowledge and his instigational attitude served him well during promos. He formed a dynamic team with John Morrison and the duo held both the WWE and World Tag Team Titles between 2007 and 2009. On October 5, 2009, The Miz won the U.S. Title and became a double-champion when he captured the WWE Tag Team belts with The Big Show. He also won the 2010 Money in the Bank ladder match and cashed it in to beat Randy Orton on November 22, 2010 to win the WWE Championship. In subsequent defenses, he showed to be an intelligent champion with the wits to do what was necessary to retain his belt. He maintained that credo in wins against Orton, Jerry Lawler, and, in the biggest match of his career, John Cena at WrestleMania XXVII. During the summer of 2011, he formed a tag team with R-Truth, and the two were impact players, even headlining the Survivor Series against Cena and The Rock.

Photo Courtesy of George Tahinos

Born:	September 10, 1976
Height:	6'9"
Weight:	320
Real Name:	Matthew Thomas Morgan
Parents:	William and Patricia Morgan
Wife:	Larissa Morgan
High School:	Fairfield High School (CT)
Colleges:	Monmouth University, Chaminade University
Finisher:	Hellevator
Groups:	Fortune (2010)
Career Span:	2002-Present

PPV Record:	14-20, 1 DDQ
WWE *Smackdown* TV Record:	5-7, 1 NC
Titles Won:	6
Best Opponents:	Kurt Angle, Samoa Joe, A.J. Styles

Morgan, Matt

Athletically gifted and immense in size, "The Blueprint" Matt Morgan has come close to becoming a TNA World Champion on a number of occasions. His ring weaponry is as punishing as it gets, and his Carbon Footprint finisher looks as if it will knock the head off his foe. A basketball player in high school and college, Morgan finished up his schooling in Hawaii, and trained at Ohio Valley, a WWE Developmental in Louisville. In 2004-2005, he reigned as OVW Heavyweight Champion on two occasions and had a brief run on the main WWE roster. Morgan debuted in TNA during the summer of 2007 as a bodyguard for Jim Cornette. He teamed with Hernandez to win the World Tag Team Title on January 17, 2010, but his partnership ended violently with Morgan injuring his teammate. From there on, he was the sole defender of the belts, and it was a solid gimmick while it lasted. An injury sidelined him in 2011, but he returned to feud with Samoa Joe, and then won the TNA World Tag Team Title with rival, Crimson.

Photo Courtesy of Dr. Mike Lano—Wrealano@aol.com

Born:	March 6, 1971
Height:	6'2"
Weight:	240
Real Name:	Sean Allen Morley
High School:	Markham District High School (Ontario)
Trained by:	Ron Hutchison, Dewey Robertson, Dory Funk Jr., Tom Prichard
Identities:	Scott Borders, Steel, Sean Morgan, The Big Valbowski
Nickname:	The Pornstar
Groups:	The Right to Censor (2000)
Career Span:	1995-Present

Morley, Sean

PPV Record:	16-13
WrestleMania Record:	0-2
WWE *Raw* TV Record:	36-81, 7 NC
WWE *Smackdown* TV Record:	23-25, 1 NC
Titles Won:	14
Days as World Champion:	Around 136
Age at first World Title Win:	26
Best Opponents:	The Rock, Mankind, Steve Austin

A talented and colorful wrestler, Morley is widely known as "Val Venis," for his controversial pornstar gimmick in the WWF. Originally from Oakville, Ontario, he wrestled all over the world from Japan to England, and won the CMLL World Heavyweight Title from Rayo de Jalisco in April 1997 in Mexico City. While in the WWF, he won the Intercontinental Championship on two occasions, beating Ken Shamrock on February 14, 1999 for his first reign and then beating Rikishi on July 4, 2000 for his second. He also held the European belt and the World Tag Team Title with Lance Storm. Many of the outside-the-ring segments he participated in drew fire from conservative groups, especially when off-color jokes were made about his "occupation" in the adult industry. In 2002-2003, he served as the "Chief of Staff" on *Raw* under general manager Eric Bischoff. Morley left the WWE in 2009, toured New Japan, and then appeared on Hulk Hogan's tour of Australia. He briefly worked for TNA in early 2010, and then returned to WWE as a "producer."

Photo Courtesy of Mike Mastrandrea

Morrison, John

Born:	October 3, 1979
Height:	6'1"
Weight:	220
Real Name:	John Randall Hennigan
Parents:	Brian and Karen Hennigan
High School:	Palos Verdes Peninsula High School (CA)
Trained by:	Trainers from SPW, Tough Enough, and Ohio Valley
Identities:	Johnny Blaze, Johnny Spade, Johnny Nitro
Finisher:	Starship Pain
Tag Team:	MNM w/ Joey Mercury
Career Span:	2003-Present

PPV Record:	17-36
WrestleMania Record:	1-2
WWE *Raw* TV Record:	45-71, 2 DDQ, 5 NC
WWE *Smackdown* TV Record:	68-52, 1 DCO, 2 NC
Titles Won:	10
Days as World Champion:	69
Age at first World Title Win:	27
Best Opponents:	Rey Mysterio Jr., Jeff Hardy, The Miz

A product of Palos Verdes in the Los Angeles area, John Morrison wrestled through high school and was a film major at the University of California. He attended a wrestling camp before landing a spot as a cast member of Tough Enough III, and his previous training as a gymnast and in martial arts worked in his favor throughout the series. Morrison displayed the heart and agility of a pure athlete, and won the competition along with Matt Cappotelli on January 23, 2003. He was ushered to the WWE Developmental territory, Ohio Valley, and there formed MNM with Joey Mercury and Melina. The trio had an organic compatibility that led them to *Smackdown* in 2005—and three reigns as WWE Tag Team champs. As a singles grappler, he won the Intercontinental belt three times before winning the ECW World Heavyweight crown in June of 2007. Known for his exaggerated ring entrances, Morrison also formed a successful tag team with The Miz, holding the World Tag Team Title in 2008-2009. He departed the WWE in late 2011.

Born:	September 21, 1956
Height:	5'11"
Weight:	225
Real Name:	Rickey Wendell Morton
Parents:	James and Lucille Morton
Trained by:	Paul Morton
Identities:	Richard Morton
Groups:	The York Foundation (1991-1992)
Finisher:	Diving Crossbody
Career Span:	1978-Present

PPV Record:	10-11, 1 DCO
WrestleMania Record:	0-1
Titles Won:	83
Days as World Champion:	189
Age at first World Title Win:	35
Best Opponents:	Ric Flair, Brian Pillman, Jushin Liger
Halls of Fame:	1

Morton, Ricky

An entertaining high-flyer, Ricky Morton was a member of one of the most successful and influential tag teams of all time, the Rock and Roll Express. Since his debut in the late 1970s, he has been a perennial fan favorite and has showcased a wealth of athletic maneuvers, with his patented dropkick being considered textbook. Originally from Tennessee, Morton joined Robert Gibson to form the Rock and Roll Express around 1983, and the duo were the youthful idols for scores and scores of fans in the expanding Jim Crockett promotional territory. Between 1985 and 1987, they won the NWA World Tag Team belts four times, and would later capture numerous other championships, including ten Smoky Mountain titles. In 1991, he turned heel and joined the York Foundation, becoming known as "Richard Morton." For a majority of the last twenty years, he's been a favorite on the independent circuit, and in March of 2011, won the AIWF World Heavyweight Title from Jimi Love in a cage match.

Photo Courtesy of George Tahinos

Born:	March 6, 1976
Height:	6'2"
Weight:	230
Real Name:	Kenneth C. Anderson
Parents:	James and Sheryl Holmes
Wife:	Shawn Anderson
High School:	Washington High School (WI)
Trained by:	Eric Hammers, Michael Krause
Identities:	Two Rivers Jack, Kamikaze Ken, Ken Kennedy
Finishers:	Mic Check, Green Bay Plunge
Career Span:	1999-Present

PPV Record:	17-18, 1 DCO
WrestleMania Record:	1-1
WWE *Raw* TV Record:	19-20, 2 NC
WWE *Smackdown* TV Record:	27-24, 1 DCO, 2 NC
Titles Won:	15
Days as World Champion:	64
Age at first World Title Win:	34
Best Opponents:	Sting, The Undertaker, Shawn Michaels
Movies:	2

Mr. Anderson

In today's wrestling environment, personality is as important as in-ring abilities, and when a special performer can combine a variety of mat styles and an outgoing attitude that connects with audiences, they usually are on the fast track to superstardom. Ken Anderson of Two Rivers, Wisconsin demonstrated these rare qualities and shot to the top of the ranks as "Mr. Kennedy" in the WWE, and is now one of the top grapplers in TNA. His sense of humor and poise in front of crowds developed in high school, where he was involved in drama and broadcasted his school's basketball games. After graduation, he served in the Army before attending the camp of Brad Rheingans. He followed standard protocol for newcomers in the business by touring the indie scene, honing his techniques, until 2005 when he entered the Ohio Valley WWE developmental territory. He made it to *Smackdown*, and exploited a colorful gimmick that had him making his own ring introductions on a house microphone dropped down from the rafters.

An injury slowed his rise, but by the summer of 2006, he was clearly heading toward bigger and better things. He captured the U.S. Title and feuded with The Undertaker, Bobby Lashley, and Batista, even challenging the latter for the World Title at the 2007 Royal Rumble. On April 1, 2007, he emerged victorious in the Money in the Bank ladder match, earning a future World Title shot, but lost the opportunity to Edge. Injuries continued to haunt Anderson and many fans were disappointed when they heard he was released from the WWE in May of 2009. He toured Australia later in the year, and in January of 2010, he found a new home in TNA. A year into his stint in the promotion, he overcame Matt Morgan and World Heavyweight Champion Jeff Hardy in the same night to annex the TNA belt on January 9, 2011. His reign came to an end at the next pay-per-view, on February 13, 2011, when Hardy regained the title. On June 12, 2011, he captured the TNA World Title a second time from Sting at Slammiversary. Sting won a rematch in July.

Born:	December 23, 1962
Height:	6'1"
Weight:	240
Trained by:	Hiro Matsuda
Identities:	The White Ninja, Super Black Ninja
Nickname:	Pearl of the Orient
Finisher:	Moonsault, Cork Screw Elbow
Groups:	The J-Tex Corporation (1989-1990), New World Order (1997), The Dark Carnival (2000)
Career Span:	1984-Present

PPV Record:	7-11, 1 NC
Titles Won:	26
Days as World Champion:	1,833
Age at first World Title Win:	29
Best Opponents:	Shinya Hashimoto, Yuji Nagata, Genichiro Tenryu
Tournament Wins:	14
Halls of Fame:	1

Mutoh, Keiji

When Keiji Mutoh as the Great Muta arrived in WCW in 1989, many new fans were exposed to the Japanese style of grappling, and were enthralled by his unique abilities. His colorful face paint, green mist, and moonsault made watching wrestling on TBS even more interesting and added a unique dynamic to WCW that the WWF couldn't claim. It has been more than twenty years since that initial showing, and Mutoh has firmly established his legacy as an international superstar. After studying Judo in his youth, Mutoh attended the New Japan wrestling school, and wrestled in Texas and Florida before arriving in WCW under the management of Gary Hart. In September of 1989, he won the World TV Title from Sting. Back in Japan, he won the first of four IWGP Titles from Riki Choshu on August 16, 1992, and remained champion for more than a year. On January 4, 1993, he added the NWA World crown to his list of achievements, defeating Masa Chono at the Tokyo Dome.

Mutoh's second IWGP run began on May 3, 1995 when he went over Shinya Hashimoto and his third reign started when he conquered Scott Norton on January 4, 1999. Genichiro Tenryu ended the latter reign on December 10, but that loss was avenged on June 8, 2001 when Mutoh won the AJPW Unified Triple Crown from Tenryu, becoming the third man in history to hold both the Triple Crown and IWGP Titles. Mutoh transferred his base of operations completely to All Japan and won the Triple Crown twice more, the final time on September 28, 2008 with a win over Suwama in Yokohama. That same year, Mutoh also regained the IWGP Title with a victory over Shinsuke Nakamura, and held both championships simultaneously. Mutoh appeared a number of times in the U.S., including for WCW and TNA, and currently is the President of AJPW. In June of 2011, he teamed with KENSO to win the Unified World Tag Team Title. A legendary competitor and athlete, Mutoh influenced a generation of fans across the globe.

Photo Courtesy of Bill Stahl

Mysterio, Rey Jr.

Born:	December 11, 1974
Height:	5'6"
Weight:	175
Real Name:	Oscar Gutierrez
Parents:	Roberto and Maria Gutierrez
Family:	Nephew of Rey Misterio Sr.
Wife:	Angelica Gutierrez
High School:	Montgomery High School (CA)
Trained by:	Rey Misterio, Super Astro, La Gacela, Cavellero 2000
Identities:	El Colibri, Green Lizard
Finisher:	619, Diving hurricanrana
Groups:	Latino World Order (1998), The Filthy Animals (1999-2001)
Career Span:	1989-Present

PPV Record:	50-65, 3 NC
WrestleMania Record:	4-3
WWE *Raw* TV Record:	38-22, 2 NC
WWE *Smackdown* TV Record:	173-86, 1 DDQ, 13 NC
Titles Won:	35
Days as World Champion:	140
Age at first World Title Win:	31
Best Opponents:	Eddie Guerrero, Dean Malenko, Shawn Michaels
Halls of Fame:	3

In the case of Rey Mysterio, Jr., his astounding athleticism has been rewarded with international popularity. He's certainly earned the support of the thousands of fans who cheer him relentlessly on any given night by performing an intriguing array of high-risk maneuvers, taking the breath away from witnesses of his speed and agility. His innovative style differs greatly from his ring competitors, setting him far apart from the competition. Add the fact that he is about a foot shorter than many WWE superstars, and wears a colorful mask; Mysterio is truly a one-of-a-kind pro wrestler. His explosive charisma and multitalented physical abilities have demonstrated time after time that his size is not a handicap. In fact, he takes advantage of the differences in size, and really helped shatter the myth that smaller wrestlers couldn't rise to the top of the heavyweight ranks and be world champions. It is well understood that Mysterio can beat any wrestler in the WWE, regardless of the size difference. His underdog status is a treasured part of the promotion.

Mysterio is an immense hero and his trademark masks are worn by people of all ages. Having debuted as a young teenager, he was a confirmed veteran by the time he entered WCW in 1996. He bedazzled viewers with his acrobatics and his presence was a considerable boost to the cruiserweight division. His match on the program was often the most talked about, and he had many outstanding contests against Chris Jericho, Dean Malenko, and Billy Kidman. In 2002, he signed with the WWE and captured the tag team title with partners Edge, Rob Van Dam, Eddie Guerrero, and Batista. Following Guerrero's death in 2005, Mysterio dedicated many of his victories to his fallen friend. At the 2006 Royal Rumble, he overcame great odds after entering the ring at number two and remained at the end only to win the event. A few months later at WrestleMania, he beat Randy Orton and defending titleholder Kurt Angle to win the World Heavyweight Championship. It was a glorious moment for Rey and his legion of fans, shared in the ring by Eddie Guerrero's widow Vickie and brother Chavo.

Mysterio was dethroned by King Booker on July 23, 2006 after Chavo turned on him. Over the next couple of years, he was haunted by injuries, but remained in the hunt for championship gold. He beat JBL in twenty-one seconds for the Intercontinental Title at WrestleMania XXV, then traded it with Chris Jericho before finally losing it to John Morrison in September of 2009. In matches against powerhouses Batista and The Undertaker, Rey was no pushover, and always appeared to be a step away from regaining the World Title. On June 20, 2010, he prevailed over CM Punk, Big Show, and champion Jack Swagger to win his second World championship. Mysterio retained against Swagger on July 18, 2010 in a tough match, only to see Kane cash in his Money in the Bank briefcase and pin him for the belt in less than a minute. On July 25, 2011, he beat Miz in a tournament final to win the vacant WWE Title, but lost it the same night to John Cena. A short time later, Mysterio was again injured with Alberto Del Rio taking the credit.

Nash, Kevin

Born:	July 9, 1959
Height:	6'11"
Weight:	325
Real Name:	Kevin Scott Nash
High School:	Aquinas High School (MI)
Identities:	Steele, Oz, Vinnie Vegas
Nicknames:	Big Daddy Cool, Big Sexy
Finisher:	Jackknife Powerbomb
Groups:	New World Order (1996-1999, 2002) (Black and White/ Wolfpack), The Millionaires Club (2000), The Natural Born Thrillers (2000), Kings of Wrestling (2004), Main Event Mafia (2008-2009)
Tag Teams:	The Master Blasters w/ Steele, The Vegas Connection w/ Dallas Page, The Insiders w/ Dallas Page
Managed by:	The Great Wizard
Career Span:	1990-Present

PPV Record:	48-50, 1 Draw, 1 NC
WrestleMania Record:	1-1
WWE *Raw* TV Record:	7-4, 1 NC
WWE *Smackdown* TV Record:	0-2
Titles Won:	21
Days as World Champion:	456
Age at first World Title Win:	35
Best Opponents:	Bret Hart, Shawn Michaels, The Undertaker
Movies:	11

Kevin Nash was an original member of the New World Order, and led a ground-breaking "invasion" of WCW that was full of colorful angles and what appeared many times to be kayfabe-breaking in-ring promos. His ability to deliver powerful, personality-driven verbal segments was always important to the development of feuds, and once in the ring, he dominated opponents with his massive size. With deliberate and crushing maneuvers, he was effective in establishing himself as one of the best big men in the business. Nash was from the Detroit suburbs and attended the University of Tennessee, where his sport of choice was basketball. He played pro ball in Europe, but a leg injury cut his experience short, and served in the Army after his playing days. Trained for wrestling by Jody Hamilton at the WCW Power Plant, Nash entered the promotion using a variety of less-than-stellar gimmicks. He was reinvented when he went to the WWF in 1993, becoming "Diesel," a bodyguard for Shawn Michaels.

At the 1994 Royal Rumble, his potential was showcased when he eliminated seven competitors and went on to win the Intercontinental, Tag Team, and WWF World Heavyweight Championships. The latter was captured from Bob Backlund on November 26, 1994, at a house show at Madison Square Garden. For 358 days, he remained titleholder, and finally lost his grip on the belt to Bret Hart at the 1995 Survivor Series. Nash returned to WCW six months later, but unlike his first run in the promotion, this time history was going to be made. Along with Scott Hall and Hulk Hogan, Nash formed the rebellious NWO, initiating a tremendously successful period for the organization. In fact, the New World Order was a golden concept that has since been often imitated, but never duplicated. Together, Nash and Hall were known as the "Outsiders" and won the WCW Tag Team Title five times. Between 1998 and 2000, he also won the WCW World Title five times and held the distinction of ending Bill Goldberg's long winning streak.

A brief tour of the WWE, where the NWO was briefly reformed, concluded in 2003, and Nash joined TNA in November of 2004. He partnered with Scott Hall and Jeff Jarrett as the Kings of Wrestling, but continued health problems put a damper on any sustained effort. He preyed on members of the popular X-Division in April of 2006, and later advised Kurt Angle and his wife as "Dr. Nash." He feuded with Angle, but the two ultimately banded together as part of the Main Event Mafia in 2008. On July 19, 2009, he beat A.J. Styles for the TNA Legends belt, and in May of 2010, he captured the TNA Tag Team Title with Hall. The following January, he reemerged in the WWE at the Royal Rumble, and participated in a unique three-way feud involving Triple H and CM Punk during the Fall. Many insider shoot references were used in promo segments between Nash and Punk, and Nash brutalized both rivals in deliberate attacks. He lost a sledgehammer ladder match to Triple H at the TLC pay-per-view on December 18, 2011.

Photo Courtesy of Dr. Mike Lano—Wrealano@aol.com

Born:	February 8, 1955
Height:	6′1″
Weight:	280
Real Name:	James Henry Neidhart
High School:	Newport Harbor High School (CA)
College:	UCLA
Identities:	Who (Masked)
Finisher:	Anvil Flattener
Career Span:	1979-Present

PPV Record:	13-10
WrestleMania Record:	3-3
WWE *Raw* TV Record:	0-1
Titles Won:	12
Best Opponents:	Steve Austin, Triple H, Curt Hennig
Halls of Fame:	1

Neidhart, Jim

A product of Southern California, Jim Neidhart was a shot put expert in school. He attended the training camp of the Dallas Cowboys in 1978, but only to be cut after three weeks. Taught by Stu Hart, Neidhart married his mentor's daughter and formed a famous tag team with his brother-in-law, Bret Hart. The Hart Foundation, as they were known, won the WWF World Tag Team Title twice, and Neidhart backed Hart during the reformation of the group in 1997. Possessing a trademark goatee, Neidhart was known for his high-energy interviews, and was aggressive in the ring. He also wrestled for WCW, and his daughter Natalya currently works for the WWE.

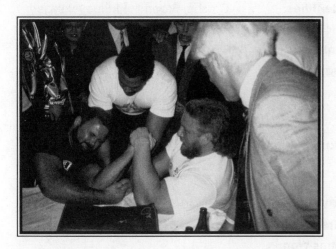

Norton, Scott

Born:	June 15, 1958
Height:	6'3"
Weight:	360
Real Name:	Scott Michael Norton
High School:	Patrick Henry High School (MN)
College:	Anoka-Ramsey Community College
Trained by:	Brad Rheingans, Verne Gagne
Nickname:	Flash
Finisher:	Powerbomb, Shoulder Breaker
Tag Teams:	Jurassic Powers w/ Hercules Hernandez, Fire and Ice w/ Ice Train,
Career Span:	1989-2008

PPV Record:	5-10
Titles Won:	7
Days as World Champion:	126
Age at first World Title Win:	40
Best Opponents:	Great Muta, Vader, Eddie Guerrero

A former bouncer and construction worker from Minneapolis, Scott Norton won innumerable championships in arm-wrestling competitions. In 1986, he beat the 600-pound Cleve Dean for the International Arm-Wrestling Title. Part of that tournament was filmed in association with Sylvester Stallone's film about the sport, *Over the Top*, which Norton was briefly featured. Extremely powerful, Norton bench-pressed in excess of 650 pounds. He held the coveted IWGP Title twice in Japan, and teamed with Tony Halme and Hercules Hernandez for reigns as IWGP Tag Team Champion. While in WCW, he formed the team "Vicious and Delicious" with Buff Bagwell and was also an intimidating member of the New World Order. Norton has occasionally returned to the mat on independent programs and often works as a bodyguard.

One Man Gang

Born:	February 12, 1960
Height:	6'8"
Weight:	450
Real Name:	George Anthony Gray
High School:	Dorman High School (SC)
Trained by:	Joe Gilbert, Jerry Bragg
Identities:	Crusher Broomfield, Blue Avenger
Nickname:	The African Dream
Finisher:	Big Splash
Managed by:	Jim Holliday, General Skandor Akbar, James J. Dillon, Sir Oliver Humperdink, Jim Cornette, Gary Hart, Slick
Career Span:	1977-2009

PPV Record:	3-10, 1 DCO
WrestleMania Record:	2-3
Titles Won:	12
Days as World Champion:	161
Age at first World Title Win:	26
Best Opponents:	Steve Williams, Bruiser Brody, Hulk Hogan

An impressively-sized man named George Gray began training to be a pro wrestler before he was out of high school, taking part in athletic programs coordinated by Joe Gilbert in the Spartanburg, South Carolina area around 1977. Along with Gilbert, Gray tutored others, and then became a wrestler on a small-time circuit under the banner of the "Independent Wrestling Association," appearing under his real name. He went to Georgia, Florida, Texas, and the Mid-South territories, winning championships and solidifying his stature as one of the best big men in the sport. He took the name "One Man Gang" and cruised to the UWF World Title on November 9, 1986 by forfeit over Terry Gordy. In the WWF, he became known as Akeem and formed the Twin Towers with the Big Bossman. On December 27, 1995, he beat Kensuke Sasaki for the WCW U.S. Title and was one of the competitors in the gimmick battle royal at WrestleMania in 2001. After going into semi-retirement, he worked as a prison guard in Louisiana.

Born:	October 29, 1949
Height:	5'11"
Weight:	250
Real Name:	Paul Parlette Orndorff Jr.
Parents:	Paul and Eileen Orndorff
Family:	Brother of Terry Orndorff
High School:	Brandon High School (FL)
College:	University of Tampa
Tag Team:	Pretty Wonderful w/ Paul Roma
Career Span:	1976-2000

PPV Record:	11-8, 2 DCO, 1 NC
WrestleMania Record:	0-1, 1 DCO
Titles Won:	18
Best Opponents:	Hulk Hogan, Ricky Steamboat, Ted DiBiase
Halls of Fame:	4

Orndorff, Paul

A pivotal player in the wrestling business during the 1980s and 1990s, "Mr. Wonderful" Paul Orndorff was an accomplished football player in high school and college. In addition to racking up yardage on the field as a running back, he was successful in the discus and shot put events. In 1973, he was drafted in the 12th round by the New Orleans Saints, but after leaving camp in July, there were already reports circulating that he was considering wrestling. Orndorff instead signed with the Chicago Bears in 1974, then the Jacksonville Express of the World Football League in 1975. Finally, he became a grappler after training in Tampa under Eddie Graham and Hiro Matsuda. He made the rounds of the southeastern territories of the NWA, winning championship gold wherever he went. In the Mid-Atlantic region, he teamed with Jimmy Snuka for the World Tag Team Title and captured the National Heavyweight crown three times in Georgia.

The always entertaining Orndorff went to the WWF and was a challenger to Hulk Hogan's heavyweight title in 1984. He co-headlined the first WrestleMania with Roddy Piper against Hogan and Mr. T, and in August of 1986, his match against Hogan drew over 70,000 to a stadium in Toronto. After a layoff of several years, he became one of the Dudes with Attitudes in WCW in 1990, and feuded with the Four Horsemen. On March 2, 1993, he beat Erik Watts in a tournament for the vacant WCW World TV Title. He also teamed with Paul Roma to capture the WCW World Tag Team Title on two occasions. Orndorff participated in a number of feuds and angles until injuries caught up with him, forcing him to retire. For years, he was a trainer at the WCW Power Plant and coached many future superstars. At the 2000 Fall Brawl pay-per-view, he came out of inactivity to wrestle, but injured his neck delivering his patented piledriver. The WWE honored Orndorff by inducting him into its Hall of Fame in 2005.

Orton, Randy

Born:	April 1, 1980
Height:	6'4"
Weight:	245
Real Name:	Randal Keith Orton
Parents:	Robert and Elaine Orton
Family:	Grandson of Bob Orton Sr.
High School:	Hazelwood Central High (MO)
Trained by:	Bob Orton Jr., WWF Developmental Territories (OVW)
Nickname:	The Legend Killer
Finisher:	Full Nelson Slam, Wheelbarrow Suplex, RKO
Groups:	Evolution (2003)
Career Span:	2000-Present

PPV Record:	44-47, 1 DCO, 1 NC
WrestleMania Record:	4-4
WWE *Raw* TV Record:	136-107, 1 DCO, 23 NC
WWE *Smackdown* TV Record:	38-32, 1 DCO, 4 NC
Titles Won:	13
Days as World Champion:	558
Age at first World Title Win:	24
Best Opponents:	John Cena, Triple H, The Undertaker
Movies:	1

The Orton name has been synonymous with wrestling for more than sixty years; and today, Randy Orton is thrilling audiences much like his father and grandfather had decades before. Fans have watched his progression from preliminaries to winning the WWE championship six times and the World Heavyweight belt three—and his ring demeanor and physical skills are as sharp as anyone in the industry. Orton was popular in the role of a babyface, but was even more hated as a heel, working his gimmick to perfection and drawing the ire of international viewers. It wasn't long before he was out from under the shadow of his father, Bob Orton Jr., and grandfather Bob Orton Sr., and making history. His feuds with Triple H, John Cena, and The Undertaker were stunningly violent, and Orton demonstrated his versatility time after time. Being able to apply an RKO in a flash is one of his trademarks, leaving his foes, and sometimes friends, out for the count.

A product of St. Louis, Orton made an impressive WWE TV debut on April 25, 2002 and was initially established as a crowd favorite. Soon, though, he turned his back on the fans and became a member of Evolution with Triple H, Batista, and Ric Flair. On December 14, 2003, he began a seven-month reign as Intercontinental titleholder after a victory over Rob Van Dam. A month after losing the belt, he raised the bar to another level when he beat Chris Benoit for the World Heavyweight Title at SummerSlam. It was an achievement, at twenty-four-years-old, that few wrestlers accomplish in their entire careers. Orton proved he was the real deal and the future of pro wrestling. He wanted to add to his credentials by ending The Undertaker's streak at WrestleMania XXI, but was turned away. He faced another legend, Hulk Hogan, on August 20, 2006, and was also defeated. Following a run as tag champion with Edge and a feud with DX, Orton reestablished himself as a top contender to the WWE championship.

On October 7, 2007 at No Mercy, he was awarded the vacant championship because titleholder John Cena had been injured. However, that same night, he was defeated by Triple H and lost the belt, only to regain it in the main event, which was a rough Last Man Standing match. In the months following, he held off challenges from Shawn Michaels and Jeff Hardy, and then faced off with Cena and Triple H at WrestleMania on March 30, 2008—a match he won. A month later at Backlash, Orton lost the belt to Triple H. He recovered from a broken collarbone and formed Legacy with Cody Rhodes and Ted DiBiase, two other multi-generational stars, and the trio created plenty of havoc. Orton won the 2009 Royal Rumble, but couldn't take a WrestleMania victory from Triple H. He did leave a six-man match on April 26, 2009 with the WWE championship when the stipulation allowed the title to change hands. He would end up trading it with Batista, and often relied on his Legacy mates to interfere when the chips were down.

Before the end of 2009, he also traded the title back and forth with Cena, winning a Hell in a Cell match on October 4, 2009 in Newark. Cena won an iron-man match at Bragging Rights, taking a firm hold on the WWE Title. Orton, on September 19, 2010, won his sixth WWE Title by winning a six-man elimination contest at Night of Champions, and was successful in defenses against Sheamus and Wade Barrett. He was able to get by Barrett in a grueling affair on November 22, 2010, then forced into a second defense when The Miz cashed in his "Money in the Bank" briefcase and pinned him. In 2011, he went to *Smackdown* following WrestleMania and had a long and intense feud with Christian, winning the World Heavyweight Title twice. Mark Henry proved to be his fiercest challenger, and downed Orton at Night of Champions for the belt. Orton traded victories with Wade Barrett in a feud that remained hot through the end of the year.

Page, Dallas

Born:	April 5, 1956
Height:	6'5"
Weight:	245
Real Name:	Page Joseph Falkinburg, Jr.
Parents:	Page and Sylvia Falkinburg
Family:	Husband of Kimberly
High School:	Point Pleasant High School (NJ)
Colleges:	Ocean County College, Coastal Carolina College
Trained by:	WCW Power Plant, Jake Roberts
Groups:	The Diamond Exchange (1988, 1991), The Millionaires Club (2000), The Alliance (2001)
Tag Teams:	The Vegas Connection w/ Vinnie Vegas, The New Jersey Triad w/ Bam Bam Bigelow and Chris Kanyon, The Insiders w/ Kevin Nash
Managed:	Bad Company (1988-1989), Diamond Studd (1991), The Fabulous Freebirds (1991), Badstreet (1991)
Career Span:	1991-2005

PPV Record:	34-39
WrestleMania Record:	1-0
WWE *Raw* TV Record:	1-2, 2 NC
WWE *Smackdown* TV Record:	7-5, 1 NC
Titles Won:	12
Days as World Champion:	29
Age at first World Title Win:	43
Best Opponents:	Sting, Randy Savage, Curt Hennig
Movies:	14

"Diamond" Dallas Page was a major success in WCW, winning the World Heavyweight Title for the first time six days after his 43rd birthday on April 11, 1999. The triumphant victory came over Ric Flair during a four-way match at Spring Stampede, and was a defining moment in his rise to superstardom. Originally from Point Pleasant, New Jersey, Page began as a manager and TV announcer in the AWA, claiming to have been a rich diamond miner from South Africa. Fans loved to hate his arrogance, and Page continued that theme when he migrated to WCW as the manager of the Fabulous Freebirds. In 1991, he made his pro debut as a wrestler at thirty-five years of age, and for several years, he toiled around the promotion as an enhancement performer. He got a break in 1995 with mid-card feuds against Johnny B. Badd and Jim Duggan, and slowly won over fans with his likeable attitude and popular Diamond Cutter finisher.

Page was also involved in a number of angles and feuds that crossed over into the mainstream. During his feud with Raven, their hatred for one another boiled over onto the set of *MTV Live*, and involved a stop sign. In 1998, he teamed with basketball star Karl Malone and Jay Leno at separate pay-per-view events, garnering lots of attention for WCW and for Page himself. He'd also later figure into the David Arquette angle, rounding out his celebrity association in the ring.

After winning the WCW World Title in 1999, he was defeated by Sting on April 26, only to regain it the same night by outlasting Sting, Bill Goldberg, and Kevin Nash in a four-corners match. On April 16, 2000, he advanced to the finals of a week-long tournament for the vacant WCW Title, but came up short against Jeff Jarrett. Eight days later, he beat Jarrett for his third WCW championship in a cage match. Page would also team with Nash to capture the WCW World Tag Title on two occasions.

Between 1999 and 2001, Page was involved in wars with Scott Steiner, Ric Flair, Mike Awesome, and Kanyon. Once WCW was sold to the WWF, he joined the latter organization as a heel, and during the summer of 2001, he appeared in a mystery stalker angle involving The Undertaker's wife Sara. "DDP" teamed with Kanyon to win the WWF World Tag Team Title from The APA on August 7, 2001. They would hold the championship until August 19 when they lost a WWF Tag vs. WCW Tag unification cage match to Kane and The Undertaker. On January 29, 2002, Page beat Christian for the WWF European Title. Bothered by injuries, Page retired in June 2002, and returned briefly in 2005. All during his tenure as a wrestler, he was committed to helping others, teaching kids about dyslexia and acting as a role model. In recent years, he's created a "Yoga for Regular Guys" fitness program and has pursued film roles.

Pillman, Brian

Born:	May 22, 1962
Height:	5'10"
Weight:	225
Real Name:	Brian William Pillman
High School:	Norwood High School (OH)
College:	Miami University (OH) (Grad. 1983)
College Ach.:	All-American, Mid-American Conference Football Defensive Player of the Year (1983)
Football Position:	Defensive Lineman, Linebacker
Pro Sports:	National Football League—Cincinnati Bengals (1984) Canadian Football League—Calgary Stampeders (1986)
Identities:	The Yellow Dog (Masked)
Nicknames:	Flyin'
Finisher:	Flying Dropkick, Crossbody from the Top Rope
Career Span:	1986-1997
Died:	October 5, 1997, Bloomington, MN 36 years old

PPV Record:	13-16, 1 Draw, 1 NC
Titles Won:	7
Best Opponents:	Steve Austin, Lex Luger, Jushin Liger
Halls of Fame:	1

As an inspiring high-flyer or an off-the-cuff heel, Brian Pillman was a thrilling superstar, creating all kinds of buzz and memorable moments. Pillman was an undrafted free agent signed by the Cincinnati Bengals in 1984, playing six games, and won the NFL's Ed Block Courage Award overcoming long odds. After his career was sidetracked because of injury, Pillman went to Calgary and trained to be a wrestler in the famous Hart Dungeon, then wrestled throughout the Stampede territory. In 1989, he turned up in WCW, where his aerial attack earned him a strong following. Along with Tom Zenk, he captured the U.S. Tag Team Title and won a tournament over Richard Morton for the initial WCW Light Heavyweight crown. His astounding series of matches against nimble Jushin Liger altered the way many Americans viewed non-heavyweight workers, and are still fondly talked about today. Pillman, in 1993, formed the Hollywood Blonds with Steve Austin, and duo won the WCW and NWA World Tag Team Titles.

Before the Blonds fully hit their stride, Pillman suffered an injury, only to return as a babyface later in the year to feud with Austin. He joined the Four Horsemen and became more and more unpredictable in and out of the ring. In promos, he made cryptic comments and defined what it meant to be a "Loose Cannon," which became his nickname. Things came to a head at SuperBrawl on February 11, 1996 when he told "booker-man" Kevin Sullivan that he respected him and left the ring. Fans were left to wonder how much of it was a work and how much was real. Pillman left WCW for a brief stint in ECW, then signed with the WWF, but a car accident and ankle injury put him out of action. He still knew how to make things exciting, particularly as he resumed his feud with Austin—spawning their infamous "gun incident" on *Raw* after Austin broke into his Cincinnati home. On the morning of the 1997 Bad Blood pay-per-view, Pillman passed away of arteiosclerotic heart disease and tributes were held on both *Raw* and WCW *Nitro*.

Photo Courtesy of Dr. Mike Lano—Wrealano@aol.com

Polaco, Pete

Born:	October 16, 1973
Height:	6'0"
Weight:	225
Real Name:	Peter Joseph Polaco
Wife:	Jill Polaco
High School:	Holy Cross High School (CT)
Finisher:	That's Incredible
Career Span:	1992-Present

PPV Record:	16-21, 2 NC
WWE *Raw* TV Record:	3-9, 2 NC
WWE *Smackdown* TV Record:	5-3, 1 DDQ
Titles Won:	20
Days as World Champion:	260
Age at first World Title Win:	26
Best Opponents:	Jerry Lynn, Shane Douglas, Tommy Dreamer

As the "Portuguese Man 'o War," Aldo Montoya, Pete Polaco was a masked fan favorite with a flashy array of dropkicks. As Justin Credible, he was a cane-wielding heel and ECW World Champion. What his ring name is doesn't necessarily matter, but what does is that he's been on top of his game for nearly twenty years. A soccer player in school, Polaco trained in Calgary under the Harts and Lance Storm, and spent a good chunk of the 1990s with the WWF as Montoya. He debuted in ECW in 1997 and defeated Tommy Dreamer for the World Title on April 22, 2000. He ruled the promotion until October 1 when Jerry Lynn won the belt. Teaming with his former mentor, Storm, he formed the Impact Players, and won the ECW World Tag Team Title twice in 2000. He affiliated himself with the Alliance upon his return to the WWF in 2001 and, between May and July of 2002, won the WWE Hardcore crown eight times. Since then, he's appeared for ROH and a host of other organizations, and wrestled at TNA's Hardcore Justice in 2010.

Born:	October 28, 1973
Height:	6'2"
Weight:	250
Real Name:	Hassan Assad
Trained by:	Norman Smiley, Soulman Alex G
Identities:	Antonio Banks
Career Span:	2002-Present

Porter, Montel Vontavious

PPV Record:	9-26
WrestleMania Record:	0-4
WWE *Raw* TV Record:	25-22, 1 DCO, 1 NC
WWE *Smackdown* TV Record:	44-78, 2 Draws, 1 DCO, 7 NC
Titles Won:	6
Best Opponents:	Chris Benoit, Kane, Matt Hardy

A product of the Miami area, MVP joined the WWE developmental system in 2005 and debuted on *Smackdown* during the summer of 2006. As part of his gimmick, he was touted as a coveted sports star, and he really had the athletic ability to match the hype. He won the United States Heavyweight Championship from Chris Benoit on May 20, 2007 and held it with distinction until the following April. He also reigned as the WWE Tag Team Champion with his perennial rival, Matt Hardy. In late 2010, he departed the WWE and joined New Japan Pro Wrestling. He was victorious in a tournament for the initial IWGP Intercontinental belt on May 15, 2011.

Raven

Born:	September 8, 1964
Height:	6'1"
Weight:	235
Real Name:	Scott Levy
High School:	Lake Worth High School (FL)
College:	University of Delaware
Trained by:	Larry Sharpe, Jake Roberts
Identities:	Scotty the Body, Scott Anthony
Finisher:	Evenflow DDT
Groups:	The Flock (1997-1998), The Alliance (2001), Sports Entertainment Xtreme (2003), The Gathering (2003)
Career Span:	1988-Present
Website:	www.theraveneffect.com

PPV Record:	45-50, 1 Draw
WrestleMania Record:	0-1
WWE *Raw* TV Record:	13-19, 2 NC
WWE *Smackdown* TV Record:	10-16, 1 NC
Titles Won:	57
Days as World Champion:	614
Age at first World Title Win:	31
Best Opponents:	Tommy Dreamer, Rhino, Dallas Page

Raven was wrestling's symbolic representative to the grunge era, a brooding intellect, yearning for respect and admiration. Verbally gifted, he expressed himself in ways other wrestlers couldn't, making feuds seem much more personal, and adding a unique element to the wrestling world. College-educated and owning the discipline of the U.S. Marine Corps, Raven made his bones in Memphis and Portland, and then appeared in WCW as Scotty Flamingo in 1992. Months later, he went to the WWF, where he managed the Quebecers, actually helping them win the WWF World Tag Team Title from the Steiners and Adam Bomb. Then known as Johnny Polo, he displayed his talents behind the microphone as a commentator, and many people were becoming aware of his well-rounded abilities. In 1994, he was back on the indie scene, where he found a new home in Philadelphia working for Extreme Championship Wrestling.

ECW was the launching pad for a new dimension of his wrestling persona, and saw the birth of Raven, an introverted soul searching for purpose. Part of his gimmick was luring weak-minded and lost souls to his camp, almost like a cult leader, and creating a universe that he was the center of. In 1995, he joined Stevie Richards to win the ECW Tag Team Title on two occasions, then toppled The Sandman on January 27, 1996 for the ECW World belt. He then went to WCW, where he beat Dallas Page for the U.S. crown in 1998, and over a two-year period, captured the WWE Hardcore Title twenty-seven times. He also had success in TNA, defeating A.J. Styles for the NWA World Heavyweight Title on June 19, 2005 in a King of the Mountain bout. In 2010, he was part of the EV 2.0 faction but left TNA before the end of the year. Raven has wrestled all over the world, taking part in violent feuds against Tommy Dreamer, Abyss, and CM Punk, and solidified his standing as a complex mat personality.

Photo Courtesy of George Tahinos

Born:	February 5, 1986
Height:	5'3"
Weight:	125
Real Name:	Ashley Nichole Simmons
High School:	Ridgewood High School (OH)
Trained by:	Jeff Cannon
Identities:	Ashley Lane, Lexi Lane
Career Span:	2005-Present

PPV Record:	5-10	
Titles Won:	7	
Days as World Champion:		299
Age at first World Title Win:		24
Best Opponents:		Tara, Mickie James, Angelina Love

Rayne, Madison

Full of personality and a dynamic performer in the ring, Madison Rayne has been wrestling only seven years and already has the credentials of a battle-tested veteran. She's a three-time TNA Women's Knockout champion, a former member of the illustrious Beautiful People, and has been embroiled in intense feuds with Tara, Angelina Love, and Mickie James. Rayne, who is from West Lafayette, Ohio, began her career in Ohio Championship Wrestling and debuted in TNA in 2009. She initially won the Knockouts belt in April of 2010, was awarded her second title that July after a controversial bout with Love, and beat Tara in October of 2010 to start her third reign.

Born:	July 11, 1954
Height:	6'2"
Weight:	265
Real Name:	Bruce Reed
High School:	Warrensburg High School (MO)
College:	Central Missouri State University
Pro Sports:	National Football League—Kansas City Chiefs (late 1970s) (camp)
Nicknames:	Hacksaw
Career Span:	1978-2006

PPV Record:	6-4, 1 DCO, 1 NC
WrestleMania Record:	1-1
Titles Won:	15
Days as World Champion:	5
Age at first World Title Win:	38
Best Opponents:	Ron Simmons, Ric Flair, Randy Savage

Reed, Butch

Powerfully built and an imposing presence in the ring, Butch Reed was a football star in high school and college in Warrensburg, Missouri. He was recruited into wrestling by Ronnie Etchison and made his debut in 1978. On the NWA circuit, he appeared in a number of territories and received a good push by Bill Watts in the Mid-South region, defeating Dick Murdoch for the North American Title in 1985. He entered the WWF late in 1986, dyed his hair blond, took Slick as his manager, and became known as the "Natural." A few years later, Reed formed a distinguished tag team with Ron Simmons known as Doom, and won the WCW Tag Team Title in 1990. They fended off challenges from the Horsemen and Rock and Roll Express before losing the belts to the Freebirds. In 1992, he beat Junkyard Dog for the USWA Unified World belt and then, in 2001, captured the WLW Title. He was a force on the Midwestern indie circuit until his retirement in 2006.

Born:	May 10, 1968
Height:	6'2"
Weight:	240
Real Name:	Darren Kenneth Matthews
Trained by:	Marty Jones, Bobby Barron
Identities:	Roy Regal, Steve Regal, Lord Steven Regal
Nicknames:	Lord, The Real Man's Man
Finisher:	Regal Stretch
Career Span:	1983-Present

PPV Record:	18-36, 3 Draws, 1 DCO
WrestleMania Record:	0-2
WWE *Raw* TV Record:	62-74, 1 DCO, 5 NC
WWE *Smackdown* TV Record:	22-53, 5 NC
Titles Won:	18
Best Opponents:	Chris Benoit, Ricky Steamboat, Dave Finlay

Regal, William

William Regal is more of a throwback warrior of the ring than a modern villain. His European uppercuts are brutal, and he constantly mixes a technical style with that of a sheer gladiator. Originally from England, he made his mark on the U.S. scene beginning in 1993 by posing as a member of the royal elite in WCW. He won the World TV Title four times and was a member of the Blue Bloods along with "Earl" Robert Eaton and "Squire" David Taylor. In 1998, he entered the WWF, and would later serve as both commissioner and the general manager of *Raw*. He was also the first member of Vince McMahon's infamous "Kiss My Ass" club. Regal formed tag teams with Lance Storm, Eugene, and Tajiri, winning the World Tag Team Title four times and also holding the Intercontinental belt twice. His trademark facial expressions, mannerisms, and comedic timing make him one of the most entertaining grapplers outside of the ring.

Born:	December 13, 1953
Height:	6'0"
Weight:	245
Real Name:	Bradley Bert Rheingans
Parents:	Willard and Lois Rheingans
High School:	Appleton High School (MN)
HS Ach.:	Two-Time Minnesota Wrestling Champion (1970-1971) (175)
College:	North Dakota State University
College Ach.:	NCAA Division II Champion (1975) (190)
Amateur Titles:	Two-Time Senior Greco-Roman Champion (1977, 1979) (220)
Olympics:	Greco-Roman Wrestling (1976) (220) (4th Place)
Trained by:	Verne Gagne
Tag Team:	The Olympians w/ Ken Patera
Career Span:	1981-1995

Titles Won:	2
Best Opponents:	Nick Bockwinkel, Larry Zbyszko, Rick Martel
Halls of Fame:	2

Rheingans, Brad

The superior legitimate wrestling skills owned by Brad Rheingans made him one of the best trainers in the business and many future superstars attended his school to learn the fundamentals. His outstanding amateur background as a Greco-Roman grappler drew the attention of Verne Gagne, who was always on the lookout for talented pure wrestlers. Rheingans was an NCAA champion and two-time member of the U.S. Olympic Team, although he did not compete in 1980 due to the U.S. boycott. He joined Gagne's AWA and was an influential coach to wrestlers Curt Hennig, Vader, and Tom Zenk. On March 25, 1989, he teamed with Ken Patera to win the AWA World Tag Team Title from Bad Company in Rochester. He went out with an injury during the summer and the title was eventually declared vacant. In the early 1990s, he wrestled for New Japan Pro Wrestling and later acted as a special advisor to Antonio Inoki's UFO group.

Born:	October 7, 1975
Height:	6'3"
Weight:	270
Real Name:	Terrance Gerin
High School:	Annapolis High School (MI)
Trained by:	Scott D'Amore, Mickey Doyle, Doug Chevalier
Identities:	Terry Richards, Rhino Richards
Groups:	Thug Life, The Alliance
Career Span:	1995-Present

PPV Record:	34-34, 2 NC
WrestleMania Record:	0-1
WWE *Raw* TV Record:	22-24, 3 NC
WWE *Smackdown* TV Record:	22-31, 4 NC
Titles Won:	18
Days as World Champion:	Around 90
Age at first World Title Win:	25
Best Opponents:	Abyss, Christian, Kurt Angle

Rhino

Rhino, an outstanding brawler, was a perfect fit in ECW in 1999. His rough-and-tumble style demonstrated his willingness to battle on the most primitive of levels, leading up to his powerful Gore, a running spear that he drove through opponents. A former amateur wrestler from Dearborn Heights, Michigan, Rhino was trained at the Can-Am Wrestling School in Windsor and grappled for various indie promotions and in Germany prior to landing a spot for ECW. In the years that followed, he won the TV Title twice and captured the World Heavyweight belt from Sandman in 2001. He also wrestled for the WWF prior to suffering a near career-ending neck injury that shelved him for more than a year. In October of 2005, while in TNA, he beat Jeff Jarrett for the NWA World Title, and was a member of the ECW reunion group EV 2.0 in 2010.

Born:	June 30, 1985
Height:	6'1"
Weight:	225
Real Name:	Cody Garrett Runnels
Parents:	Virgil and Michelle Runnels
Family:	Brother of Dustin Rhodes
HS Ach.:	Georgia State Wrestling Champion (2003) (189), (2004) (189)
Trained by:	Dusty Rhodes, Al Snow, Bob Holly
Finisher:	Cross Rhodes
Groups:	Legacy (2008-2010)
Career Span:	2006-Present

PPV Record:	11-17
WrestleMania Record:	1-1
WWE *Raw* TV Record:	60-52, 1 Draw, 1 DDQ, 4 NC
WWE *Smackdown* TV Record:	29-29, 1 NC
Titles Won:	9
Best Opponents:	Rey Mysterio Jr., Randy Orton, Daniel Bryan

Rhodes, Cody

The naturally charismatic Cody Rhodes began wrestling when he was five years old, and went undefeated as a junior at Lassiter High in Marietta, Georgia, winning the state championship. He won the title again a year later, and considered acting for a living after graduation. Instead, he joined the family business, following his father Dusty and brother Dustin into pro wrestling. Rhodes not only carried on the tradition in name, but in athletic talent, and made a dent early in his WWE career by winning the World Tag Team Title with Hardcore Holly in late 2007. He turned heel and joined Ted DiBiase Jr. and Randy Orton to form the dastardly trio, "Legacy." In 2010, he pushed a self-absorbed gimmick in which he was known as "Dashing," but that came to an end when he suffered a facial injury in a bout with Rey Mysterio. For awhile, he wore a face mask, which he often used as a weapon, and won the Intercontinental belt in August of 2011. An impressive champion, he turned back the challenges of DiBiase, Sheamus, and John Morrison.

Born:	April 11, 1969
Height:	6'5"
Weight:	240
Real Name:	Dustin Patrick Runnels
Parents:	Virgil and Sandra Runnels
Family:	Brother of Cody Rhodes
Trained by:	Dusty Rhodes
Identities:	Dusty Rhodes Jr., Marilyn Mansondust, Artist formerly known as Goldust, Dustin Runnels, Seven, Gold Dustin, Black Reign
Nicknames:	The Natural, The Lone Star
Finisher:	Bulldog Headlock
Career Span:	1988-Present

Rhodes, Dustin

PPV Record:	36-58, 3 Draws
WrestleMania Record:	0-5
WWE *Raw* TV Record:	25-40, 1 DCO
WWE *Smackdown* TV Record:	3-1
Titles Won:	22
Best Opponents:	Rick Rude, Steve Austin, Ricky Steamboat

For many second generation wrestlers, breaking out from underneath the shadow of their fathers is a painstaking chore. Even more difficult is trying to establish an identity enveloped by the shadow of a wrestling legend, and in the case of Dustin Rhodes, he's successfully achieved his own persona separate from his father, Dusty . . . particularly when dressed as Goldust, a strange and complex wrestling gimmick. As Goldust, he bears little resemblance to the ring stylings of his father outside of some of the same maneuvers. Rhodes played football at East Mecklenburg High in Charlotte after transferring from Austin and won his consolation final at the Southwestern 4A state wrestling championships. Seven months later, he turned pro in Florida, and learned a great deal about the business from Dusty. The relationship between father and son has been severely strained at times, yet they've come together to participate in angles and matches in the WWF and WCW.

With partners Ricky Steamboat and Barry Windham, Dustin won the WCW Tag Team Title, and then captured the U.S. Title on January 11, 1993, beating Steamboat in the finals of a tournament. A few years later, he migrated to the WWF and established the "Goldust" character. Flaunting an eccentricity and locked into an identity crisis, Goldust was lavish in his ring introductions and was deliberate in his overly peculiar behavior. Initially disturbing, Goldust became known more for his comedy factor, and annexed the Intercontinental championship three times, also winning the World Tag Team Title with Booker T. Rhodes had two stints in TNA and returned to the WWE after each tour, appearing on *Smackdown* as late as 2010. In December of that year, he suffered a serious shoulder injury that necessitated surgery. His autobiography, *Cross Rhodes*, was released around the same time. Through all of the different gimmicks and personal trials, Rhodes has had a successful career and created a legacy all his own.

Photo Courtesy of Dr. Mike Lano—Wrealano@aol.com

Born:	October 9, 1971
Height:	6'1"
Weight:	230
Real Name:	Michael Manna
High School:	Frankford High School (PA)
Trained by:	Mike Sharpe, The Sandman
Identities:	Dr. Stevie
Nickname:	King of Swing
Finisher:	Superkick
Managed by:	Beulah McGillicutty
Managed:	Bull Buchanan (2000-2001), The Good Father (2000-2001), Ivory (2000-2001), Jazz (2002), Victoria (2003)
Career Span:	1992-Present

Richards, Stevie

PPV Record:	6-8
WWE *Raw* TV Record:	12-45, 1 NC
WWE *Smackdown* TV Record:	2-9, 2 NC
Titles Won:	38
Best Opponents:	Tommy Dreamer, Sabu, CM Punk

   Wrestling favorite Stevie Richards has excelled in the business for nearly two decades, appearing in colorful roles and offering many comedic performances. He's been a hardcore superstar, a member of the Blue World Order, and a lackey for Raven. A product of the Port Richmond section of Philadelphia, Richards gained lots of esteem while working for ECW, teaming with Raven to win the World Tag Team Title on two occasions in 1995. Venturing through the independents, WCW, and the WWF, he gained plenty of ring experience and confidence behind the microphone. As the smug leader of Right to Censor, Richards managed Buchanan and The Good Father to the WWF Tag Team Title in November of 2000. Between April and August of 2002, he captured the WWF Hardcore Championship a whopping twenty-two times. He also seconded women's champions Jazz and Victoria. While a part of TNA, he became known as Dr. Stevie, feuded with Abyss, and joined the ECW reunion group EV 2.0 in 2010.

Born:	September 8, 1960
Height:	5'9"
Weight:	145
Real Name:	Victoria Lynn Richter
High School:	Bossier High School (LA)
Career Span:	1979-2005

PPV Record:	1-0
Titles Won:	8
Days as World Champion:	819
Age at first World Title Win:	23
Best Opponents:	Fabulous Moolah, Leilani Kai, Madusa Miceli
Halls of Fame:	2

Richter, Wendi

The first woman to achieve superstar status in Vincent K. McMahon's nationally expanding WWF was Wendi Richter of Bossier City, Louisiana, a supremely popular heroine who was much more than just a pretty face in the ring. She was proficient in actually wrestling, and was able to distinguish herself as a world champion, which she was three times over—twice in the WWF and once in the AWA. Richter was the goddess of the WWF's Rock n' Wrestling era, and appeared both on MTV and in the family friendly cartoon. She was also managed by music icon Cyndi Lauper in 1984-1985. After being double-crossed out of her title by Fabulous Moolah in 1985, she departed the WWF and only returned when she was inducted into the WWE Hall of Fame in 2010.

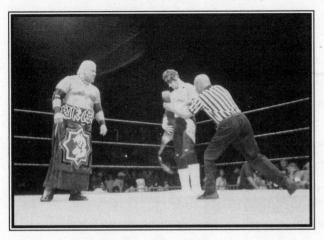

Born:	October 11, 1965
Height:	6'1"
Weight:	375
Real Name:	Solofa Fatu
High School:	Balboa High School (CA)
Trained by:	Afa
Identities:	Fatu, The Sultan, Kishi
Finisher:	Rikishi Driver
Career Span:	1995–Present

Rikishi

PPV Record:	18-30, 1 NC
WrestleMania Record:	2-2
WWE *Raw* TV Record:	31-25, 1 DCO, 1 DDQ, 3 NC
WWE *Smackdown* TV Record:	67-56, 1 DCO, 5 NC
Titles Won:	13
Best Opponents:	Steve Austin, The Rock, Bret Hart

A member of the famous Anoai family, Rikishi is the nephew of Samoans Afa and Siki, and cousin of Samu, his longtime tag team partner. His brothers, Jamal and Tonga Kid, were also wrestlers of note. In 1987, along with Samu as the Samoan Swat Team, he appeared all over the globe. They won titles in Puerto Rico and Texas, and, in 1994, captured the WWF World Tag Team Title as the Headshrinkers, managed by Afa and Captain Lou Albano. In 1999, he adopted the Rikishi persona, wearing modified sumo gear, and gained popularity for his dancing in the ring. He was also known for giving rivals the uproarious "Stinkface." He held the Intercontinental Title in 2000 and the World Tag Team Title with Rico two years later. In 2004, he partnered with Scotty 2 Hotty to win the WWE Tag Team Title. He left the WWE that same year.

Road Dogg

Born:	May 20, 1969
Height:	6'2"
Weight:	230
Real Name:	Brian Girard James
Parents:	Joseph and Gail James
Family:	Brother of Scott, Steve, and Brad Armstrong
Trained by:	The Armstrong Family
Identities:	Brian Armstrong, The Roadie, Jesse James, B.G. James
Career Span:	1993-Present

PPV Record:	60-49, 2 NC
WrestleMania Record:	1-2
WWE *Raw* TV Record:	34-27, 11 NC
WWE *Smackdown* TV Record:	27-17, 4 NC
Titles Won:	23
Days as World Champion:	A few days
Age at first World Title Win:	32
Best Opponents:	Steve Austin, The Rock, Kane

The youngest son of Bob Armstrong, "Road Dogg" Brian James joined his father and brothers in wrestling after proud service as a Marine during the first Gulf War. He was associated with Jeff Jarrett during his first stint in the WWF, but didn't gain significant status until forming the rogue New Age Outlaws with Billy Gunn. In addition to winning the World Tag Team Title five times, the unruly pair were members of popular anti-establishment group, D-Generation X. As a singles competitor, he captured the Intercontinental Championship from Val Venis in March of 1999 and was known for his colorful promos and popular catchphrases. On TNA, he partnered with Ron Killings and Konnan as 3Live Kru and was twice a tag team champion. He also wrestled all over the indie scene, and, in 2001, became the initial WWA World Champion during a tour of Australia.

Rock, The

Born:	May 2, 1972
Height:	6'5"
Weight:	250
Real Name:	Dwayne Douglas Johnson
Parents:	Rocky and Ata Maivia Johnson
High School:	Freedom High School (PA)
HS Ach:	High School All-American Football Player (1989)
College:	University of Miami (FL)
College Ach:	Member of the 1991 National Champions Football Squad
Trained by:	Rocky Johnson
Nicknames:	Brahma Bull, Rocky, The Most Electrifying Man in Sports Entertainment, The People's Champion
Finisher:	Rock Bottom, People's Elbow, Sharpshooter
Tag Team:	The Rock and Sock Connection w/ Mankind
Career Span:	1996-2011

PPV Record:	36-35, 2 Draws
WrestleMania Record:	4-4
WWE *Raw* TV Record:	86-40, 14 NC
WWE *Smackdown* TV Record:	62-36, 12 NC
Titles Won:	18
Days as World Champion:	394
Age at first World Title Win:	26
Best Opponents:	Steve Austin, Hulk Hogan, Mankind
Halls of Fame:	1
TV Appearances:	Over 150
Movies:	20

"The Rock" Dwayne Johnson is an internationally recognizable actor and a third generation professional wrestler. His active career lasted only eight years, but during that time, he displayed a mastery of performances, connecting to the audience with remarkable flair and saturating the WWE Universe with entertaining segments. His ability to convert humdrum angles and scenarios into amusing content was uncanny. In the ring, he was just as skilled, appearing in high-tension matches against the likes of Hulk Hogan,

Steve Austin, Triple H, and many other big-name superstars. The Rock's catchphrases united audiences as they repeated the sayings along with him, electrifying arenas, and spotlighting his natural charisma. Winning the WWE World Title a total of seven times between 1998 and 2002, The Rock was instrumental in helping the organization win the ratings war against WCW.

Born in Alameda County, California, Johnson was the son of wrestler Rocky Johnson and the grandson of wrestler "High Chief" Peter Maivia, as well as the nephew of Jimmy Snuka. He played football in college at the University of Miami and made the practice squad for the Calgary Stampeders of the CFL. Finding his pursuit of football to be less than desirable, he entered the wrestling business in 1996, touring the USWA out of Memphis as Flex Kavana. Before the end of the year, however, he was on the main stage in the WWF, wrestling as Rocky Maivia Jr., a tribute to his father and grandfather. At the Survivor Series on November 17, 1996, he was the sole survivor for his team, making his first pay-per-view appearance a successful one. In February of 1997, he beat Triple H for the Intercontinental Title and joined the Nation of Domination later in the year as a heel. He continued to build momentum in his rise up the bill, and on November 15, 1998, he beat Mankind in the finals of a tournament to win the WWF World Heavyweight Title.

The Rock's first WWF championship win was tainted by a screwy finish, and marked his transition to the "Corporation Champion," a henchman of Vince McMahon. He feuded with Mankind over the belt, and the two traded the title twice. At WrestleMania XV on March 28, 1999, The Rock was unsuccessful in his defense against Steve Austin, and lost the title, leading to him being fired from the Corporation. The angle turned Rock into a fan favorite again, which worked out nicely as he began to achieve some mainstream success. In addition to the release of his autobiography, he appeared as a guest host on *Saturday Night Live*. With help from Austin, Rock regained the WWF Title from Triple H on April 30, 2000, but lost it back to him in an iron-man match on May 21. A month later at the King of the Ring, Rock pinned McMahon in a six-man tag team match, and won his fifth WWF Title. Former Olympian Kurt Angle beat him for the belt, but Rock regained it in February of 2001, becoming the first ever six-time champion.

Austin again dethroned Rock at WrestleMania X-Seven, this time with some unexpected outside help from McMahon. Shortly thereafter, he was put out of action in an injury angle, and spent several months filming *The Scorpion King*. The movie was a prequel to *The Mummy*, and a continuation of the story of his character featured in *Mummy Returns*, which opened to a $65 million weekend in May of 2001. He returned during the WCW/ECW Invasion and feuded with Booker T. At SummerSlam, he won the WCW World Title and proceeded to trade it with Chris Jericho before dropping it to the latter on December 9, 2001. In what was considered a dream match for many fans, The Rock faced off against Hulk Hogan on March 17, 2002 at WrestleMania X-Eight in Toronto, and the 68,237 in attendance chanted feverishly for their heroes in an emotionally charged match. The back-and-forth drama saw Rocky score the pin and take the proverbial torch.

On July 21, 2002, he won his seventh WWF Title, and held it until SummerSlam. The Rock battled Austin at the following WrestleMania, but this time around, he was victorious. Retiring from wrestling to meet the growing demands of his film career, he appeared in twenty movies between 2001 and 2011 and made a few rare appearances on WWE programming. He returned "home" to the promotion on February 14, 2011, and ignited a feud with John Cena. It was announced that he'd be the guest host for WrestleMania, which gave him and Cena the opportunity to escalate their war of words. Finally, the two agreed to face off in the main event of Wrestlemania XXVIII in 2012. In the meantime, Rock and Cena teamed up at the Survivor Series in a win against The Miz and R-Truth, and touted their anticipated match every chance they got. The Rock is as popular as ever, and he will enter WrestleMania, held in the Miami area, as the hometown hero—and the spectacle will be enormous.

Born:	January 1, 1977
Height:	6'0"
Weight:	230
Real Name:	Robert F. Roode Jr.
High School:	Kenner Collegiate High School (Ontario)
Trained by:	Sean Morley
Identities:	Lee Awesome
Groups:	Fortune (2010-2011)
Career Span:	1998-Present

Roode, Bobby

PPV Record:	42-41, 1 Draw, 1 DCO
Titles Won:	22
Days as World Champion:	66
Age at first World Title Win:	34
Best Opponents:	Kurt Angle, A.J. Styles, James Storm

Bobby Roode of Peterborough, Ontario realized a dream on October 26, 2011 when he beat James Storm to capture the TNA World Heavyweight Championship. A hockey player in his youth, he entered the business in 1998 and worked on the indie scene and in Puerto Rico before joining TNA in 2004. He was associated with Team Canada prior to teaming with Storm beginning in 2008 and the two won the World Tag Team Title four times. During the feud with Immortal, Roode's passion for the business was evident in promos, and it was clear he sought success as a singles grappler. In September of 2011, he triumphed in the Bound for Glory series, but came up short in his October 16 bout with TNA champion Kurt Angle. Two days later, Storm won the title—but his reign was short-lived, thanks to Roode and the latter's use of a beer bottle in what was supposed to be a friendly match. Roode turned heel, upgraded his style, and did just about anything to retain his belt. He closed out 2011 as TNA World titleholder.

Rotundo, Mike

Born:	March 30, 1958
Height:	6'3"
Weight:	240
Real Name:	Lawrence Michael Rotunda
High School:	Newark Valley High School (NY)
College Ach.:	Four-Time letterwinner in wrestling (1977-1979, 1981)
Identities:	Mike Rotunda, Irwin R. Schyster, Michael Wall Street, V.K. Wall Street
Finisher:	Airplane Spin, Stock Market Crash
Groups:	The Varsity Club (1988-1989), The Corporation (1994-1995), New World Order (1996), The Varsity Club (1999)
Tag Teams:	The Young Lions w/ Barry Windham, The U.S. Express w/ Barry Windham, The U.S. Express w/ Dan Spivey, The Varsity Club w/ Steve Williams, Money Inc. w/ Ted DiBiase
Managed by:	Captain Lou Albano, Ted DiBiase
Career Span:	1981-2008

PPV Record:	9-25
WrestleMania Record:	1-2
WWE *Raw* TV Record:	0-1
Titles Won:	18
Best Opponents:	Rick Steiner, Bret Hart, Razor Ramon

An amateur wrestler at Syracuse where he won the Eastern championship as a heavyweight in 1981, Mike Rotundo was lured into pro wrestling by another member of the school's alumni, Dick Beyer, who gained international fame as The Destroyer. After initial success in Florida and becoming known as one of the best young athletes in the business, he headed for the WWF along with tag team partner Barry Windham. Outside the ring, Rotundo married Barry's sister Stephanie. During that first stint in the WWF, Rotundo and Windham won the World Tag Team Title twice, and he'd personally return to the promotion again in the early 1990s to have similar success with Ted DiBiase as his partner, known as Money, Inc. A neck injury a few years later slowed his career, but he'd make appearances in the WWE through 2008, where he works as a road agent. Rotundo is also a successful businessman,, and his two sons, Windham and Taylor, are both pro wrestlers themselves.

Born:	January 19, 1972
Height:	6'1"
Weight:	220
Real Name:	Ronnie Aaron Killings
High School:	Harding High School (NC)
Trained by:	Manny Fernandez
Identities:	Ron Killings, K-Kwik, K-Krush
Finisher:	Hang Time
Groups:	3 Live Kru (2003-2005)
Career Span:	1997-Present

PPV Record:	49-58, 6 NC
WrestleMania Record:	0-1
WWE *Raw* TV Record:	24-29, 2 DDQ, 2 NC
WWE *Smackdown* TV Record:	31-32, 3 NC
Titles Won:	12
Days as World Champion:	119
Age at first World Title Win:	30
Best Opponents:	Chris Jericho, CM Punk, Curt Hennig
Movies:	2

R-Truth

An exciting entertainer from Charlotte, R-Truth became the first African American to win the NWA World Heavyweight Championship when he defeated Ken Shamrock on August 7, 2002. Considering the title had lineage stretching back more than a half century, it was a superb achievement. Two years later, he won the title again in a four-way match. He teamed with pro football player Adam "Pacman" Jones to capture the TNA World Tag Team Title in 2007 and returned to the WWE, where he'd worked earlier in the decade, the following year. He supplemented his wide athletic range with his ability to rap, and his catchy song, "What's Up," inspired lackluster crowds innumerable times. On May 24, 2010, he won the U.S. Title, but lost it a few weeks later on *Raw*. He shocked many by turning heel in April of 2011, but his new attitude was gold, especially when he ranted about the "Little Jimmys" in the audience. He also formed a tag team with The Miz.

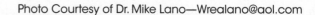

Rude, Rick

Born:	December 7, 1958
Height:	6'4"
Weight:	246
Real Name:	Richard Erwin Rood
Parents:	Richard and Sally Rood
High School:	Robbinsdale High School (MN)
Trained by:	Eddie Sharkey
Identities:	Halloween Phantom
Nicknames:	Smooth Operator
Finisher:	Reverse Neckbreaker (Rude Awakening)
Groups:	Pringle's Dynasty (1985), The Dangerous Alliance (1991-1992), D-Generation X (1997), New World Order (1997-1998)
Tag Team:	Ravishing and Raging w/ Manny Fernandez
Managed:	Triple Threat (1997), D-Generation X (1997), Curt Hennig (1997-1998)
Career Span:	1982-1994
Died:	April 20, 1999, Alpharetta, GA 40 years old

PPV Record:	15-10, 2 Draws
WrestleMania Record:	2-0, 1 Draw
Titles Won:	14
Days as World Champion:	336
Age at first World Title Win:	27
Best Opponents:	Ric Flair, Sting, Ricky Steamboat

"Ravishing" Rick Rude of Minnesota drew immense heat from audiences for his arrogance, and was adept at chastising fans, opponents, and whoever else got in his way. During the late 1980s, he used a gimmick that portrayed him as the ultimate ladies man, often kissing women from the crowd before matches. His colorful personality, chiseled physique, and profound toughness were a grand slam in terms of marketability, making him a top superstar and routine champion. He gained experience and success in many territories, which included Memphis, Dallas, and Tampa, before landing in the WWF in 1987. At the time of his jump to the northeast, he was co-holder of the World Tag Team Title in the Mid-Atlantic region along with

Manny Fernandez. Rude entered a heated feud with Jake Roberts after trying to kiss the latter's wife. In 1989, he pinned the unbeatable Ultimate Warrior, with help from his manager Bobby Heenan, to win the Intercontinental Title, and the following year, chased Warrior's World Title.

Rude went to WCW, where he captured the United States belt and enjoyed a fourteen-month reign as titleholder beginning in November of 1991. He also won the WCW International World Title three times, first taking the gold belt from Ric Flair on September 19, 1993. In March of the following year, he traded the title with Hiroshi Hase, and then lost it to Sting on April 17, 1994. Before more than 53,000 fans in Japan on May 1, 1994, Rude regained the belt, but suffered a serious back injury that ended his active career. A few years later, he made appearances for ECW and then the WWF, where he was one of the original members of DX, along with Shawn Michaels, Triple H, and Chyna. During a taped edition of *Raw* on November 17, 1997, Rude, sporting a beard, made a showing with his cohorts on an attack of Sgt. Slaughter. That same night, a clean-shaven Rude appeared on WCW's *Nitro*, live from Cincinnati, as a member of the NWO—marking one of the most notable promotional jumps of the Monday Night Wars.

Born:	December 12, 1963
Height:	6'0"
Weight:	220
Real Name:	Terry Michael Brunk
Trained by:	The Sheik
Identities:	Sabu the Elephant Boy
Finisher:	Moonsault, Arabian Facebuster
Career Span:	1985-Present

PPV Record:	19-24, 1 Draw, 3 NC
WrestleMania Record:	1-0
WWE *Raw* TV Record:	0-2
Titles Won:	37
Days as World Champion:	Around 670
Age at first World Title Win:	30
Best Opponents:	Terry Funk, Shane Douglas, Rob Van Dam
Halls of Fame:	1

Sabu

Sabu, the "Most Homicidal, Suicidal, Genocidal Man in Wrestling," has been at it since 1986. As the nephew of The Sheik, he's lived up to the family reputation of violence and extreme ring methods, including the use of weaponry. He has proven many times over to be indestructible, by performing spectacular maneuvers and working through injuries that would've sidelined a lesser man; even once applying super glue to an open wound as a way to continue participating in the sport he loves. Sabu has combined the terrifying antics of his uncle with a high-flying athleticism that makes him a sight to behold every time he steps through the ropes and into the ring. His stunts, like moonsaulting through empty tables, are always crowd pleasers. Early in his career, after toiling around the Michigan independents, he made appearances in the Memphis-based USWA and Tri-State Wrestling in Philadelphia before going to Japan for FMW.

Two years later, in 1993, Sabu was a major figure in the upstart Philly organization, ECW, which prided itself on a hardcore style of grappling. It was a perfect fit for the daredevil Sabu, who won the ECW Heavyweight belt from Shane Douglas on October 2, 1993, and then the TV Title the following month. On July 23, 1994, Sabu beat Al Snow in a ladder match for the initial NWA World Independent Title. In addition to winning the ECW World Title in 1997, he won an array of honors in Japan to include the IWGP and UWA World Junior Heavyweight championships. He captured the NWA World Title from Mike Rapada in November of 2000 and the XPW Title in Los Angeles. He's also appeared for the WWE, WCW, and TNA. In 2010, he appeared at TNA's Hardcore Justice show and was defeated by Rob Van Dam. Sabu was also involved in the Extreme, Version 2.0 angle until being fired after losing a ten-man tag match on November 7 of that year.

Born:	March 17, 1979
Height:	6'3"
Weight:	300
Real Name:	Nuufolau Joel Seanoa
High School:	Ocean View High School (CA)
Trained by:	UIWA's West Coast Dojo—Johnny Hemp, Cincinnati Red
Identities:	King Joe
Nickname:	Samoan Suplexing Machine
Finisher:	Island Driver, Dragon Suplex, Muscle Buster
Career Span:	1999-Present

Samoa Joe

PPV Record:	36-27, 1 NC
Titles Won:	15
Days as World Champion:	771
Age at first World Title Win:	24
Best Opponents:	Kurt Angle, CM Punk, Kenta Kobashi

Samoa Joe is a highly regarded superstar of Samoan descent. Originally from Orange County, California, Joe has the ability to become world champion in either one of the big two promotions in the near future. A powerful grappler, he mixes strength with ingenuity, and is well-versed in Judo, as well as other martial arts. These aspects make him a dangerous grappler with submission knowledge, and if he's not trouncing an opponent with violent blows, he's got them twisted up and forcing them to tap out. As a child, he performed a Polynesian dance at the opening ceremonies of the 1984 Olympic Games in Los Angeles, and later became a California State Junior Judo Champion. He trained to become a wrestler and one of the major feuds was against John Cena in UPW in 2000. With experience in Japan under his belt, Joe went to the Ring of Honor promotion, and became World Champion on March 22, 2003, with a victory over Xavier.

For the next twenty-one months, Joe reigned as ROH titleholder, successfully defending his belt against some of the best independent grapplers in the world, including Christopher Daniels, CM Punk, and A.J. Styles, though was dethroned by Austin Aries on December 26, 2004. Joe had a memorable bout against Japanese legend Kenta Kobashi when the latter toured the U.S. in 2005. That same year, he made his debut for TNA, winning the Super X Cup tournament and then the first of four X Division titles. In 2006, he was named "Mr. TNA," and continued to battle up the card. On April 13, 2008, Joe beat Kurt Angle for the TNA World Title in a match that he threatened to retire if defeated. Joe survived a lengthy feud with Booker T and the challenge of Angle and Christian and became the first champion to successfully retain in a King of the Mountain bout. He ran into the "Icon," Sting on October 12, 2008 at Bound for Glory and dropped the championship. Since that time, Joe has been unable to recapture the World Title, but has fulfilled a number of different roles in the organization through 2011.

Born:	June 16, 1963
Height:	6'4"
Weight:	245
Real Name:	James Fullington
Family:	Husband of Peaches
High School:	Marple Newtown High School (PA)
Trained by:	Tri-State Wrestling Academy (Larry Winters)
Identities:	Mr. Sandman, Hak
Nickname:	Hardcore Icon
Finisher:	DDT
Career Span:	1989-Present

Sandman, The

PPV Record:	17-31, 2 NC
WrestleMania Record:	1-0
WWE *Raw* TV Record:	2-7
Titles Won:	16
Days as World Champion:	545
Age at first World Title Win:	31
Best Opponents:	Cactus Jack, Raven, Shane Douglas
Halls of Fame:	1

The longtime backbone of Extreme Championship Wrestling, The Sandman is known for carrying a Singapore cane and smoking a cigarette while guzzling beer on the way to the ring. It is definitely a unique approach, one that differs greatly from the mat technicians of yesteryear. Sandman represents a generation of extreme competitors, thus dubbed the "Hardcore Icon," a wrestler who will put his body on the line for the sport. During his years in ECW, he had memorable feuds with Shane Douglas, Sabu, and Raven, but his feud with Tommy Dreamer was the most brutal. A football player in high school, Sandman won the first of five heavyweight championships on November 16, 1992 when he beat Don Muraco in Philadelphia. He won his fifth title on January 7, 2001, beating Steve Corino and Justin Credible. Since that time, he's wrestled for both the WWE and TNA, and is still making headlines on the independent scene.

Born:	May 10, 1953
Height:	6'1"
Weight:	230
Real Name:	Merced Solis
Pro Sports:	National Football League— Kansas City Chiefs (1975) Canadian Football League— British Columbia Lions (1976)
Identities:	Richard Blood, El Madator
Nickname:	Chico
Finisher:	Flying-forearm smash, Figure-four leglock
Career Span:	1977-2010

Santana, Tito

PPV Record:	7-17, 1 DCO
WrestleMania Record:	1-7
Titles Won:	22
Best Opponents:	Greg Valentine, Randy Savage, Don Muraco
Halls of Fame:	2

The multi-sport high school athlete Tito Santana became a star tight end at West Texas State University, playing alongside quarterback Tully Blanchard. Having admired the Funks, he became a wrestler after a stint as a pro football player, and trained under Hiro Matsuda in Tampa. He made the rounds of several territories, and then went to the northeast to work for the WWF, adopting the name "Tito Santana" in the process. On October 22, 1979 in New York, he teamed with powerful Ivan Putski to dethrone the Valiants for the WWF World Tag Team Title, but were later beaten by the Wild Samoans, losing the belts. A popular star, Santana won the Intercontinental Title from Don Muraco in Boston on February 11, 1984, becoming the youngest man to hold the championship. He traded the belt with Greg Valentine, and then was pinned by Randy Savage for the title on February 8, 1986 after the latter used a foreign object.

Santana's unique balance of technical and high-flying skills sustained his status as one of the best wrestlers in the promotion. He teamed with Rick Martel to win the WWF World Tag Team Title from the Hart Foundation on October 27, 1987, and established another internal record by becoming the first wrestler to win both the Intercontinental and tag team titles on two separate occasions. Strike Force lost the belts to Demolition at WrestleMania IV, and Santana feuded with his former partner. On October 14, 1989, Santana won the annual King of the Ring Tournament with a finals victory over Martel. In the vacant Intercontinental Title tournament, Santana made it to the finals in April of 1990, only to be beaten by Mr. Perfect. Santana was a longtime member of the WWF Spanish-language commentary team and wrestled occasionally, even appearing for one night on WCW *Nitro* in January of 2000. He still makes independent appearances.

Born:	August 4, 1966
Height:	5'10"
Weight:	260
Identities:	Power Warrior
Tag Team:	The Hell Raisers w/ Hawk
Career Span:	1986-Present

PPV Record:	1-4
Titles Won:	25
Days as World Champion:	894
Age at first World Title Win:	31
Best Opponents:	Kenta Kobashi, Toshiaki Kawada, S. Hashimoto
MMA Record:	2-0

Sasaki, Kensuke

Powerhouse Kensuke Sasaki is one of the most decorated wrestlers in Japanese wrestling history. Raised in Fukuoka, he was a student of Riki Choshu, and was also educated in Stu Hart's famed Dungeon in Calgary. He found success with partners Hiroshi Hase and Hawk, winning the IWGP Tag Team Title, and capturing the gold seven times altogether. Sasaki, as a singles wrestler, was even more impressive. He won the IWGP Title five times, the AJPW Unified Triple Crown, and the GHC Heavyweight belt. While in WCW in 1995, he beat Sting for the United States Heavyweight Championship. His wife, Akira Hokuto, was also a professional wrestler.

Severn, Dan

Born:	June 9, 1958
Height:	6'2"
Weight:	250
Real Name:	Daniel DeWayne Severn
Parents:	Marvin and Barbara Severn
High School:	McCloy High School (MI)
College:	Arizona State University
Amateur Titles:	Thirteen-Time National AAU Champion, Junior World Champion (1977), Greco-Roman Wrestling Champion
Trained by:	Al Snow
Finisher:	Armbar Submission
Career Span:	1992-2010

PPV Record:	0-2
Titles Won:	9
Days as World Champion:	1,559
Age at first World Title Win:	36
Best Opponents:	Ken Shamrock, Owen Hart, The Rock
Halls of Fame:	2
MMA Record:	100-18-7

A world class wrestler and MMA fighter, Dan "The Beast" Severn won the National Wrestling Alliance World Heavyweight Title on two separate occasions, helping the fledging organization regain credibility during its lowest point in history. Severn began wrestling in his youth and won a score of amateur titles. Over a two-year period from 1992-1994, he went into pro wrestling and mixed martial arts. On February 24, 1995, in Erlanger, Kentucky, Severn beat Chris Candido by submission for the NWA World Title on a Smoky Mountain Wrestling program. He went on to win the UFC V tournament on April 7. He was NWA titleholder for 1,479 days, the third longest reign in history, and finally lost the belt to Naoya Ogawa on March 14, 1999. Severn won his second NWA Title from Shinya Hashimoto on March 9, 2002. On May 29, the NWA stripped him of the belt because he was unable to defend at the initial NWA-TNA pay-per-view in June of 2002. He remains a trainer and often makes appearances for the Price of Glory promotion in Michigan.

Born:	February 11, 1964
Height:	6'1"
Weight:	230
Real Name:	Kenneth Wayne Kilpatrick
Parents:	Richard and Diane Kilpatrick
High School:	Lassen High School (CA)
Trained by:	Buzz Sawyer, Nelson Royal
Identities:	Wayne Shamrock, Vince Torelli
Nickname:	World's Most Dangerous Man
Career Span:	1990-2004

Shamrock, Ken

PPV Record:	17-17, 2 NC
WrestleMania Record:	0-2
WWE *Raw* TV Record:	8-9, 5 NC
WWE *Smackdown* TV Record:	2-2, 1 NC
Titles Won:	4
Days as World Champion:	49
Age at first World Title Win:	38
Best Opponents:	Shawn Michaels, The Rock, Steve Blackman
Halls of Fame:	1
MMA Record:	28-15-2

With the heart of a champion, Ken Shamrock helped popularize mixed martial arts fighting in the United States and around the world, and was at the core of the UFC when it was lifting off the ground in 1993. His spectacular battles against Royce Gracie and Dan Severn drew an abundance of interest in MMA, and with his UFC 6 victory over the latter, he earned the title of "Superfight Champion." In 1997, he joined the WWF and won the Intercontinental Title. He also was triumphant in the 1998 King of the Ring tournament, and teamed with Corporation ally Big Bossman to capture the WWF World Tag Team Title. In June 2002, he won a battle royal final to become the NWA World Heavyweight king at TNA's initial pay-per-view. Shamrock was inducted into the UFC Hall of Fame in 2003 and had his last MMA fight in 2010.

Born:	January 28, 1978
Height:	6'6"
Weight:	270
Real Name:	Stephen Farrelly
Trained by:	Larry Sharpe, Jim Molineaux
Identities:	Sheamus O'Shaunessy
Finisher:	Brogue Kick
Career Span:	2002-Present

Sheamus

PPV Record:	9-14
WrestleMania Record:	0-1
WWE *Raw* TV Record:	43-24, 1 DDQ, 6 NC
WWE *Smackdown* TV Record:	21-13, 1 DCO, 2 NC
Titles Won:	6
Days as World Champion:	161
Age at first World Title Win:	31
Best Opponents:	Triple H, John Cena, Randy Orton
Movies:	3

Sheamus might be the first ever Irish-born WWE heavyweight champion, but he's not the first ever Irish claimant to the World Heavyweight Title in the United States. Seventy-four years earlier, Danno O'Mahoney became the undisputed champion and earned that special distinction. O'Mahoney and his famed "Irish Whip" finisher took the industry by storm, much like Sheamus in recent years. By watching him wrestle, it is not shocking that he's already had much success, which includes two reigns as WWE champion and winning the King of the Ring tournament. A former bodyguard for musician Bono, Sheamus attended Larry Sharpe's famed Monster Factory Wrestling School and ventured through a number of independent promotions before landing in the WWE developmental program in Florida. His athletic background, which included rugby, gave him the dexterity and discipline to hurdle the initial obstacles to be a leading wrestler, and he was on the fast track to glory.

Initially turning up on the ECW brand and then graduating to *Raw*, Sheamus made a big impact at the 2009 Survivor Series, then winning a battle royal the next evening, earning him a future title shot. Sheamus made the most of it on December 13, 2009, when he beat John Cena for the WWE Title in a tables match. The "Celtic Warrior" had arrived in a big way. In the Elimination Chamber match at the February pay-per-view, he didn't leave the building with his title intact, but soon entered a feud with Triple H. On June 20, 1910, he beat Cena again for the WWE belt, only to lose it to Randy Orton on September 19. A few months later, on November 29, 2010, he won the King of the Ring tournament. On March 14, 2011, he won the U.S. Title from Daniel Bryan, and was champ until May 1, 2011, when he lost it to Kofi Kingston in a tables match. Later that year, he became a fan favorite, and feuded with Mark Henry and Christian. His distinct look uniquely separates himself from his peers, and his athletic ability cannot be questioned.

Born:	May 15, 1958
Height:	6'2"
Weight:	260
Real Name:	Ronald Simmons
High School:	Warner Robins High School (GA)
College Ach.:	Two-Time All-American Football Player (1978-1979)
NFL Draft:	Cleveland Browns (1981) (6th Round)
Pro Sports:	Canadian Football League— Ottawa Rough Riders (1980-1983) United States Football League—Tampa Bay Bandits (1983-1985)
Nickname:	All-American
Finisher:	Spinebuster
Groups:	The Ministry of Darkness (1999), The Acolyte Protection Agency (2000)
Career Span:	1986-2010

Simmons, Ron

PPV Record:	27-37, 1 DCO, 1 DDQ, 2 NC
WrestleMania Record:	1-5
WWE *Raw* TV Record:	36-32, 10 NC
WWE *Smackdown* TV Record:	29-26, 2 NC
Titles Won:	9
Days as World Champion:	150
Age at first World Title Win:	34
Best Opponents:	Vader, Butch Reed, Cactus Jack
Halls of Fame:	3

While in college at Florida State University, Ron Simmons of Perry, Georgia was a two-time All American nose guard. His number, 50, was retired by the school, and in 1986, he was inducted into the Seminole Hall of Fame. After playing some pro football, he chose to give wrestling a chance, and trained under Hiro Matsuda before joining the Florida circuit in October of 1986. He toured a handful of regions before settling into WCW in late 1989. As part of a masked tag team known as Doom, Simmons and Butch Reed were bent on taking care of the Steiners for Robin Green, also known as Woman. Doom were unmasked at Clash of the Champions X by the Steiners, but rebounded after taking Teddy Long as their manager, and winning the WCW World Tag Team Title. They reigned until February 24, 1991, when they were defeated by the Freebirds. Simmons then turned babyface and feuded with Reed and Long, gaining a large following of fans.

On August 2, 1992 in Baltimore, he beat Big Van Vader to win the WCW World Heavyweight Title, and placed his name among the other great African American champions, including Seelie Samara, Jack Claybourne, Bobo Brazil, and Bearcat Wright. Simmons nearly survived the year with his title intact, but lost a rematch to Vader on December 30, 1992, also in Baltimore. During a tour of Europe, he suffered a broken leg and eventually left WCW. He briefly worked for ECW, but then signed with the World Wrestling Federation and changed his name to Faarooq. He entered the gang wars of 1997 and 1998, joining the Nation of Domination. In 1999, Faarooq formed a successful card-playing tag team with Justin Bradshaw known as the "Acolytes," and were a team for hire, prepared to go wherever the money took them. Simmons made the catchphrase "Damn" a hit, and remained in the WWE until 2009.

Photo Courtesy of Dr. Mike Lano—Wrealano@aol.com

Born:	November 27, 1962
Height:	5'11"
Weight:	260
Real Name:	David Smith
Parents:	Sid and Joyce Smith
Trained by:	Ted Betley
Identities:	Young David
Finisher:	Running Powerslam
Career Span:	1978-2002
Died:	May 18, 2002, Invermere, British Columbia 39 years old

PPV Record:	31-28, 3 Draws, 1 DCO
WrestleMania Record:	4-2, 1 DCO
WWE *Raw* TV Record:	1-5, 2 NC
WWE *Smackdown* TV Record:	4-6, 3 NC
Titles Won:	16
Best Opponents:	Bret Hart, Shawn Michaels, Owen Hart
Halls of Fame:	1

Smith, Davey Boy

The popular "British Bulldog" was from Leeds, England and made his debut in the Calgary promotion as an eighteen-year-old in May of 1981. Already owning several years of pro experience and time under the watchful eye of his future father-in-law Stu Hart in the famed "Dungeon," Smith teamed with Hart Brothers Bruce and Bret and his cousin Dynamite Kid. He also won the World Mid-Heavyweight championship in the summer of 1982 and the North American Title twice. Continuing his development in Japan, Smith competed in a junior heavyweight tournament there in 1983 and formed an impressive tag team with Dynamite Kid. Smith and Kid debuted in the WWF in 1984, and two years later, they won the World Tag Team Title. As a singles performer, he beat Bret Hart on August 29, 1992 for the Intercontinental Title before 80,355 fans in London. Extremely built, Smith had a 56" chest and 21" bicep, and trained his son Harry for the ring.

Snow, Al

Born:	July 18, 1963
Height:	6'1"
Weight:	230
Real Name:	Allen Ray Sarven
High School:	Lima Senior High School (OH)
Trained by:	Jim Lancaster
Identities:	Steve Moore, Avatar, Shinobi, Leif Cassidy
Nickname:	Simply Sensational
Finisher:	Snow Plow
Groups:	The JOB Squad (1998-1999)
Tag Teams:	The Fabulous Kangaroos w/ Denny Kass, The Motor City Hitmen w/ Mickey Doyle, The Dynamic Duo w/ Unibomb
Career Span:	1982-Present

PPV Record:	9-19
WrestleMania Record:	0-2
WWE *Raw* TV Record:	16-39, 5 NC
WWE *Smackdown* TV Record:	17-27, 2 NC
Titles Won:	41
Best Opponents:	Sabu, Shane Douglas, Chris Benoit

For most of the first decade of Al Snow's wrestling career, he was an underrated talent and ignored by the major promotions. He made some headlines while in SMW around 1994 and had several short stints in the WWF, using different gimmicks, but none were exceptionally notable. In the late 1990s, he began to see his popularity increase, and rightfully so, as part of the JOB Squad. In ECW, the Lima, Ohio product carried a styrofoam mannequin's head as part of his oddball character, which was a home run with audiences. More and more people began learning about Snow and paying closer attention to his talents as a wrestler. In 2001, he gained national attention after appearing as the lead trainer for the WWE's Tough Enough series on MTV, remaining in that role for three seasons. The martial artist was a fixture in the WWE through 2007, winning several titles, and appeared on the independent scene before landing a gig as an agent for TNA in 2010.

Sopp, Monty

Born:	November 1, 1963
Height:	6'3"
Weight:	260
Real Name:	Monty Kip Sopp
High School:	Oviedo High School (FL)
College:	Sam Houston State University
Trained by:	Harris Brothers
Identities:	Kip Winchester, Rockabilly, The Outlaw, Kip James
Nicknames:	Bad Ass, The One
Career Span:	1992-Present

PPV Record:	43-50
WrestleMania Record:	1-3
WWE *Raw* TV Record:	39-35, 9 NC
WWE *Smackdown* TV Record:	40-42, 1 DDQ, 1 NC
Titles Won:	19
Best Opponents:	Shawn Michaels, Steve Austin, The Rock

Always an entertaining performer, Monty Sopp of Central Florida was a key figure in the WWF's late 1990s resurgence, and was part of both D-Generation X and the New Age Outlaws tag team. Billy Gunn, as he was known, and the Road Dogg, always delivered cutting-edge promos, and the Outlaws' disorderly behavior carried them to five World Tag Team Championships. Sopp also teamed with Bart Gunn and Chuck Palumbo to capture the WWF belts, making him a ten-time titleholder. In 1999, he won the King of the Ring tournament, and beat Eddie Guerrero for the Intercontinental strap the following year. Between 2005 and 2009, he appeared for TNA, and currently wrestles on the independent circuit. Considering all of his success, it's hard to believe that Sopp nearly took a different path, and devoted his life to the rodeo.

Born:	February 28, 1953
Height:	6'0"
Weight:	230
Real Name:	Richard Henry Blood Jr.
Family:	Brother of Vic Steamboat, father of Richie Steamboat
High School:	Boca Ciega High School (FL)
Trained by:	Verne Gagne, The Iron Sheik
Identities:	Sammy Steamboat Jr., Dick Blood, The Dragon
Nicknames:	The Dragon, Steamer
Finisher:	Flying Crossbody
Tag Teams:	The Great Warriors w/ Jay Youngblood, The South Pacific Connection w/ Jimmy Snuka
Career Span:	1976-2009

Steamboat, Ricky

PPV Record:	12-15, 1 Draw, 1 NC
WrestleMania Record:	3-2
WWE *Raw* TV Record:	1-0
Titles Won:	26
Days as World Champion:	76
Age at first World Title Win:	35
Best Opponents:	Randy Savage, Ric Flair, Rick Rude
Halls of Fame:	3

High-flying and technically proficient, Ricky "the Dragon" Steamboat wrestled in one of WrestleMania's greatest matches in 1987 against Randy Savage. It is still commonly referenced as a classic; full of excitement, drama, and athleticism, which are the aspects that combine to forge a true mat memory. That was a prime example of what Steamboat brought to wrestling, and his matches were constantly heralded for his ability to create powerful exhibitions against even lackluster opponents. A talented sportsman in high school, he attended the grueling wrestling school of Verne Gagne in Minnesota, and made his pro debut in 1976. With a purported relation to former wrestler Sam Steamboat, Ricky's career progressed naturally, and he learned the tough lessons of the business from the ground up, and by the late 1970s, he was a hot commodity in the Mid-Atlantic region for the Crocketts. Steamboat captured the U.S. and Television titles, plus formed a World championship tandem with Jay Youngblood, warring regularly with the Brisco Brothers in 1983.

Owning the distinction of appearing the initial Starrcade and first WrestleMania, Steamboat wrestled in some of the most gripping matches of the 1980s against Ric Flair, defeating the latter for the NWA World Heavyweight Title on February 20, 1989. He was a fighting champion for his seventy-six days as king, and

Flair was the only one who could best him, on May 7, 1989. Over the next several years, he appeared for the WWF and WCW, and won a number of honors while in the latter organization between 1991-1994; among them being the WCW World Tag Team Title with Dustin Rhodes and Shane Douglas. A devastating back injury forced him off the mat, and he made sporadic appearances until joining the WWE as a road agent in 2005. Steamboat returned to the ring to battle Chris Jericho in a special handicap elimination match at WrestleMania on April 5, 2009. Despite a heroic effort, he was defeated. He was also named to the WWE Hall of Fame. Steamboat's energetic ring style will influence professional wrestlers forever.

Photo Courtesy of Pete Lederberg—plmathfoto@hotmail.com

Born:	March 9, 1961
Height:	5'11"
Weight:	245
Real Name:	Robert Rechsteiner
Family:	Older brother of Scott Steiner
High School:	Bay City Western High School (MI)
College:	University of Michigan
College Ach.:	Wrestling Letterman (1981, 1983-1984)
Trained by:	Steve Fraser, George Steele, Eddie Sharkey
Groups:	Hyatt and Hot Stuff Incorporated (1986-1987), The Varsity Club (1988-1989, 1999), The First Family (1989), Dudes with Attitudes (1990), The Magnificent Seven (2000-2001)
Career Span:	1984-2008

PPV Record:	44-25, 2 Draws, 1 NC
WrestleMania Record:	1-0
Titles Won:	27
Best Opponents:	Scott Steiner, Mike Rotundo, Booker T
Halls of Fame:	1

Steiner, Rick

The "Dogfaced Gremlin," Rick Steiner was a powerful wrestling superstar and his version of the clothesline, known as the Steinerline, was one of the most hard-hitting moves in the business. Always wearing his amateur-style head and ear protector during matches, Rick began wrestling with his brother Scott as a kid, and gained formal training in high school and college at the University of Michigan. He initially made a name for himself in the UWF and then joined WCW, where he was part of the Varsity Club with Kevin

Sullivan and Mike Rotundo. As a singles competitor, he held the World TV Title, but things really picked up once he began teaming with his brother Scott. The Steiners won seven WCW and two WWF World Tag Team Championships, and added two IWGP Titles to their record while in Japan. They were a perfect mesh of athletes, and their versatile offense was far too much for most opponents.

Few brother duos in history experienced anywhere near their success, but the Steiners ultimately broke up in February of 1998. Remaining popular with fans, Rick teamed with Buff Bagwell to win the WCW World Tag Team Title, but after Bagwell turned on him, he picked Kenny Kaos to be his new partner. In 1999, he beat Booker T and Chris Benoit for two separate stints as WCW World TV Champion and captured the United States crown from Shane Douglas in February of 2001 before losing it to Booker at the final WCW pay-per-view in March. Rick made numerous TNA appearances, including a reunion of the Steiners in a heated war with Team 3D. Away from the squared circle, he was elected to the Cherokee County, Georgia School Board, and today serves as the chairman after being reelected in 2010. In addition to being an active member of the community, Rick sells real estate.

Photo Courtesy of Pete Lederberg—plmathfoto@hotmail.com

Born:	July 29, 1962
Height:	6'1"
Weight:	255
Real Name:	Scott Carl Rechsteiner
College Ach.:	All-American Wrestler (1986), Wrestling Letterman (1982-1983, 1985-1986)
Trained by:	Don Kent, Dick the Bruiser, Jerry Graham Jr.
Nicknames:	White Thunder, Big Poppa Pump, Big Bad Booty Daddy, Genetic Freak
Finisher:	Steiner Recliner
Groups:	Dudes with Attitudes (1990), New World Order (1998-1999, 2000), The New Blood (2000), The Magnificent Seven (2000-2001), Main Event Mafia (2008)
Career Span:	1986-Present

Steiner, Scott

College Record:	125-51-2
PPV Record:	56-47, 1 Draw, 2 NC
WrestleMania Record:	1-0
WWE *Raw* TV Record:	18-16, 1 NC
Titles Won:	30

Days as World Champion:	Around 584
Age at first World Title Win:	24
Best Opponents:	Booker T, Samoa Joe, Bill Goldberg
Halls of Fame:	1

After years of being part of a legendary brother tag team, Scott Steiner broke free and established himself as one of the most colorful and unpredictable grapplers in the world. His promos are a league apart from his peers, seemingly intermixing kayfabe-breaking commentary with the regular hullabaloo. Upon first glance, you'd suspect he was a nothing more than a bodybuilder because of his mammoth size, but Scott has shown his amazing athleticism throughout his career, particularly early on when the Steiners were dominating competition on both the North American and Asian continents. His pure grappling knowledge was fostered at Western High School in Bay City, Michigan and later at the University of Michigan, where his older brother Rick also wrestled. After becoming an All-American in 1986, Scott turned pro, working for Dick the Bruiser's WWA based out of Indiana. On August 14, 1986, he beat the Great Wojo and captured the promotion's World Heavyweight Title. Scott was only twenty-four years of age.

Three years later in May of 1989, Scott joined his brother in WCW, and the two formed a tag team that naturally clicked in the ring. They quickly garnered a following, and upended The Fabulous Freebirds for the NWA World Tag Team Title on November 1, 1989. They feuded with the Andersons, Nasty Boys, and Doom over the course the next year, losing the belts to the latter in May of 1990, but winning the U.S. Title from the Midnight Express in August. In 1991, they added to their list of accomplishments by regaining the World Tag Team Title, then beat Hiroshi Hase and Kensuke Sasaki for the IWGP crown. At that point, they held three championships and six belts, simultaneously. A serious bicep injury suffered during the summer of 1991 put Scott on the shelf, but The Steiners returned to regain the WCW and IWGP Titles. The duo also toured the WWF and added two more World Title reigns there, while still making routine trips to Japan. They appeared briefly in ECW before returning to WCW in 1996.

The Steiners feuded with the Road Warriors, Harlem Heat, and The Outsiders, remaining fan favorites through late 1997. In January of 1998, Scott turned on Rick at SuperBrawl and joined the NWO. He proceeded to dye his hair blond, concentrate more and more on his physique, and adopted a more punishing ring style. Steiner's volatile interview segments were both vicious and comical, and over the next year and a half, he won the TV and U.S. belts. On November 26, 2000, he won his first major World championship when he beat Booker T for the WCW Title.

After WCW was sold, Steiner appeared in the WWE and feuded with Triple H. Off and on since 2006, he's worked for TNA, and appeared in various capacities—more recently as a fan favorite in January of 2011, then as a member of Immortal. Scott's innovative Frankensteiner, imaginative suplexes, and supreme power have set him apart from his peers during a career lasting a quarter of a century. No one quite knows what he will say or do next.

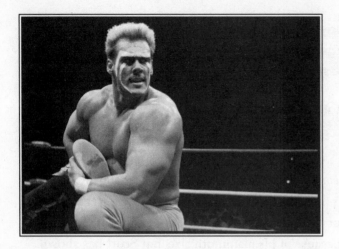

Sting

Born:	March 20, 1959
Height:	6'2"
Weight:	260
Real Name:	Steven L. Borden
High School:	William S. Hart High School (CA)
College:	College of the Canyons
Identities:	Blade Runner Flash
Finisher:	Stinger Splash leading into the Scorpion Deathlock, Scorpion Deathdrop
Groups:	Power Team USA (1985), Hyatt and Hot Stuff, Inc. (1986-1987), The Four Horsemen (1990), Dudes with Attitudes (1990), New World Order (Wolfpack) (1998), The Millionaires Club (2000)
Tag Team:	The Blade Runners w/ Rock
Career Span:	1985-Present

PPV Record:	87-49, 2 Draws, 4 NC
Titles Won:	25
Days as World Champion:	1,002
Age at first World Title Win:	31
Best Opponents:	Ric Flair, Kurt Angle, Rick Rude

Eternally charismatic, the wrestler known as Sting has enthralled audiences for decades. He was long the backbone of World Championship Wrestling and today, performs a similar function in TNA. In 2011, Sting reinvented himself yet again, portraying an off-balance animated tweener that is drastically different from his dark, brooding character seen in years past. His popularity has remained constant throughout the 1990s and 2000s, and twice in 2011, he enjoyed reigns as TNA Heavyweight Champion— making him a fifteen-time World Titleholder. Through a career full of great success, hard-fought matches, and classic feuds, Sting is the one major wrestler who has never jumped to the WWE, and that decision has never inhibited his Hall of Fame career, which is solidified in the minds of his legion of "Little Stingers." His path to superstardom began in 1985 when he joined Rick Bassman's Power Team USA, and was trained by Bill Anderson and Red Bastien along with Jim Hellwig, the future Ultimate Warrior.

Sting gained experience in the Mid-South and UWF territories, joining Eddie Gilbert's Hyatt and Hot Stuff, Inc.; a group of heels. With the more experienced Gilbert, Sting captured the UWF Tag Team Title on two occasions and feuded with the popular Fantastics. He also partnered with Rick Steiner to win the belts, only to eventually turn fan favorite and feud with Gilbert and Steiner. His transition to a widely acknowledged hero was furthered by his actions on January 26, 1988, when he called out to NWA champion Ric Flair during a Four Horsemen party. When Flair refused to respond and James J. Dillon tossed champagne in his face, Sting gave the latter a splash in the corner. In that instant, he became a huge crowd favorite and was an immediate contender for Flair's NWA World Title. That led to the match that made him a star at Clash of the Champions in March of 1988. That night, he held Flair to draw after more than forty minutes, and nearly saw him win the belt.

Over the next two years, he continued to rise up the ladder, winning the TV Title and the Iron Man competition at Starrcade 1989—pinning Flair in the finals. As his destiny to become NWA champion was about to be realized, Sting suffered a ruptured left patella and was out of action for five months. The inevitable was only delayed, and on July 7, 1990 at the Great American Bash, Sting pinned Flair and won the World Title. Flair would regain the championship the following January at a house show in New Jersey. In February of 1992, Sting won his first WCW World Title from Lex Luger, and had an ongoing feud with Big Van Vader, which saw the title change hands several times. Hulk Hogan's arrival in WCW in 1994 changed the dynamics of the organization, and Sting's place in the pecking order shifted. Although he was still supremely popular, he was somewhat overshadowed by Hogan. The NWO came to prominence in 1996, and, at one point, it appeared that Sting had defected to the rogue operation.

But he hadn't. Instead, there was an imposter Sting working on behalf of the NWO, but the angle saw Sting declare himself a "free agent," and distancing himself from his old character. He reinvented himself to be a dark and ominous figure, often carrying a baseball bat and staring down at the ring from the rafters. The shift in attitude and appearance didn't mark his full-fledged turn to heel, but Sting's motives were sometimes unclear. Prior to Starrcade '97, he missed fourteen straight pay-per-views, but returned at that show for a much-hyped match against Hogan for the WCW Title, and using his patented Scorpion Deathlock, he won the belt. Sting feuded with the members of the NWO, and then joined an offshoot of the group known as the Wolfpack in 1998. After defeating Flair in July of 1999, he became WCW President, and then turned heel for the first time two months later. Fortunately for the fans, it didn't stick. In April of 2000, Sting was lumped into the "Millionaire's Club" because of his veteran status, then participated in a violent feud with Vampiro.

Following the sale of WCW in 2001, there were scores of rumors that he was joining the WWF, but it never materialized. He toured Europe and Australia with the WWA in 2002 and 2003, holding the world title of the promotion, and then joining TNA in June of 2003 on a temporary basis. When he reappeared in 2006, it was more permanent. Sting won the NWA Title before the year was out, and added four TNA World Championships in the years that followed, defeating the likes of Jeff Jarrett, Kurt Angle, and Jeff Hardy. In 2011, he underwent a drastic metamorphosis into a Joker-esqe personality, complete with cackling and a heavy dose of unpredictability. The change added a unique edge to TNA that was unexpected from the longtime star. The gimmick displayed his versatility as a performer, and his matches were as entertaining as ever. But it ran its course, and Sting settled on a role, sans makeup, as the commissioner of all on-camera programming for *Impact*.

Born:	June 1, 1977
Height:	6'0"
Weight:	240
Real Name:	James Allen Cox
High School:	Franklin High School (TN)
Trained by:	Shane Morton
Career Span:	1997-Present

PPV Record:	86-70, 2 NC
Titles Won:	16
Days as World Champion:	8
Age at first World Title Win:	34
Best Opponents:	Kurt Angle, Robert Roode, Sting
Movies:	1

Storm, James

An engaging personality in the business, "Cowboy" James Storm of Williamson County, Tennessee, was an amateur wrestler and transitioned to the local professional affiliates before getting a job with WCW in 2000. Two years later, he entered TNA and formed a long-running partnership with Chris Harris. As "America's Most Wanted," the duo dominated competition and won the NWA World Tag Team Title six times. In 2006, Storm briefly went out on his own before teaming with Robert Roode as "Beer Money," and, again, was very successful. The pair won the TNA belts four times, and in 2010, they joined Fortune. On October 18, 2011, two days after Roode came up short against TNA champion Kurt Angle, Storm pinned the titleholder and won his first world singles title. In what was supposed to be a match between friends, Roode blasted Storm with a beer bottle on October 26 to capture the belt, effectively destroying their bond.

Storm, Lance

Born:	April 3, 1969
Height:	6'0"
Weight:	228
Real Name:	Lance Evers
College:	Wilfrid Laurier University
Finisher:	Canadian Maple Leaf
Groups:	Triple Threat (1997-1998), Team Canada (2000-2001), The Alliance (2001), The Canadians (2002), The Un-Americans (2002)
Tag Teams:	Sudden Impact w/ Chris Jericho, The Thrillseekers w/ Chris Jericho, The Impact Players w/ Justin Credible
Career Span:	1990-2006
Website:	www.stormwrestling.com

PPV Record:	19-22
WWE *Raw* TV Record:	27-39, 4 NC
WWE *Smackdown* TV Record:	10-17
Titles Won:	27
Best Opponents:	Booker T, Rob Van Dam, Jerry Lynn

Lance Storm was a smooth wrestler who let his outstanding ability speak for itself in the ring. After ending a pursuit to play volleyball in college, he went to Calgary to train under the Hart Brothers, and made his pro debut on October 2, 1990 against his future tag team partner, Chris Jericho. Astutely technical, Storm developed his skills in Asia and Europe, and then became better known to American fans while in SMW and ECW in the 1990s. He went to WCW in 2000 and was given a push as part of Team Canada, winning the U.S. championship three times. Further success in the WWE followed, as Storm captured the World Tag Team Title on four occasions and the Intercontinental belt once before going into semi-retirement in 2004 because of injuries. He was a trainer at WWE's Ohio Valley until opening his own wrestling school. He offers insightful commentary on his official website.

Born:	December 18, 1975
Height:	5'4"
Weight:	120
Real Name:	Patricia Anne Stratigias
Trained by:	Ron Hutchison, Fit Finlay
College:	York University
Finisher:	Bulldog Headlock
Career Span:	2000-2011
Website:	www.trishstratus.com

PPV Record:	23-16
WrestleMania Record:	3-2
WWE *Raw* TV Record:	66-56, 8 NC
WWE *Smackdown* TV Record:	8-8, 2 NC
Titles Won:	8
Days as World Champion:	828
Age at first World Title Win:	25
Best Opponents:	Jazz, Victoria, Lita

Stratus, Trish

A native of the Toronto area, Stratus is a seven-time WWE Women's World Champion and is much more than just a blonde bombshell. She's an athletic wonder, a yoga enthusiast, and exceptionally charitable, devoting her time and energy to numerous causes. The oldest of three sisters, she broke into the business after working as a fitness model, featured initially in *MuscleMag International*, and trained at Ron Hutchinson's Toronto gym. Upon signing a WWF contract in November of 1999, and furthering her training, she became the psuedo-manager behind Test and Albert. Stratus demonstrated her dedication for the sport by working long hours, learning the ways of the ring, and yearning to improve . . . and improve she did. Within a short time, she was one of the most talented divas on the promotion's roster, and her popularity skyrocketed. Fans could see that Stratus had the attitude and drive to be successful, not only as a wrestler in the ring, but within the madcap and drama-filled wrestling soap opera.

Stratus had on-screen romances with Chris Jericho, Carlito, and Jeff Hardy. However, her ring wars with Jazz, Lita, Victoria, and others were much more memorable. At the 2001 Survivor Series, she won a six-way match to capture her first WWF Women's Title. Many grueling battles for the belt occurred in the years that followed, and in 2002, she was honored as WWE's Babe of the Year. She was also recognized as the Diva of the Decade. Trish retired from the ring in 2006, and made sporadic appearances on *Raw* or *Smackdown*, particularly when the WWE visited Toronto. In 2011, she became a trainer for the revived *Tough Enough* series and returned to the ring at WrestleMania XXVII in a six-man tag team match, with her team being victorious. Stratus has spent time as an actress, performing in the 2011 film *Bail Enforcers*, and running a yoga studio. In just a little more than a decade on the mat, she's placed her name among the greatest women wrestlers in history, and secured her future place in the hall of fame.

Born:	June 2, 1978
Height:	5'10"
Weight:	215
Real Name:	Allen Neil Jones
Parents:	Troy and Betty Jones
Identities:	Mr. Olympia (masked)
Finisher:	Styles Clash
Groups:	Fortune (2010-2011)
Career Span:	1998-Present

Styles, A.J.

PPV Record:	96-72, 3 Draws, 7 NC
Titles Won:	30
Days as World Champion:	407
Age at first World Title Win:	25
Best Opponents:	Christopher Daniels, Samoa Joe, Kurt Angle

The youthful spirit and basically the nucleus of TNA since its inception, A.J. Styles is a proven innovator in the ring. Owning technical knowledge, a repertoire of flashy high-flying maneuvers, and growing confidence behind the microphone, he is the prototype of the modern superstar akin to this generation's Shawn Michaels or Bret Hart. He doesn't stand 6'5" and weigh 250 pounds, but he doesn't need that size to be successful. He utilizes the entire ring to his advantage, showing quickness and intelligence, and a developed psychology, all of which have earned respect throughout the world. There is a reason why TNA has pushed him consistently since 2002, from the X Division to the NWA and TNA World Heavyweight Titles—an honor the "Phenomenal" one has achieved four times. Styles' matches against Christopher Daniels, Abyss, Sting, Jeff Jarrett, and Low-Ki confirmed that he was truly one of the best in the business, and with ninety-six victories, he's the winningest wrestler in pay-per-view history.

At Johnson-Gainesville High School, Styles was a standout football player and wrestler, winning two Class AA wrestling championships at 160 pounds. He earned a scholarship to Anderson College in South Carolina, but was lured into professional wrestling, training under Rick Michaels at a school run by the NCW co-founder. He began his successful career in 1998 around Georgia and started collecting championship belts, including the NCW TV and NWA Wildside Heavyweight crown. Following brief runs in WCW and the WWA overseas in Australia, Styles passed up an opportunity to join the WWE developmental league and eventually ended up in the budding TNA. He became the initial TNA X-Division champion on June 19, 2002 with a victory over Jerry Lynn in the finals of a four-man double-elimination match. The X-Division, which spotlighted many styles of wrestling with an emphasis on high-flying and death-defying maneuvers, was seemingly created with athletes like Styles in mind.

Styles' feud with Jerry Lynn created lots of buzz and gave TNA some of its earliest headlines. While in the midst of their war, the two teamed up to win the vacant NWA Tag Team Title in July of 2002. There was no absence of excitement in X-Division bouts and they were often the highlight of TNA programs. Styles won a three-way match on June 11, 2003 for the NWA World Heavyweight Title, and at the age of twenty-five, he was the third youngest man to hold the coveted championship after Chris Candido and Tommy Rich. He'd captured the NWA belt two additional times, and on September 20, 2009, he finally won the TNA World Title in a five-way match, and then turned heel in early 2010 with Ric Flair as his manager. Styles was heavily influenced by Flair, wearing suits to the ring, and began using the figure-four leglock as his finisher. He joined the group Fortune, and feuded with Immortal in 2011. During the summer, he resumed his longtime feud with Christopher Daniels, and they displayed more of their great ring chemistry.

Photo Courtesy of Mike Mastrandrea

Born:	March 24, 1982
Height:	6'5"
Weight:	260
Real Name:	Jacob Hager
High School:	Perry High School (OK)
College:	University of Oklahoma
Trained by:	Steve Keirn
Finisher:	Ankle-lock submission hold
Career Span:	2006-Present

PPV Record:	8-22
WrestleMania Record:	1-0
WWE *Raw* TV Record:	19-46
WWE *Smackdown* TV Record:	20-31, 1 DCO, 1 NC
Titles Won:	4
Days as World Champion:	186
Age at first World Title Win:	26
Best Opponents:	Christian, Chris Jericho, Rey Mysterio Jr.

Swagger, Jack

Oklahoma has produced innumerable wrestling champions, and Jack Swagger of Perry earned honors as both an amateur and a pro. A two-time high school champion, he continued his success at the University of Oklahoma, where he went on to become an All-American. Through Jim Ross, he signed with the WWE, and spent time in the promotion's developmental territories before landing on the ECW roster in 2008. Swagger played up his amateur background, billing himself as the "All-American American," and was hated for his cockiness. He went over Matt Hardy for the ECW World Title on January 12, 2009, and reigned for four months. At WrestleMania XXVI on March 28, 2010, he won the Money in the Bank match, and used that to take advantage of a hobbled Chris Jericho two nights later to win the World Title. He lost the belt on June 20, 2010 in a four-way bout. In 2011, he played a role in the Jerry Lawler-Michael Cole feud and joined a heel clique headed by Vickie Guerrero.

Tara

Born:	February 10, 1971
Height:	5'8"
Weight:	130
Real Name:	Lisa Marie Varon
College:	UCLA
Other Titles:	NPC Inland Empire Middleweight Title (1995) (bodybuilding), 1st Place in the 1997 ESPN2 Fitness America Competition (1997) and numerous other fitness awards and achievements
Finisher:	Moonsault, Widow's Peak, Black Widow
Groups:	Revolution (2001-2002)
Career Span:	2000-Present

PPV Record:	14-21, 1 NC
WrestleMania Record:	1-2
WWE *Raw* TV Record:	47-64, 1 DDQ
WWE *Smackdown* TV Record:	13-21
Titles Won:	7
Days as World Champion:	362
Age at first World Title Win:	31
Best Opponents:	Trish Stratus, Awesome Kong, ODB

Tara is one of the most talented women wrestlers in the world today. For years prior to becoming a pro grappler, her outstanding athleticism was on display in cheerleading and in various fitness competitions. She received some advice from Joanie Laurer and Torrie Wilson, and initially trained at UPW's Ultimate University in California before her 2000 debut. She later developed further at Ohio Valley before joining the WWE as "Victoria" in 2002. On November 17, 2002, she beat Trish Stratus to capture her first WWE Women's World Title. She'd win the belt a second time, and then capture the TNA Knockouts championship a total of four times in 2009-2010. She became known for carrying her pet tarantula to the ring and placing it on downed opponents. In July of 2011, she teamed with Miss Tessmacher to capture the TNA Knockouts Tag Team Title.

Born:	August 12, 1955
Height:	6'1"
Weight:	225
Real Name:	Paul W. Taylor
Parents:	Paul and Jacqueline Taylor
College:	Guilford College
Trained by:	Eddie Graham
Identities:	The Red Rooster, Terrence Taylor, Dr. Feelgood (Masked)
Nickname:	The Taylor Made Man
Groups:	The York Foundation (1991)
Tag Team:	The Fantastic Ones w/ Bobby Fulton
Career Span:	1979-2006

PPV Record:	6-14
WrestleMania Record:	1-0
Titles Won:	28
Best Opponents:	Ric Flair, Ted DiBiase, Curt Hennig

Taylor, Terry

Named Rookie of the Year by the National Wrestling Alliance in 1980, the popular Terry Taylor was seen by many fans as a potential successor to Ric Flair as World Heavyweight Champion. Among his early ring honors were the NWA World Junior Title and the Southern championship. By 1985, he was on the big stage, challenging Flair at the Superdome in New Orleans before 11,000 fans, and for more than thirty minutes, he looked every bit like the next NWA king. Unfortunately, it never materialized. Despite that fact, in his twenty-seven years on the mat, he appeared around the globe, and had plenty of success, including powerful backstage roles that influenced many careers. Taylor was also an important figure in training grapplers, working at the WCW Power Plant and operating his own wrestling school in Georgia. Originally from Vero Beach, Taylor was more recently employed by TNA as a director of talent relations.

Born:	October 11, 1969
Height:	5'9"
Weight:	245
Real Name:	Peter Senerchia
Family:	Cousin of Chris and Joe Chetti
High School:	Franklin K. Lane High School (NY)
Identities:	Kid Krush
Finisher:	Tazmission, Katahajimi
Groups:	The Alliance (2001)
Tag Team:	The Tazmaniacs w/ Joe Chetti
Career Span:	1987-2006

PPV Record:	19-9, 1 NC
WrestleMania Record:	3-0
WWE *Raw* TV Record:	19-22, 2 NC
WWE *Smackdown* TV Record:	17-24, 3 NC
Titles Won:	15
Days as World Champion:	261
Age at first World Title Win:	29
Best Opponents:	Sabu, Bam Bam Bigelow, Kurt Angle

Taz

A powerfully built grappler with legitimate skills, including knowledge of judo, Taz has been much more than a television commentator to the wrestling world. From Red Hook, Brooklyn, he was tutored in the fundamentals by Johnny Rodz and bounced around the independents before landing in Philadelphia for a budding promotion known as Eastern Championship Wrestling, where he was known in 1993 as Tazmaniac. Legendary Jimmy Snuka passed a symbolic "torch" to him the following year, and had a nine-month reign as ECW TV Champion between June 1997 and March 1998. On January 10, 1999, he beat Shane Douglas to capture the ECW World Heavyweight Title at the Guilty as Charged pay-per-view. Taz was a fighting champion for nine months, and lost the belt to Mike Awesome in a three-way match also involving Masato Tanaka on September 19.

The "Human Suplex Machine" signed with the WWF in early 2000, and on April 13, he returned to ECW to take the World Title off Mike Awesome, who had signed a contract with rival WCW, and did so with a submission victory. Taz appeared on WWF TV with the ECW belt and had a champion vs. champion match against Triple H on April 18 in Philadelphia. He lost the strap a short time later to Tommy Dreamer. Taz served as a commentator on *Smackdown* with Michael Cole from 2002 to 2006, and proceeded to perform the same role on the ECW program. In 2009, he left the WWE and joined TNA, debuting as commentator on August 20, and working alongside Mike Tenay on its weekly show on Spike. Taz has also been a influential trainer, working with up-and-comers at ECW's House of Hardcore wrestling school and was a coach on the first season of *Tough Enough*.

Born:	February 2, 1950
Height:	6'1"
Weight:	235
Real Name:	Genichiro Shimada
Finisher:	Northern Lights Bomb
Promoted:	Wrestle Association R (WAR) (Japan)
Career Span:	1976-2010

PPV Record:	1-2
WrestleMania Record:	1-0
Titles Won:	24
Days as World Champion:	713
Age at first World Title Win:	38
Best Opponents:	Jumbo Tsuruta, Keiji Mutoh, Stan Hansen
Tournament Wins:	4
Halls of Fame:	1

Tenryu, Genichiro

In the last thirty-five years, there have been few wrestlers more successful than Japanese legend Genichiro Tenryu. Transitioning from the Sumo ranks, he was trained in Amarillo by the Funk Brothers, and returned to All-Japan to work for Giant Baba. In February of 1984, he captured the vacant United National Championship from Ricky Steamboat in Tokyo. That title would later be unified into the coveted AJPW Triple Crown, which he'd win from Jumbo Tsuruta on June 5, 1989 before 15,000 fans. Ten years later, on December 10, 1999, he defeated Keiji Mutoh at the Osaka Prefectural Gym and won the IWGP Title. With the victory, he became the second man in history to have held both the AJPW Triple Crown and the IWGP Title. Tenryu lost the IWGP belt to Kensuke Sasaki on January 4, 2000 at the Tokyo Dome. Tenryu regained the AJPW Triple Crown on October 28, 2000 in Tokyo, winning an eight-man tournament.

Tenta, John

Born:	June 22, 1963
Height:	6'7"
Weight:	425
Real Name:	John Anthony Tenta
Parents:	John and Irene Tenta
High School:	North Surrey Secondary School (Surrey, B.C.)
Sumo Name:	Kototenta, Kototenzan
Identities:	Avalanche, The Shark, Golga
Groups:	Dungeon of Doom (1995-1996), The Oddities (1998-1999)
Tag Team:	The Natural Disasters w/ Typhoon
Career Span:	1987-2004
Died:	June 7, 2006, Sanford, FL 42 years old

PPV Record:	12-13
WrestleMania Record:	4-0
Titles Won:	5
Best Opponents:	Randy Savage, Sting, Hulk Hogan

The affable John Tenta was from North Surrey, British Columbia, where he took up amateur wrestling at fifteen years of age, winning many championships. After some college at LSU, he was courted to Japan to compete as a Sumo, and his size and athletic prowess garnered him an undefeated record in twenty-one matches. He retired prematurely in 1986, and entered pro wrestling for Giant Baba, spending two years working for All-Japan. Tenta turned up in the WWF as "Earthquake," a heel grappler managed by Jimmy Hart. He was most remembered injuring Hulk Hogan in 1990 and for his shocking splash on Jake Roberts' snake, Damien. He adopted a slew of gimmicks through the end of the decade, including a run as a member of the Oddities. In 2000, he ran a wrestling school in Florida, and two years later, he teamed with Genichiro Tenryu and had a good run in the annual Real World Tag League Tournament.

Born:	November 27, 1957
Height:	5'8"
Weight:	200
Real Name:	Satoru Sayama
Trained by:	Karl Gotch, Antonio Inoki
Identities:	Sammy Lee, Tigre Enmascarado, The Tiger, Super Tiger, Tiger King
Nickname:	El Tigre Enmascarado
Finisher:	Tiger Spin, Moonsault, Tiger Suplex
Career Span:	1976-Present

Titles Won:	7
Best Opponents:	Dynamite Kid, Kuniaki Kobayashi, Black Tiger
Halls of Fame:	1

Tiger Mask

For many years, the prototypical wrestler was mammoth in size and intimidating in all aspects. Most non-heavyweight stars were ignored by the mainstream until Tiger Mask helped lead a revolution in the early 1980s, transforming wrestling in the U.S., Mexico, and Japan into a culture that admired lighter, more nimble wrestlers. The colorful persona, created after a popular cartoon character in Japan, debuted in 1981, and Tiger Mask influenced a generation of performers with his quick-moving and inventive style. In his vibrant matches against the Dynamite Kid, an amazing amount of athleticism was demonstrated, and their bouts are still talked about with great esteem today. Three versions of Tiger Mask have followed in his footsteps, and the name symbolizes a high benchmark of wrestling skill that few can equal.

Born:	October 25, 1965
Height:	5'11"
Weight:	220-230
Real Name:	Charles Scaggs
Identities:	Black Wazuma
Finisher:	Twist Legdrop, Sommersault Splash
Groups:	The JOB Squad (1998-1999)
Career Span:	1985-Present

PPV Record:	9-12, 1 DDQ
WrestleMania Record:	0-1
WWE *Raw* TV Record:	0-1
Titles Won:	16
Best Opponents:	Sabu, Shane Douglas, Chris Benoit

Too Cold Scorpio

A product of Denver, Colorado, Too Cold Scorpio is a polished high-flyer and internationally known for his outstanding grappling abilities. In late 1993, he teamed with Marcus Alexander Bagwell to capture the WCW World Tag Team Title from the Nasty Boys, but lost the belts in a rematch at Halloween Havoc. Scorpio was a mainstay in Extreme Championship Wrestling during its heyday, winning the promotion's TV championship four times, defeating the likes of Jason and Eddie Guerrero. His four reigns were the most by any wrestler. Overseas in Japan, Scorpio also found a lot of success. He spent several years with the WWF between 1996 and 1999 as "Flash Funk," dazzling fans with his quickness and wide-ranging moveset. In August of 2010, he participated in TNA's Hardcore Justice pay-per-view that featured wrestlers from the old ECW promotion In his victory over C.W. Anderson, his aerial attack was as enjoyable as it had been fifteen years earlier.

Triple H

Born:	July 27, 1969
Height:	6'5"
Weight:	260
Real Name:	Paul Michael Levesque
Parents:	Paul and Patricia Levesque
Wife:	Stephanie McMahon
High School:	Nashua High School (NH)
Identities:	Terra Rising, Jean-Paul Levesque
Nicknames:	Cerebral Assassin
Finisher:	The Pedigree
Groups:	D-Generation X (1997-2000), Evolution (2003)
Career Span:	1992-Present

PPV Record:	80-68, 1 DDQ, 1 Draw, 3 NC
WrestleMania Record:	8-7
WWE *Raw* TV Record:	151-107, 2 Draws, 2 DCO, 2 DDQ, 32 NC
WWE *Smackdown* TV Record:	57-38, 13 NC
Titles Won:	24
Days as World Champion:	1,155
Age at first World Title Win:	30
Best Opponents:	The Undertaker, Shawn Michaels, Steve Austin,
Halls of Fame:	1
TV Appearances:	Over 20
Movies:	4

A native of Nashua, New Hampshire, Triple H is a foremost pro wrestling superstar and still establishing himself as a future WWE icon. He is known for his intense, knock-down drag-out ring combat, and has amassed thirteen World Title victories during his nearly two decades in the business. Nicknamed "The Game," he has drawn comparisons to Ric Flair throughout his career, but with the frame of a bodybuilder. In fact, he was more interested in training with weights than participating in organized sports, and after high school, he worked as a manager at a local Gold's Gym. He received some timely advice from bodybuilder and ex-wrestler Ted Arcidi, and decided to follow through with a path to becoming a pro grappler. Having always been a wrestling fan, Triple H attended Killer Kowalski's Malden school and debuted in 1992. Within two years, he broke free from the independents for a job in WCW, where he fashioned himself as a British aristocrat.

There was little future in WCW, he quickly ascertained, and ventured to the WWF. It was there that he took the name, "Hunter Hearst Helmsley," the full designation of the moniker, "Triple H," and received his first significant push. In October of 1996, he won the Intercontinental belt and came up victorious in the 1997 King of the Ring tournament. That same year, he teamed with Shawn Michaels, Chyna, and Rick Rude to form the first incarnation of D-Generation X, a rebellious group that would become immensely popular. He won his first WWF Title on August 23, 1999, and viciously battled Vince McMahon. A storyline was enacted that saw Triple H marry Vince's daughter Stephanie, which became reality in October of 2003. He collected championship wins from The Big Show and The Rock, and then feuded with Steve Austin before losing to The Undertaker at WrestleMania X-Seven. After befriending Austin and winning both the Intercontinental and tag team titles, he suffered a left quadriceps muscle tear during *Raw* on May 21, 2001.

The serious injury cost him the remainder of the year. He made his triumphant return on January 7, 2002 and proceeded to win both the Royal Rumble and the WWF Undisputed World Title at WrestleMania X-Eight from Chris Jericho. During the summer, he entered a surprisingly violent feud with his old DX buddy Shawn Michaels. Eric Bischoff, on September 2, 2002, awarded Triple H the initial World Heavyweight Title, which, at the time, was exclusive to *Raw*. He was champion for more than nine months and formed Evolution with Ric Flair, Batista, and Randy Orton—although he'd eventually feud with all three. He traded the championship with both Michaels and Goldberg before finally losing the title to Chris Benoit at WrestleMania XX. A few months later, on September 12, 2004, Triple H won his fourth World Title from Randy Orton. The belt was declared vacant in December, but he rebounded to win it back on January 9, 2005. Batista went over at WrestleMania XXI and Triple H soon took a hiatus from the ring.

Notable feuds with Flair, John Cena, and the McMahons followed, and Triple H even reformed DX with Michaels in 2006. He was sidelined by another severe injury, this time a torn right quad, in January of 2007, and missed a huge chunk of the year. On October 7, 2007, he beat Orton for his sixth WWE Title at No Mercy in what would be the first of three matches that night. He successfully retained against Umaga in the second contest, but then lost a Last Man Standing bout to Orton, meaning that he'd won and lost the championship in the same night. He beat Orton in a Fatal-Four way match on April 27, 2008 and kept the title until November when he was dethroned by Edge in Boston. On February 15, 2009, he captured his eighth WWE Title in an Elimination Chamber match at No Way Out. Of all his matches and feuds, Orton would be his most heated opponent, and the latter turned the dial up when he RKO'd Stephanie on *Raw*.

Orton beat him for the WWE belt on April 26, 2009, ending his final run. From there, he went on to reunite with Michaels against the members of Legacy and captured the Unified Tag Team Title from Big Show and Chris Jericho. At WrestleMania XXVI, he beat Sheamus, and a year later, he again challenged The Undertaker's undefeated WrestleMania streak—but ended up with another loss. In July of 2011, he assumed the role of on-camera "Chief Operating Officer" from Vince McMahon, apparently closing the door on one chapter of WWE history and opening a new one. Behind the scenes, he worked as a senior advisor to McMahon and overlooked talent development. He's appeared in a handful of films and has given many mainstream interviews, including *Jimmy Kimmel Live!* and *Late Night with Conan O'Brien*. A talented wrestler with considerable knowledge, Triple H will be a major player for years to come, whether it's in the ring or behind the curtain.

Born:	June 16, 1959
Height:	6'3"
Weight:	280
Real Name:	James Brian Hellwig
Trained by:	Bill Anderson, Red Bastien
Identities:	Justice, Blade Runner Rock, Dingo Warrior, The Warrior
Finisher:	Splash, Gorilla Press
Career Span:	1985-2008

PPV Record:	17-4
WrestleMania Record:	4-1
Titles Won:	7
Days as World Champion:	293
Age at first World Title Win:	30
Best Opponents:	Rick Rude, Randy Savage, Hulk Hogan

Ultimate Warrior, The

A high-energy, muscle-bound superstar, the Ultimate Warrior was enormously popular at the height of his WWF run. Exploding with unparalleled enthusiasm on the way to the ring, he mixed an unorthodox style with brute force and became a ring idol for many grappling fans. Originally from Indiana, he was a bodybuilder prior to joining a unique squad in 1985 known as "Power Team USA." Led by Rick Bassman and trained by Red Bastien, this quartet also featured Steve Borden, who'd gain future fame as Sting. After the group disbanded, Warrior and Sting ventured to the Mid-South Territory and the UWF as a tag team. Following a stint as a member of the Blade Runners, Warrior went to Dallas, where he appeared as the Dingo Warrior. That gimmick morphed into the "Ultimate Warrior" in 1987 for the World Wrestling Federation. Accompanied by a booming guitar rift, he sprinted to the ring, usually demolished his opponents in quick time, and vanished to the cheers of the crowd.

The Warrior engaged in an early feud with Hercules before entering contention for the Intercontinental Title. On August 29, 1988 at SummerSlam in New York, he toppled the Honky Tonk Man in twenty-eight seconds to capture the championship. In 1989, he traded the title back and forth with Rick Rude, and his popularity began to rival that of the promotion's number one face, Hulk Hogan. While no one expected the WWF's top two fan favorites to feud with each other, that is exactly what ended up happening. The two confronted each other at the 1990 Royal Rumble that concluded in a double clothesline, leveling both. Their war intensified in the weeks that followed, building toward their eventual match at WrestleMania VI at Toronto's Skydome. Hogan's WWF Title was on the line against the Warrior's Intercontinental Title, and after twenty-two minutes, Hogan missed a legdrop, and the Warrior landed a splash for the pin. It seemed at the time as if a symbolic torch had been passed and a new era of Warrior dominance had begun.

Surviving another feud with Rude, Warrior remained champion through the end of the year, and lost the belt to Sgt. Slaughter at the Royal Rumble on January 19, 1991 after being hit with a scepter by Randy Savage. Warrior feuded with Savage and the Undertaker in 1991, and after SummerSlam, he disappeared from the sport only to return eight months later. He chased Savage for the WWF Title and beat him by countout at SummerSlam 1992, but didn't win the title. Once again, he vanished from the business and a succession of appearance rumors followed. He reemerged in 1996, going over Triple H at WrestleMania in a short match. The Warrior remained active through the first part of the summer, only to part ways from the organization in an abrupt fashion in July 1996. Two years later, he tried to launch a revolution in WCW with his OWN group, but the stay in the promotion was brief. In 2008, he wrestled his final match in Spain, winning over Orlando Jordan.

Photo Courtesy of Dr. Mike Lano—Wrealano@aol.com

Born:	March 24, 1965
Height:	6'9"
Weight:	320
Real Name:	Mark William Calaway
Parents:	Frank and Betty Calaway
Trained by:	Ox Baker, Don Jardine
Finisher:	Heart Punch, Chokeslam
Tag Team:	The Brothers of Destruction w/ Kane
Career Span:	1987-Present

Undertaker, The

PPV Record:	91-64, 4 NC
WrestleMania Record:	19-0
WWE *Raw* TV Record:	54-30, 1 DCO, 15 NC
WWE *Smackdown* TV Record:	118-40, 3 Draws, 3 DCO, 22 NC
Titles Won:	17
Days as World Champion:	469
Age at first World Title Win:	24
Best Opponents:	Shawn Michaels, Triple H., Mick Foley
Halls of Fame:	1

By remaining undefeated through nineteen matches at WrestleMania, The Undertaker currently holds one of the most exciting records in wrestling history. When the streak finally comes to an end, it will undoubtedly be at the end of an intense ring war, climaxing an extraordinary run and capping a hall of fame career. The Undertaker was sprung on the wrestling world in 1990, and his dark persona fit well into the colorful character-driven landscape of the WWF. Since that time, he's risen above the symbolism of any particular gimmick and has become a living, breathing icon for the promotion. Exceptionally agile for a large wrestler, he left fans in awe with his tight-rope walking, and his tombstone piledriver still appears to be one of the most powerful moves in the industry. Beginning his career in Texas, the Undertaker used several different names, winning the USWA Unified World Title as the "Master of Pain" on April 1, 1989. Before the end of the year, he was working for WCW as "Mean" Mark Callous.

Callous developed the chilling heart punch as his finisher and briefly teamed with Dan Spivey as a member of the Skyscrapers. He demonstrated his singles ability as a challenger to Lex Luger's U.S. championship, but ended up in the WWF by the end of the year, initially imported by Brother Love. Paul Bearer assumed managerial rights to the Undertaker, and an early feud occurred against the popular Ultimate Warrior—even locking the latter in an "airtight" casket at one point as a display of his willingness to injure his opponents by whatever means. He was fast becoming immensely hated, and on November 27, 1991, he shocked the world by defeating Hulk Hogan for the WWF World Title. His reign lasted only six days, but affirmed his status as an impact player. Over the next few years, he began to develop a core base of fans and feuded with heels Kamala, Giant Gonzales, Yokozuna, and King Kong Bundy. Initially without much fanfare, his WrestleMania win streak built year after year until it was too exceptional to ignore.

On March 23, 1997 he pinned Sid Vicious for his second WWF Title and successfully turned back the challenges of Mankind, Steve Austin, and Vader in the months that followed. Upon losing the title to Bret Hart, Undertaker entered a feud with Shawn Michaels, and on October 5, they wrestled a classic "Hell in a Cell" match in St. Louis. Michaels was victorious after the Undertaker's purported brother Kane attacked him. The "siblings" fought a number of high-profile matches, including an "Inferno" bout in April of 1998 with the ring surrounded by flames. On June 28, 1998, Undertaker fought Mankind in his second "Hell in a Cell" match, a bout that was seared into the minds of fans by the latter's wild bumps. On May 23, 1999, he beat Austin for the WWF belt and the next month, on June 27, pinned The Rock. The next night, however, Austin regained the belt.

In 2000, the Undertaker rose from the dead, after recovering from an injury, and made a spectacular return to the ring. Instead of his usual dead man gimmick, he was wearing a leather jacket and rode a motorcycle to the ring. The "American Bad Ass" emerged and his popularity flared to new heights. Back in action against Kane, Chris Benoit, and Kurt Angle, the Undertaker was stronger than ever, and by early 2001, he reconciled with his "brother" and formed a successful tag team. Following the onset of the WCW invasion a short time later, the Undertaker battled Dallas Page in an angle that involved the 'Taker's wife, Sara. On May 19, 2002, he beat Hulk Hogan for his fourth WWE World Title, only to lose it the next month to The Rock in a triple threat match in Detroit. On November 16, 2003, he was defeated by Vince McMahon in a "Buried Alive" match after Kane interfered, putting the Undertaker out of the business for a short time.

Of course, The Undertaker returned in time for WrestleMania XX. Using his "dead man" gimmick again with Bearer back at his side, he toppled Kane, continuing his winning streak. Heavy ring wars against JBL, Booker T, Randy Orton, and CM Punk followed. He beat Batista for the World Title at WrestleMania XXIV and had successive WrestleMania matches against Shawn Michaels in 2009-2010, winning both in dramatic fashion, with the second victory ending Michaels' wrestling career. In February of 2011, he returned to the WWE, setting up a his WrestleMania XXVII match against Triple H, who he'd beaten ten years earlier on the same stage. The result was the same, and The Undertaker earned his nineteenth WrestleMania victory. He was carried from the ring after the hard-fought win and remained out of action for many months. As his twentieth match approaches, fans wait and wonder who his opponent will be, and if the Undertaker's streak will ever be silenced. The fact is that it will never be broken.

Vader

Born:	May 14, 1955
Height:	6'4"
Weight:	425
Real Name:	Leon Allen White
College:	University of Colorado
NFL Draft:	Los Angeles Rams (1978) (3rd Round)
Pro Sports:	National Football League—Los Angeles Rams (1980-1985)
Trained by:	Brad Rheingans
Identities:	Baby Bull, Bull Power, Big Van Vader, Super Vader
Nickname:	Mastodon
Finisher:	Vaderbomb, Moonsault
Career Span:	1985-2010

PPV Record:	20-30, 1 DCO, 2 DDQ
WrestleMania Record:	1 DCO
Titles Won:	19
Days as World Champion:	2,252 (including overlapping reigns)
Age at first World Title Win:	31
Best Opponents:	Antonio Inoki, Ric Flair, Shawn Michaels
Halls of Fame:	1

An amazingly agile and powerful big man, Vader won World championships in Europe, Mexico, Japan, and the United States. Following a pro football career that was hampered by injury, he developed his wrestling abilities, and with his unique look, rose up the ladder quickly. In Austria, he ended Otto Wanz's nearly nine-year stint as the CWA champion on March 22, 1987. That December, he shocked Japanese fans with a quick win over the legendary Antonio Inoki, and would go on to win the IWGP Title on three occasions. Vader toppled Sting for the first of three WCW World Titles on July 12, 1992, and in 1994, he won the UWFI World Title. Five years later, on March 6, 1999, he pinned Akira Taue for the vacant AJPW Triple Crown, adding another monumental achievement to his record. His feuds with Hulk Hogan, Sting, Shawn Michaels, Ric Flair, and The Undertaker were immensely heated, and Vader lived up to his monster heel billing. His son Jesse is an up-and-coming pro wrestler.

Photo Courtesy of Dr. Mike Lano—Wrealano@aol.com

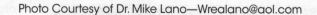

Born:	December 18, 1970
Height:	6'0"
Weight:	230
Real Name:	Robert Alexander Szatkowski
Identities:	Robbie V
Groups:	The Alliance (2001)
Tag Team:	Aerial Assault w/ Bob Bradley
Career Span:	1990-Present

Van Dam, Rob

PPV Record:	50-30, 1 Draw, 1 DCO, 1 NC
WrestleMania Record:	4-0
WWE *Raw* TV Record:	89-56, 6 NC
WWE *Smackdown* TV Record:	44-22, 1 Draw, 2 NC
Titles Won:	27
Days as World Champion:	156
Age at first World Title Win:	35
Best Opponents:	Sabu, Jerry Lynn, John Cena
TV Appearances:	Over 10
Movies:	4

Combining a natural athleticism with a kickboxing and martial arts background, Rob Van Dam has been a spectacular performer for over two decades. His ability to propel himself through the air to deliver his lethal Five-Star Frog Splash or the Van-Terminator is uncanny, and few peers can compare in terms of high-flying. Known as "RVD" and the "Whole F'n Show," Van Dam's popularity has been well-earned, and not many wrestlers hold pinfall victories over The Rock, Steve Austin, Sting, Kurt Angle, Ric Flair, and John Cena. Originally from Battle Creek, Michigan, he was trained by the master of the hardcore style, The Sheik, and wrestled in WCW and many independents before making a big name for himself in ECW. For 700 days, Van Dam held the ECW World TV Title from April 1998 to March 2000, elevating the championship to one of the most prestigious in the world. Along with Sabu, he won the ECW World Tag Team Title twice.

During the summer of 2001, Van Dam was part of an ECW invasion angle of the WWF along with Paul Heyman and others. He eventually unified both the European and Hardcore Titles with the Intercontinental Championship in 2002. He was also a top challenger to the heavyweight crown and on June 11, 2006, he went over John Cena for the WWE belt. Two nights later, he was awarded the ECW World Title, making him the first wrestler to hold both belts simultaneously. On March 8, 2010, he arrived in TNA, and within weeks, won the promotion's World Title from A.J. Styles. An ECW reunion pay-per-view was set up, entitled "Hardcore Justice," that featured many of the organization's regulars. On the show, Van Dam beat his old partner, Sabu. In August, he was injured in an attack by Fortune and Abyss, forcing officials to vacate the TNA Title. He got retribution over Abyss in a special Monster's Ball match. Van Dam feuded with the Immortal group and Jerry Lynn in 2010-2011, but wasn't able to regain the TNA World Title.

Born:	September 1, 1961
Height:	6'8"
Weight:	275
Real Name:	Sidney Raymond Eudy
Identities:	Lord Humongous, Vicious Warrior, Sid Justice
Nicknames:	Psycho, The Original Psycho, Y2S
Career Span:	1987-Present

PPV Record:	17-23, 1 NC
WrestleMania Record:	0-2
Titles Won:	13
Days as World Champion:	382
Age at first World Title Win:	32
Best Opponents:	Shawn Michaels, Chris Benoit, Bret Hart

Vicious, Sid

The towering Sid Vicious was a major impact player in wrestling from his early days as one of the Four Horsemen to being a top challenger to the NWA, WCW, and WWF World Titles. Trained by Tojo Yamamoto, he earned a name for himself as a member of the Skyscrapers with Dan Spivey in 1989, but suffered an injury before winning any gold. He joined the Four Horsemen in 1990 and was a serious threat to Sting's NWA Title. His crushing powerbombs of Brian Pillman during War Games was one of the defining moments of the 1990s. In November of 1996, he beat Shawn Michaels for the WWF World Heavyweight Title and won it again in early 1997. A few years later, in January of 2000, he became the eighth man to win both the WWF and NWA/WCW Titles with a victory over Kevin Nash for the WCW World belt. At Sin in January of 2001, he suffered a horrific leg injury during a match. Over the next few years, he made sporadic appearances on the indie scene, mostly as a special referee.

Born:	July 22, 1958
Height:	6'6"
Weight:	230
Real Name:	David Alan Adkisson
Parents:	Jack and Doris Adkisson
Family:	Brother of Chris, Kerry, Kevin, and Mike Von Erich
Wife:	Patricia Adkisson
College:	North Texas State University
Finisher:	Clawhold
Career Span:	1977-1984
Died:	February 10, 1984, Tokyo, Japan 25 years old

Titles Won:	20
Best Opponents:	Harley Race, Ric Flair, Jack Brisco
Halls of Fame:	1

Von Erich, David

The tallest of five brothers, David Von Erich was a basketball standout at Lake Dallas High School and was twice All-State. Under the guidance of his father, Fritz Von Erich, he turned pro, like his brother Kevin before him, and joined the wars of the Sportatorium. Considered to be more similar in appearance to his father than his siblings, David displayed immense talent, and his career began to skyrocket. During a tour of Florida in 1981, he proved his versatility by turning heel. He took James J. Dillon as his manager, and beat Jack Brisco for the Southern championship. Von Erich won the cherished NWA Missouri Heavyweight crown from Ric Flair, and on February 3, 1984, he wrestled the United National Title away from Michael Hayes. He went to Japan for a scheduled three-week tour, and shortly after arrival, was found dead in his hotel of acute intestinal inflammation. His death stunned the wrestling community.

Born:	February 3, 1960
Height:	6'3"
Weight:	260
Real Name:	Kerry Gene Adkisson
Parents:	Jack and Doris Adkisson
Family:	Brother of Chris, David, Kevin, and Mike Von Erich
High School:	Lake Dallas High School (TX)
Nicknames:	The Modern-Day Warrior, Texas Tornado
Tag Team:	The Cosmic Cowboys w/ Kevin Von Erich
Career Span:	1978-1993
Died:	February 18, 1993, Denton, TX 33 years old

Von Erich, Kerry

PPV Record:	5-3	
WrestleMania Record:	1-0	
Titles Won:	42	
Days as World Champion:		242
Age at first World Title Win:		24
Best Opponents:		Ric Flair, Curt Hennig, Jerry Lawler
Halls of Fame:		1

Another one of Jack Adkisson's popular and talented sons, Kerry Von Erich was a spectacular athlete, excelling in football at Lake Dallas as a running back and a linebacker, becoming All-State. He went to the University of Houston, where he was a noted discus thrower, and also turned pro in 1978. As part of the Von Erich clan, he participated in many exciting matches in Dallas at the Sportatorium. Following the shocking death of his brother, David, he beat Ric Flair for the NWA World Heavyweight Title on May 6, 1984 at Texas Stadium before 40,000 cheering fans, dedicating the win to his fallen sibling. Flair regained the belt later in the month in Japan. In 1990, he defeated Mr. Perfect for the WWF Intercontinental Title, using a clawhold and tornado punch to secure the victory. In addition, he was a four-time WCWA World and American Champion, and in 1983, he held the Missouri State Title.

On June 4, 1986, along US 373 in Argyle, Texas, he was in a near-fatal motorcycle accident. He suffered a very serious right ankle injury as well as a dislocated hip and lacerations to his right knee. His right foot was amputated and, unbeknownst to the wrestling world, he wore a prosthetic foot during his in-ring performances. When he headlined the AWA pay-per-view, SuperClash III, on December 13, 1988 in Chicago, there was an attempt by the WWF to have the Illinois Athletic Commission prevent Von Erich from wrestling due to his physical condition, but his match against Jerry Lawler went on as planned. He worked for the GWF, a local Dallas promotion, after leaving the WWF in the summer of 1992. Following his death, the GWF held a benefit show for his daughters on April 2, 1993. Among those who participated in the event were Kevin Von Erich, Chris Adams, and Michael Hayes. His daughter, Lacey, entered the profession and gained success while a member of the Beautiful People in TNA from 2009-2010.

Von Erich, Kevin

Born:	May 15, 1957
Height:	6'2"
Weight:	235
Real Name:	Kevin Ross Adkisson
Parents:	Jack and Doris Adkisson
Family:	Older brother of Chris, David, Kerry, and Mike Von Erich
Trained by:	Jack Adkisson
Finisher:	Clawhold
Tag Team:	The Cosmic Cowboys w/ Kerry Von Erich
Career Span:	1976-1995

Titles Won:	33
Days as World Champion:	313
Age at first World Title Win:	29
Best Opponents:	Ric Flair, Bruiser Brody, Chris Adams
Halls of Fame:	1

The oldest wrestling son of Fritz Von Erich, Kevin Von Erich was a standout fullback at Lake Dallas High School and as a tight end at North Texas State. He followed his father into the wrestling business, and, along with his brothers, was a hero at the Sportatorium in Dallas. Between 1978 and 1983, he held the American Title five times and also captured the all-important Missouri State crown in St. Louis. In 1986, he beat Black Bart for the WCWA World Title. With his siblings, he held an incredible number of tag team championships in Dallas. In honor of his late brother, David, he challenged Ric Flair for the NWA Title at the 2nd Annual Parade of Champions on May 5, 1985, but the match ended in a double countout. Following his retirement in 1995, he made a number of appearances, and was on hand to accept the honor as his family was inducted into the WWE Hall of Fame in 2009.

Born:	July 13, 1972
Height:	6'2"
Weight:	205
Real Name:	Sean Michael Waltman
Trained by:	Eddie Sharkey
Identities:	The Lightning Kid, The 1-2-3 Kid, Syxx, X-Pac, Syxx-Pac, Pac
Finisher:	Buzz Killer
Groups:	New World Order (1996-1997, 2000) D-Generation X (1998-1999, 1999-2000)
Career Span:	1990-Present

PPV Record:	35-47, 1 DCO
WrestleMania Record:	0-2
WWE *Raw* TV Record:	55-38, 1 DDQ, 13 NC
WWE *Smackdown* TV Record:	33-28, 1 DDQ, 6 NC
Titles Won:	25
Best Opponents:	Bret Hart, Eddie Guerrero, Shane McMahon

Waltman, Sean

A gifted mat wrestler with high-flying abilities, Sean Waltman grew up in Tampa and became a well-known grappling sensation while still a teenager. Trained by the Malenkos, he made a splash in the GWF in Dallas and was viewed as an underdog because of his lanky form. He maintained that status in the WWF and won some unexpected victories on *Raw*. Waltman captured the WWF World Tag Team Title four times with partners Marty Jannetty, Sparky Plugg, and twice with Kane. In WCW, he was a member of the NWO and held the World Cruiserweight Title; with the GWF and WWE Light Heavyweight Titles and the TNA X-Division Championship among his other achievements. In addition to his work as a member of the NWO, he was a part of another dominant faction: D-Generation X. He was engaged at one time to Joanie Laurer, and the two made a brief appearance during an episode of the *Anna Nicole Smith Show*.

Born:	June 4, 1973
Height:	5'7"
Weight:	185
Real Name:	John Michael Watson
High School:	Sayville High School (NY)
Trained by:	Sonny Blaze
Finisher:	Whippersnapper
Career Span:	1994-Present

PPV Record:	3-10
Titles Won:	17
Days as World Champion:	42
Age at first World Title Win:	22
Best Opponents:	Cactus Jack, The Sandman, Steve Austin

Whipwreck, Mikey

In a world of behemoths, the 5'7" Mikey Whipwreck seemed to be an implausible heavyweight champion. In fact, he was commonly acknowledged as the underdog when he wrestled for ECW, where he began in 1994. Fans couldn't help but be awestruck by his well-rounded ring skills and ability to take hardcore bumps from much larger grapplers. Whipwreck proved indestructible, winning the ECW World TV Title twice, the World Tag championship three times, and, on October 28, 1995, he beat The Sandman for the World Heavyweight crown. The Sayville, New York athlete also held various indie belts and mentored the likes of Amazing Red and Jay Lethal.

Williams, Steve

Born:	May 14, 1960
Height:	6'1"
Weight:	265
Real Name:	Steven Franklin Williams
Parents:	Gerald and Dorthy Williams
High School:	Lakewood High School (CO)
College:	University of Oklahoma
College Ach.:	Big Eight Wrestling Champion (1980-1982) (HWT), All-American Football Player (1982), All-American Wrestler (1978-1981)
Pro Sports:	United States Football League— New Jersey Generals (1982) United States Football League— Denver Gold (1982)
Finisher:	Oklahoma Stampede
Groups:	The Varsity Club (1988-1989, 1999)
Career Span:	1982-2009
Died:	December 30, 2009, Lakewood, CO 49 years old

PPV Record:	8-7, 2 Draws
WWE *Raw* TV Record:	0-1
Titles Won:	22
Days as World Champion:	435
Age at first World Title Win:	27
Best Opponents:	Kenta Kobashi, Mitsuharu Misawa, Bubba Rogers
MMA Record:	0-1

Williams was a powerhouse wrestler, known as "Dr. Death," and entered the business with outstanding amateur credentials. Under the tutelage of Bill Watts, he quickly made a splash in the Mid-South region, and on July 11, 1987, he beat Bubba Rogers for the UWF World Title in Oklahoma City. As a member of the impressive Varsity Club, he teamed with Mike Rotundo to beat the Road Warriors for the World Tag Team Title in April of 1989, but they were stripped of the belts in May. In Japan, Williams established a strong legacy, forming a superlative tag team with Terry Gordy, and winning the All-Japan Tag Title five times between 1990 and 1993. The duo also won the NWA and WCW Tag Team Championship in 1992. On July 28,

1994 in Tokyo, Williams captured the coveted AJPW Japanese Triple Crown from Mitsuharu Misawa. Back in the U.S., Williams was a competitor in the WWF's Brawl for All tournament in 1998. He remained active into 2009 and passed away that December.

Photo Courtesy of Pete Lederberg—plmathfoto@hotmail.com

Born:	July 4, 1960
Height:	6'5"
Weight:	250
Real Name:	Barry Clinton Windham
Parents:	Robert and Julia Windham
College:	West Texas State University
Identities:	Blackjack Mulligan Jr., Dirty Yellow Dog, The Widowmaker, The Stalker
Finisher:	Bulldog Headlock, Superplex, Clawhold
Groups:	The Four Horsemen (1988-1989, 1990-1991), The Xtreme Horsemen (2001)
Tag Teams:	The Young Lions w/ Mike Rotundo, The U.S. Express w/ Mike Rotundo, The New Blackjacks w/ Bradshaw, The West Texas Rednecks w/ Kendall Windham
Career Span:	1980-2008

Windham, Barry

PPV Record:	14-18, 1 Draw, 1 NC
WrestleMania Record:	0-2
Titles Won:	37
Days as World Champion:	147
Age at first World Title Win:	32
Best Opponents:	Ric Flair, Lex Luger, Steve Austin

The pride of Sweetwater, Texas, Barry Windham has been one of the most successful wrestlers of the last thirty years. Trained by his father, Blackjack Mulligan, he initially began as a referee and developed into a fundamentally sound and entertaining grappler. During the 1980s, he chased Ric Flair for the NWA championship, and finally won the strap from The Great Muta on February 21, 1993. Between 1988 and 1998, he was a three-time World Tag Team Champion with Lex Luger, Dustin Rhodes, and Tully Blanchard. Windham also held the WCW World Tag Team Title on three occasions with Rhodes, Curt Hennig, and his brother Kendall. In 1988, he beat Nikita Koloff in a tournament final for the vacant U.S. Heavyweight Title.

He also won the WCW World TV Title from Steve Austin in 1992. Earlier in his career, he formed a highly successful tag team with his brother-in-law, Mike Rotunda. They won the U.S. Tag Title in Florida twice before jumping to the WWF, where they won the World Tag Team Title on two occasions in 1985.

Photo Courtesy of Dr. Mike Lano—Wrealano@aol.com

Born:	October 2, 1966
Height:	6'4"
Weight:	590
Real Name:	Agatupu Rodney Anoai
Trained by:	Afa
Identities:	Great Kokina, Kokina Maximus, Samoan Kokina
Finisher:	Splash
Career Span:	1984-2000
Died:	October 23, 2000, Liverpool, England 34 years old

PPV Record:	9-12, 1 DCO, 1 DDQ	
WrestleMania Record:	3-3	
Titles Won:	5	
Days as World Champion:	280	
Age at first World Title Win:	26	
Best Opponents:	Bret Hart, Vader, Shawn Michaels	

Yokozuna

Nephew of the legendary Wild Samoans, Yokozuna was one of the most talented big men in wrestling history. From the Island of American Samoa, he weighed more than 500 pounds and made a huge impact on the World Wrestling Federation shortly after his debut in 1992. He used his bulk to win the 1993 Royal Rumble and earned a World Title shot at WrestleMania on April 4, 1993 in Las Vegas. WrestleMania, however, would see both success and failure as he initially won the heavyweight title from Bret Hart, at the time becoming the youngest WWF champion in history at age twenty-six. Minutes later, he was pinned by Hulk Hogan after an impromptu challenge was accepted and he lost the belt. Yokozuka beat Hogan to regain the belt on June 13, 1993 with some help from a ringside photographer, but dropped the title to Hart at WrestleMania X on March 20, 1994. In April of 1995, he teamed with Owen Hart to win the WWF World Tag Team Championship. He died during a tour of England in 2000.

Born:	November 30, 1958
Height:	6'2"
Weight:	230
Real Name:	Thomas Erwin Zenk
High School:	Robbinsdale High School (MN)
College:	University of Minnesota
Trained by:	Eddie Sharkey, Brad Rheingans
Nickname:	Z-Man
Finisher:	Top Rope Dropkick
Career Span:	1984-1995

PPV Record:	4-9
Titles Won:	6
Best Opponents:	Arn Anderson, Bobby Eaton, Steve Austin

Zenk, Tom

The popular Tom Zenk of Minnesota made a name for himself while in the Pacific Northwest working for Don Owen, and formed a standout tag team with Rick Martel known as the Can-Am Connection in the WWF. The "Z-Man," as he was known, was a finalist in the vacant AWA World Title battle royal in 1989, and turned up in WCW a short time later, partnered with Brian Pillman. The high-flying duo won a tournament for the U.S. Tag Team belts over the Freebirds on February 12, 1990. Later in the year, Zenk defeated Arn Anderson for the World Television Championship in Atlanta, winning the strap on December 4, 1990. He lost the belt in a return bout with Anderson on January 7, 1991. He was also a member of a World Six-Man Tag championship squad along with Big Josh and Dustin Rhodes.

Born:	July 27, 1980
Height:	6'0"
Weight:	225
Real Name:	Nicholas Theodore Nemeth
High School:	St. Edward High School (OH)
College:	Kent State University
Trained by:	Lance Storm, Steve Keirn
Identities:	Nicky
Finisher:	Sleeperhold
Career Span:	2004-Present

Ziggler, Dolph

PPV Record:	8-15, 1 NC
WrestleMania Record:	0-2
WWE *Raw* TV Record:	23-39, 5 NC
WWE *Smackdown* TV Record:	37-47, 1 Draw, 1 DCO, 1 NC
Titles Won:	6
Days as World Champion:	0
Age at first World Title Win:	30
Best Opponents:	Edge, Rey Mysterio Jr., Kofi Kingston

Ohio's own Dolph Ziggler was a talented amateur grappler, capturing three MAC championships while at Kent State, and entered the WWE developmental system in 2004. Two years later, he was buried among the five-man unit known as the Spirit Squad, and, in conjunction with the other members of the group, held the World Tag Team Title. Full of potential, Ziggler reemerged as a singles grappler in 2008 and formed a scripted relationship with Vickie Guerrero. He beat Kofi Kingston for the Intercontinental Title in 2010, and then defeated him again for the United States Championship in June of 2011. Also, for a very brief moment in February of 2011, he held the World Heavyweight Title, crowned by Guerrero, but was quickly dethroned by Edge on *Smackdown*. Ziggler's ultra confidence, athleticism, and crafty in-ring skills make him one of the WWE's top rising stars.

Statistical Notes

+ The WWE *Raw* television records include the time period of January 1, 1999 to December 31, 2011. The WWE *Smackdown* records are from April 29, 1999 to December 31, 2011.

+ Abbreviations: DCO is Double Countout, DDQ is Double Disqualification, and NC is No Contest.

+ Win/loss records include wins and losses incurred in tag team matches, handicap bouts, and any matches determined by disqualification or countout.

+ Loss count includes eliminations from battle royals or the Royal Rumble.

+ The ending year in "Career Span" is the final year they actively participated in a wrestling match—not counting any work done behind the scenes.

+ The title reign days of current champions have a cutoff of December 31, 2011.

+ The IWGP Heavyweight and AJPW Unified Triple Crown are included in "Days as World Champion" tabulations.

+ Professional wrestling is a sport in which match finishes are predetermined. Thus, win/loss records are not indicative of a wrestler's genuine success based on their legitimate abilities—but how much, or how little they were pushed by promoters.

Acknowledgments

As strange as it might sound, professional wrestling history is a complex labyrinth that has mystified researchers for decades. The aura of secrecy that has shrouded the business keeps those who partake in unraveling the sport's heritage quite busy; and it seems that as each year passes, more and more is finally revealed. I can only imagine where wrestling research will be in ten years, particularly as more historical databases appear online.

Of course, for me, a project of this magnitude could never have been accomplished without the help of many people. First and foremost, I would like to thank Amy Miller and everyone in the Interlibrary Loan department of the Broward County (FL) Library System, who provided me with a wonderful opportunity to research newspapers from all over the world—and trust me, I took advantage of the service, with over 500 requests over a period of several years. Days of research at the Jack Pfefer Collection housed at the University of Notre Dame was also pivotal, and curator George Rugg was helpful beyond belief.

The outstanding dedication and contributions of my fellow researchers was also crucial. Much gratitude goes out to historians J. Michael Kenyon, Don Luce, and Steve Yohe, who all have an unlimited knowledge on the subject, and promptly responded to my queries, regardless of the topic. These guys can write volumes on pro wrestling and have contributed to countless projects documenting its history. Yohe's penetrating biography of Ed "Strangler" Lewis is required reading for anyone interested in the sport's history.

I also have to thank historians and researchers Mark Hewitt, Fred Hornby, Steve Johnson, Greg Oliver, Dan Anderson, Koji Miyamoto, Tom Burke, Kit Bauman, George Lentz, Chuck Thornton, Haruo Yamaguchi, Daniel Chernau, Jim Zordani, Matt Farmer, Jim Mandl, Rich Tate, Dick Bourne, Hisaharu Tanabe, Glenn Helwig, Becky Taylor, Michael Norris, Karl Stern, Yasutoshi Ishikawa, Wayne Sine, Ronald Grosspietsch, Gerhard Schafer, and last but not least, the late Jim Melby, who was universally admired for his kindness and knowledge. He influenced me a great deal.

A special thanks to historians Libnan Ayoub and Scott Teal for not only being available to answer my questions, but for providing photos for this project from their vast collections. Libnan is the son of wrestling legend Wadi Ayoub, and is the author of *100 Years of Australian Professional Wrestling*. He is currently working on a documentary that will spotlight WCW in Australia between 1964 and 1978, and has a new website, www.worldwrestlinghistory.com.

Since 1968, Scott Teal has been documenting wrestling history and has over 100 publications to his credit. His company, Crowbar Press, has published fifteen autobiographies, and Scott has co-written nine of them, as well as has edited the others. Among them are highly recommended books by Lou Thesz, Nikita Koloff, and Ole Anderson. You can order his extraordinary works at his website, www.crowbarpress.com.

I must also thank John Pantozzi, Bob Bryla, and everyone affiliated with the Professional Wrestling Hall of Fame in Amsterdam, New York. Check out their website at www.pwhf.org, and make plans to visit this wonderful institution soon.

Dave Meltzer's ground-breaking *Wrestling Observer* newsletter was also a valuable resource as well as Graham Cawthon's website, www.thehistoryofwwe.com, which is a must see for any wrestling fan. Hours can also be spent at www.wrestlingclassics.com, a site that offers tons of history and has one of the best wrestling message boards on the Internet.

The professionalism of expert photographers Dr. Mike Lano, Peter Lederberg Bill Stahl, Dan Westbrook, Mike Mastrandrea, and George Tahinos made my job of obtaining pictures for this project easier than I could have ever imagined. I can't thank them enough for their unwavering assistance throughout this process. I recommend them to anyone in need of wrestling photography.

Dr. Mike Lano, wrestling's dentist journalist/historian, had his first newsstand magazine article with photos published in 1966. From that moment on, he's shot and covered nearly all the North American territories in their prime, plus Mexico, Japan, and Australia. His images have been featured in many magazines, including freelancing for the WWE, books, documentaries, and TV programs. He currently hosts a nationally syndicated radio show. You can contact Dr. Lano at Wrealano@aol.com.

Beginning in 1976, Pete Lederberg began collecting wrestling photos, and may possibly have the largest organized collection of photographs, negatives, and slides in the world. An accomplished photographer in his own right, he started shooting pictures for Paul Heyman and Eddie Gilbert in Continental in 1988, and continues to shoot at wrestling events around the country to this day. Check out his listings at his website, http://home.bellsouth.net/p/PWP-flwrestlingpix.

Bill Stahl picked up his first 35mm camera almost thirty years ago, and never could have imagined it would turn into a lifelong passion. Having refined his skills over the years by shooting sports and concerts, he is now ready to expand to portrait, fashion, and family photography. Check out his fantastic photos and contact him through his website, www.billstahlphotography.com.

Dan Westbrook has spent nearly thirty years photographing and writing about pro wrestling. Working out of the Los Angeles area, he served as the chief foreign correspondent for a number of Japanese newspapers and magazines beginning in 1972, and is currently putting together the highly anticipated book, *An Illustrated Archive of Southern California Wrestling in the 1960s*, which will cover both the WWA territory and the JWA in Japan.

Mike Mastrandrea is the SLAM! Wrestling staff photographer. The Toronto-based lensman has been shooting wrestling for over fifteen years. His work has been seen in publications across North America, Europe and Asia. http://slam.canoe.ca/Slam/Wrestling/Gallery/mastrandrea.html.

George Tahinos has been a wrestling photographer since 1993 and has worked for magazines in the United States, United Kingdom, Japan, Mexico, and Australia. He's photographed for many promotions, including ECW, TNA, ROH, WCW, 3PW, CZW, Shimmer, DGUSA, and other organizations throughout the NY-NJ-PA area.

The Wrestling Revue magazine archive is a spectacular resource, and with an online catalog of 6,000 images, www.wrestleprints.com, is definitely a place to spend time browsing. Brian Bukantis was of great help.

George Schire, an accomplished wrestling historian and author of the fantastic book, *Minnesota's Golden Age of Wrestling*, came through with a few needed photos at the last minute. I'd also like to recommend Jeff Leen's comprehensive biography of women's wrestling legend Mildred Burke entitled, *The Queen of the Ring*.

John Rauer, who also helped with some last minute pictures, is the producer of a Historic World Champions card collection. This enjoyable and informative series is a must-have, and can be seen at www.wrestlingsbest.com/collectibles/wrestuffcards017.html.

Additionally, there are many people involved in the business, family members of wrestlers and promoters, and other individuals who I consulted through the years. I'd like to thank: Dorothy Mondt Baldwin, Penny Banner, Richard Baumann, John Kim Bell, Mike Bothner, Richard Brown, Jane Byrnes and both the Byrnes and Riley families, Roger Carrier, Frank Cody, D'Angelo Dinero, Dr. Bruce Dunn, John Edgecumbe, Tom Ellis, Tina Farmer at the Boone County Library (AR), Viva Foy, Dory Funk Jr., Bob Geigel, Paul George, Holly Gilzenberg, Leilani Kai, Michael S. Karbo, John Ketonen, Dave Levin, Richard Longson, Ken Lucas, Eve Manoogian, Petros Manousakis, John McFarlin, Richard Muchnick, Sid Munn, Tommy Needham, Mark Nulty, Russell Owen, Geoff Pesek, Kevin Pesek, John Rohde, Bob Sand, Billy E. Sandow, Sandy Sparley, Dick Steinborn, Lou Thesz, Bob Thye, Diane Tourville, Bill and Nick Tragos, Maurice and Paul Vachon, Carol Walker, and Mikey Whipwreck.

On a personal note, I want to thank my editor, Jason Katzman, as well as Mark Weinstein and everyone at Skyhorse Publishing. Their guidance and recommendations turned fifteen years of research into a book I always hoped would be possible. The late Jim Cypher was a terrific literary agent and always offered sound advice. He is greatly missed.

Finally, a very special thanks goes out to my wife, Jodi, who believed in this project even before I did. I'd also like to thank Timothy and Barbara Hornbaker, Melissa Hornbaker, Virginia Hall, Frances Miller, and John and Christine Hopkins.

For more information on the history of professional wrestling, questions, or comments, go to www.legacyofwrestling.com.

Hardcore History

The Extremely Unauthorized Story of ECW

by Scott E. Williams

Photos by George Tahinos

Foreword by "The Franchise" Shane Douglas

Extreme Championship Wrestling (ECW) was one extreme contradiction piled on top of another. It was an incredibly influential company in the world of professional wrestling during the 1990s, yet it was never profitable. It portrayed itself as the ultimate in anti-authority rebellion, but its leadership was working covertly with the two wrestling giants, the WWF and WCW. Most of all, it blurred the line between real life and the fantasy world of professional wrestling like no other company, and many of those who thought they were conning others ended up being victims of the ultimate con.

Hardcore History: The Extremely Unauthorized Story of ECW offers a frank, balanced look at the evolution of the company, starting even before its early days as a Philadelphia-area independent group called Eastern Championship Wrestling and extending past the death of Extreme Championship Wrestling in 2001. Writer Scott E. Williams has pored through records and conducted dozens of interviews with fans, company officials, business partners, and the wrestlers themselves to bring you the most balanced account possible of this bizarre company.

$14.95 Paperback

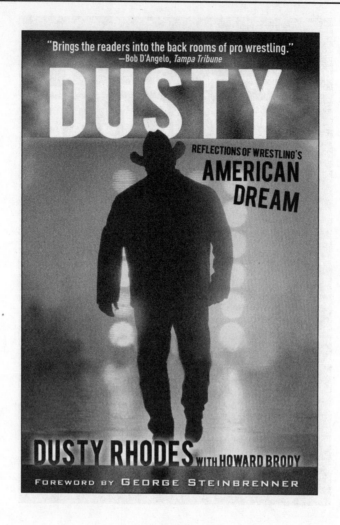

Dusty

Reflections of Wrestling's American Dream

by Dusty Rhodes with Howard Brody

Foreword by George Steinbrenner

For over two decades of pro wrestling, Dusty "the American Dream" Rhodes dominated the ring. Known for his jaw-dropping antics and bone-crunching skills, Rhodes became one of wrestling's first superstars. In this riveting narrative, Rhodes chronicles his journey through an industry plagued with political infighting, greedy promoters, destructive personalities, multi-millionaires, and great leaders.

$14.95 Paperback

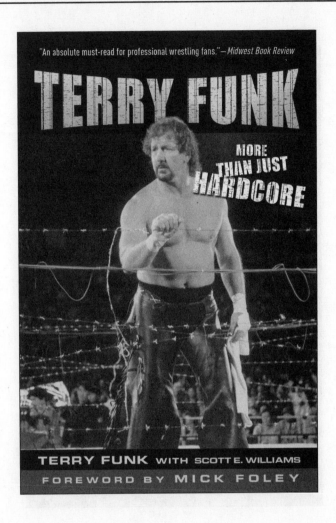

Terry Funk

More Than Just Hardcore

by Terry Funk with Scott E. Williams

Foreword by Mick Foley

He's been a fixture in professional wrestling for five decades. He helped introduce a hardcore wrestling style that you see in the WWE and Japan today. He's made his mark in Hollywood. He's Terry Funk, and this is his story. In this captivating look at the life of a living legend, Funk opens up about growing up in a wrestling family, working with various entertainment companies (including the ECW, WWE, and WWF), and so much more.

$16.95 Paperback

King of the Ring

The Harley Race Story

by Harley Race with Gerry Tritz

Foreword by Bret Hart

A true legend, Harley Race has enjoyed almost unparalleled success in the world of professional wrestling. Having turned pro in 1959 at the age of fifteen, he had a work ethic and innovative style that allowed him to become one of the three biggest names in wrestling during the 1970s and early '80s. He won the National Wrestling Alliance (NWA) championship on eight occasions and was dubbed World Wrestling Entertainment's first "King of the Ring" in 1986. His incredible journey from farm boy to international superstar is captured within the pages of *King of the Ring*. In addition to his legendary ring career, Harley Race also became a successful promoter in the Midwest during the mid 80s with a wrestling organization seen on thirteen television stations covering five states. Although injuries and a car accident in 1995 effectively ended his wrestling career, he decided to give back to the sport he loved. Race opened the World League Wrestling (WLW) organization in 1999, which serves both as a training camp and as a touring organization for young wrestlers. *King of the Ring* explores Race's life and career, both in and out of the ring, detailing everything from the grind of traveling 300 days a year to the glory of being a world champion. From the pitfalls and vices associated with professional wrestling to overcoming career threatening injuries and the death of his first wife, the Harley Race that readers will meet in *King of the Ring* is as candid as he is successful.

$14.95 Paperback

Becoming a Personal Trainer

2nd Edition

by Shannon Austin, M.S.

Becoming a Personal Trainer For Dummies®

Published by: **John Wiley & Sons, Inc.,** 111 River Street, Hoboken, NJ 07030-5774, www.wiley.com

Copyright © 2022 by John Wiley & Sons, Inc., Hoboken, New Jersey

Published simultaneously in Canada

For general information on our other products and services, please contact our Customer Care Department within the U.S. at 877-762-2974, outside the U.S. at 317-572-3993, or fax 317-572-4002. For technical support, please visit https://hub.wiley.com/community/support/dummies.

Wiley publishes in a variety of print and electronic formats and by print-on-demand. Some material included with standard print versions of this book may not be included in e-books or in print-on-demand. If this book refers to media such as a CD or DVD that is not included in the version you purchased, you may download this material at http://booksupport.wiley.com. For more information about Wiley products, visit www.wiley.com.

Library of Congress Control Number: 2022942839

ISBN 978-1-119-89148-2 (pbk); ISBN 978-1-119-89149-9 (ebk); ISBN 978-1-119-89150-5 (ebk)

SKY10035652_080922

Contents at a Glance

Table of Contents

Introduction

Maybe you're a fitness buff who would like to help people get healthy for a living. Or maybe you're already a professional personal trainer, and you want to boost your business or update your skills. Either way, *Becoming a Personal Trainer For Dummies* is for you.

You're in the right place at the right time. According to U.S. Bureau of Labor Statistics, the job market for personal trainers is expected to grow by 39 percent between 2020 and 2030. The COVID-19 pandemic shook up the fitness industry when 19 percent of boutique fitness studios and 14 percent of traditional gyms shut their doors for good, forcing all of us to rethink how we exercise. Working remotely made it easier for people to exercise at home, and according to the International Health, Racquet & Sportsclub Association (IHRSA), 68 percent of Americans plan to continue using online fitness services. This is great news for personal trainers! More people than ever are prioritizing exercise, and the sky's the limit for personal trainers looking to start or expand their businesses.

About This Book

Personal training requires more than the ability to bench-press your own body-weight or sprint without breaking a sweat. Personal training is a business, just like, say, a coffee shop, a doctor's office, or a grocery store. You need to have a solid grasp not only of exercise, but also of marketing, business structures, legal issues, accounting, customer service, certification, and more.

Not to worry! I know that's a lot to think about and I'm here to help. In *Becoming a Personal Trainer For Dummies,* I give you the scoop on everything you need to know to start, run, and even expand your personal training business.

This book tells you all the stuff you really want to know, such as:

- >> How do I know if personal training is for me?
- >> How do I become certified?
- >> How do I write a business plan?

- » Should I go solo or work for someone else?
- » How do I get clients?
- » Do I need an accountant, lawyer, and insurance broker?
- » How do I perform an initial consultation and fitness assessment?
- » How do I create exercise plans that will get results for my clients?
- » How do I keep my clients motivated?
- » What are some ways to expand my business?

Foolish Assumptions

They say that to assume makes an ass out of you and me, but I'm going to take that risk — because I assume certain things about you, dear reader. I assume that you're interested in personal training. I also assume that you have some basic knowledge of anatomy and physiology, cardiovascular exercise, and weight training. You may already be certified, or you may be studying for your certification. Or you may even be a full-fledged professional personal trainer who wants to build your clientele or motivate your clients. Whether you're thinking about becoming a personal trainer or you're already training clients, there's something for everyone in this book.

How This Book Is Organized

Becoming a Personal Trainer For Dummies is divided into five parts. The chapters within each part give you more detailed information on each topic within that part. Here's an overview:

Part 1: Shaping Up to Be a Personal Trainer

So you want to be a personal trainer. What type of trainer do you want to be? What kinds of clients do you want to work with? And most important, how do you get started? If you don't know the answers to these common questions, this part is for you. I give an overview of the personal training business and tell you how you can get a piece of the action, including tips on developing your personal training identity, finding your niche, getting certified, interning and apprenticing, and weighing the pros and cons of going into business for yourself.

Part 2: Becoming a Successful Personal Trainer

Before you start training clients, you need to have all of your business ducks in a row — like a business plan, a business name, a record-keeping system, a marketing plan, and a support system of professionals, such as a lawyer and an accountant. If you jump into training without these basics, you can land in trouble when, say, the taxes are due, you want a business loan, or you have so many clients that you can't keep track of them (because you don't have a record-keeping system!). That's what this part is all about. I also tell you not only how to bring in clients, but how to keep them coming back with tips and tricks that will help keep them happy and motivated.

Part 3: Putting the Personal into Personal Training

Clients — they're the people who make your business a business. Without them, you'd be doing deadlifts all by your lonesome. That's why in this part, I tell you all about how to understand, work with, and advance your clients. You'll find out how to perform an initial consultation and a fitness assessment, plus how to create individualized exercise programs and how to advance your clients to the next level.

Part 4: Growing Your Personal Training Business

When you're ready to get big — and we're not talking about your muscles — this part is for you. To expand your business, you may need to hire employees — and in this part, I tell you how to hire, motivate, and alas, fire workers. You can also expand by offering additional services like online training, workshops, and nutrition coaching services, or by selling products like exercise equipment. In this part, I show you how.

Part 5: The Part of Tens

You may notice that *Becoming a Personal Trainer For Dummies* is chock-full of valuable information. In this part, I put that information into easy-to-read lists for your convenience. I offer ideas to expand your services, highlight equipment that will help your clients reach their goals, and outline ways to be the best personal trainer you can be.

Icons Used in This Book

Icons are those little pictures you see in the margins of this book, and they're meant to grab your attention and steer you toward particular types of information. Here's what they mean:

The Tip icon points you to great strategies for running your personal training business.

I use this icon to give you helpful reminders. This is information that you may already know but that's easy to forget.

This icon flags information about potential pitfalls to your business, from business snafus to common exercise mistakes to client-relations gaffes.

This icon flags information that's great to know but isn't mandatory for your success as a personal trainer. You can use this information to impress your buddies in the gym, but if you're short on time, you can skip this material without missing anything critical.

I use this icon to tell a story about my adventures in personal training. You can discover a lot from these stories!

Beyond the Book

In addition to the abundance of information and guidance related to starting your career as a personal trainer that I provide in this book, you get access to even more help and information online at Dummies.com. Check out this book's online Cheat Sheet. Just go to www.dummies.com and search for "Becoming a Personal Trainer For Dummies Cheat Sheet."

Where to Go from Here

If you want to know everything there is to know about becoming a personal trainer, read this book from cover to cover. You'll get a thorough overview of what it takes to start and run a successful business, and you'll even find out about things you may not have thought of, such as how to write a marketing plan, how to name your business, and where to find a mentor who can guide you to success. You'll also find out what training clients actually entails, from taking a brand new client through an initial assessment to advanced program design for your experienced clients.

If you want to find out about a specific topic, flip to that page and start reading. For example, if you plan to take your certification test, you can turn to Chapter 2 to get study tips. You can read any section in the book without reading what comes before or after — though I may refer you to other parts of the book for related information.

And with that, it's time to dig into what it takes to become a personal trainer!

1

Shaping Up to Be a Personal Trainer

So you've decided to become a personal trainer. Congratulations! This part is for you.

First, I give you all the basics you need to get started. I tell you what it takes to be a personal trainer — and I don't mean muscles. Mental agility, listening skills, and professionalism are all important traits. I also give an overview of personal training, information on how to get certified, and details on how to find out more by interning or apprenticing.

Do you want to work with the general population? Pregnant women? Seniors? Kids? In this part, I help you decide what kind of personal trainer you want to be and whom you want to work for. I also help you answer that most important of questions: Do you want to work as an employee or as an independent contractor?

IN THIS CHAPTER

» **Understanding what personal trainers do**

» **Assessing your strengths and limitations**

» **Learning what's involved with getting certified**

» **Helping your clients reach their goals**

» **Planning to start and build your business**

Chapter 1

Introducing the World of Personal Training

When it comes to choosing or changing your career, you probably want to do something you enjoy, right? Well, here's news that should interest you: Most personal trainers love their jobs. According to a 2021 survey of 837 personal trainers by the Personal Trainer Development Center (an online fitness business education company), respondents were asked to rate their job satisfaction on a scale of 1 to 5. The average response was 3.7 — good news considering that in 2021, two-thirds of personal trainers were laid off, furloughed, or otherwise lost income due to the COVID-19 pandemic.

Numbers don't lie — personal training is indeed a fulfilling and rewarding profession. Helping your clients improve their health and fitness as a result of your guidance is an incredible experience.

To an outsider, personal training may look pretty easy — you just stick your client on a piece of equipment, throw some weight on the stack, and count reps for an hour, right? Not exactly. This chapter gives you the scoop on what it takes to become a personal trainer and how you can get started in this challenging and rewarding field.

Determining Whether You and Personal Training Are a Good Fit

If I asked you what a successful personal trainer looks like, what would you envision? Someone in great shape, with California good looks, a bright white perma-smile, and an everlasting bronze tan? Now what if I asked you what an unsuccessful personal trainer looks like? Maybe you'd think of your local gym rat, perched on top of the piece of gym equipment you want to use, glorifying the benefits of the latest fad supplement.

Truth be told, you can't tell a "good" trainer from a "bad" trainer based on looks alone. No matter how much a person looks the part on the outside, what makes trainers good is what they have on the inside — solid skills, knowledge, experience, intuitiveness, dedication, professionalism, and understanding. Take all those attributes, roll them up with the ability to teach, and — voilà! — you have the stuff great trainers are made of.

The question is, do *you* have that stuff?

Defining the role of a personal trainer

By definition, a *personal trainer* is a fitness professional who uses the body's response to exercise to improve clients' overall physical health. Trainers do all the following:

>> Perform in-depth evaluations of their clients' base fitness levels.

>> Prescribe exercises appropriate for their clients' level of conditioning and specific fitness goals.

>> Show clients how to properly implement the prescribed exercises.

>> Monitor and record clients' progress, making adjustments as necessary to ensure clients reach their goals in a safe and healthy manner.

REMEMBER

Think that's the whole shebang? Not quite. Personal trainers wear many hats! When working with clients, personal trainers act as friend, teacher, motivator, accountability partner, troubleshooter, therapist, equipment rep, and wellness advisor, all wrapped up in one. When working alone, personal trainers take on the roles of secretary, salesperson, student, accountant, business owner, and customer-service rep.

Knowing what skills you need

Being a personal trainer requires more than knowing exactly where your gluteus maximus is, or what the best exercise is to keep it from drooping. As a trainer, you need many skills to match the many roles you play for your clients. Here are some of the skills you need to hone before putting up your shingle.

You need to be accountable

You alone — not your clients, not your mother, not your annoying neighbor with the yappy dog — are responsible for yourself and your actions. If you're continually coming up with reasons (read "excuses") as to why you were late, why you didn't write out the new travel program, or why you had to cancel, clients and employers will lose trust in you. Being able to own up to the truth of your actions and working to prevent those snafus from happening in the future gains you trust and credibility in the eyes of your peers.

REMEMBER

When you're a trainer, your credibility and reputation will make or break you.

You need to be agile

No, I don't mean physically agile! (I *know* you can touch your toes!) In this case, I mean *mentally* agile — as in, able to come up with a completely different course of action on the fly if the original plan isn't working out. Working with people's bodies requires insight and the ability to identify problems and come up with solutions. Each client is unique, and what works for one client may not work for another.

TRUE
STORY

These days, many of my clients are cancer survivors and still have lingering side effects from treatment. Even when they are physically able to exercise, some days they're just too tired. It's hard to know ahead of time if a client isn't going to feel up to exercising, so I always have a backup plan for low-energy days. We work hard when energy is high, and when it's not, maybe we spend time walking and stretching instead. This might seem like a waste of time, but meeting clients where they're at and adjusting to their needs helps me earn their trust and encourages them to keep showing up, even when the going gets tough.

You need to be a good teacher

Good teachers understand that not all students learn the same way. Some are visual learners, some do better with verbal instructions, and others need a hands-on approach. They watch their students carefully to discover how they learn and match their teaching methods to their students' learning needs.

TIP

As a personal trainer, you need to understand each client's learning style if you expect them retain what you teach. Getting to know people is a process and it takes some time to figure out how to make information stick. That's okay.

You need to be a good leader

Good leaders inspire people to do their best by walking the talk, and a good personal trainer should be a positive role model for their clients. The old "do as I say, not as I do" adage doesn't cut it in this biz. You won't be getting any repeat business if you expect your clients to show up when they're busy and stressed out if you're constantly bailing on your workouts when life gets in the way. People naturally want to follow someone who is confident and relatable. In this profession, that means supporting your clients, even when they have setbacks, and they inevitably will. Life happens. We're all human (yes, even you) and your clients will appreciate that you know that.

You need to be a good listener

Sometimes, being a personal trainer feels like being a therapist — the closer you get to your clients, the more they open up about themselves. By listening more than talking, you'll find out a lot about who your clients really are. That can help you understand where they're coming from, why they're really working with you, and what some of their challenges might be.

You need to be a good observer

In addition to being a good listener, you need to be a good observer. Sometimes, your clients will tell you something different from what they're *really* thinking or feeling. Figuring out how to read your clients' body language, tone of voice, and physical cueing will help to improve your communication with your clients and the exercise programs you create for them.

You need to be knowledgeable

These days, trainers are expected to know the answers to just about everything related to health and wellness. Should I try the (fill-in-the blank diet)? What's cryotherapy? Why do I need to stretch? Of course you have to master the technical aspects of training, but you should know what science is saying about the latest trends. Being able to separate fact from fiction — and explain the difference — helps you help your clients. And by the way, it's okay to say "I don't know, but I will find out and get back to you."

You need to be likeable

Have you ever met someone who rubbed you the wrong way from the start? You can't quite put your finger on what it is about them that bugs you, but for some reason you two simply don't hit it off. For one reason or another, not every client is going to like you — and you aren't going to love every client. It's okay not to like a client; just remember that you are a professional and this person deserves the same high level of service all your clients expect from you.

TIP

Being likeable doesn't mean everyone will like you. Developing rapport with clients *is* easier if they like you, and sometimes helping them feel more comfortable with you is all it takes to create a smooth start to the relationship. Gauging their personality type and communication style helps. If your client is the strong-but-silent type, recognize this, and don't blab away about the latest strongman competition on ESPN. See Chapter 9 for information about assessing clients' personality types and learning styles to help you provide the best program for them.

You need to be passionate

Caring about what you do and the people you do it for is essential to being a good trainer. That means being present with your client, with every ounce of your attention focused on them. It means always giving 100 percent. It means being upbeat and positive, and showing your clients how enthusiastic you are about helping them achieve success.

Have you ever been in a gym and witnessed a trainer sitting down on the floor or on a piece of equipment, staring off into space while their client struggles through an exercise? Have you also watched a trainer taking a client through what looks to be a pretty challenging workout, all the while smiling and offering encouragement? Which trainer would *you* want to work with?

You need to be professional

Being professional in a plush corner office with a view looks easy. It's not so easy when you're a personal trainer on your tenth client of the day, completely exhausted, and running late because of a traffic accident. Your client yells at you (even though it wasn't your fault) and now you're boiling mad. No matter how badly you want to walk out, professionalism means you apologize for the inconvenience and get on with the session.

You need to be positive

Much like that nasty strain of the flu that goes around every year (but without the nausea), enthusiasm is contagious. If you maintain an upbeat outlook, you'll be able to keep yourself and those around you motivated. Working out is hard enough for your client without having to deal with a grumpy trainer on top of it. Your clients aren't paying you to lament about your woes of the day. They hired you to help them, not be a sounding board for your current woes.

You need to be understanding

Sometimes your clients are at the top of their game, they are consistently making time for exercise, they follow your programs to a t . . . and sometimes life happens. You wanted to be a personal trainer so you could help people, right? Being understanding means recognizing when your clients are struggling and offering support instead of lecturing them when they are already stressed out. Your job is to help your clients fit fitness into their lives. Not the other way around.

REMEMBER

When your clients don't follow your plan, it's probably not about you. More likely, what you suggested doesn't work for them for whatever reason. You need to understand what went wrong — why they didn't/wouldn't/couldn't stick with the program. When you understand why the plan isn't working, you'll be able to adjust it so your client can be successful.

Assessing your skills

No matter how much you know about adenosine triphosphate or how well you can demonstrate the clean and jerk (if you think that's a system for getting your significant other to pick up their dirty socks, you're in trouble), knowledge and technique are only a small part of what makes a successful personal trainer. How you do your job on a day-to-day basis and doing the right things consistently will make you successful and your work enjoyable.

For all the aspects of personal training that you can control — like your attitude and your knowledge — there are twice as many intangible things that you can't — like your schedule, your work location, the type of people you work with, your management, and so on. These are the little things that you can't plan for and that make any job loveable or leave-able. The personal training industry has quite a few intangibles that have been known to break a trainer or two. So before you sign up for the job, take an honest look at yourself and decide whether you have what it takes.

Answer *true* or *false* to the following statements to determine whether you've got the goods for personal training:

>> I am at my best any time of the day.

>> I get along with most people, and I can treat the others with respect and professional courtesy.

>> I can do several things well at once. (Walking and chewing gum doesn't count.)

>> I have a flexible schedule.

>> I enjoy working with different types of people.

>> I enjoy a fast-paced life.

>> I perform well under stress.

>> I am organized.

>> I am good at planning.

>> I am a self-starter.

>> I am detail-oriented.

>> I can communicate my thoughts clearly and concisely.

>> I enjoy explaining "why."

>> I enjoy being challenged.

>> I enjoy helping others.

>> I have a thirst for learning.

>> I enjoy being mobile.

If you answered false to five or more of these statements, you may find the demands of being a personal trainer challenging. These statements represent typical, day-to-day life for a trainer — and I'd hate to see you invest all your time, energy, and effort breaking into the field, only to find out that it's not what you thought it would be.

Hitting the Books: Getting Certified

So you know how to perform a perfect squat? That's great, but knowing how to do a squat doesn't mean squat when it comes to being a good personal trainer. Before you jump into the job, you'll need to practice, study, cram for exams, rehearse, train, and drill. (Okay, I'll back slowly away from the thesaurus now and keep my hands where you can see them.) You'll also need a sheet of paper from an accrediting agency proving that you did all the above.

These days, personal trainers are looked to as experts in the field of fitness — not just gym rats who can bench-press their own bodyweight and yell, "No pain, no gain!" Apply for the position of personal trainer at any gym, and the first thing they'll ask is, "Are you certified?" Certification is a badge of honor — it tells prospective employers or clients that you know what you're doing. Being certified also builds your credibility — and credibility attracts clients.

TIP

Finding the right certification for you is important — you don't want to pay for a test that's geared toward athletic training when you're looking to work with seniors, or one that requires a four-year degree in kinesiology if you don't have one. In Chapter 2, I provide all the information about certification that you need.

Getting Started

Are you ready to get out there and train the heck out of those people who need your services so badly? Great! So what's stopping you? Time's a-wastin'! Go on, get to it!

"Wait just a second," you say. "How can I get started if I don't have anyone to start with?" All dressed up but no place to go? Don't quite know where to find those people who need your services so badly? Never fear. Keep reading, and that little obstacle will soon be but a fading memory.

Creating your plan of attack

All the training, reading, studying, and practicing you do to hone your personal training skills to perfection won't make a darn bit of difference if you don't have any clients to use them on.

TIP

Lay out your goal in advance, then work backward from there. For example, if you want to train clients at a gym, your plan of attack may look like this:

1. Contact a few area gyms and ask what certifications and experience they require.

2. Decide which certification you are getting and sign up for the exam. (See Chapter 2 for more details.)

3. Study for and take the exam.

4. Fulfill any other job prerequisites (CPR training, for example).

5. Apply for the position you want. (See Chapter 4 for the scoop on résumés and interviewing.)

6. Intern or get the job. (Chapter 3 tells you all about apprenticing.)

7. Train clients! (See Part 3 for the scoop on training clients.)

PREPARING FOR SUCCESS

The power of the mind is an awesome thing. Stepping into a new career or taking on new responsibilities can be scary, and maybe you're a little doubtful that you'll succeed. We've all been there before — we look over what's involved, shake our heads, and ask, "Can I do it?" If you feel that kind of doubt creeping up on you, shake it off and set your mind straight. Even though you may need to step back and reevaluate what you're doing once in a while, don't let the little voices in your head convince you that you won't be successful.

Having a positive mindset and the core belief that you *can* succeed and *will* succeed keeps you going on the tough days, energizing you to push on toward your goal. *Remember:* What the mind can conceive the body will achieve!

When you lay out your plan step-by-step, staying on track and identifying any potential pitfalls before they occur is much easier. This habit is a good one to get into, because you'll be using this method frequently with clients, outlining step-by-step how they can reach their goals.

REMEMBER

Right now you're probably champing at the bit to get your hands on some "body" to work on! But personal training is definitely an art — and one that has to be practiced to get it right. Taking bodyfat measurements, spotting an exercise, and estimating VO_2max are not skills that anyone is born with. Don't be shy about asking friends and family if you can practice on them while you are honing your skills, creating your plan of attack, and building your base.

Personal trainer for hire: Getting work

TRUE
STORY

Getting your first client is a momentous occasion. I can still remember how I got mine over 20 years ago. At the time I was teaching group fitness classes at the YMCA and a student from one of my classes asked if I was also a personal trainer. I told her that I had just passed my personal trainer certification exam and hadn't yet worked with any personal training clients. She was happy to be my first client and I worked out a deal with the Y where I was able to offer personal training to members and the Y received a percentage of my fee.

No matter how it happens for you, getting hired for the first time is exciting. All you need to start is one client — one single, solitary person who wants to get healthy through exercise. People will see you working with your client and approach you, or, if you're training in a private setting, your client will tell their friends about how wonderful you are (and you *are* wonderful!). Trust me — referrals are the best clients (more about that in Chapter 8) and nothing boosts your business faster than psyched clients pumping you up to their friends.

If your services aren't stellar or if a client is dissatisfied, word-of-mouth or a negative online review can damage your business way more than a positive review will help it.

Building your base

After you have a few clients on board, you'll be a bona fide personal trainer, managing multiple exercise programs for multiple clients. Thinking about your time constraints (How many people can you train in a day?), examining your career goals (Do you want to make lots of moolah? Work part-time? Hobnob with celebrity clients?), and choosing how you work with clients will help you lay the foundation for a viable personal training business. For instance, if you're going to make this a full-time deal, do you want to keep your client base small and concentrate on long-term clients? Or do you want to work with people short-term so that you can continually work with new clientele? After gaining experience with in-person clients, maybe you will find that online personal training is the best fit for you. There are so many options and no right or wrong way to do it — you get to decide what's best for you and your clients. When you know what that is, you can gear your service offerings and build your client base accordingly.

Performing Your Art

As I've said, personal training involves much more than knowing one muscle from another. Customer service, planning client programs, following up, and everything in between are the elements that will take your personal training from so-so to so great!

Making a great first impression

Did you know that most people have a solid impression of who you are within the first seven seconds of meeting you? That means your first client meeting is *the* most important meeting in your client relationship. You want to start out on the right foot, because you are — hopefully — going to be working very closely with this person for a long time. No matter what happened that day, even if your cat ate your goldfish and you got a speeding ticket, leave it at the door. It's time to take a deep breath, smile, and introduce your best self to your new client.

THE MIDAS TOUCH

Clients might choose you for your knowledge and enthusiasm, but it's the little touches — and consistent attention to those touches — that will keep them coming back. When I opened my first studio, the space was small and I didn't have much equipment. I worried that my clients would miss the amenities from the big health club that I left. To my pleasant surprise, they were happier in my little 800-square-foot studio that I started on a shoestring budget. Why? Because my attention to details made their experience great. It was easier for me to give each client my full attention without the crowded gym scene. It was also possible to keep my equipment clean and organized when nobody else was using it. We didn't have to wait in line to use machines. I could stop to fill their water bottles mid-session without losing valuable training time running across the big gym to the water fountain. I put a couch and coffee table by the front door so they could unwind for a few minutes when they arrived after a busy day at work. These are a few of the small things that made a big difference and made my clients feel at home in my business.

REMEMBER

If you're happy, you exude confidence and excitement, and your client will pick up on your positive outlook. If you're blue, getting your client excited about doing crunches and lat pulldowns will be difficult.

I delve deeper into the topic of making a good first impression in Chapter 10.

Evaluating your client

Before you start your client on a program, you need to evaluate their medical history, current fitness level, and lifestyle habits. Knowing as much about your client as possible is important — after all, their health is in your hands. If you prescribe an exercise program that doesn't account for your client's schedule or their *current* fitness level, they'll probably feel discouraged when it doesn't work. You can't expect a woman with three young kids to succeed with a two-hour-per-day routine, or a client who's mainly concerned with heart health to get excited about doing exercises to build bigger biceps.

TIP

Put on your investigator hat and ask your clients as many questions as you can think of. For example, you can query them about their:

>> Exercise habits (past and current)

>> Medical history

>> Lifestyle

>> Health goals

A lot of trainers skip this step. I can't overemphasize the importance — from both a professional and liability standpoint — of evaluating your clients. For more information on client evaluations, see Chapter 10.

Establishing a program for your client

If you liked science in school, you're going to love this — creating programs is like coming up with a new hypothesis for each client you work with. You come up with a theoretical program based on your assessment of the client, and then you get to test your theory and see if it holds up. You need to take into account your client's time availability, equipment availability, strengths, weaknesses, and goals to create a program that they'll not only find doable, but also enjoy. Here is where you, the trainer, get to shine as you take your client from where they are to where they want to be. (And if you didn't like science, don't worry — I make it easy for you in Chapter 12.)

Conducting a training session

If you ask any trainer what the best part of their job is, you'll most likely hear "training clients." Taking clients through training sessions is fun! After all, that's why you got into personal training in the first place — to work with clients hands-on, showing them the proper way to exercise, encouraging and supporting them, and helping them achieve their fitness goals. And now that the hard work — finding your client, assessing their needs, planning the program — is behind you, you can actually put your plan into motion and see how it works!

REMEMBER

The only trick is, you'll need to create plans for your clients that break their goals into manageable steps, that keep them motivated, and that get results. More on how to do this in Part 3.

Staying in touch

Every good salesperson knows that the follow-up is crucial to making sales and keeping customers happy — and so should you.

TIP

Call or text your clients, whether they're active with you or not. Follow-up calls or texts to active clients can help you determine the effectiveness of your previous training sessions, or provide an opportunity to answer questions about a new workout routine. Follow-up calls or texts to inactive clients can bring them back to you for more training. However you decide to handle following up, remember that it's a key to maintaining healthy client relations. The personal training industry is based on relationships, and nurturing your client relationships is vital to the success of your business.

Meeting your clients, evaluating them, planning programs, conducting training sessions, and following up — these are the basics of performing your art, and I delve into these topics more in Parts 2 and 3.

Our Little Trainer's All Grown Up! Growing Your Business

Eventually, you may want to kick your personal training business up a notch. Growing your personal training business means different things to different people. It could mean accepting a management position at a gym, or leaving a gym to start your own studio. However and whenever the bug bites, you need to plan, plan, and plan some more in order to be successful.

Preparing for growth

Getting ready to grow is exciting and invigorating. The prospect of tackling new business and career challenges excites a lot of trainers. But before you jump into anything, do your homework to make sure your vision is viable. Your future is at stake here, and a mistake at this point in the game can be costly.

TIP

List the pros and cons of making your change. Talk with people who have been in your shoes and ask how they handled the decision. Make sure you have everything you need — financial support, skills, knowledge, and the right tools — should you decide to make the change. Involve those close to you so they can give you the emotional support you need.

For more information on determining your career path, check out Chapter 4.

Adding additional income streams

If you're looking to increase your income — and who isn't? — you don't necessarily have to increase your working hours. Trainers have plenty of ways to add dollars to their bottom line without spending more time. Selling fitness-related products that clients can use on their own, such as heart-rate monitors or foam rollers, is a great way to make extra cash while helping your clients. Offering online training is another option and one that became very popular during the pandemic.

I'll give you the 411 on adding profit centers in Chapter 16.

Duplicating yourself

Another way to grow is to bring on trainers who can handle additional clients. Because no one will be an exact duplicate of you (and if someone is, be afraid, be very afraid), before hiring, you need to create a list of attributes and qualities you feel the candidate should possess. Check with your lawyer and accountant to understand your state's laws regarding employment. Create a job description for the position so your new hires will have a clear understanding of what is expected from them.

You can find more information on hiring staff in Chapter 17.

Maintaining consistency within your business

A successful business provides its customers with consistent quality and service. (And I probably don't need to say this, but the quality and service must be consistently *good*.) Have you ever noticed how you can order your favorite drink at any Starbucks location and it's always the same? That's because there are systems in place that are consistent no matter which location you visit. You can expect the same experience every time.

REMEMBER

If you can't give dependable service, your clients won't be around for long. You need to strive to create a great experience for your clients each time they work with you. That means you must provide the same training to all your staff members; document your rules and policies; make sure everyone on board understands your company's vision, mission, and objectives; and most important, make sure that that you are the embodiment of what you preach — that you lead by example. You have to walk the talk.

Chapter **2**

Getting Certified

L ots of people dream of becoming a personal trainer so that they can help other people. Some are former athletes and others changed their own lives by getting fit and want to help people like them do the same. Whatever your reason is, the fact that you've picked up this book shows you know that there's more to personal training than just enjoying your daily workouts. Success is in the details. What kind of a trainer do you want to be? Who is it you want to train — kids, seniors, elite athletes? Do you want to train your clients in groups or one-on-one? And, most important, why do you want to train them?

Once you have an idea of what kind of personal training you want to do, you'll need to decide which letters you want after your name — that is, what kind of certification you should get. No two certifications are exactly alike, and clients and employers take some more seriously than others.

In this chapter, I help you figure out which clients you'd like to work with, consider whether you want to train individuals or groups (or both), choose the best certification for you, study for (and pass) the test, and keep your credentials up to date. Think of the information in this chapter as the foundation for your career as a personal trainer — if you cut corners where these decisions are concerned, your house might fall down around you. But if you give these decisions the attention they require, your strong foundation will last you for many years to come.

IT'S A GOAL!

A goal is more than a point in hockey — it's something that will help you decide who to work with, where to work (at a health club, say, or a corporate facility), and whether to work for yourself or for someone else. Do you dream of training athletes someday? Then you probably should focus on learning as much as you can about training active people. If your goal is to help kids become healthy adults, then becoming certified to work with children is a smart choice. And if the thought of being your own boss makes your heart go bang-shang-a-lang, you'll probably take a different path from someone whose goal is to work at a posh health club.

Take a minute to write down your goals — the reasons you want to become a personal trainer — and keep them in mind as you read the rest of this chapter. They'll help you decide which certification is best for you and what type of personal trainer you want to be.

Finding Your Niche

The type of certification you seek is directly tied to the kinds of clients you hope to work with. In this section, I help you find the place where you can best put your skills and talents to use.

Considering the possibilities

When personal trainers talk about their businesses, they often use the term *client population*, which is just a fancy name for the type of people they work with. Each client population has its own needs, advantages, and disadvantages. In the following sections, I cover some of the most common types of client populations. As you read these descriptions, make a mental note of the groups that most appeal to you.

Apparently healthy adults

This population is the one you'll probably encounter the most —adults who want to lose a few pounds or get into a regular exercise routine to improve their overall health. These clients might have a few aches or pains; for the most part though, they have a clean bill of health. That's why I'm referring to them as apparently healthy — you'll still need to do a complete assessment to find out exactly what you're working with. Generally, your primary personal training certification covers everything you'll encounter in training this population, including when you need to ask for a physician's clearance.

TIP

Apparently healthy adults are a great group to get your feet wet with, even if your goal is to eventually work with one specific client population. After you're comfortable working with these clients, you might decide to study for a specialty certification and focus on training one specialized group, like some in the following sections.

Seniors

Working with seniors is a lot of fun and so rewarding. Older adults don't require a completely different set of skills from you as a trainer, but you do need to understand how aging affects the body. Have you ever noticed an older person dragging their feet or "shuffling" when they walk? Shuffling is a common cause for falls because dragging feet tend to catch and trip on stuff. That's just one example; there's a lot more to keep in mind if you're training older adults, and a certification specific to this group will teach you what you need to know.

WARNING

It's common for older people to have chronic medical issues that can become worse if you don't know what you're doing. And with seniors having less range of motion and strength than they did when they were younger, they can easily injure themselves without proper exercise instruction. *Remember:* This shouldn't discourage you from working with seniors — it just means that, before you start working with them, you need to understand their unique needs.

Check out the Appendix for a list of recommended senior fitness specialty certifications.

Kids and teens

If you like spending time with kids, training young clients could be a great option for you. Kids and teens need an hour of physical activity every day to be at their best, and teaching them early that being active is fun will set them up for a lifetime of healthy exercise habits. You should focus first on making physical activity fun and then getting creative when you include structured exercise (think teaching them how to start lifting weights safely). Learning what they like to do is the key to making exercise something that they will actually want to do.

WARNING

Unlike adults, children have underdeveloped thermoregulatory systems, which is just a fancy way of saying they're more prone to overheating. Pay extra attention if you're training kids when it's hot out and always make sure they're staying hydrated.

There are specific guidelines for training kids and teens; see the Appendix to learn more.

Pregnant women

Don't assume that pregnant women can't or shouldn't exercise. That used to be common advice, but we know now that being physically active is beneficial for all women with healthy and uncomplicated pregnancies. If you're going to train pregnant or postpartum women, make sure you're familiar with the guidelines (yes there are specific exercise guidelines for pregnant women) and understand how to structure their exercise programs to match their individual goals and needs.

WARNING

Like kids, pregnant women are more prone to overheating when they exercise and it's important for them to stay hydrated. It's also not uncommon for fatigue and nausea to limit exercise options, especially during the first trimester. Pregnancy isn't the best time to expect major fitness gains, and a good rule of thumb is to encourage pregnant women to avoid contact sports or activities where they could fall.

Specializing in pre- and postnatal fitness requires mom-savvy knowledge and skills gained from a specialty certification. The Girls Gone Strong prenatal and postnatal coaching certification is the most comprehensive one I've seen.

Athletes

If your clients are weekend warriors with weekday desk jobs, they'll need exercise programs to keep them fit while also improving their golf swing or running a faster 10K race (for example). These clients are usually already in decent shape and need your to help to get better without getting hurt. It's also not uncommon for elite athletes to work with a team trainer and then hire a personal trainer to help them individually in their off-season. You don't have to be an expert in the sport to train these athletes, but you do need to understand their unique needs. This involves more than knowing which muscles do what — training athletes is challenging because they won't see the same dramatic improvements that your beginning clients achieve. A beginning client may go from walking a mile in 15 minutes to jogging a mile in 10 minutes in just a few months. For your elite athlete, shaving a second off their 40-yard dash time in a year can be the difference between another year of college football and being picked in the NFL draft. You'll need to get creative with advanced training programs and techniques if you're working with elite athletes.

Your basic certification will teach you a lot about training general population adults, but if you're serious about specializing in training elite athletes, I recommend finding a mentorship where you can get hands-on experience. I cover this more in Chapter 21.

Deciding which client group you're best suited for

TIP

Even if you eventually want to specialize in a client population like athletes or kids, you should probably start out working with healthy adults. Not only will you build a bigger client base to help get your business off the ground, but many certifying bodies also recommend earning a primary certification in personal training before testing for a specialized certification. For example, to be certified as a Performance Enhancement Specialist (PES) through the National Academy of Sports Medicine (NASM), you don't have to be certified as a personal trainer first, but it'll be tough to get through the exam without at least the baseline knowledge that a personal training certification provides. Skipping these basics would be kind of like trying to learn a new subject in a language that you don't speak. Sounds frustrating, right?

After you have your personal trainer certification and you're finding out who you enjoy working with from training a broad client base, you can zero in on training one client population and then focus on getting really good at it.

TIP

Still not sure which client population is right for you? Here's a quick quiz that may help:

1. Which of these adjectives defines you best?

   a. Patient

   b. Careful

   c. Gung-ho

   d. Enthusiastic

   e. Slow and sure

2. If you weren't a personal trainer, you would be a:

   a. Teacher

   b. Doctor

   c. Drill sergeant

   d. Customer-service manager

   e. Eldercare nurse

3. Your favorite exercise style is:

   a. Hula hoop!

   b. Pilates

   c. CrossFit

   d. Endurance training

   e. Gentle yoga

If you answered mostly As, consider training kids; mostly Bs, try prenatal and postnatal women; mostly Cs, train athletes; mostly Ds, go for healthy adults; and mostly Es, seniors may be your client population.

TIP

Specializing in one client population isn't required and being a "generalist" could actually be your specialty. Even if training one type of client is your goal, you'll still be expected to have at least some knowledge about things like nutrition, sleep, managing stress — basically understanding how to help your clients to become overall healthy people no matter what their fitness goals are.

Becoming Certified

Watch out! It's the attack of the acronyms! ACE, ACSM, NASM — the choices in certifications are enough to make any aspiring personal trainer's head spin. In this section, I cover the various certifications available and help you decide which one is best for you.

Knowing your ABCs: The personal training alphabet

You're probably wondering which certification is the best one, right? Ask ten personal trainers this question and you're likely to get ten different answers! Do a Google search for "personal trainer certifications" and you'll find a million (yep, I counted) different certificates, programs, books, courses . . . you get the idea. Fitness is a multi-billion-dollar industry so naturally there's going to be some serious competition for your money. Sifting through the giant sea of information online when you're just getting started feels overwhelming if you don't know what to look for — knowing when it's best to just keep scrolling helps too.

THREE'S A CROWD: CHOOSING PERSONAL OR GROUP CERTIFICATION

Personal trainers can choose to work with individuals, groups, or both, and many organizations offer certifications in both of these options. If playing to a crowd gets your motor running, becoming a group fitness instructor may be for you. Teaching group fitness classes means leading different groups of people through pre-planned workouts. That's not a bad thing and it works well for lots of people, but it's not the same as working with individual clients and giving them your full attention. You can also offer small group personal training sessions where each client is following their own program and your attention is shared equally among the group. You can earn more money per hour by training several people at once while charging your clients less per session than you would for an individual session. Some clients love group personal training and others prefer individual sessions. It's up to you to decide what works best for you and your clients.

My introduction to group personal training happened on a Monday night in 2006 when I accidently double-booked myself during primetime (those are the busiest hours at the gym). Yes, I'm human too. Luckily both of my clients were understanding and one of them asked if I could just work with both of them since they were already there. That's exactly what we did, and to my surprise, they wanted to keep training together. They were each following their own program and I was easily able to coach one while the other was resting between sets. And there was some friendly competition that pushed them to work a little harder. When I opened my first personal training studio the following year, I only offered semi-private training with groups of two to four clients. There's nothing wrong with training clients individually, but I have found that most of my clients enjoy the camaraderie that group training provides without losing the individual attention they expect from me. It's also great for me because I can schedule more clients in fewer hours, which helps me to manage my time and energy. Again, it's up to you to decide what's best for you and for your clients.

It's also an option to be a group fitness instructor and a personal trainer if you like doing both. Teaching group fitness classes is fun and it's a great way to meet people who might also be looking for a personal trainer. Inviting personal training clients to try your group fitness classes is a great way to encourage them to exercise more often too.

One of the best places to start your search is the National Commission for Certifying Agencies (NCCA) website. The NCCA is an independent, non-governmental organization whose role is to develop standards of excellence for voluntary healthcare certification programs. Simply put, they set the bar for certifying agencies and only recognize those who meet or exceed industry standards. The NCCA accreditation is the gold standard for personal trainer certifications and many employers require you to have a certification with the NCCA stamp of approval before they will hire you. Check out the NCAA-accredited program search feature at `https://ice.learningbuilder.com/Public/MemberSearch/ProgramVerification`.

The best certification is the one that's best for you and your career goals.

Choosing a certification

Now comes the important part: choosing which certification you want to pursue. The tips in the following sections will help you make the decision that's right for *you*.

Ask for advice from personal trainers you respect

If you're looking for a good restaurant, chances are you'll ask for recommendations. Do this when you're comparing personal trainer certifications too.

Start by talking to personal trainers in your area. Ask them about their certification experiences. Don't be shy — most personal trainers love talking about their work!

Have you ever noticed how online reviews tend to be really great or really terrible? Most people won't take time to write neutral reviews, so you can bet that reading online reviews of the certifying organizations you're interested in will tell you a lot about why people love them or why they loathe them. Just keep in mind that online reviews aren't always objective and shouldn't be your only resource. Asking personal trainers who have gone through the certification process about their experience is helpful too. Ask them if they would recommend their certification to others. Why or why not?

Find out which certification is required at the places where you'd like to work

Dropping hundreds of dollars and spending lots of time getting a certification only to find out that the certification you received doesn't help you get a job would be more than annoying.

If you're planning to work in a health club or other business (as opposed to working for yourself), contact potential employers in your area or check their websites to find out which certifications they require or accept.

Find out what additional requirements the organizations have

You'd think that after you paid the fee, crammed your head full of facts, and passed the exam, you'd be all set. But most certifying bodies require that you be certified in CPR and/or Advanced First Aid, and some require having a college degree, or even having work experience in addition to passing their exam before you can be fully credentialed by their organization.

TIP

Check out the organizations' websites for specific information, and make sure you'll be able to meet their additional requirements before getting started.

Preparing for the Test

No matter which certification you choose, you'll need to pass an exam that shows you have what it takes to be a personal trainer. Organizations that require in-person (as opposed to online) testing offer exams on different dates in different testing centers around the country. Check out the organizations' websites for information on test dates and locations.

REMEMBER

If a certifying organization doesn't require you to take an exam, run — don't walk — in the other direction. The purpose of the exam is to weed out those people who give personal trainers a bad name. Your certification won't mean anything — to you or anyone else — if you don't have to pass an exam in order to get it.

Understanding the exams

To give you an idea of what you will need to know on test day, the following sections include a brief description of the content you can expect to see on five different NCCA-accredited personal trainer certification exams.

American Council on Exercise

The ACE personal trainer exam has 150 multiple-choice questions, and you have three hours to complete the in-person exam. The four types of questions you have to answer are "interview and assessment," "program design and implementation," "program modification and progression," and "professional conduct, safety, and risk management."

American College of Sports Medicine

The ACSM exam is also taken in person and you have two and a half hours to answer 135 multiple-choice questions (120 scored questions and 15 unscored questions). Questions are in the areas of "initial client consultation and assessment," "exercise programming and implementation," exercise leadership and client education," and "legal and professional responsibilities."

National Strength and Conditioning Association

To earn certification as an NSCA-CPT (Certified Personal Trainer), you have to pass a three-hour in-person examination that includes 140 scored multiple-choice questions and 14 non-scored multiple-choice questions focusing on client consultation/assessment, program planning, exercise techniques, safety/emergency procedures, and legal issues. Between 24 and 35 questions will be presented in a video or image, which assesses knowledge in the areas of exercise techniques, functional anatomy, and fitness testing protocols.

National Academy of Sports Medicine

The NASM exam has 120 multiple-choice questions (20 are research questions and aren't counted toward or against your total exam score) and covers these six domains: basic and applied sciences and nutritional concepts, client relations and behavioral coaching, assessment, program design, exercise technique and training instruction, and professional development and responsibility. You can take the exam online with a proctor (someone who will monitor you remotely while you are testing) or in person at an approved testing site, and either way you have two hours to finish.

International Sports Sciences Association

The ISSA's exam for their NCPT-CPT (that's short for National Council for Certified Personal Trainers-Certified Personal Trainer) certification consists of 140 multiple-choice questions (125 questions are scored and 15 questions aren't scored). Topics you'll need to understand for this exam include applied science (anatomy, kinesiology, physiology), nutrition, intake and ongoing evaluation, program design and implementation, exercise selection, technique and training instruction, and professional practice and responsibility. You'll need to find a Prometric testing center if you're taking this exam.

Making the grade

Unless you were born with expert knowledge of exercise science, fitness assessments, and human behavior, you'll need to study for the certifying examination.

Cramming the night before a test may have worked in high school, but this technique probably won't cut it for the personal training exam. Starting a few months before the exam, set aside an hour or two every day to study.

Getting ready to study

Make sure you have a quiet place — whether that's your kitchen or maybe a coffee shop with your noise-cancelling headphones turned on — where you can concentrate on the course materials. Turn off the TV, your music (unless listening to classical music or white noise helps you focus), and your internet connection (unless you're using online course materials). Silence your phone and make sure your study area is equipped with pencils, paper, and plenty of light.

REMEMBER

If your house resembles Grand Central Station, consider going to the library or a quiet cafe to do your studying — find a place where you can concentrate without distraction.

Finding course materials

Each certifying organization offers its own course materials to help you study for the exam. When you sign up to take the test, you may receive (or be able to purchase) textbooks, online study guides, sample tests, and access to live seminars and courses. Check out the certifying organizations' websites for information on the course materials that are available.

Take a look at — and practice taking — sample tests

Many of the certifying bodies have sample tests available on their websites. Check them out and ask yourself the following questions:

- **Do I understand the language?** For example, do you know what a quadratus lumborum is, if that's mentioned on the test?

- **Am I capable of performing everything that is required in the test?** For example, can you demonstrate the proper spotting technique for a flat dumbbell bench press, if that's a requirement on the test?

- **Can I recite the Karvonen formula while hopping up and down on one foot?** Okay, just kidding about that one.

- **Is the exam challenging enough to weed out those who would be better off simply working out in the gym versus teaching other people how to work out in the gym?**

NOT YOUR MAMA'S STUDYING TIPS

When I was studying for my certification exam, I didn't just bury my nose in a book. Boring! There's a ton of material to cover and I needed to find lots of different studying techniques to help me remember it all. Here are some of the tricks I used to ace the exam:

- **Learn by doing.** Studying anatomy is an active process — getting up and moving your body helps to understand how it works. Performing movements and feeling the muscles involved will help you remember where they are and what they do. Which muscles do you use when you kick? How about when you're doing a bench press or a biceps curl?

- **Rest.** Just like during a workout, take short rest breaks. Taking a five-minute rest break every hour to move your body and rest your mind can increase information retention (meaning you'll actually remember more of what you study).

- **Use flash cards.** Making flash cards with definitions and formulas is great because you can test yourself whenever you have a free minute — in line at the grocery store, in the waiting room at the dentist's office, while you're stuck in traffic. Or have a friend flash you (the cards, that is).

- **Pick up a copy of the Anatomy Coloring Workbook.** Using the Anatomy Coloring Workbook to memorize body parts and systems is really helpful — I've had mine for over 20 years and still refer to it! Be sure to get a box of colored pencils with as many different colors as you can find too.

After you've examined the contents of the test and what's involved, try taking a practice test. The answers are usually provided so you can see how well you do. Taking a practice test is a good way to see exactly what you do — and don't — know.

Maintaining Your Certification

Most certifying organizations will require you to keep your credentials up to date by earning Continuing Education Credits (CECs). For example, to renew and maintain your ACE personal training certification, you must earn 1.5 CECs every two years through ACE-approved courses or professional activities. You can generally earn CECs through correspondence courses, online courses, practical and comprehensive training, and live classes. Most certifying organizations also require you to keep your CPR or Advanced First Aid training current — this is a good idea even if it isn't required to maintain your certification. Check out the website of your certifying organization for detailed information about how to maintain your certification.

TRUE STORY

Taking more courses after you earn your certification can feel like a waste of time, especially as your business grows and you're busy training clients, but I can tell you from experience that keeping your skills updated and your memory sharp matters — it can even save lives. I've had clients pass out due to low blood sugar; one time I helped a gym member going through a grand mal seizure (I knew what to do because I had learned about it from continuing education course); and because I recognized the signs of a possible eating disorder, I found a gym member alone and unconscious in the hot tub one night because she had been gone for a long time and I knew to keep an eye on her. Fortunately the member was okay and I don't like to think about what could have happened. These are just a few examples of what I have seen over the past 20-plus years and I guarantee that you too will eventually find yourself in a situation where you're really glad that you remember what to do.

Chapter **3**

Building Your Skills

The only way to become a stellar personal trainer is to get out there and train. But if you're not employed yet and you don't have any clients, exactly how do you go about doing that? It's the old catch-22 — you can't get clients until you have experience, but you can't get experience without clients.

Except that you *can*. In this chapter, I give you the lowdown on interning, apprenticing, and practicing on your friends (and how to do it so that they *remain* your friends).

Getting the Scoop from Those in the Know

A great way to get real-world experience before hanging your personal-trainer shingle is to be an intern or an apprentice first. Internships and apprenticeships allow you to learn the technical aspects of the job by working with people who have been there and are still doing it — and who can show you how to do it. It's your opportunity to experience firsthand what you want to be doing — you'll probably find out what you don't want to do too.

Interning

When you think of interns, do you imagine someone running around serving coffee to spoiled executives as a low-paid gofer yearning to climb the corporate ladder? As an intern in the personal training industry, you'll do your fair share of filling water bottles for clients and wiping down sweaty gym equipment, and that's part of the job, but you'll also get to experience firsthand what personal training is really like.

A personal training internship is a temporary work experience where you receive training and gain experience in your field. If you have no practical experience under your belt, interning will:

>> Give you in-the-field experience that you can't get in a classroom or a book

>> Allow you the opportunity to explore and understand the industry before committing to it full-time

>> Let you create relationships with potential employers

>> Help you earn credit toward your certification or degree

>> Help you acquire the skills necessary to perform your job well

>> Teach you valuable new skills with which to build your résumé

>> Establish vital career networks and mentors

>> Enable you to collect references for future employment

Many internships provide compensation through stipends or hourly wages. Others are unpaid but do provide perks and invaluable experience. Internships vary in duration and sometimes lead to employment. I know of some fitness business owners who will only hire interns and then they'll either bring them on permanently or part ways after the internship ends depending on how things go.

TIP

The best places to start looking for an internship are local gyms and boutique fitness businesses (personal training studios, bootcamps, and so on). Ask the owner or manager if you can shadow one of their trainers or maybe start working the front desk to learn the business. Also, don't hesitate to contact independent personal trainers to see if they would be open to taking you on as an intern. It's a great way for a busy personal trainer to get some help while training another person in the way they want things to be done — and it works for you too, because you get to learn the ropes and you could end up landing a permanent gig!

INTERNING RESOURCES

If you'd like to learn more in general about interning or finding your first job, check out these articles:

- https://www.dummies.com/article/business-careers-money/careers/job-searches/importance-securing-internships-251880

- https://www.dummies.com/article/business-careers-money/careers/job-searches/leverage-facebook-first-job-search-252056

- https://www.dummies.com/article/business-careers-money/careers/job-searches/networking-linkedin-first-job-search-252051

Ready to start looking for an internship or a job? Try these:

- **FitnessJobs.com:** Here you can post your own ad looking for internships and search for job openings. If you're posting an ad seeking an internship, be sure to include your contact information, the region you're looking to work in (so you don't get calls from people in Peoria when you live in Seattle), and a description of your experience or education.

- **LinkedIn:** If you don't have a LinkedIn profile yet, now's the time to set it up. LinkedIn is *the* social media platform for professional networking. You can search for jobs and share that you're looking. Check out this article for tips on using LinkedIn effectively: https://www.themuse.com/advice/linkedin-profile-tips.

- **Online job boards:** These are websites where you can find a list of open job positions and apply to them directly from the site. Some popular ones are www.indeed.com and www.ziprecruiter.com. You can find salary information and actual (anonymous) employee reviews at www.glassdoor.com.

Apprenticing

Apprenticing provides education and on-the-job training. Typically, you work in a structured apprentice program for a company under the watchful eye of one of their veteran staffers. Unlike internships, apprenticeships are *always* paid positions. The benefits of apprenticing include the following:

>> Paid on-the-job training, under the guidance of a skilled employee

>> Additional instruction, classroom theory, and hands-on training

>> Progressive, increasing wages as your skill level increases

TIP

If you're interested in finding an apprenticeship and don't know where to look, try contacting community colleges or universities in your area with Exercise Science degrees. Students in these programs are typically expected to complete an internship or an apprenticeship before graduating and for this reason, most schools have relationships with local businesses and can point you in the right direction.

Shadowing other trainers

Another option is finding a job at a small personal training facility where you'll learn by working closely with an experienced trainer.

TRUE STORY

Before opening my own personal training facility, I learned a lot from working for eight years in several different health clubs. I was really lucky that I got to watch and learn from some excellent personal trainers, especially at my first job where I shadowed a trainer who had been at the gym for ten years. She took me under her wing and showed me how to be successful when I was brand new and had more enthusiasm than knowledge. To this day I credit her for showing me how to take good care of my clients.

Even before going out on my own I learned a lot by shadowing other professionals. If I didn't completely understand some aspect of training, especially how to work around an injury, I would go with my clients to their physical therapy appointments whenever I could. This strategy helped me develop a network of advisors who had more experience, knowledge, and education than me. I still go back to these people all the time with questions.

TIP

Be a lifelong learner. Sometimes you don't know what you don't know, especially when you're learning something new. Even after 20-plus years in the fitness industry I learn something new every day.

Training to train

TIP

If you haven't done it yet, you might want to think about coughing up a few bucks to work with a personal trainer yourself. Although you want to be training other people — not be trained yourself — spending time with someone who's been doing it for a while and is successful at it can be worth way more than the money you shell out for the session. Trust me, if you tell your trainer that you're interested in being a personal trainer, too, and you'd like to work with them for a couple of sessions to get a feel for it, they'll be flattered. For the most part, trainers are very supportive of one another — a good personal trainer will want to see you succeed.

A bonus to working with another trainer is that, when you do get certified and start training clients, you have a colleague whom you can call when you need help troubleshooting or you just need a quick answer to a question.

To this day, I still hire other trainers for myself. Sometimes the trainers I work with are more experienced than I am, and sometimes they're not, but either way, other trainers always know something I don't.

Taking advantage of other learning opportunities

If you belong to a gym, work out with a friend with less knowledge and experience than you. While you're working out, practice your training and spotting skills. I guarantee your partner won't mind getting some free advice!

If you can't find anyone to work out with, try role-playing. (And no, that doesn't mean meeting your significant other at the local watering hole wearing a wig and dark glasses.) While you're working out, run through a mental dialogue of what you would say to yourself if you were the client. Practice explaining what the exercises do and which muscle groups are involved in the exercise. Just be sure to do this in your head, not out loud — unless you want to gain a rep as "the crazy person on the treadmill." Practicing your dialogue prevents you from being tongue-tied when you're working with a live, flesh-and-blood client. The last thing you want when you're on the job is to draw a blank and forget the names of the body parts you're training!

Attending conferences is a great way to meet people and learn from industry leaders. You can check out the annual events put on by different certifying bodies or groups such as the IDEA Health and Fitness Association or the American College of Sports Medicine (ACSM), but I recommend starting with regional and local events before heading to a national convention as these events can be overwhelming even for seasoned professionals. Attending regional and local events is much more affordable and you'll have more opportunities to meet local people who you can follow up with in person.

Study or practice at least one of your training skills every day. Read up on medical literature, listen to a lecture at the hospital on relieving back pain, practice stretching a friend. However, whatever, and whenever you decide to practice, when the time comes that you actually need that skill or tidbit of knowledge, you'll be glad you did!

Finding Folks to Practice On (Or, Getting Your Family and Friends to Jump When You Say Jump)

Who knows you better or loves you more than your friends and family? (If you said "the pizza delivery guy," you're in trouble.) You can bounce your business ideas off of them and practice your techniques on them when they're willing.

WARNING

Because your friends and family members have no problem with telling you that your teaching skills stink or that you don't know your gluteus maximus from your elbow, they can be tough to work with. Don't take their "feedback" too seriously, and remember that their suggestions will get you used to dealing with straight-talking clients! Your friends and family are also the same people who care about you and might say you're awesome to avoid hurting your feelings. It's a nice gesture, but it won't help you to identify your blind spots or improve your skills.

TIP

There's more to training than, well, training. You need to pinpoint all the other areas where you may need improvement. Ask the people you've been practicing with to give you feedback on things like:

>> **Your professional demeanor.** Do you seem like a professional, or like their goofy sibling/spouse/friend?

>> **Your ability to explain the exercises.** Do they understand what the exercises are for and how to do them correctly?

>> **Your ability to demonstrate the exercises.** Do your demonstrations help them understand the proper form?

>> **Your spotting technique.** Do they feel like they're in good hands, or are they afraid that they're going to wind up dropping a barbell on their heads?

>> **The overall quality of the session.** Was your session something they'd shell out money for, or do they feel like they'd get the same value for free from a trainer on YouTube?

>> **Your overall knowledge and ability to communicate what you know.** Do you seem like someone in the know or someone who needs to go to the back of the class?

Make a list of the skills you need to brush up on, and build time into your schedule to devote time in your schedule to strengthening those skills. With practice and good feedback from your clients, you'll have this personal training thing down in no time!

Training Yourself

Have you ever noticed how people naturally gravitate toward the buff trainer in the gym? That's because the trainers with washboard abs *look* like they know what they're doing, even though that may be the farthest thing from the truth. People typically want to get fit and look lean — so they figure, "Well, if that person knows how to look like that, then they'll know how to make *me* look like that too."

Now, the reality is that this is not reality. What you look like doesn't really have any correlation with your skill as a personal trainer. You need to be able to prescribe different exercise programs for different people, based on their unique needs and abilities. Looking the part does help; your own health and fitness are a great advertisement. But more important than talking the talk, you have to be able to walk the walk. You also have to be able to help other people who might need to crawl before they can walk.

TIP

Guess what? Lots of people don't like to exercise. And you know what else? Many of these folks aren't working out to get flat abs. They just want to feel good and stay healthy. They aren't interested in living a life that revolves around the gym or their bodyfat percentage. Keeping this in mind is helpful, especially if you're someone whose life does revolve around the gym or your bodyfat percentage. There's nothing wrong with that either, but always remember that your clients will have different goals and reasons for exercising. And they won't stick around long with a trainer who doesn't understand that.

Practicing what you preach

You don't necessarily need to have the physical strength to demonstrate any type of exercise to any type of client you take on, but you shouldn't expect them to do things that you *wouldn't* do yourself, even if you could. That means you need to learn and practice every exercise that you plan on being able to teach, and if there's an exercise you can't demonstrate for whatever reason, you better to be able to explain exactly how to do it correctly and safely.

Reading up on it

Check out your library's fitness section for exercise and weight-lifting books. Your certifying body will have publications along those lines as well. After sifting through them, pick out the exercises you're going to master first, write them out in your workout log, and practice them until you're confident that you're able to properly demonstrate and teach them to someone else. Keep incorporating a few new exercises at a time into your own routine and soon you'll have an enviable exercise repertoire to choose from.

Getting moving

Despite popular opinion, personal training entails more than pumping iron. Start getting to know the cardio equipment in your gym. Knowing how to set the programs is helpful if you're looking to change up a client's workout with a little interval training. Trust me, this recommendation comes from personal experience — throwing a client on a piece of cardio equipment that's unfamiliar to you and then not being able to get the darn thing to work won't impress anyone (at least not in the way you *want* them to be impressed).

Dear diary . . . Keeping a workout log

Keeping a workout log while you're in your experimental phase and you're discovering new exercises and training styles is extremely helpful. You can record the elements that got you the results you were looking for and keep notes about those that didn't. Make notes about how you felt and how quickly you recovered. Record how many reps and sets you completed so you know where to start next time and always remember that what you measure you can improve. You'll need to teach your clients how to document their workouts when they're not with you, and using your workout log as a teaching tool is a great way to lead by example.

Being a not-so-mad scientist: Experimenting on yourself

Every person's body is unique, and what works for one person may not work for another. When you train clients, think like a scientist. You have to step outside of your normal thought process and ask "What if?" (What if I increased the pace? What if I slowed down this movement? What if I had the client start with that exercise first?)

On top of knowing every exercise there is to know, being well versed in a variety of training styles is a good rule of thumb, especially before trying them with your clients. You should know how different tempos feel, how increased weights and/or reps affect the sensation of your workout, how changing your recovery time affects your performance. These are all things you can experiment with personally so that one day you'll be able to say to your client, "Let's try this instead," and you'll be able to describe what you're doing from personal experience.

Demonstrating your professional skills

According to some guy named Webster, a *professional* is somebody who shows a high degree of skill or competence. Becoming a professional doesn't occur overnight. Professionalism is a combination of your technical skills, practical skills, people skills, business skills, and that little indefinable something called *finesse*.

It's the ability to perform your job as a trainer in a proficient and skilled manner. To do that — and to do it well — takes time and practice. And the good news is these are all things you can learn and get better at with practice.

REMEMBER

Your speaking style and manner are extremely important when working with clientele, both paying and nonpaying; they indicate how well versed you are in your technique, how comfortable you are in your role as a trainer, and how disciplined you are as a professional.

Here's a list of traits that demonstrate professionalism.

A professional trainer:

>> Is responsible and reliable

>> Has exercise programs written out for clients ahead of time

>> Stays knowledgeable and current

>> Is focused on the client 100 percent of the time

>> Admits to not knowing the answer to a client question

>> Is early or on time for training sessions and meetings

>> Keeps clients on task without too much talking

>> Performs all requirements of the job

>> Completes duties fully and in a timely manner

>> Offers to help out other staff members

>> Doesn't gossip about others, with clients *or* staff

>> Is respectful of coworkers

>> Takes responsibility for their own actions

>> Maintains appropriate boundaries with clients

>> Doesn't blame others for problems or shortcomings

>> Takes up any problems or issues with the appropriate person — and nobody else

>> Takes clients and staff out for ice cream on a regular basis (Okay, I made that one up.)

I could probably come up with 20 more ways to be professional. These are the ones that come to mind first and that I deal with most often.

A CAUTIONARY TALE

Here's a story from a trainer I know (we'll call her Angie) that underscores the importance of being professional.

Shortly after Angie expanded her service offerings to include massage therapy, her masseuse called in sick 30 minutes before she was to meet one of Angie's first — and best — clients. Not wanting to cancel and disappoint her client, Angie thought, "I'll go myself!" With that, she grabbed the portable massage table and massage cream and loaded up her car.

The client met Angie at the front door. She looked behind Angie. "Where's your masseuse?" she asked. "Well, she's sick, so I'm going to give you your massage," Angie answered. The client looked surprised. "Have you ever given a massage before?" "No," Angie replied. "Have you ever *gotten* a massage?" the client asked, her eyes even wider. "Well, no," Angie replied. Looking doubtful, the client led the way to her bedroom, where Angie proceeded to set up the table without sheets (the client brought out her own towels and placed them on the table so she could cover herself).

To make a long story short, the client knew that Angie didn't know what she was doing, and even though Angie thought the session went fine, it wasn't until three years later, when she got her first massage, that she realized the errors she had made with her client. Boy, was her face red! Angie realized that she had compromised her relationship and her professionalism by trying to do something she wasn't qualified to do.

Make sure when you're meeting with a client — whether for the first time or the fiftieth — you're prepared and know what you're doing.

REMEMBER

No matter who you are practicing on or working with, take it seriously. If you don't, no one else will. If you're practicing with friends and family, stay in character. As easy as it is to joke around and gab about the latest reality show, keep in mind that you need to develop two skills: how to keep your client moving through a session, and how to keep yourself focused and on track while you direct your client. The whole purpose of practicing with friends and family is to find your *training rhythm* (the manner in which you'll be most comfortable working with clients).

Chapter **4**

Planning Your Start

Y ou're certified, your skills are up to game speed, and you're raring to go. Go where? Some personal trainers work as employees at health clubs and other facilities, while others work for themselves.

Being your own boss may sound like a dream come true. But if you're not prepared, it can be a nightmare. In this chapter, I help you decide whether to work for yourself or for someone else, figure out what kind of facility you'd like to work at, find your dream job, or figure out where to train your clients if you're a lone ranger.

Assessing Your Lifestyle Needs

If you're like most people, you just want to dive right in and get working. But taking some time up front to really think about what you want from your life and your career is helpful when you're planning your start. So, grab a pen and paper, and write down your answers to the following questions:

» Are you a night person or a morning person?

» How many hours per week can you work?

>> How much money do you need to earn to support the lifestyle you want?

>> How often would you like to go on vacation, and for how long?

>> How much time do you like to spend with family and friends?

>> What are your hobbies? What hobbies would you like to have?

REMEMBER

These questions don't have right or wrong answers. They're just supposed to get you to think about your priorities.

TIP

Refer back to your answers as you read about the realities of starting your own business and working for someone else. You'll find that, for example, if you like to take two months of vacation time every year, you can do that more easily as an independent personal trainer. But owning your own business can be time-consuming, so if spending lots of time with your family and friends is important to you, owning your own business may not leave much time for anything else, at least not when you're getting started.

Being Your Own Boss

Who doesn't sometimes dream of telling their boss to "take this job and shove it," and forging their own path as a freelancer or business owner? No more getting up at 5 a.m., no more fighting traffic, no more surly bosses, no more tiny paychecks.

WARNING

Hold on a second . . . before you decide that you want to go it alone, you need to be aware of the pros and cons. Running your own business isn't a surefire way to wealth or free time — if it were, everyone would be doing it.

Keep reading to find out the truth about going it alone. Being a successful business owner takes a certain kind of personality, and sometimes the disadvantages can outweigh the advantages. And I can tell you from personal experience that owning a business is not even kind-of the same thing as being a personal trainer. At all.

Figuring out if you have what it takes

You need more than an independent spirit to make it on your own. To find out if you have what it takes, answer the questions in the following sections. If you answer "no" to any of them, think long and hard about how you can change the answer to "yes" — or whether you should maybe rethink your plans.

Are you a self-starter?

When you work for yourself, you don't have a boss breathing down your neck (or docking your pay) when you punch in late. The only thing that makes you get out of bed on time, focus on your work, balance your books, and create new client programs is — wait for it — you. Be truthful: Are you motivated enough to do your own marketing, programming, accounting, and everything else you need to do to keep a business running (at least until you start making enough money to hire other people to do some of it for you)?

Do you get along well with different personalities?

As a business owner, you'll deal with insurance agents, journalists (who can give you good PR), doctors (who can give you referrals), accountants (when you can afford one), landlords or health-club owners (you need *somewhere* to work!), and — don't forget — clients. You need to be able to communicate and get along with a wide variety of people.

Are you good at making decisions?

If the idea of choosing between PB&J and chicken noodle soup for lunch sends you into a tailspin, you're in trouble. You'll need to make decisions galore, from what to name your business and what color your logo should be, to whether you should take on a new client. And sometimes you'll need to make snap decisions, such as when a client has a complaint or how to respond when a reporter from a local news station emails asking you for the ten best pieces of equipment for a home gym — and it's due by 5 p.m. tomorrow. (Don't think this will happen to you? Check out the information about appearing in the press in Chapter 8.)

Do you have money in the bank?

Unless you find some magic formula for getting clients to pound down your door, your business will probably start out slowly as you gain a reputation and get refer-rals. This isn't bad — it's just par for the course. But in the meantime, you'll need money to live on.

TIP

Most experts suggest that you have at least six months' worth of living expenses socked away before making the leap.

Are you good at organizing?

When you work for an employer, somebody else sets your schedule, supplies client forms, provides exercise equipment for you to use, and so on. When you work for yourself, you need to be able to create, use, file, and find all sorts of documents.

You'll probably have a list of contacts on your phone, as well as contact-organizer software — and you'll use them to keep track of clients, doctors, and other contacts. You'll also need to keep track of how much money you're making, who owes you money, and how much you owe. All of this requires you to be more organized than Martha Stewart's fruit preserving calendar.

Are you a leader?

If your business takes off, you may want to hire other trainers to boost your income and to be able to serve more customers. Now *you'll* be the boss whom everyone wants to tell to "take this job and shove it." Can you give orders without creating a mutiny? Can you inspire people to give 100 percent?

REMEMBER

In addition to potentially leading a staff, you'll need to be a leader to your clients. They look to you for instruction and advice, and you need to be able to lead them to better health.

Do you have management skills?

If you own a company with employees, you may find yourself doing more managing than training. Can you deal with constantly keeping an eye on your employees — and cutting down on your training hours to do so? Can you discipline an underperforming employee?

Do you have a supportive family and understanding friends?

When you start your own business, at first you'll be working overtime to lay the foundation and get the business off the ground. Will your family and friends understand that your schedule will be different; that you'll need privacy during certain hours while you work on marketing, creating client programs, and other tasks; and that you may not be able to handle all the household chores on your own? If your family and friends aren't already on board with your new business venture, you'll want to get them there — and fast.

Understanding the pros and cons of going it alone

Think you have what it takes? If you read the questions in the last section and answered yes to all of them, read on about the pros and cons of owning your own business to find out whether you really want to make the leap into entrepreneurship.

The pros:

>> **Unlimited income potential.** When you work for yourself, you set the rates and you work as much as you want to. If you can charge $100+ per session and you can handle training ten or more clients per day, that's nobody's business but your own. If you work for a health club, you'll probably be paid an hourly wage for working the floor, plus a commission for bringing in new clients and re-signing existing clients, and a set fee for personal training sessions serviced. Your employer decides how much you get paid, when you work, and how many sessions you can conduct in a day.

>> **You choose your clients.** If someone rubs you the wrong way, you don't have to take them on as a client. If you work for an employer, sometimes you'll have to grit your teeth and deal with — and even be nice to — rude or annoying clients.

>> **You choose your hours.** No 9 to 5 for you! If you want to be there to walk your kid home from the bus stop, that's your choice — as long as you can schedule your clients around it. And if you want to take off to Tahiti for a week, you can do it (as long as you don't mind not getting paid for that week).

>> **Your income lines your own pockets.** Your hard work and long hours directly benefit you, as opposed to increasing profits for some CEO in an ivory tower. Many successful business owners are people who had a "bad attitude" at work because they resented busting their buns to support someone else's dreams.

>> **Going it alone is exciting.** Nothing makes your heart go pitter-patter like signing on a new client, scoring a public-relations coup, or finding a new way to help a client beat back pain through exercise. Every day is a new learning experience as you figure out how to best serve your clients while boosting your bottom line.

>> **You can work where you like.** Instead of getting paid to "walk the floor," you can walk wherever you like! Design T-shirts with a snazzy logo and your business name and go to the beach — you're advertising, not slacking. Work at different gyms that allow independent trainers. Travel to out-of-town fitness-industry conferences. The *world* is your floor to walk!

>> **You get to keep (almost) every penny you earn.** When you work for someone else, in many cases the business owner pockets up to 50 percent of what you earn. When you work for yourself, you get to keep everything you earn (minus taxes, of course). No middlemen need to be paid, but you'll have more expenses to cover, like keeping the lights on and toilet paper in stock.

>> **You get to deduct your expenses.** As a business owner, you can deduct expenses related to your business from your taxes, such as exercise equipment, office supplies, computer equipment, and more. Consult your accountant for more information.

The cons:

>> **No company health-insurance plan.** Most working people take health insurance for granted — but not those who work for themselves.

When I was a young and single new business owner, I didn't want to be without health insurance, so I paid a few hundred dollars per month for COBRA coverage from my last employer until I could find a private plan for myself — which was about $500 per month for very limited coverage. Some industry associations offer health insurance to members, but it usually isn't cheap.

>> **No company-sponsored retirement plan.** Traditional retirement plans such as 401(k) plans, where employers often match your retirement contributions, are for employees. If you want to put aside money for retirement, you'll have to set up an Individual Retirement Account (IRA) and remember to contribute to it regularly. No employee match for you!

>> **Higher taxes.** When you're an employee, your employer pays half of your Social Security tax. If you're self-employed, you have to cough up the entire 15 percent on your own.

>> **Feast or famine lifestyle.** If you work for yourself, you can kiss your regular paychecks goodbye. Being self-employed means when you don't work, you don't get paid. You don't get paid to walk the floor, you don't get paid when you're sick, you don't get paid when you take a break.

When you have a lot of clients — like in January, when people are trying to stick to their New Year's resolutions — you work like a dog but get paid like a prince. When times are lean, so is your paycheck. Most of your clients will vacation in the summer and many will spend less time with you when the sunshine calls their names. You need to be able to put aside money when you're flush to tide you over when clients are scarce.

>> **No paid vacation or sick days.** Can't work because you're laid low with the flu? Too bad, you don't get paid. Want to go on vacation for a week or two? Hope you don't mind taking a pay cut, because you don't get those two weeks per year of paid vacation time like your 9-to-5 brethren. (Of course, you can vacation as long as you like — as long as you can afford it — a definite advantage.)

>> **No equipment and supplies.** When you work for someone else, all the equipment and all those pencils and paper clips are provided by the Business Supply Fairy. When you work for yourself, all those supplies — not to mention the computer, printer, sticky notes, internet access, ink cartridges, paper, toilet paper, towel service, and electricity — come from your *own* magic wand. And unless you rent space in a gym or a personal training center, you may even have to supply your own exercise equipment. These goodies are tax deductible, but that's small consolation when they used to be free.

>> **No breakroom chitchat.** Forget Friday morning gabfests in the breakroom. Even if you hate working for an employer, working for yourself often gets very lonely — so lonely that you can suddenly find yourself down at Starbucks making small talk with anybody who gets within five feet of your Americano. Sure, you have your clients — but you can't tell *them* how exhausted you are or how you're afraid to raise your rates.

Trading spaces: Finding a place to train your clients

After you've asked yourself the tough questions and been honest with yourself about the answers, and after you've considered all the pros and cons of going it alone, if you still want to do it, you're off to the right start.

Now's the time to get down and dirty. Although you don't have to apply for a job when you pursue the solo path, you do have to deal with some other details, such as where you'll work. When you don't work for a gym, where are you supposed to train your clients?

In the following sections, I cover some of your options for places to train clients when you work for yourself.

GETTING OTHER PEOPLE ON BOARD

Before you make your final decision about whether to strike out on your own, put together an informal advisory board of friends and family members, health professionals, small business owners, and personal trainers you may know (you probably called a few when you were deciding which certification to pursue — but if you didn't, now is the time to make some connections). These people can give you honest feedback on your strengths and weaknesses, true tales about working for yourself or for someone else, and advice on where to start and how to get started.

Gyms

Some gyms will let you train clients there — for a price. They may ask for a percentage of your fee, a set amount per client, or a set amount per month. The bonus is that you'll have all the equipment you need, and your clients will have use of the locker rooms, showers, and so on. Contact local gyms and ask if they rent space to personal trainers.

Your clients' homes

Some of your clients will have fully outfitted home gyms — about half of my clients had at least some fitness equipment in their homes when I was training full time and a few had complete home gyms. Some people will be happy to pay you to train them in their own homes and even if they have nothing but a rug on the floor, you can do a lot with just a set of dumbbells and some resistance bands.

WARNING

When you work in a client's home, behaving like the professional you are is even more important than usual. You may get the urge to slack off because you're not in a professional environment, and this is a definite no-no.

REMEMBER

If you're driving from house to house for training sessions, you probably won't be able to book as many sessions in a day, because you'll be spending a lot of time cruising down the freeway or waiting in traffic.

Local businesses

TRUE STORY

Sometimes you can rent space from compatible businesses. I moved my personal training business to a physical therapy clinic when I was between leases and building out my second location. There was plenty of open space for small group training and I was able to stock it with my own equipment.

The advantage to renting space from a business is that it won't break your bank and you don't have to worry about a lease. The drawback is that you'll be at the mercy of your landlord's schedule and rules.

Personal training facilities

Many cities have small independent gyms or personal training facilities where you can rent space — just like a hairdresser rents a station from a salon. A quick Google search for "gyms in my area" or "personal training" will give you an idea of what's available near you.

Working the 5 to 9

If you want to get hired at a gym or other facility, this section is for you. I give you the scoop on places that are looking for trainers like you, the pros and cons of working in various places, and how to get your foot in the door at the facility of your dreams. And yes, you read that right. Expect to see job openings with varying schedules because most people work from 9 to 5 and exercise outside of those hours. It's not uncommon for personal trainers to start their days as early as 5 a.m. or end them at 9 p.m. to accommodate clients' schedules.

Knowing whether you're the ideal employee

Answer the questions in the following sections. If you answer "no" to any of them, ask yourself how you can change your answer to "yes" — and if you can't, you may want to consider going solo. (Turn to the beginning of this chapter to find out if being a lone ranger — er, I mean trainer — is for you.)

Can you take direction?

As an employee, you'll need to take directions from your boss, whether that's the business owner or a manager. This doesn't mean, of course, that you have to blindly follow instructions, but too much questioning can land you in the soup.

GOING FROM EMPLOYEE TO EMPLOYER

If you really want to start your own personal training business, but you answered no to our questions earlier in this chapter, don't worry! Working for an employer will help you get your skill set up to snuff — especially if you work at a facility where you're able to get involved with all parts of running the business.

I worked for a large health-club chain for six years before going out on my own and developed a lot of useful skills during that time — such as how to hustle for work, how to treat clients, and how to sell personal training services — that helped me build a successful business.

Do you play well with others?

See those other people working at the gym you hope to work for? If you get hired there, you'll be interacting with them for the majority of your waking hours. Do you get along with all types of people? Can you handle working with someone who thinks or works differently from you?

Are you punctual?

Of course, being punctual is important whether your self-employed or an employee — but as an employee, excessive lateness or tardiness can land you in the unemployment line. Do you have the willpower to get up when your alarm goes off and be at your workplace, bright-eyed and bushy-tailed, at the appointed hour?

Can you stick to someone else's schedule?

Your employer will make up a schedule for you, and chances are they won't care that Monday is trivia night at your favorite sports bar. If the boss says you work Monday nights, guess what? You work Monday nights. If you need a certain day off, you'll need to let your boss know well ahead of time so they can work it into the schedule.

Can you do it someone else's way?

Your employer may have a different outlook on exercise programming, client relations, employee relations, or business operations than you do. A good employer will give you leeway to do your job your own way, but you'll probably have to make some changes to your preferred way of doing things to fit in your place of employment.

Identifying the pros and cons of being an employee

If you answered "yes" to all the questions in the preceding section and you're thinking about going to work for someone else, read on to find out about the pros and cons of your decision. Just like any other situation, working for someone else has its advantages and disadvantages.

The pros:

>> **Your company pays for your health insurance.** Self-employed workers have to shell out megabucks in some areas to get insured — but not you! If

you work full-time for your employer, chances are you'll be offered health insurance as part of your benefits package.

>> **You may get a company-sponsored retirement plan.** You can have a certain percentage of your paycheck automatically deposited into your retirement account so your savings will grow — and it will be painless, because you probably won't even notice that the money is gone. If you're lucky, your employer will match your retirement contributions up to a certain amount — that's free money (something you should definitely take advantage of, if you can).

>> **You get a regular paycheck.** Every week (or every two weeks), like clockwork, your employer will put a check in your hands — unlike freelancers, who get paid when they have clients, and get zilch when they don't.

>> **Your employer provides everything you need.** Need a particular form? Your employer has a whole drawer full of them. Not sure what to wear? How about that snazzy polo shirt your employer gave you? Want to start your client on a new exercise? Have them hop on that brand new treadmill, courtesy of — you guessed it — your employer. As an employee, you don't have to drop money on supplies, equipment, or other work-related goodies.

>> **You can make new friends.** As an employee, you'll always have someone else to talk to, whether it's to trade ideas for client programming or chat about the latest news. You'll never get lonely with other employees around.

>> **You get paid vacation and sick days.** Unlike self-employed workers, if you get sick and have to stay home, you still get paid (as long as you still have sick days left). Your employer will most likely also give you paid vacation time, so you can relax on holiday without worrying about how the bills are going to get paid.

The cons:

>> **Your income potential is limited.** You can make only as much as your employer pays you (except when you get a raise). Unlike business owners, you can't make more moolah by raising your prices, adding more clients, adding more services, or working more hours.

>> **You don't choose who you work with.** Don't like that new client? Too bad. You'll be expected to work with — and be nice to — all clients, no matter how frustrating they may be. You also don't choose your colleagues, and may get stuck with a stinker of a coworker.

>> **You work set hours.** Working set hours can make it hard for you to do the things you like. For example, if you're scheduled to work the 9-to-5 shift, you'll have to find some way to do your errands after hours or during your lunch

break. If you're scheduled for Tuesday night and that's the night your son has a baseball game, you're out of luck unless you remember to ask your employer for the day off weeks ahead of time.

>> **Your employer takes a cut of what you make.** If your employer charges clients $75 for an hour-long session, why do you make only $25 per hour? Because your employer has to take a cut of what you earn from each client to pay for *overhead* — things like heat, light, rent, and other operating expenses. Employers also pay additional taxes on their employees, as well as matching employees' Social Security withholdings.

Picking from the job jar

Don't think that because you're a personal trainer your working options are limited to gyms. Plenty of businesses that deal with health are willing to hire a sharp specimen like you. In the following sections, I give you a guided tour of some of your options.

Hospital-based wellness centers

Hospital-based wellness centers operate like any other gym, except that your client base will consist of a lot of doctors, nurses, and patients (though members of the community are also welcome to join). The good news is that being surrounded by medical professionals will be a great learning experience for you.

REMEMBER

A lot of doctors and nurses don't know nearly as much as you think when it comes to physical fitness and they need *you* to help them with adopting a healthy lifestyle!

University gyms

Many large universities have gyms for their students and faculty. You'll be working with plenty of brainy people, and the benefits package is usually impressive.

Chain health clubs

You know these places — they're the ones with super-fit people in designer sportswear in their ads. In this large gym environment, you have plenty of opportunity for advancement. However, much of your salary is based on sales, so you'll feel the pressure to sell, sell, sell — whether you're pushing nutritional supplements or personal training sessions.

If the words "sales" and "spiders" give you the same dreaded feeling in your gut, you may feel uncomfortable working in a large health club setting. In order to boost your income, you'll have to get comfortable with handing new and existing members a slick sales pitch for your personal training services.

Independent or small health clubs

Because the staff is small, you'll wear many hats in an independent or small health club — such as working the front desk, answering phones, scheduling clients, cleaning, taking part in marketing campaigns, and, oh yeah, conducting personal training sessions.

If you hope to own your own personal training business someday, this may be the best workplace for you, because you'll get to see all aspects of running a business.

Private personal training studios

Private personal training studios do nothing but personal training. Clients don't go there to work out on their own, use the whirlpool, or use the sauna. You may also be sent out to train clients in their home gyms or in small corporate facilities.

YMCA/YWCA

The YMCA, immortalized by the Village People, caters to families (as does the YWCA). This employer will give you a good, solid base of experience. If you want to work with a diverse group of people, then the Y's for you. And it's a great place to start if you're looking to get a feel for what the gym industry is like, as it typically offers everything from badminton to martial arts, so you can test your skills in different areas of fitness services.

Senior centers

If you want to work at a senior center, you'll need to be aware of the changes the body goes through as it ages and you may need advanced certification as well. State-run senior centers may not pay as much as other fitness facilities. The good news is that even if your local senior center doesn't offer a fitness program, they may be open to new ideas, so you can propose a program or a class to them.

Fitness management companies

These companies are like staffing agencies for fitness professionals. Management fitness companies outsource personal trainers to corporate fitness centers and other businesses that need staff but that don't want to take on staffing themselves. These employers have very stringent requirements; you'll probably be required to know CPR, turn in a résumé, and even take a test.

Alternative healthcare centers

Alternative healthcare centers are into natural care and an Eastern philosophy of medicine, so they offer treatments like acupuncture, massage therapy, naturopathy, and chiropractic services. Clients may be trying to avoid surgery or medication, and they may have ailments they're trying to resolve. Personal training fits in with this environment perfectly, because clients are looking for natural ways to improve their health — and what's more natural than exercise? Only those with open minds need apply.

Physical-therapy businesses

Some physical therapists hire personal trainers to work with patients after they get past the acute stage of an injury, to regain strength and mobility. You'll be teaching exercises under the supervision of the therapist to help patients improve their physical fitness and prevent re-injury. Because you'll be working for a licensed or registered therapist, you're in for a great learning experience.

Health resorts

These are the exclusive playgrounds of those with a lot of cash to drop. They usually boast a full-blown gym in addition to spa services, healthy meals, and activities. Most health resorts require trainers to show proof of certification plus a résumé, and they'll likely expect you to be certified in CPR as well. Because these are vacation spots, you won't have long-term clients, and you'll have to pack a lot of information into a short amount of time.

Day spas

Day spas are like toned-down health resorts. Clients usually visit for a few hours or a day to get massages, facials, and other treatments. The difference between working at a day spa and working at a health resort is that you'll see clients on a more continuous basis.

Evaluating potential workplaces

Before you go to all the trouble of convincing an employer to hire you, make sure that *you* want to work for *them*. Nothing's worse than knocking yourself out to get hired and then finding out that you're working for Satan himself.

WHERE THE JOBS ARE

Surf to these job sites to find personal training jobs in your area:

- **LinkedIn:** Most employers post openings here and on multiple job sites, and because LinkedIn is the most popular professional social networking site on the internet, you'll be able to connect with employers or recruiters directly about jobs you're interested in applying for.

- **Indeed.com:** This popular job-search site lets you search keywords or browse job categories. For personal training jobs, select the categories "Personal Care and Services" and "Healthcare — Other."

- **The International Health, Racquet & Sportsclub Association (IHRSA):** Job seekers can choose to browse through all available job listings on IHRSA's website or search for jobs by using specific criteria. The ads are mostly for directors and managers, but why not contact the businesses you're interested in working for and offer your services?

- **Exercisejobs.com:** This site has a good selection of fitness-specialist/personal-trainer jobs. You can also post your résumé (preferably in a way that stands out from the dozens of pages of other trainers' résumés). The site also includes career resources, such as interview tips and a résumé guide.

TIP

Head to the facility and take a look around. You can even ask for a day pass or a week pass so you can work out there yourself. Do you like the equipment? Do the employees seem happy, bored, miserable? What kinds of clients do they cater to — women, men, bodybuilders, young adults, seniors?

TIP

Corner a personal trainer and ask some questions. If they're busy or can't talk while on the job, ask if you can get coffee sometime (your treat) soon. Don't be shy — personal trainers love to talk about their jobs! Here are some questions you want to be sure to ask:

- » How is the facility's management to work with?

- » What's the pay like? Do you get a commission for bringing on new clients?

- » Is there a lot of pressure to bring in new clients or push products like nutritional supplements?

- » What are the hours like?

- » Do you like the equipment?

- » Does the employer take good care of the equipment?

>> What are the clients like?

>> What kind of certification do you need to work there?

>> Do you find it difficult to get clients?

>> What are the pros and cons of working for this employer?

Getting hired

Finding out where you'd like to work is the easy part. The hard part is convincing the owner or manager that you're the best darn personal trainer this side of the Mississippi and that they should hire you right away (preferably for a lot of money).

TIP

Unless you're applying online and the instructions specifically say to submit your application online, your best bet is to visit the facility of your choice in person, hand your résumé to the person behind the counter, and ask to make an appointment with the manager or owner (if it's a small facility). But don't make a move before sharpening the tools in the following sections.

Polishing your résumé

REMEMBER

Your résumé is you — on paper. Is the résumé sloppy? This tells an employer that you may do a sloppy job. Is it riddled with typos? This shows a lack of attention to detail. Is it well-organized? You'll probably be just as organized when dealing with client programs.

A résumé is also a sales tool. You're presenting information about yourself in such a way as to convince someone to hire you.

Here are some tips that will take your résumé from "ho-hum" to "hire me!":

>> **Start with your most impressive credentials.** If you studied physiology or exercise science in college but have no job experience, start your résumé with a section that describes your education. If you have no formal training but you've worked in the fitness industry, put your job-experience section first.

TIP

Résumés can be chronological or functional in format. A *chronological résumé* lists your jobs and education from most recent to least recent. A *functional résumé* focuses on skills rather than job titles. A functional résumé is best if you want to highlight skills and strengths that your most recent jobs or education don't necessarily reflect. If you don't have much experience in the fitness industry, a functional résumé may be the way to go.

>> **Use active verbs and phrases to give your résumé punch and help the employer understand how you can benefit the facility.** Rather than weak verbs (as in "Was a trainer for Club X" or "Was responsible for training at Club X"), use strong, active verbs that stress accomplishments (as in "Trained clients at Club X"). Here are some active verbs you can use:

- Trained (clients, employees)
- Implemented (programs)
- Reduced (costs, accidents)
- Increased (profits, sales, safety)
- Improved (clients' fitness levels, customer service)
- Managed (employees, programs)
- Helped/assisted (clients, management)

>> **Fake it 'til you make it.** Never worked as a personal trainer before? Stress the responsibilities you held at previous jobs that will help you in your new position. For example, if you worked in retail, you know how to treat customers and handle complaints. If you worked in sales, you have the skills you'll need to bring in new clients. Just make sure that your résumé is truthful — lying on a resume is a firing offense in pretty much any business!

>> **Check it over.** Much like Santa, you should check your résumé twice — not to find out if you've been naughty or nice, but to make sure your résumé is free of typos and misspellings. Don't rely on spell check, which can't tell the difference between *you're* and *your*. If you have time, put your résumé in a drawer for a few days so you can look at it with fresh eyes before turning it in. Even better, have a friend look it over for you. Or, if you have a little extra time and money, consult a freelance editor who can take your résumé up a notch.

Knowing what to wear

Even though you're applying to be a personal trainer, you shouldn't wear your sweats when dropping off your résumé or during the interview. You don't need to don a suit, but do dress professionally and comb your hair — your professionalism will shine through.

Brushing up on your interview skills

You don't want to lose your cool when you're being grilled by a potential employer. Follow these tips to become an ace interviewee:

>> **Research the employer thoroughly.** This strategy will help you ask intelligent questions and show your enthusiasm for the job.

>> **Ask a friend to pretend they're an interviewer and ask you questions.**
Typical questions you may have to answer are:

- Why do you want to become a personal trainer?

- What are your strengths and weaknesses?

- What would you do if a client hurt herself while doing a squat or deadlift?

- What certifications do you have?

- Why did you leave your last job?

- Why should we hire you?

>> **Use your phone to record yourself answering interview questions.**
Check for mumbling, slouching, fidgeting, wandering eyes, and saying things like "um" and "y'know."

TIP

For many more tips, check out *Job Interviews For Dummies* by Joyce Lain Kennedy (published by Wiley).

2

Becoming a Successful Personal Trainer

Personal training is about more than pumping iron and doing cardio. You're a business, which means that you need to think like a businessperson. In this part, I tell you all about how to create a business plan, project your income and expenses, develop your fee structure, and develop a marketing plan — just like a Fortune 500 company!

Next, I help you hire other professionals, such as an accountant and a lawyer (yes, you do need them). I also tell you how to create a business name and logo and how to determine your business structure (that's those modifiers that come after your business name like *Inc.* and *LLC*).

Keeping with the business theme, the following chapters describe how to develop sound business practices that will keep your business running smoothly, how to bring clients in the door, and how to keep those clients happy and motivated so they keep coming back.

Chapter **5**

Creating Your Business Plan

S ome trainers, eager to strike out on their own, jump feet-first into business ownership. They have a vague idea of what they need to do — go out, get clients, train them, collect money — but no real plan.

Success doesn't happen by accident; you need to plan for it. In this chapter, I show you how to develop a business plan, fee structure, and marketing plan, plus how to project income and expenses so you don't find yourself in a financial hole.

Developing a Road Map for Success

Before you rent a space, before you start advertising for clients, before you decide how much you're going to charge, you need a plan — a business plan, that is. A *business plan* is a detailed blueprint of how you're going to reach success. You can — and should — refer to it occasionally to make sure you're on the right track. (You also need a business plan if you ever decide to apply for a business loan.)

TIP

Here are some of the questions you answer in your business plan:

>> **What are your personal goals?** Do you want to make more money, have a flexible schedule, work with celebrity clients?

>> **Where do you want your business to be six months, a year, five years from now?** Do you want to stay solo or hire additional trainers?

>> **Whom do you want to train?** If you're not sure about the answer to this question, turn to Chapter 2, which offers information on the different types of clients you can work with.

>> **Where do you want to train your clients?** Do you want to travel to their homes or gyms, meet them at their offices, or have them come to you?

>> **What services or products will you provide your clients?** Will you offer specialty services like half-marathon training programs? Will you sell nutritional supplements or fitness equipment?

>> **How are you going to let clients know that you're available?** Read more about marketing yourself in Chapter 8.

>> **Why will clients hire you?** What makes you and your services different from Big George's Deep Discount Personal Training?

For a sample business plan to help you get started, check out *Creating a Business Plan For Dummies* by Veechi Curtis (published by Wiley).

TIP

For more information on writing business plans, visit the Small Business Administration (SBA) website at www.sba.gov. In particular, check out the "Write your business plan" page at www.sba.gov/business-guide/plan-your-business/write-your-business-plan.

Sounds like a plan to me: Writing your business plan

After you've thought about what services and products you want your company to provide (your goods), who you want to provide those services to (your clients), and where you're going to provide them (your location), your next step is to create a business plan.

TIP

The business plan contains seven parts:

>> **Executive summary:** The executive summary is an overview of your entire plan, highlighting all key strategic points. You typically write this last but list it first.

>> **Company description:** The company description is, well, a description of your company — your vision and mission statements, a company overview, and an overview of your legal structure (the letters that come after your business name, such as *Inc.* or *LLC*). You can find more information on legal structures in Chapter 6.

>> **Products and services:** This section describes in detail the types of products and services your business will offer, any research and development that you may have done to support them, how much they'll cost, and how you plan to deliver them to your clients.

>> **Marketing:** In this section, you define the market you'll be operating in (the health and fitness industry), the type of client you expect to service (your target market), your competition (Big George's Deep Discount Personal Training), and your strategy for attracting clients.

>> **Operations:** This section describes your business's physical location, any equipment you need, the kinds of employees you need, your inventory requirements, and any other applicable operating details, such as a description of your *workflow* (how your business will perform its day-to-day activities). For more information on workflow, turn to Chapter 7.

>> **Management:** Here you outline your key employees (even if you're the only one), external professional profiles (that's your accountant and lawyer, as well as any other professionals you've hired to help you with your business), the members of your advisory board (if you don't have one yet, include this section for the future), and your human-resource needs (how many staff members you'll need to run your business and service your clients).

>> **Financials:** This section contains financial projections that will show whether your concept is viable or whether you need to head back to the drawing board. The projected financial statements — the income statement, the cash-flow projection, and the balance sheet — are estimates based on research of your start-up costs and projected sales.

For even more information on this huge topic, check out *Business Plans Kit For Dummies* by Steven Peterson, PhD, and Peter E. Jaret (published by Wiley).

Developing your mission statement

Having a mission statement is important because it's how you'll introduce your business to the world. The mission statement isn't the full story about you and your business. It's a brief description of who you are, what you do, and why you're in business. Apple's 2022 mission statement is a great example:

Apple's more than 100,000 employees are dedicated to making the best products on earth, and to leaving the world better than we found it.

The statement doesn't say anything about computers or iPhones, but it does tell us who they are (100,000 employees), what they do (make the best products on earth), and why they do it (leaving the world a better than we found it).

REMEMBER

Your mission statement is an important part of your identity and should convey the image of your business that you're trying to create.

Here are some tips for writing a strong mission statement:

>> Keep it short (two to three sentences are plenty).

>> Consider your long-term goals ("leaving the world a better place than we found it").

>> Ask for feedback. If your family, friends, or clients aren't loving it, ask why and try again.

>> Remember that it's okay to change it. Your company will change and grow and your mission will probably evolve too.

TIP

You can start formulating your mission statement by answering these questions:

>> Who are my clients? What is my client population, and what do they want?

>> Who are my competitors, and what makes my business different?

>> What can my business do for my clients?

>> How do we do this for the clients?

>> Why am I in business? What do I want for myself, my clients, my family?

Now compose a brief paragraph incorporating who you are, what you do, how you do it, and who you do it for.

TIP

Before you start framing your mission statement and hanging it all over the walls, put it to the test:

>> Ask your clients if they would want to do business with a company that has your mission statement.

>> Ask your friends if they understand the mission statement and if they would support it.

>> Ask vendors you buy products from (like equipment suppliers and supplement vendors) if it helps them understand your business.

Incorporate feedback you get from your clients into the mission statement, and then repeat the testing process until you have a mission that you can live and work by.

TIP

Your mission statement clearly articulates what your business is all about. Post it on the wall, include it in your marketing materials, and put it on your website.

Researching your market

When you were a kid, didn't you dream about being a spy? C'mon, you know you did. Well, here's your chance. Here's where you go undercover to get the dirt on your potential clients and your competition.

Gathering demographic data

If you don't know the demographics of your chosen location, you need to do research to determine whether the area you want to do business in can support your personal training prowess. You need to know your area's population, a breakdown of the ages and genders of the inhabitants, and the average income of the area. If you're planning to open a personal training business that caters to seniors, you probably don't want to open it across the street from a college campus.

TIP

A great — and free — place to find information about your chosen location is the Census Bureau website (www.census.gov), which lets you look up the demographic makeup of towns, states, or zip codes. You can search for specific information about the location you're considering by zip code or you can look at a town or city as a whole.

REMEMBER

Don't forget your own eyes and ears. If you're interested in opening a business in a particular part of town, drive around and see what kinds of businesses are already located in the area. Spend some time there and get a feel for the atmosphere.

Scoping out the competition

Another important aspect in determining your venture viability is having a strong awareness of your competitors. Your competitors are the personal trainers and personal training companies in your area that are already catering to the people you hope to train one day. The ones you want to scope out are the successful businesses, not the poseurs who think that *lat pulldown* is short for *lateral pulldown*.

TIP

The best way to know your foe is to "shop" them. Call as a prospective client and ask for information about their services. You'll want to know things like:

- ❯❯ What type of services do they offer?
- ❯❯ How much does it cost?
- ❯❯ Are their trainers certified? If so, how?
- ❯❯ How many trainers do they have?
- ❯❯ How long have they been in business?
- ❯❯ Are they insured and bonded as a business?
- ❯❯ When are they open?
- ❯❯ Do they travel to clients' homes or offices?

Not only will you get the information you need to compete in your marketplace, but you may also pick up an idea or two for yourself.

TIP

Pinpoint all your competitors within a five-mile radius of your proposed business location. (An industry survey by the International Health, Racquet & Sportsclub Association [IHRSA] reported that consumers generally travel to fitness facilities that are within five miles of their homes or workplaces.) Make a chart listing the competitors you want to call and the specific items you want to know. This chart will make it easier to compare and contrast.

WHERE TO FIND YOUR COMPETITION

Don't know where to go to find the competition? Start by searching online for personal training businesses in the area. You'll find a list of businesses and you can check out other personal trainers' websites and social media profiles. Get friendly with your local gym manager — gym managers typically have the scoop on the training scene and where to go to find people in the know. Also try your local fitness-equipment store — personal trainers often leave business cards on their counters, and the managers there can fill you in on who's a poseur and who's the real deal.

Another great tip: Search for every URL you can think of that includes the name of your town or neighborhood + "trainer," "personal trainer," "fitness coach," and so on. If someone already has one of the URLs, go there to see who they are and what they do. Chances are, they'll be your primary competition because they were there first and knew to grab a valuable URL. If one of the URLs isn't registered, snap it up so someone else doesn't.

Selecting a location

Now that you know everything about everyone — including where your target market lives, where your competitors are located, and what Big George had for breakfast this morning — selecting a location should be a snap.

If you're still having a hard time deciding, use Google Maps to look up a map of the area you live in. Outline the zip-code boundaries, then label the map with the demographic information you turned up for each zip code — the average household income, the number of households, the predominant gender and class — and take a step back. Does anything jump out at you? Do you notice certain areas with similar profiles that are close together? If you see similarities in certain areas, and those similarities match your objectives, that is most likely where you want to be!

Deciding How Much to Charge

You know about how much a computer, a car, or a house should cost. But how do you put a price on something as intangible as your personal training services? One of the ways your prospective client determines the value of your services is through your fee structure. Whether you realize it or not, what you charge says a lot about you. If your prices are too low, your prospect will think that you're not too confident with your skills as a trainer or that you're not really a pro. If your prices are stratospherically high, your prospect might think that you're a little *too* confident or won't be willing to pay that much for your services. Setting your fee structure at the right level is imperative — both for you and for your client.

Make a list of how much your competitors are charging. Add together all the prices, and divide that number by the number of companies you surveyed. Round up to the nearest dollar, and — voilà! — you have an average price per session. You should be fine as long as your prices are close to that average — you don't want to be too far under or too far over. Just like Goldilocks, you want your price to be "just right."

If you don't have many competitors in your area to help you set your price point, first do a dance of joy. Then log on to the IHRSA website at www.ihrsa.org for industry statistics — such as average session price by state or club type — to point you in the right direction.

Too often, newbie trainers are so hungry for clients that they'll do just about anything for the business — from offering multiple free sessions to charging bargain-basement rates. Be confident that you're offering a valuable service. After all, what can be more important than keeping people healthy? Recognizing and standing by your worth tells your client that you know what you're doing and you know what it's worth. Charging fair prices even helps your clients — the confidence that you exude gives your clients the confidence to let you help them.

To Market, to Market: Getting the Word Out about Your Services

Owning a personal training business is not like *Field of Dreams* — if you build it, they may *not* come. You can go ahead and open your business, but you won't have any clients if they don't know you're there. Marketing is simple. It's about offering a top-notch service and then telling people about it. And that's where your marketing plan comes in.

You versus the competition: Knowing what sets you apart from the crowd

Before coming up with your marketing plan, think about what makes you different from your competition. How will you convince clients to sign up with *you*? What do you offer that sets you apart? By understanding and establishing your *unique selling proposition* (USP), you'll form the foundation on which you'll base your marketing strategy.

TIP

Consider each of your competitor's selling points. Do they have a good location? Are all their trainers certified? Are they bottom-of-the-barrel cheap? Make a comparative list of their selling points versus your selling points.

Developing a marketing plan

A marketing plan outlines the specific actions you need to take for getting in front of potential clients. In your marketing plan, make sure you detail:

>> **Your services and what makes them unique:** Refer to the preceding section, "You versus the competition: Knowing what sets you apart from the crowd."

>> **Your pricing strategy:** Refer to "Deciding How Much to Charge" earlier in this chapter.

>> **Your sales and distribution plan:** How are you going to get your services and products to clients — online or in person? Will you accept credit card payments? Will you offer refunds?

>> **Your advertising and promotion plan:** See Chapter 8 for more-detailed information on advertising.

Doing the Math: Projecting Your Income and Expenses

The last section of your business plan is the most important: your financial plan. The financial plan tells you whether you can do what you hope to do — that is, whether your business will make money.

Estimating expenses

Here's where you get a grip on what you're going to have to shell out to be in business for yourself. Divide your expenses into two groups: *start-up expenses* (typically, one-time costs) and *operating expenses* (which occur on a regular basis).

Start-up costs

TIP

Think of your business as a car: Before you can get anywhere, you have to fill up the tank. Start-up costs are all the things you have to pay for to get your business started. Start-up costs include the following:

>> Business registration fees

>> Business licensing and permits

>> Rent deposits

>> Equipment

>> Promotional materials

>> Your website (domain registration, hosting fees)

>> Utility setup fees (phone, internet, electricity)

REMEMBER

This list is just a small sample of possible start-up costs. You'll find that, as you write down your own start-up costs, the list will seem to grow faster than the national debt.

Operating expenses

A full tank will get you moving, but as with your car, your business requires regular infusions of cash to stay in gear. Your operating expenses may include the following:

>> Payroll (your salary and/or staff salaries)

>> Rent and building maintenance expenses

>> Loan payments

>> Phone and utility bills

>> Advertising

>> Continuing education

>> Equipment maintenance

Again, this is just a sample list to put you on the right track. After you've completed your list of operating expenses, add up all the expenses to know how much dough you'll need to come up with each month.

Projecting income

Now that you have a clear idea of how much you'll need to pay the bills, you have to figure out how many clients you need in order to earn that money! Bear in mind when you're projecting your session load for the week that you need to leave room for:

GETTING HELP ESTIMATING EXPENSES

If you're having a hard time estimating expenses, turn to the International Health, Racquet & Sportsclub Association (IHRSA) for help. IHRSA performs extensive surveys every year of the entire health-club industry. They publish industry-specific periodicals and custom reports geared toward very specific sectors of the population. You need to be a member to access some of their information, but you can purchase their reports and books through their online store.

>> **Travel time:** If you travel to your clients' homes or workplaces, you need to factor in that driving time.

>> **Cancellations:** People inevitably cancel, and you have to figure that it'll happen — you're better off planning for at least some of your clients to cancel. That way, if they all keep their appointments, you'll be ahead of the game.

>> **Administrative time:** Your clients don't pay you for the time you spend writing their programs, but you have to do it anyway.

>> **Personal time:** If you don't want to burn out within six months, I recommend you build time off into your schedule now.

TIP

Okay, here comes the fun part. Break out your calculator and use this formula to determine how many sessions you need to conduct per week to meet your monthly income goal:

1. **Add your total monthly expenses (see "Operating expenses" earlier in this chapter) to the amount you want to make as a profit.**

   Be realistic! This profit has to pay for your mortgage, food, entertainment, and all other nonbusiness expenses.

2. **Divide the number you came up with in Step 1 by your session price (refer to "Deciding How Much to Charge" earlier in this chapter).**

   The resulting number is how many paid sessions you need to conduct per month in order to pay your bills.

3. **Multiply the number you came up with in Step 2 by 12 (the number of months in a year).**

4. **Divide the number you came up with in Step 3 by 52 (the number of weeks in a year).**

   This figure is how many paid sessions per week you'll need to conduct in order to make your desired monthly income.

REMEMBER

   If you plan to take vacation time, you need to account for this in your calculations. For example, if you plan to take two weeks of vacation time, divide by 50 rather than 52.

Now that you know how much you need to make, project your entire financial scenario — by month for the first year, then by year for the following years.

» Creating a board of advisors

» Determining your business structure

» Naming your business

» Getting registered

Chapter **6**

Setting Up Shop

You have a client. Now you're a full-fledged personal training business, right? Not quite. As you probably know, personal training involves more than just the training. You need to get all your ducks in a row in terms of handling taxes, registering your business, and deciding on a business structure. And you have to work with more people than just clients to get your business off the ground. Professionals such as lawyers, accountants, physical therapists, and other trainers will serve as your advisory board, mentors, and networking group. In this chapter, I show you how to connect with the people who will help you reach the pinnacle of personal training success.

Shakespeare said a rose by any other name still smells as sweet. But will a personal training business called Lazy Louie's Personal Train-o-rama still bring in clients? Probably not. In this chapter, I also help you come up with a winning business name (and come up with a logo to match).

A Little Help from Your Friends: Forming Your Support System

You'd think that an independent professional like yourself would be — how should I put this? — independent. Far from it. No matter how much of a take-charge person you are, to get your business up and running (and lifting, and stretching, and jumping rope), you'll need to rely on lawyers, accountants, bankers, insurance brokers, health professionals (physical therapists, orthopedists, and so on), friends and family, athletic directors or coaches for local schools and sports teams, and other trainers. Sure, you can aspire to be the next Oprah Winfrey, an uber-entrepreneur with her hands in a thousand pies — but even Oprah has a team of assistants doing her bidding behind the cameras.

Drafting your professional team

At first, hiring a team of professionals probably feels out of your league — after all, you're not Oprah. But at the very least, you need to rely on a lawyer and an accountant to help move your business beyond the field of dreams and make it a reality. And because your business (like all businesses) will change with time — whether you're hiring new employees, moving across town, or opening additional locations — you'll need the advice of some pros to keep yourself on the up-and-up.

In the following sections, I tell you about the people you need and how to find them, and which questions you should ask before you put someone to work for you.

REMEMBER

You need to interview these professionals just like you would a potential employee. Finally, I let you know whether going it alone, without a team of professionals, is an option.

Knowing which players you need

Before you start drafting your team, you need to know which players you need (that is, which professionals have the kind of expertise that can help you out). In the following sections, I tell you about the four biggies: lawyers, accountants, insurance brokers, and bankers.

HIRING A LEGAL EAGLE

What do you need a lawyer for? You're not planning to sue anybody, are you? Despite the impression you may get from TV shows like *Law & Order*, lawyers do a lot more than represent you when clients mysteriously disappear after hitting on your spouse or missing a payment. A lawyer can

>> Help you make sure your business is registered and licensed properly.

>> Defend you if someone decides to bring legal action against you.

>> Give you legal advice related to the operation of your business (such as when you hire and fire employees).

>> Create and interpret contracts and leases — even the small type!

>> Choose the right business structure (such as a limited liability corporation, partnership, sole proprietorship, or corporation — more on this in "Structuring Your Business" later in this chapter).

TIP

Don't know where to start your search for a lawyer? Try these tips:

>> **If you already have a banker, accountant, or insurance agent — professionals that I recommend hiring — ask them for recommendations.**

>> **Go to the U.S. Chamber of Commerce website (www.uschamber.com) and search for small business attorneys in your state.**

>> **Ask your friends, family, and clients for suggestions.** Who knows? One of them may actually be a lawyer who would be willing to trade advice for training.

TRUE STORY

When I was planning to start my business, I turned to an attorney who was a long-time client of mine for advice about which business structure to choose for growth and personal liability protection. Starting here helped me to avoid potential pitfalls in my business that I wouldn't have known about if I hadn't asked for help.

GETTING ACCOUNTED FOR

They're often called bean counters — though you shouldn't call them this to their faces if you want them to help you — but accountants do a lot more than count legumes. In fact, they can make the difference between a personal trainer who thrives and one who gets tossed into jail for tax fraud. An accountant can

>> **Work with your lawyer to help you decide what type of business structure to have.**

>> **Design and set up your accounting system so that year-end financial reporting will be easier.**

>> **Keep Uncle Sam off your back by making sure you pay the correct types of taxes in the right amounts.**

>> **Make sure that you send out W2 and 1099 forms to the right people at the right times.** If you hire independent contractors, the accountant will make sure that they actually fit the criteria for independent contractors

(who get 1099s) and are not considered employees (who get W2s) by the government.

>> **Let you know whether that smoothie or pair of sneakers is a legitimate business expense.**

>> **Show you how to separate your personal and business expenses, from home offices to work mileage to foam rollers.**

>> **Advise you through the process if the IRS ever audits you.**

>> **Help you decide whether you're better off leasing or buying that exercise equipment or office machine.**

>> **Compile your financial records for the past period.**

>> **Advise you regarding tax shelters or direct you to professionals who specialize in investing and protecting your hard-earned income.**

>> **Help you understand your financial statements.**

TIP

Even if you have an accountant making sure your finances and taxes are on the up-and-up, you should be able to understand your business's finances so that you'll always know how your business is doing. Check out *Accounting For Dummies* by John A. Tracy and Tage C. Tracey, and the latest edition of *Taxes For Dummies* by Eric Tyson, Margaret Atkins Munro, and David J. Silverman (both published by Wiley) for more help.

TIP

Start your search for an accountant by following these tips:

>> **Check with the Professional Association of Small Business Accountants (PASBA).** The PASBA website lets you search for accountants in your area. Check it out at www.pasba.org.

>> **Ask your friends, family, and clients who their accountants are.**

>> **Ask local small businesses, such as salons, for their recommendations.**

INSURING YOURSELF

No matter how careful, thoughtful, and just plain wonderful you are, a claim of personal injury, bodily injury, or sexual harassment can wipe out your bank account — even if it's not true. That's why you need to find an insurance agent. An insurance agent can help you determine how much coverage you need if you set up your own place of business.

The type of insurance you'll need depends on whether you're working in someone else's facility or leasing you own space. Either way, you need to carry professional liability insurance. If you're ever involved in a lawsuit claiming you made a mistake in the service you provided (for example, if you aren't paying attention and a client is injured while training with you), this type of insurance will help to cover legal expenses. Most personal trainers can purchase this insurance, which is relatively inexpensive, through their certification body.

It goes without saying, of course, that just because you're insured doesn't mean you have a free pass to do things that are irresponsible (just like car insurance doesn't mean you can drive as fast as you want). Ideally, you'll never need to file an insurance claim — but you still need the insurance in case an accident happens.

Most small-business owners seek out independent brokers in their area; brokers are independent businesspeople who deal with different types of insurance from different companies. Your insurance broker will be able to find the best liability insurance as well as health insurance and other policies.

Personal trainers can also find fitness-instructor insurance through credentialing organizations and insurance agencies that specialize in the fitness industry.

Check out these resources for finding an independent insurance agent:

>> **Search the Independent Insurance Agents & Brokers of America (IIABA) website at** www.independentagent.com. The IIABA has a database of agents that you can search for by name or location.

>> **Check with your local Chamber of Commerce for recommendations.**

>> **Ask other local businesses whom they use.**

BANKING ON IT

Most small businesses (like you!) have banks, but no bankers. But a banker — the person who handles your account at the bank — can help you get credit, avoid fees, and enhance your business opportunities through the banker's extensive personal contacts.

Personal trainers rarely bother with bankers at all — and when they do, they don't understand how to cultivate an alliance with them. Follow these tips to build a good relationship with your banker — after all, good rapport is like money in the bank!

>> **Invite your banker to tour your facilities.** Just don't do this right before asking for a loan, because you don't want to look like you're pleading for sympathy or special favors.

>> **Let your banker know when something important occurs** — for example, when you've landed new clients, reached a profit goal, or faced a new competitor.

>> **Don't ask for favors at the beginning of your relationship.** First create goodwill by giving the bank your business.

>> **If something bad happens in your business** — for example, if you lose several clients — try to determine the cause and develop a plan of action *before* contacting your banker.

TIP

The best way to find a banker who will help keep the money flowing is to ask other small business owners in your area which banks they use, and then research the banks to figure out which one fits your needs. If you want to bank online, does the bank offer this service? How long does getting a loan approved usually take? How much red tape will you have to go through to, say, replace a missing ATM card?

Separating the good from the bad

Have you ever been stuck with a bad haircut because you walked into a hair salon without checking it out first?

WARNING

If you hire a lawyer, an accountant, or any other professional without doing some research first, you could end up being sued or in trouble with the IRS, which is a lot worse than a bad-hair day.

TIP

Ask to meet with the professional for a consultation (many will do this free of charge) and make sure that person:

>> **Has experience working with small businesses like yours.**

>> **Asks more questions than Barbara Walters.** The person should interview *you* in addition to being interviewed *by* you. They may ask you where you want to be in five years, what your goals are, how you expect to reach those goals, what your major concerns are, and what you expect from a lawyer/accountant/banker/insurance agent. Be prepared to answer these questions so your interview is productive.

>> **Has time for you.** A lawyer or accountant who constantly interrupts your meeting to answer her phone and deal with crises probably won't have the time to give you the attention you need.

>> **Explains their fee structure so that you understand it.**

>> **Defines industry terms you need to know,** such as *LLC* and *1099,* in plain English.

Going it alone: Should you or shouldn't you?

Maybe you took a tax-preparation class, or maybe you were a lawyer before you realized that you'd rather pump iron than push papers. Can you save money by handling the accounting or legal tasks yourself?

It depends. Every hour you're sweating over tax filings or contracts is an hour that you're not making money or building your business. Sure, you may save money by filing that form yourself, but you're simultaneously *losing* money because you could have been training a client in that hour. The question is: How much will you save by doing these tasks yourself, and how much will you lose by not being able to spend the time training clients?

REMEMBER

When you're training a client, you're building goodwill and giving that person something to tell all their friends about (and referrals are the lifeblood of the personal training business — see Chapter 8 for more information on referrals). While you're hassling over a form, you're building nothing but a headache. You can also be spending that time working on meeting your business goals by networking, marketing, and dreaming up new ways to bring on more clients.

TIP

If you're strapped for cash when you first start out, doing as much as you can yourself may make sense. But as soon as you're able, hire professionals to do their thing so that you have time to do *your* thing — that is, train clients and build your business.

Someone to look up to: Mentors

A mentor isn't just someone who will tell you, "Jane, I prefer this logo to that one" or, "Bob, I think you need to drop that client to save your sanity." A *mentor* is someone you trust, who has an interest in you and your business, and someone who will tell you what you need to hear (not always what you want to hear). It's also someone who's a little further along than you are in your career who can relate to the challenges and opportunities you're facing. A mentor can be:

>> A friend

>> A professional, such as a former teacher or professor

>> Your spouse, son or daughter, parent, or sibling

>> The owner of a local business

>> Another personal trainer

You can create a formal mentor-mentee relationship, but you don't necessarily have to; in other words, no one needs to sign on the dotted line. But as you develop your network, you'll find people whose opinions you trust and whose success you'd like to emulate. You'll naturally gravitate toward these people when you have a question or a problem.

I recommend finding mentorship early and having at least one mentor at every stage of your career.

Building your network

Networking is a low-cost and effective way to build your reputation, grow your professional contact list, and earn personal training referrals. Like marketing, networking involves getting the attention of people you want to do business with, but there's more to it than that. Networking is less about pitching your services to prospects and more about establishing and nurturing relationships. It gets your name out there, but more importantly, you will have professionals you can call on when you need to. For example, let's say you have a prospective client with an injury. Instead of turning the client away, or "referring out" to a physical therapist, you call a physical therapist in your network and help the client to schedule an appointment.

Having a strong professional network to call on is invaluable, but keep in mind that you are one half of your professional relationships. You too need to be available when someone in your network needs personal training advice. Being a good partner in your professional relationships goes both ways!

I am super lucky to have an awesome network. I have the best physical therapist, dietitian, orthopedic surgeon, massage therapist, and many more in my circle and consider myself even luckier to call most of them friends. I didn't set out to market my services to any of these people; instead, I have always taken a genuine interest in what they do so I could to get to know them and learn about what they do. This has given me so many opportunities to expand my knowledge and I have received a lot of personal training referrals from my network over the years. More important though, I have helped countless personal training clients by referring them to the best professionals in my area.

Networking with your peers

Your peers are the people who are doing what you're doing: personal training. "Peers? You mean competitors," you gripe. "Why should I network with them?"

Being active in the fitness community and networking with other trainers will keep you up to date on industry happenings, help you generate new ideas for running your business, and give you understanding ears to bend when your spouse is sick of hearing about gym drama. In addition, personal trainers often refer potential clients to other trainers when they have too many clients to handle or when a client is looking for specialized services they don't normally provide.

REMEMBER

You can't be all things to all people and there are plenty of clients to go around!

TRUE STORY

Networking with your peers can give you more than a convenient sounding board — it can also boost your business. When I decided to go back to graduate school full-time, I sold my personal training business to a peer. It was a win-win for both of us and I was able to pursue the next chapter in my career knowing that my clients were in good hands.

TIP

To get in on the networking loop, you can:

>> **Attend industry conventions.**

>> **Talk to other trainers in your area.** You can find many of them online through their websites or on social media.

>> **Participate in Facebook or other online social networking groups for personal trainers.**

TIP

Your network doesn't only have to consist of healthcare and fitness professionals. Look to other industries for services that you or your clients might need and that could benefit from you. This could include attorneys, accountants, real estate agents, and many more.

You may also want to consider forming an advisory board for your business. An *advisory board* is simply a group of people you go to for advice on running your business, and it can be as formal or as informal as you like. With their expertise, these people can help you get funding, make smart business decisions, and avoid costly mistakes.

An advisory board can consist of:

>> Your lawyer

>> Your accountant

>> Your mentors

>> Professionals in related fields (such as physical therapists or orthopedic surgeons)

>> Public relations (PR) people

>> Other small-business owners

TIP

To form your advisory board, simply ask these people if they'd like to serve on your board. Be clear as to what this means — do you expect to contact them only when you have a problem or a question, or do you expect more hands-on advising?

You're already paying your accountant and lawyer; if you feel bad asking other people to advise you for free, you can offer them personal training sessions in exchange for their counsel. In addition, if they agree to meet you in person, you can treat them to a cup of coffee or a nice lunch.

Structuring Your Business

Y'know those letters businesses have after their names, like *Inc.* or *LLC?* They aren't there just because they sound cool. They indicate the legal structure of the business. The legal structure has an impact on how much you pay in taxes, the amount of paperwork you have to do, the personal liability you face, and your ability to raise money for your business.

Liability, taxation, and record-keeping are all things to keep in mind when choosing your type of business entity. The following sections offer a brief look at the differences between the most common forms of business entities.

REMEMBER

A lawyer can help you to decide which of these entities is best for your business:

Sole proprietorship

A *sole proprietorship* is the most common form of business organization among small business owners. In this type of business, you're the proprietor and you have complete managerial control of the business. The drawback to sole proprietorship, however, is that you're personally liable for all financial obligations of the business. If someone sues your business, they can come after you personally to ante up the dough from your own personal bank account.

Partnership

A *partnership* is a business relationship between two or more people who share the profits and losses of the business. The partners report any losses or profits on their individual income-tax returns. The benefit of this business structure is that it's easy to set up and operate. Unfortunately, as in a sole proprietorship, the partners remain personally liable for all financial obligations of the business.

Corporation

A *corporation* is taxed (just like an individual is) and can be held legally liable for its actions. The corporation can make a profit or take on a loss. The key difference between a corporation and a sole proprietorship is that, if someone sues your business, your personal assets remain safe at home underneath the mattress. In other words, your personal finances are separate from your business finances. The drawback is that running a corporation requires extensive record-keeping.

Limited liability corporation

TIP

Want to have it both ways? The *limited liability corporation* (LLC) is the one to pick. It's taxed like a partnership but has limited liability like corporations (meaning your personal finances are separate from your business finances).

Getting Registered and IDed (Even if You're Over 21)

When you start a business, you need to get the proper licenses, permits, and ID numbers so that all those government officials can look busy when the boss walks by. The permits, licenses, and IDs required of you depend on where you live, but I offer some general guidelines in the following sections.

TIP

This is only a sampling of the licenses, permits, and ID numbers you may need to do business in your city or state. A lawyer will be able to help you navigate the maze of requirements in your particular location.

Employer Identification Number

The Employer Identification Number (EIN), also known as a federal tax identification number, is used to identify a business entity. You'll use the EIN in place of your Social Security number on tax forms. You can find instructions to apply for an EIN on the IRS website (www.irs.gov).

Business license

No matter where you decide to set up shop, you'll likely need a business license to operate legally. If your business is located within an incorporated city's limits, you should get a license from the city; if you're outside the city limits, you'll probably get your license from the county.

TIP

For more information, contact the county or city office in your area. You can find links to individual states' business-license forms on the Small Business Administration (SBA) website.

Certificate of occupancy

If you plan to occupy a building with your new business, you may have to apply for a Certificate of Occupancy from a city or county zoning department. For more information, contact the county or city office in your area.

Fictitious business name

Businesses that use a name other than the owner's must register the fictitious name with the state. This rule doesn't apply to corporations doing business under their corporate name or to those practicing any profession under a partnership name. For more information, contact your state or local government.

A Rose Is More than a Rose: Naming Your Business

Can you imagine people referring their friends to "that personal trainer, um, what's his name, the guy down the street"? Probably not. That's why you need a catchy, memorable name for your business.

Your business name should convey your expertise, value, and uniqueness. You want something that will tell potential clients that you're a personal trainer, and a darn good one (so "Doughnuts and Dumbbells Personal Training" is out). Don't stress — in the following sections, I show you how it's done.

Playing the name game

The first step to finding a business name that will have clients beating down your doors is to decide what you want your name to communicate. In Chapter 2, you started thinking about what your client population will be, how you'll position yourself (an affordable alternative? trainer to the stars?), and whether you'll concentrate on individuals or group classes. Your name should convey this information in as few words as possible while avoiding potential misunderstanding by prospective clients. (For example, if you chose the name "We Pump You Up," people may not know if you're a personal training company, a balloon manufacturer, or a tire retailer.)

TIP

Many experts say that your business name should be made up of real words or combinations of words rather than made-up monikers. Sure, Xerox and Nike work for those companies, but those companies also have million-dollar marketing budgets to help their names stick in consumers' minds. If your marketing budget consists of spare change and pocket lint, you're better off going for actual words that people will recognize.

WARNING

Think carefully before going with constrained names that limit you to certain locations or services. For example, say you name your business "San Antonio Personal Training." What if you move to Walla Walla, Washington? And if you choose the name "Fun and Games Fitness for Kids" you won't be able to expand into another client population.

WARNING

Think carefully before using your own name for your business name. It's probably fine if you know for certain that you don't want to grow your business beyond just you, but if you do hire additional trainers down the road, everyone who walks in the door will want to train with the person whose name is on the sign (yes, that's you). And if you ever want to sell the business, you're going to have to explain why the brand has value even without you staying involved.

TIP

Ask yourself the following questions to decide on a moniker for your business:

>> What is my target market? (See Chapter 8 for more information.)

>> What problems do I solve for my target market? Do I help them lose weight, get healthy, increase their confidence?

>> What words or phrases appeal to my target market? Perhaps words like *healthy, fit,* or *strong*?

>> What are the best benefits my business brings to customers?

>> What kind of name would differentiate me, in a positive way, from my competitors?

When you have a few contenders, run them by friends, family, and potential clients to get their reactions. Be sure to say the names aloud. Can you imagine answering the phone with this business name? If it doesn't roll off the tongue, 86 it.

TIP

If you're having trouble deciding on a name, try using a free business name generator. You can find several by searching online for "business name generator."

Marking your territory: The trademark

Any word or image (or combination of words and images) used to distinguish your business or services from other businesses or services can be a trademark. You don't have to officially trademark the name, but doing so ensures that someone else can't start using it next week.

Making sure your name isn't already taken

Earlier in this chapter, I recommend hiring a lawyer to handle your legal matters. But in the case of searching out names, you can easily do this yourself.

TIP

Search the trademark filings on the U.S. Patent and Trademark Office (USPTO) website (www.uspto.gov) to ensure your name isn't already trademarked. Their Trademark Electronic Search System (TESS) contains more than three million pending, registered, and dead federal trademarks. They also have other helpful resources, such as instructions on how to submit your trademarks and information about how much it will cost to send in an application.

In addition, search online to make sure nobody else has already staked a claim on your preferred name.

Filing a trademark application

You can file your application online with the USPTO at www.uspto.gov/trademarks/apply.

REMEMBER

You don't have to have a lawyer submit your application, but if you do it yourself, you're responsible for complying with all requirements of the trademark statute and rules. If you do use a lawyer, the USPTO will correspond only with the lawyer, not with you directly.

As they say, nothing in life is free, and that includes trademark applications. As of this writing, submitting an application costs $350.

TRUE STORY

Several years after starting my personal training business, I decided to re-name it. We were preparing to move into a larger facility and the timing was right to separate my personal name from my business name. About three years later, a very large and recognizable company with similarities to my business announced that they were re-branding. This included a new name — the same name as my small business with a slightly different spelling. After expressing my concerns to one of the company's vice presidents, I was told that they didn't see their new name as a conflict of interest and would not be changing it. Fortunately, because I had followed the advice from my attorney to file a trademark application when I changed my business name, I was able to legally support my claim of trademark infringement. I never could have anticipated something like this happening, and had I not trademarked my name, that big company with much deeper pockets than mine could have simply waited until I ran out of money before running me out of business.

Image Is Everything: Creating Your Look

When you see a pair of shoes with a swoosh on the side, you know they're Nikes without reading the label. That's the power of a logo — a graphical depiction of your company. Your logo will help people recognize and remember your business. A logo gives you an image of substance and stability. It also shows you're serious about what you do.

But choosing a logo design is only one part of creating your image. Your logo design is part of your brand and should express the personality of your business to your audience. Your potential clients should have an idea of what you do just by looking at your logo, and ideally your logo will become recognizable on its own over time. Did you know colors also influence how people perceive your business? In this section I show you how to decide on a logo design and how to choose the right colors for your branding materials.

Branding that works

Branding is simply the process of creating your company's image. This includes things like your logo, the colors you use in your marketing materials, and your company mission statement. Putting some thought into your branding matters because you want people to have a positive perception of you and your company.

There's not a right or wrong way to start the process, and if you're not sure where to begin, I recommend working on your logo design first. Asking yourself questions about your business and the image you want to project will help you to envision what your overall look will be, including what you want your logo to look like.

Here are some criteria of a good logo for your brand or company:

>> **Readability:** A busy design may make it hard for people to understand your logo or read the name of your business.

>> **Memorability:** You want your logo to create interest, not yawns. When potential clients see your logo, they should think of your business.

>> **Uniqueness:** If your logo looks like the logo of the personal trainer down the street, it won't distinguish your services from your competitor's.

>> **Appropriateness to your business:** Weights, healthy bodies, training shoes? Good. Flowers, puppies, cookies? Bad.

>> **Professionalism and stability:** You want to look like a professional business, and not some fly-by-night with a clip-art logo, so cutesy cartoons are out.

>> **The ability to convey the message in any size and any medium:** You should test your logo to make sure it looks good in email, on your website, and on your Facebook business page.

>> **A design that's not too trendy:** A trendy logo will quickly go out of date and make you and your business look out of date as well.

REMEMBER

You don't have to answer *all* the questions about your business in your logo design.

When you're designing your logo, keep in mind the message you want your business to convey and who your customers are.

TIP

Not too long ago, unless you had graphic-design experience, logo design had to be done professionally if you wanted it to look, well, professional. These days you can use various programs and apps to create a stellar look on your own without spending big bucks. I recommend checking out Canva if you want to give DIY logo design a try. If you would rather stay in your own lane and let someone with graphic-design experience turn your vision into the perfect logo, check out Upwork or Fiverr. Or you can try contacting art and design schools for students who would be willing to design your logo in exchange for a few bucks. Who knows? Maybe someday you'll become a globally recognized brand. After all, the iconic Nike swoosh logo was created by a graphic-design student for $35.

Giving your logo some color

In addition to the graphic design of the logo — the image you choose — you'll need to decide on colors. Color conveys emotions, so the colors you choose for your logo, your office or gym (if you have one), and your branded apparel (especially if you employ other trainers and they wear your branded apparel) are important aspects of your image.

TRUE STORY

Choosing a logo for my business didn't come easily to me until I really thought about how I wanted the image to represent my vision. The logo I ended up using included a prominent orange circle — because in psychology, round shapes represent community (like "circle of friends") and orange is the color of vitality, good health, and energy.

Okay, so you decide on a three-color logo incorporating a duck-billed platypus lifting weights. You go all out and spend several thousand dollars getting some big-shot designer to draw it up for you. And the first time you print your logo on a black-and-white printer, that beautiful, expensive logo ends up looking like a big blob.

That's why you need to make extra sure that the logo you go with works in black and white, as well as in all different sizes. The solution: Keep it simple. The most common mistake made by anyone designing a logo is creating a symbol that is much too complicated and difficult to read — especially in smaller sizes.

TIP

You can trademark your logo if you like; this will ensure that other businesses can't "borrow" your awesome design. You trademark your logo in the same way that you trademark your business name (see "Filing a trademark application" earlier in this chapter).

Chapter 7

Developing Sound Business Practices

'm guessing you probably want to be a personal trainer because you love physical action and you'd rather do push-ups than push papers. But alas, every personal trainer must push some paper, from legal forms to client session notes and activity logs.

In this chapter, I show you how to keep your business organized and running smoothly. Here, you discover everything you need to know about setting policies, maintaining documentation, tracking your cash, and more.

Crossing Your T's and Dotting Your I's: Legal Forms for Your Business

Personal training is an injury-prone profession, and we're a litigious society. Add these together and what do you get? Clients who sue if they get a hangnail when they're doing battle rope waves. Okay, maybe that's a bit of an exaggeration. But when people get hurt, they tend to sue, so you need to do everything you can to make sure you don't wind up on *Judge Judy*.

Three kinds of forms will help you keep yourself out of hot (and by hot, I mean legal) water — incident-report forms, liability waiver forms, and disclaimer and informed-consent forms.

Disclaimer and informed-consent form

The disclaimer and informed-consent form states that the client understands that there is a risk involved with personal training, and that they have disclosed all relevant medical, physiological, and lifestyle information that you need to create their exercise program. It also gives you permission to work with the client based on the information the client has given.

TIP

You need to collect detailed health history information for every client from the very beginning and update your records if anything changes. I show you how to do this in Chapter 10.

REMEMBER

If you have the client write out any past injuries and sign the disclaimer and informed-consent form, you're somewhat protected if the client tries to sue you for causing an injury they already had. Not only that, but having this information allows you to design a program around the client's previous injuries and illnesses. Here's a link to the consent form I use and recommend from the American College of Sports Medicine (ACSM): www.acsm.org/docs/default-source/certification-documents/b_exprescripreferral_pdf.pdf?sfvrsn=45ad4f30_0.

Incident-report form

The incident-report form is the one you'll need to fill out if a client gets injured on your watch.

ATTORNEY (N): YOUR NEW BEST FRIEND

In Chapter 6, you learn why you need a good attorney on your professional team. An attorney can help you create forms that reduce your liability and can represent you if you get sued. If you haven't found an attorney yet, follow the advice in Chapter 6 on how to find the one who's right for your business.

TIP

The incident-report form should include the following information:

>> **Identification information:** Record the date and time, the name of the person in charge, the activity that was going on, the names and contact information for all witnesses, and the name of your insurance company. (See Chapter 6 for more information on getting liability insurance — a must.)

>> **Location of incident:** Take note of the area where the accident or injury took place plus the location of any witnesses and other participants.

>> **Action of the injured party:** Describe in detail what was going on and specifically what action caused the injury.

>> **Sequence of events:** Describe when, in the course of the workout, the injury happened (for example, during the warm-up).

>> **Preventive measures that could have been taken by the injured party:** Detail what the client could have done to prevent the injury.

>> **Procedures followed in giving aid:** Write down what first-aid measures were taken and by whom, including who called for help and when the help arrived.

>> **Disposition or follow-up:** Follow up with the doctor or hospital and record how long the medical professional said the client must refrain from exercise after the injury. Be sure you ask your client if it's okay to follow up; you'll need their written permission.

>> **Person completing the accident report:** Record the name of the person completing the report, along with the person's position and whether that person witnessed the incident.

REMEMBER

You should keep completed incident forms for seven years, although this number varies by state. Contact your lawyer for advice.

Liability waiver form

Before you go skydiving or take a dance class (or do just about anything these days), you have to sign a form that says you promise not to sue if you plummet to your death while skydiving or lose an arm while tap-dancing. That's a *liability waiver form*, and you need one for your personal training business. It's not foolproof, but a liability waiver form can go a long way toward keeping you out of court.

TIP

Consult your attorney for help developing a liability waiver that you can have clients sign. You can draft the form yourself, but you should still have your attorney review it before you use it to make sure all your i's are dotted and t's are crossed. You can check out a sample liability waiver form at https://ncaaorg. s3.amazonaws.com/championships/resources/common/NCAAChamp_Volunteer WaiverofLiabilityForm.pdf.

Going with the Flow: Determining in What Order to Conduct Your Business

When a prospective client comes to you and eventually (you hope) becomes a paying client, things happen in a certain order. A stranger doesn't just walk in off the street and start doing goblet squats. And a client you've seen for five years doesn't walk in one day and expect you to do an initial assessment. This order in which things happen is referred to as *client flow* — it's literally just the way your clients *flow*, or progress, through your business operations. Step 1, for example, may be when a prospective client expresses interest and you fill out a client lead sheet. Step 2 may be an initial consultation, and so on through the life cycle of a client.

In order for everything to run smoothly and efficiently, you need to plan what to do and when to do it. For example, what if someone expresses interest but then doesn't end up becoming a paying client? Will you call in two weeks or send a card in a month — or both? When will you do a fitness reevaluation? When will you make stay-in-touch calls to former clients? Putting *standard operating procedures* and *systems* in place for tracking all these details will help you stay on top of things. I show you how to create them here.

REMEMBER

Much of this information comes from your business plan (see Chapter 5), which tells you who your client population is, how you plan to target them, and what you'll do when you have them.

SOPs and Systems: Maintaining a well-oiled machine

Have you ever noticed how your favorite Starbucks drink or Subway sandwich or (insert chain restaurant name and item here) is always exactly the same every time no matter where you order it from? That's because your go-to place has *standard operating procedures* or SOPs that every employee at every location follows. SOPs are clear step-by-step instructions that ensure your drink is made exactly the same way by every single person every single time.

TIP

SOPs are important for all businesses and you can learn a lot from other industries about how to create yours. Here's a great article to get you started: https://medium.com/the-mission/building-a-business-machine-the-ultimate-guide-to-standard-operating-procedures-1cc4cc473aca.

Consider creating a client flow SOP to keep track of your client flow. These days I use Google Docs to keep track of everything from administrative actions and client care, and when I had my training facility, I also included trainers' responsibilities for each client.

Your client flow SOP may have data like what you see in Table 7-1. *Remember:* This table is just to give you an idea of what kind of information your client flow SOP may contain — it doesn't contain all the steps or possible scenarios.

TABLE 7-1 What You May Include on Your Client Flow SOP

Situation	Administrative	Client Care	Trainer
Prospect buys a package and pays up front.	1. Take the client's picture. 2. Schedule a fitness assessment. 3. Collect the payment.	1. Assign the client a client ID. 2. Set up a service contract. 3. Have the client sign the waiver, cancellation policy, and service contract. 4. Give the client a tour of your facility. 5. Give the client a copy of the waiver, contract, and What to Expect sheet.	N/A
The client shows up for the initial fitness assessment.	1. Greets the client and alerts the trainer assigned to them that the client is here. 2. After the assessment, schedules the next session. 3. Rings up sales.	N/A	1. Has the fitness assessment equipment, blood-pressure cuff, heart-rate monitor, and towel ready. 2. Greets the client. 3. Performs the assessment. 4. Enters a follow-up call two days out in planner.

(continued)

TABLE 7-1 *(continued)*

Situation	Administrative	Client Care	Trainer
Two days after the first session.	N/A	N/A	**1.** Calls to follow up with the client. Asks the client how they're feeling and asks if the client has any questions. **2.** Confirms the next appointment. **3.** Makes notes in client file.

TIP

Notice how detailed the chart is? This extra detail is there to ensure that every client gets the same exact treatment and that you (or your employees) don't skip any steps.

REMEMBER

Did you know that all airline pilots complete the same safety checklist in the cockpit every single time before they fly? And that your entire flight crew follows several SOPs every time you fly? You know, "flight attendants prepare for landing." And how many times have you learned how to fasten your seatbelt on an airplane? That's because most plane crashes are caused by human error. Just like you wouldn't want a pilot to skip any steps on the safety checklist, be sure that you don't skip steps in your order of operations. If you skip the fitness assessment because the client is eager to begin, and then the client gets injured, you're in big trouble. Or if you send a thank-you note or special offer to one client and not another — and that second client finds out — you'll create hard feelings.

Every step you take, every move you make . . .: Keeping track of everything you and your client do

Keeping notes on everything you do with a client from day 1 can keep you out of court. For example, if a client claims you charged them for a session they didn't complete, you can whip out your client file that shows when the session happened and exactly what you did. Or if a client is unhappy with your services and cancels the credit card charge, you'll need to send the credit card company a record of everything you've done with the client. If you have no documentation, the credit card company will likely take the money from you.

TIP

Make a record of every time you have contact with a client and keep it in their file. For example, you may write something like, "March 2, 2022: Talked with Eric about his interest in our services," "March 3, 2022: Made appointment for initial consultation," and "March 4, 2022: Sent follow-up email. Eric will come in next Wednesday to sign up for 10 personal training sessions." If there's an issue that might come up again (like the credit card cancellation example), you can send yourself an email documenting your conversation so it's date stamped.

REMEMBER

You don't have to write the Great American Novel (besides, this isn't fiction!). You just have to write enough so that you know what you and your client have done and when.

Putting Policies in Place

Don't you hate it when you ask for a little flexibility somewhere — for example, to get onion rings rather than fries with the Super Gulp Meal at your local fast-food joint — and you're told, "We can't do that — it's against the policy"? Well, the time is ripe for revenge — now you get to set policies of your own.

Of course, the purpose of policies isn't to wield power over clients or to make them jump through hoops. It's to make sure that everyone is treated the same way and that you have a set way of dealing with every process in your business, from payments to refunds.

REMEMBER

Your policies are in place for a reason, but you're also in the business of serving your customers. You don't want to become a dictator, shouting, "It's against our policies!" every chance you get. Instead, you want to try your best to adopt policies that make sense, and then explain them to your clients so that they understand that you aren't just setting rules for the sake of setting rules.

Setting a payment policy

Asking for money makes many people feel uncomfortable. People who go into personal training generally want to help people. When they ask for money, they feel greedy, miserly, like Ebenezer Scrooge on Christmas Eve. But money is, if not the main point of being in business, a big part of it. Without money, you wouldn't be able to run your business and you wouldn't be able to help your clients.

TIP

You have two basic options when it comes to accepting payment from your client:

>> You can charge up front.

>> You can charge for each session on an individual basis.

Although getting some or all your money from a client up front is a good idea, some states prevent you from collecting over a certain dollar amount without being *bonded*. (Being bonded means you pay an insurance company or bonding agent an annual fee to cover costs if you don't finish the job — bonding is a kind of insurance.)

TECHNICAL
STUFF

In the 1980s, some gyms collected for lifetime memberships and then folded, leaving their lifetime members in the lurch. The government created this law to protect consumers from such snafus. Personal training falls under the recreation/ gym category, which means that this law applies to you. Contact your lawyer to find out how the law affects your business (read more about finding and hiring a lawyer in Chapter 6).

Charging for a month's worth of sessions at a time has many benefits. Clients don't feel trapped as they may with a long-term package, and you get a steady monthly income. Also, because you're collecting less money at a time, you may not need to be bonded.

Another option is to collect for one session at a time. Of course, if you do this, you have no guarantee that the client will sign up for another session.

WARNING

If you're allowed to charge for sessions up front and choose to do so, budgeting your money is especially important. Some months you'll get $50,000 because many clients are signing up for packages and paying up front, and other months you'll take in nothing because the clients are still working on the sessions they already paid for. In the business world, this is called *feast or famine*. Make sure you save enough from your feast to get through the famine!

TIP

Try collecting a small amount of money up front and then collecting for services either every six sessions or monthly. That way you get some money right away but still keep the cash flowing. Also, this method eliminates the hassle of refunding a whole truckload of money if the client buys and pays for a huge package up front and then decides to cancel after a few sessions.

TIP

See Chapter 5 for information on how to set your fees.

Show me the money: Collecting fees

Now that you know how you plan to charge your clients, you have to have a way to actually collect the money. You can use any one or more of the following methods.

Checks

Checks used to be a popular way to accept payments, and you can still accept them, but it's less common now for people to pay by check than it used to be. If you do decide to accept checks, you'll get the money fairly quickly, and you're not charged a fee as you are with credit cards and electronic funds transfers (more on these in the sections that follow). You also don't need to have a special setup to accept checks — just take them and deposit them in your business account.

TIP

Sometimes, whether on purpose or by accident, people bounce checks. When this happens, as unfair as it seems, your bank will charge *you* a small fee. Setting up a policy of charging clients to cover this fee if they bounce a check is perfectly within your rights. Just be sure that the client gets a copy of your check-bouncing policy in writing — do this the moment they sign on with you, *before* they bounce a check.

Peer-to-peer (P2P) platforms

I'm sure you've heard of these and probably use at least one of them already to send and receive money. Some of the more popular ones include Apple Pay, PayPal, Venmo, and Zelle. P2P payments have replaced checks and cash for a lot of folks, including many service providers (personal trainers, massage therapists, hairdressers, and so on).

REMEMBER

Keep in mind that P2P business income is no different from any other transaction from the IRS's point of view. You'll need to report any payments you receive through PayPal, Venmo, and so on as taxable income.

Credit cards

Most of your clients will probably expect you to accept credit or debit card payments. Although using credit cards is easy for your clients, it can be complicated for you.

Before you can accept credit or debit card payments, you need to get a merchant account. A merchant account is a type of business bank account that allows your business to process credit and debit card payments. Providing credit-processing services to merchants is risky for financial institutions. Credit card users can return items or dispute charges, which means the bank loses money. And if the merchant goes out of business, the financial institution is responsible for the charged amounts. That's why, before approving your application, the financial institution asks such questions as:

>> Will you electronically authorize all credit cards?

>> How long have you been in business?

>> What prior experience do you have in managing a business?

>> What type of refund or return policy does your business have?

>> What is your anticipated *credit card volume* (that is, how many credit card payments do you expect to accept each month)?

If you're approved, you'll need to buy, rent, or lease credit card processing equipment from the financial institution if it's not included in your merchant agreement.

Accepting credit cards and debit cards isn't free. The financial institution will charge you a transaction fee for every payment you receive. Merchant fees vary by provider but typically the merchant will keep a percentage of each transaction (typically 2 to 3 percent) and some will also charge an additional fixed rate (for example, 2.5 percent + 10 cents) per credit and debit card transaction. You may also be charged for your monthly statement and for chargeback fees.

TIP

An alternative for accepting credit and debit card payments without a merchant account is to use a credit card processor for small businesses. Some popular options include Square, PayPal, and Intuit QuickBooks. You'll still pay transaction fees, and although these providers' fees are higher than most merchant account fees, I still like this option for small business owners because you only pay for the processing you use. You don't have to pay additional annual or monthly fees and there are no long-term contracts (meaning you can pay as you go and stop when you want).

EFT

Electronic funds transfer (EFT) lets you debit fees directly from your clients' bank accounts. Your client will need to fill out a form that includes their bank name and address, routing number, bank account number, and signature to approve funds transfers. The bank will likely charge you a small processing fee for each transfer (much like with a credit card), as well as setup and monthly fees. Contact your bank for more information on how to set up EFT capabilities for your business.

TIP

Most gyms require members to pay for their membership dues either through EFT or automatic charges to a credit card that is kept on file. EFT is less common for personal training services but it's an option.

Cash

You can always accept cash, but beware the allure — walking down the street with $500 in your pocket and not spending it can be tough! Also, having a lot of cash hanging around your place of work is an invitation to thieves. I recommend depositing all cash payments in your business bank account as soon as possible and keep all cash in a lockbox or safe if you can't get to the bank right away.

Billing your clients

Now that you know how you'll accept payment from your clients, you have to decide how you'll bill them.

Accounts on file

Y'know how you can go to a bar, order a drink, and say, "Can I start a tab?" The server holds your credit card and then charges the total amount you owe when you're ready to leave rather than charging you each time you order something. You can start a tab for your clients by keeping an *account on file*.

Some clients will allow you to keep their credit card number on file and charge them for sessions they use. Each credit card company will tell you what they need to have to validate the receipt. Generally, you write "signature on file" on the receipt and email the client a copy of the receipt.

REMEMBER

You're responsible for protecting the client's credit card number from prying eyes.

Invoices

You may want to mail or email your clients invoices that they can pay within a certain period of time, such as two weeks or a month. Make sure your invoices include the following information:

>> **The name of your business**

>> **The client's name**

>> **The date**

>> **An invoice number:** This will help you keep track of your invoices.

>> **The services rendered:** What kind of sessions? How many? On what dates?

>> **The amount due:** You may want to break this down for the client — for example, "Ten sessions @ $80/session = $800."

>> **The due date:** Expecting payment in two to four weeks is fair.

Determining a cancellation policy

Sometimes clients get sick, or they have work emergencies, or they're too tired to return to a vertical orientation after lying down on the couch. In other words, sometimes clients cancel sessions. You need a plan for what will happen when a client misses a session.

When a client cancels on short notice, that session time is gone, and you get paid nothing for it. If the client gives you enough notice, however, you may be able to schedule a last-minute session with another client and recoup your losses. That's why deciding how much heads-up time you need when a client wants to cancel is important. Will you let a client cancel an hour before the session without charging them? Or will you require 6 hours' notice, or 24 hours' notice?

TRUE
STORY

I require 24 hours' notice to avoid being charged for cancellations and my "missed session fee" is $50 for cancellations with less than 24 hours' notice. Stuff happens, clients get stuck at work, kids get sick. I get it. Charging a cancellation fee ensures that I am still being paid and demonstrates to my clients that my cancellation policy is firm. It's up to you to decide how you will handle cancellations. Be up front about it and make sure you consistently enforce it.

REMEMBER

Whatever you decide, put your cancellation policy in writing and have all your clients sign it.

Maintaining Records

If the very thought of paperwork makes your hair stand on end, you're not alone — keeping records and maintaining files is probably not on any personal trainer's top-ten list. But don't worry — in the following sections, you see how to make record-keeping as easy and painless as possible.

Understanding why records rock

You may become a fan of record-keeping when you discover that keeping good records can save you hundreds of dollars. For example, suppose you forgot to record a $20 business expense, which would have taken you a mere five minutes to record had you remembered it. This oversight raises your business's net income by $20, for which you will now be taxed. As a result, your federal, state, and Social Security taxes go up — even if I'm very conservative in my estimate, the taxes may go up by $5. If you had recorded the deduction, you would have saved $5 in taxes in five minutes — which comes out to a whopping $60 per hour!

TIP

If that's not enough to convince you, I have more. Accurate, well-maintained records:

>> Provide a record of your business's financial performance so you always have a handle on the health of your business.

>> Give you income-tax data, which will make your life easier come April 15.

>> Give you ammo for when you're applying for a loan or a merchant account.

Keeping the books

Part of maintaining records is keeping the books, which will help you:

>> Keep track of your income and expenses

>> Have the data you need on hand to file tax returns

Whenever you're feeling overwhelmed by the daunting details of keeping your books, keep those two simple goals in mind.

You can keep your financial records in any way you want, as long as they work for you — but I explain the common methods that will make your life easier.

"I'm no number cruncher!" you cry. "I'm a personal trainer!" Well, have no fear — keeping books consists of just three easy steps:

1. **Keep receipts and records of every payment and expense.**

2. **Summarize these records on a regular basis.**

3. **Use these summaries to create financial reports, which will help you determine the financial health of your business.**

Keeping receipts

Unfortunately, Uncle Sam won't just go by your word when you claim that you spent $3,000 on a piece of equipment — or even $5 buying a smoothie for a potential client. Whenever you make or spend money, you need to have the transaction backed up with receipts or other records that show the amount, the date, and other relevant information.

Legally, you can keep all your receipts under a rock in your yard if you want, but choosing a system that fits your needs makes more sense. If you handle only a few clients, you can get by with a low-key system; if you have lots of sales and expenses, you'll need something stronger.

Make sure you have a place to keep all your records and to handle bookkeeping duties — an inexpensive filing cabinet or file box works well. You can scan receipts directly into your bookkeeping software too. You also need a desk or table, a comfortable chair, and good lighting for when you need to do some number crunching.

How long do you have to hold onto these pieces of paper? According to the IRS, you need to keep your records as long as they may be needed for the administration of any provision of the Internal Revenue Code. In plain English, most financial advisors recommend keeping all tax-related materials for seven years. After seven years have passed since your first year filing taxes as a business, you can throw a bonfire in the yard and burn your tax records for your first year of business if you want — unless you file a fraudulent return or don't file a return at all, in which case the IRS can come after you at any time.

Summarizing your records

You'll need to keep a summary of your income, expenditures, and anything else you need to track, all entered according to category and date. This wonderful document is what accountants call a *ledger.* This summary will help you determine, at a glance, how your business is doing — how much money you're making versus how much you're paying out.

Using a piece of ledger paper (you can get ledger pads at an office-supply store), transfer the amounts from your receipts and records into the ledger. You can keep one journal for receipts and one for *disbursements* (expenditures). Recording receipts and disbursements in the journals is called *posting.* You can do this as often as you like, but make sure it's often enough that you won't feel overwhelmed with a mountain of receipts to enter. If you have just a few transactions every month, you can post weekly or monthly.

If you're a total bookkeeping newbie, check out *Bookkeeping All-In-One For Dummies* by Lita Epstein and John A Tracy (published by Wiley) for more information. I also recommend using a software program like QuickBooks for managing your financials records and keeping them up to date. To learn more about this popular program, check out *QuickBooks 2022 All-In-One* by Stephen L. Nelson (published by Wiley).

Creating financial reports

Financial reports bring together everything you've recorded in your ledger. Sure, you can see how much cash came in from your ledger, but you can't get the big picture about how your business is doing without measuring your income against total expenses. This is where the financial report comes in. The report will also tell you whether money from clients is coming in quickly enough to allow you to cover your bills.

THERE'S NO ACCOUNTING FOR PERSONAL TRAINERS: HANDLING YOUR MONEY LIKE A PRO

People who become personal trainers and people who become accountants are typically two very different kinds of people. You may not be excited by numbers — unless they're the number of reps and sets your client has completed — but you can still manage your money wisely. Here are some suggestions:

- **Open a separate checking account for your business.** Don't make the mistake of using your personal checking account for business purposes.

- **Pay your bills by check or electronic check through your bank, and note on the check what you purchased.** This tactic will help you keep track of expenditures.

- **Deposit checks and cash often.** Keeping checks and cash hanging around your place of business is an invitation for theft.

- **Record all your sales by using invoices, duplicate receipts, or some other method.** This approach will help you keep track of who has paid and who owes you money.

- **Keep records neat and tidy, the way your mom wanted you to keep your room.** You probably couldn't find your favorite baseball glove or Barbie doll when your room was a mess — and messy records will keep you from finding the data you need for tax purposes. (Your parents were the only people you had to contend with as a kid, but now you have Uncle Sam breathing down your neck. How's that for motivation?)

TIP

If you're using software such as QuickBooks, you can have it generate reports for you with the click of a button. Pie charts, bar graphs — you name it, the chart is there.

Developing an accounting method

Choice is good. The red or the blue? Small or large? Today or tomorrow?

Well, you'll be happy to know that you also get a choice in accounting systems: cash or accrual. These methods are different sets of rules for the timing of income and expenses. Usually, you report income and expenses in the year in which they're paid. So if you buy a piece of equipment in January 2023, you can't include it as a deduction on your 2022 taxes, even if you haven't filed your taxes yet. But what if you bought the equipment in 2022 but paid for it in 2023? The year in which you'll take this deduction depends on which accounting method you choose.

Cash

Using the cash system, you record an item of income or expense when it's paid. So when you receive money from your clients, you report it in that tax year. (Even if you invoice them for it in 2022, if they pay you the money in 2023, you report it in 2023.) And if you buy that piece of equipment in 2021, but you don't pay your credit card bill until 2023, you can't deduct it on your taxes until 2023. Most businesses that sell services (such as yours) use this method of accounting.

REMEMBER

Even though it's called the *cash* method of accounting, it actually covers any kind of payment, such as credit card, check, or even barter.

WARNING

In some cases, you must report income as soon as it becomes available, even if you don't have it in hand. For example, if someone gives you a check in December 2022 and you don't deposit it until January 2023, you still must report the income for 2023. You're also not allowed to take a deduction for the current year for items paid for but not yet received.

REMEMBER

Check with your accountant to make sure you're always on the right side of the tax law. (See Chapter 6 for more information on finding and hiring an accountant.)

Accrual

Many C corporations, businesses with inventories of products, and manufacturers use the accrual method of accounting. It may not be the best for your service business, but I want you to know what it is just in case.

With the accrual method, you count the money as received as soon as it's earned, even if it isn't actually in hand. (That means if you've had a session with your client and invoiced them for it in 2022, but the invoice isn't paid until 2023, you still report it on your 2022 taxes.) You record expenses when the obligation arises, even if you haven't actually paid it yet. This means if you buy a piece of equipment on your credit card in 2022 and don't pay for it until 2023, you still need to report the expense on your 2022 taxes.

REMEMBER

If you decide to use the accrual method, you'll definitely need to consult your accountant to get set up and stay on the right track. (See Chapter 6 for the scoop on hiring an accountant.)

The Tax Man Cometh

Think paying taxes once a year is bad? Well, I hate to scare you, but as an independent contractor or business owner, you need to pay taxes four times per year. That's right, I said four. But don't worry — in this section, I tell you how to breeze through these quarterly tax payments without breaking a sweat.

TECHNICAL STUFF

If you're curious about why you need to pay taxes more often when you're an independent contractor or a small-business owner, here's the lowdown: Essentially, when you're an employee of someone else, your employer withholds enough to cover your federal and state income taxes. (That's why your paychecks are always less than you think they'll be!) When you're working for yourself and your client writes you a check, no one is withholding anything for tax purposes. As an employee of a company, your tax dollars are going to the federal and state governments all throughout the year — every time you get a paycheck. So to even out the playing field a bit, when you work for yourself, you have to pay taxes four times a year. (Lucky for you, you don't have to pay taxes every time someone writes you a check!) Also, when you work for an employer, the employer is required to pay half your Social Security tax; the other half is deducted from your paycheck and turned over to the government. When you work for yourself, you have to pay the whole Social Security tax yourself. And you thought being your own boss was going to be all fun and games. . . .

TIP

Before I get started on the tax talk, I want to let you know about the IRS Small Business and Self-Employed Tax Center. Here you'll find all the resources you need for staying on the up-and-up with the IRS as a small business owner or self-employed taxpayer. Check it out at www.irs.gov/businesses/small-businesses-self-employed.

Computing your estimated tax

To avoid an underpayment penalty, your estimated tax must be at least the lesser of the following:

>> **Ninety percent of the tax liability shown on the return for the current year:** This means that you predict how much you're going to earn (minus deductions), and you pay 90 percent of that estimated amount over four quarterly payments.

>> **One hundred percent of the tax liability shown on the return for the prior year:** This means that you pay the same amount of taxes that you paid last year over four quarterly payments.

For example, say you paid $10,000 in taxes in 2022. For 2023, you can either predict what you're going to make and how much you'll owe in taxes and be sure to pay at least 90 percent of that amount in four quarterly installments, or you can pay $2,500 per quarter, which will add up to $10,000 — which is 100 percent of your liability from 2022.

In general, unless you expect your income to fluctuate dramatically one way or the other, your best bet is to pay 100 percent of what you paid last year. It's the surest way to avoid an underpayment penalty, even if your income skyrockets.

Knowing when to pay

Most businesses use the calendar-year accounting period, meaning that their business year ends on December 31 every year. You may also use a fiscal-year accounting period, which is a 12-month period ending on the last day of any month *other than* December.

Unless you have a reason to do so (for example, your accountant recommended it), using the calendar-year accounting period makes the most sense.

If you use the calendar-year accounting period, you need to pay your quarterly payments on:

>> April 15

>> June 15

>> September 15

>> January 15 of the following year

The idea is that your April 15 payment will cover what you earned January through March, your June 15 payment will cover what you earned in April and May, and so on. Don't ask why the payments aren't evenly spaced (in April, July, October, and January) — it's just a quirk of the IRS.

If you also earn a salary or wage in addition to your self-employment income — for example, if you have a "day job" in addition to your personal training clients — you can get around the whole quarterly tax deal by asking your employer to withhold more tax from your earnings. To do this, you need to file Form W-4 with your employer.

CONTACTING UNCLE SAM

Want to contact someone at the IRS to ask tax questions, get the status of your refund, or just shoot the breeze (okay, maybe not)? You can find everything you need from ordering forms to tax FAQ's online at www.irs.gov.

Filling out the forms

You'll use federal Form 1040-ES to determine the amount of your estimated taxes. You can get this form from the IRS website. After you file the form, it'll automatically be sent to you in following years. Your state will have a similar form — check with your state's income-tax authorities for more information.

Saving for taxes

TIP

To get a head start on paying your taxes and avoid last-minute panic, why not do what an employer does and deduct taxes from every check? Using last year's figures, determine what percentage of your income goes to taxes. Then deduct that percentage from every check and deposit it in a special savings account set aside just for taxes. If you expect to make way more this year, up the percentage accordingly.

WARNING

This is not a vacation fund or a Christmas-gift fund or an I-really-need-those-new-shoes fund! Resist the temptation to dip into your tax savings account.

Tracking Your Clients

No, I don't mean heading off after your clients with bloodhounds. I *do* mean that you need to document all sorts of information about your clients to help you create the best programs for them (and also to help you remember who's doing what).

Creating client forms

TIP

These forms are the ones you need to run your personal training business well:

>> Prospect lead sheet

>> Initial consultation form (you can also include your informed consent and liability waiver forms here)

>> Medical history form

>> Fitness assessment form

>> Workout log

>> Session log

>> Exercise prescription form

TIP

Search online for sample forms that you can either replicate or use to create your own forms that fit your way of doing business.

Putting together a client file

The client file will include all the forms listed in the preceding section. This way, you'll have the client's contact information and medical information, plus be able to track their fitness status and progress through the personal training sessions. Your files can be hard copies or electronic; it's up to you.

TIP

Keep the files consistent from client to client. For example, if the first page in one client's file is the prospect interest lead sheet and the second page is the initial consultation form, it should be that way for every client file. This setup makes it easier for you to find what you need pronto — and if you ever hire employees, they'll all be on the same page (pardon the pun).

Maintaining client files

Maintaining client files entails more than sticking them in carefully labeled, alphabetical folders. After all, what good are the files if they have clients' old addresses or don't note new injuries or other medical issues?

TIP

Go through your files quarterly and update the information. Make sure clients' contact information is up to date and that you have their most current medical information. The files should also specify the date of the last fitness assessment, when you need to do a follow-up, and so on.

» Building a solid reputation

» Getting new clients through referrals

» Marketing on a shoestring

Chapter **8**

Flexing Your Marketing Muscles

Before you can convince prospective clients to hire you, they need to find you. That's where marketing comes in. Marketing doesn't require a fortune or a specialized college degree, at least not right away — most independent professionals and small-business owners do their own marketing until they can afford to pay someone else to do it for them.

In this chapter, I show you how to identify your ideal customers — in other words, the people you should be marketing to. You can successfully market your business when your marketing budget is small and I can show you how.

TIP

This chapter is just one chapter on marketing — for a whole book dedicated to the topic, check out *Small Business Marketing Strategies All-in-One For Dummies* presented by the U.S. Chamber of Commerce (published by Wiley).

Ready, Aim . . . Focusing on Your Target

In marketing-speak, the people you want to target with your marketing efforts are called your *target market*.

TIP

Figuring out who your target market is will save you bundles of money. For example, if your target market is seniors who want to prevent heart disease, Snap Ads (paid advertising on Snapchat) would probably be a waste of money.

Developing a specialty

Pinpointing a specialty within the personal training industry will help you identify your target market — and will make you stand out in people's minds to boot. For example, maybe you want to be known as the Goat Yoga Trainer (which you can check out at www.goatyoga.net if you're curious).

TIP

In Chapter 2, you get an idea of different client populations you can work with as a personal trainer. Knowing who you want to work with will help you target your marketing efforts and that's a good place to start. You also need to understand what your target market wants if you want your marketing plan to work.

Part of your specialty is your persona. Some clients will want you to stand on the sidelines and cheer them on — "You're doing great! Just one more set! I know you can do it!" Others will prefer the drill-sergeant approach — "Okay, drop and give me 50. Move, move, move!" Which fits your personality? And which group of people do you think would most appreciate that approach?

Which of the following is your personal training personality:

>> **Drill sergeant:** If your teaching style is to yell, "Faster! C'mon, no slacking!" you're a drill sergeant. You may be best off training competitive athletes and healthy, gung-ho adults.

>> **Cheerleader:** If your favorite phrase is, "Awesome! You got this!", the cheerleader is your type. You'll be great with clients who are looking for lots of encouragement.

>> **Teacher:** If you're a patient soul who can handle a barrage of questions from your client, you're a teacher. You would be great as a trainer of kids or for adults who are new to exercise.

TIP

Whatever your "personality," it needs to mesh with your market. For example, the senior population may need more of a cheerleader personality rather than drill sergeant, whereas an athlete may need the drill sergeant rather than a cheerleader. Though some people may prefer the teacher personality, what really matters is what *you're* most comfortable being. Clients who like your persona will find their way to you — always be yourself!

REMEMBER

Don't worry, you won't have to try too hard — you'll find your style after working with a few clients when the nervousness that comes with being a "newbie" goes away.

Targeting your market

The next step is to delve deep into the psyches of the people you want to work with to figure out who your target market is, what makes them tick, and how you can get them interested in your services. Ask yourself the following questions about your prospective clients.

What's their gender?

Do you want to work with men, women, both? For example, if you want to work with women only, you'll want to advertise your services in places where women will notice. For example, if your target market is working moms with young children, ask the schools in your area if you can send their families a monthly email newsletter with simple fitness tips for busy moms.

How old are they?

Within your chosen category, what age range do you prefer? Perhaps you want to focus on young men in their 20s, or women approaching 50, or kids between the ages of 7 and 12. If your focus is on older people, for example, you'll want to emphasize in your marketing how exercising helps the aging body.

What kind of income do they have?

Would your target market prefer less-expensive group classes, or do they expect pricier one-on-one sessions? If you plan to target people who are looking for low prices, your marketing needs to emphasize the value you deliver. If you're targeting people who are willing to pay more, your marketing can focus on the high-end services you provide.

WARNING

Be careful not to confuse "less-expensive" with "cheap." You can offer an excellent service for less money with group classes or semi-private personal training sessions. Emphasize "value" instead of "price" in your marketing.

Where do they live?

Do they live in the city, suburbs, country? Do they live in houses, apartments, dorms? Knowing where your potential clients live helps you to know where to concentrate your marketing efforts. Also, if you target people who tend to live in apartments or dorms, you can emphasize in your marketing that clients don't need to have a home gym to work with you.

What are their main concerns?

Are your clients mostly interested in looking or feeling better, improving their golf swing, preventing cardiovascular disease? How can your personal training business help them with their concerns? Make sure you mention this in your marketing. For example, if your clients are people who put in a lot of time at work, you can stress your flexible hours and quick workouts.

The Power of Publicity: Spreading the Word about Your Services

Want to get people talking about your personal training business? Then publicity is for you. In this section, you find out how to get media attention, garner positive word of mouth, and turn your clients into walking billboards for your business.

Breaking the news

If you dream of seeing your name in print or online (more about online marketing later), success is only a press release away. A *press release* (sometimes referred to as a *news release*) is a document you email to members of your local media in the hopes that they'll put it online, or call you for an interview. Even if members of the media don't use your press release, they may keep you on file as an expert they can call when they're writing an article about health or fitness — and that's just as good.

In the following sections, I give you some tips for writing a stellar press release that will land in the press instead of in a spam folder.

Be newsworthy

News releases are for news, not advertising — so don't try to pass off a self-serving ad as news. When an editor or producer reads such a release, they'll see that you're trying to get a free ad and toss it.

TIP

Here are some examples of real news:

>> The opening of a new business (like yours!)

>> Health stories, such as a new study linking exercise to longevity (you can quote yourself as an expert)

>> An event, such as a seminar or demonstration (more on these topics later in this chapter)

>> Community service (donating free fitness classes to at-risk youth, for example)

>> A move to a new location

>> A new product or service (but *only* if it's truly new and unique to your community, such as offering the first underwater bench-pressing class or being the first person in your area to use a new type of equipment)

Follow the proper format

TIP

A standard format is key to press-release success. Check out this article to learn how to write a press release and tips for getting the recipient to open your email: `www.dummies.com/article/business-careers-money/careers/general-careers/prepare-a-personal-or-business-press-release-171981`.

REMEMBER

You could have a great news story on your hands, but if you don't follow the format that editors and producers are used to seeing, they'll likely ignore you.

TIP

To follow the latest health & fitness industry news, you can check out current press releases at `www.prnewswire.com/news-releases/health-latest-news/fitness-wellness-list`.

Get it out there

After you've created a press release that will have editors champing at the bit to share it, it's time to email it out to the media. But who should you bless with this paragon of publicity perfection?

REMEMBER

You don't need to spend a fortune to have someone distribute your release (though you can if you want); you can compile your own list of media outlets for nothing. Just be sure to make it targeted. If you want to get coverage for a new personal training service you're offering, for example, don't send a press release to *The Beekeepers' Journal*.

Most people get their news online, but the internet doesn't have a lock on the news — send your release to the producers at all the radio and TV stations in your area as well. Local news outlets are often looking for interesting stories to tell.

TRUE STORY

Once in 2012 a local media outlet contacted me for a story about P90x simply because I wrote a news release about Paul Ryan's P90x workouts on the campaign trail.

Sitting for an interview

If you follow my instructions for creating a press release, you may actually have a journalist, podcast, or even a local radio or TV station contacting you for an interview. Kind of a scary thought! Have no fear — the tips in the following sections will turn you into a veteran media personality in no time.

If possible, have interviewers visit you in your workplace. This will help them get a better idea of what you do and you'll feel more comfortable on your home turf.

Be prepared

Preparation is the key to success in any interview. To get yourself ready, think about some of the basic questions you can expect the reporter to ask. Make sure you have interesting, concise answers to these questions.

If you're stumped for an answer, say, "That's a great question." That response will buy you some time while you wrack your brain for an answer. Don't stop with the basic queries. Be ready for the obvious questions, but also for the kinds of questions that give even seasoned press jockeys sweaty palms. For example, a reporter may ask you, "What do you think of so and so celebrity's diet that they swear by?"

As you may have discovered from watching political debates, *what* you say sometimes matters less than *how* you say it. Distill your message into a few memorable words — what's called a *sound bite* — and practice saying it with conviction.

Answer the questions you're asked — and don't be afraid to admit when you don't know the answer

Despite all your preparation, you're bound to be asked a question that you don't have an answer to. When this happens, don't fake it. It's perfectly acceptable to say, "I'm not an expert on that, but I can tell you someone who is." You can also offer to get back to the reporter later with the information.

You were asked for an interview for a reason, and you owe it to the reporter (and to your reputation) to answer the questions you're asked. Using the interview for self-promotion or free advertising for your business is a big no-no. If you sidestep the reporter's questions and only talk about how wonderful you and your business are, you'll only make it difficult for the reporter to do their job — and not only will you not get any coverage, you'll also blow your chances of ever being contacted again by that reporter.

Dress the way you normally do

If you normally work in spandex, don't go pulling your lone suit out of its dry-cleaning bag for the TV reporter. If you feel uncomfortable, you'll look uncomfortable, and the audience won't take you seriously. For television, avoid pure white shirts or suits with stripes, checks, or small patterns, which don't mix well with the cameras.

TRUE STORY

Once I gave an interview early in the morning wearing sweaty workout gear with my hair in a messy ponytail. My gym was doing a 24-hour indoor "bikeathon" fundraiser for cancer research and a local TV station ran the story. The reporter showed up ready to go after I had been cycling for 2 hours. I admit that I wasn't thrilled to appear on live TV without taking a shower first, but giving a live interview during the event had a positive impact on our fundraising efforts.

Going to the head of the class: Giving free seminars or webinars

One way to get the word out about your business is to give free educational seminars, webinars, and demonstrations. Potential clients get free information, and you get the chance to promote your business, establish yourself as an expert, gain credibility — and maybe even land a new client or two.

Picking your project

Here are some ideas for educational programs you can offer potential clients:

>> Give a talk about the benefits of exercise for stress relief, osteoporosis, or heart disease.

>> Demonstrate how to use resistance bands.

>> Give a seminar or webinar about nutrition for healthy living.

>> Give a talk about starting an exercise program to a local business's employees.

Finding a venue

When you have an idea of what you want to offer potential clients, consider hosting a webinar. Webinars are virtual seminars that people can attend from anywhere with an internet connection. If you would rather present in-person, you'll need to find a place to do it. Here are a few ideas to consider:

>> Browse the websites of local colleges and universities to see if any of them offer seminars or lectures by local experts — like you!

>> Reach out to medium to large businesses in your area and ask if you can give your demonstration or seminar to their employees. Don't forget to mention that healthy employees take fewer sick days!

>> Contact a venue that your client population frequents — such as a community center or high school — and offer your expertise.

Getting the word out

Tell people about your talk, seminar, or other program by sending a press release to your local media outlets, posting flyers on public bulletin boards, and leaving flyers at health-food stores, doctors' offices, and other places where your potential clients hang out. You should also use social media to spread the word. You can buy micro-targeted Facebook ads, post on your personal and business pages, and/or reach out to moderators of Facebook groups focused on your community or activity (a local runners' group, for example).

TIP

Social media is probably your best bet for making direct contact with a journalist or other media personality in your area unless you've already established contact via email. You can send a direct message (DM) to media personalities you follow on social media who might be interested in what you're offering.

Standing on your soapbox

Now's the time to brush up on your public speaking skills. Here are some tips that will give you the gift of gab:

- >> **Know your audience.** If you read Chapter 2, you know who your target audience is. Keep their interests in mind when you're developing your presentation. Think about who they are and what they want to know.

- >> **Practice, practice, practice.** Grab a friend or family member and practice your presentation in front of them. Ask for feedback. Do you speak loudly enough? Is your presentation interesting? Ask them for honesty — and remember not to take criticism personally. (If you do, not only won't you learn anything, but they won't tell you the truth the next time you ask.)

- >> **Repeat yourself.** Adhere to the public speaking maxim "Tell 'em what you're gonna tell 'em, tell 'em, then tell 'em what you told 'em."

TIP

Public speaking is a huge topic — way too much to cover completely in this chapter. Before taking the stage, pick up a book like *Public Speaking Skills For Dummies* by Alyson Connolly (published by Wiley). Toastmasters International is another excellent resource for developing your public speaking skills. Check them out at www.toastmasters.org.

Reaching Your Clients through Referrals

The idea behind referrals is to get trustworthy people to give your business a little word of mouth. Referrals are a powerful — and free! — way to build your personal training business.

HAPPY CLIENTS ARE LIKE WALKING BILLBOARDS

There's no better publicity for your business than satisfied customers. Your role? To make your clients happy and keep them that way. Give your clients 100 percent, ask how you can make their personal training experiences better, and show them you care. You know the saying "people don't care how much you know until they know how much you care?" It's true. Some of the most successful personal trainers I know aren't the most experienced or credentialed, but they do have the most loyal clients. These train-ers show their clients that they care by listening to them, remembering important things about them like their kids' or grandkids' names, sending them birthday cards . . . they become an important part of their clients' lives.

Say you have to choose between two hairdressers — one who has a few positive Yelp reviews and one who was recommended by a trusted friend (who also happens to have great hair). Which would you pick? If you're like most people, you'd go with the hairdresser your friend referred you to. That's how referrals work.

Earning referrals

How do you get referrals? Well, you ask for them! More important though, you need to earn the right to ask people to recommend your business to others. I suggest building and nurturing relationships with other businesses with the same clientele you're looking for. When someone sends you a referral, send them a handwritten thank-you card. Refer your friends and clients to businesses that you like and trust. Be the kind of person that people want to do business with!

GIVING TO GET

TIP

Google Ads and getting people to follow you on social media can be part of your overall marketing plan, but only a small part. Before asking people to buy something from you, give them something of value for free. This could be free articles, a cookbook with sim-ple and healthy recipes, a basic exercise plan with an instructional video, or anything else your target market could benefit from. If it seems counterintuitive to give away what you're trying to sell, I get it. Some people will take your freebies and never become clients. And some will become paying clients when they see how much value you offer for free. They figure if your free stuff is that good, your paid services must be amazing!

TIP

Local healthcare professionals (physical therapists, massage therapists, chiropractors, and so on) can become some of your best referral partners. Start with your own healthcare providers. Ask for a ten-minute meeting to explain what you do and to develop a professional relationship. Ask your friends, family, and even your clients if they can introduce you to their healthcare providers too — scoring a meeting with a busy provider will be easier if you have a connection!

REMEMBER

You may not get to meet with the provider, but an office manager or receptionist is just as good. Treat these gatekeepers well and be sure to leave literature with your contact information they can give to patients or leave in the waiting area.

Here are a few healthcare providers who are the most likely to send you referrals:

>> **General practitioners (GPs):** These family doctors are the front line against disease for many people. Because exercise can prevent problems like diabetes and heart disease, GPs are likely to send their patients to personal trainers.

>> **Physical therapists:** Recovering from knee surgery? Suffering from back pain? Physical therapists help people reduce pain and regain function. After a patient recovers, exercise helps prevent reinjury.

>> **Obstetricians/gynecologists (OB/GYNs):** OB/GYNs deal with women's health and changes associated with aging, pregnancy, hormones, and so on. Exercise can alleviate symptoms related to hormonal changes, reduce cancer risk, and prevent age-related muscle and bone loss.

When a healthcare provider refers a patient to you, make sure you do the following:

>> Send a thank-you note.

>> Follow any exercise instructions sent along with the referral.

>> **Return the favor — refer back!** As you become more established, your clients will start asking if you can recommend a doctor, physical therapist, and so on.

>> **Make sure you're clear on the medical needs of your referral.** If you have any doubts, call and ask the provider about your client's medical issues before making any exercise recommendations.

Getting referrals from other people whose recommendations count

People talk — and you want to get them talking about your business in a favorable way. Doctors are great, but don't pass up these other opportunities for referrals:

>> **Health-food stores:** People who shop at these stores tend to be health conscious — and you're just the person who can help them get fit. Ask the store manager if you can leave flyers at the register.

>> **Spas:** Clients of health and beauty spas want to look and feel their best — and they're willing to spend money to do it. Establish a relationship with the manager and ask to become referral partners.

>> **Friends and family:** Who *better* to advertise your business than the people who already think you're the greatest thing since sliced bread? Tell everyone you love about what you do, and ask them to spread the word.

>> **People you do business with:** Your hairdresser, your mechanic, your tax accountant — all these professionals come into contact with dozens of people each week who could be getting fitter with your help. Talk up your business with the people *you* do business with.

Turning referrals into clients

Congratulations! You've gotten your first referrals. Treat them right and watch your business boom. Here's how:

>> **Offer a free strategy session.** This will give you a chance to establish good rapport with your referrals, find out what they're looking for, and show them how you can help.

>> **Follow up with each potential client who has been referred to you three times — one week, three weeks, and six weeks after your initial contact.** Call or email any more frequently than that, and you could be mistaken for a stalker.

>> **If you have no luck after three calls or emails, take the potential client off your contact list, but keep them on your email list (if they have opted in) so they get occasional updates, newsletters, and offers from you.** One time I had a prospect turn into a client *four years* after first meeting her — don't give up!

Marketing on a Shoestring

Coca-Cola, Apple, and Nike have multibillion dollar marketing budgets, and they spend it on celebrity spokespeople, billboards, multipage magazine spreads, and TV spots during the Super Bowl.

You? If you're just starting out as a personal trainer, chances are your marketing budget jingles when you shake it. But don't let your tiny budget get you down! Smart business owners know how to market on the cheap. The publicity tips I provide earlier in this chapter are a good start, but you have plenty more ways to get the word out without spending a mint.

Establishing your internet presence

You might be asking yourself why you need to be online if your personal training business is offline. Well, the answer is simple. We live in a technological world and most consumers (over 90 percent) find businesses or services they're looking for on the internet. Reaching your target market will be tough if you're not online — and it's hard to say how many new customers you could miss out on.

The good news is that you don't need a multi-billion-dollar marketing budget to establish an internet presence for your small business. Setting up a simple website with information about your services and how to contact you is a great place to start. You also need to make sure your target market can find you when they search online for local personal trainers. This is where *local search engine optimization* (local SEO) comes in. Local SEO involves adding local listings about your business to search engines like Google and to local online directories like Yelp. It's worth taking some time to work on your local search visibility because you'll reach more people who are already online looking for a local personal trainer.

TIP

The internet is a big place and search engine optimization is a way bigger topic than what I'm covering here. It's not necessary to become an expert in SEO, but I do recommend understanding it well enough to make finding you online easier for your target market. Check out *Search Engine Optimization All-in-One for Dummies* by Bruce Clay and Kristopher B. Jones (published by Wiley) to learn more.

WARNING

Your potential clients will probably read online reviews about your business before deciding if they want to do business with you. Positive reviews on popular online directories like Yelp might attract people to your business, but a negative Yelp review can seriously damage your reputation.

TIP

No matter how amazing you are, eventually someone isn't going to like you and might write a negative online review of your business. Some things are out of your control, including what people say about you online. But you can control your reaction. Responding to online reviews (positive or negative) shows that you care, and even if a review feels unfair, ignoring it says more about you than a respectful reply ever could.

Today, connecting with your target market through social media is another way to establish yourself online. Social media can be an extremely useful marketing tool, but it can just as easily become a distraction. Before setting up any social media accounts for your business, I recommend figuring out which social media platforms your target market uses and only focus on those. To learn more about using social media to boost your business, check out *Social Media Marketing All-in-One* by Michelle Krasniak, Jann Zimmerman, and Deborah Ng (published by Wiley).

TIP

Make sure all your online content (website, social media posts, and so on) has a clean, attractive layout with relevant and clear graphics or photos.

Donating your services

Want to feel good about yourself and generate positive word of mouth at the same time? Of course you do! Consider donating your services to charitable causes.

Offering a training package to be auctioned off at a fundraiser where the proceeds go to a charity is one way to donate your services. Your clients may ask you to participate in an auction, but if you want to be proactive, you can look up the head of a local charity organization and offer to donate your services for their next fundraiser. Places like private schools, hospitals, and social groups often hold black-tie charity events with auctions.

Putting it in print

For the cost of paper and a little time, you can create printed materials like newsletters and flyers that will educate your clients and potential clients about your business. Most of your marketing and advertising will probably be done online, but it's still a good idea to have some printed material to hand to people if they ask.

GIVING YOUR SPIEL

Write down a description of your business and its benefits — a description you can recite in 30 seconds or less and ideally with real examples of people you have helped. This little spiel is called an *elevator speech,* because you can give it in the time it takes for the elevator you're riding in to reach your floor. Practice your speech until you've memorized it and until it sounds natural — not like a pitch. For example: "I help people over 60 to get active and move better so they can feel great and keep up with their grandkids." Then whenever you meet someone, you're prepared to tell them who you are and what you do. *Remember:* Never miss an opportunity to spread the word about your services.

Newsletters

Newsletters are a great way to gain credibility, put your name in front of potential clients on a regular basis, and spread the word about your product or service. If you're sending a newsletter, you should email it to everyone on your email contact list, and you can mail a copy to clients, prospects, businesses, or anybody else who hasn't opted in to receive emails from you. If you're mailing copies of your newsletter, be sure to budget for envelopes and postage.

TIP

Here are some tips on how to create a newsletter that your prospective clients will look forward to receiving:

» **Collect the mailing addresses and email addresses of your clients and of all the people who have shown an interest in your business and use this as your mailing list.**

» **Decide how often you'll send out your newsletter.** A weekly newsletter sounds great, but will you really have time to create new content every week, especially when your business picks up? Monthly, bimonthly, and quarterly newsletters are probably more realistic.

» **Come up with a name for your newsletter that will grab your readers' attention.** You want to start with a hook that keeps your audience reading. Don't make the mistake of sticking with your company's name — or you'll be throwing away prime newsletter real estate. For example, if your company's name is Perfect Personal Training, don't call your newsletter *Perfect Personal Training News*. A name like *The Health Success Guide* is more likely to pique the interest of all readers.

» **Share your knowledge.** Is there anything people like more than getting something for free? Filling your newsletter with free helpful information, tips, and resources will make you a valuable resource to your readers and create the kind of goodwill that all the ads in the world can't buy.

» **Include special offers like a discount for first-time clients or incentives like one free session to clients who get a friend to sign up.**

» **Give the heave-ho to the hard sell.** A newsletter full of sales propaganda will get sent straight to the spam folder. Focus on sharing information instead. If you make your newsletter a valuable resource rather than a boring sales tool, your audience will read it and maybe even file it away for future use. Can you say that much for an ad?

» **Tell them how to contact you.** Let your potential clients know how they can set up a consultation with you or become a client.

» **Liven up your articles with quotes.** People love to hear what other people have to say. Quoting experts lends credibility and quoting clients or the "man on the street" gives the newsletter a newsy, human-interest feel. Who can you quote in your newsletter?

- *Your clients:* If you're writing a newsletter article about exercise tips for busy professionals, for example, you could quote a client who lost 50 pounds in six months through healthy eating and exercising for 30 minutes a day. You can even include a different client success story in each issue. Clients love to see their names in print, and they're sure to show off your newsletter to others.

- *An expert in a related field such a physical therapist:* Write an information piece on how exercise helps to prevent a certain condition and quote the appropriate practitioner. Or try writing about nutrition and interview a local nutritionist for quotes.

- *Your employees:* If you have employees, why not include a question-and-answer session with one of them in each issue, addressing their specialties.

- *A local celebrity:* Perhaps a popular restaurant owner serves up low-fat, organic cuisine — what a great idea for a short newsletter article! If someone in your area ran the Boston Marathon or won a power-lifting contest, they would also be perfect to interview.

Another bonus to using quotes: Instead of doing the hard sell, you can quote other people's great opinions of you or your product. It sounds less like hype if a third party is saying it for you.

Flyers

A *flyer* is a single sheet of paper printed on one or both sides. You won't be able to fit every detail about your business on a flyer, and that's ok. The purpose of a flyer is to have something you can hand to prospective clients so they'll remember how to reach you.

NEWSLETTER NEWS SOURCES

If you'd like to include health news in your newsletter, check out EurekAlert (www.eurekalert.org), a science news site that includes press releases about health advancements, and PR Newswire (www.prnewswire.com), a media site mentioned earlier in this chapter that posts press releases on health-related topics.

You can also read health magazines like *Health, Fitness, Prevention, Oxygen, Men's Fitness,* and *Men's Health.* You can find all these magazines online, but you'll need a subscription to see all the articles. Using these magazines to find topics for your newsletter is okay, but be aware that you can't publish the articles in your newsletter without getting permission from the copyright holder first.

TIP

Include this information on your flyer (much of which can be taken from your newsletter):

>> **A catchy headline.**

>> **The name of your business.**

>> **A list of benefits of going to a personal trainer:** Some benefits you may want to include are more energy, more confidence, increased strength, better heart health, lowered risk of disease, and better sleep.

>> **Any special offer you want to make:** For example, a discount for first-time clients.

>> **How people can reach you.**

YOU ARE YOUR BEST ADVERTISEMENT

The best marketing medium is also the cheapest, and the one you have the most control over — it's you. The way you look, talk, and act, and the things you say, can make a potential client drool over the prospect of working with you — or run the other way.

The last thing people want to see in the person who's supposed to get them healthy is a frowny-faced trainer with their arms crossed over their wrinkled shirt. People go to personal trainers in part to improve the way they look and feel, and they need you to serve as an example of someone who likes the way they look and feel.

Your appearance should be neat and stylish, but stylish doesn't have to mean expensive or trendy. Choose clothes that fit properly and that you feel comfortable and confident in. See more about dressing for success in Chapter 10.

If you're confident, if you're happy, if you love personal training, it shows. Do everything you can to stay as healthy as possible, including eating well and getting adequate rest. You don't have to be perfect, but do be an example for your clients of a confident person with healthy habits.

Love your work — if you don't, something has to change. Your clients can tell if you're unhappy and they won't stick around for long if you give them about as much attention as that bored kid flipping burgers gives to his customers. Hopefully the tips in this book will help you build a career that you love!

Chapter **9**

Retaining Your Clientele

G etting clients is easy. Keeping them — ah, there's the rub. As a personal trainer, you have to use every trick in the book (this book!) to keep your clients happy, motivated, and on the track to living an active and fit life. Social media is full of trainers like yourself, and if you don't make an effort to retain your clients, they just may click on over to one of your competitors down the street.

In this chapter, I give you the basics for keeping clients coming back, including how to motivate them, how to adjust your training sessions to their personalities, how to keep them excited about fitness, how to connect with them on a personal level, and how to resolve conflicts when they arise (alas, the road to fitness is never a straight line).

Keepin' It Real: Putting Fitness within Your Clients' Reach

Say you're using a computer for the first time. Your teacher tells you, "Okay, by next week I want you to write a ten-page document with tables and clip art in Google Docs, create a slide deck, and, while you're at it, write a program that will control all the electronic appliances in your house." Chances are, you'd be so frustrated that you'd give up hope before ever even trying to open Google Docs or use email.

TIP

The same principle goes for your clients, many of whom are learning how to exercise for the first time in a long time. Maybe even for the first time ever. If you tell a new client, "You need to overhaul your diet, stop smoking, exercise five times per week before work, sleep for eight hours every night, and meditate for 30 minutes every night before bed to manage your stress," they won't be a client for long. Getting to know your clients and learning what makes them tick helps you to help them tackle their fitness goals one step at a time.

Knowing who you're dealing with

Before you can give your clients what they need, you first have to understand their reasons for hiring you, their likes and dislikes, their strengths and weaknesses, what they had for breakfast this morning . . . . Getting to know your clients will keep them coming back — and knowing your clients means meeting them where they're at today, not where they want to be someday. When you understand where your clients are starting *and* where they want to go, you'll be able to create exercise programs that help them to reach their fitness goals at a pace they can handle.

But how do you get to know your clients without taking them out for dinner, going for long walks on the beach, or reading their memoirs? (Hey, who *doesn't* have a memoir these days?)

You start with your initial consultation, where your job is to ask question after question until you feel like a job interviewer for the CIA. (You can find out more on initial consultations in Chapter 10.) In the following sections, I show you how to take it beyond those first consultations and develop great relationships with your clients.

Getting to know you: Personality types

People tend to fall into distinct categories of personality types, and recognizing your clients' individual personality types will help you to coach them effectively. If you're not familiar with personality typing and want to learn more about it, I recommend starting here:

>> **The Myers-Briggs Type Indicator (MBTI)** divides people into 16 types of personalities, such as "The Scientist" and "The Executive," based on four main traits: introversion/extroversion, intuitiveness/sensing, thinking/feeling, and judging/perceiving. (The trait names have nothing to do with what career the person has; you may have a "Scientist" client who hasn't touched a Bunsen burner since high school.) Knowing the different types of personalities and how to recognize them is actually a lot of fun, and you can use this knowledge to communicate effectively with your clients. If your client is a "Scientist" type,

for example, knowing how the exercises work and what muscles are involved can spur his enthusiasm. An "Executive" type of client, on the other hand, may be motivated more by research demonstrating that entrepreneurs who exercise daily are more likely to meet income goals. For an explanation of the 16 personality types and to take a test to find out *your* personality type, check out www.myersbriggs.org.

» Discovering whether your client is **Type A or Type B** will help you determine how much you can push him and how long you can spend on one exercise before moving on to the next. The Type A person is competitive, impatient, and goal-oriented, and thrives on challenges. These types of clients probably expect you to change up their program frequently, and they'll want to achieve fitness milestones quickly. The Type B person, on the other hand, is more laid back, patient, noncompetitive, and maybe not as driven as the Type A person. They'll want to take things nice and slow. Push them too hard, and they may quit in frustration, despite making progress.

TIP

Taking inventory of your own personality type will help you understand how other people perceive you. And understanding how your clients perceive you will help you to communicate with them effectively.

Reading you right the first time: Learning styles

Unlocking the secrets of how your clients think and learn will help you to make meaningful connections with them. By gathering information about people's personality types, temperament, discipline, and various other qualities that make individuals who they are, you'll be able to create a "profile" of each one of your clients. When you have a clear profile of your clients, you'll understand how to best support them when they need you to.

TIP

Can I tell you a secret? This may surprise you, but most of your clients really won't care how much you know about exercise physiology. Sure, they want you to know enough to help them get in shape, but that alone won't get you far in this field. Some of the best personal trainers I know are great because they can read people well. Sure, they know how to get results for their clients, but more important, they recognize their clients' unique personality traits. And they understand each individual client's preferred learning style. The best trainers I know coach their clients according to how they like to learn. Some people are visual learners (they learn by watching), some are auditory learners (they learn by listening), and others are kinesthetic learners (they learn by doing). When your training approach matches your client's preferred learning style, you'll get really good at demonstrating exercises, explaining assessment results, and much more. On the other hand, if your approach doesn't match your client's learning style, they'll probably either feel overwhelmed by too much information, frustrated by a pace that's too fast or too slow, or otherwise underwhelmed by your inability to connect with them.

Let me hear your body talk: Understanding body language

Think that what you say is more important than the way you say it? Not so. Fifty-five percent of the impact of what we say comes from our body language and other visual cues, 38 percent from the way we sound, and a piddling 7 percent of the meaning comes from our words.

You can use this knowledge to your advantage by reading your clients' body language. Even if they never say a word, you'll be able to tell whether they're bored, excited, angry, or happy — and whether you should offer some positive reinforcement, push them a bit harder, or keep mum.

The cues in Table 9-1 will help you understand what your clients are saying — even when they say nothing at all.

TABLE 9-1   **Understanding Body Language**

Body Language	What It Means
Leaning forward Standing with open arms	They're engaged in what's going on.
Standing with their arms behind their back	They're paying attention to what's going on.
Moving backward Crossing their arms in front of their chest	They're rejecting what you're saying or you're being too aggressive and making them uncomfortable, regardless of what you're saying.
Tapping their fingers or foot	They're feeling combative.
Looking around Pointing their feet toward the door	They're eager to leave or they're self-conscious and feel you're drawing too much attention.
Blinking quickly Tilting their head	They're listening to what you're saying.
Clenching their hands	They're feeling defensive.

Coaching your clients

You might think that your job as a personal trainer is simply to design exercise programs and teach people how to use them. This is definitely a key part of what you do, but you'll soon find that your role in your clients' lives goes far beyond teaching them how to bench press. Your clients look to you for coaching — someone who can show them how to succeed in improving their health and how to fit exercise into their busy lives. And if doing this were simply a matter of following instructions, people wouldn't be looking to personal trainers for help.

Now, if you're wondering how you're supposed to come up with a different training approach for each individual client's personality and learning style, never fear. Understanding your clients for the unique individuals they are matters, but you don't need a new approach for every client to be a good coach. Fortunately, most people can be sorted into categories by "type" and I show you how to do it in this section. But first let's talk about what it means to be a coach.

In sports, a coach works with athletes to develop their full potential. The coach analyzes the athlete's performance and teaches them relevant skills to maximize their strengths and improve their weaknesses. At the same time, the coach encourages their athletes and guides them in their chosen sport and in their lives. In other words, coaches create the right learning conditions for their athletes to be successful human beings. In personal training, a coach (that's you!) helps to overcome obstacles that stand between their clients' health and fitness goals and what they need to do to reach those goals.

In a nutshell, being a coach means providing sound advice and personal, thoughtful solutions — rather than textbook answers — to your clients' problems. That's why you need to understand the human side of lifestyle change in addition to being able to teach your client how to do a proper deadlift.

So how do you sort your clients into categories that you can use to guide your approach to coaching them? I recommend using the Skill–Will Matrix, a tool popularized by author Max Landsberg in his book, *The Tao of Coaching* (Profile Books, 1996). The Skill–Will Matrix, shown in Figure 9-1, combines a person's skills (can they do it) and motivation (do they want to do it) to determine how you should coach them. The four quadrants in the matrix categorize clients into four general "types" based on their combined skill/will level. Table 9-2 provides a breakdown of each.

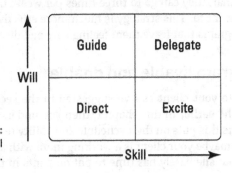

FIGURE 9-1:
The Skill-Will Matrix.

TABLE 9-2　　　　**Understanding Client Types**

Client Type	Coaching Style	Description
High skill/High will	Delegate	Typically good at everything and motivated to improve
High skill/Low will	Excite	Good at things but loses interest
High will/Low skill	Guide	More enthusiasm than skill
Low skill/Low will	Direct	Often quiet, shy, and introverted

TIP

Here are three key tips to remember for coaching your clients:

» Always listen — *really* listen — to your clients' questions and problems. Don't formulate a response in your head while your client is still talking.

» Don't interrupt, and don't jump in with your quick fix as soon as sounds cease to come out of your client's mouth.

» Take the time to formulate a customized solution, even if it means you have to get back to your client in a day or two.

Setting your clients up for success

If your client loses those 20 extra pounds, lowers their blood pressure, or feels more energetic than they have since high school, they're sure to keep coming back. In other words, if you want to retain clients, you need to help them succeed at their fitness goals.

Planning one step at a time

REMEMBER

Nothing is more frustrating for a client than getting nowhere because the trainer has given them too much to do. Any program needs to be broken down into manageable steps. For example, if your client wants to start exercising but doesn't know how, start by having them exercise twice a week as opposed to three times a week. After mastering that, they can go to three times per week; then maybe four times per week if they want to. This strategy is much more effective than starting clients off on tough programs that leave them feeling sore and discouraged.

Making the program livable and doable

If you've gotten close to your client as I've suggested in the section "Knowing who you're dealing with" earlier in this chapter, then you understand their lifestyle and any constraints this puts on their schedule and ability to follow a fitness program. For example, maybe your client is a working mom with a high-powered career and is so busy that she barely has time to put on pants in the morning let alone trying to work out for an hour. You need to work within the confines of how your client lives her life and create her fitness program accordingly.

TIP

Something is always better than nothing. If a client continually has reasons for why they can't fit a workout into their schedule, listen carefully to figure out why they're struggling. Some days there really isn't an extra hour available, but there's probably a way to sneak in 15 minutes of exercise. More often than not, you'll be able to come up with a solution to help your client stay on track *if* you understand their barriers. The longer you let a client slide by on excuses for skipping workouts, the farther away they'll be from their goals — and they may turn the blame on you, losing you both a client and your reputation.

Motivating Your Clients

Great motivational speakers (like Tony Robbins) make their audiences believe that they have the power to change their lives for the better. Great motivational trainers do the same for their clients. Being an example of a healthy and fit person, keeping things interesting (people who are bored are rarely motivated), providing positive reinforcement, and substantiating their progress are all things you can do to keep your clients interested.

Being a role model

You want clients to look at you and think, "Seeing this healthy, vibrant person motivates me to work hard to meet my fitness goals." You *don't* want them to look at you and think, "It looks like my trainer slept in that shirt, and now I'm ready for a nap." In other words, be a good role model for your clients.

TIP

It sounds like a lame cliché — okay, it *is* a lame cliché — but the reason people keep saying it is it's true. To be a good role model and keep your clients motivated, you have to practice what you preach. You need to:

>> **Be fit.** You should look reasonably healthy. (Looks can be deceiving, but appearances do count. You want to project fitness to your clients so they can look to you for inspiration.)

>> **Be strong.** Spotting clients, handing them weights, and putting plates on the machines takes a lot of strength. Make sure you have it.

>> **Be a nonsmoker.** I can't think of anything worse than a trainer who teaches clients how to be healthy while they reek of stale stogies — except maybe a trainer who bums cigarettes off a client!

>> **Eat healthfully.** Even though your clients may not see what you eat, it's the principle of the thing. You can't, in good conscience, tell your clients to deep-six their favorite goodies while you eat fast food for every meal.

Changing up the program

Would you want to eat egg whites for breakfast, a salad for lunch, and a grilled chicken breast for dinner *every day of your life?* Your clients feel the same way about their personal training sessions. Doing the exact same exercises in the exact same order on the exact same days of the week gets stale pretty fast. Not only that, but their progress will soon plateau, which can be discouraging.

TIP

To keep clients interested, motivated, and coming back for more, you can't stick with the same ol' same ol'. Throw them a few curveballs without changing the program so dramatically that they feel lost. Here are some ways to do this:

>> **Up the weights.** Increase the weights as your client gains strength. They'll always be challenged and will be super-motivated when they now bench-press way more weight than when they first started!

>> **Decrease rest time** with active recovery. If your client's program calls for two minutes of rest between sets, try filling the rest time with corrective exercises.

>> **Superset it.** It sounds like what you do in a fast-food joint when you upsize your fries and drink for a nickel, but *supersetting* is actually putting two exercises back to back without a rest period in between. This technique is for more-advanced clients. (Read more on advanced programming techniques in Chapter 15.)

>> **Periodize it.** Talk with your clients about where you're taking them. Are you taking them from a fat-loss/endurance program lasting from three to six weeks, moving on to a hypertrophy phase for six weeks to build muscle, and then going into a strength phase to help them get stronger for their outdoor adventures? Periodizing — and telling them what they stand to gain from it — helps your clients set goals and look forward to new programming. Depending on what their goals are, be sure to tell them whether they can expect to lose more fat or add more muscle during one period than in another. You can stick to a fat-loss phase for a good chunk of time, but shaking things up will help both mentally and physically.

>> **Mix it up.** Even something as simple as changing your client's schedule can keep things interesting. For example, try changing the days of the week that you do strength training and cardio, or change the order of the exercises in a session.

Providing positive reinforcement

People thrive on feedback. Your client will appreciate a pat on the back for finally getting their deadlift form right or a high-five for doing their first chin-up. You need to create a positive environment that fosters growth and mastery for your clients to stay motivated. Sport and exercise psychologists base these techniques on *principles of reinforcement*.

There are positive and negative ways to reinforce behavior. The positive approach means rewarding your client for their achievements. Focusing on what's going well (even if there's a lot that's not going so well) increases the likelihood of the client repeating the thing that earned the reward. This could be as simple as a "way to go" for showing up ten minutes early to do a dynamic warm-up and foam roll. The negative approach focuses on what's wrong and tries to change unwanted behaviors through punishment or criticism. For example, if your client shows up ten minutes late for a training session, you criticize them for it, hoping your punishing words will lead to the client showing up on time in the future.

WARNING

Reinforcement is more complex than you might think. Sometimes the same reinforcement will affect two people completely differently, which is why it's so important to get to know your clients and understand their personalities. For example, a lecture for showing up late might feel like punishment to one client and recognition to someone else.

TIP

Take a positive approach with your clients. Here are some ways to encourage and motivate them:

>> **Make a comparison to a past performance.** For example, you could say, "You did five more reps than last time. Awesome job!"

>> **Compliment their form.** Focusing on form is a subtle reminder that it's not just about the end result.

>> **When you record workouts in their training log, include encouraging notes about what they're doing well.**

>> **Send your clients an occasional greeting card or email, or give them a call, to say you're proud of them.** Everyone likes to get things in the mail or email besides bills and spam (and phone calls from people who aren't trying to sell them something). Your clients want you to be proud of them (sounds cheesy, but it's true) and an encouraging note or text might motivate them more than you realize.

WARNING

Don't overdo the gushing — people can sense insincerity a mile away.

Reward effort. People are more willing to try new things when they know they'll be recognized for trying instead of being criticized for falling short.

TIP

We all have days when we feel like we can't do anything right. If a client is feeling down, try turning their negative comments into positive ones. For example, if they say, "I'm doing horribly today," give a gentle reminder that, "even though you're not feeling at your best today, you're doing your best and getting stronger every week." Training logs can really help on days like this — showing your clients how much they've improved since starting will help them through down days and keep them focused on their long-term goals.

TIP

The ability to motivate their clients, rather than technical knowledge about personal training, is what separates very good trainers from average ones. All the personal training knowledge in the world means zilch if you can't get your clients to follow your programs. Motivation is a vast subject and I could write an entire book describing the various points of view on the role motivation plays in sport and exercise. I hope you'll put some time into learning more about it, and about sport and exercise psychology in general. When you do, you'll become a personal trainer who knows how to get your clients results because you'll understand what makes your clients tick.

Following up for follow-through

If you're a parent, you know that sometimes getting your kids to do their chores takes some nagging. "Please take out the garbage." "When do you plan to take out the garbage?" "Have you taken out the garbage yet?"

Parenting a kid is good training for working with clients, except with clients, we don't call it *nagging* — we call it *following up*. Following up with your clients holds them accountable for following the plan you've laid out for them and gives them little motivational boosts.

TIP

Following up with your clients doesn't mean calling them every five minutes between sessions to ask if they've done their workout yet. Follow these tips for following up:

>> **Lay out a plan.** Give the client specific directions, such as, "You will do exercises X, Y, and Z on these days, drink eight glasses of water per day, and eat a fruit or vegetable with every meal."

>> **Put it in writing.** Ask your client to record their workouts (exercises, sets, reps, and so on) in a log.

>> **Check in once or twice while your clients are between sessions (depending upon how often you see them).** A quick call or email to make sure they're on track and to see if they have any questions is all you need.

>> **Be a problem solver.** If your client reports that they haven't been sticking to the plan, ask why. For example, if they're crunched for time after work, you could suggest getting a quick workout in before work or going for a walk at lunchtime.

>> **Schedule sessions.** Plan to see your clients at regular intervals to re-assess goals, measure body composition, and other measures of progress.

Getting Connected: Fostering Good Relationships with Your Clients

If you've ever been on a dud of a first date (and who hasn't?), you know that sometimes you just don't feel a connection with someone. Maybe they didn't share any personal information, or maybe they only shared personal information. Maybe they were just really boring to be around. In any case, you probably didn't want to see that person again.

REMEMBER

Your clients are trusting you with their most important assets— their bodies and their health— and you need to establish a connection with them based on trust, sharing, and rapport. Keeping a connection alive will keep your clients coming back.

Knowing when to listen and when to talk

They say talk is cheap, but they're dead wrong. Saying the right thing at the right time (and knowing when not to say anything at all) will help you forge a connection with your clients that will keep them happy and motivated — not to mention paying.

TIP

Open up a little bit about yourself. When you do, you're telling your client, "I hear you, and I experience the same things as you." For example, you might have a client who is trying to cut back on sugar but struggles at night with chocolate cravings. You can offer tips like eating a piece of fruit to curb a sugar craving or you can teach your client how to incorporate chocolate into their diet without sabotaging their fitness goals. Also, don't pretend you're not human. Tell this person that sometimes it's hard for you to make healthy choices too.

Sometimes your client needs to vent, and you happen to be the person who's nearby at the time. You don't need to be a problem solver in this situation. If your client shows up late and starts complaining about their jerk of a boss, for example, don't tell them to take that job and shove it. Just listen and let them know that you can relate.

WARNING

Be careful not to fall into the trap of commiserating with your clients — remember that you're at work when you're with your clients. Your time with them is their time and I guarantee that clients don't want to listen to you complain about your job.

REMEMBER

If your client is normally talkative but is suddenly glaring at you and giving monosyllabic answers to your questions, don't take it personally. They're probably having a bad day and need some space (and some silence). No need to fill the silence with small talk. Sometimes silence truly is golden.

TRUE STORY

Many of my clients had high-stress jobs and often their time with me was the only hour they had to themselves all day. Some days these clients would come in and chat away, and other days they would barely mutter two words. At first, I thought I had done something wrong, but I eventually understood that a client's silence wasn't a personal slight — sometimes they just had a lot going on and didn't feel like talking.

Say this, not that

Certain words and phrases should never come out of a personal trainer's mouth (at least when the client is within earshot). Naturally, you want to avoid cursing, talking smack about other clients, or insulting a client. But even such seemingly innocuous terms as *overweight* should be purged from your patois. Check out Table 9-3 to know what not to say, and for suggestions of what to say instead.

Respecting your clients' privacy

Would you like it if your hairdresser told another client exactly how not natural your blonde is? Or if your accountant told all your neighbors how much your tax bill was last year? No? Then please understand why your clients' doings — even the positive ones — should be marked "Strictly Confidential" in your mind.

TIP

Here are some suggestions for keeping the lid shut on your clients' private affairs:

>> **During the initial consultation, assure the client that anything they say and do in the training sessions stays between the two of you.**

TABLE 9-3   ## What Not to Say to Your Clients

Instead of . . .	Say . . .	The Reason
Overweight	Nothing	Weight isn't an indication of a person's health status and unless your client specifically tells you they want to lose weight, it's not your place to tell them how.
Inflexible or not flexible	Shortened range of motion	Inflexible sounds so . . . inflexible, as if the client can do nothing to fix it. Referring to it as a shortened range of motion lets the client know that the range of motion can be increased.
Weak	Not strong yet or not strong on this exercise	Telling the client they're not strong *yet* indicates that eventually they will be. Or perhaps they're not strong on a certain exercise because they're using a small body part — on the next exercise, they may be stronger.
No stamina	Low lung capacity	If you say that a client has no stamina, they may think that's just the way they are, that nothing can change that. If you say low lung capacity, that sounds like something that can improve.
Out of shape	Deconditioned	The word *deconditioned* says that your client's current state of fitness is temporary.

>> **If you have employees, have them sign a nondisclosure agreement that states that they won't disclose information about clients, including their names, to anyone.** You can have your lawyer draw one up for you.

>> **If your client gets tight lipped about a subject, back off.** If they want to talk about it, they will.

>> **If you're in a client's home and you see or hear an argument or anything else the client would rather you didn't see, keep mum and don't pry.** Don't even share details about the client's belongings or decorating style. Even raving about the client's beautiful home isn't wise — if they hear you've talked about them in *any* way, they'll wonder what other things you've said about them.

>> **Never talk about one client with another client.** If a client hears you talk about others, they'll probably wonder if you talk about them too.

>> **If a client asks about another client, simply tell them you can't talk about your other clients because you don't want to violate their privacy.** Remember in your first meeting when you said what happens between you and your clients is confidential?

RECOGNIZING THE SOURCE OF YOUR CLIENTS' FRUSTRATION

A normally cheery client snaps at you during a workout. What did you do wrong?

Maybe nothing. Sometimes people have a bad day, and they take it out on the people closest to them. Psychologists refer to this as *transference*. Your cranky client may have had a fight with their spouse, had a bad day at work, or been cut off by a rude driver, and they're taking it out on you.

The best way to deal with transference is to use simple words: "You seem angry. I'm sorry. How can I help?" Chances are, they'll cool down.

If your client seems too angry to focus on the session, offer to reschedule, but suggest that a good workout could be just what they need to work out those negative feelings!

Remember: Just because you work in a gym doesn't mean you have to be your client's punching bag. You deserve to be treated with respect and civility; if your client can't grant you the minimum of human decency, you can — and should — ask them to leave and come back when they can.

If asking someone to reschedule or leave seems harsh, sometimes it is, but it's also effective. Most of the time the client will apologize for behaving badly and it won't happen again. Remember, if you don't insist that people respect your boundaries, they won't.

Resolving Conflicts and Addressing Concerns

You know that you rock, and I know that you rock, but every once in a while a client will think that you do *not* rock — and you'll have to take action to make things right.

Figuring out what went wrong

TIP

The minute you sense something is wrong, start asking the client questions to dig up the root of the problem. You can come right out and say, "You seem upset — is anything bothering you that I can help you with?" Or you can ask questions that will help uncover the problem, such as, "Are you achieving your goals? Are you happy with my services?"

Why wrack your brain if you don't have to? If a client is unhappy with your services, ask what you can do to make them better. Often, the client will tell you exactly where you're going wrong and how to fix the situation.

Acknowledging your mistakes

We all make mistakes. That's right, even the esteemed author of this book has made *lots* of mistakes. So you're not alone if you've made mistakes. In fact, you're alone if you *haven't!*

If you make a mistake, you have two choices: You can compound the mistake by denying it or blaming someone else, or you can do the right thing, fess up, and do what you can to make things right. You may feel that admitting to a mistake will lower you in the eyes of your client, but in truth they'll respect you for owning up to your actions.

Many trainers commit the faux pas in the following list. If you're aware of their mistakes, you have a better chance of avoiding them yourself:

>> **Not following through:** For example, if you tell a client that you'll research a certain piece of equipment and then you don't do it because you were busy watching the season finale of your favorite reality show and forgot, apologize, then do what you promised ASAP.

>> **Giving the client incorrect information:** For example, if you tell a client an exercise will work their biceps when it will really work their triceps, correct yourself as soon as you realize your mistake.

>> **Not admitting that you don't know the answer to a question:** When you don't know the answer, you're much better off telling your client that you'll have to find out and get back to them. They'll respect you for it in the long run — and even if they don't, you'll still be able to respect yourself.

>> **Showing up late:** Time is money — and this holds true not only for you, but also for your clients. If you're late to your appointments with your clients, the message you're communicating is that your time is more important than theirs. And that's the last thing you want your clients to feel. If you can't avoid being late, call ahead of time to apologize and explain the situation, and make sure you extend the session to make up for the lost time.

>> **Not showing up at all:** Worse than being late is not showing up. If you have an emergency and you have to cancel your appointment, be sure to call your client and explain the situation. And make sure you don't make a habit of it. Emergencies don't happen every day.

>> **Not being prepared for your sessions:** For instance, if you were supposed to update your client's program but you didn't, your client will wonder how much you really care about their progress. Apologize and do what you promised — pronto.

Making things right

If you make a mistake, the first thing to do is apologize. Then try to fix the problem. Remember you can try asking the client what you can do to make it right. If you really messed up, a free session or two may be in order.

TRUE STORY

Before sharing this story, I have to tell you that it happens once to all of us. And if you're anything like me, it will only ever happen once. Thinking about it over 20 years later still makes my stomach drop. One morning I woke up to my phone ringing at 6:20 a.m. It was the gym calling to ask if I was okay and to let me know my client was there waiting for me. Yep, you guessed it. I slept right through my alarm and no-showed my 6 a.m. client. Fortunately, my client forgave me, despite being stood up at 6 in the morning. To make amends, I offered the client two free sessions — one to make up for the missed one, and one more to say thank you for understanding that I, too, am human.

"BUT YOU PROMISED!" GUARANTEES AND WARRANTIES

Sure, promising clients they'll definitely lose 20 pounds in three months or that your plan will lower their blood pressure might keep them coming to you. But is this a good tactic? Not really. You may offer the best workout sessions around, but you have no control over what clients do outside of the sessions. Maybe they go home and down two pints of Ben & Jerry's. Maybe they sit on the couch watching eight hours of TV every day. You simply can't guarantee that a client will lose weight, be free from back pain, or lower their cholesterol.

A better idea is to do what salespeople call "under-promise and over-deliver." In other words, downplay what you can do for the client. For example, you can tell your client that your workouts will make them stronger and more flexible — you know this will happen if the client is working out with you regularly, even if they don't do it at home. If you give your clients exactly what you promised, they'll be happy. If you give them more — say, they do lose pounds or their back pain goes away — you're golden.

If you can't resolve a problem, the best option may be to refund the client's money for any unused sessions and refer them to another trainer. In fact, you should have a refund policy in place for such situations.

TIP

Many experts recommend a simple refund policy: 100 percent satisfaction or your money back. And why not? If you're good at what you do, you should be able to back it up with a strong refund policy. Of course, you should refund only for those sessions the client hasn't used yet. (See the nearby sidebar, "'But you promised!': Guarantees and warranties.")

Breaking Up is Hard to Do: Setting Your Client Free

Whoever said "All good things must come to an end" must have been talking about personal training. And the person who said "If you love something, set it free"? Well, that person was talking about unicorns (if the posters bearing this slogan are any indication). But we can pretend this applies to personal training too. In other words, sometimes you have to let a client go.

Time to spread your wings and fly

Sometimes you can easily tell when it's time to set a client free — they can work out successfully on their own, and you don't think they need you anymore. Or maybe a client has gone as far as they can with you, and it's time to start working with another trainer (for example, maybe they want to start doing sport-specific workouts and you know a trainer who would be a better fit for their goals).

TIP

If you've determined that your client is ready to move on, and you've had a good relationship with them, you can either suggest that they visit another trainer (you can refer them to a trainer you know) or that they start working out on their own more often and with you less often. For example, if you're seeing a client three times a week, cut back to two times a week and have them work out once on their own between sessions. Continue to taper off the sessions until you're seeing the client only once every couple of months to check progress and change the program as needed.

It's not you, it's me

Sometimes deciding to cut a client loose isn't so easy — you may be burned out on a client or you just don't click with them. If any of the items on the following list are true, it may be time to let go:

>> The client regularly cancels sessions at the last minute or doesn't show up at all.

>> You find yourself wanting to end workouts early, or you no longer have the passion to make the training sessions as engaging as possible.

>> The client has started to complain a lot (or a lot more than usual).

>> You don't look forward to seeing the client.

Sound mean? Well, think of it this way: In order to give all your clients your best effort, you need to care about what you do. If you start feeling burned out because you and a particular client aren't a good match, everyone suffers if you continue hanging on.

Letting a client go requires an abundance of tact and grace. Try saying something like, "I sense that you're not getting as much as you can from our training sessions. I really think that Trainer X can offer you more than I can, and you'd enjoy working with them more." This puts the blame on your shoulders rather than the client's — you can't meet their needs — and eases the blow.

STAYING IN TOUCH WITH CLIENTS AFTER THEY'VE MOVED ON

Y'know how you get notes in the mail from your dentist, your mechanic, and your cat's veterinarian reminding you that it's time for a checkup? Or how you changed from one cell provider to another, and now your old provider sends you email every once in a while (or every five minutes) with a new offer?

These companies know that staying in touch with former clients is a good business practice. If you have clients who've moved on, shoot them an occasional email to touch base and make sure they're on track. You never know — they may decide to come back to you!

Try these little reminders to keep former clients thinking about how wonderful you are:

- **Holiday cards:** Holiday cards are a great way to stay in touch. Just be sure they're nondenominational so you don't offend clients who don't celebrate a particular holiday. Sending a "Happy New Year" card in the last week of December is a good approach — plus, you'll catch your former clients at a time when lots of people think about getting or staying in shape.

- **News clippings:** If a former client is a florist and you run across an article about new flower arranging techniques, clip it and send it along. This method drives home the importance of getting to know your clients.

- **Newsletters:** Turn to Chapter 8 for more information on creating winning newsletters.

- **Coupons or gift certificates:** Special offers like these may prompt your former clients to give you another try.

- **Thank-you notes:** Right after the client heads for other pastures, send a hand-written thank-you note for doing business with you. They'll remember you for it.

3

Putting the Personal into Personal Training

IN THIS PART . . .

You're ready to meet your first client. Yipes! What to wear, what to do, what to say? No worries — I talk all about this in Chapter 10.

Next, Chapter 11 describes the fitness assessment, where you prepare your clients for their first session and take baseline measurements like resting heart rate and range of motion.

And finally, starting with Chapter 12, I get to the good stuff — the actual training of clients! It's time to figure out how to plan your client's program, such as determining which exercises to prescribe, how intense they should be, and what order the client should do them in. I also tell you how to conduct the client's first session and how to advance your client when the time comes.

Chapter **10**

Getting to Know You: Performing Initial Consultations

ave you ever walked into a restaurant, sat down, and had a server put a plate in front of you without first asking what you wanted from the menu? I hope not! Before you can help your clients, you need to find out what they want.

How do you find out what a prospective client wants? Simple — you ask! Before someone hires you to be their personal trainer, you need to find out about their goals, lifestyle, expectations, and so on. This is typically done in the *initial consultation*. The information you collect during this meeting helps you to make sound, safe, and effective recommendations.

Before you meet face-to-face with a prospective client, they will probably call or email to inquire about you and your services. Think of this as a job interview. If the prospective client likes what they hear, they will come in for a consult and hire you to be their personal trainer. In this chapter, I show you how to sell your services (and yourself) and how to conduct effective and efficient initial consultations that convert prospects into clients.

Hello, My Name Is . . .

I'll bet that if you're talking with a potential client, they have already read all about you online. They probably know what you look like, how your training program — or programs — work, how much your services cost, and so on. Selling yourself online first helps, but you still have to convince your prospects to take the next step and schedule a face-to-face initial consult.

"No sweat," you think.

Not so fast! Picking up the phone or sending an email is easy, but convincing the person on the other end, through one conversation, that you are different from every other trainer they have checked out is a lot harder. On an inquiry call or email, your objectives are:

>> To establish rapport

>> To qualify your prospective client

>> To schedule an initial consultation

Polishing your "netiquette"

There may be times when your phone rings with a potential client inquiring about your services, but more often than not, your first communication will happen over email.

TIP

Make sure you reply within one day when you receive an email inquiry. I also recommend sending an auto-reply thanking the person for their interest and letting them know when you will get back to them. Keep your emails brief and professional, check for spelling and grammar errors, and avoid typos.

Figuring out what you're going to say

Instead of coming up with what to say every time someone calls or emails, use a script. Your script should be a well-thought-out checklist of answers to commonly asked questions about your services. A script helps to guide your conversations and will also save you time once you have it down.

REMEMBER

Your script is like your elevator speech and is only effective if you are comfortable with it. Start by describing who you are and what you do in a few sentences. Then make a check-list of common questions and answers, including why you are different from your competitors.

Here are some common questions that prospective clients ask:

>> How long have you been a personal trainer?

>> What do you charge for your services?

>> Do you offer group or family discounts?

>> Do you have other clients my age and with similar goals?

TIP

Write out the answers to these questions and anything else you think someone might ask you; then practice saying it out loud until you have it down. Whether you are talking on the phone or writing an email, you need to convey confidence in your choice of words and your tone. Be concise and definitive in your answers. You don't have to recite from a prepared script every time you talk to someone, but practicing your answers in advance will help you to avoid stumbling over your words or pausing to think of the right answers. You will come across as confident and knowledgeable when you know what to say, and you will be able to keep the focus of the conversation on the prospective client's needs.

You'll usually need to gather some information from the prospective client, but some people are reluctant to give the details you need. So you need to practice the art of getting information without being pushy.

TIP

If the caller seems reluctant to share personal information, offer to schedule a face-to-face consultation instead so they can get to know you. I have always referred to my initial consultation as a strategy session and I explain to potential clients that it's an opportunity for them to ask questions and for me to thoroughly evaluate their needs and goals so I can make a sound training recommendation. This is a free, no-obligation meeting.

If the person doesn't want to schedule a consultation, you can still give a brief overview of your services and pricing, and then offer to email them with more information. If they're interested, they will be back in touch when they're ready. You can also ask for permission to follow up in the future.

Building credibility . . . fast!

A person is showing interest in your services by contacting you, but they might still need to know more about you before committing to training with you.

REMEMBER

You can use this conversation to gain credibility, but establishing good rapport — and fast — is vital. Did you know that most people will have a solid impression of who you are within seven seconds of meeting you? Prospective clients can read about your credentials online, but it has been my experience that people don't care how much you know until they know how much you care. You need to be passionate about what you do and about helping people with their fitness goals. Someone might believe you're an expert, but if they don't trust you, they probably won't feel comfortable sharing personal information with you. First impressions are everything!

TIP

Here are some ways to quickly establish rapport, but remember to be yourself; you don't have to use all these ideas.

>> **Listen more than you talk.** When someone reaches out to ask for help, listen. Something prompted them to call you, and most of the time, people just need to feel like they are being heard.

>> **Don't take yourself too seriously.** You can take what you do seriously without taking yourself too seriously. People feel more at ease when you come across as relaxed.

>> **Use layperson's terms when you are talking.** Most people won't be familiar with technical anatomy and physiology terminology and will have no idea what you're talking about if you over use it. For example, don't say patella. Say kneecap.

>> **Be relatable.** You are the expert. You are also human. You won't always feel like working out, competing demands will make it hard for you to prioritize yourself, sometimes you make mistakes. You don't have to highlight your shortcomings, but your clients will appreciate your transparency and the example that you set for them by doing your best to stay on track with your fitness goals in the midst of everyday life.

>> **Share your experience with similar clients.** Tell your prospective client about people you have worked with who started with similar goals.

>> **Mention other respected providers in your area (doctors, physical therapists, massage therapists, and so on) with whom you work.** If you are meeting with a prospective client after they have recovered from an injury, knowing their physical therapist and learning how to work around injuries will boost your credibility.

Qualifying a potential client

You will learn with experience that not all clients are a good fit for your business and that you are not a good fit for all clients. You could be someone's first choice, but your location and schedule are inconvenient for them. Or, maybe your rates are outside of their budget. It's tempting to work with anybody and everybody when you're getting started, but don't offer a service that you can't deliver.

You need to ask *qualifying questions* to see whether you and the potential client are a good fit before scheduling an initial consultation. You don't want to waste your time or a potential client's time with a consult if they want a type of training that you don't offer or if your schedule won't work with theirs.

Here are some qualifying questions you could ask:

>> What type of training are you looking for? (Is it something you offer?)

>> My rates range from X to Y. Does that work for you?

>> When are you available for training sessions? (Does their schedule work with yours?)

>> Where do you live or work? (Are you in a convenient location?)

Knowing what to say before you hang up or hit send

Now that you have gone through your script, learned what the caller is looking for and how you can help them, ask to schedule an initial consultation even if they are ready to get started right away.

If you're talking on the phone, take notes and summarize key points of the conversation. Tell the caller that scheduling a free initial consultation is the next step. Do the same thing when you reply to an email inquiry, and in both situations, be sure to explain what the initial consultation entails and why it's important.

Sending a follow-up email the same day

Even if you schedule a consultation, send a follow-up email to thank the person for their interest and tell them you are looking forward to seeing them. If you don't schedule a consultation, send an email to thank the person for their interest and include more detailed information about your business. You might include an attachment with a detailed overview of your services and links to your website and social media accounts. Set a reminder to send another follow-up email in a week to ask if they are ready to schedule a consult.

Getting to Know You: Preparing to Meet for the First Time

Getting ready for your first meeting with a new client is a lot like preparing for your first day of school. That day was a long time ago, but I'll bet you can remember it. The night before, you probably had your backpack filled with new school supplies, clothes laid out, lunch waiting downstairs in the fridge — all in anticipation of meeting your new classmates and teachers for the first time. You wanted to make sure that you made a good impression and that everyone liked you.

That's just what you need to do before meeting a potential client for the first time. Taking a little time beforehand to make sure you have your ducks in a row will give you the extra boost of confidence of knowing that you're well prepared.

WARNING

Don't skip the initial consultation! Some trainers skip this step, eager to show their clients how great they are, and it will come back to haunt them. The client could get injured if the trainer isn't aware of previous injuries, or the client might head for the door early if the trainer doesn't understand the client's needs and expectations.

The time, energy, and effort you devote up front to learning everything you can about your client will benefit you in the long run. The more you know about the client, the better your service will be — which means your clients will get the results they are looking for.

Making a good first impression

Good or bad, the first impression is the one that lasts. Either you're going to wow the prospective client with your amazing professionalism and knowledge, or you're going to completely underwhelm them with your lack thereof.

Don't despair, grasshopper! Whether this consultation is your 1st or your 50th, I'll share with you my time-tested tips that are sure to leave your new client all aglow afterward. These tips are simple — no studying required.

Practice punctuality

Always be on time. Better yet, plan to be ten minutes early, even if you risk sitting in your car in front of the prospective client's house for nine of those ten minutes. Besides, you can do a lot during those nine minutes. You can:

>> Review the notes from your earlier phone conversation with the prospect.

>> Make sure you have your paperwork in order.

>> Mentally rehearse your presentation.

Planning to arrive early allows time for the unexpected — a traffic jam or a lost client form — to happen without causing you to be late. Nothing is worse than greeting a potential client with, "Hi! Sorry I'm late! The funniest thing happened to me on the way over here . . . ."

Dress for success

Granted, personal training lends itself to spandex work apparel, but you should still strive to look professional. Is it possible to look professional in workout clothes? Of course! Whether you're working solo or planning to have a whole fleet of trainers, picking the right attire matters and can make or break your professional image.

TIP

Keep these tips in mind when choosing your personal training uniform:

>> **Choose fabrics with some stretch.** This will allow the garment to retain its shape and for you to be able to move comfortably.

>> **Opt for high-quality shirts with breathable fabric.** Add your logo for a more professional look.

>> **Make sure your clothes fit well.** It's ok for your clothes to accentuate your physique, but don't wear revealing clothing when you're at work. My motto has always been "no boobs, no butts, no bellies."

>> **Make sure you don't have any rips or stains (like sweat) on your clothes or shoes.** Save your old workout clothes for mowing the lawn or cleaning the house. Just as you wouldn't wear torn or stained clothes if you worked in an office, you shouldn't wear them when you meet with clients. You might want to get a new pair of shoes that you only break out for assessments or other meetings. You can wear (slightly) older shoes for your actual training sessions. Same with the rest of your clothes. Set aside the best stuff you own for sales meetings and assessments. Eventually, when your best stuff gets a few scuffs, they'll become your regular clothes, and you'll buy new ones to replace them.

Be enthusiastic

Smile, smile, and smile some more! Your smile is your best asset for putting your potential client at ease. Naturally, they'll probably be nervous about sharing personal health information with a stranger. Your pleasant demeaner will help set the tone for a successful first meeting.

REMEMBER

Smiling can help *you*, too! If you're feeling nervous about conducting your initial consultation, it's ok to crack a joke or use small talk to break the ice. Sometimes you have to fake it 'til you make it.

Being prepared

Being prepared can save you headaches and embarrassment while you're presenting your services to a potential client. The more organized you are, the more smoothly the whole consultation will go. Knowing you have everything in place ahead of time lets you concentrate solely on your consult.

Before setting out for the initial consultation, consider putting together a *consult packet* to give to your prospective client. This packet will contain information about you and your services that the prospect can keep after the consultation is over. Your packet can include copies of your:

» Company overview or personal bio

» Services and rates

» Training philosophy

» Client testimonials

TIP

Remember when you put reports in plastic folders to score brownie points with your high-school teacher? You can do the same with your consult packet. Put the copies in a folder that has a slot for your business card, or you can take the copies to an office-supply store and have them spiral-bound with a clear cover. Professional presentations help establish your credibility.

TIP

In addition to your consult packet, before leaving for the consultation, make sure you have the following items in your attaché (yes, you should carry a backpack or a nice bag, not a duffel bag like the one you throw your gym clothes in):

» Forms and information on your prices and policies (such as your liability policy, your cancellation policy, and your refund policy), as well as information on what to expect during the client's first training session

» Forms you use to record information on your prospective client, such as health history and exercise history

» Clipboard

» Notepaper

» Pens and pencils

» Business cards

TIP

Arrange your paperwork in a clipboard in the order you'll be using it. I recommend filling out the forms yourself during the consultation, using them to guide your conversation.

The order of your paperwork should be:

1. Informed Consent and Waiver of Liability
2. Physical Activity Readiness Questionnaire (PAR-Q+)
3. Health History and Present Medical Condition Questionnaire
4. Comprehensive Client Information Sheet (goals, preferences, and so on)
5. Readiness for Change Questionnaire
6. Typical Day in the Life Questionnaire
7. Social Support Questionnaire
8. Cancellation policy
9. Refund policy
10. What to Expect During Your First Session sheet

REMEMBER

No matter how good you are, you must set your ego aside during an initial consultation. You need to find out as much as you can about your prospective client, which means asking insightful questions and being a good listener. The initial consultation is all about the other person and how you can help them with their fitness goals.

Conducting the Initial Consultation

You've arrived ten minutes early in your clean polo, clipboard in hand. It's go time! You're about to meet with your prospective client for the first time — take a deep breath, relax, and go for it! You've done most of the hard work already. Now is the time to relax and enjoy getting to know your client-to-be.

Setting the tone

Say you meet someone at a party, and before you can even say, "So, come here often?" they launch into an interrogation about your health problems and eating habits. You'd probably bolt for the door, right? That's why setting the tone with a potential client is so important.

Upon greeting your consult, shake hands and make small talk about the weather or driving conditions to break the ice. Settle yourself in a position where you can look them directly in the eyes while you're speaking. You should be close enough to share your clipboard with them when you're presenting your services, but not so close that you invade their personal space.

Reviewing the client's health and medical history

The health history form contains important information that will help you to determine how you'll train your client and note how exercise might affect them.

Preparticipation health screening

The purpose of preparticipation health screening is to identify risk factors for cardiovascular, pulmonary, and metabolic diseases and any other health conditions that you should be aware of (like pregnancy or previous injuries). I recommend screening all prospective clients regardless of age or health status as part of your initial consultation. This way you can determine if the person should consult with their physician before starting an exercise program. You don't need to bring this up with a prospective client until they have decided to become an actual client, and I'll tell you later in this chapter when and how to ask for a physician's clearance.

PAR-Q+

The *Physical Activity Readiness Questionnaire* (PAR-Q+) is a simple medical history and health risk appraisal questionnaire that anyone can access online and use for free. I recommend using the PAR-Q+ in your initial consultations to gather information from your prospective clients. Check out the current version of the PAR-Q+ online at `www.acsm.org/docs/default-source/files-for-resource-library/par-q-acsm.pdf`.

Medications

Some medications affect heart rate or blood pressure, or can make a person dizzy from exertion, among other side effects. That's why you need to know the type of medications your client is taking.

TIP

If you don't know what a medication does, or what the side effects are, ask a local pharmacist. You can also look up medication information in the *Physicians' Desk Reference* online at `www.pdr.net`.

Previous surgeries

You'll want to know about any surgeries your client has been through — especially if the surgery involved a joint, muscle, tendon, or cartilage. If you're unsure of the training parameters for a client who has had a surgery involving *soft tissue* (muscle, ligament, or tendon), ask for permission to contact their surgeon or physical therapist for guidance. *Remember:* you'll need written permission from the client before their healthcare provider will share patient information with you.

TIP

Don't hesitate to contact the surgeon's office or physical therapy clinic to ask for exercise parameters — it will show your prospective client that you care enough to make sure you have the right information to work with them safely. And, as a bonus, you may also develop a new professional relationship with the provider.

Muscle aches, strains, and pulls

When asking your potential client about any aches, strains, or muscle pulls they experience frequently, pause and give them a chance to think about it. People will often forget about nagging aches and pains, or they just think it's no big deal and don't mention it. It's a good idea to ask about each joint specifically during the initial consultation because often times you'll trigger a memory of waking up with a stiff back or having knee pain when walking down steps.

Be sure to make a note of which side the person is experiencing pain or soreness and how frequently it happens. Use this part of your consultation to flag any movements that may cause problems during the actual workout.

Learning about a day in the life of your potential client

You need to know about your potential client's daily lifestyle, from their eating and sleeping habits to their stress levels. Using a "typical day" questionnaire, ask the person to verbally take you through a typical day, starting from the time they wake up, and explaining in as much detail as possible everything they do until going to bed at night.

TIP

Some questions you'll want to ask include:

>> Do you wake up in the morning feeling rested and refreshed? Or do you wake up feeling tired?

>> How many meals a day do you have? Do you typically eat each meal around the same time each day?

>> Do you have lasting energy throughout the day?

>> Do you feel stressed throughout the day?

>> How many hours of sleep do you get?

>> What kind of job do you have? Is it active, or do you sit in a chair all day?

These types of questions will help you determine exactly where your client is starting from in terms of lifestyle. Understanding how a person is feeling and why will help you determine how to get them started with making healthy lifestyle adjustments that are in alignment with their goals.

Identifying your client's goals and reasons why

After asking typical day questions, have your prospective client describe their goals to you. Ask specific questions to get to the root of what they want and why it matters. When you feel like you understand your client's goals, repeat them back in your own words. Doing this demonstrates to the client that you understand what they want, or it allows them to correct you if you didn't quite get it right. Keep talking through it until you're sure you're on the same page.

Discussing your client's exercise history

After you've identified your prospective client's goals, move on to the exercise history questions. This will allow you to find out what your prospect's experience has been with exercise, what they liked or didn't like about it, and other information that will help to guide your recommendations.

Before You Say Goodbye

Now you know everything there is to know about your prospective client, down to what brand of toothpaste they prefer (okay, maybe not that), and it's time to say goodbye. Before you head for the door (or show your prospective client out), summarize everything you've discussed and answer any remaining questions. Then show your prospect how you can help and which of your services you recommend.

Outlining solutions that will meet your prospect's goals

TIP

Propose a plan for the potential client to reach their goals, and using their goals as your objectives, outline how you can help. (This is where all that stuff you studied for in your certification comes in handy!) For example, you might say:

I believe that if we start training together twice a week, we can steadily progress to your goal of exercising three times a week on your own in four to six weeks. I wouldn't want to start you working out three times a week immediately, because you haven't exercised consistently before and your schedule is really busy. Starting slowly will help you get into the habit of exercising without feeling overwhelmed by it.

REMEMBER

Your plan isn't set in stone and it's important to communicate this to your prospective client. You can make sound recommendations, but can't predict with certainty how the client will respond to a program before trying it. You can say, "I don't know you or your body yet, but if you respond well to your fitness assessment, this is what I envision for you . . . ." Then lay out the plan.

Explaining your prospect's options

After you propose your solution, explain your services and go over your rates. For example, if you only offer one-on-one personal training, you might recommend starting with eight personal training sessions so your new client can exercise with you twice per week for their first month. If you offer personal training and group training, make your recommendation based on your client's needs and preferences.

Requiring a physician's release

Occasionally, you'll meet with a prospective client who should undergo a medical evaluation to obtain a physician's release before they start working with you. This *physician's release* is important both for the client's safety and yours. For most people, physical activity is safe and the benefits of regular exercise far outweigh the health risks associated with being sedentary, and you don't need to require a physician's release from all your clients. You do however need to understand when you should and shouldn't ask for it. A basic personal trainer certification will prepare you to work with apparently healthy adults, and most will provide at least some information about when to require a physician's release, but some won't. Either way, your clients' safety is your responsibility, and so is knowing how to identify who could benefit from a medical evaluation. I recommend following the American College of Sports Medicine's (ACSM's) exercise preparticipation health screening recommendations, which you can download for free from their website at www.acsm.org/docs/default-source/files-for-resource-library/acsmprescreening101.pdf?sfvrsn=bc703144_4.

TIP

The ACSM's recommendations were updated recently to reduce barriers to exercise and encourage more people to adopt an active lifestyle. These guidelines recognize that physical activity is safe for most people. No doctor's appointment required.

Setting the stage for the first appointment

If all has gone well, the next step is to set up your first appointment with your new client. Explain that the first session is a fitness assessment, where you'll be measuring your client's baseline fitness levels.

REMEMBER

After you've set the appointment, you'll need to collect payment based on your payment policy. *Remember:* You're not charging for the initial consultation (which you're just wrapping up); you're charging for the first appointment.

TIP

After you've set up your first appointment and collected your fee, make sure before you leave that you have your new client sign your:

>> Client agreement form

>> Waiver of liability

>> Cancellation policy

>> Refund policy

Before the client signs each one, briefly explain the purpose of each policy and answer any questions they may have. Have the client sign two copies— one for your records and one for theirs.

You're almost done! The last step is to explain to your new client what happens next. Clarify what they should wear to the first session, whether or not to eat beforehand, whether they should purchase anything (like a pair of sneakers if they don't have any), and remind them to bring a water bottle and towel if you don't provide these. This helps to alleviate anxiety the new client may have before their first appointment. It also sets you up for a great first session — one that will leave a positive impression in your client's mind. Let them know that everything you covered is also in their consult packet on the "What to Expect During Your First Session" sheet.

KNOWING WHEN TO BACK OFF: LETTING THE CLIENT THINK ABOUT IT

When you go car shopping, you don't open your wallet for the first car you look at — you tell the salesperson you'll think about it, then head out to look at other options. In the same way, some prospective clients would rather think about all the information you've gone over with them before signing on the dotted line. If your client seems unsure or combative, give them some space to make a decision.

Remember: Your time is limited and precious — you want clients who are champing at the bit to get in shape, not ones whose arms you have to twist. Leave your consult packet with the potential client to peruse on their own time, and let them know that you'll follow up in a few days to answer any questions they may have.

If a prospective client isn't interested, don't push the issue. Personal training is a service that clients will buy when they're good and ready. By being gracious and professional and respecting a person's space, you'll create a good first impression — and when that person is ready to start working with a personal trainer, you'll probably be the first one they call.

IN THIS CHAPTER

» Getting your client started

» Preparing your client for the session

» Recording baseline measurements

» Assessing your client's fitness

» Going over the results

Chapter **11**

The First Session: Performing the Fitness Assessment

Before you take your new client into the gym and get their heart pumping, you need to know what they're ready to do, and what you should avoid. That's where the client assessment comes in. The client assessment is where you record baseline measurements and safe working ranges for the client's starting sessions. The baseline measurements provide an excellent motivational tool to use when showing your client their progress, and the safe working ranges ensure that your client does enough without doing too much.

You can measure baseline fitness levels in many different ways, and some methods are easier than others. Some require expensive equipment that's not all that portable, while others call for a PhD in exercise physiology to interpret the results. In this chapter, I cover some of the most practical assessment methods — ones that you can administer safely and effectively with little equipment (and without a PhD).

Prepping the Client

When your client arrives for their appointment, before you jump into the assessment, take a few minutes to go over your fitness assessment forms. Thoroughly explain each section of the form, detailing what the client will be doing in this initial session, what you're looking for, and why it's relevant. Having your client sit for a few minutes before getting started should help to lower their heart rate and blood pressure, as well as calm any jittery nerves before starting the fitness assessment.

Introducing the tools of your trade

After you've fully explained how the session is going to work, it's time to break out all the fun toys that you'll be using with your client!

REMEMBER

You don't have to own the most expensive gadgets to be a good trainer! Start with the bare essentials, and as you build profits you can upgrade your equipment if you want.

TIP

When purchasing equipment, consider factors such as safety, warranties, portability, durability, and cost. Ask other professionals in your area what they recommend — you don't need to reinvent the wheel.

The following list includes some low-budget tools that can increase your professionalism and profitability. Explain what each of the following tools does and when and where you'll be using it:

>> **Tape measure:** You won't believe how handy a tape measure is. You can measure girth, range of motion, flexibility, distance — and the stacks of money you'll earn as a personal trainer. Inexpensive and portable, tape measures with a *lanyard* (a string so you can hang it around your neck) and a self-retracting wheel will work best for you. (You don't want to spend all your time rolling and unrolling it!) You can find them for as little $2 or $3 in the arts-and-crafts departments of major discount stores or at online retailers, or you can check your local craft, sewing, or hobby store. Make sure the tape measure you choose is inelastic (not stretchy) too.

>> **Skinfold calipers:** Skinfold calipers are used to measure the thickness of skinfolds on various points of the body so you can estimate a person's bodyfat percentage. If you're going to include skinfold testing in your assessments, I recommend investing in a Lange Skinfold Caliper. At around $200, the Lange Caliper isn't the cheapest option, but you'll get more accurate measurements because the arms are spring-loaded and provide constant standard pressure

(which basically means you're less likely to mess up). You can also calibrate the Lange Caliper each time you use it, meaning that you can be certain that your starting point is the same every time. You can get an inexpensive plastic skinfold caliper for around $20, but I wouldn't recommend using one of these for the same reasons that I *do* recommend using the Lange Caliper. If you're going to do skinfold testing, you need to make sure your measurements are accurate every time. If you're not using a caliper that can be calibrated every time, you won't get accurate measurements.

» **Body-weight scale:** You'll need a scale to measure body weight. When purchasing a scale, ask yourself these questions:

- How portable is the scale?

- Is it thin and flat or big and bulky?

- Is it solar powered with battery backup, or just one or the other?

- What's the maximum poundage it can measure (and will I someday take clients who weigh more than that)?

Scales can range from $30 to $200, with the more expensive models being marketed to the medical community. I recommend scales made by Tanita, which are available online at www.tanita.com or at your local home store.

» **Heart-rate monitors:** Taking a heart rate manually can be tedious and time-consuming, especially if you're trying to get an active heart rate! Buying a heart-rate monitor to use with your clients is a good investment — the reading you get from it is immediate and accurate. Prices range from $50 to $350. Check out your local fitness-equipment stores for pricing, or do an online search for "heart-rate monitor." The most popular manufacturer is Polar, and you can check out their products at www.polar.com.

» **Blood-pressure cuffs and stethoscopes:** With prices ranging from $30 to $300 for a stethoscope and $20 to $80 for a blood-pressure cuff, you have a lot of options. Your best bet is to order from a medical-supply company like Quick Medical (www.quickmedical.com). You don't need anything fancy, but I wouldn't go with the cheapest. You'll need to listen to your client's heartbeats when you're measuring their blood pressure and it's hard to hear with cheap equipment. If you're not sure what to order, chat with one of the customer-service reps. Explain what you're looking for and they can offer advice about which products will best suit your needs.

TIP

While you're explaining the tools, go ahead and put your heart-rate monitor on your client. Have them sit down to relax, because your first step in the fitness assessment will be to measure their resting heart rate, which will be more accurate if your client is calm and relaxed.

Explaining the purpose of assessments

While your client rests for the heart-rate reading, let them know that the assessment isn't meant to test the limits of their physical ability. You're not looking for them to Hulk-out and pop veins in their forehead; you just want to determine a starting point for what they can do *comfortably*.

TIP

Playing down the assessment is critical because many clients will try to impress you with how much they can do, sometimes going above and beyond their safe working limits.

Using rate of perceived exertion scales

A good way to teach your clients how to manage the intensity of their workouts is to explain how easy or difficult a particular activity should feel. This method of letting your client evaluate their own working intensity is called *rate of perceived exertion* (RPE). (Ring a bell? This is one of the basic training principles taught in most certification courses.) Pair this technique with a heart-rate monitor, and you have a great method for showing your client how to evaluate workout intensity.

TIP

Teaching your client up front — at the initial fitness assessment — about perceived exertion will help you later on, because they'll be able to provide feedback as to how they're feeling compared with the actual intensity of the exercises you prescribed. You'll be able to make simple adjustments that make sense to your client based on how the exercises feel. This can be especially helpful with beginners because their perceived exertion might be much different from what the heart-rate monitor says. In other words, they'll probably feel like they're working much harder than they actually are at first. You can also set intensity levels for your client by using the same method when they're not with you (for instance, "When you're performing your circuit sets, you should be working around a level 6").

Another simple method for helping your clients understand how an exercise should feel is the talk test. This works especially well with aerobic exercise where you want the client to maintain a certain intensity level for several minutes. For example, you could say, "You should feel like carrying on a conversation would be challenging, but you could do it. If you can easily have a conversation, push yourself a little harder. If you're gasping for air and couldn't talk even if you had to, you're working too hard."

You may want to prepare something like the chart in Table 11-1 that you can use with each new client to describe how their exercises should feel.

TABLE 11-1   The Perceived-Rate-of-Exertion Scale

Cardio-respiratory Conditioning Level	Perceived Exertion Rating Level	Workout Intensity	Similar to . . .
No Effort	0	Not exercising	Sitting down and relaxing
Very little effort	1	Very easy	Standing up
Warm-up or recovery effort	2	Somewhat easy	Walking
Warm-up or recovery effort	3	Moderate	Walking moderately
Aerobic effort	4	Somewhat hard	Walking uphill moderately
Aerobic effort	5	Moderately hard	Jogging slowly
Aerobic effort	6	Hard	Jogging fast
Anaerobic effort	7	Hard	Running moderately
Anaerobic effort	8	Very hard	Running
Anaerobic effort	9	Very, very hard	Sprinting
Anaerobic effort	10	Maximal	Sprinting maximally

Recording Baseline Measurements

All-righty then! You have your client relaxed and ready to begin, your assessment tools are laid out and ready to be put into action, your pencil is sharpened, and your clipboard is at the ready. What are you waiting for? Let's get started!

Taking your client's resting heart rate

You can use either one of two easy methods for measuring heart rate — the palpation method or the heart-rate-monitor method. I cover each of these in the following sections.

Palpation method

Palpation is the most common method for taking heart rate. It's also the least expensive — all you need are your index and middle fingers and a stopwatch. The three commonly used sites for this are the radial artery, brachial artery, or the carotid artery. I recommend using the radial artery (located near the thumb side of the wrist) because it's the least invasive and easiest to palpate for most people. Here's how you do it:

1. **Using the tips of your index and middle fingers, locate the radial artery.**

   Avoid using your thumb, because it has its own pulse and may confuse your count.

2. **Using your stopwatch or the second hand on your watch, keep time while counting the beats for either 30 seconds or 60 seconds. (If you're counting for 30 seconds, multiply the final count by 2 to calculate the one-minute resting heart rate.)**

   If you start your stopwatch simultaneously with a beat, count that beat as 0. If your stopwatch or secondhand is already running, count the first beat you start your time measure on as 1.

TIP

When measuring heart rate, make sure your client is calm and still, and remember that the *white-coat effect* (elevated heart rate due to nervousness from being around an analyst) may skew the results.

Heart-rate-monitor method

Heart-rate monitoring is easy and painless — the equipment does all the work for you! A monitor is always on, giving you continuous feedback. To use a chest-strap monitor, follow these instructions:

1. **Attach the transmitter to the elastic strap.**

2. **Moisten the two grooved electrodes.**

3. **Adjust the strap length to fit snugly and comfortably.**

4. **Secure the strap around your client's chest, just below the chest muscles at the *xiphoid process* (the area where the two halves of your rib cage meet at the bottom of your breastbone), and buckle it.**

5. **Make sure the area under the electrodes are wet as well, or that the transmitter has snug contact with the wet fabric/skin.**

6. **Check the specific manufacturer's directions on the interaction of the watch (receiver) and the chest strap (transmitter).**

Measuring your client's blood pressure

Measure blood pressure when your client is in a full resting state for at least five minutes. A normal resting blood pressure is below 120 systolic and 80 diastolic (120/80). "Hypertension," or high blood pressure is a condition where resting blood pressure is chronically elevated above normal. If your client's resting blood pressure exceeds 130/80 at rest, they may have hypertension. Slightly elevated blood pressure isn't cause for alarm; however, a reading of 180 or higher systolic and 120 or higher diastolic (180/120) is considered a hypertensive crisis and the client should seek medical care right away.

WARNING

Hypertension can't be diagnosed with one blood pressure reading. That requires several measurements on different days. If your client's resting blood pressure is elevated during the assessment, check it again at their next session. Sometimes you'll get a high reading if the client is nervous or overly caffeinated that day. If you measure again a few days later and it's still elevated, you don't have to send your client away, but you shouldn't blow it off either. Tell your client that, for their safety, you recommend sharing the information with their doctor.

TIP

Follow these tips to take your client's blood pressure:

1. **Have your client sit upright in a chair that supports their back, with either the left or right arm exposed, palm facing up and supported at heart level.**

2. **Select the appropriate cuff size for your client.**

   The large adult cuff size is for people whose arm circumference is 13 to 16½ inches (33 to 42 cm). The adult standard cuff size is for people whose arm circumference is 9½ to 12½ inches (24 to 32 cm).

3. **Place the cuff on your client's arm so that the *air bladder* (the cuff that goes around your client's arm) is directly over the *brachial artery* (the large pulse point on the inside of the arm) and the edge of the cuff is 1 inch above the *antecubital space* (the crease where your arm bends on the inside of the elbow).**

4. **With your client's palm facing up, place the stethoscope directly over the antecubital space.**

   Do not press so hard that the stethoscope indents the skin.

5. **Position the *sphygmomanometer* (the dial on the cuff you use to measure blood pressure) so that the center of the dial is at eye level.**

   Be sure that all tubing is free and not in contact with anything else.

6. **When everything is in place, quickly inflate the air bladder to 160 mmHg.**

7. **Upon maximum inflation, turn the air-release screw counterclockwise to release the pressure slowly, at a rate of 2 mmHg per second.**

8. **Mentally note the mmHg at which you hear the first *Korotkoff sound* (a heartbeat-like sound).**

   This is your systolic number.

9. **Mentally note the mmHg where the Korotkoff sounds disappear.**

   This is your diastolic number.

10. **Continue to observe the manometer to ensure the sounds stay disappeared.**

11. **When you've confirmed the absence of sound, rapidly release the pressure and remove the cuff.**

TIP

If you feel uncomfortable using these tools, buy an automatic blood-pressure cuff similar to the ones used in drugstores. Use it until you get more practice with the sphygmomanometer.

Measuring body composition

Your clients will all have their reasons for hiring you, and for many, their goals will include losing fat, putting on muscle, or both. Because body weight consists of muscle, fat, organs, bones, and fluids, tracking only scale weight can be a very disheartening and misleading assessment tool for monitoring change. A client's body weight can fluctuate a lot, and for many different reasons, and sometimes by several pounds in a day— and for a fat-loss client, it's not very motivating to step on the scale at the high point of those extra pounds! A more accurate way to measure your client's progress (fat loss or muscle gain) is to include a body composition analysis in your initial assessment. A body composition analysis can tell your client roughly how many pounds of fat versus fat-free mass they have. Personal trainers have several options for measuring body composition and I review the most common methods in this chapter.

Skinfold assessment

The least expensive and most reasonably accurate method for use in the field is the *skinfold* assessment, which analyzes body composition by measuring the thickness of skinfolds at several points on the body using a skinfold caliper (this is where you'll use your Lange Caliper). This method assumes that there is a pre-dictable relationship between subcutaneous fat and total bodyfat, and when administered properly, a skinfold assessment can predict bodyfat percentage fairly well (within 3 to 4 percent). Several formulas for analyzing bodyfat exist, from three-site methods to nine-site methods. The more sites that you're able to read from, the more accurate a picture you're going to get. Depending on the method you use for measuring bodyfat, the number of locations and site locations themselves vary. Refer to your certification manual for the specifics on how to locate, measure, and mark each site based on the formula you will be using.

Follow these tips for skinfold testing:

>> **Take all skinfold measurements on the right side of the body.**

>> **Take all measurements pre-exercise, when the client's skin is dry and free of lotions or oils.** Exercise causes hydration changes in the skin that significantly affect skin thickness, therefore affecting the skinfold reading.

WARNING

The skinfold method isn't appropriate for everyone. For example, if you have a client with a lot of excess bodyfat, it's likely that you'll take an unreliable measurement due to the large size of the pinch and the inability to pull the skin away from muscle. Try a few random pinches on different areas of the body that may be thin enough to measure correctly so you can establish some sort of baseline. Or try to find a formula that may work with the pinches you can take on that person. Another consideration is that skinfolds need to be taken directly on the skin (not through clothing) and some people aren't comfortable with this. Also, because you'll be pinching the client's skin, this method is somewhat invasive and it can be painful. Make sure you're up front with your clients about what the skinfold assessment entails and then ask if they wish to proceed.

Bioelectrical impedance analysis

In this method, a small electrical current is sent through the body via a device that measures the amount of time it takes for the signal to return to it. Fat tissue doesn't contain a lot of water, making it a poor electrical conductor and providing an impedance to the electrical current. Lean mass is mostly made of water (about 70 percent) and is a good electrical conductor. Bioelectrical impedance assumes that the volume of fat-free mass in the body is proportional to the electrical conductivity of the body. Bioelectrical impedance analysis is a noninvasive and easy method for assessing body composition, and because it doesn't cause any physical discomfort, it can be a better option for some clients.

TIP

Keep in mind that bioelectrical impedance is sensitive to hydration status and the accuracy of this method can be affected by the client's hydration status.

To improve the accuracy of bioelectrical impedance analysis, give your client the following instructions ahead of time:

>> **Don't eat or drink within four hours of the analysis.**

>> **Avoid exercise within 12 hours of the analysis.**

>> **Empty your bladder completely within 30 minutes of the analysis.**

>> For females, reschedule the analysis if you're in a stage of your menstrual cycle where you're retaining water.

There are various devices available for bioelectrical impedance analysis and instructions will vary based on which one you use. Be sure to follow the instructions specific to the device you're using to improve accuracy and avoid user errors.

Hydrostatic weighing

Hydrostatic weighing (also called *hydrodensitometry*) isn't typically used for body composition analysis in fitness settings and is more common in clinical or research settings. This method is based on the Archimedes' principle, which states that a body immersed in water is buoyed by a counterforce equal to the weight of the water that is displaced. Basically this means that fat mass and fat-free mass act differently in water. Fat mass is less dense than water and buoyant. Fat-free mass is more dense than water and sinks. So, a body with a lot of fat will float and a body with a lot of lean mass will sink.

The process involves getting into a dunk tank while a technician drops you completely under the water and instructs you to blow all the air out of your lungs. The accuracy of this method requires complete cooperation by the person being tested, and finding a facility with a hydrostatic weighing tank can be challenging.

Ultrasound

Ultrasound devices are becoming an increasingly popular alternative to skinfold assessments in fitness settings. You can measure subcutaneous skinfold thickness with an ultrasound device, and unlike skinfold calipers, it can also analyze deeper fat deposits. Ultrasound devices are portable and relatively inexpensive, but there are disadvantages to this method, including reliability of the device (some are higher quality than others). There's also not a standardized testing protocol available yet, meaning that you can't follow the instructions and expect consistent results like you can with a skinfold assessment.

Dual-energy x-ray absorptiometry (DXA)

DXA works by measuring x-rays as they pass through the body and quantifying three components of body composition: bones, lean mass, and fat mass. DXA technology is typically used to measure bone density in medical and research settings, and because it can predict bodyfat percentage with near perfect accuracy, it's considered the gold standard for body composition analysis, and more medical private practices are offering DXA assessment as a service. DXA isn't feasible in most fitness settings because it's an expensive test ($100 or more) that requires specialized training, and DXA scanners aren't widely available for commercial use. Other advantages of DXA are the minimal effort needed from the patient or client — there aren't any instructions they need to follow before the test — and it only takes a few minutes.

Circumference measurements

Circumference measurements (also called girth measurements) are useful for identifying how a person's bodyfat is distributed. This matters because some circumference measurements can predict a client's health. For example, someone with excess fat in their trunk — the technical term being *android obesity*, otherwise known as the "beer belly" — has an increased risk of developing hypertension, metabolic syndrome, type 2 diabetes, and other chronic conditions. You can quantify "excess fat" with a circumference measurement of the waist. Health risk increases when waist circumference is more than 88 centimeters for women and 102 centimeters for men.

TIP

Circumference measurements are also useful for tracking changes in a client's bodyfat distribution. You can estimate a client's bodyfat percentage by plugging various circumference measurements into a translational equation, but it's not very accurate, which is why it's a good idea to also include a body composition analysis in your assessment protocol.

It's also important to include *anthropometric measurements* in the assessment and for you to understand the difference between these and body composition analysis. Anthropometrics will give you information about your client's external proportions — things like height, weight, and circumferences (this is where your tape measure comes in). These measurements won't tell you about your client's internal body composition — like how much fat versus how much lean mass they're starting with. That's why for most clients, especially those with fat-loss goals, tracking body composition is a good idea so you can see what's happening on the inside. But there's still value in anthropometric measurements for a couple of reasons. First, they give you more information about your client than you would otherwise have, and too much information is always better than not enough. You can also empower your clients to monitor their progress by teaching them how to take these measurements accurately on their own. Circumference measurements are helpful because they don't typically fluctuate nearly as much or as often as the scale does.

Including both body composition analysis and anthropometric measurements in the assessment can give your client a total picture of their body's physical state. You can refer to your certification manual for descriptions of circumference sites and instructions for measuring them.

Here are a few additional tips for consistency in your circumference measurements:

1. **Have your client stand in the correct anatomical position with arms relaxed by their sides.**

2. **Ask the client to relax the area to be measured — no flexing!**

3. **Always take measurements from either the right side or the left side of the client's body. Either side works; just make sure you're doing it the same way every time.**

TIP

Practice taking circumference measurements on your friends and family before you start seeing clients. You'll be more comfortable when you know what you're doing and with practice, you'll get better and faster at it.

Assessing Your Client's Fitness

Imagine taking an English class and being tested on, say, how to dissect a frog or how to solve a quadratic equation. You would likely fail the test — and feel pretty rotten to boot.

TIP

In the same way, you have to make sure that the tests you give your clients won't injure them physically or damage their pride. For instance, you may have a 55-year-old female with weak legs whose only recent exercise has been changing the channel on her TV. Knowing that she's deconditioned and has some possible joint problems with her knees, would you administer a step test? Most likely not. How about a walk-run test? No again.

What you *can* do, however, is take what you've learned from the clinical aspects of testing and create your own individualized cardiovascular test just for your client. When you retest her, you'll need to re-create the test exactly as you did it the first time — and that's okay, because the point of testing with most of your clients is to show them that they're improving and getting stronger.

REMEMBER

Most clients won't know what VO_2max is — and they won't really care. What they *will* care about, however, is how much easier it is for them to perform a five-minute march, how quickly their heart rate comes down, and how they now consider a certain exercise to be a perceived rate of exertion level 3, whereas the first time they did it they rated it a 6.

REMEMBER

When testing your client, apply only the tests that are going to be the most useful for you and beneficial for that person.

Run, don't walk: Testing cardiovascular endurance

A key component to any exercise prescription is aerobic conditioning. Most clients will be concerned about their heart health and overall cardiovascular endurance, and the tests in the following sections will show them where they stand (or walk, or run).

The walk-run test

The walk-run test is a great field test to measure a client's cardiovascular capacity. All you'll need is a stopwatch and a measured mile. Here's how to make it work:

1. **Mark off a one-mile route.**

2. **Have your client warm up for three to five minutes prior to starting the course.**

   Your client can warm up by walking at a comfortable pace.

3. **Instruct the client to finish the course as quickly as they can — walking, jogging, running, whatever they can do.**

4. **Give the client a countdown for starting the test, and start your stopwatch with their first step.**

5. **After the client finishes the course, either immediately take their pulse for ten seconds, or use a heart-rate monitor to record exercise heart rate.**

6. **One minute after stopping the test, record the client's heart rate again.**

   This number is their *recovery heart rate* and refers to how long it takes for the heart rate to return to baseline following a bout of exercise.

TIP

You can also perform this test on a treadmill, or with a shorter distance if one mile is too long. Just follow the same testing procedures.

The step test

Another great field test, the step test can be done with an actual 12-inch platform step or with any step available — such as a stair in your client's home, an aerobic step, or an outside step (as long as the step is no higher than 12 inches and you use the same one every time you re-test). Here's how to do it:

1. **Explain to your client that they're going to be stepping "up, up, down, down" (up with one leg, up with the other, down with one leg, down with the other) at a pace a little faster than one second per step.**

2. **Have them step to a cadence of 96 beats per minute (or more slowly if necessary) for three minutes.**

You can count cadence if you have a stopwatch by counting on the seconds: "up, up, down, down, up, up, down, down . . .". You can also set a metronome so that you don't have to worry about counting at the right pace.

3. **When the client has stepped for three minutes, take their heart rate manually for ten seconds or read the heart-rate monitor.**

This is their exercise heart rate.

4. **One minute after stopping exercising, take their heart rate again.**

This number will be their recovery heart rate.

This test isn't appropriate for everyone and you should avoid using it with people who have back, knee, or hip problems.

Stretch marks: Testing flexibility

A long muscle is a strong muscle — so testing flexibility is important in evaluating your client's overall fitness. Because the hamstrings are among the most commonly understretched muscles and have a direct impact on the health of the back, it's a good test to include in your fitness assessment.

The sit-and-reach test

For a lot of beginning clients, touching their toes is out of the question. Although fitness experts have recently debated the usefulness of the sit-and-reach test, it's an easy test to administer in the field and flexibility is an important component of a person's overall physical fitness. The only equipment you need is a nonelasticized tape measure and your client. Be sure to perform this test only after you've thoroughly warmed up your client (for example, after completing the cardiovascular test). Conducting the flexibility test after your client is warmed up reduces their risk of pulling any muscles. You'll be able to find guidelines and fitness categories for the sit-and-reach test in your certification manual.

TIP

Getting down and up from the floor is challenging for some people. If you're unsure about asking a client to get down on the floor because you're not confident that they'll be able to get back up, have them sit in a chair instead and follow the same guidelines as you would if they were seated on the floor. Just make sure you document if you use a chair so you'll remember to use it when you re-test later.

Testing muscular strength and endurance

Let's face it — a lot of personal training is about building muscles, or as Hans and Franz said on *Saturday Night Live,* "We vant [clap!] to pump you up." As a personal trainer, much of your time will be spent dealing with your client's muscular strength and endurance, which is why it's really important to put some serious time into this portion of the fitness assessment.

Explaining the difference between muscular strength and muscular endurance as you demonstrate each test will be helpful to your client — no need to overwhelm them with too much detail here, but they'll appreciate understanding why you're asking them to do certain exercises and how they're beneficial.

Muscular *endurance* is the body's ability to exert a submaximal force for a sustained period of time. Muscular *strength* is the body's ability to exert a maximal force for a very short period of time.

The push-up test

The push-up test is frequently used in the field, because it requires no equipment. Plus, for some clients who aren't strong enough to do sustained repetitions, it can be used as a measure of strength rather than endurance. Refer to your certification manual for push-up testing procedures.

Remember how some people have trouble getting up from the floor? Good news, a wall works really well for testing these clients. Follow the same procedure as you would for push-ups performed on the floor. You can also use a modified push-up position (from the knees instead of from the toes) if your client doesn't yet have the upper body strength to perform a proper push-up. If push-ups are completely out of the question (say your client has an injured wrist), you can use a set of dumbbells and have them perform chest presses instead. Again, just be sure to use the same protocol consistently for each individual client.

Don't hesitate to use this part of the assessment to "test" starting weights for exercises you're planning on using with the client. After each test set of 10 to 12 reps, ask your client for a rating of perceived exertion. When your client rates the set a 6 or 7, you've found your starting weight for that exercise.

The weakest link: Uncovering asymmetries and identifying poor movement patterns

Functional movement assessments have been used in physical therapy and by coaches for a long time to assess joint mobility and stability, and to identify any risk factors that a patient or player may have for musculoskeletal injuries. Functional movement assessments have become increasingly popular in fitness settings in recent years as a way to monitor improvements or problems with clients' movement patterns.

The most common of these, the Functional Movement Screen (FMS), was designed by physical therapists Gray Cook and Lee Burton in the 1990s to predict a person's musculoskeletal injury risk by identifying asymmetries in seven fundamental movement patterns. The FMS is a screening tool with seven individual movement pattern assessments and three clearing tests. Movement assessments are scaled on a scale of 0 to 3 and the total score is then used to determine whether a client should be cleared for exercise or referred to a physical therapist (or other healthcare professional) for further assessment. Personal trainers can use the FMS to identify a client's "weakest link" to guide program design decisions and to reduce injury risk by adding load to an asymmetry or training a faulty movement pattern. To learn more about the FMS and how to become certified if you're interested in using it in your fitness assessment protocol (which, by the way, is required if you're going to use it), visit www.functionalmovement.com.

TIP

Doing a movement assessment is a quick and simple way to screen your clients for risk factors that may lead to injuries. They'll appreciate understanding how to get fit without getting hurt!

Discussing the Results with Your Client

After you're done with your fitness assessment, take the time to review your client's results with them. Start by setting realistic goals that can be achieved in one month's time. If you reassess the client's fitness level at the beginning of every month, they'll know when to expect it — and it's extra incentive to stay committed to the program when there's a looming deadline!

TIP

Give your client accurate assessments of normal ranges for people with similar body types, ages, and conditioning levels as theirs. When you re-assess in a month, you can measure progress in percentages improved rather than against the norms.

Referring to a Professional in Your Network if Necessary

As much as I want to encourage you to remove as many barriers as you possibly can for your clients, a lot of situations are beyond your scope of practice as a personal trainer. Some specific examples include diagnosing or attempting to treat musculoskeletal injuries, medical nutrition therapy, recommending drugs (not even Advil), mental health care, and really anything that requires a medical degree or other higher education. Understanding when to refer a client to a professional for further evaluation or treatment is in everyone's best interest — your client's because you're getting them the help they need, and yours because working outside of your scope of practice is a liability risk and can get you in serious hot water.

TRUE STORY

I'm really lucky to have an amazing professional network. It's always been important to me to nurture these relationships so I can serve my clients as best I can. My advice to you is to start making connections with professionals in your area right away, even if you don't have any clients yet, and even if you're not even certified yet. My own network includes physicians, the best physical therapists I know, a dietitian, a chiropractor, a massage therapist, an acupuncturist, and more. When you have a strong network, you won't have to "refer out" when a client needs to see a professional. You'll be able to find that client the healthcare or other professional they need and help them to make an appointment with someone you know and trust, and going above and beyond for your clients like this will mean way more to them than your vast fitness knowledge ever could.

Chapter **12**

Before We Meet Again: Planning the Program

W hen you're planning out your clients' programs, you of course need to consider how you're going to help them achieve their fitness goals. Sometimes a plan looks great on paper, but as the saying goes, even the best laid plans sometimes go awry. Your programs need to align with your clients' goals, but more importantly, a plan has to realistically fit into the life of the person who is working that plan. Your job is to do everything possible to set your clients up for success, and that includes planning exercise programs that are enjoyable, livable, doable, and achievable.

REMEMBER

Before you start planning a program for your client, you need to have the initial consultation and do the initial fitness assessment, covered in Chapters 10 and 11.

Now it's time for the fun stuff — planning your client's program, which means deciding what exercises your client will do, how many of them, and for how long — the stuff that personal training is all about. So get ready to make your client's fitness dreams a reality!

Get with the Program: Considering Your Client's Programming Needs

If creating an exercise program were based solely on the results of a fitness assessment, prescribing exercises wouldn't be so challenging — in fact, it would be the easiest part of a personal trainer's job. The problem with using data to create a program is that a human being shows up. If your program is too time consuming, too intense, too easy, too boring, too complicated . . . you name it . . . your client probably won't be around for long.

A comprehensive exercise program isn't only about the physiological benefits that your client seeks. You need to consider many other factors besides the results of your client's fitness assessment. Issues such as time availability, where and when your client is planning to exercise, what equipment they'll have available, and what equipment they may need are important parameters to consider. Also, you need to keep in mind intangible aspects like your client's lifestyle, personality, exercise likes and dislikes, motivation levels, and commitment to train.

When you have a strong grasp of all these important parts, you'll be able to successfully piece together a sound (and successful!) fitness formula for each individual client.

Understanding your client's goals

It's the reason your client came to you in the first place — a motivating desire to make a change. Your client's goals become *your* goals — that's why you need to understand your client's goals and why they matter to them. Programming specifically to reach those goals, is key.

REMEMBER

Your client's goal is their "fuel" — it's the driving force that feeds them mentally, keeping them motivated and on track. Your job is to sustain that fuel by prescribing a program that works.

For example, if a client came to you saying that they wanted to run a marathon, would you have them bench-pressing one and a half times their body weight? Probably not.

TIP

As you're planning your client's program, think of ways that you can explain how each exercise or activity contributes to reaching their goals. Your clients will be more compliant and dedicated when they understand the why's of the program.

Location, location, location: Knowing where your client will be exercising

When you sit down to plan your client's exercise program, you need to know where they'll be exercising. Each location — such as the gym, home, office, or outdoors — has its own unique set of variables that you'll need to consider so you can choose exercises accordingly.

Table 12-1 provides a quick overview of the pros and cons of different training locations.

TABLE 12-1   **The Pros and Cons of Different Locations**

Location	Pros	Cons
Gym	Optimal environment for strength training	May be difficult to travel to
	Large variety and selection of equipment	Client may not feel "ready" to train in a gym
		Can be crowded during peak hours, requiring you to wait for equipment
Home	Can exercise any time	May not be enough space to exercise
	Easy and convenient to get to	Limited equipment availability
	Clients can exercise in the comfort of their own homes	Clients may find exercise easy to put off because of other household responsibilities
Office	Allows clients to exercise during their working hours without having to leave work	Clients may find exercise easy to put off because of work-related responsibilities
		May not be enough space to exercise
		Limited equipment availability
		The client may not be comfortable exercising at work
Outside	Optimal environment to train for aerobic endurance	Pollution, bugs, potential safety issues
		Very limited equipment availability
	Fresh air, nice views	Weather constraints

Knowing what equipment your client will (or won't) be using

After determining your client's exercise location, the next step is finding out what equipment they have access to.

If your client is training in a gym

Gyms typically have the largest selection of equipment — be sure find out beforehand what equipment they have. A good rule of thumb is to be sure you can cover each exercise in the program with at least one piece of equipment or dumbbell movement.

TIP

If your client has hired you to create a program to use in a gym you aren't familiar with, visit the gym ahead of time to see if it's set up to accommodate personal training. Is there enough room for you to coach your client? Will you be able to alternate between multiple exercises without having to compete for equipment or space? If you can, work out there yourself — it'll help you to get a feel for the equipment and make your job a lot easier when it comes time to train your client there. Also, knowing where everything is and how it works makes you look more professional. Your client will appreciate that you took time to do some research.

If your client is training at home or the office

You can design a very effective workout with very little space and very little equipment. If your client doesn't have any equipment to start, you may want to recommend a few key pieces such as:

>> Resistance bands

>> Adjustable dumbbells

>> TRX suspension trainer

>> Gliding discs or fitness sliders

>> Foam roller

>> Foam pad or mat

REMEMBER

Your client doesn't need to have any of this to start — you can actually do a full routine with everyday objects like chairs and stairs and bodyweight exercises. You could recommend starting with one or two pieces, and then gradually add to the collection and diversify the program with new equipment.

If your client is exercising in the great outdoors

Equipment here varies greatly depending on the type of program you're looking to set your client up on — the outdoors *is* one big piece of equipment! You're limited only by your imagination — from walking or running a hilly course to obstacle-coursing it through the local park.

We've got your number: Considering how many sessions your client has purchased

Another very important factor to consider in your initial program-planning stage is how many sessions your client has purchased. If your client has purchased a small number of sessions (one to three), you need to determine what you can realistically teach in that amount of time. Start thinking about the progression of your sessions — this will help you to determine which exercises you can safely teach someone to do without you within that time frame.

The same holds true if your client has purchased a large number of sessions. Even though you have more time, you still need to determine ahead of time at approximately what points you'll progress the program.

REMEMBER

Be sure not to overwhelm your client with too much information at once. By knowing how many sessions you have to work with each client, you'll be able to break down the exercise progression you're teaching into stages, allowing you to deliver your information in small, easy-to-understand "bites" that allow your client to "digest" the information before moving on to the next session.

WARNING

Just as you wouldn't crush your client under bucketloads of weight in the first session — that's a fast way to lose a beginner — the same applies with how much information you unload on them the first time through. Information overload can be as much of a turnoff as pushing someone way too hard on day one! Educate your clients as you would train them — briefly explain what they'll be doing that day, and then focus on coaching them through the session.

Keeping injuries and medical conditions in mind

When planning out your client's exercise program, don't forget about any aches and pains they told you about, no matter how minor. And always keep at the forefront of your mind any major physiological issues (injuries, chronic conditions, and so on) that were covered during your initial consultation. When you're choosing exercises for a new client, double-check their medical history to make sure that you're not recommending anything that could be potentially harmful.

TIP

If you aren't sure what impact a particular exercise will have on an old injury, err on the side of caution and choose something else. If the client has seen a physical therapist or other rehab specialist, ask for permission to contact the provider for guidance.

Using Assessment Results to Create a Baseline Program

You've already done a good chunk of the work for this part (and if you haven't, you need to). By using your client's fitness assessment results, you can recommend starting weights for their resistance training exercises, training heart rate range for the aerobic program, and corrective exercises to address any imbalances or asymmetries that were identified during the functional movement screen if you did one.

Before you start madly concocting the best gosh-darn exercise program in the history of exercise programs, you need to determine the order of operations for your client's training plan. These factors include the following:

>> Type of exercises for the program

>> Order of exercises for the program

>> Working exercise intensity

>> Session duration

>> Exercise frequency

Your clients' training plans will vary, but the components of the training *session* should not. All comprehensive exercise programs should — at a minimum — address cardiorespiratory fitness, muscular fitness (including muscular strength and endurance), movement skill and exercise competence, conditioning, mobility, and flexibility. Keeping this in mind will lend structure to your exercise training sessions. Current American College of Sports Medicine (ACSM) guidelines recommend always following this format:

>> **Warm-up:** Five to ten minutes of low-to-moderate-intensity cardiorespiratory and muscular endurance activities.

>> **Conditioning:** A total of at least 20 to 60 minutes of aerobic, resistance, neuromotor, and/or sports activities. Continuous exercise or ten-minute bouts of various exercises work here as long as the client accumulates a total of 20 to 60 minutes of daily aerobic exercise.

>> **Cool-down:** Five to ten minutes of low-to-moderate-intensity cardiorespiratory and muscular endurance activities.

>> **Flexibility:** Ten minutes or more of stretching exercises after the warm-up or cool-down.

Following this framework, you'll choose exercises for your client based on their:

>> Specific goals and objectives

>> Likes and dislikes of various aerobic activities

>> What type of equipment they have access to

>> How much time they're able to commit to an exercise program

>> Conditioning level and mobility

TIP

The initial consultation is a good time to discuss your client's exercise preferences. Ask them what type of exercise experience they have and what types of activities they prefer. If a client has been sedentary for a long time and doesn't have any preferences yet, that's okay too. Be sure to take detailed notes — they'll come in handy for this part of the process, and when your clients enjoy the activities you recommend, they'll look forward to them and are much more likely to make exercise a priority.

Aerobic Exercise Programming

In personal-training-speak, *cardiorespiratory* endurance refers to how well the circulatory system (heart and blood vessels) and the respiratory system (lungs) can provide oxygen to your body during sustained activity. Any type of activity that uses the body's large muscle groups in a sustained, movement-oriented manner that increases respiration for a prolonged period of time requires sufficient oxygen. Another common term for this is "aerobic" fitness, which makes sense because aerobic literally translates to "with oxygen." Aerobic exercise can either be done continuously or in intervals. Continuous, or "steady state" aerobic exercise is exactly what it sounds like. In a gym setting, it usually involves traditional fitness equipment like a bike or treadmill. Biking and walking can of course be done outdoors too.

You can offer many options for cardiovascular exercise — from traditional fitness equipment, such as a bike or elliptical trainer, to nontraditional methods, such as running bleachers at a local high school or college stadium (when there's no game, that is).

TIP

However, prescribing aerobic activity for your client is more than deciding to use a treadmill or walk outdoors, though that is an important part of it. You need to be able to recommend:

>> **Training mode:** Which activity will they do? Will it be equipment-based (such as the treadmill), or will walking outside be a better option?

>> **Training method:** What type of training method will they be doing while exercising? Will it be continuous training, where they maintain a steady heart rate for a sustained period of time, or will it be interval training where they'll alternate short bursts of high intensity effort with longer periods of recovery, when the client does the same movement at a slower pace?

>> **Working intensity:** Exactly how hard should they be working? Should they be able to gab with a friend on the neighboring treadmill, or will barely be able to carry on a conversation?

>> **Exercise frequency:** How often will your client exercise over a predetermined time period? Will it be four times a month, three times a week, every other day?

>> **Exercise duration:** How long is each exercise session? 20 minutes? An hour?

I cover each of these key questions in the following sections.

Choosing the proper training mode

The *mode* (or type) of exercise you prescribe for your client should be easily accessible and convenient (so extreme skydiving is probably out). It should be an activity that your client likes and a mode that you can *progress* or *regress* — the factors contributing to the workload (typically resistance, speed, and/or incline) can be incrementally increased to provide greater exercise intensity as your client's conditioning level increases or decreased on days when they're overly tired.

On a broad spectrum, equipment-based aerobic activity is preferable for most clients for multiple reasons — primarily because of the ease of use and easy access. You may know a few people who *absolutely love* to do cardio, but they're typically few and far between. The advent of cardio machines such as treadmills, elliptical trainers, and stationary bikes have made the boring task of getting healthy less boring by adding variety. Whereas, back in the olden days, if you wanted to get healthy, you had to worry about getting struck by lightning, tripping over a pothole, or swallowing a bug, now clients can listen to a podcast, watch TV, listen to their favorite music, *and* exercise without fear of being run over! Imagine that!

Table 12-2 provides a quick reference chart of several common aerobic training modes, all of which can be done in any location.

TABLE 12-2 ## Common Aerobic Training Modes

Activity/ Equipment	Client Level	Pros	Cons
Walking or running *Optional equipment:* Treadmill or elliptical machine	Beginning to advanced	On machine, multivariable speed and resistance settings can accommodate all fitness levels. The client can control their movements easily — they'll be working on a fixed plane of movement, so there's no choice but to push the machine where it is designed to go. Walking has a low perceived exertion value, meaning clients don't think of it as a hard workout. The intensity level can be modified easily. Walking or running outside gives the client a dose of fresh air and nice scenery.	Can be difficult or unsafe for clients with balance problems or hip/knee/ankle/foot issues. Can be difficult or unsafe if performed outside in unfamiliar territory.
Stair climbing *Optional equipment:* Stair stepper	Intermediate to advanced	Equipment doesn't take up much room. More demanding exercise mode with higher perceived exertion value, meaning the client thinks of stair climbing as a harder workout. If performed outside, without a machine, the client can easily control the intensity of the workout.	Continuous same-plane movement on a machine, which can place a strain on the lower back, knees, ankles, and feet.
Cycling *Optional equipment:* Upright bike or *recumbent bike* (where your feet are out in front of you, rather than underneath you)	Beginning to advanced	Low perceived value of exertion, meaning the client doesn't perceive bicycle riding as a hard workout. Moderately inexpensive equipment to own. Recumbent position takes stress off lower back and hips.	Upright model can place stress on lower back in some people.
Rowing *Optional equipment:* Rowing machine or upper-body *ergometer* (bicycle for the upper body)	Beginning to advanced	Offers clients an upper-body aerobic workout. Very challenging.	Clients with neck, shoulder, or lower back problems should be careful on this machine.

Choosing the best aerobic training method

When you've chosen what mode of aerobic exercise your client will be performing, the next step is determining what type of aerobic training method they'll be using. You have a choice of two types of training methods for cardiovascular conditioning: steady-state and interval training. Both options will allow for similar improvements in cardiorespiratory fitness, and you can determine which method is best suited for your clients based on their goals and preferences.

Steady-state aerobic training

Steady-state training is a method of aerobic training that maintains a moderately elevated heart rate for a sustained period of time. As implied by its name, steady-state training does not allow for a rest period during the working phase. Continuous training is well suited for all types of clients — from beginners to elite athletes.

The work is performed at a moderate intensity level (usually 60 to 80 percent of the client's maximum heart rate), and because of its lower intensity level, it can be done every day and for a longer period of time.

TIP

Clients who benefit most from continuous training are those who:

>> Are just starting to exercise aerobically on a regular basis

>> Have cardiovascular disease

>> Are older and have joint issues

>> Want to increase their cardiovascular endurance and stamina

Interval training

Interval training is a method of aerobic training that intersperses short, high-intensity bursts of maximal effort with intermittent recovery bouts. Interval training, such as high-intensity interval training (HITT), takes less time than steady-state training to accomplish the same training objectives, but it's also much more challenging.

TIP

Interval training is best suited for:

>> Clients who can no longer elevate their heart rate into a satisfactory working zone with continuous training.

>> Clients who are more conditioned and who want to increase their maximal oxygen consumption capacity (lung capacity).

>> Athletes who need to train at a maximum aerobic capacity for their sport or competition.

>> Clients who can't sustain moderate cardiovascular activity for long periods of time. Working hard for short periods of time followed by a long recovery period allows them to perform a greater total volume of work.

I cover various ways to incorporate interval training into the program in more detail in Chapter 15.

Determining working intensity

To the client, *working intensity* is how hard they'll work during the aerobic session. To you, it means the heart-rate training zone that the client will maintain during an aerobic session.

There are several methods for calculating working intensity. The most common is the *Karvonen formula*, which is a mathematical formula that uses an estimate of maximal heart rate based on a client's age and resting heart rate to determine optimal lower and upper aerobic training ranges.

REMEMBER

Tracking a client's heart rate during training is an objective measure of intensity, but it's not always the best option, especially for beginners. When a person has been sedentary for a long time, their rate of perceived exertion (RPE) is often much higher than their target heart-rate numbers suggest. You can set a target heart-rate training range, but also recommend a number on the RPE scale. With time, the client's RPE should correlate with their target heart rate.

REMEMBER

Achieving working intensity is the net result of how long the session lasts and at what pace. Other factors, such as resistance and training method, as well as exercise frequency, also contribute to the client's perception of intensity.

Specifying exercise frequency

Exercise frequency (or how often your client exercises) depends primarily on how much time they can set aside each week for exercise. You'll find that some clients will have no problem training three times a week, and others will be lucky if they can get in three times a month. Your job is to make fitness fit into your clients' lives, not the other way around.

REMEMBER

Too often, trainers tell their clients, "You need to be exercising three times a week for an hour," even when a client clearly isn't able to do that. Telling your clients what they *should* be doing is easy — but if they *could* do what they *should* be doing, they wouldn't have hired you in the first place. You're a professional fitness troubleshooter — your job is to look at and evaluate each client's unique fitness needs and come up with a customized solution that works with their lifestyle. Let's say you have a client who travels every week and squeezing in workouts on the road is difficult. But that person *is* home on the weekends and can do an intense cardio session once a week. If that's what they *can realistically* do, that's what you prescribe. It's not the textbook three times a week, but at least it's some exercise — and some exercise is better than no exercise.

That said, the American College of Sports Medicine recommends doing cardiovascular exercise at least three days per week. Meet your clients where they're at, even if they can't meet the recommended guidelines. Some activity is better than none and you can always work with your clients to find ways to sneak extra activity minutes into their daily routines.

Make sure you're taking into account how many other activities your client is participating in outside of their training sessions and include enough rest and recovery.

Designating duration

The *duration* of your client's session, or how long they will be exercising at one time, is ultimately determined by their personal fitness goals, the intensity level you have prescribed for, and how often they're training. On average, you should for having your clients exercising for between 20 and 40 minutes per session.

The higher the intensity level of a training session, the less time it takes to complete it.

Creating a Strength Program

Putting together a strength program involves more than slapping some plates on a weight machine. You'll need to consider several factors as you're creating the ultimate resistance training workout for your client.

Choosing the exercises

One of the first steps in setting up a weight-training program is choosing which exercises your client is going to perform. You can choose from a multitude of equipment and methods; determining the best one for your client takes some time and effort.

TIP

To figure out which exercises are best for your client, consider the following:

>> **Their fitness goals:** Generally, you train your client in a specific way to produce a specific change or result to achieve specific goals. Keep in mind that only the muscles that are trained will change, and that's why your resistance training program has to target all the muscles that you're trying to change. This approach refers to *specificity of training*. (Did I mention that all this should be specific?) For example, if you were training a swimmer who wanted to be stronger, you would probably choose upper-body exercises for the back, chest, shoulders, and arms.

>> **Training location:** Where your clients will be training will help determine which exercises they can realistically and safely do in that particular training environment.

>> **Available equipment:** Resistance training can be done with little-to-no equipment, but eventually you'll need at least some equipment — whether it's a set of dumbbells, resistance bands, *selectorized weight machines* (a machine that has a stack of plates, where you select the weight by sticking a pin into the plate), or any other equipment that you can use for resistance training (there's a lot). Knowing what type of equipment the client has access to will help you determine which exercises you can include in their program.

>> **Previous exercise experience:** Knowing how much exercise experience your client has saves time and frustration during your sessions. Your number-one goal is to ensure that your client understands the exercise and can perform it safely and correctly when you're not there. If you have a beginning client with no weight-training experience, you may choose to start with machines rather than free weights, because mastering the exercise motion through a fixed-plane mechanism such as a selectorized machine is easier than using free weights, which require more skill and control.

>> **How much time they have available to train:** The amount of time the client has to train affects which exercises make the most sense. If the client is time-strapped, you probably aren't going to focus on exercises like alternating dumbbell curls or single-arm kickbacks — these aren't optimal for a limited-time program. Instead, choose exercises that target several muscles at once (think squats, deadlifts, upper body pushing, and upper body pulling). You'll get more bang for your buck with these.

Specifying how often your client will work out

Training frequency refers to the number of times a client will exercise each week. Training frequency is determined by the client's personal fitness goals, available training time, and other activities such as sports or aerobic activities.

Here are some suggested guidelines for strength-training frequency:

>> **Beginner:** Two to three times per week

>> **Intermediate:** Three to four times per week

>> **Advanced:** Four to six times per week

Less-conditioned clients need more recovery between their workout sessions than more-conditioned clients, who can work more frequently within the week with fewer rest days in between.

REMEMBER

It's a good idea to allow at least one full day of rest before training the same muscle groups again — no matter how conditioned the client is.

Determining the order of the exercises

Deciding in which order your client will do the exercises goes hand in hand with selecting the exercises themselves. You need to keep in mind your client's training goals, previous training experience, and conditioning level.

REMEMBER

Choosing the best exercise order for your client is important. Your goal is to arrange the exercises you're prescribing in a way that matches your client's goals.

For example, if a new client wants to increase upper-body strength, you most likely wouldn't prescribe triceps extensions as their primary movement. To exhaust the client's triceps first would be counterproductive, because the triceps are *synergistic,* or secondary, muscles for multijoint movements such as the chest press or overhead press. These compound movements are more goal-specific for your client because they involve the larger muscle groups of the upper body, and lend themselves to developing upper-body strength — exactly what the client wants!

Table 12-3 provides some suggested guidelines for choosing exercise order based on client goals.

TABLE 12-3   ## Choosing Exercise Order

Exercise Order	Benefit
Multijoint movements first, then single-joint movements, working from largest muscle groups down to small muscle groups	Helps to prevent injury, because larger muscle groups need assistance from smaller muscles to perform the exercise correctly. Great for beginning clients.
Alternating push and pull exercises (for example, chest press [push]; then seated row [pull])	Allows for adequate muscle-group recovery by not allowing the same muscle groups to be used consecutively, reducing muscular fatigue. Good for clients who are deconditioned and can't sustain a progressive multijoint to single-joint method.
Alternating upper-body exercises with lower-body exercises (for example, chest press [upper body]; then leg press [lower body])	Allows clients who can't sustain consecutive upper-body or lower-body work to perform more total work volume by completely resting the upper body while lower-body work is being performed, and vice versa. Great for clients with minimal muscular endurance.

TIP

Check out Chapter 15 for advanced programming techniques. There I provide examples of these types of workouts.

Planning sets, reps, and rest

Okay, you've learned where your client is going to train and decided which exercises they'll be doing, with what equipment, and in what order. Next, you need to determine how much total work they'll do — also known as *volume* — during the session.

Volume is the number of sets and reps you prescribe for your client. A *repetition* (or *rep*, for short) is a single-movement count that, when performed consecutively, makes up a *set* of repetitions. For example, if you perform a squat one time, then rest, that is one rep, making it a one-rep set. If you perform a squat 15 times before resting, that is considered one set of 15 reps. If you perform a squat for 15 reps, rest, then perform 15 squats again, you will have completed two sets of 15 reps each.

Sets and reps depend on your client's specific training goals, training frequency, conditioning level, and recovery between exercises. As a general rule, the training volume directly correlates to the client's conditioning level (see Table 12-4).

Client Level	Goal	Reps	Sets (per exercise)	Rest (between sets)
Beginner	General fitness	12 to 15	2 to 3	1 to 2 minutes
Intermediate	Muscular endurance	12 to 15	3 to 4	45 seconds
Intermediate	Muscular size	10 to 12	3 to 4	45 to 90 seconds
Intermediate	Muscular strength	8 to 10	3 to 4	1 to 2 minutes
Advanced	Muscular endurance	12 to 20	4 to 6	30 to 45 seconds
Advanced	Muscular size	8 to 12	4 to 6	30 to 90 seconds
Advanced	Muscular strength	6 to 8	3 to 6	2 to 5 minutes

TABLE 12-4   **Approximate Sets and Reps Based on Fitness Level and Goals**

Setting the starting weight

After you've determined the total training volume for your client, have a look at their initial fitness assessment results. Use the results from the assessment exercises to recommend baseline starting weights.

TIP

Looking at your client's perceived exertion rate for each exercise will help you to determine reasonable starting weights. As you go through the actual session with your client, you can adjust the weights based on how they're performing and responding.

IN THIS CHAPTER

» **Preparing your client for the session**

» **Warming up your client**

» **Stretching your client**

» **Exercising your client**

» **Cooling down your client**

Chapter **13**

Taking Your Client through the First Workout

Finally! It's the moment you've been waiting for. You're up and running as a personal trainer. You've gotten your first client, done the fitness assessment, planned their program, and now you're ready to do the thing that brings in the dough — take your new client through their first full-fledged workout with you.

In the last chapter, you reviewed the format that your training sessions should follow: warm-up, conditioning, cool-down, flexibility. If you've studied for your certification exam already (see Chapter 2), you probably have an idea about how to incorporate the components of a workout session into the session format. However, this chapter is a handy reference that shows you options for each part of the workout. Here, you also see how to communicate with your clients during their training sessions and how to help them stay motivated and moving along toward their fitness goals.

Checking Up So Your Client Doesn't Check Out

Before you hand your client that 20-pound dumbbell, ask a few quick questions to check in. Their response will indicate how ready they are to work with you today and whether or not you'll need to make any-last minute adjustments.

Asking the right questions

The following sections include some sample questions that can help you to read your client's readiness.

How are you feeling today?

If your client has slept well and has had a normal day so far, they'll probably respond with "good," or something along those lines.

WARNING

Pay attention when a client answers otherwise — anything less than an "okay" response is your indication to do a little digging to determine what's going on. It's normal for people to feel mentally exhausted or stressed after a long day at work. Once they get into the workout, they usually start feeling better. But if a client isn't feeling great physically (didn't get enough sleep, feeling under the weather, and so on) ask if they're feeling up to training today. You don't have to cancel a session every time a client is tired — you'll be cancelling a lot of sessions if you do — but sometimes rescheduling is in everyone's best interest. If a client is running a fever, feeling achy, or if they have visible symptoms of a head cold (runny nose, cough, and so on), you should reschedule the session. Your client will benefit much more from rest than a workout, and you'll avoid catching the crud from them.

TIP

If your client is determined to work out even if they're not feeling great, tell them that you appreciate their diligence and enthusiasm, but working out when you're sick isn't a good idea. The session won't be productive and they'll probably end up not feeling well for even longer than if they had rescheduled and opted to get some rest.

How did you feel after our last session?

This is a good question to ask *every* session, especially if you haven't been in touch with your client since the last session. If your client says, "I was sore for days!" you may want to temper this workout. On the other hand, if they come back with "I felt great — it didn't even feel like I worked out!" it might be time to kick the intensity up a notch.

TIP

Even when a client tells you "I felt awesome after our last workout! You rock!" you may want to ask some direct questions, such as, "Did you experience any unusual pain in your joints and muscles, other than some soreness?" Or if they're just getting over an injury, ask a follow-up question related to that injury — for example, "Did you have any trouble with your shoulder after your last workout?" Even if it feels like you're asking too many questions, it's better than not asking enough. Sometimes a more specific question will get a different answer. For example, maybe the client did experience something unusual after the last workout, and then it passed and they simply forgot about it.

When was the last time you ate?

This question is *tres importante!* If your client hasn't had anything to eat within the last three to five hours, chances are their energy won't be great. Worse yet, low blood sugar can cause some people to become dizzy, nauseated, or even faint when they train too hard without enough fuel. This isn't the case for everyone; some people are fine with exercising on an empty stomach, and that's why asking about eating habits during the assessment is helpful.

REMEMBER

It's helpful to remind your clients, especially when they're new and haven't been active in a long time, that eating nutritious food consistently will keep their motor running through their workouts.

TIP

Keep a sugary drink or some hard candy on hand to get some quick sugar back into your client's system if they become nauseated or dizzy because their blood sugar is low. If they faint, call 911, then elevate their feet above heart-level to get their blood moving.

Explaining what will happen during the first session

Imagine that it's your first time, say, taking a martial arts class. You don't know how to tie your belt. You don't know when and how to bow. You certainly don't know how to block, punch, or kick. You don't even know how to put on your gi (yes, there is a right way to put on your gi)! You feel lost — and a little scared.

That's probably how your new client is feeling before their first real training session. Sure, *you* know the gym like the back of your hand, and you know a dozen ways to work every muscle group. But your client doesn't. They might not even know how to step onto a treadmill without flying off the back end of it, much less what to expect during a training session. That's why offering an overview of what will happen during the session, before it actually occurs, is important. Your clients will have less "beginner's anxiety" when they know what to expect.

In the following sections, I cover some things you should explain to your clients before the first training session.

What activities they'll be doing and in what order

For example, you might start by telling your client:

> Today, you're going to start your training session warming up on the treadmill. After you're warm, we're going to lightly stretch all your muscles to help prepare them for the work we're going to do with the weights and also to help prevent them from being injured. After you're fully stretched out, you'll be ready to start your strength exercises, which I'll demonstrate to you before you actually perform them. We're doing a full-body workout today, which means you'll do one strength exercise for each muscle group. After you complete your strength training, we'll end the workout with some abdominal work and lower-body stretches that will serve as your cool-down, which will help prevent any muscle cramping and breathing problems. Cooling down helps to return your body to the way it normally breathes — the way it was when you first walked in here, before you started exercising.

What they can expect to feel like during the training session

For example, you might tell your client:

> While you're exercising, your heart rate will increase slightly, and your body will become warm — you may start sweating. During your warm-up, your breathing will become faster and heavier, but you shouldn't feel uncomfortable and you should still be able to hold a conversation with me. If you do feel uncomfortable, please don't hesitate to let me know. During the strength exercises, you may experience a light "burning" sensation in the muscle groups we're working. Don't be alarmed — this is completely normal. When you're through with your entire workout, your body will feel slightly fatigued, but not to the point of being exhausted.

What they can expect from you

For example, you might say:

> During your workout, I'll demonstrate every movement first, giving you verbal and visual instruction of how to do it. After I've demonstrated what you'll be doing, you'll perform the movement. I'll be giving you pointers as you go through the exercise to help you get the form right.

What you expect from them

You may say something like the following:

> While you're training, I'll be asking you to rate how hard you feel like you're working on a scale of 1 to 10. A rating of 1 would be equivalent to you sitting in a chair, whereas a rating of 10 would be the way you'd feel if you were pushing your car uphill in the middle of winter. During this first workout, I *don't* want you trying to perform at a level of 10. That's all-out, maximal exertion and effort, which at this point isn't necessary to reach your fitness goals. Also, this is my first time working with you, and I'm still learning your body and what you're capable of doing. As we work together longer, I'll know you and your body better, and I'll be able to push you harder in a safer manner. For today, the intensity level of your workout will be slightly lower than your normal working intensity. I do expect, however, that if at any point you feel dizzy, nauseated, or uncomfortable in any way, you'll let me know immediately. Also, please don't hesitate to interrupt me or stop me at any time to ask questions. My goal is to make sure that you completely understand what you're doing, and that you do it well.

So Hot It's Cool: Warming Up the Client

Now that your client is clear on what's going to happen during the session, it's time to warm up!

Sometimes clients want to skip the warm-up and get right into the fun stuff. You don't want your client injured during her very first session — that's not exactly motivating! So explain to your eager-beaver client that warming up is very important (and necessary!). If they skip the warm-up, their muscles will need a lot more time to get the greater blood flow they need. Cold muscles with less blood flow don't move as well as warm muscles with increased blood flow — which also increases their risk of pulling or straining a muscle.

TIP

Warming up doesn't have to happen on a machine; that's just one of many options. Whether you're training in a gym with lots of equipment or training in someone's home, try mixing up the warm-up with different activities to keep it interesting.

Showing them what's what

For your clients who will be exercising at least some of the time in a gym, you'll need to show them what to do and make sure they know their way around.

You'll want to show your client:

» How to safely get on and off of the machine if they'll be using one

» How to increase and decrease the intensity

» How to slow down and stop the machine

Believe it or not, I *have* seen more than one person fly off the back of a treadmill because they started it while standing on it, instead of straddling the machine, turning it on, holding the handrails, and then hopping on.

When putting a client on a piece of cardio equipment for the first time, show them how to use the machine by first hopping on yourself. Explain what all the buttons do, and where to place their hands and feet. Demonstrate the proper form for that machine — and what *isn't* proper form.

Never assume that using fitness equipment is intuitive for your clients — what's obvious to you is probably completely new and not obvious to them.

Lay out each action as a set of steps and verbally describe the action as you're demonstrating it. Most clients will need to hear you say it and see you do it to learn how to do the activity properly themselves.

Here's an example script for teaching your client how to use a treadmill:

1. **Walk up to the console on the side tracks that run the length of the tread.**

   At this point you'll be straddling the tread.

2. **Start the treadmill.**

3. **As the treadmill slowly starts, put both hands on the side rails or front hand bar for balance.**

4. **Lightly step onto the tread, still holding on to the machine for balance.**

5. **When you're comfortable matching your walking stride to the pace of the machine, take one hand off the treadmill and press the up arrow to increase the treadmill's speed so that the machine mimics your natural walking pace.**

6. **When you're comfortable walking at that pace, let go of the handrails.**

   Make sure that, as you walk, you pick up your foot and extend your leg, swinging your leg from your hip. As your leg lowers and your foot comes down, be sure to land heel-first. Also, be sure to swing your arms in a normal walking motion.

7. **To decrease your speed, put both hands back onto the handrails.**

8. **Holding on with one hand, use the other hand to press the down arrow, which will decrease your speed.**

9. **When the treadmill slows down, press the stop button.**

10. **When the treadmill has come to a complete stop, get off the machine.**

   Be sure to wait for the treadmill to come to a complete stop. As you dismount the treadmill, be sure to hold onto the handrail as you step down. Your body may feel a little strange walking on a nonmoving floor after being on the treadmill.

Providing constructive feedback

REMEMBER

It's okay to correct a client's form — you won't offend them and they'll appreciate learning how to exercise safely and efficiently.

Letting your client do it on their own

Teaching your clients well from the beginning sets them up for success, which is really important because you'll eventually have to let them fly. Ideally your clients will reach a point where they train with you because they want to, not because they need to. As your clients develop the skills and confidence to exercise regularly on their own, your role will evolve too — it's rewarding and a lot of fun to create advanced programs for your once-novice clients. More on that in Chapter 15.

REMEMBER

Every *body* is different and so is the amount of time it takes for clients to warm up before diving into their workouts. For some, five minutes is enough. Others may need 20 minutes to prepare their bodies for work.

HOME IS WHERE THE WARM-UP IS

If you're training your clients in places without a selection of exercise equipment at your disposal, try including some of these options in your warm-ups:

- Walk up and down the stairs three to four times; then do alternating walking lunges with upper body rotations.

- Alternate bodyweight squats with bench push-ups (hands on the bench, toes on the floor).

- Try two to three rounds of this circuit: ten bodyweight squats, ten easy TRX rows, ten bodyweight lateral alternating lunges, ten bench push-ups, ten dead bugs, ten medicine ball rotations.

TIP

You can also take your client through a series of *dynamic mobility* exercises where they'll be moving and stretching at the same time. This serves two purposes. First, any type of movement works for increasing the body's core temperature, which you already know is important. The other reason for dynamic stretching is that it prepares the body for the specific activities that you'll be doing after warming up. I'll cover pre-workout stretching later in this chapter, but to give you an idea of why it's useful, consider a baseball pitcher. Have you ever noticed a pitcher doing arm circles before throwing the ball? They do this to warm up while simultaneously preparing the shoulder to work — a warmup that makes better sense than jogging a few laps around the diamond.

Going for the Stretch

When a client has limited time to train, it's tempting to focus all your time and attention on conditioning, leaving stretching out entirely, or tacking a few stretches onto the end of the training session as an afterthought. Having worked with many busy clients myself, I can certainly relate! If you haven't studied for your personal trainer certification yet, you might not fully understand *flexibility* as a component of health-related fitness. Flexibility in this context refers to a joint's ability to move through a normal and pain-free range of motion (ROM). People with inadequate flexibility often say they feel pain or stiffness in the affected area, making it hard for them to move or to get comfortable when they're sitting or lying down. If a client has limited ROM in one or more joints, be extra mindful of the exercises you prescribe. Limited ROM isn't a reason not to train someone, but it can become worse if you exacerbate it with the wrong exercises. If you're not sure how to proceed, it's always okay to ask for guidance from a physical therapist or even a more experienced personal trainer.

Stretching is the simplest and most common method for increasing joint ROM, and as a personal trainer, you need to understand how and when to work it into your clients' programs.

Before the workout

As I mention earlier in this chapter, you can incorporate dynamic stretching into your client's warm-up. Dynamic stretches are controlled, rhythmic movements that gradually move a joint through its full ROM, ideally mimicking the movements that you're preparing your client to do later (remember the baseball pitcher from earlier?) After the warm-up and before moving into the conditioning component of the training session, a full-body *static* stretching routine is also appropriate for some clients, depending on their flexibility status. Static stretching involves moving slowly into a stretch and holding it at peak tension for 10 to 30 seconds. After you're done with the workout, a more concentrated stretching segment is recommended, because your client is as warm as they're going to be at that point, which is the safest and most effective time for most people to stretch.

REMEMBER

A person's flexibility level is influenced by several factors, including age, sex, and physical activity level. Generally speaking, flexibility tends to decrease with age, women are typically more flexible than men, and active people are more flexible than sedentary people. Be sure to take all these factors into account when you're planning your clients' programs.

After the workout

Here are two techniques for post-workout stretching that can effectively stretch your clients above and beyond the static stretching that you do pre-workout:

>> **Proprioceptive neuromuscular facilitation (PNF):** This type of stretching is commonly called PNF because the name that PNF stands for — proprioceptive neuromuscular facilitation — is a mouthful. In English, this technique consists of an isometric contraction (squeezing a muscle as hard as you can) followed by a static stretch for the same muscle group. PNF increases joint ROM, but the reason why is not well understood. It's possible that PNF stretching triggers a "relax" response from the neuromuscular system, which in turn allows a muscle to stretch further. It could be that PNF stretching simply increases a person's tolerance for deeper stretching.

>> **Passive stretching:** This type of stretching can be done with a prop (like a stretching strap) to slowly move into each stretch. Instruct the client to relax as they move into each position.

WARNING

PNF stretching should only be performed by experienced personal trainers with training in this technique. Without fully understanding PNF, you'll risk injuring the client by overstretching. PNF stretching is intense, but it should *never* be painful. A good rule of thumb is to only use stretching techniques that you understand completely. Also, if your client can't tell the difference between tension and pain with stretching, stop immediately and choose a different method.

TIP

For some great stretches your client can practice on their own, check out *Fitness For Dummies* by Suzanne Schlosberg and Liz Neporent, MA (published by Wiley).

Now for the Main Event: Exercising Your Client

You've probably already decided which exercises you want your client to do based on their fitness assessment results (see Chapter 11). However, the way you present the exercises is just as important as the exercises themselves. After all, when you were in high school, your math teacher didn't teach you algebra by tossing you a book or barking orders, did they?

Strong but not silent: Teaching strength exercises

If you could toss your client an Olympic bar, tell them to do a chest press, and collect your $100, your job would be simple. But because each client is different and learns in different ways, you need to modify your teaching techniques for each client.

TIP

Here are some tactics for teaching your clients strength exercises. Use whichever techniques work best for the client you're working with:

>> **Use analogies.** Some clients need to have a mental image of the exercise, so try using analogies. For example, when explaining a chest fly, you can tell the client to imagine they're hugging a big beach ball and can't quite get their arms around it.

>> **Demonstrate what you're looking for.** Your client may learn visually, which means you should show them how to do the exercise by doing it yourself, instead of simply by describing it.

>> **Ask your client to do a move while looking in the mirror, and then while turned away from the mirror.** This way they can see and feel how to do the move properly.

>> **Try saying the same thing several different ways until the client grasps the concept.** For example, you can say, "During a seated chest press or a lying dumbbell press, you're working your chest, so keep your elbows at 90 degrees." Then you can say, "To keep your elbows at 90 degrees, you have to keep your shoulders down." That way you're drilling into the client's mind that the elbows need to be kept at — guess what? — 90 degrees.

REMEMBER

Spotting your client helps with teaching proper form, especially during the first few training sessions when they're getting the hang of their exercises. Keeping your hands on or near your client allows you to guide their form in the moment. After a few sessions, you can start taking your hands away more and more as the client gains confidence. Make sure you explain what spotting means and *always* ask permission before putting your hands on a client.

TIP

Be as verbal and descriptive as possible while talking your client through each exercise. Use action verbs such as *pause, push, pull,* and *lift.* Explain what to do, how to do it, and how much energy to put into it.

Getting feedback

During your session, ask the client for feedback and use it as a guide. Client feedback lets you know how well the client thinks the session is going, how they're feeling, and whether your programming is on track. Feedback can come in a variety of forms, but here are the two main types:

>> **Verbal feedback:** Grunts, groans, and the always beloved "I can't believe you're making me do this!" indicate that your client is working hard. On the other hand, if you get more than the occasional "Do I have to?" or a flat out "No!" you may want to rethink your approach.

>> **Physical feedback:** If your client is breathing hard and sweating, you're doing something right.

WARNING

Pay attention to physical cues. If the color suddenly drains from your client's face, they're probably either working *too* hard or their blood sugar has dropped. If this happens, stop the workout and let your client recover. When they're ready to resume, try lowering the intensity.

REMEMBER

With experience, you'll get better at guessing how hard your clients are working just by watching and listening to them.

Cooling Down and Recovering from the Workout

The cool-down is the period of time after conditioning involving similar activities as the warm-up, only now instead of preparing the body for work, you're gradually moving back towards resting status by decreasing the client's heart rate and blood pressure.

REMEMBER

Cooling down should take at least five to ten minutes and longer for higher intensity workouts.

TIP

Whenever possible, I like using the same movements for the warm-up and the cool-down. It's a great teaching strategy for starting and ending every session at baseline. After the cool-down, I like to do a few minutes of PNF or passive stretching. It's relaxing for my clients and I can feel good knowing that they stretched. Remember that stretching shouldn't replace the cool-down; they're two different things with distinct purposes.

TRUE STORY

Stopping exercise abruptly without cooling down can cause *blood pooling*, which happens when blood pools in the lower extremities and can't return to the heart fast enough. I have seen this happen first-hand when clients are in a hurry and skip the cool-down. One time at the end of a particularly intense 6 a.m. indoor cycling class, I had a client hop off the bike and walk out as we were beginning the cool-down. Without warning, he fell backward onto the floor and fainted. He was okay, but it was scary — and served as a reminder to the entire group not to skip the cool-down!

Chapter **14**

Choosing Exercises and Teaching Your Beginning Client

B y now you can see that a personal training session involves more than randomly prescribing deadlifts, pull-ups, and sprints and expecting your client's highly motivated inner athlete to show up. In Chapter 12, I outline the steps personal trainers take to design training programs. In this chapter, I show you how to choose exercises for your clients, when to progress them, and why getting it right matters.

REMEMBER

The key to a successful training program lies in your ability to deliver results.

Program Design Basics

The training program is your step-by-step plan for getting a client from where they are now to where they want to be. And like most things, training is just guesswork if you don't have a plan. Sometimes your best guess isn't wrong, but it might not be the best option, either.

Planning a training program is like using your car's GPS to plan a trip. You might already know several ways to get to your destination, but GPS shows you the most efficient way to get from point A to point B. It also gives you the ETA and re-routes you as information changes or if a better route becomes available. All you have to do is follow the directions.

A successful training program works the same way *if* it meets two criteria: physiologic rationale (simply put, you need to choose appropriate exercises for your client and make changes when necessary) and the client's willingness to follow your directions.

TIP

Choosing exercises is one part of the program design process; the best program is the one your client will follow.

Your program design choices depend on each client's unique needs and goals, and no matter what those are, you should be able to answer the following questions before choosing even one exercise:

>> What is the *main* goal of the resistance training program? Your client can have more than one goal, but what is the priority?

>> What movement patterns does the client need to train?

>> Which energy systems (anaerobic, aerobic, or both) need to be trained?

>> What muscle actions make the most sense for the client (isotonic, isometric, and so on)?

>> If the client isn't currently injured but has been injured in the past, where was the injury and how did it happen?

Beyond the assessment, this is really all you need to know to get started. If you're missing any information, go back and get it before you start plugging exercises into your client's program.

Focusing on your client's goals

Without a goal, your client (and you) won't have direction. Some common resistance training goals include getting stronger, improving endurance, adding muscle, and losing fat. Chapter 12 notes that effective exercise programs start with understanding why your client hired you in the first place. Getting clear about what your client wants to accomplish will guide your program design decisions.

REMEMBER

Always keep your client's goals front and center in your planning. Guide them toward what *they* want, not what *you* think they need.

TIP

All clients have their reasons for starting an exercise program — and you won't know what they are unless you ask. Never design a client's program based on your assumptions!

Also, keep in mind that goals can change and goal setting with your clients doesn't have to be a one-time thing. Some people start out simply wanting to adopt a regular exercise habit and later set their sights on a bigger goal. For example, maybe they love running and decide to train for a half-marathon.

Evaluating your client's progress regularly matters too. You need to determine from the beginning how and when you'll measure progress. If you're not tracking your client's progress, you won't know if (or when) it's time to change the program (cue the GPS analogy). You'll also learn the hard way that people become frustrated and lose motivation if results don't meet their expectations — even if you think they're making significant progress.

TRUE STORY

Sometimes you need more than one way to measure results. One of my favorite client success stories of all time is of a woman who came to me with a weight loss goal and ended up gaining 5 pounds. At 55 years old, she had never set foot in a gym or lifted a weight in her life. She had lost 30 pounds over the previous year through healthy eating and walking, but her progress stalled, so she asked me to help her lose "the last 10 pounds." She continued eating healthfully and walking, and she started seeing me twice weekly for full-body resistance training sessions.

Six months later, her energy was through the roof, she had six-pack abs, and she was down *four* clothing sizes, but she was frustrated. She was 5 pounds heavier instead of 10 pounds lighter. Fortunately, I was prepared for this. I took photos of her on day one and recorded circumference measurements every six weeks so I could show her tangible evidence that the scale doesn't always tell the whole story. Muscle doesn't weigh more than fat, but it does take up less space! Fortunately she decided that six-pack abs and smaller clothes mattered more than the number on the scale and that *nothing* mattered more than how strong and energetic lifting weights made her feel.

Considering your client's abilities

Sometimes it's obvious what a client can or can't realistically do. For example, your 5-foot, 6-inch 43-year-old client probably isn't a strong NBA prospect, but he *can* shoot hoops with his friends a few times a week to stay in shape. Or maybe your 65-year-old client with no previous running experience wants to train for a 5K. She probably won't be running her first race next weekend, but she *can* gradually work her way up to completing a 5K six weeks from now.

TIP

Part of your job is helping your clients to set realistic and obtainable goals.

But what do you do when a client has a lofty goal, and even though they're capable of doing what it takes to achieve it, you know it isn't realistic? For example, suppose your client wants to look like a specific celebrity with a very lean physique. They might actually have the fitness level and genetic potential they would need to get ultra-lean, but they also have a full-time job, a family, and a serious taco habit. They might like the idea of looking like a celebrity, but do they realize what's involved? How looking that way is practically a full-time job? And that it's the celebrity's job to rock a ripped physique, which almost always involves a team of people behind the scenes making it possible (personal trainer, personal chef, and so on)? Is the client able *and* willing to do what it takes?

I'm all for dreaming big, but I have also learned from personal experience — and from training a *lot* of clients — how unrealistic goals that require habits nobody can sustain forever (not even celebrities) eventually lead to burnout and frustration. I'm not telling you to discourage your clients from setting big goals — training for a race, getting super lean, whatever — just make sure they understand exactly what they're committing to. And then help them to adjust their expectations if they decide to start with something a bit smaller (also totally okay!). Precision Nutrition has a great infographic on its website that describes different bodyfat percentages and what it takes to achieve them. Check it out at www.precisionnutrition.com/cost-of-getting-lean-infographic.

Movement Patterns

Now that you and your client are on the same page about goals and expectations, let's get into the nitty-gritty of choosing exercises. Keep in mind that a main goal of resistance training usually involves improving musculoskeletal fitness, and that the three primary structures of the musculoskeletal system that we (personal trainers) deal with are bones, joints, and muscles. Understanding how these structures interact to make bodies move should inform your exercise choices. In other words, you need to understand how to choose exercises based on the abilities and limitations of your client's musculoskeletal system.

TIP

If you don't have a solid understanding of anatomy and kinesiology yet, that's okay! There are lots of resources available for in-depth study, including — and beyond — your personal trainer certification. Also, there's Google. The human body has around 600 muscles and it's okay if you can't name all of them off the top of your head. I know I couldn't!

Now's the time when a movement assessment (like the Functional Movement Screen [FMS] discussed in Chapter 11) comes in handy and why I encourage you to include one in your fitness assessments. You'll quickly get a clear snapshot of how a person is moving in their everyday life so you can see what you're working with and where to start with each client. Assessing your client's ability to move properly before choosing exercises is like building your house on a strong foundation. A solid brick house might look strong from the outside, but if you look closer and find cracks in the foundation . . . see where I'm going with this? You can teach your client a bunch of exercises without assessing their movement quality first, but if you do, you'll learn the hard way about any cracks in their foundation.

REMEMBER

When you move well your body is more efficient. And efficiency with exercise means getting more done with less effort *and* you're less likely to hurt yourself in the process.

Movement patterns refer to the various ways that our bodies move through motions. Considering how many muscle and joint actions the human body is capable of — from simple tasks like scrolling through text messages to more complex tasks like swinging a kettlebell — we can create *a lot* of movement patterns. Try doing a quick Google search for "movement patterns" and you'll get about 534,000,000 results (really; I just tried it).

For personal trainers, the main components of movement patterns that we work with are mobility and stability. *Mobility* refers to the body's ability to move freely, and *stability* refers to how well your body can maintain balance *and* support your joints during movements. All our joints can be classified by their primary role (mobility or stability), and it's good for you to know which joints do what, but don't miss the forest for the trees here. Look at the body as a whole structure instead of a sum of its parts. Then start by training fundamental movement patterns, giving extra attention to areas that need work. Repair the foundation before piling on more bricks.

Matching exercises to movement patterns

If you ask ten personal trainers which movements are the most important to master you'll get ten different answers. That's because there's more than one right way to prioritize movement, but I think most trainers would agree that all or most of these five movement patterns guide the bulk of their exercise choices: squat, hinge, push, pull, rotation.

Movement patterns can happen in more than one *plane of motion*, meaning that you can match countless exercises to a few movement patterns. The human body has three anatomical planes:

>> Sagittal plane (right/left)

>> Frontal plane (front/back)

>> Transverse plane (top/bottom)

Check out your personal trainer certification manual for visuals of all three planes of motion and descriptions of the fundamental movements that happen in each one.

Keeping it simple

Here are a few basic guidelines that you can follow to avoid overcomplicating things:

>> Balance your client's movement patterns. If you choose a horizontal pushing exercise (like a push-up), balance it with a horizontal pulling exercise (try a TRX row or a dumbbell row). For each lower-body anterior movement (front dominant exercises, like a lunge), balance it with a posterior-dominant movement (try a deadlift or a bridge).

>> If you're prescribing a full-body workout, choose four to eight exercises that target large muscle groups and emphasize movement patterns that need the most attention.

>> Put bigger lifts (squats, deadlifts, and so on) first while your client is fresh and able to perform them with proper form.

>> Focus on doing a few things well and do them consistently.

Choosing Exercises

Typically for a client who hasn't weight-trained before, you need to condition all large muscle groups in a slow and safe manner before progressing to higher intensity exercise.

By starting this way your client will develop *base-level conditioning*. To accomplish this successfully, you typically start with a full-body workout based on your client's past exercise experience and current fitness level.

Your client's experience level

Training a complete beginner with no previous exercise experience takes a lot of time and patience, but you're also starting with a blank slate. There's nothing to "unlearn" and no bad habits to correct. Experienced exercisers can be some of the most challenging training clients, especially if they're in decent shape but have some bad gym habits. These are typically the "no pain, no gain" folks and convincing them to follow a repetitive program full of basic exercises can be challenging.

REMEMBER

Sometimes unlearning old habits is harder than learning new ones.

For a brand new lifter, start with the most basic exercises possible. Choose exercises that you can explain easily and that your client can perform without thinking too much. This helps your client to grasp what you're teaching without feeling overwhelmed by information overload.

If your new client has some past experience but hasn't worked out in a while, you'll still want to start with basic exercises. The difference is in how you teach. This client will probably be familiar with the names of most exercises and know how to perform them.

TIP

Never assume that someone with previous experience has a lot of knowledge. Sometimes clients know how to perform exercises but they don't know the names of them.

The flipside of this is a client with a lot of knowledge but no recent experience. Choose this client's exercises wisely. These clients typically think they're more advanced than they actually are. They still need to start with a basic routine and you need to explain *why* more than *how* when you're training them.

REMEMBER

Knowledge and experience are two different things. Knowing how to exercise helps but it doesn't replace doing the work.

Your client's fitness level

This might seem obvious but knowing how hard to push a client is an important consideration. You have to take your client outside of their comfort zone to get results. If you want to get technical here, applying the *overload principle* leads to improved musculoskeletal fitness. The overload principle states that you have to continually increase the demand placed on muscles to get results. In other words, if you want to get stronger, you have to progressively lift heavier weights.

REMEMBER

"Methods are many, principles are few. Methods often change, principles never do." This saying is adapted from a quote from engineer and business theorist Harrington Emerson that I keep in a frame on my desk.

Challenging your client is necessary, but pushing someone just for the sake of pushing them isn't. It's never a good idea to push a client beyond what they can do safely. That's a fast way to injure people and not everyone enjoys grueling workouts.

Always meet people where they're at today. Not last year, ten years ago, or where they want to be tomorrow.

Tailoring the Program with Progressions and Regressions

Over time you'll find that most beginning clients tend to start with similar exercises that you'll tailor based on your assessment results. You do this by making an exercise harder (progression) or easier (regression). Some options for modifying an exercise include changing the weight (make it heavier or lighter), change the surface (try moving from a stable surface to an unstable surface), change the tempo (faster or slower), add isometrics (for example, try adding a wall sit into the mix), or you can challenge stability with single-sided exercises like single-leg squat or a single-arm chest press. Some examples of making an exercise easier include doing push-ups on the knees instead of the toes or elevating the upper body on a bench or a wall and using a band for assisted chin-ups.

Sometimes modifying an exercise isn't enough and you need to be able to recognize when it's necessary to substitute an exercise. For example, if your client physically can't do an exercise, choose a different one. If an exercise is painful, stop immediately and try something different. You'll also need to consider equipment availability (gym versus home) and make sure your client feels confident about doing the exercises you assign on their own. Make adjustments as needed.

TIP

A good rule of thumb is to choose exercises that you can progress twice and regress twice. If you make an exercise more challenging twice and it's still too easy, you might need to try something different. If you make an exercise easier twice and the client still can't do it, you definitely need to try something different.

Chapter **15**

Taking Your Client to the Next Level

According to the SAID principle (short for *Specific Adaptations to Imposed Demands*), the body will adapt to overcome a demand that's greater than what it is capable of performing at that time. What does this mean in plain English? Your client may not be able to perform 15 goblet squats with a 30-pound dumbbell *today* — but with repeated training, their body will continually grow stronger until it can achieve that workload. At some point, your client's once-seemingly-weak muscles will inevitably become stronger. And when they do become stronger, the initial programming you designed won't seem as strenuous or challenging.

So, true to the SAID principle, you need to change your client's program to increase demand on the body so that they can continue progressing. The question is, how do you know *when* to progress your client, and exactly *how much* progress is needed?

You may be tired of hearing this by now, but it's true: Each program you create is unique to that particular client's current level of conditioning and specific training goals. So it only stands to reason that your program decisions depend on the client — and what works for one person might not work for someone else. In this chapter, I show you some different methods and techniques you can use to take your clients' programs up a notch.

Taking the Next Step

Progressing your client is a skill and an art — one that's polished over time and with lots of client experience. Each client will respond in their own way to program change. As you gain working knowledge of your client's physiological responses to different workload scenarios, you'll soon be able to masterfully manipulate exercise prescriptions to keep them continually progressing toward their goals.

TIP

In Chapter 14, I offer some ideas for progressions and regressions with your beginning clients. Here are some additional techniques to create change in your client's program:

>> Increasing or decreasing rest time

>> Increasing or decreasing repetitions

>> Adding sets

>> Adding exercises

>> Changing the type of exercises

>> Changing the order of exercises

>> Increasing exercise frequency

In the following section, I show you ways to identify when the time is right to help your client advance and how to come up with next steps in your plan.

Ch-ch-ch-changes: Knowing when to change it up

If you go through a session with a client, only to have them look at you and say, "That's it?" that's usually a sign that it's time for something a little more challenging.

Of course, the signs aren't always that obvious — not all clients love exercise, and not all clients will want to let you know that the workout was less than challenging. Most of the time, you're going to need to look for signs from your client — mostly nonverbal signs — that it's time for a new challenge.

TIP

Here are a few signs that it's time to advance your client:

>> They can easily talk through an entire set.

>> They don't appear to be exerting much effort.

>> Their perceived exertion rate is less than 6.

>> Their breathing doesn't increase.

>> Their heart rate no longer reaches the target training range during a set.

Patience, grasshopper

WARNING

No matter how eager your client is, you need to advance the program appropriately. Improper progression can result in injury, undue fatigue, and an overall unmotivating effect that can lead to your client saying, "No way," every time you try something new. Your job is to manage your client's program progression so that their muscles, ligaments, tendons, and cardiovascular system get stronger safely, before pushing the next training level.

TIP

Here are some key points to remember when planning a program progression so that you end up with successful results (rather than a burned-out client):

>> **Always put safety first.** If your client can't perform an exercise with acceptable form, you may want to introduce a different exercise rather than increase the weight or intensity for that one.

>> **Change one aspect of the program per session.** If you were to change the weight, sets, reps, and rest periods for a client all in one session, you could end up injuring your client — and then you're not only not gaining ground, you're losing it. You also won't know what's working and what isn't if you change everything at once. By changing one aspect of the program at a time, your client's body can safely adapt to the new element.

>> **Increase intensity, weight, or duration levels by no more than ten percent.** For instance, you might increase the weight by five pounds for a few sets — but not all of them. Or you can increase the number of reps per set without increasing the weight.

>> **Give each phase of the program at least two weeks before increasing intensity, weight, or duration again.** For example, you may choose to increase their tempo of lifting after increasing reps two weeks earlier.

>> **When advancing a client's exercises, make sure you advance them logically.** You don't want to jump a beginning client who's never worked with free weights before from a machine-based program to a complete free-weight program. Try switching one machine-based exercise to one that uses free weights each time over the course of a few sessions.

If you're changing exercises from machines to free weights (or vice versa), make sure you're sticking with the same movement pattern. For example, you might try moving from a machine chest press (horizontal pushing) to a dumbbell chest press (horizontal pushing that requires greater stability).

Providing direction for clients you see less often

If your client has purchased a long-term training package and you've been working together on a frequent basis, you'll have the luxury of knowing that client's capabilities well and you can continually monitor and advance the program. Unfortunately, that ideal scenario won't be the case for all clients. For clients you're seeing intermittently, you need to provide direction on how and when to advance their program on their own, as well as set follow-up appointments so you can reevaluate them and make solid recommendations for updating their program.

For clients you see less frequently, document everything when you're giving them a new program. You can even create a specific form just for program changes, with areas sectioned off to make notes so the client remembers what to do.

Here are areas to cover when prescribing program changes for an intermittent client:

>> **If/then scenarios:** Envision a few possible scenarios and tell your client what to do in each case. For example, you may say, "If this set is too easy, then next time increase your weight by five pounds."

>> **Benchmarks for increasing intensity:** You want to make sure your client doesn't get hurt by being overeager. So you may say something like, "After your third week on this program, raise your repetitions to 15, keeping your weight the same."

>> **Appointment for program change:** You need to tell your client how long to stick with this program before you'll recommend changes. For example, you may say, "We'll need to reevaluate you for a new program in six weeks."

>> **Recording workouts:** It's important that your client records what they actually end up doing for each workout. You'll need this information when you reassess so you can see what's working and what isn't.

>> **Recording intensity level during workouts:** Ask your client to gauge how hard they're working and make a quick note of it. If you see that most workouts were a perceived exertion rate of 4, you'll know that the program wasn't challenging enough.

Put it in writing! When you make program changes for an intermittent client, you end up giving a lot of information in one session, which can be overwhelming. Most of the time, clients won't remember everything you've told them — put it all in writing so they can walk away with a program they understand and feel confident about following on their own.

Use the same workout template every time to avoid confusion.

Strengthening Your Strength Techniques

You truly are only limited by your imagination when it comes to advancing your client. In the following sections, I provide some basic programming techniques to get you started. But remember, you're not limited to what you see here — be creative. Your clients will thank you for it!

Strength-training routines

One strategy for taking your client to the next level is to move from total body workouts to training the body in smaller and smaller parts. For example, you might start with a full-body routine and progress over time to a five-day split where the client exercises a different body part each day.

The full-body routine

The full-body routine assigns one exercise to each muscle group. This routine is an excellent format for beginning clients, because it provides a consistent format for creating a strong baseline conditioning level. When you're advancing the client within this routine, you can increase sets, weights, and intensity. This program can easily take your client from beginner to intermediate status. You'll still want to prioritize movement patterns but you can include additional exercises.

Typically, beginning clients who are training two to three times per week will use this type of programming for *at least* their first three to four weeks of training. You can vary a client's exercises within the full-body-workout format, helping to keep the program fresh and interesting even though you're still training the entire body with the same movement patterns during each workout.

The two-day split

The two-day split is the next logical program progression after a client has mastered the full-body routine. When you're implementing the two-day split, you'll typically have your client devote one workout solely to upper-body exercises, then on the next workout, concentrate on lower-body movements.

By dividing the body into upper and lower regions, you enable your client to increase *volume* (total amount of work completed) per session and per body part without increasing injury risk or overtraining. Alternating the body's regions each workout allows for adequate recovery time before you train the next region again.

The three-day split

The three-day split builds on the premise of the two-day split routine. After a client has adapted to the two-day split, their body will be ready to increase workload volume for more-specific body parts. Dividing the body further and adding an additional session to the program cycle allows the client to devote more training volume to each muscle group worked that session.

You can divide body parts in a three-day-split routine in a few different ways.

How you choose your client's split depends on their training goals.

REMEMBER Here's one example of a three-day split by body part:

>> **Day 1:** Chest, shoulders, triceps

>> **Day 2:** Back, biceps, core

>> **Day 3:** Legs

And here's another example:

>> **Day 1:** Chest and back

>> **Day 2:** Triceps and biceps

>> **Day 3:** Shoulders and legs

The four-day split

With a four-day split, you can go even further by dividing the body into smaller segments. The intensity of this type of programming is useful for increasing strength and power if that's the primary goal.

Here's a way to group movement patterns for a four-day split program:

» **Day 1:** Horizontal push and horizontal pull

» **Day 2:** Quad dominant (squats, lunges)

» **Day 3:** Vertical push and vertical pull

» **Day 4:** Hip dominant (deadlifts, kettlebell swings)

And here's another approach if you want to try a four-day split by specific body part:

» **Day 1:** Chest and shoulders

» **Day 2:** Back and biceps

» **Day 3:** Legs

» **Day 4:** Triceps and abs

The five-day split

The five-day split divides the body into even smaller regions to be worked out one day at a time. This type of routine isn't for everyone, but it can be beneficial for advanced lifters who are short on time.

By dividing the body into even smaller regions, you put more intensity into training each muscle group. Although it might seem time-consuming to train this way, the five-day split actually saves time because you're only training each body part once a week and training sessions become much shorter.

Push-pull routines

A *push-pull routine* (in which you alternate a pushing movement with a pulling movement) can work well for any level client because it allows for adequate muscle recovery. How you manipulate your client's rest and reps is what makes this program challenging.

Push-pull routines are a popular alternative for clients who have plateaued or who have been on a particular program style for an extended period of time. Push-pull training forces opposite muscle groups to work intensely back-to-back and is another way to increase volume.

Advanced training techniques

In addition to giving your client new routines, you can also include advanced training techniques *within* the training routines. Coming up is a rundown of some popular advanced training techniques.

Supersetting

Supersetting is when opposing muscle-group exercises are paired (such as a push-up and cable row) and performed back to back, without rest in between. After your client has performed the two back-to-back exercises, they'll rest, and then perform the same set again.

This type of exercise pairing raises intensity without overloading the same muscle group. You extend the duration of the activity overall without overstressing the active muscle group because one muscle group rests while the other one works.

TIP

This method is great for advanced beginners because it increases their intensity level without over-stressing the musculoskeletal system.

Compound sets

Compound sets are based on the same principle as supersets. The only exception is that same-muscle-group exercises are paired rather than opposing-muscle-group exercises. For example, you may pair a deadlift with a glute bridge.

TIP

This method is slightly more advanced because you're working the same muscle groups for a longer duration without rest. This method isn't appropriate for your beginning clients.

Strip sets

Strip sets are also known as *drop sets* or *breakdown sets.* When you strip a set, you have your client perform all assigned reps in a set. Then you "strip" a certain amount of weight (such as five or ten pounds) and the client continues to perform as many reps as possible. Then you "strip" some more weight off; this continues on until the client can't do another rep, even with no weight. Save this technique for the end of the workout because there won't be any gas left in the tank when you're done!

WARNING

This technique is advanced and should only be used with clients whom you know very well and who are highly conditioned. If your client isn't that advanced, and you would like to try this technique, you still can. Just *don't* take it to failure. Instead, try doing one or two "strips."

Negatives

A *negative* is the eccentric phase (the relax phase of a muscle contraction); typically, it's the easiest part of a movement. Eccentric strength is 130 percent of concentric strength (the lifting part of a movement), which means a client can handle 30 percent more weight with an eccentric action. In other words, can *resist* 30 percent more force than they can *lift*.

Negative training is when you apply manual resistance during the lowering phase of a movement and the client resists the additional force, slowing the return to the start position, or when you help your client lift a weight that's 30 percent heavier than they would normally train with, and then have them resist the weight as they lower it.

See Spot run: Spotting techniques

Spots on your uniform: bad. Spotting your client: good. Any trainer will tell you that a good spot helps your clients to learn good form. It also goes a long way toward boosting their confidence to try lifting heavier weights, knowing you'll be there to help if it's too much. You need to recognize *when* and, more important, *where* to spot.

REMEMBER

A spot doesn't help your client if you aren't in a position where you can help to control the movement.

TIP

The most difficult movements to spot are free-weight and body-weight exercises. To spot free weights:

>> Always spot from a position of strength.

>> Place your hands by (never on) the joint closest to the weight.

>> Make sure you have stable body position.

>> Make sure you can handle your client's weight yourself if they lose control.

TIP

To spot body-weight exercises:

>> Spot from the client's nonmoving body part.

>> Place yourself in a position to protect the client from falling.

>> Watch the client's posture.

TIP

You can use spotting to increase your client's intensity. For example, you can apply additional light pressure to the arm of a machine to very gradually add extra resistance. Or, you might take the momentum out of a movement by slowing the lift at the top. These are all good methods that can gently ease your client into more intense training methods over time.

Let's Get Physical: Progressing Your Client's Cardio Program

Strength training isn't the only piece of a program that needs progression. Your client's aerobic fitness will adapt to training too. Here, I'll show you how to apply the *FITT-VP principle* to bump up the intensity of your client's cardio workouts and how to use interval training appropriately.

The FITT-VP principle

You can make a client's aerobic exercise program more challenging by manipulating the *FITT-VP principles of exercise prescription*. FITT-VP stands for *frequency* (how often), *intensity* (how hard), *time* (how long), *type* (mode of exercise), *volume* (total amount of work completed in a session or during a time period), *and progression* (advancing the program). The FITT-VP principle is a helpful framework for monitoring progress, but make sure you're only changing one thing at a time; otherwise you risk not knowing what worked and what didn't. There's also a good chance your client will end up doing more work than necessary to get the same results. And everyone loves doing extra cardio for the sake of doing extra cardio . . . said nobody ever.

You can also use the FITT-VP principle to challenge new clients who are experienced and already in good shape (like athletes).

Introducing your client to interval training

Interval training uses moderately paced work interspersed with short, high-intensity work periods. Typically, the goal with interval training is to challenge your client's cardiorespiratory system enough to increase aerobic capacity without overstressing them physiologically.

Whereas steady-state cardiovascular training is a common starting point for beginning clients, interval training may be the next program type you want to incorporate into your intermediate client's programming repertoire. There are two types of interval training: aerobic interval training and anaerobic interval training. Aerobic interval training is when your client works to a level that is harder than what they are used to but not maximal during their interval phase (higher-intensity work). Anaerobic interval training means pushing to the limit during the high-intensity bout.

I'm guessing you're most familiar with *high-intensity interval training* (HIIT), which alternates short bouts of a high intensity anerobic exercise with short bouts of less intense recovery. This type of interval training doesn't allow for full recovery between bouts, just enough to catch your breath before going all out again. HIIT has gained popularity in recent years because it's a very efficient way to increase aerobic fitness. In other words, it's hard work, but it doesn't take much time.

Some people get great satisfaction from pushing their limits and going all out during their workouts — the key word being *some*. Pushing your body above its lactate threshold means going 100 percent all-out until there's nothing left and you have to take a rest . . . not that you *want* to stop, you actually have to stop because you truly can't continue. Most people can push to this level for a few seconds, maybe a minute at most, and it's not a comfortable feeling.

WARNING

Please don't prescribe HIIT training to clients with little experience or those who have been sedentary for a long time. It's not necessary and you risk turning them off to exercise if they believe this is the only way to get in shape.

Table 15-1 shows a sample interval program on the treadmill, for both an aerobic program and an anaerobic program. Notice that the anaerobic program's speeds are higher, meaning that the client is going to be working harder during those cycles.

TABLE 15-1   ## Sample Treadmill Interval Program

Time	Aerobic Program	Anaerobic Program
Minutes 1:00 to 7:00	Warm-up (Speed 3.3)	Warm-up (Speed 4.0)
Minutes 7:00 to 8:00	Jog (Speed 5.0)	Run (Speed 8.0)
Minutes 8:00 to 10:00	Walk briskly (Speed 4.0)	Jog (Speed 6.0)
Minutes 10:00 to 11:00	Jog (Speed 6.0)	Sprint (Speed 10.0)
Minutes 11:00 to 13:00	Walk briskly (Speed 4.0)	Jog (Speed 6.0)
Minutes 13:00 to 14:00	Jog (Speed 6.0)	Sprint (Speed 10.0)
Minutes 14:00 to 20:00	Cool-down (Speed 3.5)	Cool-down (Speed 4.3)

REMEMBER

Interval training is also great for:

>> Breaking training plateaus

>> Increasing VO$_2$max (lung capacity)

>> Increasing stamina

>> Boosting metabolism

4

Growing Your Personal Training Business

It's all about getting big. This part describes everything you need to expand your business. First, I outline the basics on preparing for growth — how to document your systems and automate your processes so everything you need will be in place. Then, I describe all the ways you can expand your business, such as by adding massage services, nutritional services, and group classes; by giving seminars; and by selling fitness equipment.

When you start expanding, you'll likely need some help. That's why I also give you the scoop on hiring and — gulp! — firing employees, including information on placing want ads, conducting interviews, and staying on the right side of employment law.

Finally, I talk about how to build your business culture — that is, how to make the environment and atmosphere of your business conducive to great business, happy clients, and motivated employees.

Chapter **16**

Preparing for Growth: Automating and Documenting Your Workflow

The moment you realize, "Oh my gosh, I need help!" is a defining moment in your personal training career. Needing help typically means that you're at capacity and can't take any additional clients on yourself. Congratulations — this is a good "problem"! But before you run and post your help-wanted ad on LinkedIn, consider this scenario:

> You hire your first employee. (Find more on *how* to hire your employees in Chapter 17.) You say, "Here's your staff shirt, your first client is Monday at 9 a.m. Don't be late."

How well do you think that employee will fare? Most likely, not too well. Studies have shown that the more energy and time you invest into on-the-job training, the more successful your new employee's career with you is going to be. So yes, hiring employees means being accountable for your clients' success and for the success of your personal training team.

In this chapter, I go over the prep work that's necessary to make this important decision a successful one.

Planning for Growth

So how do you make sure that your team of trainers have the tools they need to be successful? You plan for it! You developed your business plan to be a successful business owner, and now you'll need to develop your operating plan to be a successful employer. Your *operating plan* outlines how your employees will carry out their responsibilities, defined by the steps needed to complete each task — the order of operations for your business, also referred to as *workflow*.

Before you even think about hiring some help, you need to have an overall plan of how that employee is going to operate within your business, the role and responsibilities they'll have, and how they'll contribute overall to the growth of your company. Sound like a lot? It is — and making the leap from personal trainer to employer isn't for everyone. Knowing what's involved, including the work you'll need to do up front as you map out your plan, will help you to decide if becoming an employer is right for you.

Thinking strategically

Strategic thinking sounds like a term you would hear thrown around in the Mergers and Acquisitions office of GiganticCo, Inc. Actually, strategic thinking is the process of developing your end vision for how your business will look when it's up and running successfully. It's a tool used by successful entrepreneurs — and no matter how large or small your company is, it's one that you should learn to use well.

Strategic thinking is a technique for framing and solving problems. Your first step is to assess your industry and your business — where you are currently — then identify where and how your efforts can be applied to reach your end goal.

Envisioning the end

If I were to ask you right now, "What is the end goal for you and your business?" would you be able to answer? When you plan for growth, you need to envision your ultimate goal as the end result, then work backward from there, planning what steps you need to take to reach your end goal successfully.

TIP

Break out a pen and paper and write down your ultimate goal for your business. Don't be afraid to describe, in detail, what it will look like. This goal statement will be very useful to you later on as your business changes and evolves, to help keep you on track toward reaching your goal.

Here are some things to keep in mind as you write:

>> What will your business look like? Will you have two employees or 20? Or 200?

>> What type of business structure do you need (LLC, sole proprietorship, and so on)? If your business is already established, will the current structure still work?

>> What type of employees do you need? Personal trainers? Front desk staff?

>> How many employees will you need?

>> What roles will they have in your company?

>> What skill sets do your employees need to have?

>> What types of problems should you be prepared to handle?

>> What types of obstacles will you need to overcome?

TIP

Every four years, the Small Business Administration (SBA) updates its strategy document, a resource that you can access for free to outline your current and future business goals and objectives. You can find it on the SBA website at www. sba.gov/document/support-sba-strategic-plan.

Working backward

Now that you've envisioned your goal for your business, write down the steps you'll need to take to get there. (Does this sound familiar? This process is just like creating your business plan.) Working backward, think of everything you need to put in place to support your end vision. Try doing some free-form brainstorming to help stimulate the old gray matter.

For example, say your goal is to own a 10,000 square foot personal training facility with 20 employees. That means you'll eventually be hiring 20 people. To do that, you'll need to have enough revenue to justify bringing on more staff. To do *that*, you'll need to do enough effective marketing to attract new clients. That's working backward.

This subject is one that a mentor, or someone who has grown a business before, can help you with and I highly recommend reaching out to SCORE for guidance. SCORE is a network of volunteer business mentors that entrepreneurs can connect with for free. In addition to mentorship with an expert in your field, you'll also have access to a treasure trove of educational content to help you succeed in business. To learn more about SCORE, check out its website at www.score.org.

Follow the Leader: Creating a System for Others to Follow

Now that you've defined your business goal, and you understand the type of support you'll need to get there, you're ready to create the how-to of your business — your business's rules and regulations, as well as the basics of how your company will run with others working in it.

Offering your clients consistent service

You have a special way of doing things — it's *your* way, the way that has worked so well that you now need to bring on other people to handle all the new clients clamoring for your stupendous services. And although you can't work with each client personally, you still want your clients to have the same exceptional experience with your new trainers as they would with you.

That exceptional experience is the result of your *consistency of service*. Consistency of service is what keeps your clients coming back. You want a team with the same mindset and upbeat, positive attitude for each client. You should also expect your trainers to dress the same way, spot clients the same way, perform initial consultations and fitness assessments the same way, and so on.

To deliver consistent service, you need to:

>> Consider how you hope clients will perceive your business and make sure your entire team understands it.

>> Document your business's *standard operating procedures (SOPs)* — that is, the exact way and order in which you expect your team to carry out their duties.

Developing your workflow

Without knowing it, you already have workflow systems in place. For example, when you perform an initial consultation or a fitness assessment, you follow specific steps unique to each of those sessions. Each step has a specific order that you execute it in for accuracy and for consistency. Each step and the order you execute it in are considered *workflow steps*.

When your staff performs those activities instead of you, outlining each step of a task, listing the details of how each step is performed, and identifying what happens after each step is important. The way your staff members perform is reflected in your attention to details. It's on you to develop your workflow so you can train your staff to do their jobs successfully and to your standards.

REMEMBER

You want your business to run smoothly as much as you want your clients to receive excellent service. You also need to provide your employees with a good working environment, where expectations are laid out well and they don't have to guess what to do.

TIP

Take a moment to think about the recurring things that you do as a personal trainer. Then list the steps needed to complete each one.

For example, suppose you want to outline for your employees how they should answer the phone and handle a call from a prospective client. Your workflow may look something like this:

Referred callers: The bulk of our clientele is obtained through client and physician referral. Some of these people may want to speak to the referred trainer directly. If the trainer is not available, let the caller know that you have the trainer's schedule and would be more than happy to set up an initial consultation. If they still want to speak directly with the trainer, take their name, number, and ask who referred them. Tell them their call will be returned as soon as possible.

Email inquiries: When prospects find our ad online, they'll typically fill out an inquiry form or email us for information about our services and pricing.

How to reply: Usually, when prospects inquire online about our services, price is the first question. Rather than giving a list of prices for each service, we let them know that we offer several services with pricing starting at $99/month for unlimited group classes. Then we invite them to schedule a free consultation to learn about what we offer and how we can help them.

Email script: We're a personal training and nutrition company, offering one-on-one and group personal training and nutrition services to clients at our private facility, in your home, or the gym you belong to. To get started the first step is to set up a free initial consultation where we will discuss your goals and background.

We offer several training options and I can help you decide on the right one for you based on your goals and your budget. The consultation lasts from 45 minutes to an hour. There won't be any physical exercising during this session, just discussion. For your convenience, our appointment availability is on our website and you can schedule a time online that works with your schedule. (Slight variations of this are fine; this is the general idea of how we handle new client inquiries.)

Who to book the consult with: If you're on the phone with a prospect, try to schedule the initial consultation before hanging up instead of directing them to the website. You can pull the schedule up online while you're on the phone and book the appointment during any available time slot. If the caller requests a specific trainer, please schedule the consultation with that trainer. If the trainer doesn't have an immediate opening, tell the prospect that you'll ask the trainer to get back to them right away with their availability.

Give directions to the facility over the phone or email directions to the prospect, especially if your location isn't easy to find.

If the prospect doesn't schedule an initial consult, ask if you can email them with additional information.

This is just one example of an everyday situation you should document for your employees. You can apply this approach to other scenarios too, such as:

>> Booking and rescheduling training appointments

>> Handling cancellations

>> Performing the initial consult

>> Selling a personal training package

>> Collecting payment

>> Performing a fitness assessment

>> Performing a personal training session

Once you've outlined steps for each task that your employees will be doing, the next step is to map out how all tasks and steps integrate with each other in the everyday flow of your business, including who will handle each one.

Mapping your workflow

Try drawing a flowchart of the daily activities in your business and how they integrate with one another. This chart will give you a bird's-eye view of your business so you can spot potential conflicts before you actually have other people following the steps in your plan. See Figure 16-1 for a sample flowchart.

Administrative			Trainer		
Opening					
Reception AM			**Trainer AM**		
1. Check voice mail.			1. Disarm alarm.		
—Return all calls and distribute messages.			2. Turn on lights, fans, radio.		
2. Complete items on to-do report.			3. Check AND save messages.		
3. Confirm next day's new appointments.			—Respond to urgent ones.		
Mid-day					
Reception AM—End of Shift			**Trainer AM—End of Shift**		
1. Validate sessions in schedule.			1. Pick up cups and towels.		
2. List to-do's.			2. Wipe down showers.		
3. Face front.			3. Wipe down equipment.		
4. Stock bathrooms.			4. Stock bathrooms.		
5. Bag towels.			5. Bag towels.		
6. Check trash.			6. Check trash.		
Administrative Manager			**Head Trainer—End of Team Trainer Shift**		
1. Count bank.			1. Approve team trainer leave.		
2. Approve reception AM leave.					
Reception PM—Beginning of Shift			**Trainer PM—Beginning of Shift**		
1. Review and complete to-do's.					
2. Validate sessions in schedule.					
Closing					
Reception PM			**Trainer PM**		
1. Enter next day's appointments on daylog.			1. Pick up cups and towels.		
2. Print out trainer schedules.			2. Wipe down showers.		
3. List to-do's.			3. Wipe down equipment.		
4. Face front.			4. Stock bathrooms.		
5. Stock bathrooms.			5. Bag towels.		
6. Bag towels.			6. Check trash.		
7. Take out trash.			7. Turn off lights, fans, radio.		
			8. Arm alarm.		

FIGURE 16-1:
A flowchart can help you and your employees manage the day-to-day operations of your business.

TIP

You can create flowcharts for any system in your business, such as selling, training, hiring, and so on. Simply list out the steps and actions involved, who performs them and when — and you have the meat and potatoes of your operations manual!

Writing Job Descriptions

Now that you have all your systems mapped out, and you know which employee will be doing which tasks, you need to write job descriptions for each position you're planning to hire for.

A job description is important because it defines what the job entails. You'll want to include a transparent description of the work involved and the minimum requirements for applying (education, experience, skills, and so on). An accurate job description is crucial — you need qualified candidates to apply! That, and a clear job description will avert the oh-so-familiar "but it isn't in my job description!"

TIP

A well-written job description provides a concise summary of everything important about the job, such as:

>> **The job title**

>> **Individual tasks involved**

>> **Methods used to complete the tasks**

>> **The job objective:** This statement is generally a summary designed to orient the reader to the general nature, level, purpose, and objective of the job. The summary should describe the broad function and scope of the position and be no longer than three to four sentences.

>> **The purpose and responsibilities of the job**

>> **The relationship of the job to other jobs**

>> **Qualifications needed for the job**

>> **The relationships and roles relevant to the employee's position within the company, including any supervisory positions, subordinating roles, and other working relationships.**

>> **The job location (that is, where the work will be performed)**

>> **The equipment to be used in the performance of the job:** For example, does your company's computers run in a Mac or Windows environment?

>> **The range of pay for the position (include this to avoid interviewing applicants with salary requirements outside of your pay range)**

REMEMBER

Keep in mind that the job descriptions you're creating now are a starting point. They're the base for future employees' job development and training and you'll want to be sure to update them regularly. As your business grows and evolves, so must the team that you rely on to keep it running like a well-oiled machine.

TIP

When writing a job description, keep each statement short and clear. Be sure to structure your sentences in classic verb/object and explanatory phrases. Figure 16-2 shows a sample job description.

Job Description
Team Trainer Position

1. Description
The UltraFit Team Trainer (TT) position is a part-time, salaried training position. The TT reports to the Manager.

2. Qualifications
The TT is required to have current personal training certification from one or more of the following certifying bodies: ACSM, NSCA, or ACE. The TT must also maintain current CPR certification from the American Red Cross or the American Heart Association. The TT must have two years of practical experience prior to employment.

3.Duties
The duties of the TT include, but are not limited to:

3A.1 Personal Training/Nutrition—General Duties

Maintaining and promoting client relationships

The TT will provide all clients with an exceptional, five-star training experience. To do this, the TT will:

   i. Be ready 5 minutes prior to all training sessions.

   ii. Train clients no fewer than 45 minutes, or no more than 75 minutes (unless otherwise agreed upon by management).

   iii. Train each client uniquely and specifically for his individual goals.

   iv. Be a positive source of encouragement, education and feedback for each client.

3A.2 Personal Training/Nutrition — Specific Duties

   i. Become completely knowledgeable about the exercise and nutrition methodologies practiced by the company.

   ii. Become completely knowledgeable about each new client's needs, goals, location of training, package purchased, and assessment parameters prior to assessment.

   iii. Provide fitness and nutrition assessment, evaluation, prescription, education, and follow-up to clientele of the company, utilizing company-set protocols.

   iv. Accurately record each workout in client's workbook, providing date of session, session number, exercises performed during session, and weights and repetitions performed per set per exercise per session.

   v. Provide accurate, detailed notes of client progress in client files.

3B. Administrative

Maintain all paperwork critical to the operations of the company

The TT is responsible for all paperwork pertinent to the daily functions and overall health of the company and the company's clientele.

3C. Maintenance

Maintain equipment and fixtures of facility

The TT is responsible for the maintenance of the company's equipment and facilities on a daily basis.

4. Compensation
Compensation for this position is $64,000.00 annually.

I acknowledge and agree to the above statements and terms:

Signed:

Employee: _____   Date: _____

Manager: _____   Date: _____

FIGURE 16-2:
Have your new hires sign a job description to keep on file in case you ever need to gently remind an employee what your expectations are.

Charting Your Progress: Creating Your Organizational Chart

An organizational chart shows who's in what position and their relationships to one another. The *org chart* shows employees who they report to, who reports to them, and what positions they could advance to within the company.

TIP

When you build your own org chart, you need to make the level of each position clear to your employees. Too often, org charts can become confusing, so keep it as simple as possible.

Here's how to build your own org chart:

1. **Start with yourself — create a box and enter your name and your title.**

2. **Create a row of boxes below yours for all the positions that will report to you; enter the title and position for each one.**

3. **Create connecting lines between your box and those of the people who report to you.**

4. **Create smaller boxes below the row of boxes directly beneath you to demonstrate the positions that report to your subordinates.**

Figure 16-3 shows an example of an organizational chart for a personal training company.

TIP

Here are some tips for creating org charts that will help — and not confuse — your employees.

» Draw your org chart on paper or create one in Microsoft Word.

» Make the box sizes correspond to the ranking in the company. Boxes are usually larger for higher-ups, the same size for peers, and smaller for subordinates.

» Draw all positions, even if you don't have an employee in place for that position yet. Show the position as TBH (to be hired) or TBD (to be determined).

» For positions that report to you for direction but report to another position primarily, use a dashed line rather than a solid line to connect their boxes to yours.

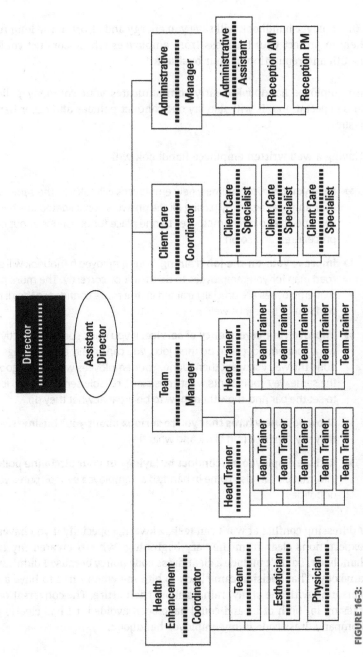

FIGURE 16-3:
An organizational chart helps everyone know their relationship to everyone else.

Creating Your Employee Handbook

An employee handbook will save you energy and effort in the long run. It will also help to protect your business from employees whose conduct could damage the health and reputation of your business.

An employee handbook clearly communicates your company policies, benefits, and expectations. It will also lay out conduct policies and other hard-to-address issues.

TIP

Having a well written employee handbook will:

>> **Save you time.** Most times, new employees will ask you the same questions over and over again. By having all the answers consolidated in a handbook, you'll be able to refer employees to one place for questions about office procedures, and so on.

>> **Improve your on-the-job training.** Your employee handbook will serve as a road map for your employees to do their jobs correctly. The more procedures that employees are officially trained in, the more confidence they'll have in performing their jobs well.

>> **Improve your consistency of service.** If you don't spell out exactly how you want your employees to do their jobs, you can't really expect things to get done the way you want them done. Your employees want to do good work the same way your clients want consistent, reliable service — and it's on you to set the bar and show them how to be great at what they do.

>> **Show your new hires that you're serious about your business.** After all, as they say, "There it is in black and white"!

>> **Reduce employee misconduct by laying out your discipline policies.** This information can also come in handy if an employee ever disputes your rules or policies.

TRUE STORY

Addressing conflict at work can feel awkward, especially if you haven't made your expectations clear from the very beginning. When I created my first employee handbook, I didn't include a clear dress code policy because I didn't want to offend anybody. That decision came back to bite me when I had to have a difficult conversation with one of my trainers about their attire. The conversation was embarrassing for both of us and could have been avoided if I had clearly explained the company dress code in my employee handbook.

Chapter **17**

Hiring Additional Staff

For years, you were probably someone else's employee — working hours you didn't choose for a paycheck that you didn't set. Now it's payback time — time for you to hire employees of your own!

But you'll soon find that there's more to hiring trainers than posting a "help wanted" ad online. You need to understand the employment laws in your state, learn how to find the best trainers, and understand how to keep employees whistling while they work. That's what this chapter is all about.

Even if you aren't hiring other trainers, you probably *are* hiring other professionals like accountants and attorneys. In this chapter, you discover how to find the best professionals for your business.

Outsourcing Is In: Hiring Professionals

Even if you don't need employees, you need employees. Does that make sense? Well, let's put it another way: Even if you don't plan on hiring other personal trainers in your business, you need to outsource certain tasks to professionals.

You can take the time to master the skills needed to handle these tasks yourself, but your clients probably aren't looking to hire a personal trainer/lawyer/painter/tailor just like you're probably not looking to hire a jack or jill of all trades to keep your business on the up and up. Your clients want a personal trainer who knows their stuff inside and out, so focus on being the best professional personal trainer you can be and leave the rest to the other professionals.

TIP

Consider hiring the professionals listed in the following sections. For more information on hiring an attorney, accountant, and insurance agent, check out Chapter 6.

Graphic designer

As you find out in Chapter 8, you can create your own logo and build your online presence yourself. But if you want to look truly professional, I recommend hiring a designer as soon as your budget allows to create (or update) your logo, website, and any other branding materials you will use to promote your business.

To find a designer who can create graphics that will have clients flocking to your doors, try these suggestions:

>> Look online at fitness websites and blogs (yes, blogging is still a thing) to get an idea of what you like. Usually if you look at the bottom of the homepage, you can find out who designed the website and you can contact them to see if they're a good fit for your business.

>> Ask other small-business owners and personal trainers who they use.

>> Search your LinkedIn network. You'll find more information about the graphic designers you're considering and you can see who other professionals in your network recommend.

>> Do a Google search for "graphic designer" — just be prepared to sift through a massive list of options.

TIP

Can't afford a designer? Try these tips:

>> **Barter your services for the services you need.** If you're just getting started and don't have a lot of cash, you might be able to find someone who's interested in trading personal training sessions for professional design services. Think carefully about bartering before doing it though. Some states consider bartered hours as taxable income, and you need to make sure you understand your state's rules so you don't get yourself into a bind at tax time. I'm telling you about bartering so you know it's an option, but I don't recommend making a habit of it. Your business needs revenue to survive and you can't live off of bartered time.

>> **Contact a design school to find designers-in-training.** Students are usually willing to charge less than full-time professionals to gain experience and credentials. You can also find freelancers who charge less on Fiverr or Upwork.

SEO specialist

Hiring a designer to build your website won't pay off if nobody can see it. A *search engine optimization* (SEO for short) specialist can identify strategies for increasing traffic to your website by *optimizing* it for search engines. In other words, this person can make your business appear closer to the top of search engine results pages when a prospective client searches online for personal trainers. That being said, I recommend starting with some very basic steps that won't cost you anything before working on SEO. Make sure your business is set up for Google search and set up a Facebook business page.

Social media manager

If your website is your virtual business card, think of social media as your online living room. Being active on social media is necessary for building your online presence, and more important, you can use it to interact with current and prospective clients. If trying to figure out how to use all the different social media channels feels daunting, you're not alone. It seems like there's a new one to figure out every day, and just when you think you're getting the hang of one, it's not relevant anymore. Not only that, but posting regularly to social media and engaging with your audience can be a full-time job, and it actually is a full-time job for a *social media manager*.

Hiring a social media manager will free you up to run your business without having to worry about managing your online presence. They'll put your business on several social media channels and can manage them for you. This means posting regular content, but more importantly, they'll be your online voice. They can respond to comments on your posts, reply to messages, and they'll keep you informed about what people are saying online about your business.

Handyperson

If you own your own facility, what happens when the air conditioning breaks or you need someone to assemble your new equipment? You don't need to have a professional waiting in the wings, but knowing who you can contact to fix things and build stuff from time to time will save you from lots of headaches down the road. Ask friends, family, or your clients for referrals. You can also search for help on Thumbtack, a website where a variety of local service providers advertise their services. Searching for services on Thumbtack is free.

REMEMBER

Find a good handyperson and build a good relationship before you actually need them.

Internet service provider

If you plan to have a website, send out an email newsletter, or answer email inquiries, you need an internet service provider (ISP) to keep you connected to the web. Depending on where you live, you'll be able to shop around for the best ISP for your business. Some areas have more options than others and you can ask around or check online to see what your options are.

TIP

Many ISPs also offer phone and cable TV service and you'll save money if you bundle services with one provider. It's worth your time to shop around a bit to find the right fit for your business.

Payroll service

A payroll service cuts checks or manages direct deposits for your employees' pay and also handles tax withholdings. You can find payroll services online, or ask other business owners for referrals. You can also use QuickBooks to manage payroll yourself if you don't want to use an outside service, but if you do, I strongly recommend hiring a bookkeeper to help. Even if you only have one employee, keeping your financial records current and paying your employee on time is time consuming. And you need to pay your employees on time, no exceptions. A part-time bookkeeper can do this for you and at the same time keep your financial records organized — which your accountant will appreciate when tax-time rolls around.

Pumping Up Your Ranks: Hiring Other Trainers

So you're ready to expand your business and take on more trainers. Congratulations! This is what many trainers dream of. You can't add more hours to the day, after all, so hiring help who will let you serve more people (and make more money) than you can by yourself is almost always a boon.

Don't write that want ad just yet, though. First, you need the scoop on hiring, dealing with, and (gulp!) firing employees.

Uncovering where trainers hide out

Unfortunately, walking into the local gym and shouting, "Who wants to quit this dump and come work for me?" is bad form. But I have the scoop on how you can find trainers who would be happy to join you and pave the way toward your goal of world domina — um, your goal of a healthy world for all:

>> **Post your job opening on LinkedIn.** Be sure to outline exactly what you expect so your network can refer the right candidates. For example, if you want someone with a four-year degree and CPR certification who can work a 40-hour workweek, say that in your job description.

>> **Use word of mouth.** Your clients know you well and can suggest people who will fit in with your culture. Some of your clients might even want to be personal trainers, and considering that they chose to pay you, they're on board with what you do and they're familiar with your training methods and your gym culture.

TRUE STORY

Sometimes the best trainers aren't trainers at all. One of my best-ever hires was a Starbucks barista who I convinced to give personal training a try. Every morning, I would watch her greet her regular customers by name and have their drinks ready without them having to tell her what they wanted. One day, she mentioned to me that she was thinking about becoming a yoga instructor, and I asked if she had ever thought about becoming a personal trainer. The rest is history, and not only did the barista give personal training a try, she went on to build a successful personal training business that she still owns today. Always keep your eyes open and ears peeled for people who you think would be great personal trainers because you can teach someone with a great personality how to train clients, but you can't give a boring personal trainer a new personality.

Evaluating a trainer's potential

In a perfect world, you'd be able to pull random trainers off the street and they'd be model employees. But alas, the world is not perfect — so if you want good employees, you have to do some research on the people who are applying to work with you.

I have always sought out people with personality and a positive attitude above all else, even if they didn't have personal training experience, and I had a simple two-step process to help me understand everything I needed to know about a potential trainer before hiring them.

Step 1: The phone screen

Before scheduling an interview, I would schedule a 30-minute phone call with a candidate. Talking on the phone first allowed me to gauge their enthusiasm — and how my clients might perceive this person.

If the candidate was an experienced personal trainer, I didn't ask anatomy and physiology questions to test their knowledge. Instead, I asked them to describe how they would handle typical situations like a client showing up late for a training session or not following their program. Their answers to these questions told me a lot more about their character than their practical knowledge ever could.

After the phone screen, I either scheduled an interview or let the candidate know they would not be moving forward to the interview.

Step 2: The interview

During the interview, I ask the typical questions (more on that later). Candidates with prepared answers indicate to me that they are serious about making a good impression. I also ask them why they would be a good fit for our team, and if they talk about our core values and training philosophy — information freely available on my website — I know they had done their research. Attention to details and showing up prepared are key attributes I look for in personal trainers and I use the interview to determine whether the candidate already had these qualities or if trying to instill them would even be worth my time and energy. I give you more information about interviews later in this chapter.

Being your own human-resources officer

Major companies have human-resources officers who hire employees and make sure that everything regarding the hiring and firing of employees is on the up-and-up. You don't have this luxury, so it's up to you to hire and fire employees, do interviews, and understand employment law. In the following sections, I show you how.

Understanding labor or employment law

Labor law and *employment law* are the same thing — statutes found at all levels of government, from county to federal, that determine the rights and obligations that arise out of an employment contract. Labor law regulates everything from the initial hiring process and benefits to job duties and termination of employees, and protects employees from discrimination and unfair labor practices.

DOING BACKGROUND CHECKS

If you've ever tried renting an apartment, you know that the landlord does a background check to make sure you're not some sort of psychopath (and that you can afford the rent). In the same way, you may want to do some sleuthing into your applicants' criminal backgrounds before you hire them.

You generally have the right to access arrest and conviction records that are public information, but whether you can use such information for hiring decisions varies from state to state. Some states allow employers to discriminate based on criminal convictions but not on arrests. Other states apply varying rules depending on the position or industry the candidate is applying for. Check with your lawyer to find out what the rules are in your state.

REMEMBER

Your lawyer (see Chapter 6 for tips on finding one) can help you understand labor law as well as write up employment contracts and other contracts and forms you need in your business relationship with an employee.

Knowing the costs of hiring others

Think that wages are your only employee-related cost? Think again. You also have to pay for workers' compensation insurance, unemployment tax, and Social Security tax:

>> **Workers' compensation insurance:** Workers' compensation insurance (or as the cool kids say, *workers' comp*) covers your employees if they get sick, injured, or even killed on the job. The benefits they receive include medical expenses, lost wages, vocational rehabilitation, and death benefits. Workers' comp doesn't protect just the employee — it also protects the employer (that's you). Before workers' comp existed, a serious injury to an employee could put you out of business. Now, all the lost wages, rehab, and so on are paid by the insurance, no matter who's at fault.

Workers' comp requirements vary from state to state, so check with your state's insurance commissioner's office for more info (you can find contact information online). Your insurance agent can also help you with the details.

>> **Social Security and Medicare taxes:** Social Security (also known as FICA) taxes provide for benefits for retired workers and the disabled and their dependents. Medicare taxes provide medical benefits for certain people when they reach retirement age. Not only are you required to withhold Social Security and Medicare taxes from your employees' paychecks, you also have to match their contributions. So if the employee owes $7,000 in Social Security

and Medicare taxes, you deduct half of that from the employee's paycheck and pay the other half yourself as the employer. (You may have noticed that if you were self-employed, you would have to pay the whole $7,000 yourself.)

>> **Federal unemployment tax:** Most employers have to pay federal unemployment tax, though if you're a sole proprietorship or partnership, you don't have to pay the tax on your own compensation.

WARNING

Before you start putting out want ads, you should know that all these taxes and benefits can cost you an additional 20 to 35 percent over and above an employee's gross wages.

TIP

I could write another book just to explain all the taxes and other costs associated with hiring employees! Contact your accountant for more detailed information.

Identifying when an independent contractor is really an employee

You may find hiring independent contractors (sometimes called *freelance trainers*) more convenient. But the government sets strict rules on who is an employee and who is an independent contractor, and the distinction is important because it determines how you handle taxes and what laws govern your relationship with the person you hire. For example, if the person you hire is an independent contractor, you don't have to match their Social Security and Medicare contributions. That might look good on paper, but you should also know that an independent contractor has more autonomy than an employee. Simply put, this means independent contractors don't have to follow your company policies the same way an employee does.

TIP

How do you know if the person you hired is an employee or an independent contractor? Independent contractors:

>> Are in business for themselves

>> Make quarterly federal and state income-tax payments

>> Pay the entire contribution for Social Security and Medicare taxes

>> Provide their own insurance and benefits

>> Are not subject to wage and hour regulations

>> Have no employer-employee relationship with you

REMEMBER

If you're confused about whether someone you've hired counts as an employee or an independent contractor for tax purposes, consult your lawyer or accountant.

Interviewing Potential Employees

So many times you've been interviewed for jobs, and now it's your turn to put someone in the hot seat. But it can be just as nerve-wracking to be the person on the other side of the desk. Here I tell you everything you need to know about planning for and conducting interviews.

Arranging and setting up interviews

Set up the interview in a place you're comfortable in. You can interview applicants:

>> In your home (make sure you have a desk and chairs set up)

>> At your gym

>> At a cafe — as long as you pick up the tab!

TIP

As for what time to conduct the interview, try to be accommodating; many people have full-time jobs and can't get away during the 9-to-5 workday. If finding a time becomes too challenging, consider conducting the interview over Zoom or other online video platform either before or after regular business hours.

Conducting the interview

When you're interviewing a potential employee, it's okay to be nervous, but you need to be confident! Here are tips that will help you conduct a great interview and make the right hiring decisions for your business:

>> **Dress for success.** Wearing business-casual attire or your training uniform for interviews makes you look professional and reflects the dress code policy in your employee handbook.

>> **Write out your questions.** You won't be reading from them like a robot, but having your questions in front of you will help you remember what to ask and will ensure that you ask all applicants the same questions so you can compare apples with apples. Avoid questions that can be answered with a simple "yes" or "no." (More on what questions to ask — and not ask — is later in this chapter.)

>> **Make a mental note of your first impression.** How is the applicant dressed? Did they have a firm handshake? Do they smile and sound enthusiastic about the job?

>> **Put the candidate at ease.** Try some friendly small talk to break the ice. A good way to do this is to share your company's background and details about the job the candidate is applying for.

>> **Ask your questions, and give the applicant time to formulate answers.** Ask follow-up questions such as "Why did you do that?" and "How did that happen?"

>> **Take notes during the interview.** After the dust clears, remembering whether it was Applicant A or Applicant B who said such-and-such can be difficult. A big advantage of doing a Zoom interview is that you can record it. You can go back and listen more intentionally when you don't need to take detailed notes.

>> **Near the end of the interview, ask the applicant what questions they have for you.** This gives the applicant a chance to clarify details about the job and it shows you who's done their research. Does the applicant ask questions about things they should already know (such as what client population you service), or do they ask intelligent questions about your training process? There's a big difference between the applicant who asks, "I noticed on your main competitor's website that they offer in-person and online training. Have you considered offering online training?" and the one who asks, "How many vacation days do I get?"

>> **Let the applicant know what to expect. When (and how) will you let them know if they got the job or not?**

What you should ask

They're what make an interview an interview — the questions. But how do you know what to ask? Here are some suggestions:

>> What made you choose personal training as a career path?

>> What experience have you had training people?

>> Tell me about a mistake you made with a client and how you handled it.

>> What interests you most about this company?

>> What is your greatest strength? What's one thing you could be better at?

>> Tell me about an accomplishment in your last job that you're proud of.

What you should never ask

WARNING

In a nutshell, you can only ask about the applicant's skills and experience as they relate to the job. Other questions can be considered discriminatory — as you probably know, strict laws prohibit discriminating against job applicants based on sex, race, disability, religion, marital status, and so on. Here are some questions that are taboo:

>> **Do you have any disabilities?** Ask this question, and you can run afoul of the Americans with Disabilities Act.

>> **Do you plan to have children?** Although it's true that parents sometimes have to take time off to care for their kids, basing a hiring decision on this fact is considered discrimination.

>> **Are you married?** If you ask this question, it can be interpreted that you discriminate against married or unmarried employees.

>> **How old are you/what is your date of birth?** Age discrimination is another no-no. However, if you're interviewing a teenager, you can ask if the candidate is at least 16 years old.

>> **Have you ever filed a workers' compensation claim or been injured on the job?** This question is considered a disability-related one.

>> **What is your sex/race/creed/color/religion/national origin?**

>> **When were you discharged from the military?** Discriminating based on military duty is illegal.

>> **What is your maiden name (for female applicants)?** This is just another way of asking whether the applicant is married and is just as illegal.

>> **Are you a U.S. citizen?** However, you *can* ask if they can legally work in the United States.

>> **Have you ever been arrested?** You may, however, ask if the person has been convicted, as long as the question is accompanied by a statement saying that a conviction will not necessarily disqualify an applicant for employment. A safer option is to require a criminal background check, which is particularly important if your employees will be interacting in any way with minors.

Payday! Dealing with Compensation

The best things in life may indeed be free, but those people you hired will expect something from you besides a hearty "Good morning!" and the occasional pat on the back. It's called money. Here, I tell you how to develop a payment plan that will tickle your employees pink without putting your business in the red.

Developing a pay/commission schedule

Determining what to pay your employees can be difficult. You want to be fair and for them to make a decent living — and at the same time, you don't want to go broke yourself.

REMEMBER

Your business plan (see Chapter 5) will help you make a decision. According to the plan, what are your overhead costs? What are your taxes and other expenses? Figure out exactly what your overhead costs are — meaning, how much of your total monthly revenue does it take to keep the doors open and the lights on? Then you need to factor in taxes and other expenses (like money for emergencies, savings, and your own salary). Looking at what's left, you'll be able to figure out what you can comfortably pay your employees.

TIP

Find out how much other personal trainers are charging clients and paying employees. You should have a range of numbers. Where do you want to land on that scale?

Have you ever noticed how you can walk into certain stores and the sales clerks are all over you like ants on a donut crumb? And the sales clerks make sure you know their names when they help you? These employees are working on commission — they get a percentage of every sale they make. The good news is that commissions can motivate your employees to work harder, and you pay only for results. The bad news is that working on commission can be stressful for employees and annoying for customers. Also, determining how to pay commissions can be difficult. If a trainer sells a $2,000 package and collects only $1,000 before the client quits, do you pay commission on the $2,000 or the $1,000?

REMEMBER

Your accountant and mentor (see Chapter 6) can help you decide whether to pay commissions, and if so, how to do it.

Motivating employees

A client walks in, and the trainer, after finishing a conversation with another trainer about the latest *New York Times* bestseller, saunters over and greets the client with a grunt. That's one unmotivated employee.

REMEMBER

Unmotivated employees — employees who don't feel valued, appreciated, or challenged — are usually unhappy employees, and unhappy employees equal unhappy clients.

TIP

Believe it or not, motivation isn't only about money. Even if you pay your employees sky-high rates, if they're working in a toxic environment or if you let clients treat them badly or you don't praise them for a job well done, they'll quickly lose their motivation to do their best. Read on to find out how to keep your employees engaged and productive.

Rewarding employees with perks and benefits

Which employer would you work harder for: the one who offers a paycheck and that's it, or the one who rewards you above and beyond the expected paycheck for doing a good job? If you're like most people, you'd prefer the job with the rewards.

TIP

Here are ways to motivate your employees through perks and benefits.

>> **Offer extra paid time off, such as an extra 30 minutes for lunch or a paid day off.**

>> **Offer benefits like a 401(k) plan and health insurance.** Talk to your accountant and insurance agent for more information.

>> **Give praise.** Employees appreciate knowing they're appreciated. A thank-you note or even a simple "You handled that situation really well!" can go a long way toward keeping an employee motivated.

>> **Give employee discounts on products you carry.**

>> **Give gift cards for local businesses.**

Creating sales incentives

Many businesses, both personal training and otherwise, motivate employees with sales incentives. For example, the employee who sells the most personal training packages may get a cash bonus or other prize.

WARNING

Based on my own experience, I don't recommend sales incentives. The personal training industry is sales-driven enough as it is, and sales incentives can turn your employees from caring trainers into hard-sell machines whose goal is not to recommend what their clients need, but instead to sell them the biggest personal training packages and the most products.

TIP

Ask your employees what they want. They might actually prefer a sales bonus over extra paid time off. You won't know if you don't ask!

Offering flexible and part-time schedules

If you can swing it, offer part-time and flexible schedules to trainers who love working with you but don't love the hours. For example, if one of your trainers is a single parent or has a second job, they may appreciate being able to work odd hours.

TRUE STORY

I once hired a trainer who had recently retired after working for years as an executive for a large company. She wanted to only train part-time and no early mornings. I decided to give her a shot, and she was one of the best trainers I ever hired — she loved her work and she was happy because she could work on her own terms. If I could have had ten clones of this woman working only part-time rather than five other people working 40-hour weeks, I would have.

Providing a happy place to work

TIP

A toxic work environment will lead to unhappy employees. Would *you* be motivated to go to work in a dank, smelly gym full of rude coworkers? If you have your own workspace, follow these tips to keep it pleasant for your employees (and your clients).

>> **Keep it clean!** Make sure the equipment and other surfaces are dust-free, that the bathrooms are clean and sanitized, and that the air is fresh. Everyone (even you) has to step up here, but staying on top of day-to-day cleanliness just takes a little effort from everyone. For deep cleaning, unless you want to do it yourself, I recommend hiring a cleaning service to come in after hours as soon as you can afford it. Depending on the size of your facility and how many people are using it every day, you might be able to get away with only having it cleaned a few times each week, especially if everyone is doing their part to tidy up during business hours.

>> **Make sure the equipment is in good shape.** After all, what trainer wants to train clients on equipment that's rusty or falling apart?

>> **Keep a small fridge stocked with water and healthy snacks for everyone to share.**

>> **Make sure employees have a breakroom or other space they can go to eat lunch and take breaks in private.**

>> **Set the tone for the environment that you work in.** If you want the atmosphere of your facility to feel fun and upbeat, try playing background music with a good beat.

>> **Celebrate birthdays and have fun together.** Everyone deserves to be celebrated on their birthday and it means a lot when your coworkers remember your special day. Consider taking the entire team out to lunch to celebrate birthdays. I hosted an annual holiday party at my house for my team and we all looked forward to it every year. We enjoyed good food and wine together and had a white elephant gift exchange. The best white elephant gift I ever got was a shake weight. Remember those?

Parting Is Such Sweet Sorrow: Firing and Laying Off Employees

Downsize, lay off, pink slip — no matter how you say it, it's an unpleasant task. But reality is, at some point you may have to fire an employee. Maybe they had disciplinary problems, like showing up late for sessions, or maybe your job training isn't sticking and they're less competent than you would like (though if you read the earlier section on hiring the best employees, you may improve your chances). Here, I show you how to make the process as painless as possible.

Understanding the law

Before you take on an employee, you explain the job requirements and make a deal: "You do X for me and I'll pay you Y dollars per month." If the person is not able to do X, you're not obligated to keep that person on the payroll; you're entitled to find someone else who can do the job.

TECHNICAL STUFF

Under the *at-will* employment doctrine, either the employee or the employer can terminate employment at any time, for any reason, except for reasons involving illegal discriminatory action. Talk to your lawyer for more information.

If you implied or expressed job security for a certain amount of time (that is, you gave the employee reason to believe they would have a job for a certain length of time — for example, you said the job would last one year), you need proper justification for letting the employee go sooner. Examples of proper justification are neglect of duty, dishonesty or unfaithfulness, misuse of trade secrets, and theft.

REMEMBER

As always, consult your lawyer, who can help you draw up employment contracts and make sure you're staying on the right side of the law.

Documenting disciplinary actions

Remember when you were in high school and your teacher threatened to put a negative note in your permanent file? Well, now that you're a personal-training-business owner, you too must create a paper trail when it comes to disciplinary actions. If you don't record your employees' violations and the actions you took as a result, you have no way to justify the steps you took to avoid firing that person. And if you're sued for wrongful termination, it's your word against theirs if you can't produce a written timeline of events.

TIP

Make sure you have a plan for handling employee violations. For example, consider using a three-strikes policy like this one (you can modify it however you want):

>> **Strike 1:** The employee gets a verbal warning, which lasts for 30 days.

>> **Strike 2:** The employee gets a written warning, which goes into their permanent file.

>> **Strike 3:** The employee gets paid time off — or *decision-making leave*. The employee is to use this time off to either choose to change the problematic behavior or to leave the company. If the employee leaves, it's voluntary. If they stay on, they'll be required to sign an agreement stating that their employment will be terminated immediately if the problem behavior happens again.

Making the break

TIP

It's time to do the deed — you just can't keep that employee on any longer, and you need to let them go. Here's how to do it with as little emotional (and legal!) trauma as possible:

>> **Think hard before you do it.** Remember that even a very weak job performance can be brought up to snuff with enough effort, especially if the person is eager to learn. Remember also that firing someone can have a traumatic impact on your staff and exposes you to potential lawsuits. Do you really need to fire this person?

>> **Give the person a chance to change.** Don't fire someone out of the blue — make sure you give them every chance to improve. If you do and they don't, you're less likely to be hit with a lawsuit. If you document all employee violations and disciplinary actions, they won't be surprised when you show them the door.

>> **Talk to your lawyer.** If you have any doubts or questions about firing someone, talk to your lawyer. It may seem like a hassle, but compare that to the hassle of a lawsuit!

>> **Plan what you're going to say, and stick to it.** Believe it or not, if you offer kind words about the employee's performance to soften the blow, you open yourself up to potential lawsuits. After all, if you liked the employee's performance enough to compliment it, why are you firing them? Plan what you're going to say — and don't even hint at anything positive regarding the employee's performance.

>> **Stay cool.** Soon this person will be gone from your business forever, so don't let them get to you if they lash out or become verbally abusive.

>> **Be nice.** Although you shouldn't say anything positive about the employee's job performance, that doesn't mean you have to be cruel. Being fired is a traumatic experience for most people. Be kind.

IN THIS CHAPTER

» Leading by example

» Taking responsibility for your business

» Managing micromanagement

» Understanding and communicating your mission

» Training your employees

Chapter **18**

Establishing Your Business Culture

B usiness culture — it sounds like your personal training company is traipsing around European museums *ooh*ing and *aah*ing over Picassos and Matisses. But really, your business culture is everything that makes your business what it is — your leadership skills, your mission, your attitude, your team. It's your beliefs and values, the unwritten rules in your company, the "way we do things here."

In this chapter, I show you how to establish a business culture that keeps clients and employees — and yourself! — happy and excited to come to work.

THE BUCK STOPS HERE

Realizing that the health and well-being of your entire business — including your clients, your employees, and yourself — rests squarely on your well-conditioned shoulders-can be scary. Your business will succeed or fail based on your own behavior.

Your employees may love you, they may adore your business — but if your company were to go belly up, they'd simply find different jobs. They don't have as much invested in the business as you do. That's why you need to take responsibility for your business — because nobody else is going to do it for you. For example:

- **If an employee continuously makes mistakes, fails to follow up with clients, or comes in late, you need to take quick action to put a stop to the bad behavior and to reinforce the behavior you want.** You can't just let it slide, hoping the problems will go away. They won't. And when other employees see what one staff member is getting away with, they may decide to try it for themselves.

- **If sexual harassment occurs in your workplace, you may be held liable if you knew about it and didn't take steps to stop it.**

- **If clients continue to make the same complaints — for example, that your training space is too hot or that they don't like one of your policies — it's up to you to fix the problem if you want your clients to keep coming back.**

- **If an employee is out sick, you need to make sure that the tasks they usually do are taken care of by someone else (even yourself if it comes to that).** Yes, this means you have to take out the trash sometimes.

This doesn't mean that you have to do everything yourself, from cleaning the toilets to plotting your business growth. Later in this chapter, I give advice on delegating tasks to your employees.

Lead, Follow, or Get Out of the Way

Guess who your employees are looking to for leadership? Don't look around like that — of course I mean you. Now that you have a business and employees, you're a leader. You've got the power!

No one can really define what leadership is, but they know it when they see it and they miss it when it's not there. In the following sections, I help you become a leader employees will want to follow.

Envisioning your vision and philosophizing on your philosophy

Most people say they'll follow a leader who stands for something, who has good values and a good business philosophy. Think about why you're in business, where you want to go, and how you hope to help people. You may even want to break out some paper and write this down.

Maybe the vision of your business is "to educate clients through hand-tailored exercise and nutrition prescriptions while improving their lives through successful lifestyle-modification strategies." Who wouldn't stand behind that? A philosophy to go with this might be something like, "Success happens with hard work, integrity, and knowledge. We believe in educating our clients so that they feel empowered to make well-informed, positive lifestyle decisions."

REMEMBER

The key is to write a vision statement and philosophy that works for you and your business.

Living your core values

We're all driven to some extent by our beliefs and ideals. Your *core values* are your deepest beliefs. They're the root of who you are and how you see the world–and how the world sees you. Defining your company's core values will help you to explain your vision, and more importantly, you'll have a guiding set of principles for every decision you make. Whenever there's conflict, you can run all possible solutions through the filter of your core values to find your answer. Your company core values will probably reflect your personal core values, and this makes sense because you're the heart and soul of your business. Check out *Dare to Lead*, by Brené Brown (published by Random House) for more on defining your values and understanding the behaviors associated with them. Here's a list of commonly held values to get you started: https://brenebrown.com/resources/living-into-our-values.

Leading by example

If your employees see you doing something, they'll do it too. If they see you snapping at clients, forgetting to follow up, and cutting corners, guess what? They'll probably do the same. If, on the other hand, they see you providing service with a smile, acting like a professional, and putting all your energy into doing a good job, they'll be inspired to do the same.

Here are some ways you can lead by example:

>> **Dress the way you want your employees to dress.** Your employees will hate wearing that yellow company polo shirt if you show up every day in jeans and a T-shirt that reads, "Born to fish."

>> **Eat right.** No snacking on candy bars while on the job!

>> **Don't call in sick if you aren't actually sick.** Yes, they *will* find out.

>> **Show up on time.** Why should employees bust their rear ends getting to work on time if you always saunter in at 9:30?

>> **Treat people well.** Put on your best smile and show your employees, by example, how you want them to treat clients and each other.

Communicating effectively

Leaders (that's you, remember?) must to be able to communicate clearly. They have to say what they want done and expect that it will be done.

REMEMBER

Most people think of communicating as a one-way process. One person talks, and then when there's a pause, the other person talks. Where's the listening? When someone talks, you need to listen. Don't think about what you're going to say next or wait impatiently for a pause so you can jump in. Actually listen to what the other person is saying and ask for clarification if you need it.

TIP

Your body language says a lot about you. For example, if you're tapping your finger on the desk, chances are you're feeling impatient or combative. If you're leaning forward, you're seen as open and engaged. That's why it's important to make sure your body language matches the message you want to give. For example:

>> **When talking with someone, make sure you look directly into the other person's eyes.** (But don't stare — that's just creepy.) Wandering eyes signal wandering attention.

>> **Mirror the other person's body language, which keeps the two of you in harmony.**

>> **Don't cross your arms or lean away from the other person.** Either of these behaviors indicates hostility or that you're rejecting what they're saying.

>> **Keep your hands open with your palms showing to signal openness and warmth.**

You can also decipher other people's body language to figure out how they're really feeling.

If you don't know the answer to something, say so; people will respect your honesty. On the other hand, if you fake it, people will think you're, well, a fake.

To make sure you're understanding what the other person is saying, say it back to them in your own words — for example, "So, if I'm understanding you correctly, what's concerning you is that we don't have heavy enough kettlebells. Is that right?"

Try to understand and address how the other person is feeling. For example, "It must be frustrating for you that you need the day off on Thursday but no one can stand in for you. I appreciate the fact that you're missing the log-toss competition to be here today."

Asking questions shows that you're listening and heads off problems before they happen. Questions also offer great learning opportunities — after all, if you don't ask, you'll never know! Here are some tips on asking (and receiving!):

>> **Try to ask questions before stating your point.** You may discover something that changes what you planned to say.

>> **Don't just stick question marks on the ends of statements.** Think about what you can find out from someone or from a situation and formulate questions accordingly.

>> **Question, don't interrogate.** Make sure you're asking because you want to find out more, not because you want to attack or cast doubt on someone's idea.

For more information on improving your communication skills, check out *Communication Essentials For Dummies* by Elizabeth Kuhnke (published by Wiley).

Considering what other people want

Some really hard-core trainers just don't know — or care — where their employees and clients are coming from. They think, "If I can do chin-ups why can't my clients?" (Maybe because they've been injured?) Or, "If I can arrive at 6 a.m. and work until 10 p.m., why can't the other trainers?" (Perhaps because the other trainers have lives?)

TIP

Bulldozing your way to what you want isn't the way to build a positive business culture — or to be a good leader. To get the most from your employees and clients, you need to find out what they want and figure out how you can reconcile that with what *you* want.

For example, if a client tells you that they love yoga and hate lifting weights, you probably shouldn't design a "heavy weight lifting only" program for them. Instead, come up with a "yoga focused" program that incorporates a variety of resistance training exercises and explain how they'll help the client reach their goals *and* become a better yogi.

Or say an employee wants the evening off to watch the season finale of *Shark Tank* and you're short-staffed. You can ask the employee to find a replacement, let the employee take a dinner break while the show is on, or offer to record the show because you just can't give them the evening off.

Now, isn't that better than telling a client, "Just lift the weights, yoga is dumb!" or saying to your employee, "Look, we're short-staffed. You'll be here and you'll like it"? A little empathy goes a long way, and it's an important skill for building and maintaining a positive culture. It's also what a true leader does, instead of bullying people to get what they want.

Managing micromanagement

If you haven't had time to think about where you want your business to go because you're too busy trying to get the copy machine to work, if you view excessive employee supervision as "mentoring," if you check up on your employees on an hourly basis, you may be the dreaded micromanager. A *micromanager* is a business owner who has to manage every aspect of the business, from bringing in the mail to writing the business plan, even though they've hired employees to take on some of the work.

You may have several reasons for micromanaging your employees:

>> **You didn't hire right.** If your employees can't do the job, then you'll have to do it for them.

>> **You don't trust your employees.**

>> **You feel you can do a better job yourself.** After all, it *is* your business.

>> **You're used to doing everything yourself because you didn't used to have employees.**

>> **You're afraid that something will go wrong if you're not there to fix it.**

Keeping a close eye on your business is a good thing, but micromanaging your team goes beyond keeping an eye on things and brings several risks:

>> **You can stunt your business's growth.** After all, you can't do strategic planning if you're busy taking out the trash and tracking your employees' every moves.

>> **You'll eventually burn out.** Running a business all by yourself is tough!

>> **Your employees will feel unmotivated.** How would *you* feel if your employer didn't trust you to do your job?

Follow these tips for delegating work to your team — so you have the time and energy to attend to growing your business:

>> **Appreciate people's strengths and accept help.** Your goal should be to surround yourself with exceptional people and train them to be even better than you! Think about it. If you can identify where everyone's strengths lie, you can play to them and delegate tasks accordingly. Your team will be more eager, committed, and loyal when they know you appreciate them. Make sure everyone understands their role and how the business is great because they're all bringing their best.

>> **Create a vision.** Determining goals for the future, making plans for new products or services, and setting sales targets will help you see where your talents are needed the most — so you can stop mismanaging your time and skills. As you delegate more and more, you can start looking at the company's future needs rather than running around putting out fires.

>> **Hire the right people and pay them well.** Even if every cell in your cost-conscious brain is telling you to hire cheap — don't do it. Remember that you get what you pay for. Don't consider it spending money on an employee — instead, consider it investing in your business. Because skilled employees free you up to do the things that generate more income for your business, they're worth every dollar you pay them. (You can find more on hiring employees in Chapter 17.)

>> **Make a list of every task you don't want to do, and then write out the steps required to accomplish each task so you can delegate.** The resulting policies-and-procedures checklist will help you let go, because it's a guide for employees on how to handle the small things — so you don't have to.

>> **Trust your employees.** After you've trained your employees, trust them to do what needs to be done. Take comfort in knowing that you hired good people and the business won't crumble if you're not doing everything yourself.

Higher Education: Encouraging Your Employees to Grow

What would happen if experienced personal trainers stopped learning about the personal training industry? Chances are, they'd miss out on all sorts of important developments and would also be way behind on their skills and knowledge. That's why personal training business owners need to foster a learning environment in the workplace.

Having a growth mindset

Having a *growth mindset* means you believe that your skills, talents, and even your intelligence are qualities that you can improve. You're willing to try new things that challenge you. If you try and fail, you say to yourself "I can't do that . . . yet." When someone with a *fixed mindset* tries something new and fails, they say "I can't do that because I'm not smart enough . . . or talented enough." They don't try again because to the person with a fixed mindset, intelligence and talent aren't things you can change. You either have them or you don't. There's nothing wrong with being a beginner! Even the best personal trainers in the world were beginners once, and I can almost guarantee you that they didn't get to where they are now simply by being smart enough. Your success depends on your willingness to learn and grow — not on how much you think you already know.

Staying certified

As I mention in Chapter 2, most certifying organizations require trainers to keep their credentials up to date by earning continuing education credits (CECs). For example, to renew and maintain ACE personal training certification, trainers must earn 20 CECs every two years through ACE-approved courses or professional activities. That's about ten hours of continuing education each year.

TIP

Be sure that your trainers have what they need to stay certified. For example, you can:

>> **Find out about the certification standards for each of the certifications you accept in your business and include this information in your employee manual.** This way, your employees will be kept up to date on what they need to do to maintain their certifications.

>> **Encourage your employees to attend professional activities that will count toward their CECs.** Give them time off to do so, and better yet, consider hosting continuing education courses at your facility if you have one.

>> **Keep a list of upcoming professional activities, such as seminars, and post it somewhere where employees will see it.**

>> **Make sure your employees keep their CPR certifications current.** They'll need to send proof of their current CPR certification along with their CEC certificates to their certifying body when it's time to renew.

Creating a learning atmosphere

TIP

If you expect your trainers to continue to grow, you should be committed to fostering a learning environment at work. For example:

>> **Subscribe to fitness-industry and science magazines and loan them out to employees.**

>> **Keep health books, fitness books, and business-management books on a shelf that employees can access.**

>> **Keep health and fitness magazines available for employees to read.** These can be a great way to glean useful bits of information about content your clients might be curious about. No fitness professional should pick open one of these magazines and see something they didn't already know, but they do offer insight into the type of content readers (like your clients) are interested in. Such magazines include *Shape, Men's Health, Runner's World, Prevention,* and any others you like.

>> **During staff meetings, encourage your team to share things they've learned since the last meeting.** Other trainers (and their clients) may benefit from knowing this information.

Continuing your own education

Not only do you need to keep your own certification up to date, but you should also continue learning as much as you can about business management. Here are some ways to keep the learning going:

>> **Subscribe to small-business magazines like *Inc.* and *Entrepreneur.***

>> **Read small-business-management books like the following:**

- *Small Business For Dummies* by Eric Tyson and Jim Schell (published by Wiley)

- *The E-Myth Revisited* by Michael Gerber (published by Harper Collins)

- *Built to Last* by Jim Collins and Jerry Porras (published by Harper Business)

- *The Ultimate Small Business Guide: A Resource for Startups and Growing Businesses* (published by Basic Books)

>> **Take continuing education classes in business management and entrepreneurship online or at your local college.**

Be sure to tell your employees about all the continuing education you do yourself. You'll set a good example and may inspire them to do the same.

REMEMBER

Training Your Employees

Training your employees — and training them well — is the best business investment you'll ever make. Most people want to do good work and are happier when they know what's expected of them and how to do their jobs — and clients are happier when they're looked after by well-trained, competent personal trainers.

Creating a training manual

Imagine taking a six-hour course on how to run a dentist's office. At the end of the six hours, how much do you think you'd remember about filing, reception, answering the phone, handling patients, filling out insurance forms, cleaning, and handling receipts? Not much, I'd wager.

That's why having an employee training manual that spells out your business procedures is so important. This is a separate manual from the employee handbook, which is designed to teach employees the specifics of their role. The training manual is where details about the day-to-day operation of your business are housed. Whenever a trainer (or any employee) has a question about how to maintain a piece of equipment or fill out an assessment form, they can just flip open the training manual and find the answer.

Writing out all the procedures in your business will show you where they may be lacking. For example, maybe you don't have any procedures in place for handling declined credit cards, or maybe you'll discover that you need some sort of chart that shows who's responsible for cleaning what.

TIP

Here are some of the procedures you'll want to include in your training manual:

>> **Instructions on filling out forms:** Personal training requires a lot of forms, and remembering who fills out what when, as well as what you do with the

forms after they're filled out, can be difficult. Along with the instructions, you should include copies of each form.

» **Client retention information:** This is information about how to keep clients happy. For example:

- How to handle an unsatisfied customer: Do you offer a free session? Call in the supervisor?

- When and how to follow up on clients: This includes check-in phone calls as well as thank-you notes, special offers, and so on.

- How to keep clients motivated.

- How to update a client's training program.

» **Client-service details:** This is information on how to interact with clients, and includes the following:

- How to answer the phone: Do you want your employees to answer with "Good day, Perfect Personal Training. This is Janet speaking. How may I help you?" No matter how you want people to answer the phone, write it down.

- How to take money: Do you accept cash, checks, credit cards? How many sessions do clients pay for at a time? What happens if a check bounces or a credit card is declined?

- How to fill out a receipt or invoice.

- How to answer potential clients' questions about free trial sessions, prices, and so on.

» **Equipment maintenance:** This is information on how and how often to "tune up" equipment. It includes answers to the following questions:

- Who is responsible for maintaining equipment?

- How often does it need to be maintained?

- How are different pieces of equipment maintained, where are the manuals for each piece of equipment kept, and where are the tools kept?

» **Cleaning procedures:** This gives details on how to clean everything that needs to be cleaned, from floors to equipment, and includes the following:

- Who is responsible for cleaning? Do trainers take turns?

- How often does cleaning need to be done?

- What gets cleaned — equipment, floors, the bathroom? What are the procedures for cleaning?

- Where are the cleaning supplies located?

TIP

The training manual ensures that everyone on your team is consistently trained the same way and treated fairly. Include a document that acknowledges receipt of the training manual and keep a signed copy in each employee's file.

Getting your employees up to speed

Training your employees involves more than showing them what you want and then throwing them out onto the gym floor. In the following sections, you'll find suggestions for getting your employees up to speed.

Throw the book(s) at them

Remember the employee handbook from Chapter 16? Make sure each new employee gets — and reads — a copy. It's not exactly a *New York Times* bestseller, but it will help your employees get a grasp on your business and what's expected of them. Give every employee a copy of the employee handbook and a copy of the employee training manual.

Identify their skills

An important step in working with new employees is identifying the skills they're lacking so you don't waste time focusing on what they already know.

Role-play

By *role-play* I don't mean to don a wig and hit the singles bar. Role-playing means that you and the employee being trained will act out different situations that are likely to happen in a personal training business. For example, you can pretend to be:

>> **A disgruntled client:** How can the trainer soothe your sore feelings?

>> **A potential client who has just walked in the door:** How can the trainer make you feel welcome and explain your options — *without* the hard sell?

>> **A client who doesn't comply with the trainer's exercise prescription:** What does the trainer do when he's bombarded with excuses from a client who's not improving?

>> **A client with an injury:** What exercises should the trainer avoid, and at what point should the trainer refer the client to a health care professional?

>> **A client with a health issue, such as high blood pressure:** Again, what exercises should the trainer avoid, and how do they know when to ask for a physician's clearance?

TIP

Acting out various scenarios helps the new trainer work out solutions before they're in the situation. It's also your opportunity to give feedback.

Monkey see, monkey do

TIP

Let the new trainer *shadow* (follow around and observe) a more experienced trainer (even you) to see how things are done. Let them ask questions afterward to make sure everything is clear.

It's show time: Starting new employees in their jobs

Now it's time to let the trainer fly alone — but make sure you're close by and available at first if any questions come up.

REMEMBER

Frequently observe your trainers to make sure everything's going smoothly. If you see them taking shortcuts or making mistakes, pull them aside later and give them feedback. If you see them doing something great, you should say so. Always praise publicly and correct privately.

Continuing the training long term

The training process should continue throughout the employee's career with your company. Encourage your employees to continue learning about the business so they can help make it grow and stay competitive.

5

The Part of Tens

Every *For Dummies* book has a Part of Tens, and this one is no different. In this part, I give you ten ways to add more services and products to your business, ten pieces of equipment every personal training business needs (they're not all what you think!), and ten ways to wow your clients by being the best personal trainer this side of the Mississippi.

With this section, I draw the curtain on *Becoming a Personal Trainer For Dummies.* I wish you (and your clients) much health, wealth, and happiness!

Chapter **19**

Ten Great Ways to Expand Your Services

t's inevitable — when the entrepreneurial bug has bitten you, you see things in a whole new light as a business owner. The day will come when you've mastered the art of the personal training session — and that will no longer be challenging enough for you. You'll ask yourself, "What else can I do to offer my clients more — and increase my revenue?" Or maybe you'll be talking with a client and realize there's a need outside of personal training that you can fulfill. However it happens, here are a few suggestions to help quench your entrepreneurial thirst — and, oh yeah — expand your services to grow your bottom line.

Adding Nutrition Services

Healthy eating and exercise practices go hand in hand, so this seems like an easy add-on to your existing menu of services, right? It is . . . but there's a catch. You need to be *knowledgeable* about nutrition if you're going to talk about it. Unless you're a medical doctor or a *registered dietitian* (RD), you can't diagnose medical conditions or prescribe diets to treat symptoms of medical conditions. But you *can* talk to your clients about healthy eating *if* you know what you're talking about. For example, you can encourage clients to eat lean protein and colorful veggies. You can also share simple and healthy recipes and you can educate clients about the benefits of healthy eating. There are several nutrition courses and certifications available for non-RD fitness professionals who are interested in offering nutrition coaching services. Check out the additional resources for my recommended nutrition courses and certifications.

TIP

Check with your lawyer and your state's regulatory agency to find out what you can (and can't!) do legally in terms of giving nutrition advice in your state.

Selling Supplements

Meal-replacement bars, protein powders, vitamins, and other nutritional supplements accompany personal training and nutrition services well. But make sure stocking your shelves with supplements makes good business sense before you do it. Depending on your state's laws, these types of items may be considered taxable goods, and you may have to apply for a resale tax certificate to sell them legally.

Adding Group Sessions

If you do it for one person, why can't you do it for a whole group of people? If you have the space, group classes can be a great way to extend your services to those who may not necessarily be able to afford you one-on-one.

Or you can offer group classes as an add-on service for your personal training clients, where you take five to eight people through a preset workout. This is a great option for getting your clients into the gym more often. It's also a lot of fun and you'll find that people tend to push themselves harder than they would on their own.

Giving Workshops and Seminars

In the same vein, giving workshops and seminars is a great way to add extra income. Just realize that they can take quite a few hours to plan, market, and execute.

If you're working in a gym, check with the manager about using their group exercise room for an hour or two to hold the seminar or workshop. Or, try your local hospital — hospitals typically have room available for lectures and presentations. Or try your local community college.

TIP

Contact local high schools and ask about giving seminars there. Parents are always willing to shell out a little coin to get a sports scholarship for their kid or just to help them improve in their sport. And working with kids can segue into training the parents.

TIP

In planning the topics for your lecture or workshop, think through the most common issues with clients. Better yet, ask them what they would be interested in learning more about.

REMEMBER

In preparing for your lecture or workshop, you'll want to outline your speech or presentation and prepare written materials to hand out afterward. Be sure to include your name and contact information so if anyone in your audience wants to work with you, they know how to get in touch. See Chapter 8 for more information on giving seminars.

Adding Massage Services

Another very synergistic service is massage therapy. Unless you're a licensed massage therapist, you'll need to hire or contract with one. Or if you have an extra room in your facility, you could rent it out to a massage therapist.

TIP

If adding a massage therapist to the payroll isn't for you, consider creating a dedicated R & R space in your facility. It's not an add-on service, but investing in a massage gun and some foam rollers for your clients to use after their workouts adds value to your existing service. And it's the small stuff you do to add value that will set you apart from your competition.

Selling Fitness Equipment and Apparel

A great and easy way to make extra money is to sell fitness equipment to your clients. Sooner or later, most of your clients will want some type of fitness equipment to use at home, when they're traveling, or just so they can exercise at their leisure.

You can go about selling fitness equipment in a few ways. One way is to sell the equipment directly, where you become a vendor for a manufacturer and sell their products to your clients. This way definitely requires that you have a resale license and requires a little more work come tax time; for example, you have to pay quarterly taxes on the equipment that you sell, and you need to charge your clients sales tax as well.

Another way to sell fitness equipment is to team up with a local fitness-equipment store and help them sell their products to your clients. Work out a deal where you receive a commission on whatever equipment you help to sell to your clients. This way is a little cleaner, because you don't need to worry about inventory or sales tax.

Your clients will also need to replace their workout clothes and shoes from time to time, or they'll forget to pack their socks or an extra T-shirt, or maybe they just want a new T-shirt . . . whatever the reason, why not carry a few of your favorite brands so you can turn a profit?

Typically, to become a reseller for fitness apparel, you need to provide the clothing company with proof of:

>> A valid federal tax ID number

>> A valid tax reseller's certificate

>> A bank account with your company name on it

You may also need to place a minimum order of up to $1,000 to open your account with them.

You can also earn money online by directing clients to the products and apparel you want them to buy through *affiliate marketing.* An affiliate link is a unique URL that you can post on your website, blog, or social media, and anytime someone clicks on your link and makes a purchase, you earn a commission. If you're interested in trying affiliate marketing, I recommend The Amazon Associates Program because you can create your own storefront on your website with links to all your recommended items. It's easy to use and because most of your clients are probably already shopping on Amazon, they'll be comfortable with making their equipment and apparel purchases there.

Providing Corporate Wellness Services

Corporate wellness, also known as *worksite wellness,* is providing health and fitness programs for employees of companies. With healthcare costs rising, more companies are turning to fitness to help reduce their costs. A solid worksite wellness program can:

- » Lower healthcare costs

- » Reduce employee absenteeism

- » Increase employee productivity

- » Reduce employees' use of healthcare benefits

- » Reduce workers' compensation/disability claims

- » Reduce employee injuries

- » Increase employee morale and loyalty

Here are a few ideas for different services you can provide to a company for corporate wellness:

- » Sell fitness equipment to businesses and corporations to set up their worksite fitness facilities.

- » Train employees how to safely use the fitness equipment.

- » Provide weekly workout classes

For more information on worksite wellness, visit the Wellness Council of America's website at www.welcoa.org.

Running Challenges or Contests for Members and Non-Members

Challenges or contests are fun for your clients and they're a great way to get prospective clients in to check out your programs. The possibilities are endless, but I particularly like challenges that encourage people to get to the gym more often. For example, you could challenge members (and prospective members) to attend two group classes each week for a month and everyone who completes the challenge is entered into a drawing to win an iPad. All they have to do is show up.

Encourage non-member participants to schedule an initial consultation before the end of the challenge.

Offering Training Programs Without Training Sessions for Advanced Clients

Some of your clients will come to you as complete beginners, but others will be advanced and simply looking for a new program to follow. Designing advanced training programs is fun, and as you become more experienced, it won't take a lot of time.

I personally only offer program design without personal training sessions for established or previous clients. This way I know where to start and I'm aware of any injuries or limitations the client might have so I can prescribe appropriate exercises — and avoid anything that could increase their injury risk. This is my policy and it's up to you to decide what works best for you. If you're wondering what to charge, I recommend charging your hourly or session rate. For example, if you're hourly rate is $85, you'd charge the client $85 for a DIY training program.

Offering Other Services

Y'know, this is *your* business — and you can offer any type of service you feel would benefit your clients! If you have your own place, you can even offer a shoe-shine service or car detailing. Services that save clients time while they're training with you are called *value-added services*, and as I have said before, it's those little things that keep your clients sticking around.

The moral of the story here is that no one can say what's right or wrong for you to offer with your personal training services. Only *you* will know what works best for your business!

Chapter **20**

Ten Helpful Tools

As I stress throughout this book, you wear many hats in your role as a personal trainer. You're a salesperson, scientist, friend, coach, motivator, teacher, employer, bookkeeper, and business owner, to name just a few. To be successful wearing any of these hats, you need to be well equipped — and that means you need to have the right tools in your toolbox — literally and figuratively speaking.

As you've discovered by now, your "tools" as a trainer won't always be big, heavy pieces of workout equipment! Read on for ten pieces of equipment — some essential, all helpful — to start filling your personal trainer toolbox.

Your Mindset

There is unlimited equipment available to help you be a successful trainer: mobile apps, software programs, free weights, machines, ropes, bands, suspension trainers, kettlebells, medicine balls . . . The list goes on.

But make no mistake, no matter how many tools you have (or how expensive or cutting edge they are), it won't matter if you don't have the most important one: the right mindset.

Important factors for having the right mindset are:

>> **Honesty:** You need to be honest with yourself about what you realistically can and cannot do; this flows through to your clientele as well.

>> **Determination:** Not every day is easy; you won't always have a full book, and sometimes those slow days end up being weeks. Pushing ahead and staying on track when the going gets tough takes determination and focus.

>> **Willingness:** You must be willing to change if your original course of action isn't producing the results that you want. You also need to keep an open mind and be able to set your ego aside when a client isn't happy with your services. Willingness means being flexible and doing whatever it takes to be successful — and it's not always easy. Sometimes becoming a successful personal trainer means doing things that you don't *want* to do.

Your Certification

Your certification is your personal trainer badge of honor — it tells everyone who works with you, from employers to clients, that not only do you *say* you know what you're doing, but you can also prove it. You have your sheet of paper that states, "I studied, I tested, and I passed — I know what I'm talking about here!"

Certification demonstrates to your clients that you've undergone stringent studies and testing protocols to figure out what to do and what not to do as a personal training professional — so that you can help them reach their fitness goals.

Certification is also a means of qualifying your credibility. Have you ever seen a trainer quoted online or on television who was introduced with "an *uncertified* personal trainer, John Q. Smith, states that exercise is . . ."? Most likely not! Being certified gives you the credibility you need for other professionals and clients to take you seriously. Certification helps you to build a solid rapport with the people you will be doing business with, such as:

>> Employers

>> Clients

>> Mentors

>> Media contacts

>> Physical therapists and other healthcare providers with whom you have a referral relationship

In other words: If you're not certified yet, it's time to get on it!

Your Online Presence

Whether you're using the internet to market your brick-and-mortar personal training business or to share your fitness knowledge with a broad audience, you need to be online. Establishing — and monitoring — your online presence is more important than ever because most people turn to the internet for information.

Keep in mind that your potential clients will probably already have formed a first impression of you before meeting you in person. It's a good idea to Google yourself regularly to see what the world wide web has on you. You'll need to be mindful about how people perceive you on social media too. It's one thing to share fitness tips with your audience — people love free advice, especially from an expert like you — it's another thing entirely to post a half-naked photo of yourself online with the hashtag, *#AbsAreMadeInTheKitchen*. Sure, you'll get people's attention, but probably not the kind of attention you're after. Before you post a photo online, ask yourself if you would want your grandma to see it. If the answer is no, well, I hope you get the idea.

REMEMBER

Make sure that your online presence reflects everything you want people to associate you with — professionalism, integrity, quality, and trustworthiness, and temperament. Getting into heated arguments with random people on social media will probably scare off potential clients. And you never know when you're going to meet a potential client, business associate, mentor, or referring health-care provider — use the internet to make a good first impression!

Tape Measure

The tape measure can be used for many different things, like recording your client's *anthropometric measurements* and tracking circumference changes (inches lost or gained). If you surveyed all the personal trainers in the world and asked them for the number-one reason clients come to them, the unanimous answer would most likely be "to lose weight." You know, however, that if a client loses fat and maintains muscle, the number on the scale might not change much — and it could even go up. You'll be able to show your client consistent results by tracking inches lost no matter what the number on the scale says. You can also measure degrees of flexibility and how far your client can reach in the sit-and-reach test (see Chapter 11).

Foam Roller

Foam rolling is a simple form of self-myofascial release therapy, and with regular practice, it can help your clients to relieve tense muscles and improve overall mobility. Foam rollers are widely available and there are many inexpensive options to choose from. To learn more about foam rolling, check out *Foam Rolling for Dummies*, published by Wiley.

Smartphone

A smartphone isn't a must-have for personal trainers, but once you use one, you won't want to be without it. Any mobile phone works for managing contacts so you can call or text your clients from one place. But with a smartphone, you can also email your clients, schedule appointments online, offer video consultations or training sessions, take progress photos, keep notes, download training apps, accept payments, and so on.

Resistance Bands

A solid alternative to dumbbells, resistance bands are easy to travel with because they weigh practically nothing. Resistance bands are inexpensive and typically come as a set, with different bands providing different levels of resistance — light, medium, and heavy. There are two general categories of elastic resistance: minibands (great for working all functions of hips muscles) and longer resistance bands with or without handles (for working larger muscle groups).

Bands are great for just about anybody, and they're a good long-term option for clients who may have problems with their wrists, hands, or fingers and may not be able to grasp a dumbbell. Another bonus is that almost all free-weight movements can be duplicated with them.

TIP

You can buy resistance bands at most sporting goods stores, big box retailers (like Target or Walmart), and online. You might also want to pick up a door anchor for using bands at a client's home. You can find these on Amazon for less than $10.

Adjustable Dumbbells or Kettlebells

Dumbbells and kettlebells are, in my humble opinion, the best investment you can make when it's time to invest in resistance training equipment. Sure, you can start with bodyweight exercises and resistance bands, but at some point, you'll need to increase the weight on your clients' lifts as they progress and become stronger. This is a good problem! Adjustable dumbbells or kettlebells are a perfect solution, even if you have the space and budget for a full set of free weights. Adjustable free weights save space, they're versatile, convenient (easy to store and you can transport them), and the weight can usually be adjusted in smaller increments than a full set of weights. Dumbbells and kettlebells are typically rounded in 5-pound increments, and with an adjustable set, you can adjust by 2.5-pound increments — this is especially helpful for beginning clients and smaller people.

TIP

To get the most bang for your buck, invest the most versatile set of adjustable free weights that you can afford. You'll save money in the long run when you're not constantly upgrading them and they'll be suitable for more of your clients. Choose a set with a with a high weight range (at least 50 pounds) so you can use them for compound exercises like squats and deadlifts and make sure you can adjust them in small increments (no more than 2.5 pounds).

TIP

My first big equipment purchase for my personal training business was a set of adjustable dumbbells. I didn't have enough space to store a full set of dumbbells, and even though I was on a tight budget and considered buying a starter set of adjustable weights, I saved up for a more expensive set with a weight range up to 52.5 pounds and 2.5-pound increments. That was in 2007 and I still use the same set of adjustable dumbbells today.

TRX

Chances are you're familiar with suspension training, even if you haven't yet swung through the air on a TRX suspension trainer. TRX suspension training is a type of bodyweight training that involves suspending from an anchored strap and changing body positions to increase or decrease the weight for each exercise. TRX suspension training was originally created by a Navy Seal for training his troops in remote parts of the world and has since become popular among elite athletes and beginning exercisers alike because of its versatility.

The TRX suspension trainer is the original and the one I recommend, even though there are now many cheaper knock-offs to choose from. The TRX suspension trainer is a lightweight and portable tool that anybody can benefit from, regardless of fitness level or physical ability. To learn more about TRX suspension training, check out www.trxtraining.com.

TIP

Make sure there is a sturdy place to anchor the TRX if you're using it in a client's home. You need to be 100 percent certain the setup can hold more than 100 percent of the client's body weight.

Stretching Strap

Also referred to as a yoga strap, a stretching strap is another lightweight and versatile tool that every personal trainer should have. A stretching strap is used for holding stretches with proper form and can be used to mimic partner-assisted stretching. This is particularly helpful for clients with tight hips or shoulders who might not be able to safely get into and hold stretches without assistance. A good stretching strap should be made of a durable, non-stretchy material (like nylon) and have multiple loops. You can find one for as little as $5 in stores that sell exercise equipment or online.

Chapter **21**

Ten Ways to Be the Best Personal Trainer You Can Be

Personal training is a competitive field. Big George's Deep Discount Personal Training down the street would love to take your clients away from you — and if you don't give your clients what they're looking for, they just might give George a try.

REMEMBER

Your clients want more than just a good workout. They want a personal trainer who motivates them, cares about them, and sets a good example.

That's why I give you this chapter. When all else is equal, your professionalism, your attitude, and your knowledge of business etiquette will put you ahead of the pack. These ten tips will help you be the best personal trainer you can be.

Stay In Your Own Lane

You're having a conversation with a new acquaintance at a dinner party and they start talking about the works of Umberto Eco. Instead of saying, "Who in the ever lovin' world is Umberto Eco?" you nod along, pretending that you're deeply familiar with *The Name of the Rose* and the other works of whatshisname.

C'mon, you know you've done this before. We all have.

Although you may get away with this tactic at a dinner party, you won't get away with it as a personal trainer. If you give false information (for example, confusing personal training with physical therapy and advising a client on how to work through an injury) because you don't want to look stupid, you can do more than get found out — you can injure the client.

TIP

Scope of practice refers to the services that a practitioner is competent to provide. Clearly defining personal trainer scope of practice is tricky because the prerequisites and qualifications required to become certified vary widely depending on which certification you pursue. Generally speaking though, if a client needs a service that your personal training certification didn't prepare you to deliver, it's probably beyond your scope of practice. Unless you're also a medical doctor, licensed counselor, registered dietitian, chiropractor, physical therapist . . . you get the idea . . . stay in your own lane and refer your clients to the appropriate professionals in your network when you need to.

Reserve the Right to Improve

Everyone makes mistakes. A key difference between a good trainer and a bad trainer is that the good trainer admits when they were wrong, and the bad trainer tries to sweep the evidence under the proverbial rug. It's also okay to acknowledge that you did the best you could at the time, and now you know better, so now you do better. "Reserve the right to improve" is some solid advice I once received from a friend and mentor in the fitness industry that has always stuck with me.

TRUE STORY

Sometimes doing better has nothing to do with exercise knowledge. Thinking back on my early personal training days, I didn't understand then how hard it was for so many of my clients to prioritize exercise. Especially the working moms. It's cringeworthy to admit how unwilling I was to adjust my expectations to meet their needs, even if I was doing the best I could at the time. Now I know better, and now I do better.

Be There for Your Clients

Being there for your clients doesn't mean trailing them in the gym with cold water and fresh towels. Being there means giving your complete and undivided attention to your clients during their training sessions.

Don't ever take your eyes off your client during a session; have you ever seen a trainer at the gym staring off into space rather than watching their client? Don't be that trainer. Your clients are paying you for a service and they deserve your full attention when you're on the clock.

REMEMBER

Your job is to be a motivating and enthusiastic trainer for your clients. Always show up with a good attitude, even when you're not feeling it. Your clients really don't care if you're having a bad day — it's not about you.

Respect Boundaries

You have your personal self, and your professional self. Your professional self does not offer relationship advice, does not eat candy bars in front of the client, and does not make comments about the client's home or its contents.

Personal training is just that — personal. Your client may come to think of you as a friend. That's a good thing, but it also invites unprofessional behavior. If a client starts, say, complaining that her husband doesn't pay attention to her, you need to draw that boundary line. Say, "I hear you, that sounds difficult," but don't offer advice or tell her what a jerk her husband is. If a client asks you to train her for an extra half-hour free of charge, or to drive 15 miles outside your regular area to train her daughter, tell her you can't do it. If you do, the client may come to expect this from you all the time — and it can hurt your business.

Under Promise and Over Deliver

When you tell someone you'll do something, you should do it. Sounds simple, right? Well, it's a challenging concept for many personal trainers, but probably not for the reasons you would think. Personal training is a helping profession and personal trainers are notorious for spreading themselves too thin. Trainers think they're helping their clients, but the reality is that a single person can't be everything to all people. Offering to help your clients beyond their training sessions isn't a bad thing, but make sure you follow through with your promises, and only take on as much as you can realistically handle.

REMEMBER

The best way to keep your word is to be prepared, to always be on time, and to follow the tips in this chapter about getting your bag and files ready ahead of time.

Show Clients You Care

Care is more than just a four-letter word. It also stands for "Clients Are Really Everything." You may know everything there is to know about personal training, but you couldn't exactly be a personal trainer without your clients. Clients can make or break your business. That's why you have to show them you care.

TIP

Here are some tips for showing clients that you care:

>> Return calls, texts, email, and direct messages promptly.

>> Follow up with your clients to make sure the sessions are working for them.

>> Send your clients thank-you cards for doing business with you.

>> Send clients holiday and birthday cards.

>> Always express empathy for your clients' concerns.

>> Keep your records on each client up to date so you can track them and create the most personalized programs for them.

>> Follow the rest of the suggestions in this chapter!

Always Be On Time

Imagine having a weekly appointment with someone at 4 p.m. What if the other person always showed up at 4:15, or even 4:05? It may not seem like much, but over time, the other person's tardiness would probably irritate you.

Being late shows a lack of respect for the person who is waiting. Not only that, but if you have a personal training session and you show up late, what are your choices? You can either cheat the client out of a few minutes of training so you'll be done at 5 p.m., or you can run late — which is annoying for a busy person (and who *isn't* busy?) and for your next client who you will also be running late for.

If you're always late, ask yourself why and come up with a solution. Do you get stuck in traffic? If so, find alternate routes or leave earlier. Do you have trouble getting yourself out the door? Have your bag, your client folder, and everything else you need ready by the door early in the day so you can grab it and leave when the time comes.

Do you just dread working with a particular client? Then you need to think seriously about whether that client is right for your business, or whether you're the right personal trainer for that client. See Chapter 9 for information on how to appropriately part ways with a client.

Always keep your phone with you so that if you're late despite these tips, you can call or text your client to let them know.

Dress Professionally

Which trainer inspires more confidence — a personal trainer wearing clean athletic apparel that fits properly, or one dressed in a revealing, skintight spandex top? Even if you look and feel great in spandex, consider the image you want to portray. You need to look professional if you expect to be taken seriously.

Here are some dress-for-success tips:

>> I'll say it again — no skintight spandex or revealing clothing when you're on the clock!

>> Make sure your clothes aren't too baggy either. You need to be able to move comfortably and your clients need to be able to see you demonstrating exercises.

>> Keep jewelry to a minimum. Long, dangly jewelry gets in the way when you're demonstrating an exercise or spotting a client.

>> The same goes for long, loose hair. If you have long hair, you may want to pull it back.

>> I recommend finding a uniform that you look and feel confident in. If you don't like wearing polo shirts, don't wear one. Athletic apparel that fits you properly and isn't revealing is appropriate personal trainer attire too. Several brands offer a fitness professional discount and you can find a list of some of my favorites in the resources section at the end of this book.

Never Stop Learning

As the saying goes, "when you're green, you grow; when you're ripe, you rot." This means that to keep growing as a personal trainer, you need to keep learning. Become complacent, and you'll be, well, a rotten personal trainer.

You can't be an expert in everything, but some topics that personal trainers should have current working knowledge about include medicine, fitness, business, and even psychology and nutrition. These fields are constantly changing, and researchers are uncovering new information every day.

TIP

Here are some ways to keep learning:

>> Attend continuing education courses.

>> Talk to other personal trainers.

>> Go to conferences and workshops.

>> Read industry magazines.

>> Read medical journals.

>> Read health, fitness, and business magazines (many are available at the local library).

>> Talk with doctors and other healthcare professionals.

>> Study successful businesses outside of the fitness industry.

>> Only learn from other lifelong learners — a piece of advice I received many years ago from a mentor.

Do What You Love, Love What You Do

When you love what you do, it shows. Your enthusiasm is contagious and your positive outlook motivates your clients.

Unfortunately, though, personal trainers do burn out. Burnout happens when you take on more than you can handle and start neglecting your self-care. You can avoid burning out by eating healthy food, exercising regularly, getting enough sleep, taking regular time off to recharge . . . all the same advice you give your clients. If you do start feeling burned out, do yourself — and your clients — a favor and take a time-out. Sometimes you just need a couple of days to rest and focus on something other than work, or maybe it's time to take a week-long vacation to relax. You'll learn over time what you need to do (or not do) to feel your best.

Here are some ideas beyond taking a break for changing up your work to avoid burnout:

>> Try working in a different environment, like corporate wellness.

>> Write a fitness book.

>> Write magazine articles on fitness.

>> Conduct group sessions.

>> Work with a new client population.

>> Go on sabbatical to study for a certification to learn something new.

>> Take classes in nutrition or another field related to fitness.

When I became self-employed, I learned about burnout the hard way. I had already been working full-time as a personal trainer, group fitness instructor, and personal training manager for six years when I decided to start my own business. I hadn't taken a vacation in several years and didn't take any time off before going out on my own. I loved my new-found freedom, but I ran myself into the ground with too many early mornings and late nights in the studio. I felt like an employee with the worst boss ever! After three years of self-employment, I was exhausted and quickly losing my passion for the work I had always loved.

I decided to close the studio for a month during the summer when several of my clients would be away and used the time to re-evaluate my career. It turned out that I still loved my work, but it took stepping away from it to realize that I had to take better care of myself if I wanted my business to survive. After that, I started working either early mornings or late evenings, taking a full weekend off every month, and eventually hired more trainers to work with me in the business so I could meet my clients' needs without burning myself out. Sometimes we have to learn hard lessons before we can improve, but burnout didn't have to be a part of my experience. Hopefully my story will inspire you to work hard, play hard, and rest plenty.

Index

A

accountability, 11

accountants, 81–82
  responsibilities of, 81–82
  searching for, 82

accounting methods, 111–112

accounts on file, 107

accrual accounting method, 112

ACE (American Council on Exercise) certification exam, 31, 276–277

ACSM. *See* American College of Sports Medicine

adjustable dumbbells and kettlebells, 295

advanced client programs, 140, 232–233, 290

Advanced First Aid
  maintaining certification, 34–35
  requirements from certifying organizations, 31

advisory boards
  business plans, 69
  informal, 53
  networking, 87–88

aerobic exercise program, 195–200
  exercise duration, 196, 200
  exercise frequency, 196, 199–200
  FITT-VP principles of exercise prescription, 234
  training methods, 196, 198–199
    interval training, 198–199, 234–236
    steady-state training, 198
  training modes, 195–197
  working intensity, 196, 199

affiliate marketing, 288

alternative healthcare centers, 60

Amazon Associates Program, 288

American College of Sports Medicine (ACSM)
  cardiovascular exercise frequency, 200
  certification exam, 32
  conferences, 41
  disclaimer and informed-consent forms, 98
  exercise frequency, 200
  PAR-Q+, 164
  preparticipation health screenings, 167–168
  program format guidelines, 194

American Council on Exercise (ACE) certification exam, 31, 276–277

Anatomy Coloring Workbook, 34

android obesity, 181

anthropometric measurements, 181, 293

apparel, selling, 287–288

Apple, 69–71

apprenticing, 37, 39–40

asymmetries, 185–186, 194

athletes, training, 26, 28, 118, 199, 234

B

background checks, 257, 261

bankers, 83–84

bartering, 112, 252

benchmarks, 228

bill paying, 111

billing policy, 107

bioelectrical impedance analysis, 179–180

blood pooling, 216

blood pressure, 176–178
  cool-downs and recovery, 216
  hypertension, 176–177
  measurement, 177–178
  medications, 164
  systolic and diastolic numbers, 177–178

blood-pressure cuffs, 173, 177–178

body composition measurements, 178–182
  bioelectrical impedance analysis, 179–180
  circumference measurements, 181–182
  dual-energy x-ray absorptiometry, 180–181
  hydrostatic weighing, 180
  skinfold assessment, 178–179
  ultrasound, 180

body language, 12, 136, 272–273

bodyfat percentages, 43
  circumference measurements, 181
  dual-energy x-ray absorptiometry, 180
  infographic, 220
  skinfold assessment, 172, 178

body-weight scales, 173, 178, 181, 219, 293–294

bonding, 104

brachial artery, 175, 177

branding, 93–95
  colors, 94–95
  criteria for, 93–94
  defined, 93